THE EMPEROR CHARLES V

CHARLES V

THE EMPEROR
CHARLES V

*The Growth and Destiny of a
Man and of a World-Empire*

by

KARL BRANDI

HON. D. PHIL.; LITT. D.
(Cantab)
*Professor of History at the University
of Göttingen*

Translated from the German by
C. V. WEDGWOOD

JONATHAN CAPE
THIRTY BEDFORD SQUARE
LONDON

FIRST PUBLISHED 1939
REPRINTED 1949
REPRINTED 1954
REPRINTED 1960

PRINTED IN GREAT BRITAIN BY THE REPLIKA PROCESS BY
PERCY LUND, HUMPHRIES & CO. LTD, LONDON & BRADFORD
ILLUSTRATIONS PRINTED IN COLLOGRAVURE BY HARRISON & SONS LTD,
LONDON AND HIGH WYCOMBE
BOUND BY A. W. BAIN & CO. LTD, LONDON

CONTENTS

BOOK ONE

THE DYNASTY, ITS LANDS AND KINGDOMS: THE EMPEROR'S YOUTH

CONTENTS

BOOK TWO

CHARLES MAINTAINS HIS INHERITANCE: YEARS OF GROWTH

CONTENTS

BOOK THREE

THE STRUGGLE FOR GERMANY: CLIMAX AND DECLINE

CONTENTS

ILLUSTRATIONS

The device on the binding, bearing the legend 'QUOD IN CELIS SOL HOC
IN TERRA CAESAR EST. Ao 1548', and Charles's personal motto, 'PLUS
ULTRA', is from the reverse of a medal by Hans Bolsterer. Specimens
are to be seen in Vienna, Frankfort and Basel.

TRANSLATOR'S PREFACE

PROFESSOR KARL BRANDI of Göttingen, who celebrated his seventieth birthday last year, is the greatest living authority on Charles V. In the following pages he has epitomized the results of a lifetime of research in the archives of almost every European country. Not the remotest corner appears to have eluded his minute and illuminating scrutiny. It is no easy task to compress this immensity of knowledge into the pages of a single volume. Professor Brandi has himself explained his attitude both in the dedicatory letter, and in a later passage of his work. 'Neither prejudice nor ingenious selection', he writes in Book Three, Chapter II, 'can make a convincing picture of a man, but only the strictest devotion to historic truth. Our knowledge must rest on the accumulated tradition and observation of centuries. Only by unfolding the material gradually and carefully, only by conscientiously recognizing its peculiarities and its limitations, can we draw valid conclusions. These are not to be made by rashly over-estimating, and then as rashly decrying. Only in the utmost caution and observation lies the true scientific value of historical work, and only by that can we arrive at a truer knowledge of things as they were and as they are.'

Very little can be added to that. Professor Brandi has, as it were, taken the reader into his confidence and shown by the careful examination of document after document the development of a human being, in the fulfilment of one of the most complex and burdensome tasks that ever man was called upon to bear. Professor Brandi has substituted for the external excitement of stirring events, the tenser and quieter excitement of a man's inner development. The colossal wealth of existing material, the profound scholarship and controlled imagination of Professor Brandi have combined to produce an historical work which is, and will probably long remain, unique. Few great men in history lend themselves to this microscopic treatment, for few have left the documentary material essential to it; few, very few scholars, would have the necessary gifts to carry out the task, untiring, to its end.

C. V. WEDGWOOD

To

THE UNIVERSITY OF CAMBRIDGE

THE dedication of the German edition to the Academies of Berlin, Budapest, Copenhagen, Munich and Vienna, and of the English edition to the University of Cambridge, is at the same time an expression of my gratitude and an indication of the scholastic nature of this work. It is based almost exclusively on a new and thorough examination of the best and most immediate contemporary evidence. Much of what I have to say is new; many events will be freshly illuminated.

It is the highest object, even of the scholar, to make the past live again, with all the peculiarities of its special circumstances, its opinions, prejudices and interactions. I have used the traditional narrative form, which, by approaching most nearly to the actual course of events and experiences, enables the writer to catch even the moods of an epoch. In building up the whole, I have sought not so much to describe a series of exciting events as to live over, step by step, with the Emperor, the gradual processes of his extraordinary career, with all its puzzling delays, crises, hopes and wearinesses. I have not sought to vindicate the Emperor's actions nor to paint the portrait of hero, but rather to draw the features of a man and a ruler, with his frailties and his virtues.

KARL BRANDI

INTRODUCTION: CHARLES'S
CHARACTER AND PLACE IN HISTORY

THERE are in history certain men whose productive energy is more than human. They create out of their own elemental strength and lay down the laws of thought and action for centuries to come. The Emperor Charles V was not one of these. Rather did he belong to that other group who must be called great because ancient historic forces were concentrated in their single being, because they moulded inherited ideas of power, belief and behaviour into new forms. Thereby they also resolved within themselves the eternal contradictions of humanity.

In this way he also was a builder.

Charles V carried the Hapsburg dynasty to the height of its greatness. He united and completed its possessions; mingling old Burgundian ideas of chivalry with the conscientious piety of the Netherlands, with Spanish self-restraint and the universal traditions of the Romano-German Empire, he created the attitude which was in future to be typical of his dynasty. At the same time, out of the mass of his inherited possessions he formed a new European and, in a sense, a new overseas imperialism — a world Empire dependent for the first time in history not on conquest, still less on geographical interdependence, but on dynastic theory and unity of faith.

The Emperor gave his Empire not only new foundations but new ambitions, which found expression in the conflict in the Netherlands, and in the wars in Germany, Italy and Spain.

On the younger branch of the dynasty he bestowed the old rights over the Danube lands, with their important possibilities and no less important dangers, while he shifted the weight of his own power from Germany and Burgundy to the growing state of Spain. Thus he founded within his own family that predominance of the Spanish branch which lasted for a century and a half. Resting not on Germany, but on Spain, he was able to reassert his suzerainty over the old imperial lands of Milan, Tuscany, and even Naples; thereby he turned the axis of the Empire, which had run for so long from north to south, on to the line of Madrid

13

and Rome, and sheltered Italy for many years to come from the attacks of France. Basing his imperial theory on Spain, he regained both for himself and his son that relationship with the Papacy as an Italian power within the framework of the European system, which had prevailed during the earlier days of the Empire. For reasons rooted deep in German history his relations with the Protestants were governed at least as much by political as by ecclesiastical considerations. In his world-struggle for the ancient Church, the Emperor was to experience the bitter mortification of being deserted by the Pope, and he was to be touched to the quick by the alliance of Catholic France with the Turk. For him, as for the Hohenstaufen, the spiritual office of the Pope proved to be sharply at odds with the political; because of the intensity of Charles's convictions, both religious and political, this contradiction gave rise to gigantic conflicts.

The same latent tension is to be found in internal politics. Inevitably Charles's highly centralized policy over-rode the individual territorial divisions of his lands; thereby he weaned them from outworn political forms based on disintegrating feudal and urban authority, with their special privileges, local feuds and shifting powers, and drew them towards higher political conceptions. A Burgundian of the old school, that great realist, Commines, has vividly depicted the contrast between the personal rivalries of the great lords of his time and the humanist theory of the state, supported by universal principles, which dominated the councillors of Charles V. The Emperor's dynastic policy of world-power gave to the ideas prevalent in Europe during the century which saw the rise of the nation-state, a direction which survives to-day.

In Spain this ruler, haloed with the glory of the Empire, became, not without the support of his universal theories, the architect of that national state for which Ferdinand and Isabella had laid the foundation. Charles completed it. Although he was forced to combat the separatism of the individual kingdoms, his marriage policy nevertheless made way for the subsequent ephemeral union with Portugal and for the unification of the whole Iberian peninsula, from whose shores so many men had sailed to circumnavigate the globe.

In Germany and Italy, on the other hand, the territorial states, whose development had long been hampered by the structure of the Empire to which they belonged, no less than by outworn political ideas, gained through Charles's universal policy the means to become European powers. By bringing them into contact with the resources of a world Empire, he marked out the way for their future. Yet this very Emperor, who extended the German Empire to its widest bounds, was also responsible for its dissolution. He who might so easily have re-united the Netherlands with the body of the Empire, completed their severance. He jeopardized Alsace; he side-tracked the ambitions of France from Italy to Lorraine. As ruler of the Low Countries he opposed the German Hanseatic League, and his policy towards his brother-in-law Christian II of Denmark was partly responsible for its disappearance from the ranks of the northern powers. The principalities of North Germany discovered a new force in Protestantism, and Charles left them at his death in a strong position. The Catholic states too were strengthened. Bequeathing to the Austrian branch of the dynasty both the religious problem and the Turkish menace, he left them neither Spain, Milan nor Burgundy, and thus forced them to depend more than ever before on the help of their co-religionists in Germany.

Lastly, although his relations with the Netherlands and Denmark entangled him with the northern states, his attitude to the rising commercial powers of England and Scotland remained indefinite. His changing personal alliances, as much as his political ideas, forced him to veer from close co-operation to open enmity. Here too the outcome was to strengthen the theory of the nation-state.

Many as are the seeming contradictions in the life of Charles V, it had an inner unity. His career was dominated by the dynastic principle, which found more vital and effective expression in him than in any other ruler in the history of the world. Both as a man and as a sovereign, he was subjected to the moral pressure of this principle, which beset his path with perilous temptations. The Emperor gave living reality in his own person to the doctrine of a binding relationship between the generations, of responsibility alike towards his ancestors and his descendants. For him the dynastic principle did not merely mean the theory of hereditary kingship for the permanent security of the state; it was also a profound moral, almost a religious duty. Charles was not indeed unlike other princes of his time in his physical weaknesses; but he was far above them all in the political sanctification, as it were, of his marriage, in the courtly and princely reverence which he showed to his wife, Her Serene Majesty, the Empress. No father could have displayed greater care for the spiritual and material welfare of his children than this Emperor who, in the forty years of his reign, wandered ceaselessly from land to land, waged war after war, negotiated treaty after treaty, and spent in all that time hardly one continuous year by his own fireside. We shall live through it all in his company.

A particular circumstance enables us to gain detailed insight into his character and beliefs. His native country, the Netherlands, was the home of many great teachers, theologians and humanists. His reign witnessed the rise of grave and learned councillors to the chief positions in the State. Partly owing to the impressions of a minority spent in the control of others, he was acutely conscious of his personal importance as a ruler, and refused to submit to the influence of the higher nobility and grandees in State affairs. Instead he collected about him men of learning and intelligence, spiritual energy and creative force. Under the influence of these surroundings, a prince who by inheritance might well have had no greater ambition than to live the life of a nobleman and a knight, developed gradually into an industrious worker, a punctilious compiler of letters and minutes, and at times even developed a habit of introspection and reflection. Not for many centuries can any prince compare with him in the number of revealing documents which he left behind. There are vain pedants, like James I of England, there are royal theologians and poets, but not until Frederick of Prussia was there one for whom, as for Charles, the very affairs of State became the material of a spontaneous literature. Tens of thousands of letters bearing the imperial signature have survived, and of these a not inconsiderable part are written in Charles's hand. Even in his early twenties the young ruler made a beginning, jotting down important memoranda, minutes and notes for consideration. In the prime of life he composed a dry but thoughtful account of his career, which, no less than his instructions to his son, reflects with brilliant clarity even to the minutest detail, the meticulous conscientiousness of his nature. Under his hand private letters, even those to the Empress, became official documents and fatherly admonitions, political testaments.

Through his actions and his confessions, in the motives and methods of his policy and his private life, we see the man mature and develop before our eyes. We can follow him from boyhood to premature old age; the historic type of a whole period, he is for us a man of flesh and blood. Strangest of all, through his growth and maturing, nay to his very decline, we shall find that his age is coloured still with those same desires which enflamed his youth. So also in his youth we shall find early the foreboding of age, wistful dreams of rest and thoughts of death. His life forms a circle complete within itself.

BOOK ONE

THE DYNASTY, ITS LANDS AND KINGDOMS: THE EMPEROR'S YOUTH

CHAPTER I

DUKE OF BURGUNDY

THE Hapsburg dynasty came from the Upper Rhine. It rose to princely power in Austria, whence even in the days of Rudolf of Hapsburg, its princes had looked towards the greater possibilities of the Danube basin with its natural connections with Bohemia and Hungary. But later it had fallen a victim to the fate which overwhelmed all German dynasties from the Merovingians to the Welf and Wittelsbach — self-annihilation by the division of inheritance. Powerless in the Empire, the King and Emperor Frederick III had had to divide even the Hapsburg lands with his cousin Sigismund of Tyrol, and he lost Austria itself, the very kernel of his dominions, when King Matthias Corvinus of Hungary entered his capital, Vienna, in 1485, and remained there until his death in 1490. For long enough, therefore, Frederick's only son, Maximilian, the grandfather of Charles V, would have looked forward to no very brilliant future, had he not secured the hand of the richest heiress in Europe, Mary of Burgundy.

True that the power of her father, Charles the Bold, was limited, his possessions scattered and disunited. But his dynastic and territorial connection with France and England, his position on the Channel, the commercial prosperity of his lands and the wealth of his family in treasure of every kind, seemed to ensure both to him and to his heirs high prestige as a ruler and unlimited prospects in European politics. The Medici had but newly risen, the Popes were still fighting for the control of Rome, France was recovering slowly from the English war, England drifting towards the conflicts of York and Lancaster; nowhere in Europe in the middle of the fifteenth century was there to be found such store of actual bullion, such wealth of precious stones, of gold and silver plate, of magnificent and beautiful works of art, as at the Court of Burgundy.

The family were the younger branch of the French royal house. They owned, as a fief of the French Crown, the Duchy of

21

Bourgogne,[1] with Dijon and the celebrated tombs of their ancestors in the neighbouring Chartreuse — tombs since destroyed. They had other French fiefs in the coastlands of Flanders, Artois and Picardy, with Arras, Lille, Ypres, Ghent and Bruges. As fiefs of the Empire, they held the county of Burgundy, known as Franche Comté, with Dôle and Besançon, the province of Brabant, lying eastwards from Flanders and no less rich, with Brussels, Louvain, Malines, Antwerp, and at its northernmost point Bois-le-Duc in the valley of the Meuse. South of this they owned Hainault with Mons and Valenciennes, Namur on the Meuse and farther to the east the ancient counties, now dukedoms, of Luxembourg and Limburg. Last of all the broad district in the Rhine delta and to the north with its population of mariners and merchants; more especially the flats of Holland and Zeeland, at that time still poor and water-logged, with Amsterdam, The Hague, Leyden and Delft as well as Veere and Middelburg on the southern islands. All these lands had been gradually acquired since 1369 by marriage or by purchase from the last dynasties of the Counts of Flanders and Luxembourg, the Dukes of Brabant and Limburg, the heirs of the Wittelsbach in Hainault, Holland and Zeeland. It was a loose assemblage of possessions, of a kind not uncommon in this Germano-Frankish Empire. The Duke's subjects were partly nobles long settled in their castles and estates, ruling over peasants and serfs, partly a self-conscious merchant class, already practised in universal trade to the north, south and east. His dominions were split up by ecclesiastical lands, above all by the Archbishopric of Cambrai on the borders of France and Germany — of Liège, spread out in a wide semicircle between Hainault and Luxembourg and reaching as far to the north as Maaseyk — of Utrecht whose eastern half was separated from the western by the large county of Gelderland, still a direct fief of the Empire. The bishoprics, above all Overyssel, the eastern half of Utrecht, Friesland and Groningen were technically still under the direct control of the Empire, but, like Gelderland, they had long in fact formed part of the political conglomerate of Burgundy. Even Cleves on the lower Rhine and its ruling dynasty submitted at least to the social leadership of the Burgundian Court.

[1] I use *Bourgogne* to distinguish this French part of the dominions from the more general *Burgundy* (TRANSLATOR'S note).

THE NETHERLANDS

These lands were united as little by the character of their people, of their speech, or of their economic development as they were by their political heritage. This in itself was a reason for the richness of their culture as also for the provocative variety of their political problems. Flanders, Artois and Brabant had long been devoted to manufacture; their seaports brought them into touch with the wide world and they lived on their thriving export and import trade, above all their commerce in wool and cloth. Here Italian trade from the south made contact with Anglo-Scottish and Hanseatic trade from the north. Westwards their connections stretched to Portugal and Castile, and eastwards, on the ships of the Hansa, far into the Baltic. In this eastern commerce too the Dutch and Frisians had long taken part in their own vessels; the towns of Overyssel, Kampen, Zwolle and Deventer acted in accordance with an old treaty with the Hanse, the rising merchants of Holland and Zeeland, on the other hand, in open competition. Fishermen and mariners needed salt and wood, and the whole of this flat land, so rich in cattle, had been forced for some time past to import wheat.

Politically the greater part of these lands belonged to the German Empire. Flanders, however, had fought itself free of France without emancipating itself altogether from the jurisdiction of the *Parlement* of Paris. But the treaty of Arras, the terms of which were designed to make satisfaction for the murder of Jean Sans Peur and re-establish peace with Charles VII of France, had assured an exceptional position for the Duke of Burgundy in relation to the French monarchy. Not only did he receive a definite guarantee of Boulogne, Artois and the districts of the Somme, but he was exempted from doing homage for any of his fiefs. This was tantamount to a total separation from the French kingdom. But the Burgundian dukes, for their part, continued to claim the highest place in France after the King himself. Thus the representatives of the lines of Orleans and Burgundy, Louis XI and the Duke, were both on the same level as the English King who still carried the title 'King of France'. The varying attitude of Burgundy to these two crowns was the result of a relationship

23

which, at first exclusively concerned with internal politics, had developed gradually into an external problem. Yet the Duke of Burgundy addressed the King of France as 'Your Majesty' when they met. For this very reason Charles the Bold dreamt of an independent kingdom of Greater Burgundy; it was to be created by gaining permanent hold on Gelderland, by joining the Netherlands to Franche Comté and Bourgogne through the Duchy of Lorraine, by aggression in Hapsburg Alsace and the lands of the predominantly peasant Swiss, in order to acquire a commanding position on the Vosges and the Jura. This yearning for a higher title and for European recognition brought Charles the Bold and the Emperor Frederick together, and at length persuaded the Duke to allow the betrothal of his daughter to Maximilian.

All these things played their part in the internal development of the land. The immediate goal of Charles's bold policy was the geographical completion of his estates; it was no less important for him to unite them internally, both by a closer personal tie to the dynasty and by the introduction of centralized administration in justice and finance.

Both intentions were in tune with the ideas of his leading ministers and the traditions of his family.

In many respects the growing state was essentially modern; varied economic enterprise and lively commerce brought with them highly developed forms of trade and a breadth of outlook comparable only to that of the contemporary Italian city-states. But in contrast to the Italian states with their historically generated, if unfulfilled, theory of nationality, and in still sharper contrast to the kingdoms of England and France, each well on the way to becoming nation-states — Burgundy in its political aspect still presented a truly medieval picture. Mixed in speech, the Burgundians shared with their neighbours on both sides of the Channel not only their ecclesiastical hierarchy, but a great part of their historic tradition and of their culture, both urban and feudal. So much the more was the dynastic principle to be the decisive influence in the unification of the state. This principle was strengthened by the later development of the custom of drawing State officials very largely from Franche Comté, or at least from a district different from the one in which they were to work. The learned recruits to this profession were some of them

24

drawn from the only university in the land — Louvain, but others came from farther afield. Schooled in Roman law, they in turn brought with them a higher and more universal conception of the state, which they were not altogether able to realize in practice. The feudal traditions of the Court were still too strong for them. These, combined with the chivalrous training that was still in fashion, bound the leaders of the local nobility both to the dynasty and to each other while at the same time, to a very great extent, preserving intact their relations with foreign lands. The wide network of political alliances was tightly drawn over all, and the scattered lands were brought ever closer together by a growing tendency towards the formation of a single state.

THE CULTURE OF THE BURGUNDIAN COURT

The Court itself, with its knightly tradition, was thus at first the chief factor in the unification of the Burgundian lands. These districts, the French no less than the German, were still and were long to remain under the control of the nobility. Towns and municipalities were welcomed and encouraged not only because they brought money into the land, and created or increased local prosperity, but because both as strongholds and as the seats of garrisons they had an actual military importance. But in spite of their far-reaching, if often disputed, rights of self-government, they had no part in the political direction of the country except in time of civil disturbance. Politics were the exclusive concern of the nobility; even the clergy played little part. Abbeys had nearly all become dependent on the Duke and the larger bishoprics were gradually engrossed by the dynasty. They had not of course wholly lost their independence thereby, and some, like Liège and Utrecht, could still be hotbeds of discontent. But many bishoprics were held by bastards of Burgundy, themselves with troops of children, and their submergence in the duchy was thus already foreshadowed. John of Burgundy, the Duke's brother, was Bishop of Cambrai in spite of his seventeen children; the sons of Philip the Good, David and Philip of Burgundy, succeeded in turn to Utrecht.

Only in the intellectual sphere the clergy maintained a

dominance based on their past strength. True that among the greater prelates family tradition and the secular cult of chivalry prevailed. But in the lower ranks of the clergy, in the lesser monasteries and convents, under the influence of a scholarly humanism derived from Italy, a new standard of culture, distinguished by intellectual honesty and profundity of thought, had emerged. This was the source from which the religious life of the time gained strength to resist degenerating influences and a resilience which was for ever renewed. The piety of the layman, revealed in the work of the Beguines, in the improvement of teaching and in such writings as *The Imitation of Christ*, put forth blossoms of an austere beauty. The chief centre of this religious cult was the eastern part of the old bishopric of Utrecht, the lower Frankish and lower Saxon lands.

Through its own Chapel, through its ecclesiastical activities, through the pulpit, the Court kept in touch with the possibilities of this intellectual revival, but it was nevertheless wholly dominated by the customs of chivalry. This knightly culture, in all its autumn glory, its slight but now perceptible over-ripeness, has but recently been evoked again by a latter-day offshoot of the fine intellectual stock of that land.[1] 'The Autumn of the Middle Ages' is not a general term, nor can it be used, except with certain modifications, of the towns and cities. But aristocratic society, still bound by the conventions of chivalry, was indeed mellowing fast towards decay. All that now concerns us is to discover whence those new shoots drew the strength, by which they so valiantly pushed their way from beneath the yellowing foliage.

The literary convention of Burgundian society was 'the last echo of the great medieval literature of France'. Outworn and stylized both in thought and form, here and there it yet retained a touch of its old bravura. The delight in allegory persisted. First the saints had been made to represent the various virtues; now virtues and vices were themselves personified and richly decked out with human attributes. The armour of the contemporary knight graced the limbs of Hercules, Jason, Paris and

---

[1] Professor Brandi refers to J. H. Huizinga's great work, *Herfsttij der middeleeuwen*, Haarlem, 1919. The literal translation of the title is *The Autumn of the Middle Ages*. English readers will, however, know it under the title which it bore when published in this country in 1924: *The Waning of the Middle Ages* (TRANSLATOR's note).

Alexander, no less than those of Joshua, David, Caesar, Arthur, Lancelot and Charlemagne. Honour, knight-errantry and fame were idealized in a manner as wearisome as it was natural and familiar. Ladies were creatures apart, like the jealously guarded daughters and sisters of the prince himself, for literary forms and court etiquette here reacted one upon the other. Not only Court chaplains and secretaries but the knights themselves contributed to this literature, from the major-domo, Olivier de la Marche, down to country gentlemen like Claude Bouton, who composed his *Miroir des Dames* as late as 1520. This was the reason for those celebrated libraries which the noblemen collected — that, for instance, of the *Grand Bâtard*, Antoine de Bourgogne, lord of la Roche in the Ardennes, of Bishop Philip of Utrecht, of Lodewijk van Gruthuys, First Chamberlain to Mary of Burgundy, of the dukes themselves at their palace in Brussels. French was spoken almost exclusively. Even the Fleming Chastellain wrote in French; it was used spontaneously by the German nobles who subscribed to this tradition, like the young princes of Cleves, Baden and the Palatinate, even by the Emperor's son Maximilian, and by his children and grandchildren.

The especial glory of the land at this time was the new art of painting on wood and this too must have derived its inspiration almost for certain from the miniature painting of northern France. Prayer Books of every kind now came from these provinces, Books of Hours which, with their exquisite decorations, are the showpieces of our libraries to this day. It is impossible not to feel that the warm personality of these Prayer Books bore some relation to the spiritual needs, if not of the actual possessor, then at least of the period. It was at this time that this form of art, characterized as it is by intense depth of feeling, found in the brothers Van Eyck and their successors a profundity and a radiance through which, as never before in the history of the arts, the inner warmth of the soul seems to find expression. Here as in the devout retirement of the Brothers of the Common Life,[1] the influence of the tranquil German countryside, which unrolls its green expanses from the Meuse to Flanders, may be clearly felt. Like the persuasive humanistic teachers who came from those same districts, the

---

[1] The *Fratres Vitae Communis*, founded by Geert Grote, about 1380, at Deventer (TRANSLATOR'S note).

painters too strove after an exceptional sincerity both in the observation and in the interpretation of what they had apprehended with their minds — even in painting there was an almost philological exactitude. Ghent, Bruges, Brussels, preserve to this day in their churches and almshouses the gems of this art. The career of Hans Memling proves that the best talents of the Rhineland were lured to the Netherlands; his paintings, completed in the seventies and eighties of the fifteenth century for the *Hôpital St. Jean* at Bruges, are perhaps the highwater mark of Burgundian art. In them too we have visible evidence of the interpenetration of this Franco-Burgundian culture by a German element. The sixteenth century was to bear the ultimate fruit of this union.

The influence of these masters on the famous tapestries, which were manufactured for export to all countries, cannot be overestimated. In these, too, that world of romance and myth, those figures of medieval chivalry lived again in all their radiant splendour. Nor did their influence count for nothing in the devices and processions of the dukes, in their masques and solemnities.

But the most significant and vital type of this Court and its life was its own highest honour, the Order of the Golden Fleece. This was at the same time the descendant of the Military Orders of the Crusades and the forerunner of the modern Court-decoration. On January 11th, 1430, his wedding-day, Philip the Good founded the Order, 'out of his love for chivalry and to protect and propagate the Christian faith'. The Duke collected about him the Princes of the Blood, the highest nobility of the land and one or two foreign rulers. The symbol chosen was the Golden Fleece of the Argonauts, celebrated in the story of Jason and in the whole cycle of medieval legends of Troy. It stood for adventure and knightly honour, the restless desire for action typified in the flint and steel, the *fusils* and *cailloux* which formed the chain of the Order. Converted to a Christian meaning it was the fleece of Gideon on which the heavenly dew had fallen. The knights wore scarlet robes lined with sables, and over all the heavy gold chain of the Order. They held their meetings in cathedral choirs and to this day in Nôtre Dame at Bruges or in St. Rombaut at Malines, in long rows above the choir-stalls or along the walls, there hang the coats of arms of those illustrious lords. 'Heretics, traitors and cowards before the foe' — these were excluded from the Order. The general council

28

kept watch even on the moral conduct of the knights, and at each meeting there was a general denunciation to which all, even the sovereign, were subject. One by one the knights went out and returned to hear submissively from the Chancellor of the Order the verdict of the Chapter either for praise or blame. The minutes of the Order show that for more than a century this proceeding was in force. The knights were, too, the leading councillors of the Duke; without their consent — and they had one and all the administration of justice in their own lands — he could not go to war.

The formal ideals of the Order reflected the attitude of the dukes to religion and morality. Theology played small part in them. Even towards Heaven, they bore themselves after the fashion of the Court, with formality and social correctitude. They kept the necessary fasts and vigils: they gave alms: with the same qualified generosity, they had masses read for the souls of all the Court, from a nobleman down to a scullion, graded according to rank — five hundred, three hundred or a hundred masses. The historiographer of Philip the Good once drew up the balance between the virtues and vices of his master and found, when he cast up the account, that the Duke was too good for Hell. As in the Chapter of the Golden Fleece, so also in ordinary life, the higher clergy were allowed to exercise their right of criticism freely. Once on St. Andrew's Day, at the castle of Hesdin, the Bishop of Cambrai preached before the Duke and Duchess and all their Court. He had, he said, met with a lady named 'Honour of Princes', who had been driven out of the Empire and out of France, nay out of Burgundy too, by four rude fellows. These four, whom he drew with unmistakable and graphic symbolism, were the vices of the Duke and his Court — sloth, luxury, flattery and exaction.

The *Fête du Faisan* in 1454 reflects in a manner, half grotesque and half majestic, the close cultural relationship between this Burgundian chivalry and the ideas of medieval France. It took place immediately after the fall of Constantinople, in the last year of the pontificate of Nicholas V, a time at which all Europe was filled with the idea of a Crusade. The Duke of Burgundy too wished to summon his nobility to the task; his own father, Duke John, had already lost his liberty, fighting against the Turks at the Battle of Nikopolis under Sigismund of Hungary. A series of great festivals at Court was designed to inspire the chivalry of Burgundy to new efforts in the service of Christendom. The festal Crown, conferring the presidency of the feast, was handed from one prince to another, from the Duke of Cleves to John of Burgundy, Count of Etampes, then to Duke Philip himself. Whole days passed riotously with tournaments and banquets, in the display of gorgeous robes and splendid spectacles. Adolphe of Cleves, Lord of Ravestein, appeared once in the dress of the Swan-knight, glistering white from head to foot. Velvet and silk, rich brocade, gold and silver bells, feathers, furs of all kinds, precious stones — all were shown off and made use of with a lavishness of which the portraits of the period give us but a dim reflection. The pleasures of the table were interlarded and spiced with spectacles of the most ostentatious kind. There was a magnificent representation of the Golden Fleece, with Jason on Colchis; there was the ceremony of an oath taken over the body of a noble bird — this time not over a roast peacock but over a live pheasant; this ceremony gave its name to the whole series of feasts. The walls were hung with tapestries showing the labours of Hercules, the tables gloriously spread with silken damask. Over the Duke's chair a splendid baldachino reared its height. Beside him stood a table loaded with costly gold and silver plate, crystal and glass. At the narrow side of the hall was the statue of a naked woman guarded by a lion. At the end of the table a spring of water gushed forth from a grotto encrusted with sparkling gems. The dishes were some of them brought in with ceremonial pomp, others let down from the ceiling. Without a break, without an end, one gorgeous spectacle followed another — farce and high symbolism strangely mingled. A fiery dragon flew through the room hotly pursued by a heron. After an almost wearisome series of such shows, followed the most important of all — the lament and exhortation of the Church. Olivier de la Marche, standing on the back of a huge elephant, himself recited this. To every Knight of the Order he pronounced the same command:

> Dear son, draw thou thy sword,
> For the glory of God and for thine own honour.

The herald of the Golden Fleece then read out the Crusader's oath, which was to be sworn by each knight. Each man took it to 'God, the Virgin Mary, his lady and the Pheasant'. As for the

Duke himself, he solemnly vowed to challenge the Sultan in single combat. At the very end a beautiful maiden, called 'God's Mercy', made her entrance, attended by twelve Virtues. She gave thanks to the knights and adjured them to keep their word. Immediately after dancing began, in which the twelve Virtues remained to take part.

Such festivities did not take place every day. Nevertheless the Court lived in an unreal world of fanciful imagery, of high-sounding words and braggart pretensions, and was surrounded by an immense barricade of ceremonial and formality. An order dating from this Burgundian period and doubtless from the pen of Olivier de la Marche, reappears in the Spanish language in 1545. Such forms must then have dominated Court life until far into the sixteenth century. The Court had its officers of the greater and lesser Chapel, such as the Grand Almoner, innumerable chaplains and a choir of trained singing boys and organ players; with the Chamberlain's office were connected all the personal servants of the ruler, who attended on him from the hour of his rising until his retiring, and divided among themselves the countless important privileges of handing him his shirt, or giving him the chain of the Golden Fleece. In kitchen and cellar prevailed the most detailed formalities as to how to hold a napkin or to cut and serve a loaf of bread. Then there was the marshal and all his following, and for all this army of servants and dependants a forest of regulations for their dressing, feeding, heating and lighting. Such was the impressive, sumptuous and yet wholly meaningless shell within which the Duke and his family lived out their lives.

How could the harsh reality of life penetrate into this world of dream?

If it is true of the outer circle of the devout in the later middle ages, that they did but disport themselves in the golden beams which streamed from the Holy of Holies, then it is no less true that these Burgundian tournaments were but a game of war, played with great noise and show. Faced as they were at Nikopolis with the elemental fury of a real battle, the chivalry of Europe failed. Yet it would be wrong not to recognize in this sport an education which bred fortitude and courage. Even in local feuds these lords acted with more coarseness and brutality than was to be expected from knights so finely decked with precious stones, plumes and fine linen. Philippe de Commines several times reports in his *Mémoires* that knights gained great honour to themselves by dismounting and joining in the conflict hand to hand. He hints too at the ill-concealed savagery of these uncontrolled lords, who casually burnt whole towns and villages, drowned their prisoners in hundreds, cut off the hands of poor devils and gave free rein to their lusts in a manner which shocks us even to-day. Charles the Bold is himself the type of this Burgundian knighthood — boastful, vain, recklessly brave, unbridled both in activity and in fantasy. Flaming ambition, and a sense of his own right to govern, stiffened by his education at Court, took a form in him which weighed down and utterly destroyed all other qualities.

He fought for that tract of land joining the five towns of the Somme, from Amiens to St. Quentin; he fought for the possession of Liège, for Lorraine, the connecting link between the Netherlands and Franche Comté; he fought for dominance on the Upper Rhine; he fought against the Swiss. Yet behind all these wars there was one governing idea; the formation, consolidation and confirmation of an effective state. And behind the actions of these noblemen, who dismounted and fought hand-to-hand in the mêlée, there was too the idea of organizing a self-willed nobility to take its place in this higher conception of things, for the honour of the new state.

MARY OF BURGUNDY AND MAXIMILIAN

When Charles the Bold fell before the walls of Nancy in 1477, fighting for a Lorraine which he had already won, it seemed that he had undermined rather than strengthened the Burgundian state. History has pronounced no final verdict on his character.

Not so on his country.

He had established the fundamentals necessary to its existence. Had his lands extended to Bresse and Savoy, they would have formed the natural corridor from southern to northern Europe. Yet even in their incomplete condition they survived not only the

32

violence of Charles the Bold himself, but the more serious test of a change of dynasty and several minorities. They continued to be the cradle of the great political coalitions of Europe. Holland and Belgium exist to this day, the descendants of the old Burgundian state. We need not linger over the details of the forty years war which this state managed to survive. Our only interest in this troubled time is that it showed more clearly than the peaceful reign of Philip the Good or the brief interlude of Charles the Bold, the strength and weakness of this conglomerate state. In the light of that knowledge we shall be able more easily to understand the conditions in which future rulers were to work. Nor must we overlook the fact that individual egoism or the deceptive interplay of European politics often obscured the essential needs of these lands or even concealed them altogether from the eyes of contemporaries.

A defenceless girl of barely nineteen, the princess of Burgundy, was in Ghent with her stepmother Margaret of York and her father's councillors, when the news of Charles's death was confirmed. Immediately his deadly enemy, Louis XI of France, began with unconcealed delight to make good his rights on the 'escheated' fiefs in France; he even encouraged a clumsy attempt to throw Flanders into his arms. Naturally enough the distant French duchy of Bourgogne could not be held and Lorraine reverted at once to its old ruler. In Gelderland, the important province rounding off the north-eastern frontier which Charles the Bold had won from his cousin Arnold, there appeared first John of Cleves and later Arnold's grandson, the adventurous Charles of Egmont, who set themselves up under French protection against Burgundian rule. Meanwhile in Ghent Mary's reign opened under tragic conditions, for the guilds, with scant regard for justice, brutally arrested her father's councillors Hugonet and Humbercourt, and, in spite of her entreaties, sent them both to the scaffold.

But the sky brightened with the coming of a splendid embassy from her betrothed, followed immediately by the eighteen-year-old Archduke himself, like a Prince of Fairy-tale. The people of Ghent set up triumphal arches and the crowds along the streets hailed him with cries of 'Emperor and more than Emperor!' Besides the nobility and the towns stood fast by the dynasty; the theory of a united state seemed established. In the frontier districts, too, there were valiant champions, to balance traitors like d'Esquerdes, lord of Crèvecoeur; the fate of Artois was decided more effectually by the behaviour of its nobles and townsfolk than by ancient laws. Maximilian was fortunate in the field. Both in 1479 at Guinegate, south of Thérouanne, and later, he defended the greater part of his wife's inheritance in the Netherlands and preserved it intact for his children.

These children were Philip, born in 1478, and Margaret, born in 1480. They became the centre of the political picture when on March 27th, 1482, at barely twenty-four years old and in the full flower of her youth, their mother, the Duchess, was killed in a hunting accident. She was 'lamented, wept and mourned by all her subjects and by all who knew her as never princess before' — so runs the inscription on the magnificent monument which used to stand in the lofty choir of Onze lieven Frowen Kerk at Bruges; the massive splendour of the lofty Gothic cathedral seems no more than one gigantic shrine for this single jewel.

Thus, while still a young man, Maximilian became merely guardian and regent for his children. With this his serious difficulties began; he was a stranger, not born in the land, needing foreign troops to maintain his position; moreover he was that ever unwelcome thing — a man determined to rule in earnest.

Maximilian's task was first to defend his lands against France and secondly to govern the scattered provinces, according to the intentions of Charles the Bold, as one united whole. To achieve this latter object he had to overcome one important obstacle; in 1477, under pressure, Mary had issued the 'Great Privilege', by which she had abandoned the constitutional unity of her lands, then but recently established. Maximilian must restore civil unity if he were not to see the whole state crumble asunder, as had the German Empire.

But the leading cities, above all the 'three limbs of Flanders', the ancient industrial and trading towns of Ghent, Ypres and Bruges, desired, in their short-sighted egoism, nothing so much as this disintegration. Brussels and Louvain stood by them. Very different was the feeling in the towns of the south and the remaining cities of Brabant, above all in Antwerp which was but newly rising to greatness at the expense of Bruges. Thus it was no division of race or speech which here found expression but rather one of economic interest. The people of Ghent, for instance, who allowed themselves to be politically protected and privileged by the King of France, yet demanded that Flemish should be spoken at Court. The Walloon province of Hainault, on the other hand, was second only to the northern districts, where Low German predominated, in its loyalty to Maximilian. And it was as much a sign of the waning trust which the ancient city of Bruges placed in its own future, as an insolent attack on the part of demagogues, when Maximilian, returning to the city as King of the Romans in 1488, was seized and made prisoner as soon as he confidingly set foot inside the walls. Deeper causes affected the economic attitude of the county of Flanders; of old it had been 'protectionist' in its attitude to English industry, while Antwerp, if one may use the expression, believed in free trade.

With the change of dynasty, the nobility naturally increased in importance. If it is an exaggeration to suggest that their lack of sympathy with Maximilian drove them into the arms of the French party, it is true that the greater number of them were conscious of a cultural connection with France. Maximilian was taken up with a hundred other cares, both in the Empire and in the Hapsburg lands, nor was he free from many human failings. He was not content to keep these lands both internally and externally united; swift and impulsive, he yielded to every temptation inherent in his over-sanguine temperament. Like many highly gifted men, he was altogether lacking in inner solidity of character. For instance, as soon as he was set free by the citizens of Bruges, he asserted that he had imperial warrant for breaking the terms of the peace which he had signed as the price of his liberty. This alienated the hitherto undecided members of the nobility; above all it lost him Philip of Cleves, Lord of Ravestein, who was a nephew of Philip the Good on his mother's side and ranked as the chief among the Princes of the Blood, as the descendants of the old dukes were called. It was typical of the old relationship between the county of Flanders and the dynasty, that here the Princes of the Blood regarded themselves as the natural regents, whereas they were willing to leave other districts to Maximilian.

We must linger yet a little over the Burgundian nobility of Maximilian's time, and form a clear conception both of their organization and of their cultural background. Although these noblemen played their part both at Court and in the government, yet they had not lost that ancient independence, by right of which they felt themselves the equals of the prince. Just as the Duke strove to attain full sovereignty although he was feudally dependent on France and the Empire, so also his nobility had supported the French Crown in the Anglo-Burgundian struggle for so many years that they too had in a certain sense acquired international significance.

Some of those who revolted against Maximilian left the country and returned to the French King as to their other legitimate lord. Philip of Cleves, after some wavering, withdrew to France, was made governor of Genoa, commanded a French fleet in the Mediterranean and landed once on Lesbos. Since he had also fought in the Flemish wars, he was able, when he at length returned home, to compile from his own experience a book on the art of war by sea and land — a striking monument to his wide culture. His palace has been recently restored and remains to this day the only survival of the old Burgundian nobility still to be seen in Brussels.

The nobility was thus partly internationalized, partly collected about the Court; but under the influence of this very Court the power of the nobility was further disseminated throughout the country. The Princes of the Blood married into the leading families and inherited their possessions; in the second generation they lost their 'honourable title' of Bastards and called themselves after their estates, like other noblemen. The nobles were for the most part not only rich in land and long-settled in their estates, but they had relieved the Duke of the most important offices in local administration — those of Governor, Stadhouder, *Grand bailli* and seneschal. By right of these offices they stood forth at the ducal Court itself as the hereditary representatives of the provinces. These attributes which were later to add so enormously to the importance of a Prince of Orange, an Egmont or a Horn, had already been acquired by certain of the nobility. Either by ducal appointment or by their own nomination they held the chief positions; they sat on the Council, belonged to the Order of the Golden Fleece, and were at the same time the natural leaders of their own lands.

Such were the Wassenaer in Holland, or in Zeeland the Borsele lords of Veere, who died out with Wolfart in 1487. In northern Brabant there were the Hoogstraeten and the Berghes, lords of Walhain and Zevenbergen; John of Berghes was First Chamberlain to the young Philip and governor of Namur. The southern family of Lalaing succeeded to the lands and titles of the Hoogstraeten. Antoine Lalaing, lord of Montigny, became in the right of his wife, Isabella of Culembourg, lord of Hoogstraeten and Borsele; his diary of his journey to Spain in Philip's suite shows that this youth of two-and-twenty was already a man of percipience and education.

On the Lower Rhine there was Cleves-Ravestein. In Brabant the house of Nassau had made itself rich and powerful. The office of seneschal in that province passed in 1504 from the hands of Engelbert of Nassau-Breda, who fought at Guinegate, into those of his nephew Henry of Nassau-Dillenburg. On the borders of Limburg there was the family of Horn, a scion of which house became a free prince as Bishop of Liège; so also later did Cornelius Berghes. In Flanders itself only one family is worthy of mention and it was unique in having its seat, like the aristocracy of the Italian cities, within the walls of a town; these were the lords of Gruthuys and Steenhuys in Bruges, famous for a palace which is still standing, for their books and their great wealth.

But the cradle of the great Burgundian nobility was the Walloon provinces of Hainault, Artois and Picardy. Here there was the family of Luxembourg, an offshoot of the imperial dynasty of Henry VII, which had grown great partly in France, partly in Burgundy. Hence, too, came Claude Bouton, Captain of the Guard and Master of the Household to Philip, Maximilian's son, and later to Ferdinand of Austria; in spite of his *Miroir des Dames*, written in French, his sympathies were Hapsburg and English. But the strongest supporters of the Hapsburg dynasty during these early years were the already influential families of Croy and Lannoy.

Jean de Croy, Bouteillier of France, had fallen at Agincourt in 1415, leaving his title and lands to John, lord of Chimay, and to Antoine, Comte de Porceau, Grand Chamberlain to Philip the

Good. Their sister was Jeanne de Lannoy, mother and grand-mother of many chivalrous gentlemen of this family. But the son of Antoine married Jaqueline de Luxembourg, herself a daughter of that Count de St. Pol, once Constable of France, who had ended his life on the scaffold in Paris in 1475, victim of the, for once united, animosity of Burgundy and France. Her son was Guillaume de Croy, Lord of Chièvres, on whose shoulders both the highest honours and the heaviest burdens were soon to be heaped.

Besides this strong support in the country itself, Maximilian had more resources abroad than Charles the Bold; he could rely on the wealth of the German Empire and the help of German princes — Albert, Duke of Saxony, Margrave Christopher of Baden and the Count of Werdenberg. Maximilian owed his greatest military successes to Duke Albert, whom he rewarded with the gift of Friesland, which was later inherited by his son, George the Bearded. Margrave Christopher, on the other hand, although he too, through his Hapsburg mother, was a cousin of Maximilian, made himself and his family fast in Luxembourg, where they supported the dynasty it is true, but clung none the less tenaciously to inherited ideas of independence.

All this support did not save Maximilian from many a serious defeat; still less did it shelter him from the temptations which the old relationship between Burgundy and France naturally pre-sented to him. Immediately on the death of his wife his fortune touched its nadir. The Estates, led by Ghent, allied themselves with France behind his back, by the second treaty of Arras in December 1482. By this agreement Maximilian was forced to send his only daughter, at barely three years old, to France to be educated as the Dauphin's bride. It was the price of peace. Immediately after Louis XI died. His successor Charles VIII was still a minor. Following the old Burgundian tradition, Maximilian at once united with the other tenants-in-chief of the French King in combating the pretensions of the Crown. As once Charles the Bold had allied with Guyenne and Brittany, so now Maximilian renewed the alliance with Brittany, hoping to win from the Duke, with the hand of his only daughter and sole heiress, almost the last of the great fiefs of the French Crown. Had the marriage come to pass the Hapsburg Dukes of Burgundy must have been involved even more deeply than their predecessors in the internal politics of France. But the fantastic plan was never realized. The bride, already promised, was reft away by the young King of France himself, an act which meant the shameless repudiation of his first betrothal, to Maximilian's daughter, Madame Margaret. For a little girl of nearly thirteen, who had learnt to think of herself as Queen of France, it was a deep humiliation.

But in the meantime Albert of Saxony had subdued Bruges and Ghent, Philip of Cleves had capitulated (1492), Franche Comté had been regained and peace was at hand. The terms evaded all problems by confirming political boundaries as they stood. Maximilian thus retained Artois and Charolais. On May 23rd, 1493, peace was concluded at Senlis.

PHILIP THE HANDSOME AND JOANNA OF CASTILE. BIRTH OF CHARLES

The French government had been eager for peace because Charles VIII was already imbued with the idea of a new undertaking. This enterprise, which was to mark an epoch not only in the history of France but in that of Europe, was the invasion of Italy. It was unnecessary to deck out this invasion in the guise of a Crusade. Brittany had been united to France, the French duchy of Bourgogne had been regained; when the House of Anjou became extinct the French Crown took over its fiefs and naturally enough extended the claim to Naples, itself theoretically a part of the Angevin heritage. Yet the French government was nevertheless embarking once again on a policy of universal significance. Not until 1443 had Alfonso of Aragon made ready to put an end to the incompetent Angevin rule in Naples. The French King's claim on that land involved him therefore not merely in the labyrinth of Italian politics, but brought the Valois dynasty for the first time into collision with a Mediterranean power, the House of Aragon, whose collateral branch ruled in Naples.

These events do not immediately concern us. For the moment we must stay in the Netherlands where Maximilian, shortly after his elevation to the imperial throne, had declared his sixteen-year-old son of age, and handed over to him the reins of government. The prince's task was the easier because the attention of France was for the moment fixed on Italy. Philip the Handsome, as he was called, opened his government in the traditional manner by a *Joyeuse Entrée* into Louvain on September 9th, 1494. As a native born prince he was in truth joyously received, and thanks to his father's recent victories he did not have to confirm the Estates in the Great Privilege of 1477, but was able to fall back on concessions formulated at an earlier time. In fact the salient features of a constitution covering all his lands were again confirmed. In foreign affairs too he was fortunate; after a short commercial war he concluded the favourable trading agreement with England known as the Intercursus Magnus in 1496, nor did this English friendship provoke further ill-feeling with France.

It was essential for him to avoid such ill-feeling.

But the advocates of this policy who, in order to pacify France, were prepared to go back on all that had previously been done, even in so important a question as that of Gelderland, were not so much the Duke and his circle as the nobility, who once again took their country's fate into their own hands. At Court there were of course the usual bad elements, ready to encourage Philip in every weakness, so that a new generation of Bastards of Burgundy would in all probability have to be provided for. But the government itself was in the hands of serious statesmen, the Princes of the Blood, and members of the families of Croy, Berghes and Lalaing.

Nor was Maximilian himself excluded. No longer guardian and regent, he was still head of the Hapsburg dynasty and Emperor. His policy was now almost exclusively dynastic, dominated by plans for the marriages of his children. He sought and found alliances which were to be decisive for the future history of Europe. Next to his own family, the ruling house of Spain held the highest place among European dynasties. Rich in daughters, it had already given a wife to the heir to the throne of Portugal and was shortly to do the same by the heir to the throne of England. But for his own children Maximilian thought neither of England nor of France, but only of Spain. Since French policy had taken so curious a turn in Italy, he felt that an alliance between himself and the King of Aragon was essential. As early as November 5th,

1495, he reached an agreement with this new ally in accordance with the needs of his European policy. On a visit to Innsbruck in the following year, Philip was confirmed in his father's opinion. And so came into being the most remarkable marriage contract in the history of modern Europe, a contract which was to divert the interests of the Netherlands far beyond the English Channel, far away from Germany, to remote worlds across the Ocean.

The connection with the Spanish Peninsula was not in itself new. Trading and dynastic relations had existed for generations. A princess of Portugal, Isabella, had married Philip the Good and been the grandmother of Mary; Maximilian's own mother had been a Portuguese princess. There was nothing essentially new in the agreement that Philip the Handsome should marry Joanna the second daughter of the Catholic King, and his sister Margaret, her only brother Don John. The first of these marriages was celebrated in the Netherlands on October 21st, 1496, the second in Spain early in 1497. Don John was young and sensual. Bride and bridegroom, too inexperienced for moderation, indulged their mutual passion to such lengths that Queen Isabella was warned. She refused to intervene; as Peter Martyr Anglerius tells us, she felt that man might not put asunder those whom God had joined. Within six months the prince died — of exhaustion as it was commonly reported. His memory long remained, a warning to his family.

Joanna was still not the heiress of the Spanish kingdoms. But when first her elder sister the Queen of Portugal, and shortly afterwards in July 1500 her only son Don Miguel, died, the prospect of a world-wide power opened, contrary to all expectation, before the eyes of the Duke and Duchess of Burgundy.

Hitherto the princely pair had lived in the Netherlands, chiefly at the ducal palace in Brussels. Here on November 15th, 1498, their first child, a daughter, was born. She was called Eleonore, after Maximilian's mother. Jean Molinet has left a description of the splendid baptism. A magnificent procession, rich in all the glory of old Burgundian ceremony, wound its way from the Castle to the Cathedral of Sainte Gudule, revealing to the insatiable eyes of the spectators all the joy in colour and glittering jewels which was so characteristic of the time. Towards evening the procession returned home, lit by countless torches and burning candles.

It was an occasion to which Rembrandt alone might have done full justice.

Soon the little princess had her own household. The emphasis laid on the personal importance of the royal family and its members was increasing; because of this, and because of the light it throws on the personnel of this new Hispano-Burgundian society, it is interesting to know what ladies were considered for the control of the baby's household. Two claimants came forward — Madame Halluvin, of the family of Commines and thus of old Burgundian stock, and Doña Maria Manuel who had married Maximilian's ambassador to Spain, the Bastard Baldwin of Burgundy. But in the end a third was chosen, Anne de Beaumont, who was of the King of Navarre's family and thus a Frenchwoman, although from the Spanish part of France.

In the following year the Court moved to Ghent, the ancient capital of the land and the city which had dominated Flanders for centuries. To this day the ruined Gravesteen broods above the town like a gigantic tree, about whose roots the houses huddle as though they were some honeycomb conglomeration of cells formed by an emulous but smaller breed of men. Not the Castello of the Este at Ferrara, not the palace of the Gonzaga at Mantua, tower so defiantly above their cities. Yet the Castle had long been deserted by the Court. In the pleasant open space below the Gravesteen they had built a modern palace, of which nothing now remains save the street-name *Prinsenhof* and some fragments of wall built into modern houses. There was something magnanimous in the Court's decision to return to Ghent, that irrepressible and often rebellious city which still defied their power. And it was symbolic too that here, in the very heart of the old duchy, in the shadow of the proud ancestral castle, a prince was born who was to fulfil all the traditions of Burgundy, a prince who for the first five-and-twenty years of his life had no other desire than to be a Burgundian nobleman. On February 24th, 1500, Saint Matthias's Day, the Infanta gave birth to a son; he was given the name of the last native Duke of Burgundy, Charles.

This child, who was to carry the Hapsburg dynasty to the height of its power, was hardly yet a Hapsburg. Among all his thirty-two ancestors, one line alone was derived from German stock — that of his grandfather Maximilian and his forefathers the

Emperor Frederick III, the Archdukes Ernest and Leopold who had fallen at Sempach. All his other ancestors were not of German blood; Duke Ernest's wife had been Cimbarca of Masovia, Frederick III's wife, Eleonore of Portugal, Maximilian's, Mary of Burgundy. These, with Charles's mother the Infanta Joanna, came all from the dynasties of Castile, Aragon and Portugal, of Visconti, Bourbon and Valois.

But on his mother's side Charles had another and a more sinister heritage.

In July 1501 Joanna gave birth to yet another child in the Netherlands. Then with her husband she went back to her home in Spain; on their way across France, Philip, as the first peer of the realm, presided at a meeting of the Paris *Parlement*, and when they reached Spain Joanna was solemnly acclaimed as heiress to the thrones of Castile and Aragon. At the end of a year Philip hurried back to the north, to Austria and Flanders. Joanna was expecting another child and on March 10th, 1503, she was delivered at Alcala of her second son, who was called Ferdinand after his Spanish grandfather. Although everything possible was done to spare her, she wasted away with longing for her husband. Prevented from joining him, she flew into frenzied passions with her attendants, and at the castle of La Mota near Medina del Campo, she spent night after night watching by the lowered portcullis, no one daring to come near her. In this plight her mother Isabella found her, out of her mind and wildly raving; it was a moment of unutterable anguish to the great Queen who was to leave this daughter as her only heir. At last, with every possible precaution, they allowed the young woman to go back to the Netherlands. Once more in Brussels, she gave birth to a third daughter, Mary. But more dangerous to Joanna's over-sensitive nature than the strain of these confinements, following all too rapidly one upon the other, more dangerous than anxiety and travel, was her husband's infidelity. She, on her side, made his life unbearable with her boundless jealousy and eccentric actions. She wanted him for herself alone, and when her suspicions were but slightly aroused by a pretty Flemish girl, she attacked and disfigured her with a pair of scissors. In Spain, at Torquemada, on January 14th, 1507, she bore her last child, Katherine. Like all her other children, the princess was strong in mind and body and lived to be seventy. But at the time of her birth the mother was far sunk in hopeless madness.

No doubt now remains of this fact. Neither the efforts of the Castilian Comuneros to set her up in later years as legitimate Queen in place of her son, nor the explanations of historians can alter the facts. Joanna's mind had always been unbalanced, her heritage was tainted; her Portuguese grandmother, Isabella, had died mad. Possibly a tranquil life would have preserved the frail web of her sanity longer untorn, but to add to those sufferings of which we have already spoken, the sudden death of her husband on September 25th, 1506, gave the last blow to her tottering reason. For many months she would not be parted from his corpse, but followed it night after night in ghastly procession by torchlight, stopping repeatedly to have the coffin opened that she might be sure his body was still within. Only with difficulty did her father at last persuade her to lay Philip's bones to rest and withdraw herself to the beautifully situated castle of Torde-sillas near Valladolid. Here she passed her life with a few attendants, becoming daily more careless of her own person and refusing even the ministrations of the Church.

In this condition, years later when he was King of Spain, Charles once again set eyes on his mother. His father he barely knew. As orphans, therefore, the children grew up, Ferdinand and Katherine in Spain, Charles, Eleonore, Isabella and Mary in the Netherlands. They had their little Court and their own house-hold. Among the many documents relating to the management and finances of the Court now in the Brussels archives, there are one or two notes of the expenses of the household of 'the Arch-duke Charles, Duke of Luxembourg' — this was his first title — 'of Madame Lienor and Madame Isabeau, his sisters, in Mecheln on January 27th, 1503' — the household, therefore, of three children of whom the eldest was only four. A little more informa-tion comes from the accounts of Lille; here we learn of an ABC and a doll's bed for Isabella, of a clavichord for Charles and the growing Eleonore. The earliest portraits of the children are of this period. Their parents' place was taken by high state digni-taries and carefully chosen attendants. But when Philip the Handsome died the Estates, as early as November 16th, 1506, entreated the Emperor to take over the government. At one and the same moment Maximilian appointed both a regent for the Netherlands and a foster-mother for his grandchildren, in his daughter Margaret.

THE ARCHDUCHESS MARGARET

Early tried by sorrow, the Archduchess Margaret had returned home after the death of her husband and the birth of a still-born child. Within a few years she contracted a second marriage with Philibert, Duke of Savoy. This was a time of unbroken happiness, which grew yet more radiant in the light of memory. Fate owed her some happiness, and for a space she found herself leading the life of a care-free and beloved wife in a green and beautiful land. But in 1505 her second husband too was torn from her in the flower of his youth. At twenty-four she was a widow for the second time, and childless. Her widow's dower was partly in the country near Faucigny, south of the Lake of Geneva, at the foot of Mont Blanc. But she passed her time at Bourg en Bresse on the borders of Franche Comté, occupying herself in rebuilding the church at Brou where her husband's body rested. Both then and later she devoted all her care and all her fertility of invention to the beautification of this monument to her dead love, gathering about her artists, architects and men of letters. She herself was immortalized by the sculptor Conrad Meit of Worms. 'Fortune infortune fort une' was one of her melancholy devices, referring perhaps to the fickleness of fortune, but more probably to the fact that past happiness was now nothing but the source of her present misery.

Her father and brother alike advised her to marry again. Henry VII of England sought her hand and later the Duke of Norfolk stormed her defences with wearisome persistence. But always she refused — 'be the suitor never so virtuous, rich, gifted or well-born'.

> Tant que je vive mon cueur non changera
> Pour nul vivant, tant soit il bon ou saige,
> Fort et prudent, de haut lignaige.
> Mon choix est fait; autre se ne fera.
> Tant que je vive . . .

We know much of this remarkable woman, and even the exaggerated compliments of her contemporaries cannot dim her exquisite picture. Over her tomb at Brou she was twice depicted, once as Duchess of Savoy with a crown on her head, once as a woman with long flowing curls. But neither white stone nor the monochrome reproductions of the well-known portrait in oils, which shows her wearing the muslin cap fashionable in her time, give any conception of the glittering magic of her golden hair, shining through the transparent head-dress, or of the vitality of her light brown eyes. Her features are too round for perfection, but the animation of her face makes up for all. Many of her letters have survived, among them her full and interesting correspondence with her father, the Emperor. In these the topics discussed were predominantly political; sometimes father and daughter disagreed and Maximilian often pitched his demands too high. But he had his jokes too. Newly a widower, he declared to her that 'now he could become a priest or even Pope' — an ambition which he did in fact try to realize — 'and perhaps a saint into the bargain so that after his death she would have to pray to him which would give him great satisfaction'. In the political world Margaret was later to show herself one of the greatest rulers of the century, firm in her judgments, shrewd in her knowledge of men and endowed with almost virile energy.

This was the woman to whose care the education of the royal children was now entrusted.

When Maximilian summoned her to the Netherlands in the spring of 1507, she built at Malines, opposite the old-fashioned ducal residence where the children lived, a modern palace. To judge by the inventories of her goods, it was decorated and organized with equal distinction and good taste; the wing which flanks the street is the earliest Renaissance building in the Low Countries, but the semi-Gothic halls behind were spacious and well-lit. Here she surrounded herself with books and works of art, with a Court of distinguished men. Barend van Orley was her chief painter, and she herself personally conducted artists, like Albrecht Dürer when he travelled through the town, over her apartments and through her collections. She brought with her from Savoy and Franche Comté some of her more distinguished advisers; such were the Lord of Marnix, whom Dürer

46

drew, and Laurant de Gorrevod, later an influential man at the Court of Charles V. But chief among them was Mercurino Gattinara; he had been her chief legal adviser in Savoy, a man of profound education, immense energy and an all-embracing idealism in politics. Margaret was thus equally well-armed for political government and for the direction of a large household. In her the children found not only love, but the valuable example of a truly noble lady. They addressed her as 'My lady aunt and good mother', and at Vienna an undated letter from the little Eleonore is preserved. It is written in courtly French and runs as follows: 'Since our joys are your joys, I write to tell you that our grandfather has visited us, which was a very special joy to us.' The English ambassador once caught a delightful glimpse of all three children, joyously absorbed in the festivities of midsummer day. From other sources we hear of banquets, expeditions, hunting parties. All this took place in the quiet little town of Malines over which, then as now, the massive tower of Saint Rombaut soared to Heaven, like the promise of a great future.

Charles's debt of gratitude to his aunt must rest on surmise alone, for the sources are lacking. Yet there is no room to doubt but that the debt was heavy.

The same is true of the other great figure who dominated Charles's boyhood. His great teacher, Adrian of Utrecht, was at this time deacon of Saint Peter's at Louvain and representative of the rector of the University. He was a theologian by vocation, serious, thoughtful, but kindly and conscientious in little things. From his own previous intellectual achievement, and from his and his pupil's later development we may infer what seeds the teacher sowed during those early years in the untilled mind of his pupil. Adrian was a product of that religious atmosphere which derived its quality from the Brothers of the Common Life; he was one of those to whom the conventional practices of the Church were but a means towards a life of devotion. The piety which was Charles's very being had its roots in the teaching of this man.

From his earliest youth the prince's actual instruction was entrusted to men from the Netherlands or Spain, Robert of Ghent, Adrian Wiele, Juan de Anchiata, and the distinguished Spaniard, Luis Vaca, to whom Charles later proved his gratitude. In his

47

education, history was not omitted and he read both the chronicles of his own land and the deeds of his forefathers.

But, unless we are much mistaken, the young prince, in spite of his physical delicacy, was more drawn to bodily than to intellectual exercise. Doubtless the prejudice was encouraged by the pages of honour who shared his education — young Balançon, John of Saxony, a son of Duke George who predeceased his father, Frederick von Fuerstenberg. Besides these Maximilian Sforza was sometimes his companion, as well as several members of the native nobility of the Netherlands. To his grandfather's joy he soon learnt to ride and hunt, and mastered with enthusiasm and skill all the arts of tourney, such as splintering a lance without losing his seat on horseback and every kind of shooting and fighting. These things were the talk of all about him: they were the common spectacle and admiration of his time. If Charles had any one quality which was to provoke admiration for years to come, it was his skill in horsemanship and jousting. The will dominated the fragile body.

Charles de Poupet, Lord of La Chaulx, was also among the prince's instructors; later Charles was to give him a seat on the inner council and entrust him with many an important mission. At that time, knightly exercise, service at Court and diplomacy still went hand in hand.

For his introduction into Court life and the higher spheres of politics Charles had to thank another member of the old Burgundian nobility, Guillaume de Croy, Lord of Chièvres, his governor and Grand Chamberlain. In the Brussels Museum the revealing portrait of Chièvres, with his intelligent, observant eyes, makes a fine counterpart to that of Margaret. The changing and often hostile relations between the Archduchess and the Burgundian nobility cannot have failed to make their impression on Charles; for that very reason he was probably all the more ready to fall under the spell of the single-minded Burgundian outlook of Chièvres, both on life and politics. Making every allowance for later influences, no one could reasonably expect a young man educated in such courtly surroundings, to prefer the company of noble ladies and the grave Adrian to that of an experienced man of the world, like the haughty Lord of Chièvres.

The family of Croy are not new to us. As early as Maximilian's first regency, Chièvres had been a knight of the Golden Fleece, a councillor and a Gentleman of the Bedchamber. His name occurs too in the records of the wars. But in accordance with a taste certainly more congenial to him, he was in 1500 sent for many months to France as ambassador; later, in 1501, he accompanied Busleyden, the teacher and representative of Philip the Handsome, on a mission to Lyons. For the rest he contented himself with the exercise of his own high office in Hainault until he was recalled to the Court in 1504, and in 1505, actually appointed governor during Philip's absence in Spain. He rejoiced at the same time in the trust of the French government and the Hapsburg dynasty. In 1509 Maximilian made him governor to the young Charles. Until that moment the office of governor, in the hands of the Count of Chimay, had been no more than a place of honour at Court. But now the instruction of the child, already on the threshold of his tenth year, assumed political importance. Chièvres was to establish an influence all the more effective because he remained at Charles's side until his death.

At the same time two Spaniards entered Charles's household, both in spiritual capacities; these were the almoner Doctor Mota and soon after him Alonso Manrique, Bishop of Badajoz. Michael Pavye became Charles's confessor and at Margaret's instigation the whole Court was reorganized. But the direct influence of Chièvres continued to be far more important than that of any other person. Where lay the secret of his charm, of his high repute? In his lust for power and greed for reward Chièvres was no better than any other man of his time — and no worse; no one for instance was more open to bribery than the Emperor Maximilian. But Chièvres had one exceptional characteristic: his political life was frankly guided by the ancient traditions of the old Burgundian nobility, now once again in close sympathy with the Hapsburg dynasty. He was determined to prevent devastating and costly wars with France, in Gelderland or in Liège, and he was cautious in his dealings with Margaret and her party who leaned, for economic reasons, towards an English alliance. He was clever in his handling of Maximilian, clever above all in gauging the importance of each political force, which came into the sphere of his activities either in internal or foreign politics. Many years after his death Charles once declared to Contarini that he had early learnt to value the ability of Chièvres and had therefore subordinated his will wholly to that of the minister. Meanwhile the Grand Chamberlain slept in the same room as the growing prince and had his ear at every hour of the day: small wonder that his influence was boundless.

Contemporary reports of foreign diplomats on the young Duke at this period are numerous but unilluminating. It is more important therefore in tracing his development to follow the actions which the government committed in his name and to examine the manner in which he himself was treated. Only in this way shall we understand the particular conditions which went to form his character and to determine his later independent actions.

At Lyons in the summer of 1501, on that mission at which Chièvres was present, a marriage had been arranged between Charles and Claude, the daughter of Louis XII. At that time Charles was already known to be the heir to the Spanish Crowns, and the French government were prepared to offer Brittany, Milan and Naples as a dowry for the bride — a high price. Yet this apparently mutual solution of a perennial problem proved to be no more than a mere suggestion for a possible future alliance. Both sides held to it for a couple of years and as late as 1505 the Cardinal of Amboise received at Hagenau from Maximilian's hands the fiefs of Milan and Pavia for his King — to be passed on to his daughter Madame Claude and her betrothed bridegroom Charles. Anxious to secure the Spanish inheritance without trouble, Charles's councillors sought friends on every side. When, yielding at last to the insistence of the French Estates, Louis XII quashed the Burgundian marriage and gave his daughter to wife to Francis, Duke of Angoulême, his heir, Charles's government turned at once towards England and in 1506 sanctioned even the unfavourable commercial treaty known as the Intercursus Malus and approached the question of a dynastic alliance. It was typical of the complicated diplomacy of the time that in those very December days in 1508 during which Margaret brought about the treaty of Cambrai between her father and France, she was also confirming the preliminary negotiations for a marriage between Charles and Mary, sister to that prince who in May 1509 ascended the English throne as Henry VIII.

Gradually, under the influence of Spanish politics, the relations between France and the Netherlands grew calmer. For in the struggle for the regency of Castile in which the Hapsburg dynasty and the great majority of the nobility were ranged on one side, and the King of Aragon on the other, Maximilian naturally looked for help to the neighbouring kingdom of France, itself at war with this same Ferdinand of Aragon in Naples. Nevertheless the government of the Netherlands was independent of Maximilian and remained officially neutral. It maintained this position even when the Holy League of 1511 brought into being against France that astonishing coalition between all the powers which had an interest in Italy. Even England, once again afraid that the French would induce their Scottish friends to attack her, sent troops to assist in the reduction of Navarre.

Henry VIII amused himself by following the old heroic tradition of English Kings, crossing the Channel in person and challenging the French in Artois at the head of well-paid German troops. This was the first open appearance in European politics of the King who was to become so important in the coming decade; surrounded by his German mercenaries he cut a portly, jovial figure, his manners perhaps, for a prince, almost too free. On the day on which the issue was to be decided a new-comer was suddenly and joyfully acclaimed by the German troops; it was the Emperor Maximilian himself, offering to serve the English King for a hundred ducats a day. So once again it was Maximilian who won the day at Guinegate on August 16th, 1513. The Netherlands, which had studiously remained neutral, profited the most by this war. But in a letter to his grandson written early in September 1513 Maximilian gave expression to the true state of feeling between the dynasties; here he referred to the French as the 'hereditary enemies of our house' — 'anchiens et encoires naturelz ennemis de nostre maison de Bourgogne'. On the other hand Louis XII had called on Charles to help him as his true vassal, even before the outbreak of hostilities. He later excused him his duty because of his extreme youth. On this campaign the English took possession of the two episcopal towns of the land, Tournai and Thérouanne.

But these remarkable English gains on French soil in the heart of Artois are not the chief object of the historian's attention during those autumn days of 1513. More important were the events in the background of the conflict, which were slowly bringing Charles into contact with the political life of his people. The two powers which were struggling to dominate him now stood forth openly. The old adherents of Philip the Handsome in Castile, who from that time onwards were the implacable enemies of Ferdinand of Aragon, now supported the French party in the Netherlands. Several of Charles's closest attendants belonged to this group. But as Maximilian and Ferdinand drew closer to each other again, Ferdinand began to see that it would be both advisable and possible to undermine his opponents in Burgundy. For this purpose he dispatched spies and counter-intrigants — Juan de Lanuza and the son of one of his own bastards, Juan of Aragon. These stood out in open opposition to Chièvres and his adherents. On the other hand some correspondence of the Castilians and their friends with France was discovered and the agent of these intrigues, Diego de Castro, placed under arrest. Feeling her position insecure, Margaret did not hesitate. After first discussing matters with her father and then more thoroughly with the English government, she gathered the results of both these inquiries into a coherent whole and on October 19th issued the *Ordonnance* of Lille. It was an open attack on the Burgundian nobility, for it gave to Maximilian, Ferdinand and Henry VIII, acting each through a representative, full control of Charles. The Emperor sent the Count Palatine Frederick, Ferdinand the Señor de Lanuza, Henry VIII Floris Egmont, Lord of Isselstein. Among these three, the dominating spirit was undoubtedly the Count Palatine. Great were now the political opportunities open to the Germans at Court!

Margaret meanwhile developed her policy by writing to her nephew a very flattering letter in which she painted the glories of the English Court in glowing terms. His presence, she said, was all that it lacked. These then were the circumstances in which Charles made his first journey abroad — his first State visit, to the man whom he now seriously regarded as his future brother-in-law. This visit was the earliest personal recollection of which his memoirs were later to tell. Lanky in person, reserved in manner, Charles had yet a quiet dignity which made an immediate impression at the English Court.

Strengthened by the success of her measures, Margaret dared yet more. To prove her opinions beyond all doubt to Ferdinand of Aragon, she decided to arrest the chief leader of the Castilian emigrants, Don Juan Manuel, once the closest adherent of her dead brother. Having gained her father's approval of this move, on January 17th, 1514, she had the grandee carried off prisoner to the castle of Vilvorde, north of Brussels. A storm of indignation followed this deed. But for Margaret the worst moment must have been that of receiving a deputation from the knights of the Golden Fleece on behalf of their brother in the Order: the deputation was headed by her nephew Charles himself. Dressed in the robes of the Order, he seemed, like his father before him, to be one with the nobility, body and soul. The great lords protested against a breach of the privileges of the Order; painful recriminations and heated arguments ensued. Margaret addressed herself first to her nephew, appealed to the Emperor's authority and upbraided him for intervening. Then almost scornfully she spoke to the knights. 'If she were a man and not a woman', she said, 'they might whistle for their privileges.' She refused to be intimidated, but perceptibly she was losing control of the situation.

The solution which was at length found was that of handing over Manuel to the Emperor. Thus far at least Margaret stood to her guns. But her position was not only weakened by her own wavering opinions; the passage of events played its part. Her father had, without consulting her, negotiated secretly for Charles's marriage to a French or a Hungarian heiress. The English discovered the fact before Margaret was herself informed, and did not hesitate to give Charles's bride, the now marriageable Princess Mary, to the newly-widowed Louis XII. Great was the disgust of the Netherlands, where the English marriage had always been popular. Besides which, the campaign of Tournai had provoked ill-feeling among all the nobles of the Netherlands who had entered Henry's service. Soon there was no more talk of carrying out the decisions issued at Lille. The nobility on the other hand pressed earnestly for the declaration of Charles's majority.

There were many changes at Court. The younger princesses were expected to serve Maximilian's dynastic schemes, whereas Chièvres, with greater intelligence and a clearer perception of the immediate interests of Burgundy, wished to solve the problem of Gelderland by marrying one of them to Charles of Egmont, and intended the other for the Duke of Lorraine. He planned in vain. On May 2nd, 1514, the eight-year-old princess Mary left Malines to rejoin her grandfather in Austria, whence one day she was to be married to a son of the King of Hungary. A full month later Princess Isabella was betrothed in Brussels by proxy to King Christian II of Denmark. Next summer, at the age of fourteen, the little girl left the Netherlands in the company of the Danish ambassador for her new home — or more truly for a wedded life of indescribable unhappiness of which we have not heard the last. Charles had contracted a fever at the wedding festivities and once again Margaret had to fulfil the office of a sick-nurse. But for the rest, her domestic task as foster-mother of the orphan children was at an end.

As regent, too, she had for the time being reached the end of her powers. Even earlier than this she had written despairing letters to her father, declaring once in 1511 in a sentence which she subsequently crossed out, that she did not know which way to turn. She had sacrificed everything to her task, she lamented, and now she wished she had never been born. During the last months irritation and wounded pride mingled with her plaints. Without consulting her, Maximilian agreed to the emancipation of Charles. All he stipulated was that his own pension and a considerable 'honorarium' should be guaranteed to him. With Charles's majority the regency came to an end, and Margaret's political role was for the time being played out.

CHARLES BEGINS TO RULE. CHIÈVRES

And in truth on January 5th, 1515, in the Parliament Hall at the castle of Brussels, Charles, Duke of Burgundy, was solemnly proclaimed of age. In Castile, on the other hand, he was by the terms of a treaty, to be represented by his grandfather, Ferdinand of Aragon, until he completed his twenty-fifth year.

After the declaration of his majority Charles made a royal progress through his lands to receive the homage of his subjects. His movements can be followed in the dispatches of foreign

CHARLES V AS A BOY

ambassadors, for they now flocked to his Court and were received on the course of his journey, now here, now there, so that their accounts come from almost every quarter of the land. The people of the Netherlands enjoyed the festivities no less than they had enjoyed the *Joyeuse Entrée* of Philip the Handsome twenty years before and many earlier celebrations. Life at Court, once Charles returned to Brussels, regained a focal point and a particular style. In the ducal palace, which has since disappeared, Charles and Eleonore occupied different quarters, each with their own household.

As in Philip's time the nobility controlled the government to the exclusion of almost all other influences, and again as in that time they set their mark on the outer appearance of Court life. Banquets, joustings and hunting parties were the order of the day. Henry of Nassau dispensed princely hospitality, Chièvres issued invitations to hunting dinner-parties at his castle of Heverle on the Dyle, the Count Palatine splintered a lance with Charles de Lannoy. He challenged him merely to decide a question newly raised at Court as to whether music was effeminate. Standing forth in defence of music, the Count Palatine sought to prove his point all the better by laying down the exceptionally hard conditions of the 'German tournament': this meant that instead of charging upon each other with flexible lances which splintered easily and were each tipped with a wreath, they were to use seasoned lances and heavy saddles so that both horse and rider risked life and limb. The Count Palatine was victorious but even his horse fell in the end and he bore for many years afterwards the marks of his injuries.

The whole personnel of Court and Bedchamber was re-organized. The orders and lists of 1515 and 1517, together with various other regulations, provide some picture of the scope and cost of that vast shell of ceremony in which the young Duke passed his life. Almoners and chaplains, musicians and choristers pass in procession before us; the Grand Chamberlains, Guillaume de Croy and Antoine Lalaing, lord of Montigny, with the lesser chamberlains, Gorrevod, Gaesbeck, Egmont, Beaurain and Sempy, both of the family of Croy, Molembais and Maingoval, both of the family of Lannoy; next the learned councillors, chief among them Jean de Sauvage, lord of Escaubeque in Flanders, Adrian of

Utrecht, Professor at Louvain, Philippe Naturel, Chancellor of the Order, Carondolet, Dean of Besançon, and Gerard de Pleine, lord of La Roche, who was also *Maitre des Requêtes*, or judicial adviser. Then followed the masters of the household and of the ceremonies, with the gentlemen of the *Paneterie*, of the cellar and the stable. Among these too there were many names which were to recur later — Ferry de Croy, lord of Roeulx, chief Master of the Horse, Guillaume Carondolet and Charles de Lannoy, assistant Masters of the Horse. Among the other attendants on Charles there were many ambitious scions of families already high in the ducal service — Gorrevod, Rye, St. Pol, Courrières, Sauvage, Lannoy and Montfort. As well as the Burgundians there were Spaniards, all hopeful of what the future might hold in store for them — Guevara, Juan de Zuñiga and Diego Manuel, son of the arrested Don Juan. Among the bedchamber staff there were several physicians, the best known of these being the humanist Marliano, who invented for Charles the proud device: '*Plus oultre*' — symbolic of ambitions stretching far beyond those of other men, beyond the pillars of Hercules, which are so often represented in drawings of his device, under the words *Plus Ultra*.

It would be hard to estimate the annual expenditure of so populous and opulent a Court. Figures must be accepted with the greatest caution for there were annual pensions as well as daily salaries and almost all offices were paid in kind as well. Only by converting the sums into some approximate relation to the buying power of to-day can any true conception be formed, and the accuracy of such approximations is always doubtful. But allowing that the buying power of actual bullion was about five times what it is to-day, we still have an expenditure of roughly ten thousand gold marks a day and of more than three and a half million in the year, counting pensions and payments in kind. To this figure numerous incidental expenses should be added. Reliable accounts show that Charles spent not less than three hundred thousand gold marks on his clothes in less than eight months. Furthermore, one must not forget the fantastically expensive appointments of banquets, processions and journeys for the prince and the outlay on the Order of the Golden Fleece with its feats and tourneys. By this reckoning we find that the little land parted every year with a sum of many millions for the Court alone.

Splendid works of art and costly hangings embellished every room, and in every aspect of the prince's life there was the same disproportionate outlay on sumptuous and valuable things, the same lavish indulgence of all the senses. The *Diner magnifique* at the first Chapter of the Golden Fleece held by Charles was so heavy that the greater number of the knights missed Vespers afterwards, some because they were ill, others because they were still at table. Nevertheless the Court had a good reputation; it was thought to be ostentatious but not lax.

The Archduchess Margaret at Malines was no longer regent; but she remained, surrounded by her own Court, the first lady of the land, daughter of the Emperor and Mary of Burgundy. She could still be approached for political ends, she was still favourable to her old friends, above all to the English party and the English ambassador.

But Chièvres, on the other hand, who had hitherto passed much of his time in opposition, now bore the full responsibility of the government. He was equal to the task. With Sauvage and probably also with Adrian of Utrecht, he formed the inner council, while the outer circle consisted of the knights of the Order and the higher dignitaries of the Court. Chièvres too controlled the disposition of grants voted by the Estates; having clamoured for Charles's majority the Estates proved themselves willing to support his government with unaccustomed generosity. In the country at large Chièvres made good use of Charles's initial visits to exploit all the hopes and ambitions which the emancipation of a young prince naturally evoked. On the other hand he had to reckon on probable opposition from the Emperor while, as a result of recent events, he had taken up his stand almost openly between France and Aragon.

It so happened that during those very days which saw the emancipation of Charles, Louis XII died in France on January 1st, 1515. This event brought to the throne a young ruler who was to be henceforward a decisive influence in the life of Charles himself — Francis I. As Duke of Burgundy and the highest vassal of the Crown, Charles was asked to the Coronation. He excused himself but sent as his representatives Henry of Nassau and

Michel de Sempy, with some other lords. They were to use the occasion for discussing the political relations of the two countries, the problem of Charles's fiefs in Flanders and Artois and his rights to the long-lost French duchy of Bourgogne. Cautiously they were to hint at a marriage between Charles and Renée, second daughter of Louis XII and sister-in-law to Francis. For a dowry, Charles had his eye on Milan — with Maximilian's help — as well as money and rights of inheritance. The embassy arrived too late for the Coronation and had to waste weeks in negotiations over the marriage. Illuminating reports of all that passed have survived. Francis was good-humoured but firm. At a ball at the Duchess of Vendôme's he spoke long with Nassau and Sempy. They said to him, 'Your Majesty is as young as our prince; you are both blank pages and could together do much for Christendom'. Francis did not agree merely for form; he swore on his honour as a knight that he was not second to Charles in his care for the weal of Christendom. Under the new King the ladies of the Court were already beginning to play their part in society; soon they were to trespass into politics. Now they stormed Nassau with questions about his master, his titles and his possessions. Nassau answered cautiously but clearly for he thought he had information that the King of Aragon too was seeking the hand of Renée for his younger grandson, Charles's brother the Infant Don Ferdinand. In fact Nassau's diplomacy won the field from this rival.

Nor was this triumph insignificant, for the King of Aragon left no stone unturned to secure a great future for his favourite grandchild, the Infant Don Ferdinand, who had been educated in Spain and who carried his own name. Thus years before when a French alliance had first been suggested to him — probably by the regent Anne — he had jumped at the prospect, and by ingeniously exploiting the ambitions of Maximilian in Upper Italy he had won him over to the side of his younger grandson. It was curious how the territorial greed of the two grandfathers played the cards into the hands of the French government.

For this very reason the other results of the Paris negotiations were extremely meagre. We know something of the last problems they discussed; should the French break the treaty, the towns of the Somme and the county of Ponthieu were to go to Charles, who was already to have authority over the leading officials in those districts. He also received the old *composition d'Artois* as a French fief. On the other hand should the treaty be broken by the Netherlanders, Artois and Charolais were to return to France. The revenues of Charolais and its appendages were guaranteed to the Archduchess Margaret, whose interests were defended by Gattinara. A document dated March 31st gives a list of the allies of each party. But much was concealed; on the French side only Scotland, Venice and other Italian states were mentioned, together with Gelderland, the Estates of the lower bishopric of Utrecht and the lord of Sedan. On the Burgundian side all the allies to which they admitted were Aragon — whose obligations were further modified by a private treaty — Cleves, the Bishop and town of Cambrai, the Bishop and town of Utrecht, the Swiss and the adherents of Charles in Gelderland. It is clear that neither of these states were at all decided in their views. For the rest, as soon as both parties had agreed to put pressure on the King of Aragon for the return of Navarre, the agreement for the forthcoming marriage was solemnly ratified on Palm Sunday, April 2nd, in Nôtre Dame.

The people of the Netherlands were overjoyed at this peace of Paris, because it was favourable to their trade. Henry of Nassau, a widower of thirty-two, had with the help of relations in Paris, won the hand of Claudine de Châlon, who later became heiress to the principality of Orange. When John of Egmont died in that same summer, Charles bestowed on Henry of Nassau the Stadhouderates of Holland, Zeeland and Friesland: all this was to have important consequences for the dynasty later known as the House of Orange-Nassau.

Tension with Aragon was not yet relieved. When he drew up his will in 1515, the King was still determined that the Infant Ferdinand should succeed to the regency and to the presidency of the three knightly orders of Calatrava, Alcantara and Santiago. The Burgundian government therefore thought it wisest to send to Spain as their ambassador a man in the closest understanding with Charles. They chose Adrian of Utrecht, whose mission was all the harder because he was not only expected to gain support for Charles, but, if the King of Aragon should die, it would be his duty to take over the government in Charles's name in a land to which he was a stranger. No statesman in the Netherlands at this time could have proved equal to so delicate a double task. In accordance, too, with its obligations by the Treaty of Paris, the Burgundian government sent a certain lord of Marsilles to deal with the question of Navarre; but this appears to have been the merest form.

To counteract the defensive measures taken by France and Spain, the Burgundian government needed to ensure the permanent goodwill of England. This was guaranteed by a new commercial treaty in 1516. No less a person than Thomas More played a part in these negotiations; he took the occasion to pay a long visit to Erasmus in the Netherlands. Meanwhile the reception given to the Venetian ambassador showed with what caution the government was treading. On account of strained relations between Venice and the Emperor, he was coldly received in public, but in private he was all the more warmly welcomed.

A full year after Charles came of age the whole Court gathered once again for an even more solemn occasion. This was the requiem for Charles's grandfather Ferdinand of Aragon, who had died on January 23rd, 1516. Two thousand burghers bearing torches lined the streets through which on March 13th the solemn procession of mourners passed from the ducal palace to Sainte Gudule. The Cathedral was hung with priceless brocades and tapestries, lit by innumerable flickering tapers. Michel Pavye preached the funeral oration from the pulpit — 'this is the dance of death which all must tread, even Kings and princes. This is the irrevocable law of life! Sceptres and crowns must fall. Let us not forget how swiftly joy and feasting may turn to mourning and lamentation!' Opposite the pulpit sat the young prince, dressed in black. Afterwards the herald of the Golden Fleece stepped forward and called out twice into the echoing silence of the church, 'Don Ferdinand!' And three times came the answer, 'He is dead.' At the same moment the royal standard of Aragon was lowered to the ground. Once again the herald rose and called: 'Long live their Catholic Majesties, Queen Joanna and King Charles!' Charles, who had laid by his mourning cloak, appeared now on a dais, took from the hands of the Bishop of Badajoz a dagger consecrated at the altar, and raised it to heaven. From countless throats, the air vibrated with shouts of 'Long live the King!'

It was the end of ancient Burgundy. Charles was now King of Spain. Before his eyes the world was opening, and the Netherlands were soon to be no more than a tiny fragment of that vast Empire which he ruled. Yet the land of his birth and boyhood left its mark upon him. It had given him serious principles, courtly bearing and the ambitions of a great prince. The idea of knightly honour and of fighting for the Christian faith, as embodied in the code of the Golden Fleece, were engraved deep on his mind. But the forms among which he had grown up were those of a dying age. Charles stepped forth into the world imbued with the ideals of a society which belonged, politically and spiritually, to the past. Strange how the old and the new met and clashed in him. Or perhaps not, after all, so strange. Perhaps like so much in this tremendous life, this too was but the common fate of all humanity, writ larger. For every generation in turn must find its way through the discarded achievements of the past to the creation of its own.

CHAPTER II

KING OF CASTILE AND ARAGON

IN spite of the manifold reactions of their policy on the Netherlands, the Spaniards had not hitherto wrested the decisive control
of negotiations from the Burgundian government. On the
contrary Charles's ministers had been able to maintain their
independence and coolly to withstand all the demands made by
Ferdinand of Aragon for the education of his grandchild in Spain.
This policy involved a danger which we have already indicated:
efforts might be made in Spain, either in Aragon at the Court of
King Ferdinand, or in Castile in the household of the Infant Don
Ferdinand, to play off the younger against the elder brother.
Such efforts had indeed been made, and those entrusted with the
education of the Infant, Pedro Nuñez de Guzman and Alvaro
Osorio, Bishop of Astorga, had been forced to reckon with the
Queen-mother of Aragon. But the danger never became serious.

When we recollect the shattering crises through which the
Spanish kingdoms passed between the death of Queen Isabella
in 1504 and that of King Ferdinand in 1516, we cannot but wonder
that the structure of the united kingdoms had not been far more
seriously undermined. First came the struggle for the regency
between Philip, as the husband of Joanna, according to old
Castilian law, and Ferdinand, as laid down in the will of Isabella.
Joanna's madness and consequent inability to rule added yet a
further problem. Next came the split in the Castilian nobility,
of whom the majority, inspired by a fundamental desire for
independence, ultimately joined Philip. Last of all came Philip's
early death and Ferdinand's subsequent incontestable regency
with its reactions on the conduct of his old opponents and their
exodus to the Netherlands.

One of the chief reasons for the continued solidarity of the
government was the conduct of the regent of Castile, Ximenes
de Cisneros, Archbishop of Toledo. Each new inquiry into the
history of Spain at this time serves only to throw into higher relief
the commanding figure of this extraordinary man. His character

was in a sense the epitome of those forces which were, in the course of his life, to give birth to a new Spain. He above all others had the anxious responsibility of bringing this new Spain to birth.

THE SPANISH KINGDOMS

Of old, Spain had never been united. Although the peninsula is geographically a self-contained whole, yet its political structure remained for centuries fragmentary and strained. Far from being sufficient to themselves, the separate kingdoms burst their frontiers and blazed divergent trails to the farthest quarters of the globe. Portugal turned her face to the sea and dreamed of African coasts, of engrossing that whole vast southern continent and of opening a new way to India. Great was her success but it severed her from the rest of the peninsula and from Europe. The Kings of Castile, on the other hand, had carried out the *Reconquista*, and redeemed the land from the hands of the Moors, from the mountains of Asturias to the pillars of Hercules. From the ancient holy places and cathedrals of Santiago, Leon, Burgos, they had driven forward across Estremadura and New Castile, past Toledo on the Tagus and Badajoz on the Guadiana, to Seville, Cordova, and Jaen in the angle of the Guadalquivir. At length, after the conquest of Granada, they too reached the southern shore and they too were tempted towards the unknown distances of India. Early in August 1492, from Palos, the port of Rio Tinto, the three ships of Columbus set sail towards the west. Of more immediate importance was the policing of the seas along the African coasts, opposite Cartagena and Malaga. Long before this the Aragonese, themselves monarchs in a small group of kingdoms, had sailed out into the Mediterranean. Their history reads as though they had been impelled to follow the course of the Ebro, their native river, thence to spread their rule over the coastal provinces of Valencia and Catalonia. As early as the thirteenth century they acquired Sicily, in the fifteenth Naples, for the possession of which they were now once again at war. Alfonso the Great had taken his stand beside Calixtus III in defending Europe against the Turk, making a land attack on Albania and pushing his advance by sea deep into the Levant.

But in Italy for the first time the Aragonese had felt, tingling in their blood and stirring them to fresh adventure, the mighty pulse of the western world.

Like most wars of conquest, the long conflict of the Spanish kingdoms, the struggle with the Moors in particular, had generated an aristocracy proud of their military prowess and their possessions. Through their manifold connections — their feuds as much as their alliances — they had acquired like the Burgundian nobles a consciousness of their own integral unity in the midst of the growing kingdoms. This did not prevent them from fighting among themselves, although they jointly resisted every attempt to bring them under the control of a strong central power. Here too we shall do well to seek out in their own provinces some of those great dynasties whose names we are in future so often to hear.

In old Castile there was the family of Manuel, which we already know. It was related to the royal dynasty and its scions filled the episcopal chairs of Santiago, Leon and Zamora. In the same province, north of the Douro and west of Valladolid, were the Enriquez, who held the courtesy title of admirals of Castile. A daughter of Fadrique Enriquez the elder, who died in 1493, was the mother of Ferdinand of Aragon. The family bishopric was Osma. In the more easterly part of old Castile, round the upper waters of the Ebro, lay the estates of the Velasco, Counts of Haro and Dukes of Frias. All these families had innumerable titles, scattered among their several branches, like those of their fellows in the Netherlands, only more high-sounding. The Velasco family held the office of Constable and one of them, Bernardino, married a natural daughter of Ferdinand of Aragon. Along the frontier of Aragon, there were the Hurtado de Mendoza, Dukes of Infantado, Marquesses of Mondejar, Counts of Tendilla in Guadalajara. Typical nobility of their time, they already held the bishoprics of Oviedo, Burgos, Zamora, and Valencia, and were soon to place their members on the episcopal chairs of Toledo and Jaen. The same was true of the old Castilian family of Manrique de Lara, who lived, as their ducal title of Najera indicated, near to Burgos. As early as 1490, Alonso Manrique, whom we have already met at Charles's Court in the Netherlands, was Bishop of Badajoz. Later he was to have Cordova and Seville.

The Astorga, lords of Osorio and Counts of Lemos, were no less in control of their local bishoprics. The family of Benevente came from the district of Zamora; that of de la Cueva, Dukes of Albuquerque, from the Portuguese marches north of Badajoz.

Round the Tagus there were the Silva, Counts of Cifuentes, and the Alvarez de Toledo, Dukes of Alva, whose sons were enthroned on episcopal chairs from Burgos to Granada. On occasion they were rivalled by the Zuñiga, Dukes of Bejar, who had come thither from the north. Farther eastwards were the Pacheco, Marquesses of Villena, Dukes of Escalona, intermarried with the Acuña and Puertocarrero. In the rich Andalusian south lived the important family of Cordova, of which was born Gonzalo Hernandez, the Great Captain, field-marshal and chief organizer of the armies of Ferdinand of Aragon, himself a kinsman of Puertocarrero. Alfonso Aguilar, father of the Marquis of Priego, was one of them. The title of Duke of Sessa had passed from the Great Captain to the husband of his daughter and heiress, Don Luis de Cordova. In the south too there were the Figueroa, Dukes of Feria, and the Guzman, Dukes of Medina Sidonia. They too were Counts of Niebla in the province of Seville to the east of Cadiz — but their claim to the title Duke of Medina Sidonia had been attacked by Pedro Giron of the family of Acuña.

While emphasizing the immense local importance of these families, we must not forget that their services as bishops and warriors gave them a national importance equal to that of the imperial nobility, and some of them achieved the European honour of the Golden Fleece. For long enough they remained unsubdued, intolerant, like the German princes and nobles, of any interference from a new civil power. Thus if he wished to form a united state, the sovereign had no choice but to use force, and in Spain, as in the rest of Europe, he looked for this to the towns. As fortresses, the cities offered him strategic positions, man-power and wealth. If here and there the higher nobility, or more often the gentry, the Hidalgos, exercised a certain influence within their walls, yet the industrial and trading population was the controlling element. We have not heard the last of their economic aspirations. The towns exercised political influence by way of the Cortes and occasionally gave proof of their military

E
65

strength in a *Hermandad*, a union for the better security of the land, like the Leagues of the German cities.

It is true that the Crown derived a no less important support from the Church. But the statement should be modified by the addition that the material and not the spiritual resources of the Church were what mattered. Men were tempted into the King's service by the prospect of the rich benefices of which he could dispose. More important still was the royal right, under Papal dispensation, to tax all Church foundations, while the considerable revenues of the three knightly orders of Alcantara, Santiago and Calatrava were in the King's control.

The most important source of semi-ecclesiastical power in the King's hand was the Inquisition. The word needs some explanation, for an *Inquisition*, meaning merely an inquiry, was well-known in old Frankish law and in the thirteenth century the Pope entrusted a special inquisition against heretics to the Dominicans. But the right of Inquisition granted to the Spanish monarchs on November 1st, 1478, stands in direct relation to that struggle of race and religion which was now at its bitterest in Spain. The mob anti-semitism of the Middle Ages was a by-product of the Crusades; it was directed against the enemies of the faith — though jealousy of Jewish wealth and economic competition played its part. Spain was the only country in western Europe, in which occidental civilization had made a widespread and prolonged contact with that of the east. The great mass of the Jews emigrated or were converted; but it was popularly asserted that many had been baptized for form alone, so that they were now able to marry into Christian families with consequences all the more disastrous. The new Inquisition was the State's judicial mechanism against such surface Christianity. Purity of faith and blood, *limpieza*, became the essential demand of the Spaniard, and the slightest failing in either the one or the other gave to the Inquisition, secret alike in procedure and accusation, its particular terror. Confiscation of goods, the habitual penalty, placed a dangerous material weapon in the hands of the State.

Crown and State were by this time one, and the ultimate and decisive instrument in the hands of the government was an educated bureaucracy. In spite of their frequent dependence on ecclesiastical benefices, these *letrados* were as independent of the Church as of the towns and the nobility. It is common to speak loosely of general tendencies of development, to assert for instance that judicial and civil administration, nay the very government itself, gradually passed into the hands of learned jurists and scholars. But a political structure, based on a spontaneously increasing class of professional officials, does in fact possess exceptional powers of resistance as long as its foundations remain undisturbed. It will create its own theory, as it were, its own code of ethics, and strong in this inner solidarity it will outlast the changing chances of skilful or clumsy governments. But such developments, however general they may appear, always derive their peculiar character from that originally impressed on them by a responsible ruler. And in Spain, as elsewhere, a beginning had to be made.

FROM THE DEATH OF ISABELLA (1504) TO THE DEATH OF FERDINAND (1516). CARDINAL XIMENES

There can be no doubt that the new State was built up in Spain, both from without and from within, in all its unity and completeness, in the time of Queen Isabella and under her personal influence. Isabella, rightful heiress to the throne of Castile, had given her hand to the young Ferdinand of Aragon in 1469 under the most perilous conditions. On one side she was threatened by a rising in Portugal, on the other by the pretensions of an illegitimate niece, Beltraneja, and her supporters. After 1474, when her debauched brother Henry died, she had, under her husband's protection and with the sole help of dynastic tradition and her own courage, governed a kingdom which had long been a stranger to all discipline. The circumstances brought many helpers to her side and she was great enough to let herself be ruled. Isabella's intelligence and profound sense of duty were completed by Ferdinand's energy; the subsequent union of the two kingdoms of Castile and Aragon into the one monarchy of Spain was foreshadowed in their joint rule and by their joint actions.

Ferdinand of Aragon had the misfortune to be admired by

Macchiavelli, on which account he has been too easily dubbed a knave. Popular belief is in this as unfair to him as to the great Florentine. However that may be, Macchiavelli thus describes him in the twenty-first chapter of *The Prince*: 'We have now in our days Ferdinand, King of Aragon, the present King of Spain: he in a manner may be termed a new Prince, for from a very weak King, he is now become for fame and glory, the first King in Christendom, and if you shall well consider his actions, you shall find them all illustrious and every one of them extraordinary.

'He in the beginning of his reign assailed Granada, and that exploit was the ground of his state. At first he made that war in security and without suspicion he should be anyways hindered, and therein held the Barons of Castiglia's minds busied, who thinking upon that war never minded any innovation; and in this while he gained credit and authority with them, they not being aware of it; was able to maintain with the Church and the people's money all his soldiers, and to lay a foundation for his military ordinances with that long war: which afterwards gained him exceeding much honour.

'Besides this, to the end he might be able here-among to undertake greater matters, serving himself always of the colour of religion; he gave himself to a kind of religious cruelty, chasing and despoiling those Jews[1] of the Kingdom; nor can this example be more admirable and rare: under the same cloak he invaded Africk and went through with his exploit in Italy: and last of all hath he assailed France, and so always proceeded on forwards contriving of great matters: which always have held his subjects' mind in peace and admiration.'[2]

All this shows the impression which Ferdinand made in Italy, but it is only half the truth. No one would deny that he was both a warlike and a circumspect ruler. As a husband he had all the frailties of his time, and, as in Burgundy, generations of bastards occupied the episcopal chair of Saragossa. He owed his military success to his generals, to the Great Captain and to the less reliable Pedro Navarro. But the execution of his internal policy must be ascribed largely to Isabella and to Cardinal Ximenes.

[1] Macchiavelli's original has 'Marranos', the collective name in Spain for persons of oriental origin, predominantly Moors.
[2] DACRE's translation. London, 1640.

The Cardinal too must be held partly responsible for that action which Macchiavelli regarded as Ferdinand's most 'admirable and rare' achievement — the expulsion and oppression of the Moriscoes.

It is to the eternal honour of Isabella that she first won Ximenes for her confessor and then allowed the confessor to develop into a statesman of the first rank. Francisco Ximenes de Cisneros was a man of that outstanding type which occurs but rarely in the history of the world. He was one of those who, living in a spiritual world wholly sufficient to himself, was dragged out of seclusion and forced into political life against his will. Because of their apartness, their self-sufficiency, such men are often able to work out their genius in an extraordinary mastery of the world itself. The whole career of Ximenes is eloquent witness to his strong and passionate soul. A young scholar, ordained priest in Rome, he had on his return dared to oppose his bishop by demanding a benefice which had been bestowed on him at Rome. At last, after he had lain many years in prison, his great gifts were recognized; but he was sought out and honoured only to escape again from the world, this time to the inexpressible joys of complete surrender and the conquest of the flesh, in a Franciscan monastery. Small wonder that he was again sought out, that his bishop, Don Pedro Gonzalez de Mendoza, followed him from Siguenza to Toledo, and here recommended him to the Queen. At her side he found his true vocation. He brought to politics the same determination and calm which he brought to life. Never did he execute or advise a half-measure. When in 1495, under pressure from the Pope, he accepted the Archbishopric of Toledo, he began a general reform of the Spanish Church. He had been early influenced by the philological writings of the humanists and now he saw to the printing of the scriptures and insisted on a sermon or an explanation of the gospels at every celebration of the Mass. He demanded a thorough reform of priestly life, the keeping of baptismal and confessional registers, the residence of bishops in their cathedral cities — all the principles of the Counter-reformation, long before the Reformation itself.

So it was Ximenes who decided the central question of Spanish national life, the establishment of a single faith and the final contest with Jews and Moors. He may have turned the rudder in the wrong direction; the moral and economic results of his policy were perhaps later the ruin of that very Spain which he created. Yet he acted not merely as a religious zealot, but as a national statesman and in the interest of a large section of the people. On March 30th, 1492, a decree of his Catholic Majesty brought the war on the Jews to an end with the most ruthless thoroughness, by banishing from the land at one and the same time all the unconverted or unconvertible. As a result thirty-six thousand are said to have emigrated.

Next Ximenes faced another problem. Toleration had been granted to the Moorish Mohammedan population after the fall of Granada; could that toleration continue? Spanish tradition pointed to toleration. The nobility lived on the labour of the Mudejares, who worked hard and asked little in return, and thirty years later even in Valencia the most southerly part of Aragon, men were found to argue that this Moorish population, whatever its beliefs, was necessary to the economic welfare of the country. Only the middle classes in the towns, who suffered from the successful competition of non-Christians, demanded sterner measures.

Not for an instant did Ximenes hesitate to refuse the demand for toleration. Strong in his sincere and positive conviction, he set himself at once to convert the unbelievers by preaching, teaching and discussion. Earlier he had been filled with the Franciscan spirit of the thirteenth century; now he was filled with that of the Dominicans. When his violent measures, above all the destruction of Arabic literature, aroused first a bitter outcry and finally rebellion, he advised ruthless suppression — and he had his way. If the foreign elements could not be absorbed peacefully, then, to his mind, the theory of a united state justified the use of force.

From his earliest youth Ximenes had shown that he feared no man. He had acted harshly against the Mudejares and Marranos; he acted no less vigorously against the nobility. He was determined to put an end to blood feuds and to make the roads safe for travellers. Not that his government was in any way dependent on the merchant middle classes; here too he acted as one convinced of the idea of a united Christian state, and answerable only to the judge of all mankind. He maintained royal governors, called Corregidores, even in the cities.

Yet this statesman, like King Ferdinand himself, for one instant risked the entire worldly legacy of Isabella — united Spain — on a single throw.

In his anger at the demands made by Philip the Handsome, contrary to the testament of Isabella, Ferdinand, no less than the Burgundian government, counted on the help of France. At the Treaty of Blois, in October 1505, he contracted a second marriage with Germaine de Foix, niece of Louis XII. He even made over to her parts of the kingdom of Naples, to revert to France in the event of her death without children. Had her son lived, the unity of the Spanish state itself would have been destroyed. Yet Ximenes, intent on the internal problems raised by a nobility in revolt, seems to have agreed with Ferdinand.

Since the death of Philip the Handsome, the Cardinal's position had been beset with difficulties. Nevertheless since even the most radical of them saw no other way out, the Grandees of Castile chose Ximenes as regent for the time-being. As to any further action, their opinions were utterly divided; only a minority wanted Ferdinand. Ximenes grasped the reins firmly. Drawing on the rich revenues of his Archbishopric, he raised troops with which to keep order. Although he failed to persuade the wretched Joanna into any definite decisions, he nevertheless made all ready against the coming of his absent King, to whom, like Ferdinand's old adherents, Alva and Cifuentes, he remained loyal even in the most difficult conditions. In 1507 Ferdinand came back from Naples, bringing with him as a reward for the Archbishop's services a cardinal's hat. Both now worked together to restore the kingdom to its quondam unity. The Catholic King ruled once more, at his side the Cardinal.

In 1511 the Holy League was formed; Ferdinand, his son-in-law Henry VIII, and later Maximilian, allied themselves with the Pope against France. It was then that the Spaniards, 'on the very point', as they put it, 'of continuing their war with the unbelievers', were called on by the Pope to protect Italy and the Church itself against the French invaders and their schismatical council. In 1512, with English help, they occupied Navarre, which was allied with France. But this time the Spaniards were not interested in that small section of Navarre which lies to the north of the Pyrenees and belongs geographically to France; their concern was with the very considerable kingdom which stretches from

Pamplona to Tudela on the Ebro and controls the communications between old Castile and Aragon. This was the district which they wished to absorb into the Spanish state. In Spain the idea persisted that their intervention had saved the Papacy: in fact they had not only secured Navarre and with it the connecting link between the two kingdoms, but had established for the first time their incontestable superiority in Italy. Charles's two grandfathers remained in alliance: we have already studied the reactions of that alliance in Burgundy. In Spain Cardinal Ximenes was acclimatizing himself gradually to this friendly attitude towards the Hapsburg.

The war against the unbeliever to which Ferdinand had referred in his manifesto of July 30th, 1512, dealing with the question of Navarre, was enacted on the African coasts. Ximenes was directly responsible for it. His personal intervention led to a successful assault on Oran. He promoted Pedro Navarro, who, in spite of intermittent defeat, did in fact gain ground in Algiers. When Ferdinand died in 1516, the Cardinal, now a very old man, might as he took stock of the situation, predict with confidence a great future for Spain and for the young heir to its many kingdoms.

INTERIM GOVERNMENT AND EUROPEAN POLICY

Ximenes was now regent in Castile; the Archbishop of Saragossa, in accordance with the will of Ferdinand, was regent in Aragon; Adrian of Utrecht was regent by command of Charles. This latter had the tact to come to an understanding with the Spanish prelates; he was bound to Ximenes in particular by common theological interests. On March 13th Charles was proclaimed King in Brussels; on the 21st his government asked that he might also be proclaimed King in Spain. But this was not possible, for Queen Joanna had not renounced her rights nor was Charles yet in a position to perform the customary accession ceremonies in the presence of the Cortes. At a meeting of the inner council and the Grandees, Cardinal Ximenes confirmed this view through his mouthpiece, Carvajal. Protests left him unmoved. He understood clearly enough that no doubt must be allowed to arise as to the unanimity of the government in power. He tacitly supposed that the young

King would soon come to Spain in person and in the meantime it was for the regents to act as if in the conscious enjoyment of his absolute confidence.

On every side there was tinder for rebellion. And as the King's coming was repeatedly postponed, two flames of discontent flared up into a single blaze. There is always a smoulder of unrest when a foreign ruler ascends a throne; but in Spain another fire was piled on this and with it a draught to fan the flames, for doubts were soon raised as to who was really ruling — the native regents or foreigners. Mistakes in the distribution of places and privileges added to the uncertainty. In the correspondence of Ximenes with his representative in the Netherlands, Diego Lopez de Ayala, the whole situation comes to life before our eyes.

Ramon de Cardona kept order in Naples, but unrest was reported from Sicily, and the Viceroy, Hugo de Moncada, had to fly from Palermo. Ximenes sent both ships and troops. But his anxiety for the fleet reached its height when two pirates, Horudsch and Chair ed Din, called Barbarossa, established their lair on the African coast, and, under the protection of the Sultan, threatened to spread Mohammedan dominion farther west. A Spanish relieving force failed to dislodge the pirates from Algiers. Ximenes strained all his resources to rebuild the fleet; there was talk of spending fifty-three thousand ducats a month. On September 22nd, 1516, he wrote to his representative in Brussels: 'No one can be powerful by land unless he is also powerful by sea.' He asked the Pope for the re-imposition of the old Crusading tax on Church lands, the *Cruzada*; it was abundantly justified, for the Turks insolently pushed their way even into Spanish sea-ports and threatened to cut off the vital supplies of corn from Sicily. At the same time Jean d'Albret invaded Navarre; so energetically had the Cardinal seen to the defence of the land, that the invaders failed to cross the pass at Ronceval and were later forced to evacuate St. Jean Pied du Port to the north of the Pyrenees.

The regent achieved his successes for the most part in despite of the Burgundian government. His intentions were blameless when on December 6th, 1516, having called the Cortes of the eighteen Estates of Castile, he dissolved them once again at a hint from the Brussels government. And in March 1517 he prevented an independent meeting of the Cortes. Yet when a

Hermandad of Burgos, Leon, Valladolid and Zamora sent a deputation to Charles in the summer of 1517, demanding that the King himself return to Spain, that no bullion be exported from the land, that no official positions be given to foreigners, their messengers were well received and graciously answered, nor were they reproached for taking independent action.

But soon all classes alike began to feel slighted. The Grandees, although certain individuals among them had made their peace with him, rarely had cause to praise Ximenes's government. The hopes of the townsfolk had been raised without being satisfied, for they had expected much from the new connection with the Netherlands. The clergy were indignant at the increasing taxes. At the same time the government in Spain was assailed by grave accusations against the behaviour of the Conquistadores in the Indies. In 1516 Las Casas first raised his voice in the name of the Indians, and Palacios Rubios supported him. Only one man could give help — the King. And he was far away.

A year had passed since Ferdinand of Aragon died. Why did Charles and his councillors hesitate?

Chièvres was not to be put out of his course either by good or bad news from Spain. For the time being he was fully occupied in handling problems which had arisen out of the new position of the Burgundian government relative to other European powers. Gone was that comfortable neutrality which had been possible in 1513 when England, the Emperor and Aragon had united against France. The French monarchy, too, had gained enormously in prestige, when, on September 13th and 14th, 1515, the young King won his great Italian victory at Marignano. This new importance of France in Italy might well react unfavourably on Naples. But the fear of France's great power was as strong a deterrent as the apprehension of her menacing predominance was an incentive to action. England, the Pope and the Emperor, nevertheless, were for preventive action. But Chièvres had no inducement to allow the Netherlands to be sucked into the Italian whirlpool merely on Maximilian's account. Naturally enough Maximilian himself was still meddling in the politics of the Netherlands, but the cautious politicians who governed Burgundian politics were no longer to be tempted by the intricacies of his policy. With England in particular Maximilian was playing

a curious game, at one moment offering the young King condottieri to fight his wars, and at another dropping hints to him
about the imperial throne. Moreover Charles's ministers had other
matters to attend to; the peace of Paris in 1515 had by no means
put an end to troubles in the Netherlands. The partisans of
France were still active, Charles of Egmont in Gelderland and
Robert de la Mark on the borders of Liège.

Friesland and Utrecht were repeatedly harried from Gelderland;
not only Edzard of East Friesland but many other neighbours and
factionaries intervened. On May 19th, 1515, Duke George of
Saxony had sold his rights in Friesland to Charles for 100,000
florins, and the lord of Isselstein had been made stadhouder in
the province. Here and in the lands belonging to the seignory of
Sedan, some attempt might be made to deprive the agitators of
French support and cripple their military power. The attempt
was not altogether unsuccessful. Although they did not altogether
put the agitators from Gelderland out of action, yet Nassau,
Isselstein and Wassenaer at length gained the upper hand.

In spite of all, Chièvres, with that unswerving singleness of
purpose which was typical of him, continued to work for better
relations between the French and Burgundian governments, and
enlisted for his help all the European powers friendly to the
Netherlands. The reason for his action was not merely a sentimental affection for France but the conviction that in her alliance
alone lay the solution of his immediate problems. Exploiting to
the full every possible bond of marriage and kinship, and acting
with the utmost political caution, he gradually won over to his
side most of the old anglophile party, at one time the chief
opponents of his policy, and little by little even the Archduchess
Margaret and the Emperor. It speaks volumes for the essential
rightness of his object that he not only convinced his opponents
but even made them into active allies. Yet for him too difficulties
in certain quarters had lightened or disappeared. The rivalry
at Court between Castilians and Aragonese had, for instance,
since Ferdinand's death, ceased to have any importance.

The way was now clear for a series of ticklish but skilfully
executed manœuvres with France and England. The first move
was a proposal to renew the commercial treaty with England. As
soon as discussions were under way, Chièvres opened negotiations

with the French at Noyon. These, after intermittent inter-
ruptions, were brought to a happy conclusion on August 13th,
1516. All the while Charles's representatives had used his supposed
friendship with that coalition of the English, Swiss, imperial and
Neapolitan governments, as a convenient counterpoise to sway
the balance of the negotiations in their favour. The treaties concluded at Noyon comprised the preliminaries of a marriage
alliance between Charles and Madame Louise, the baby daughter
of Francis I, who was to bring him the disputed kingdom of Naples
for a dowry. In return for this the French agreed to forgo pressing
the claims of Germaine de Foix, widow of the late King of Aragon,
until such time as Charles should himself be in Spain and able to
give the matter his personal attention. A precautionary clause
was added by which, in the event of the death of Madame Louise,
her still unborn sister should be given to Charles in her place.
Should both these potential brides fail, then he was to have
Princess Renée, the daughter of Louis XII and sister-in-law of
Francis I.

Clearly this treaty was nothing but an outward show. No one
can seriously have expected the seventeen-year-old Charles to
wait for a bride who was less than a year old. Still less was it
likely that the Spanish government would consider Naples an
adequate dowry for this potential bride; crippled as the kingdom
was with debt, it was yet incontrovertibly at the moment in their
own possession. Least of all was it probable that they would agree
to disgorge Navarre. Yet the French government seemed well-
content with the fallacious treaty and Charles's grateful letters to
his present feudal overlord and future father-in-law, the King of
France, gave substance to the facile deception. Only in Spain was
there indignation. The Bishop of Badajoz and Cardinal Ximenes
expressed their disapprobation and uttered grave warnings of the
French danger. 'The French care neither for truth nor for
friendship and it is much to be feared that they will make no
exception in their dealings with our master, for they are jealous to
see him a greater ruler and a mightier King than their own.'
Spanish pride revolted against even the outward show of their
King's vassalage to France. Unlike the Burgundians, they had
not learnt by experience to see in that very vassalage a means of
acquiring dangerous influence within France itself.

76

At the same time the English negotiations were nearing a conclusion. The young Jacques de Luxembourg, lord of Auxy,
secured a brilliant diplomatic victory when he gained not only the
friendship of England but a very considerable loan to cover the
expenses of Charles's journey from the Netherlands to Spain.
England could not afford to let France have the monopoly of
Charles's friendship.

On October 29th, 1516, the negotiations were brought to an end
by the conclusion of an alliance between Charles, Henry VIII and
the Pope. On December 3rd the Emperor Maximilian entered
the general coalition by declaring his intention at Brussels of being
included in the treaty of Noyon. All princes of Christendom
seemed thus to be united by vows of eternal brotherhood. Wrapped
in the mantle of this glorious achievement, the Hapsburg dynasty
thought to enter upon its heritage in Spain. But, speaking privately
to his grandchild after an audience in the spring of 1517, Maximilian with his usual light-hearted indiscretion let the cat out of the
bag. 'My child', he said, 'you are about to cheat the French and
I the English — or', here he hastily corrected himself — 'at least I
shall do my best.' The fulfilment of their treaty obligations Charles
and Maximilian left wholly to the future.

The feast of the Order, solemnized with the usual pomp in the
late autumn of 1516, shows how seriously the Burgundian Court
took up arms for its new task. The festivities lasted from October
25th until November 5th, intermittently interrupted by final
negotiations with the French. The Treaty of Noyon was once
more solemnly ratified: Charles received the Order of Saint
Michael from Francis, Francis the Golden Fleece. After his instal-
ment the French King was, however, specifically released from
certain duties. The general meeting of the knights in the Chapter
provided the occasion for the pronunciation of certain words of
censure; but Don Juan Manuel received full satisfaction for the
wrongs he had suffered. The knights also decided that the fifteen
vacant places in the Order should be filled and added the momentous rider that since there had been a 'mighty increase in the power
of the House of Burgundy', the Pope should be solicited to
sanction an enlargement of their number. Ten Spaniards came
into consideration for later inclusion in the Order and several
Germans in the service of the dynasty were to be immediately

elected to vacancies. Out of respect for the Emperor's feelings, his old enemy Philip of Cleves, lord of Ravestein, was not mentioned among these. Among those immediately chosen were the Infant Don Ferdinand, the Count Palatine Frederick, Margrave Hans of Brandenburg, who was to marry Germaine de Foix, the widowed Queen of Aragon, and the Counts of Werdenberg and Mansfeld. The Burgundians elected to the honour included Philippe and Antoine de Croy, lords of Porceau and Sempy, Antoine Lalaing, lord of Montigny, Charles de Lannoy, lord of Sanzelles, Jacques de Luxembourg, now lord of Gavre, and Adolphe of Burgundy, lord of Beveren and Veere. New vacancies were found for Charles's future brothers-in-law, the Kings of Portugal and Hungary, for the lords of Rappoltstein and Wolkenstein, as well as for the nobility of the northern Netherlands, the families of Gaesbeck, Wassenaer, Zevenbergen and Egmont. The old Burgundian tradition was retained, but the Order was in future to have many foreign knights.

The first half of the year 1517 was wasted in irksome delays. Although the war in Gelderland was all but ended, it continued to cost money. Not until the autumn was all ready for the Spanish journey. And then the Court had to wait weeks for a favourable wind.

They stayed close to the sea. And here in the dunes above Middelburg took place the last act of a drama whose earlier scenes had been played some months before. Now that he was of age and the head of his family, Charles not only exercised the greatest discretion in choosing a bride for himself, but also in selecting a husband for his eldest sister Eleonore. One of the most valuable assets of the dynasty, hitherto she had always been kept back. She was now eighteen years of age, and her princely suitors were as many as the countless negotiations which had been conducted on her behalf both in Brussels and in Vienna. Yet the princess, it seems, had determined to defy all political considerations by entering into what is commonly known as a love-match.

The Count Palatine Frederick had been educated at the Burgundian Court and had returned thither in 1513. As regent he had been repeatedly entrusted with important missions and had been honoured with the Order of the Golden Fleece. True that Maximilian did not find him very useful politically, but he was a pleasant companion, and, as we have already seen, a bold exponent of the tourney. The Count Palatine must have exploited to the full such rare opportunities as Court hunting-parties and balls gave him, to approach the princess. At length he pressed her for a decision in a letter which apparently took her by surprise. Hastily she hid it in her bosom, but her kingly brother, realizing at once what was afoot, first demanded it of her and then took it. Pitiful love-letter, unread by her for whom it was intended, it lies to this day among a bundle of State papers, serving no better purpose than to give the historian a momentary glimpse of the amorous conventions of that time and of the formalities of the Court. Frederick had left nothing unsaid. He addressed the princess as 'ma mie, ma mignonne', declared himself ready to dare anything for her, called on God and the Holy Virgin for help, and demanded no less than that 'he might belong to her and she to him'. Vain hope. His love-letter was degraded into a mere piece of documentary evidence and was filed with the other legal instruments in which the two lovers declared before witnesses that they had contracted no secret marriage and that they renounced each other for ever. In spite of all pleading the Count Palatine was banished the Court, a sentence which foreign ambassadors attributed chiefly to Charles's inexorable obstinacy. In such family matters decisions rested entirely with him. When the question of Eleonore's marriage to her uncle the King of Portugal was approached, the princess bowed to the inevitable.

About this time, too, Charles began to assert himself in other matters. Margaret declared that he was a different person. As far as we can tell it was during these months that he took the decision to enter German politics as a candidate for the imperial throne — that is as the successor of Maximilian. His grandfather had just left after another long visit to the Netherlands: Charles was never to see him again.

On September 8th the adverse wind gave place at last to a favourable breeze and the Court set sail from Flushing. It was a fleet of forty sail, Charles and his sister Eleonore surrounded by all the pomp and circumstance of the Burgundian Court. The passage was stormy and when, after ten days, the ships came close alongside the Spanish coast, they had already passed their intended harbour. They were forced to land as best they might, in rough weather and on a rock-bound shore, not far from the village of Villaviciosa. Terrified, the inhabitants had already prepared themselves to meet the unknown invaders — in arms.

CHARLES IN SPAIN. THE MEETING OF THE CORTES

In the historical writing of all time it has been the custom to single out certain moments as symbolic in the history of the world. The great solemnities which mark the various stages in the lives of princes are conceived, at least, in this manner. Charles's coming to the native land of his mother had hopelessly miscarried. The seventeen-year-old prince had borne the sea-journey tolerably well, but the hostility of the shores on which he landed, the lack of suitable quarters, the exhausting and comfortless journey along the coast and over cliffs and mountains, patently affected his health. Often the Court had to camp for days, resting, among the hills. Surprisingly enough they made no attempt to reach Santander, although it was close by, nor yet the slightly more distant towns of Leon, Burgos or Palencia; they even passed by Valladolid.

Men were not slow to put their own constructions on these movements. Chièvres, they asserted, had been determined to prevent a meeting between Charles and Ximenes. Hastening to meet his master, the aged regent had fallen ill of a fever at Roa, not far from Valladolid, and here he died. At eighty years old, Ximenes can have had no dearer wish than to see his King, were it only for once, and to give him good counsel. It is equally clear that Charles's Burgundian advisers neither sympathized with this desire nor recognized the importance of this extraordinary man. Yet a long journey over the mountains, with all the dangers to which it exposed the King's health and his Court for weeks on end, was too heavy a price to pay for so needless a precaution, merely out of fear of Ximenes. However much mutual distrust exacerbated feelings on both sides, the true explanation of Charles's journey is simpler and more reasonable. After they had missed the right harbour, Charles's councillors were perplexed by rumours of an epidemic of infectious disease; later their decisions were further complicated by recriminations. Besides the various parts of the

fleet had come ashore at different places and the Court had somehow to be reassembled.

Above all Charles and his sister were guided by their natural
desire to seek out their mother at Tordesillas, before receiving the
official homage of the people. Charles felt that he could not justly
exercise his royal authority on Spanish soil until he had personally assured himself of the condition of the mother whom he
had never known. On November 4th Charles and Eleonore came
at last to the high castle of Tordesillas, where their mother lived
with their ten-year-old sister Katherine. The historian Vital accompanied Charles to the threshold of the Queen's room, but
when, driven by curiosity, he tried to bring a light into the room
itself, Charles barred his way. Several times the King repeated
these visits. We shall never know what he found. The wretched
brain-sick Queen lived until 1555; all that we know is that with
the proud reserve of his family, Charles treated her always with the
same unfaltering respect and tenderness. Of her governing the
country there was no longer any question. Still less could her
way of life be altered. Nevertheless both Charles and Eleonore
decided that their little sister, Katherine, must be rescued from
the unhealthy atmosphere of the castle. At the side of Eleonore,
in her 'fabulous' finery, spectators declared that Katherine looked
like some pitiful little nun. In future she was to live more as
befitted a princess. But her mother took the parting all too hard
and it proved for the time-being impossible to take Katherine
away from Tordesillas. Instead she was given a small independent
household within the castle.

Four days after this visit, on November 8th, Cardinal Ximenes
died in Roa. He had not been well enough to travel to Mojados,
south of Valladolid, where Charles had arranged to meet him.
In his place there came another; this was that prince who, since
the death of Ferdinand of Aragon, had been carefully watched
over by the Cardinal himself — the Infant Don Ferdinand. After
the visit to the mother he had never known, Charles now met for
the first time the brother whom he had never seen, a youth nearly
fifteen years old. Ferdinand dismounted to salute him. And now
Charles was able to assure him in person, as he had already done
by letter, that he would never fall short in brotherly love towards
him. When soon after Ferdinand held the napkin for him as he

F

washed his hands at dinner, this was no humiliation of the younger prince, but rather the exercise of an honourable privilege. He was accorded due precedence in the magnificent processional entry to Valladolid which reminded the Spaniards of the gorgeous spectacles they had seen when Philip the Handsome was with them. The King, clad in shining armour and priceless stuffs, ablaze with gems, sat his fiery charger with impassive dignity; so strong already was his self-discipline.

By an old agreement Ferdinand was to leave Spain as soon as Charles arrived there, so that no faction might have time to spring up about the prince who had been born and educated in the country. In return Ferdinand was to be provided with a personal apanage proportionate to his birth, out of the wide lands of the Hapsburg inheritance. He set out almost at once and reached the Netherlands safe and sound, where his aunt Margaret, whose house had now long been empty, gave him a warm welcome. In Spain Ferdinand had been spoiled and cherished, nor did he find Margaret's affection hard to win, for he was in truth very charming.

More typical of the culture and outlook of the Burgundians than their ostentatious entry into Valladolid was the tournament which was next arranged, in order, as they declared with the greatest self-complacency, 'to display to the Spaniards the great valour of the Burgundian lords'. The lords of Beaurain and Sanzelles, of Porceau and Fiennes, scions of the houses of Croy, Lannoy and Luxembourg, led forth thirty knights on either side, 'each knight shining like Saint George'. They themselves were dressed from top to toe in priceless cloth of gold or silver, with plumes and crests which floated on the wind or swept the hind quarters of their magnificent chargers. First they fought in groups of three, then all together with naked weapons. When their lances were broken, they closed hand to hand with drawn swords. Riders and horses were wounded; soon ten horses lay dead on the ground and the knights fought on foot. Only when blood was already flowing in rivers and the spectators, the ladies in particular, were crying out in terror, 'Jesus! Jesus!' did Charles forbid further fighting. By that time the combatants were so furiously engaged that they could be separated only by force. A reception and a Court ball concluded the entertainment and for long after people still spoke of the 'wondrous tournament'.

Many other joustings were held, with lavish expense and amazing splendour, though probably no more with unguarded weapons, which the King forbade in future. Charles himself appeared in the lists, clad in the gorgeous accoutrements of a Burgundian nobleman, accompanied by an army of drummers and pipers and followed by an impressive troop of pages wearing his colours. One day he bore a shield with the device *Nondum* — not yet. This was his own youthful variant on that other proud emblem of his — *Plus Ultra*. Already he felt stirring within his bosom the possibility of a great future and he drank deep of the intoxicating wine of ambition. For he was young and proud, imbued with all the sensual loveliness of the Court. Yet he yearned for the fleshpots of the Netherlands and for his old friends. In January 1518 we find him writing from Tordesillas to Henry of Nassau. The words flow spontaneously, from the heart. He intends, he says, to answer Henry's last 'mad' letter 'with his own fair hand'. After several allusions to Lalaing and to a series of sleighing parties he comes at length to the ladies; he finds little pleasure in them here, he says, save in one only, and alas she paints herself atrociously! If he cannot have a chat with 'his beloved Henry' from time to time he will be in danger of growing as grave as Solomon — a development which might have its uses among all the cunning fellows who pester him in these parts. This then was the way in which Charles still looked at the world. Only in the Court life to which he was accustomed did he feel himself at home and free. How then did he acquit himself of his task as a ruler?

Gradually now we must turn our eyes from that world of Court and ceremony in which the young King moved with such consummate grace, and seek him out in public affairs, in which he was later to pass so much of his life. During the last months before he left the Netherlands Charles had already attended council meetings. It was said that all official letters were submitted to him — although naturally this can refer only to the most important — and that he gave his opinion of them at the council table.

Hitherto the Burgundian government had proceeded with the utmost caution in all its dealings with foreign powers; this, more than anything, contributed to Charles's undisturbed accession to the Spanish throne. The position was comparatively easy, for his grandfather, the Emperor, was on good terms with England and all other European powers were almost openly hostile to France. Yet the Spanish government soon began to feel that it had committed itself too far with the French. It was in no position to keep the terms of Noyon, at least in so far as they affected Naples and Navarre. In particular the tribute exacted for the kingdom of Naples was much too high. But long before they had to take any decision in foreign policy, Charles and his advisers had to face problems in the internal politics of Castile and Aragon which were completely new to them. And they faced them at first in circumstances of exceptional difficulty.

Ill-feeling was already rife on all sides. Modern writers have accepted Spanish complaints of the tactlessness, avarice and self-interest of the Burgundians at their face value. But most of these complaints were voiced by scholars and learned councillors or by historians whose thought was cast in the same mould — Peter Martyr, Carvajal, Zurita and their plagiarists. To these we can now add Santa Cruz, who in his *Chronicle* blames not only Chièvres and Sauvage, but Lannoy above all. The few Burgundian writers, who composed their works in the old-fashioned courtly style, cannot compete with these. Sharing the reactionary feudal theories of their lords, they do not stand out boldly as the advocates of that unity which had by this time grown so necessary to government. Yet this is the very crux of the problem. The unification of so many different states and people under one ruler inevitably produced almost insoluble problems. But the Burgundians could only act in accordance with the rules of the life they knew; only by degrees could the King learn to fit himself to the customs and needs of his new lands, without altogether abandoning the ideas which had hitherto guided his life. Comprehensible as are the bitter outbursts of the Spaniards against the foreigners, they were partly at least the natural result of the strain through which their much-divided country had but recently passed. The Spaniards were bred up in a tradition which taught them to criticize and take sides, and they turned instinctively against anything foreign. If they were not actually antagonized by everything feudal and courtly, then they were antagonized by anything which smacked of French influence. Charles's advisers prevented him from meeting not only Ximenes but most of the principal members of the interim government. These in turn complained that they were neither received in audience nor yet given leave to go.

The confiscation of the Cardinal's worldly goods is a point which has been so much discussed that no clear judgment can now be given. Chièvres being childless, the Archbishopric was bestowed on his nephew; this was a criminal folly even though the revenues went only in part to the young absentee. Otherwise, apart from the elevation of Adrian of Utrecht to the see of Tortosa and of the humanist Ludovico Marliano to that of Tuy, very few Spanish bishoprics were given to strangers. A few bishoprics were in the hands of Cardinals and members of the Curia, as for instance Orense, Leon, Cuenca, Valencia, Huesca and Pamplona; but this was an old abuse in the Roman Church and, as against the thirty Castilian and forty-odd Aragonese bishoprics, it was a dwindling evil. Not until 1521 did Cartagena go to the Cardinal of Salzburg and Valencia to the Cardinal of Liège. But the nomination of Adrian, of the youthful Croy and of Marliano, took place at the very outset and was accompanied by the advancement of those very Spaniards who had lived at the Burgundian Court, such as Manrique and Doctor Mota. Misunderstandings and causes for irritation continued to multiply.

The transactions of the first Cortes which met at Valladolid in the winter of 1517-18 perhaps best reflect the situation. Even earlier, in the winter of 1516-17, an old councillor of the High Court of Justice in Valladolid, the septuagenarian licentiate Pedro Ruiz of Villena, had presented to Charles and his advisers a memorial which may serve us for introduction to the politics and problems of Spain. Although it lacks the bitterness and clear emphasis which a political body can alone give to its writings, it deals with long-standing evils and embodies the advice of an experienced and loyal servant. In Spain, unlike Burgundy, the modern theory of the state, developed by a learned bureaucracy, had already found expression; it speaks out of the pages of this document with no uncertain voice. 'Keep God before your eyes': these are the words with which Ruiz begins his mirror for princes. Next he holds up as a model for his young master that ruler who devotes two hours of every day to prayer, two to study, two to justice and two to his army. He urges the monarch to temper justice with mercy after the example of the King of Kings: even by granting a pardon, justice may be done. False accusers should be punished as severely as the guilty. The Inquisition is to be preserved but strictly confined to experienced judges. It would be as well if the confiscation of goods by the Inquisition could be abolished, but if this is not possible then it should only come into force if the prisoner is condemned on the evidence of four witnesses and confesses his guilt without torture. Judges are very crafty in the exaction of perquisites, all of which should be abolished. First and foremost no part of confiscated goods should go to the judge; how honourable soever he may be, there will always be suspicions of foul play. It is a well-known scandal, in any case, that a bare third of the confiscated goods ever find their way to the royal treasury. Appeals in small matters should be made more difficult, and in great they should be confirmed by a new judge. A part of the money realized on grants made out of the sale of offices ought to be earmarked for the state.

Nor does Pedro Ruiz confine himself to the failings of the judicial system. He attacks both the lack of social justice and the unequal distribution of taxation. From the assessment of taxes, he passes to the devaluation of the coinage, the Maravedi in particular. Originally a gold coin, then a silver one, it had become a third of a Real, then a seventh, then a fourteenth and had now dwindled in value to a thirty-fourth. He next suggests that rich men should be restrained from appropriating more than a fair share of common land for their cattle. Among fifty peasants, he laments, not more than one or two are prosperous. The whole question of purveyance needs attention; previously the Court had only claimed a third of its expenses, now it takes half. If the King stays anywhere for any length of time he should pay for his lodging. The aim of fiscal policy should be to lower taxation for the benefit of the poor — 190,000 ducats a year should cover the expenses of a standing army of about 1000 heavy armed cavalry, 500 light horsemen and 2000 infantry; another 90,000 ducats should suffice to keep about 9000 troops in reserve; 100,000 ducats would be enough for a Court of 500 people, if salaries were properly graded. Nor are these figures Utopian; some of them even exceed the expenditure of Ferdinand and Isabella. But alas, the expenditure of the Burgundian Court had long been in excess of any such amount. The writer repeatedly emphasizes the fact that extravagance burdens not only the subject but the conscience of the prince himself.

One of the most interesting sections of the whole document is that in which Ruiz approaches the problems of the Church. The Pope ought to transfer the special privileges of the prelates to the King; he should be willing to do this in return for the services of 'so many Spaniards who have but recently poured forth their blood, not to mention their money, for Pope Julius'. Consecrated priests alone, not mere clerks, should be exempt from temporal justice; owing to the abuse of this privilege all too many crimes go unpunished. Priests should not be consecrated unless there is work waiting for them. Ruiz goes even further, complains that there are too many saints' days and suggests that plenary absolution should be given freely to all those who have conscientiously fulfilled their religious duties, but that it should be given only once a year or at the hour of death. The use of the interdict should be rigorously watched; above all a royal court of ecclesiastical justice should be set up, and appeals to Rome — where so many cases drag on for ever unsettled — should be forbidden. Annates may be used for war against the infidel and to lighten the weight of taxation on the poor. Unhappy factions and schisms in the land should end and all forces be united against the unbeliever.

This account proves that Ruiz was a man of perception but it gives a gloomy picture of conditions in Spain. We do not know how much of it reached the King. Echoes of it are to be found later in notes drawn up by Charles himself, but the same is true of many other such documents. Its importance lies rather in the impressive picture which it gives of the serious minded Catholicism and anxiety for reform of a typical councillor.

The royal government was, however, forced to adopt a positive attitude in reply to the explicit demands of the Cortes of 1518. In spite of all efforts at intimidation, one of the procurators of Burgos, Doctor Zumel, boldly defended the privileges of the Cortes. At his instigation they first refused to accept the Chancellor Sauvage as president and next formulated clear demands both as to the manner of the King's acclamation and the form of the oath which he was to take. They got their way. On February 5th the solemn ceremony was performed and on the 7th the clergy and grandees did homage.

The Cortes presented its demands in eighty-eight articles, of which some were in substance mere repetitions of those made by earlier Cortes. As in 1469 they asserted that the King was merely the representative of the people and they reiterated numerous economic demands, complaining of the export of gold, silver, horses, and of the alienation of Crown land. Other requests bore out what Pedro Ruiz had written. They asked that the judicial system be reformed, that the Inquisition be kept under control, that the King give audience daily and the council hold regular sessions. To this group too belonged the demand that the preaching and sale of indulgences be restrained, that taxes levied by clerical authority be prevented and that the Pope be urged to present no more benefices to foreigners. The remaining articles were concerned directly with the troubles of the day. The Cortes asked that Queen Joanna be suitably treated, that the King take a wife and that Don Ferdinand be allowed to remain in the country at least until the birth of an heir. All this was conceived in the narrowest dynastic sense. But the Cortes renewed the demands which they had made in the time of Ximenes: they asked that the King give neither official posts nor benefices to foreigners, that the new Archbishop of Toledo be brought to Spain, that Spaniards alone be given posts at Court. To the King personally they addressed a plea that he should learn Spanish. Their allusions to the testament of Cardinal Ximenes and the distribution of his worldly property cut nearer to the bone. But the emphasis which they laid on the necessity of holding Navarre — a province which they described as the key to the whole realm — was in strict accordance with Charles's own plans for foreign policy. In return for an exceptionally large *servicio*,[1] granted for three years and amounting to 600,000 ducats, the Cortes urgently entreated that the towns might be allowed to assess their own taxation instead of depending on tax farmers.

The royal government answered every point as favourably as possible; if there was no help for it, it did however refuse to comply, as in the case of the Infant's journey to the Netherlands, which had been settled long before. The protest against Papal interference with the Spanish Church and its revenues was likely to prove helpful in strengthening the idea of a national Church.

[1] A technical term, the equivalent of the English 'subsidy' (TRANSLATOR'S note).

Still more welcome was the willingness of the Cortes to defend Navarre; the government now felt that its foreign policy had the justification of popular consent.

On March 22nd, 1518, Charles left Valladolid in order to perform the same ceremonies, meet the same difficulties and achieve the same success in Aragon, as he had in Castile. At Saragossa the Aragonese Cortes voted him 200,000 ducats, at Barcelona the Catalans 100,000. Considering the size of these kingdoms as compared to Castile, the sums were more, rather than less, generous. But the Aragonese Cortes proved far more troublesome, their negotiations more procrastinating, their insistence on petty formality more irksome than those of Castile. When the Castilians saw that the Court, which had passed a bare four months in Valladolid and seen fit to visit no other town in the kingdom, was spending the whole of the rest of 1518 in Saragossa and almost the whole of 1519 in Barcelona, ill-feeling was at last aroused.

They had not made a grant of good Castilian money to see it frittered away in Aragon.

All this while there was discontent in Aragon. The Archbishop of Saragossa was prevented from visiting his half-sister Queen Joanna at Tordesillas; this was interpreted as a calculated insult. Complaints of the greed of the foreigners, like dust-clouds seen afar off, here too accompanied the passage of the Court. Naturally enough the long delay in Barcelona cured the Court of any wish to expose itself to the same inconveniences in Valencia, the third sub-kingdom of Aragon, a refusal which brought down upon Charles a new series of dangers and difficulties.

We look in vain among all these negotiations for any sign of the King's personal initiative. He figures only in the social life of the Court. The Chapter of the Golden Fleece met at Barcelona and elected to its ranks eight Castilians of the noblest families, together with an Aragonese and a Neapolitan; at this meeting Charles, to judge by the minutes of the Order, repeatedly opposed the opinions and wishes of Chièvres. But in the political world he had barely begun to take his share of responsibility. He gave his oath and received homage, nor were the actions of the government valid without him. His person was the sole guarantee for the unity of that government itself; yet he personally had remained so far immune from complaint and criticism.

Driven by necessity, Charles was exercising that virtue of self-effacement which is at times the most essential quality of a ruler. His action, or more truly, his inaction, was to exert a favourable influence on his future.

SPANISH OR UNIVERSAL POLICY?

Now as before, Chièvres and Sauvage, the responsible leaders of the royal government, were the targets for all attack. The situation was undoubtedly eased when on June 7th, 1518, the Chancellor Sauvage died; he carried with him to the grave some at least of the unpopularity of the government. His successor learnt in course of time to establish better relations with the Spaniards; moreover he of all men seemed made for the very purpose of weaning Charles from his limited Burgundian or Spanish outlook, and re-orientating his policy about a larger axis. This new Chancellor was Mercurino Gattinara. Although the transactions with the Cortes illuminate the problems of the moment and foreshadow those yet to come, their importance pales to nothing beside the elevation of Gattinara to a dominant position in public affairs and in the immediate surroundings of the King. Gattinara was to influence not only Charles's general policy but his character, as only Chièvres had done before, as no one was to do again.

The chance which made the Piedmontese Gattinara 'Grand Chancellor of all the realms and kingdoms of the king' on the eve of Charles's candidature for the imperial throne, is not without inner significance. Unlike all the other advisers who had hitherto served Charles, he was essentially a man of a universal outlook. For several years now both his autobiography and innumerable letters, printed and unprinted, have been available. The neat, clear handwriting of the humanist and scholar is typical of the defined and systematic character of the man. Schooled in the logic of jurisprudence, imbued both with the classic theory of the state and with the Christian doctrine of duty, his whole personality reflected a mind far above all material and personal considerations. Charles had grown up in the dynastic tradition of Burgundy and only with difficulty did he accustom himself to the secularized political theory of Spain; but it was Gattinara with his humanist conception of Emperor and Empire who first provided him with a practical formula for the consistent guidance of all his lands and peoples. The outstanding problem of Charles's life could only find an ultimate solution in the fusion of dynastic and imperial tradition. In his single person the glories of all his ancestors were concentrated and intensified; each part of his Empire was warmed by rays of reflected glory from the whole. But we must not forget that this overloading of the dynastic idea, no less than the emphasis laid on the primacy of the Emperor in Europe, was in direct contradiction to the theory of the national state, then gaining hold and expression throughout the west. The fundamental contradiction overshadowed Charles in life and long survived his death.

Mercurino Gattinara had been born of a family of lesser nobility at Vercelli in 1465; he rose to eminence as a lawyer, early entered the service of the Duke of Savoy, and accompanied the Archduchess Margaret from Franche Comté to the Netherlands as her legal adviser. As President of the *Parlement* of Dôle he had defended a personal cause with a certainty of his own rectitude reminiscent of Cardinal Ximenes, but in the end he had had to yield to the nobility, led by Maréchal Vergy. He remained nevertheless in Margaret's confidence and even Maximilian had entrusted him with important missions — one of which had kept him for a whole year (1510) at the Court of King Ferdinand in Spain. It is proof of Margaret's continued influence and of the shrewdness of Chièvres, that on the death of Sauvage, Gattinara was immediately selected for the Chancellorship. He arrived in Spain on October 8th and on the 15th took over the seals.

The relief occasioned by his coming was soon forgotten when he entered for the first time into European politics; the first opportunity afforded him for the practice of his universal theories came almost too soon.

The general lines of foreign policy had been already defined and Gattinara could not materially alter either the discontent of the Spaniards or Charles's relations with France. On the news of Maximilian's death, which the Court received at Lerida on January 28th-29th, 1519, the dangers inherent in Charles's foreign policy assumed gigantic proportions. Almost at once the Court had news that the French king was negotiating for the imperial throne. Meanwhile the discussions recently opened at Montpélier for the execution of the treaty of Noyon were prematurely interrupted by the sudden death of France's first delegate, Arthur Gouffier, Grand Maître of France. But from their very nature they were doomed to be abortive.

The greatness of Charles's government now showed itself, for the difficulties and dangers surrounding them in the Spanish kingdoms were of no effect in forcing Charles and his ministers to take up a false or ill-considered position in the altered field of European politics. Had the Court behaved with more tact during its two and a half years in Spain, some of its difficulties might have been smoothed away, but the fundamental problems would have remained. The great weakness of the old pragmatic school of historians, from Charles's contemporaries onwards, was that they always regarded single events or single men as the sole originators of political troubles whose roots lay far deeper.

A particular event may give a sudden stimulus to a general feeling of discontent, and there was much in the situation to trouble the politically conscious classes in Spain. They were subjected to the rule of a Burgundian courtier, to whom the exploitation of his opportunities was second nature, and over whom the inexperienced King exercised little control. Charles, who had not yet won the love of his people, had ascended the throne during the lifetime of a Queen-mother, herself incapable of ruling. Abroad, the new government was still, if only superficially, friendly to France; at home, out of fear and lack of sympathy, it repressed the natural forces of the country. The Spanish kingdoms were themselves split by factions. Worst of all, having once gained his *servicio*, Charles intended to leave this land, which had known no undisputed government for the past sixteen years, without making provision for a successor.

One of the most important sections of Charles's opponents although by no means the only one, was the group of Castilian towns represented in the Cortes. The inner tension of these towns gave birth to a revolutionary movement whose beginnings were already discernible when Charles left Spain. For as soon as the Court heard that Charles had been chosen King of the

Romans,[1] they dispensed with the ceremony of swearing allegiance in Valencia, and hastened instead across Castile to the north coast, there to take ship for Germany by way of England and the Low Countries.

Gattinara appears to have realized that the excitement in the towns would be aroused rather than quieted if the Cortes were called, while a demand for a second *servicio* before the expiry of the first might well fan their emotions into a dangerous blaze; but he could not convince Chièvres. Contrary to all custom the Castilian Cortes were summoned to a meeting at distant Santiago, only to be forced — not always by the most scrupulous means — to formulate their final decision at the port of Corunna itself.

In Valencia a destructive conflict had long since broken out between the nobles and the so-called *Germanía*, a league of small merchants. Matters were only made worse by contradictory decrees from the government. At the King's suggestion in May 1519 the guilds of Valencia had armed themselves against pirates and took a delight, that was not always without unfortunate consequences, in their weapons, banners and processions. By the decree of Fraga on January 31st, 1520, the King gave them some encouragement, thinking that he could have absolute confidence in the purpose for which they would use their defensive arms. They for their part recognized the monarchy as the fount of all justice. Moreover their leaders, the cloth-worker Juan Lorenzo, the more passionate Sorella, the dexterous confectioner Juan Caro and Geronimo Coll, had made their cause good at Court. But the nobility also came to Court, asked for the acceptance of their personal homage, 'for the ease of His Majesty's conscience', and were no less favourably received. The Guilds were then asked to restrain their activities. This was again contradicted in the final instructions left for Adrian and the Viceroy, which were all in favour of the *Germanía* — or brotherhood — whose membership now extended over the whole land, so that it stood ranged against the nobility both in town and country.

The rumoured departure of the King and the support given to the government by one or two deputies of the Cortes, was the

---

[1] *King of the Romans*, a title given by the German Electors to the prince chosen to succeed the reigning Emperor. For the development of this practice see BRYCE, *Holy Roman Empire*, Note C III (TRANSLATOR's note).

signal for a general rising in Castile. This rapidly assumed a serious form; all classes were drawn into the revolt and leaders were found even among the higher nobility. A deputation from Toledo headed by Pedro Laso de la Vega was not received. In Valladolid the people believed that their defenceless country was being exploited to serve the policy of foreigners and when Charles left they rang the tocsin; only by a lucky chance did the Court manage to get out at the gates. The Cortes met therefore in a tense atmosphere. Early in April the burghers and their league were victorious at Toledo and the royal Corregidor had to fly the town. At Segovia and Zamora there were yet more serious clashes. At Avila, on June 19th, 1520, the towns most deeply concerned formed themselves into a league, the Holy Junta.

On May 20th the Court embarked at Corunna.

The towns were not in agreement among themselves; the Comuneros everywhere were as hostile to the nobility as to the royal officials and the over-excited country drifted rapidly towards a general and disastrous civil war. Adrian of Utrecht, whom the King had left as regent, showed himself unequal to the task from the first, and each day added to his impotent perplexity. It had been all too easy for Chièvres to repeat what he had done in the time of Ferdinand of Aragon, and to make the deep-rooted friendship between Charles and his religious mentor a reason for imposing on the latter a burden which this time proved too heavy for him to bear.

But the time has come for us to turn our attention to that new honour which had for long enough, not without the influence of Gattinara, exerted its powerful enchantment over the young King — the imperial title. 'It is', so he wrote in his instructions to Adrian, 'so great and sublime an honour as to outshine all other worldly titles.' This belief was the sole justification which the King could advance for leaving Spain, in the midst of a rebellion, in great haste, and for three long years.

CHAPTER III

ARCHDUKE OF AUSTRIA AND HOLY ROMAN EMPEROR OF THE GERMAN NATION

HITHERTO we have hardly had occasion to notice that Charles was not only King of Castile and Aragon but, as a son of Philip of Burgundy and grandson of Maximilian of Austria, heir to the hereditary lands of the Hapsburg dynasty. Shortly before his Spanish marriage his father had paid a visit to Innsbruck, but Charles himself had set foot neither in Germany itself, nor in the hereditary lands on the Danube and Upper Rhine. These parts of his inheritance seemed doubtless as remote to him as the newly conquered Indies, which Cortes was even now piling up about the nucleus of New Spain. Charles himself could not yet speak German. But in his full title the many outlandish names of his German possessions all appeared.

These possessions included the family lands of the Hapsburg at the angle of the Upper Rhine, bordering on Franche Comté, the landgravate of Alsace with Ensisheim as its seat of government, a group of estates in the district now controlled by the strong Swiss Confederation; various countships in Breisgau and Swabia, in Vorarlberg and Tyrol. Innsbruck was the seat of Hapsburg administration in Hither Austria. Last of all there were Austria, Styria, Carinthia, Carniola and the Windish Mark, ruled over by a government at Wiener-Neustadt. These were rich lands; even the mountains were valuable for their store of precious metals and well-worked mines. They were important too because they controlled the key passes to other lands — the Arlberg, the Wormser Joch, the Brenner. Besides all these, there was the bishopric of Brixen, enclosed within Tyrol, and the bishopric of Trent on the frontier, stretching to the foothills of the Alps. On this side and in the east, the Alpine states encircled the so-called *terra firma*, the mainland of Venetia. Once a part of the Empire and called the Mark of Verona, it had, in the course of the last century, been gradually conquered by the republic of Saint Mark. Meagre result of Maximilian's last expensive wars — he had had to- renounce his claim on Verona and content himself in return with the cession of Riva, Rovereto and a few insignificant fragments to round off his frontier.

Austria itself stretched from Linz to Vienna, along the valley of the Danube, an important district both in geography and politics, for it was the connecting link between Bohemia and Hungary. To this juxtaposition it owed its political possibilities and perils, both internal and external. The two neighbouring kingdoms, after remaining for a short while under the control of the nobility alone — a fate with which Austria itself was repeatedly threatened — had fallen into the hands of the Jagellon family. At this time therefore they formed a dynastic whole with Poland.

MAXIMILIAN. THE HEREDITARY LANDS AND THE EMPIRE

Maximilian had received a bankrupt inheritance from his father. The reputation and the resources of the dynasty had been alike dissipated. But even if Maximilian in turn left the hereditary lands heavily encumbered with debt, he yet contrived to build on this derelict heritage the foundation for a brilliant future. In character Maximilian was unstable, easily tempted by wild plans, usually without patience and always without money. But those who consider or even demand that he should have had an equal measure of success in everything which he undertook, prove themselves guilty of the very faults with which they charge him.

Son of Frederick III by a Portuguese princess, husband first of Mary of Burgundy and then of Bianca Maria Sforza of Milan, Maximilian belonged in a very different way from the German Emperors of old to the now expanding world of European politics. Delighting in masquerade, he acted with passion and virtuosity any and every part which the day demanded of him. He passed his youth amid the glamorous surroundings of the Burgundian Court, but it was typical of his natural romanticism that he should later become absorbed in the humanistic atmosphere of the Renaissance. From these two sources he derived his conception of an Empire, universal in extent and resplendent with all the traditions of chivalry. The pursuit of this vision gave to his whole policy a strange air of unreality; even his military campaigns defied the dictates of common sense and assumed under his leadership the outward appearance of the tourney. A hundred half-formed conceptions revolved in his brain; he felt that the glory of his dynasty had some close connection with the special sanctity of the Emperor's person; he believed that it was his mission to expel the Turk from Europe; and he perceived dimly, although he could never clearly formulate, the connection between these two ideas and the honour and advancement of the German nation. But his contact both with Anglo-Dutch and with Italian civilization had early proved to him that kingship and honour were closely and irksomely yoked to finance. The opening years of the century were more fertile in political theory than in experimental practice and Maximilian was typical of his time in so far as his conceptions far outran his political capacity.

His literary efforts and his personal participation in the political propaganda of his government reflect these characteristics in a manner which, if sometimes distorting, is always instructive. He liked to call the Estates of the Holy Roman Empire the *Corpus Christianus*; and in commanding a prince of the Empire to war he would conjure him 'on the duty and obedience which thou owest to God, our Creator, to His Holy Faith and to us, His viceroy and thine own natural lord, to come immediately to our help, as the salvation of thy soul, thy duty and thine honour command'. His sense of nationality was still an indistinct mixture of religious formulae, supported by a common language and tradition, and — on account of his Burgundian connection — directed above all against the French. 'The Estates must consider', he said to them in 1509, 'that we, as lord of Austria and Burgundy, have for long years borne many weighty burdens and charges, have suffered much travail and expense at the hands of Frenchmen, Switzers, Gelderlanders, Hungarians and Turks.' He called the Swiss to war against the French because they spoke the German tongue, and he justified his wars in the Netherlands by saying that 'men of no foreign speech should break into Germany'. Yet this same prince spoke and wrote to his two only children in the French language alone. In an official manifesto he cited France as his chief and hereditary enemy and he insistently claimed that

Charlemagne had been a German. Yet for years he cherished no greater ambition than to marry the heiress of Brittany and thereby to make himself twice over a vassal of the French Crown. When he laid claim to Milan he acted partly as the master of the Empire but more for the sake of opposing France. So also when he marched on Venice, he acted in part to maintain his own imperial prestige but more to settle certain south-eastern frontier troubles on the Adriatic.

The German Estates had little difficulty in persuading him to the reform of the Empire; yet it is not surprising that they in return showed small desire to support him in those impulsive, varied, often brilliant, more often fantastic and always insufficiently considered plans which flitted through his mind. He did his duty indifferently towards the German nation; for he expected too much if he imagined that the princes would see eye to eye with him and accept his view that the interests of the hereditary lands, of the Hapsburg dynasty and of the Empire were one and undivided. In spite of a wild plan for making himself King of Sweden, Maximilian failed utterly both in the north-east and in Prussia, where he came up against the Order of the Teutonic Knights. He was equally unlucky in his dealings with those hereditary enemies of his house, the Switzers; unluckiest of all in Italy. Yet in spite of certain perilous crises, he did succeed with the help of his own peculiar tenacity, in solving the singularly difficult problem of Burgundy. Even if certain reforms were forced upon him rather than freely granted, he nevertheless deserves some credit for leaving the German Empire with an organization which, compared to that of earlier times, was astonishingly well ordered. Civil peace had been established, a standing court of justice, the *Reichskammergericht*, set up, the imperial administrative circles had been formed and a practical means of raising taxes, either by the *Gemeinpfennig* or the *Matrikel*, had been introduced. Maximilian had not only established his dynasty in the Spanish kingdoms, he had doubly secured their position by tempering his bold demands for participation in the regency with a skilful adaptation of his ideas to those of Ferdinand of Aragon. Lastly, during certain festive days in Vienna in July 1515, he had brought his earlier negotiations for the acquisition of Bohemia and Hungary to a successful conclusion. On July 20th he completed a transaction which is probably one of the most remarkable in imperial history; by it he adopted Louis of Bohemia, the heir of Ladislas, as his own son, and appealed to the electors to choose him Emperor. Even more astonishing was the marriage contract by which Louis was to be betrothed to the Hapsburg princess Mary, and his sister Anne to the already ageing Emperor. In the name of the Hapsburg dynasty, Maximilian was to take charge of Anne as soon as the treaty was signed. The Emperor could hardly have foreseen that these amazing agreements were to bring forth material results almost immediately. When he thus sought to unite in one dynastic bond all the resources of Christendom, so that the Turks, whose menacing advance had continued unchecked since the beginning of the last century, might at last be stopped, he was acting less as an individual than as the tool of historic circumstance. Maximilian's policy had little in common with the political nationalism of the nineteenth century. Yet the effect of his actions long survived him, and the dynastic policy which he had outlined took its place as a possible solution to the problems of a great part of Europe. Dynastic policy has as much historic justification as the theory of the national state itself. Maximilian, by arranging for Ferdinand to succeed to these various prospects of inheritance in Central Europe, had defined the frontiers of that territorial division which was later to be made between Charles and his brother.

THE IMPERIAL ELECTION

The political structure of the Austrian lands and the German Empire was more essentially medieval than that of the duchy of Burgundy or even of the Spanish kingdoms. The Hapsburg dynasty owed its dominance merely to the extent of its territorial possessions and privileges; its estates were scattered far and wide among the lands of innumerable princes, lords and free-cities, who, theoretically the vassals of the Emperor, were in fact wholly independent. The titles by which these lords, dukes, margraves and counts were known were fundamentally as little distinct one from another as the same titles in Spain and Burgundy. The distinction between a free prince of the Empire and a member of the local nobility, for instance, had no real significance before the religious and ecclesiastical conflicts of the next generation. The principalities and lordships of which Germany was made up were each individually in a higher state of political development than was the Empire of which they formed part. Indications of political theory were already to be found among them, formulated by learned councillors in recognizable forms. Perhaps this was the natural outcome of their separate patriarchal organization, perhaps the result of the long struggle for imperial reform.

There was as little evidence of any clear policy for the Empire as a whole as there was of a truly German foreign policy.

The seven Electors alone — the three spiritual Electors of Cologne, Mainz and Treves, and the four secular Electors of Bohemia, the Palatinate, Brandenburg and Saxony — possessed as well as certain exceptional rights during an interregnum, a general importance far greater than that justified by the extent of their lands. Since Maximilian's grandson was Duke of Burgundy and King of Spain, and the Kings of England and France were rivals for the imperial crown, the Electors in the last years of Maximilian's reign had achieved a European significance. Their importance was further increased by the natural anxiety of the Pope as to the choice of the future Emperor; in his capacity as ruler of the Papal States, the Pope was bound to keep careful watch on the Spanish King of Naples, no less than on the King of France who had recently grown so powerful in Italy. The acquirement of the imperial crown would give Francis I an impregnable position in Italy; besides which it would flatter his ambition and give him the idle pleasure of seeing the youthful Charles twice over his vassal. Henry VIII, on the other hand, had once been opposed to the French dynasty and had subsidized coalitions against Louis XII and Francis I, not only in Burgundy and Navarre, but even in North Italy. More recently, however, he had changed his policy and was now contemplating a marriage between his daughter and the Dauphin. By coming forward as a candidate for the imperial crown he proved that at this time even England had no conception of national *Realpolitik*. The early Tudors were dominated still by the old medieval theory of universal monarchy.

Three successive Emperors of the house of Luxembourg had

been followed by three successive Emperors of the Hapsburg dynasty. It was therefore still justifiable to consider that the German monarchy was disposed of by inheritance, as it had been in the Middle Ages. Charles of Spain was the grandson of Maximilian, a fact of which his supporters made every possible use. But he was as much a foreigner in Germany as the King of England or the King of France.

Maximilian did not deceive himself on this point. If, in the exuberance of a new friendship, in temporary annoyance with the Burgundian government, or in one of his usual financial scrapes, he promised the imperial throne now to the boy-king of Bohemia and Hungary, now to Henry VIII of England, there can yet be no serious doubt but that his thoughts were in reality fixed on his own dynasty. As late as 1551 the Count Palatine, Frederick, told Veltwyk how vividly he remembered the unconcealed efforts which Maximilian had made in 1513. In his usual fashion and with the most disarming simplicity Maximilian never lost sight of the practical uses to which the imperial title could be put in the hereditary lands, nor of the advantages to be derived from the financial resources of Burgundy and Spain. When Charles made his first appearance among the candidates for the imperial crown by sending the lord of Courteville to Germany, Maximilian's criticism of the ambassador's instructions was sharpened by his personal interest in the matter.

There was no need to harp on Charles's kinship to him, he wrote, on May 18th, 1518, 'Much money' was by far the best argument for winning votes. And since the imperial title would add to the value of the hereditary lands, there was no need to be parsimonious. No one would be satisfied with promises; hard cash alone would be effective. The princes thought more of the jingling coin of the French than of all their fair words. The Elector Palatine must have an indemnification of 80,000 gold Gulden well and truly paid to him, in return for the bailiwick of Hagenau, which did in fact belong to the Empire but would be a useful addition to the Hapsburg lands. The Elector of Saxony must be immediately satisfied with the relatively small sum of 30,000 gold Gulden for renouncing his claim to Friesland. The spiritual princes could not be fobbed off merely with promises of benefices. The sum of 4000 gold Gulden apiece — which had been decided on as suitable for the temporal Electors — was the smallest possible amount with which they could be satisfied. Some of them had already had much more than this from France. As well as the Electors, certain other princes had to be considered, the Margrave Casimir for instance.[1] The French had already offered that ubiquitous bride, Princess Renée, to the Elector of Brandenburg for his son. To outbid them, Maximilian suggested, Charles could not do better than offer his sister Katherine. Even for Sickingen[2] something more than a pension would be necessary: rather, thus shamelessly did Maximilian express himself, he must be paid 20,000 gold Gulden in return for the damage he had done to Worms. Since Duke Louis of Bavaria had refused to take Queen Joanna of Naples to wife,[3] he should be offered the daughter of Gonzalo Hernandez, his brother William, Princess Eleonore, whose betrothal to the old King of Portugal Maximilian opposed. Only by drawing on all possible resources could they hope to combat the 'monstrous practices' of the French within the Empire. The French had already sent so splendid an embassy to the Switzers that Charles could not possibly make do with sending Courteville. A more important man would have to be selected — say Zevenbergen.

A few weeks later new instructions did in fact come for Courteville. In the summer the Electors appeared at Augsburg in person and buzzed about Maximilian. Even the King of Bohemia was represented; he was still a minor but the plenipotentiaries of his nearest kinsman, the King of Poland, acted for him. On August 7th all except Saxony and Treves declared themselves ready to accept the Emperor's grandson Charles. Treves had apparently committed himself too far with France, and Saxony appealed to the Golden Bull. Nevertheless Maximilian did not lose hope of winning them both over.

But Maximilian's death on January 12th, 1519, released the Electors from all obligations and opened the last stage in the conflict for the crown.

[1] Casimir of Brandenburg, 1481-1527, Margrave of Baireuth, first cousin to the reigning Elector (Joachim) of Brandenburg (TRANSLATOR'S note).
[2] Franz von Sickingen, 1481-1523, the celebrated Rhenish knight and free-lance leader. He had attacked Worms in 1513, Mainz in 1518, and had recently been employed by the Swabian League against Ulrich, Duke of Württemberg (TRANSLATOR'S note).
[3] Widow of Ferdinand II of Naples, d. 1496 (TRANSLATOR'S note).

At this time there were, beside Charles's own council, two other Hapsburg governments, in the Netherlands and in Austria. Both depended on instructions from the Court but were forced, by its remoteness, to a certain self-reliance in State affairs. Much might hang on their immediate knowledge and their personal activity.

Matthias Lang, Bishop of Gurk, Cardinal since 1511, and later Archbishop of Salzburg, was head of the government in Austria. He had been coadjutor of Salzburg since 1514 and in the year of Maximilian's death he became Archbishop. He passed both now and later for a harsh, unsociable man, and more than one member of the Burgundian council considered him unfit to handle the negotiations for the imperial crown. His chief lieutenant was Michael von Wolkenstein, once a particular favourite of Maximilian; his name and titles may be seen to this day in the inscription which greets the eyes of travellers, pierced in the stonework above the gateway of that castle not far north of Brixen where his descendants still live. Cyprian von Serntein was Chancellor, a man of long experience, as also the treasurer Villinger and Hans Renner. Charles added the bishops of Trieste and Trent, Dietrichstein, Roggendorf and one or two other councillors to this government before he confirmed its powers. Among those whom the Hapsburg trusted within the Empire itself were the Count Palatine Frederick — in spite of his recent unwilling banishment from Court — the Margrave Casimir and Matthias Schinner, Bishop of Sitten who, like Matthias Lang, had been a cardinal since 1511.

For long enough, too, all the resources of the Burgundian government had been placed at the disposal of the dynasty in Germany. The German princes and supporters of the dynasty were assisted in their advocacy of Charles's cause by Hugo, Count of Mansfeld, a scion of the Germanic nobility of the Netherlands, and Maximilian Berghes, Lord of Zevenbergen, a leading member of one of the great Dutch families. This latter had recently received the Golden Fleece, together with Mansfeld and Wolkenstein, and he was bitterly insulted when he found that he was expected to act under orders from the Innsbruck government. On his urgent representations the position was set right; Nicholas Ziegler was restored to favour at the same time and even considered for the office of imperial vice-chancellor. As well as these,

Margaret sent her personal secretary Marnix to Zevenbergen at Augsburg early in February, there to help him in his fight against the allurements of France. He was to tell the German princes that they would have to pay fourfold for every French ducat which they took. Another leading councillor, Hugo Marmier, was dispatched at about the same time to the Electors of Treves and Mainz. As the date of the election drew nearer, Margaret redoubled her activity. The councillors whom she now had about her were Philip of Cleves, Charles de Croy, lord of Chimay, Henry of Nassau, Antoine Lalaing, lord of Hoogstraeten, and her old confidant Jean de Berghes. Little by little the Brussels government put its best men forward; Zevenbergen was followed by Charles's dearest friend, Henry of Nassau, who was to woo the counts of the Rhineland for their support; later accompanied by Gérard de la Pleine, lord of La Roche, he sought out the Electors of Treves and Cologne, and later still, accompanied this time by Johann von Armerstorf, he continued his journey to the Courts of Saxony and Brandenburg. Armerstorf himself had already visited the Electors of the Palatinate, of Treves and Mainz. Last of all Margaret thought of using Eberhard de la Mark, Bishop of Liège, in the German business. He was expecting shortly to be made a cardinal.

All these gentlemen and their secretaries worked with feverish activity and their reports, often written daily, bear witness to the intense excitement which reigned in Germany in that memorable spring of 1519. Well-founded information of the intentions of the French government mingled with the wildest rumours: King Francis was sparing neither men nor money; he intended to march at the head of an army across Lorraine to the Rhine, and had secret allies within the Empire. For their part the Electors in the Rhineland felt compelled to appeal to Charles to guarantee them from coercion.

The French menace in the Netherlands and the Empire became real with the circulation of a rumour that the French King's old protégé, Charles of Gelderland, had married at Celle the daughter of Henry of Luneburg, and was now offering assistance to his father-in-law. This Duke Henry had joined with the Bishop of Hildesheim, himself by birth a duke of Saxe-Lauenburg, in prosecuting a feud against the refractory nobility of the latter's diocese —

with the family of Saldern above all. The nobility, for their part, had found ready help with Duke Eric of Calenberg and his nephews, Duke Henry the younger of Wolfenbüttel and Duke Francis, Bishop of Minden. Hitherto this destructive conflict had been waged chiefly at the expense of the see of Hildesheim, but the bishop's friends now turned their attentions towards Minden, reduced the fortress of Petershagen and overran the whole district. In Lower Saxony, therefore — that land whose hardy breed both of men and horses was to make it for the whole of the next generation the best recruiting ground in Germany — the French party had a victorious army already on foot.

The Hapsburg dynasty, too, had military support. The Swabian League, by origin an alliance for the protection of the lesser estates, knights and towns against the aggressive rulers of Württemberg, had long been a tool of Hapsburg policy. A new opportunity to mobilize the League occurred when the Duke of Württemberg, who was already involved in the murder of Hans von Hutten,[1] attacked Reutlingen. His quarrels with his wife had meanwhile brought her brothers, the Dukes of Bavaria, about his ears. The French supported him inadequately and a brief campaign ended in the sequestration of his lands. Zevenbergen's ingenious policy in Zurich forestalled an attempt of the Switzers to come to his help; realizing that they were now in danger of being surrounded by the French, they were clamorous for the election of an Emperor who came of a German line. Thus at the end of May 1519 the disengaged troops of the Swabian League stood ready to be taken into Hapsburg pay at a moment's notice. At about the same time the Austrians detached from France and won over to Charles's side another military force which was much feared: this was the leader of Landsknechts, Franz von Sickingen.

Such was the situation in Germany in spring 1519.

Yet the success of the Hapsburg government, however skilful and energetic its efforts, depended ultimately on the will and means of the young sovereign in Spain. For the third time now we shall see how Charles himself played his part and how effectively he reimbursed his commissioners and agents for their immense

---

[1] Hans von Hutten, stabbed by Ulrich, Duke of Württemberg, during a hunting party on May 7th, 1515. He was a kinsman of the celebrated Ulrich von Hutten, who lent his literary talents to stir up the general indignation at the murder (TRANSLATOR'S note).

outlay on bribes, indemnities and pensions. All told, the election cost nearly a million gold Gulden, of which nearly half went in bribes to the Electors and their advisers. The greater part of this immense sum was released by the firm of Fugger, whose account books to this day bear witness to Hapsburg expenditure. They insured themselves against risk by steadily acquiring more imperial and dynastic lands and privileges in Swabia and Tyrol.

One day the anxious Court in the Netherlands gave Charles an opportunity to make his own point of view clear. Someone had delicately hinted that, should his position as King of Spain prove an insurmountable barrier to his election to the imperial throne, the Archduke Ferdinand, or even some other German prince such as the Elector of Saxony, should be put forward in his place. Margaret's advisers were frankly far more concerned to prevent the election of the French King than to secure that of Charles. But at the merest suggestion of this alternative Charles was up in arms. On May 5th he sent one of his personal confidants, Adrian de Croy, Lord of Beaurain, on whom he had just bestowed the Golden Fleece, with meticulous instructions and a personal letter to his aunt. Passionate and almost jealous was the intensity with which this grandson of Maximilian counted on acquiring intact the whole inheritance of his ancestors.

By this envoy he declared that he had already spent much, his prospects were hopeful and the Electors had previously expressed themselves willing to choose him. He therefore refused to forgo his candidature in favour of any other man. The Electors might well take his intervention in Ferdinand's behalf for an insult to them and a renunciation of those obligations which he had already undertaken. His advisers were to understand that he would stake his last penny, for he had no greater desire in all the world than to be elected. He had instructed his agents to spare no effort, for his reputation and honour depended on it. He had a mind to prove that his friendship was worth as much as that of the French King. The mere suggestion that Ferdinand should come to Germany to take possession of the Hapsburg lands he sharply set aside; the idea, he said, may have been put forward in all good faith and out of a praiseworthy desire to help, but he could not but express his amazement at the making of such independent plans. Matters of this nature had to be most carefully considered. He had arranged for an army both in Germany and Naples and as soon as his election had been successfully concluded he would come over for his coronation. Once he was Emperor, his prospects would be very different and he would naturally take care of his brother. But the division of the Hapsburg power at this critical moment was precisely what the French most wished to see. Whatever arrangements had been made, either for Ferdinand's candidature or for his visit to Germany, must be immediately and completely cancelled. A postscript in his own hand once again emphasized the fact that these were his own personal wishes. Moreover, he wrote to his brother to warn him against further suggestions of this kind and to assure him of his willingness to make a reasonable division of the inheritance with him later on.

Even more explicit than these letters were the instructions drawn up for Beaurain. Here for the first time Charles definitely mentioned a project for the election of Ferdinand as King of the Romans, after his own imperial election. And here, too, we find him expressing the fear that these other suggestions are the fruit of a French intrigue, calculated to separate him from his brother by means of a French marriage. Ferdinand would be in no position to maintain himself on the imperial throne, for even their grandfather Maximilian, in spite of his remarkable ability and many victories, was never free from grave anxieties. Only the union of all the Hapsburg lands under a single head would give to the imperial title an actual power strong enough to intimidate any opponent, so that the Emperor would at last be free to work for the salvation of the faith and the defence of Christendom.

These words clearly reveal the interaction between Charles's dynastic ambition, his aristocratic Burgundian pride and his high conception of imperial duty. They reveal, too, not merely the influence, but the actual penmanship, of Gattinara. Charles's feelings found expression in the appeal to honour and reputation, but the belief in imperial power as a dominant factor in the pacification of Christendom — this sprang from the mind of Gattinara.

The theory behind Hapsburg policy as expressed by its agents at Innsbruck, at Augsburg, at the German Courts, in the Netherlands and in Spain, was uniform, even if it was based on different premises and expressed with more or less vigour according to the temperament of the spokesman. But how would they carry out their intentions within the political framework of Europe? Was not Charles himself bound by sacred obligations to that very dynasty which now so haughtily opposed him? Was it not possible that France might lean again towards England, now that the brief clash of arms in 1513 had been nullified by the return of Tournai? Had not a *rapprochement* between France and the Pope recently come to pass? The Papacy had played an important part in disposing of the German kingship since the thirteenth century — and this in spite of the declaration made when Lewis the Bavarian was Emperor. Vatican policy always had an eye both to universal needs and to those of the Italian states.

The sudden death of the French ambassador had brought the discussions at Montpelier to an end, since when Paris had displayed little inclination to resume them. The Pope was unfriendly and England's attitude uncertain. The director of English policy, the gifted but vain Archbishop of York, Cardinal Wolsey, gave fair words to everyone and received a corresponding number of gifts in return. He himself hoped to become the arbiter of Christendom while his master gained the imperial title. Leo X informed him, through the legate Campeggio, that he agreed with the English government in not wishing to see either the King of France or the King of Spain on the imperial throne; but unlike the English he held the King of Spain's election for more dangerous than that of the King of France. Henry VIII had long asked for nothing better than this encouragement to press his own candidature; but on his side he emphasized the fact that should he fail, he preferred the election of Charles to that of the French King. Thus Henry and the Pope agreed to give equal encouragement to both candidates, while secretly undermining them. The instructions with which Richard Pace was sent to Germany on May 30th were conceived in these terms. The English government had cast itself for the part of *tertius gaudens*.

But the Pope did not stand by his agreement; rather he assured the King of France of his warmest support and on his behalf offered cardinals' hats to the Electors of Treves and Cologne and the post of permanent legate to the Elector of Mainz who was already a cardinal. Furthermore he sent as nuntius to Germany, where Cajetan and Carraciolo were already active, the francophile Orsini. At a meeting of the Rhenish Electors at Oberwesel,

Orsini proclaimed that Charles as King of Naples was not eligible for the Empire, owing to an obligation to which Ferdinand of Aragon had once committed himself. This declaration rent the veil which had hitherto concealed papal policy. Charles's government at once protested in Rome, whereat the Pope took no further pains to conceal his objection to Charles's election even from the Spanish ambassador.

By May all the cards were on the table. Apparently every government in Europe was against Charles and the German Electors were wavering. But in fact the very peril of the situation was an element which worked in his favour. English policy, over-subtle, nullified itself; Pace achieved nothing and could only report the sudden, inexplicable eclipse of French prospects. The open alliance of the Pope and France proved the surest means of securing the votes of the Electors for the Hapsburg dynasty. The Germans began to grow restive at the ostentation of French power and the constant emphasis laid by the ambassadors of Francis on the might and resources of their King. The credit of the Pope in these, the first years of the Lutheran movement, was waning. On the other hand national feeling had been awakened by the rise of humanism, and above all in Alsace and the Rhineland men were growing almost daily more conscious of their political entity in opposition to the French and in relation to the dynasty of the last emperor. The friendly, forthcoming, cheerful and gallant manners of Maximilian had won both the princes and the people to his side. The faults they had found in his policy were now forgotten. His picture, distributed over the country in countless broadsheets, had remained a living one, and his young grandson who would not be intimidated either by the menacing power nor the personal demands of his French neighbour, rejoiced — certainly without the least personal merit — in what is commonly called popularity. Cheap portraits of him in woodcut were scattered broadcast and a popular song asseverated:

> I hope the cause may yet be won
> If Charles, of noble house the son,
> Will take it for his own. [1]

[1] Ich hoff, die Sach soll werden gut,
So Carolus, des edel Plut
die Sach tut für sich nehmen.

Some years ago a German historian attempted to destroy the Hapsburg legend. But against the clear voice of tradition he shouted in vain.[1]

The inevitable happened. The Hapsburg government had made thorough and extensive preparations for the election. Without allowing anyone to feel the pressure they had cautiously raised an army, and they had poured out money on all sides. All that they lacked was provided by the behaviour of their opponents.

In this situation the Pope seized on one last weapon. Seeing that the election of the French King was now impossible, he still sought to prevent the elevation of Charles. He fell back on the choice of a German Elector.

Only the Elector with the highest reputation came up for consideration. This was Frederick the Wise of Saxony. He had been mentioned in this connection once many years before, only to disappear completely behind greater names. This harsh and mistrustful man stood in fact at the very heart of the political problem; he was the temporal overlord of that Augustinian monk and professor of Wittenberg who was even now combating papal indulgences with such profound sincerity and immense knowledge. Driven on by this one question, the monk Luther was soon to be forced into open conflict with the whole ostentatious being of the Church. Controlled by foreigners, guided by the lust of power, what had it now in common with the spirit of the Gospel, with the joyful news of sinful man's reconciliation with God, his father?

Frederick the Wise had listened unmoved to the overtures of Maximilian. Later Hapsburg offers had smote against the same obstinate resistance; it was not his affair to engineer an election. The offer of a Hapsburg bride with a splendid dowry for his son did not, however, find him altogether indifferent. But this as well as bribes given to his councillors and a large loan for the electoral treasury, were regarded as immaterial to the election. Even the money was nothing but an indemnity for an old debt. There is no doubt that the Elector's coyness was proof of more delicacy than was to be found in the actions of his fellows. Mainz had accepted 113,200 gold Gulden for himself and his councillors; Cologne, up to the present, 52,800; the Palatinate 184,000, includ-

---

[1] The historian was PAUL KALKOFF in *Die Kaiserwahl Friedrichs IV und Karls V.* Weimar, 1925 (TRANSLATOR's note).

ing the indemnity for Hagenau and satisfaction for the Count Palatine, Frederick. These princes had unblushingly forced up the amount of the bribes by negotiating. Judging by the books of the Fuggers the final sum paid to the Elector of Saxony was 70,000 Gulden. All the Electors therefore got their wages, save only the most insatiable of all, the Elector of Brandenburg, who went empty handed away. Although once he wavered so close to Hapsburg policy that the marriage of his eldest son to 'Fräulein Katharina von Hispanien' was all but carried out by proxy, he remained at the end unwisely loyal to France.

At the last moment the Pope and the King of France tried to influence the Elector of Saxony through the busy Karl von Miltitz. On July 14th Miltitz insinuated that, should the election of the French King prove unattainable, Frederick should stand himself. His Holiness would regard the election as valid if Frederick gained only two other voices beside his own. By this it seems that they were making the curious error of reckoning the number of electors as six only. Nor was this all: should Frederick agree, the Pope would give him leave to dispose of a cardinal's hat to whomsoever he chose. Some have thought that this offer was directed at Luther — an idea which cannot but appear ridiculous to anyone who has followed the inner activities of the Vatican at that time; a case had been already drawn up against Luther. But these overtures foundered on the immovable honesty of the old prince; he answered a French offer of marriage openly and honourably, saying that he was already negotiating with the other side. The one thing essential to his candidature was lacking — his own consent.

But matters never got so far. We have certain knowledge that the last talks of the Electors at Frankfort on June 26th and 27th brought no new developments. On the evening of the 27th they appointed the following day for the actual election. The town council informed the people that they must not be frightened if the tocsin rang three times: that was the custom at elections, and at the sound of the bell every man must pray God to send down his grace on the Electors 'that they might choose a King who would be useful to God Almighty, the Holy Empire and us all'. Charles was unanimously elected. Only the Elector of Brandenburg declared that he made the election 'out of very fear and not out of very knowledge'. But when the election was announced 'the 22 trumpeters of the Count Palatine and the Margrave of Brandenburg blew on their trumpets and then the organ rolled forth the great Te Deum Laudamus'. So wrote the town clerk of Frankfort.

Charles was the fifth of his name in the ranks of German kings and emperors and under that title he has gained immortality in history and in the languages of all peoples. He bore the old Carolingian name, a name carried only by one emperor since their time, and then by the Luxembourger Charles IV, he too a native of the lower Frankish land which had brought forth Charlemagne. The history of Germany and western Europe seemed to harken back to its beginnings, and once again a great future seemed to spread out before it.

Such at least was the prophecy of Charles's leading minister, his Grand Chancellor Gattinara. In a memorial written on July 12th, 1519, and therefore directly after the election, he entered upon the great work of his master's political education with these words: 'Sire, God has been very merciful to you: he has raised you above all the Kings and princes of Christendom to a power such as no sovereign has enjoyed since your ancestor Charles the Great. He has set you on the way towards a world monarchy, towards the uniting of all Christendom under a single shepherd.' For this reason, he went on, it was fitting that Charles should fear God and be humble, conscientiously execute the testament of his ancestors, care for the Queen-mother and be generous to his brother. He must seek out the right men for employment in Church and State and for the proper administration of justice. Like Moses he must select good advisers, like Justinian pass wise laws, and like Titus administer them with mildness. To these qualities he must add the generosity of Seneca, and moderation in all things. He must order his finances and keep discipline in his army: a hundred well-paid soldiers would be worth more to him than two hundred without pay. He must centralize and supervise his household expenditure. Gattinara warned Charles against showing preference to the Netherlanders; he suggested that the inner council be kept small, and, lest important matters should be delayed, that the Emperor should settle all pressing business as soon as he got up, if not actually while he was dressing. To relieve the pressure on the monarch and his Chancellor, he recommended that the royal

secretaries be allowed partial, the Courts of Justice total, independence of action. Towards the end of the document he added
that the king owed his especial gratitude, after his parents, to the
Marquis of Arschot, lord of Chièvres. In conclusion he reiterated
his belief that the true purpose of monarchy was to unite all
peoples in the service of God.

On November 30th at Molins del Rey the Electors ceremoniously
acclaimed Charles through a special embassy. Gattinara answered
them with a dignity suited to the occasion. A few weeks later he
received an embassy from the Austrian Estates. The Chancellor
painted the new King in the brightest colours, and even in private
conversations defended him against all unfavourable rumours.
Yet we cannot but feel that the wish was father to the thought
when he asserted, in praise of his master's industry, that he trans-
acted important business even in the early morning, in his bed,
showing an insight which often put his elders to shame.

A few weeks later the Chancellor produced his schedule of
advice on the titles, coats of arms, seals and currency to be used
by the new Emperor. Every document, he stated, should now
begin with the formula: 'King of the Romans, elected Roman
Emperor, semper augustus.' Other titles could come after. In
order to forestall all possible complaints Charles should proclaim
in Castile and Aragon that he intended in no way to lower the
dignity and honour of these kingdoms, rather the reverse. The
name of Queen Joanna, too, was still to be included after Charles's
imperial title but before his royal one. In Germany his title
should run: 'Roman King, future Emperor, semper augustus,
King of Spain, Sicily, Jerusalem, the Balearic Islands, the Canary
Islands, the Indies and the mainland on the far side of the
Atlantic, Archduke of Austria, Duke of Burgundy, Brabant,
Styria, Carinthia, Carniola, Luxemburg, Limburg, Athens and
Patras, Count of Hapsburg, Flanders and Tyrol, Count Palatine
of Burgundy, Hainault, Pfirt, Roussillon, Landgrave of Alsace,
Count of Swabia, Lord of Asia and Africa.' This grouping of
titles by strict precedence of rank, rather than by lands or peoples,
is typical of the outlook in accordance with which this new
universal Empire was to be built.

Gattinara advised Charles to sign documents in future with his
own name, not as in Spain, simply, 'Yo el Rey' — 'I the King'.

As for his arms, he could in future carry nothing but the two-headed eagle as the late Emperor had done; smaller shields could be grouped round it. Different seals could be used in different lands and by the various German chancelleries. But the Emperor must keep a great imperial seal for all secret or important transactions. This seal must be a royal seal, showing the Emperor on his throne with sceptre and orb, the imperial arms on the right, the royal arms on the left. There could be lesser seals for each department as well as a secret and counter seal for Burgundy with the cross of Saint Andrew, the flint and steel of the Order of the Golden Fleece and the device *Plus Oultre*; or else the device alone with the Pillars of Hercules. Spanish coins should bear Charles's head and the imperial eagle on the obverse, his mother's likeness on the reverse and the arms of the country. Moreover he suggested for Charles's consideration the plan of 'simplifying the currency in the Spanish fashion by making these coins valid throughout all his dominions'. Gattinara was doubtless dreaming of a Europe united even in the economic sphere.

CHANGED RELATIONS BETWEEN THE POWERS. THE FIELD OF THE CLOTH OF GOLD

The election once completed every government in Europe was forced to reconsider its political connections. Francis I had boasted too much and, inadequate as his measures had been, they had nevertheless exposed both his pride and his political reputation to a heavy blow. On the credit side, the promise of marriage made by Charles to his daughter still held good. With this in mind, his advisers gave expression to a modified joy in Charles's election, which, so it was reported, 'had cost infinitely more than the French negotiations'. Francis I forced himself to accept the bitter-sweet consolation, and even sent his congratulations to Charles, who received them gratefully.

Even Henry VIII put a good face on his losses. He recalled 'his old and friendly relations with Burgundy and Spain'. Charles thanked him in seemly fashion for his supposed help at the election, as also did Margaret, on the occasion of the reception which she accorded to Richard Pace. In fact she had good reason to be grateful both for France's defeat and for England's attitude of apparent friendship.

More timorous than the two youthful secular rulers of England and France, the Pope was less able to simulate unconcern. Yet Leo X saw that French friendship might be rather a menace than a support to his position in Italy and much as he feared the Spaniards, he felt nevertheless drawn towards them whether he would or no. He could not altogether forget that the power of the French ruler of Milan was still unshaken. The numerous and often astonishing reports of ambassadors, particularly those of the Venetians, whose government was in much the same quandary as the Pope, reveal with merciless precision the devious course which led Leo from his first exaggerated hopes to his final obsequious acceptance of the situation. These dispatches are daily commentaries, not well-prepared accounts; walls, especially those of ante-rooms, have eyes, and it was soon observed that the French, English and Venetian ambassadors used the imperial elections as an excuse to stay away from the solemnities and feasts of the Vatican. The Pope for his part declared that these three powers must stand together with the Swiss, in order to counterbalance the rising power of Charles. He was anxious not only for the papal states, among which he would gladly have included Ferrara, but above all for his native Florence, where his nephew Lorenzo de' Medici, himself bound to France by marriage, had but recently died. For long enough he hesitated to confirm the fief of Naples to the new Emperor, for both ancient and modern decretals stood in the way, to say nothing of France's claim.

Commines had dated the rise of the Swiss as a European power in the sixties of the last century. Since the French invasion of Italy, their position had been generally recognized. The Confederation controlled, in its own subjects, Europe's best mercenary soldiers, and since the acquirement of Lugano and Locarno in 1512 it had a gateway to the Duchy of Milan itself. This was of the utmost importance for not only was the duchy hotly disputed between the Emperor, Venice and France, but it was of great economic value. Hapsburg and French embassies came simultaneously or close upon each other to the federal meetings held at Zurich and Baden. But for the time being the Swiss kept clear of all entanglements.

Peace with England and France was essential for the moment at least, so that Charles would be able safely to return from Spain to the Netherlands and Germany. Negotiations with Henry VIII were entrusted to the Bishop of Elne, Bernard de Mesa, and to the secretary Le Sauch. The English expectantly awaited Charles's visit, flattered by the belief that it would be the first official visit to be paid by the newly-elected Emperor. Since Charles's government, hampered by the rapidly waning friendship of France, showed signs of holding back, Wolsey exerted additional pressure. At the beginning of 1520 he himself openly encouraged French overtures and at length arranged that personal meeting between Henry VIII and Francis I which each of these spirited princes had long ago sworn to bring to pass. The new situation found immediate expression in the presumptuous note which was handed over by the emissaries of Francis I at Burgos on February 20th; in this the French King demanded no less than the immediate execution of the treaty of Noyon.

All this was not without effect on Spain and the Netherlands. The Hapsburg government in these countries wanted nothing less than a close understanding between the Kings of England and France. Charles therefore sent a distinguished embassy, the aged Berghes, Gorrevod, La Roche and Haneton, as well as Le Sauch and Mesa, as his ambassadors extraordinary to England, to announce his arrival. This was not enough for Margaret. She hurried to meet all English overtures with outstretched arms, immediately ordered Le Sauch to hasten on ahead of the others, to repudiate the original imperial offer to meet Henry VIII on the Isle of Wight and to accept instead Southampton, the place originally proposed by the English government for the meeting of the sovereigns. Prudently Margaret added that Le Sauch was not to let it appear to the English that these offers were the result of the recent *rapprochement* between Francis and Henry; for this reason she even deleted several sentences from the instructions originally given to the secretary because they emphasized points which she thought better suppressed.

And now, strangely enough, the political issue was altogether submerged by questions of mere etiquette. For the next weeks all efforts of English, French and Hapsburg diplomacy were concerned with the formalities of the meeting. There was no talk of

Charles visiting France; it was agreed that he should land in England in mid-May, make the first official visit of his imperial reign there and then continue to the Netherlands. In the meantime Henry wished to go to Calais to see the King of France, after which interview he hoped for yet a second meeting with Charles. It was essential to clear up these points, with all the possible misunderstandings which might arise out of them, particularly in France. Delusive diplomatic letters had to be composed by all the parties concerned, whose suave tones should in no wise break the surface friendship of all parties.

Naturally several jarring notes were struck. Rightly Le Sauch thought it tactless of Wolsey when he interfered with unwanted advice in Charles's private affairs, proposing that the Archduchess Margaret should go to Spain as regent and leave Chièvres a free hand in the Netherlands. But the ruffled surface was soon calm again.

And now at last we have the answer to the question as to why Charles could barely wait for the dissolution of the Cortes in Spain; he was afraid lest he should come late to the meeting with the English King. But he had fair weather and in seven days he reached Dover. The Cardinal Archbishop of York had hastened to meet him; wisely the Spanish government had sought to content Wolsey by giving him one entire Spanish bishopric and a substantial part of the revenues of another, transactions for which the confirmation of Rome was even now being sought. On Whit-Sunday, May 27th, 1520, took place the processional ride from Dover to Canterbury, where the great royal meeting was enacted. King Henry with his Queen, Katherine of Aragon, was there, attended by her stepmother Germaine de Foix, now Margravine of Brandenburg, and Henry's sister, the dowager Queen of France, now Duchess of Suffolk. Here Charles met them with his splendid train of nobles from Spain and the Low Countries. The ladies played the gracious part allotted to them by the social convention of the time.

Many were the treaties which had already been projected; in particular that commercial pact with the Netherlands, so favourable for England, was extended for five years. But the outcome of the talks at Canterbury was the close compact of May 29th, the original of which has recently come to light at Turin. Certain details were held back in the conversations between Wolsey and Charles, for, after the meeting planned between the Kings of England and France, Henry and Charles were in fact to meet a second time, on June 11th between Calais and Gravelines.

Charles landed once again at Flushing on June 1st, journeying on the very same day by way of Bruges and Ghent to Brussels. On June 1st Henry too crossed the Channel with a suite of several thousand people in order to take part in that celebrated meeting with Francis I known as the 'Field of the Cloth of Gold'. The tents were of stuff worked through and through with gold thread, outward sign of the fabulous splendour with which each of the Kings and their followers attempted to impress the other. Once again, for three weeks on end, there was a spate of social entertainments and delusive, if not actually false, declarations of mutual devotion. The two Kings united in praise of the glorious days, of their long-expected pleasure in seeing each other. Above all the French King's mother, Louise of Savoy, excelled in gracious acts of courtesy. But Francis himself once surprised the royal friend of his heart, by coming to rouse him at daybreak and waiting on him at his levée, handing him his shirt. But apparently practical political discussions progressed not at all. Deep mutual distrust was on both sides barely muffled by the noisiest expression of its exact opposite.

Far more important was the final meeting of Henry and Charles between Calais and Gravelines. This meeting gave the lie direct to the fair words so recently spoken by the French and English Kings only a few miles away. The very sea-sands might have blushed, for unless we are much deceived Henry and Charles here openly discussed the Emperor's marriage to the English princess. When Henry sent a confidential note to Francis asserting that Charles had first approached the question, whereupon he, Henry, had recalled him to a sense of his obligations under the treaty of Noyon, we are only the more convinced of Henry's shameless duplicity. Nevertheless it is permissible to doubt the true warmth of feeling between even Henry and Charles. Talking to Chièvres, English politicians did not scruple to play on their ancient friendship with France, and Chièvres feared that the Field of the Cloth of Gold might not be wholly without consequences. Was Charles's position not in fact still very unsafe? There were enough people

who did not scruple to exaggerate the bad news from Spain.
And what might not be hidden in the heart of Italy? What in
Germany?

ACQUISITION OF WÜRTTEMBERG. CORONATION
AT AACHEN

The perennial shortage of money was the next trouble which
the Court had to face. So far it has been impossible to gain any
clear idea of Charles's finances. In spite of Gattinara's persistence,
they were still hopelessly decentralized. A mass of government
accounts, the detailed ledgers of the great banking houses, do not
make up for the total lack of evidence as to the current relations of
income to expenditure. Great sums were often raised from the
banks against the pledging or alienating of Crown lands, but every
embarrassment had its origin in the fact that the government lived
not on the revenues which had already been collected, but on the
perpetual mortgaging of future income, of domain lands and of
mines. This, it is true, is the practice of almost all states at almost
all times; but the sixteenth century was still dominated by the old
system of private credit. The constant pull between the needs of
the Crown and the loans which it had to raise at such short terms,
was still felt as an oppressive weight on the personal honour and
credit of the prince. Money could be gained from bankers,
ministers and war-lords only at the expense of the State. The
State itself suffered, for the extravagant journeys and gifts made
by the Court immediately devoured all the current yield of the
taxes, however high, leaving the demand still unappeased.

During the last months in Spain and the first in the Netherlands
a cause hung in the balance which was itself an excellent example
of this. This was the acquisition of Württemberg.

Taken at its face value the acquisition of Württemberg was a
masterpiece of political insight and activity on the part of the
Hapsburg agents. But the Court stupidly held back, for the
council at Innsbruck was opposed to the whole Württemberg
negotiation from the outset for no better reason than lack of ready
money: even the rich mines of Tyrol were already in pawn to the
Fuggers. The Burgundian councillors acted very differently.

Immediately after the initial victory of the Swabian League, more emphatically still when Duke Ulrich failed to reconquer his land, they determined to secure the country for the House of Austria. Zevenbergen was once again the driving force. He himself probably dictated the more important dispatches since, several times, they diverge into the first person. The negotiations continued until February 6th, 1520, when a treaty with the League at last came into being. First of all Zevenbergen's chief object was to prevent the League from dividing up the land; later he thought of acquiring the whole for the House of Austria, against the repayment of the League's war expenses. For this project he sought the connivance of Bavaria. There was talk of three or four hundred thousand Gulden. But the penniless Court did not wish to have to raise such a sum. The ambassadors, therefore, of whom Zevenbergen had already risked a small fortune to secure Charles's imperial election, boldly decided to buy Württemberg on their own responsibility. The document which gives their actual reasons for taking this decision has survived, and is in fact the first State paper in the German language for the reign of Charles V. It is in itself a startling example of the way in which learned and well-informed councillors could force the hand of the government.

The arguments given were intended to disarm all possible criticism of the councillors' action, whether addressed to Charles, to Chièvres or to Margaret. They well knew that they had played high, but they were no less convinced of the inestimable advantage which they had secured for the dynasty. They knew that certain people, lords and nobles, who grudged the House of Austria this success, would be ready to blame them, asserting that 'it might well provoke a war or a revolt against His Majesty, if he deprived a ruling German prince of his lands and subjects'. The councillors argued, on the other hand, that Württemberg was so favourably situated between the scattered provinces of Austria, from Tyrol to the Breisgau and Sundgau, that only the possession of the whole was really valuable; that this very land with its resources and man-power was itself a guarantee 'that the princes and Estates should obey Your Majesty, and that the master of Austria could in future always be King of the Romans and Holy Roman Emperor' if he so wished it. If they lost the opportunity of securing the land, itself worth three million and popularly known as Switzerland's

Bread Cupboard, if they even allowed the restless Duke to return, then they would have had to reckon with 'another Duke of Gelderland', a pensioner of the French King. The unprotected Estates of Württemberg for their part would probably fulfil an old threat, and 'join with the Swiss Confederation; thereafter they could not but draw Swabia and the Rhineland as far as Cologne — the district of the free cities — into their alliance; so that the German land would become one vast commune and all authority would come to an end'. For this same reason it was equally important to keep control of the bailiwick of Hagenau, for otherwise the Decapolis[1] too 'would join with the Swiss; and what would then become of the city of Strasbourg may well be conceived'.

The Hapsburg councillors read the signs of the times with extraordinary insight. They were building as if by plan a powerful territorial state stretching from the mouth of the Rhine to the Upper Danube; at the same time they were effectively damming the rising tide of urban democracy. It was as if they had the experience of the Spanish *communeros* already before their eyes, and could foresee the coming troubles with the peasants and the smaller towns. For this reason they urgently advised the continuation of the Swabian League, rightly seeing in it a support not only for the Emperor but for the dynasty. In the same group of papers these councillors, noble and learned alike, gave clear proof of the manner in which they thought government finance should be organized. A 'born nobleman' should be appointed governor, they advised, a 'learned man Chancellor' with six of the rank of knights and a few fiscal officers to collect revenues and imposts. These could be farmed out if convenient and general expenses covered by the yield.

We cannot be certain whether the Court had any clear insight into the situation, or whether they merely accepted the accomplished fact of Württemberg's acquisition. But they retained the land for the time being, and with its possession the government was able once again to envisage an imperial policy reminiscent of the days of the Hohenstaufen.

Meanwhile Germans flocked to Charles's Court bringing with

---

[1] *The Decapolis:* the Alsatian cities of Hagenau, Colmar, Schlettstadt, Weissenburg, Landau, Oberehnheim, Rosheim, Münster, Kaysersberg and Türkheim (TRANSLATOR'S note).

them a host of new and serious problems. All attention was now turned to the coronation. Charles's entry into Aachen was fixed for October 22nd, it was to be his *Joyeuse Entrée* into the Empire.

On a fine autumn day the Electors met their new King outside the town. Until that moment he had courted and made much of them. Gradually, now, his attitude was to alter. The young ruler saw for the first time the many princes of that Empire whose government was to be so great a part of his life's work. In the years he had spent in Spain he had grown up fast; he had even given occasional proof of independent ideas, and his meetings with the English King cannot have been without an effect on him. He had always had an impressive presence, and the impenetrable, somewhat haughty expression of his face gave him, in spite of his youth, the appearance of an unapproachable ruler. Added to this, he was attended by a suite of impressive magnificence, while the titles and promotion which he had it in his power to bestow evoked the wildest ambitions in the breasts of those who welcomed him. Silent and bare-headed, he received the homage of the Electors, giving answer through the Cardinal of Salzburg.

The entry into Aachen took place with military pomp: troops of horsemen were followed by counts, lords and three hundred foot soldiers under Francesco de Castelalto; next came the town-councillors of Aachen with their white staffs; the Duke of Jülich, as the prince in whose lands the town was situated, attended in person with four hundred cavalry, the Electoral suites and the servants, pages and heralds of the Court brought up the rear, while largesse was scattered among the crowds. Among the halberdiers rode the great dignitaries of Charles's realms — Spanish grandees, knights of the Golden Fleece, princes and Electors in person. Before the King rode the hereditary great Marshal, Pappenheim, bearing the imperial Sword of State. Charles himself was in the midst, in armour and brocade, resplendent, controlling his fiery horse with a firm and practised hand.

That same evening he swore his Coronation Oath, the terms of which had been settled as long ago as July 3rd in Barcelona. If documents alone could bind a government then the German Electors had indeed done their part in protecting the Empire from the dangers of a foreign rule. By the terms which the elected Emperor now swore to uphold, he declared that he would guarantee the Electors and princes in all their rights and possessions, protect them against revolt whether among the nobility or the common people, and against hostile alliances and leagues. This latter clause was not to be taken as implying any prejudice to their own Electoral College, nor to its influence on the imperial government. The Emperor was to place only born Germans in imperial and Court offices, to use only the German or Latin tongue in official writings and negotiations; he was to call no Diet beyond the imperial frontiers, to introduce no foreign armies, and not to decrease but rather to increase the Empire by bringing back lost provinces.

Chosen by free election, not by divine hereditary right, bound by the terms of an exacting oath — thus did Charles begin his imperial reign. The Electoral College and the many traditional leagues of the Empire had long converted the Diet into a mere Court of Arbitration. Whatever the outward appearance of his sovereignty, the Emperor was bound by the decisions of the majority.

Very early on the morning of the 23rd the coronation ceremony began in the great cathedral of Charlemagne. In accordance with the *ordines* of past centuries, Charles was first sworn, then anointed, robed, crowned and enthroned. Reiterating the formula *'Volo'* — *'I will'*, the elected Emperor swore in turn to preserve the ancient faith, to protect the Church, to govern justly, to safeguard imperial rights, to care for widows and orphans, to reverence his Father in God, the Pope. Turning to the congregation, symbolic representatives of the German people, the Archbishop of Cologne put the traditional question — 'whether they would be obedient to this prince and lord, after the command of the Apostle?' Loud and jubilant resounded the people's answer — 'Fiat, fiat, fiat.'

After receiving the crown from the hands of the Archbishop, Charles ascended the throne of Charlemagne, created certain knights and listened to the great Te Deum Laudamus. At midday the coronation banquet was held; in the evening there was a feast at the Rathaus. The Archduchess Margaret was present at all these solemnities and proudly indeed her heart must have throbbed to see the power of her dynasty thus gloriously confirmed. Three days later the Pope's consent arrived in Aachen, giving Charles the right to bear the title of 'elected Roman Emperor'.

GERMANY AND THE PROBLEM OF MARTIN LUTHER. DIET OF WORMS

No greater event, and none more worthy of these beginnings, could have occurred than that which now ensued. For the young Emperor was immediately brought face to face with that important religious question, with which the fate of the German nation was inextricably bound up. A Diet had been fixed at Worms for the coming winter. Besides the usual constitutional questions and the voting of the money necessary to enable Charles to receive the imperial crown in Rome, it was essential that either at this Diet or earlier the Emperor should define his attitude towards a certain problem — that raised by the Augustinian monk, Martin Luther. Grouped on Luther's side was not only the national movement which had hitherto openly supported the Hapsburg Emperor, but, driven by their own unmistakable interests, those very princes and towns from whom Charles hoped to gain concessions. The Vatican, which had worked so decisively against the young ruler and which still, to say the least of it, preserved a very guarded attitude towards him, did not tire of issuing complaints and protests against this declared heretic. Beneath these open contradictions lay hidden the fundamental oppositions of centuries, ready to cleave the world.

In vain to attempt here any picture of the German people's condition at this time; their feverish excitement was the outcome of a mighty desire, still but remotely conceived. Drinking greedily of the New Learning and of the historical knowledge which it offered them, they had become conscious of their own ancient and glorious nation; they had learnt of their own early liberation from the Romans and of many later conflicts between Emperor and Pope. Now, as never before, the whole people had access to pictures and writings, and this new preoccupation with life itself, a preoccupation in which the sense of history played an important part, spread throughout the land. Inexhaustible was the creative energy displayed in the pictorial representation even of spiritual things, while the now predominantly High German speech of the people, rich in picturesque colloquialisms, was imbued with a tense persuasiveness. Above all religious life was transfused with a new vigour; this was manifested in a new and intense sympathy of outlook, sometimes expressed with subtlety, more often with a certain crude strength. It was as though men sought to open the very heavens with their ideas and questions. All this was the outward expression of a strong and natural inner desire for life, waiting now only for its direction.

This direction might well have taken a political turn. Indeed belief in the Emperor's position had, in this last period so rich in imperial reform, often enough recalled the image of the mighty past. But if multiple and often contradictory political and material interests are to be led in a particular direction, there must be not only a firm conviction of the possibility of change, but above all some personal embodiment of the universal desire. In spite of all his charm of manner, Maximilian had failed in this.

Now, in this very autumn of 1520, Martin Luther flung himself on the mercy of the German nation in his bold appeal 'To the Christian Nobility'. Here he declared, 'God has given us a young and noble ruler to reign over us and has thereby awakened our hearts once more to hope'. But Luther was wrong. Charles, even less than Maximilian, was the leader of Germany's desire.

Tragic and fateful moment in the history of the nation! Now when she most needed a king who would knit her boundless power and ambition into one, she found a young ruler who had not one thought in sympathy with her own inner being. His heritage and his duty prepared him to act according to his belief in a purely dynastic world-Empire, and thus to oppose that very nation to whose leadership he had been called. Above all, he could find only in Rome the necessary pivot for his policy — Rome to which Martin Luther had but now renounced all faith and obedience.

Fateful both to the young ruler and his people was the tragic development which now began. The nation was to disintegrate at the very hour in which it had been ready to acclaim Luther as the single leader which it needed, in the spiritual sphere at least.

Passionately did Luther fight for the souls of his fellow-country-men, and partly because he gave voice to their immediate griefs, partly because he lifted from them the terror of eternal damnation, they hung on his words. Listening, they dimly grasped that here was the quintessence of their hopes and fears, and here too a light leading them towards some universal concept, in which trivialities would be forgotten. They were ready now to smash the brittle conventions which bounded their religious and moral beliefs, to tear open secrets long sealed up, to arrogate once more to themselves the long-forgotten message of the eternal fatherhood of God. The rediscovery of a divine significance in life itself, derived from some elemental force, from some inner conviction of the idea of life, of work, of the family, of the State, may have been con-conscious or unconscious; but it brought with it a new theology. Later it was to 'bring too the renunciation of political self-consciousness, of unity and national power. For the sake of a remote truth, half seen through the ambiguities of delusive words, all these were to be foregone.

Yet there was a new theology too, for nothing acquires true sanctity without acquiring also a tradition. Theology itself is in its origins nothing more than interpreted legend. Men acted therefore under the cloak of theology. They spoke of truth and right. Truth was conceived of scholastically; it was something which could be proved. Right was formulated after the manner of the Church and the Empire; it was a form of social order. And now appeared the papal nuncio, armed with protests against the heretic, who, with all his forty-one theses had been recently condemned in Rome by the Bull *Exsurge Domine*. At Charles's Court this office of nuncio was to be filled not only by Carrac-ciolo, but by a special ambassador, Hieronymus Aleander, a theologian as persuasive and learned as he was skilful. In the third week in September he was welcomed at Antwerp. Contrary to his expectation, the young ruler impressed him at once as a man much bound to the Church and of remarkable insight. He found help too among the Emperor's following; he spoke highly of the humanist Marliano, Bishop of Tuy, who had himself written against Luther. Soon at Louvain he was able to celebrate the first formal burning of Luther's writings. Charles ordered his chief chaplain, Alonso Manrique de Lara, to make a thorough examination of the Church in the Low Countries, having particular care to the Lutheran heresy. Later he permitted him to speak his mind very frankly on the subject.

Very different were the impressions of Aleander when he travelled in the suite of the crowned Emperor from Aachen to Cologne and farther into the Rhineland. His celebrated dispatches well reflect his varying moods of anxiety, irritation and fear. They bear witness less to the timidity of the Vatican than to the rising storm of excitement among people, knights, merchants and princes in defence of Luther. The Bishop of Liège showed him the challenging open letter written by Ulrich von Hutten, which the Emperor had secretly sent him; this horrified the nuncio. Thenceforward his journey was a path beset with bitterness and peril.

At Cologne he met the Electors. At that time those of the Palatinate and Saxony were thought to be the most dangerous. Aleander gained access to Frederick the Wise during Mass at the Franciscan monastery. He found the Elector himself a good and devout Catholic, but his suite more Lutheran than Luther. Yet he greeted the old prince reverently and with flattery well suited to the occasion, for he knew his reputation in the Empire. He demanded however that he should have Luther's writings burnt and hand over the monk himself to Rome. Only after a few hours did the Elector send back an answer — a flat refusal. There had, he said, been many clumsy attacks made on his land and he did not deserve such treatment. He was in no way bound to Luther, but the man had submitted in all reasonable matters, and he himself would keep an open mind in the event of Luther's conversion before just and learned judges.

Frederick's answer closely followed advice which Erasmus of Rotterdam had given him by word of mouth the day before. All reasonable men, Erasmus stated, must feel that Luther was behaving reasonably when he declared himself ready to participate in a public disputation before unprejudiced judges. This very disputation was the great topic of the day. It was, too, in close accordance with the Emperor's election promise to condemn no German unheard.

The demands of the Elector reached the Emperor through Chièvres and Nassau. Charles was now playing a well-defined personal part in politics. Aleander being absent, he conjured the Elector saying: 'You are to bring this Luther with you to the coming Diet at Worms.' But Charles withdrew his offer of a hearing for Luther when representations were made to him that the time limit of sixty days set down in the Papal Bull had elapsed, even if the days were only calculated from the time of the Bull's publication at Wittenberg. Aleander's letters show clearly how the mood of the Court varied in response to the demands of the Estates, to political news from abroad, even to his own well-knit and timely arguments. Thus at one meeting of the Emperor's general Council — that is of all his councillors, not merely of the Germans — the ministers decided to issue a certain mandate acting on Aleander's advice. Later they failed to draw it up, the nuncio attributing this failure to their fear of offending Frederick the Wise. At this time Chièvres seemed to be in closest sympathy with the nuncio, while Gattinara shared the opinions of Erasmus, whom he deeply admired.

In the meantime, on January 27th, the Diet of Worms was opened, Charles himself adding a few words in German to his Chancellor's official propositions. Everybody was apparently in a good humour, although the Duke of Alva, as a Spaniard, was not permitted to take part. The Estates intended to answer the imperial propositions at once, but they abandoned the first speech which they had drawn up and in the end only answered the Emperor in part. The chief objects of their deliberations were the voting of subsidies for the journey to Rome, the organization of imperial government, and the payment of the judges in the *Reichskammergericht*. Besides these there were several minor matters connected with public order — economic, administrative and judicial problems. They were also negotiating with the Swiss and French. All these concerns intersected and interwove themselves in multifarious patterns with the grievances of the German nation and the Lutheran question. Although here, too, the great lords wasted day after day in 'running and jousting' at tourneys, yet they achieved more in their four months' meeting than the Spanish Cortes had done in a year. In questions of civil government the imperial theory was almost wholly victorious. The Estates did not even demand, as they had done under Maximilian, that there should be a standing governmental body with its own president; they were content instead with the request that there should be some official government in Charles's absence, under an imperial regent. Both the Archduke Ferdinand and the Count Palatine Frederick were considered as possibilities. Charles openly formulated his own conception of the extent of his monarchic power within the Empire and it was accepted. He declared that 'our own honour and dignity is the honour and dignity of you all; it is not our desire and will that there be many lords, but one lord alone as is the tradition of the holy Empire.'

On the other hand Charles and his government came step by step to meet the Estates in the Lutheran question.

Fundamentally, the problem was different from those usually discussed at a Diet and Aleander reproached both Emperor and Empire for their weakness. Aleander would have been content with an imperial mandate only; but the Court felt that the agreement of the Estates was necessary. These contested the validity of any condemnation of Luther without a hearing. The protest led to a remarkable series of negotiations, in which the imperial confessor, Father Glapion, was actively engaged. Not that the Emperor had altered his fundamental beliefs; he was still governed by the idea of orthodoxy and heresy in which he had been bred. But he allowed his councillors a free hand to attempt in the most various ways to win over the Estates, or at the very least Frederick the Wise, while at the same time satisfying the nuncio. This latter feared Luther's appearance before the Diet as much for practical as for theoretical reasons. But it was precisely his appearance which the Estates wanted. With an eloquence only matched by his duplicity, Glapion explained to the Saxon Chancellor, Brück, that he himself had for long believed in the sincerity of Luther's projected reforms. 'I myself', he said, or so at least Brück reported, 'ask for nothing better than the reform of the Church, for which we now have a worthy head.' But Luther's book, *On the Babylonish Captivity*, had put him in the wrong. That at least Luther must withdraw; the rest could then be discussed. Much might be read into the Bible, much might be proved or contradicted; Brück should consider of it.

The Grand Chancellor Gattinara, Glapion and Aleander now tried other tactics; they tempted Nassau into their group. The negotiations, they said, could be postponed to some other place, say Ebernburg; this town was in the protection of Sickingen, by whose military strength they set great store. Glapion went so far as to declare that he had always told the Emperor that God would punish him if he did not take steps to reform the Church. Nevertheless Brück stood obstinately to that promise given by the Emperor to his master the Elector, that he would not condemn Luther unheard. Glapion protested that it would be impossible to find judges fair to both sides.

By imperial invitation on February 13th, Aleander made an impressive speech to the Estates. On the advice of his councillors, Charles was already determined to issue an Edict. Meanwhile this speech brought the matter in all its aspects once again before the Estates. At the very moment at which Aleander laid bare the weak points in their arguments with equal skill and knowledge, he was, unknown to himself, already facing a new world order. There were heated debates during those days: it was said that the Electors all but came to blows. On February 19th the Estates were still adamant: Luther must be asked to appear in his own defence, under a safe-conduct, 'for the need, welfare and the future of the German nation, our Christian faith and all Estates and Members'. This was the decisive day. In fact on March 6th, Charles V cited the Augustinian monk to appear, under a promise of safe conduct, before Empepor and Empire. Momentous decision, epoch-making alike for the dogmatic and ecclesiastical developments of the next generation.

What followed is general knowledge. The Chancellor Brück sent Luther a written list of arguments for and against his appearance at Worms. Luther swept aside all instinctive fear, even the very present recollection of what had befallen Huss on a like occasion. Courageously he made ready for the journey which was to be his great triumph. On April 16th he entered Worms, the people thronging the streets to see him. Great things were eagerly expected of the next few days. Yet Luther's first appearance before Emperor and Deit was disappointing. He pleaded, 'in a very low voice', for time to think. The chancy game seemed to be in Aleander's hands. Then on April 18th, Luther made his great speech. It was skilfully constructed, packed with knowledge, and capable of but one interpretation, and when, with the best intention, negotiations were once again opened with him, as they had been earlier with Brück, he stood by what he had said, immovable. He had warned the Estates 'not to burden the hopeful rule of a young Emperor with persecution of God's Word', and his decisive answer, given already on the 18th, ran in these words: 'So long as I cannot be disproved by Holy Writ or clear reason, so long I neither can nor will withdraw anything, for it is both criminal and dangerous to act against conscience. So help me God, Amen.'

Luther's valiant words are great in themselves. Yet this moment takes a unique place in the history of the world, because the young Emperor too realized that a mighty decision was at hand. Dominated still by the ideas of Church and chivalry which he had learnt in the Burgundian world of his childhood, surrounded on all sides by contradictory forces and advice, he had so far followed events only from the outside. But at this moment he took his place openly before the world, with a document which is recognizably the work of his own hand and his own brain. He had the original read in French and then translated. These words, uttered on April 19th, were the most significant expression of opinion to which he gave voice during the whole of his youth. 'Ye know', he declared, 'that I am born of the most Christian Emperors of the noble German Nation, of the Catholic Kings of Spain, the Archdukes of Austria, the Dukes of Burgundy, who were all to the death true sons of the Roman Church, defenders of the Catholic Faith, of the sacred customs, decrees and uses of its worship, who have bequeathed all this to me as my heritage, and according to whose example I have hitherto lived. Thus I am determined to hold fast by all which has happened since the Council of Constance. For it is certain that a single monk must err if he stands against the opinion of all Christendom. Otherwise Christendom itself would have erred for more than a thousand years. Therefore I am determined to set my kingdoms and dominions, my friends, my body, my blood, my life, my soul upon it. For it were great shame to us and to you, ye members of the noble German Nation, if in our time' — and here he used the very words which the chief Court chaplain had impressed upon him — 'through our negligence, we were to let even the appearance of heresy and denigration of true religion enter the hearts of men. Ye all heard Luther's speech here yesterday, and now I say unto you that I regret that I have delayed so long to proceed against him. I will not hear him again: he has his safe-conduct. But from now on I regard him as a notorious heretic, and hope that you all, as good Christians, will not be wanting in your duty.'

This declaration, translated into all languages, was immediately published. In Rome the Pope laid it before the Cardinals in the Consistory, and even the imperial ambassador, Don Juan Manuel, showed himself to be profoundly satisfied.

Thus did Luther and Charles take up their positions before history. The Emperor, just twenty-one years old, gave expression to his pride in his illustrious ancestry and his duty to his house. Opposite him stood the might of conscience, ready to attack his heritage. Between the ancestral and ecclesiastical pride, the deep sincerity of this apparently all-powerful ruler, and the profound and lonely grief of the reformer, strong in God alone, there could be neither compromise nor understanding.

On May 8th the council confirmed the Edict against Luther, which bears this date, although as late as May 12th the Emperor refused the nuncio's demands that he should sign it. Only after the close of the Diet on May 25th was it at length agreed on by a very diminished gathering, with the Elector of Brandenburg as spokesman; on May 26th it was signed and only then published in print.

In Greek tragedy the Chorus is often represented as seeing far into the future. At this moment in German history, the Chorus must have covered its face before the horror and bloodshed which the next century and a half were to bring upon the soil of Germany. Contemporaries guessed nothing; astonishingly enough all remained quiet at first in the land, until one day the waters, stirred at last to fury, broke their banks, first merely in sputtering streams, but gaining ever more in force and depth until the nation itself was submerged.

The Emperor and the Reformer alike withdrew from the open field of German politics. Charles threw himself into his first war, Martin Luther, protected still by his Elector, waited, gathering strength for trials yet to come.

Before the half-closed eyes of the young Emperor, lay all his lands, with their griefs and troubles. Gradually he himself began to play his part in their affairs. Plague at Worms had deprived him of his best adviser, Guillaume de Croy, lord of Chièvres. It had taken also Marliano, Bishop of Tuy, Diego Manuel and many others. Chièvres had played a decisive part in forming his master's political outlook; they spoke the same language. Now that he was gone the young ruler was left alone to work out his destiny as best he could, with a foreigner and a man with whom he was not always in sympathy — that great statesman whose political perceptions embraced the universe, the Chancellor Gattinara.

CHAPTER IV

HEREDITARY RIGHT AND WORLD-EMPIRE

THE dominions of Charles V may be called a world-empire not only because they stretched over the old and the new worlds, but because of their international and Christian character.

Yet this Empire was not imperial in any sense of conquest. It was based on the most peaceful of all foundations, on the rights of a family. It was the legacy of Maximilian, the inheritance of the House of Austria. For this reason the dynasty treated family alliances and marriage contracts with exaggerated respect, nor was this remarkable for the progress of the state, even during Charles's lifetime and certainly beforehand, may be regarded as little more than a series of marriage contracts with their results. Charles himself, from the very time of his birth, had been repeatedly betrothed, Maximilian had anxiously sought to use his sisters to gain the neighbouring northern and Jagellon crowns. With painful anxiety Charles himself had kept watch over his eldest sister Eleonore. And now she had become Queen of Portugal, a land whose sovereign controlled the other half of the New World. The youngest sister Katherine, whom we heard of last with her mother at Tordesillas, had been promised, to further her brother's plans for the imperial throne, first with every formality to the electoral prince of Brandenburg, later to the heir of Saxony, the nephew of Frederick the Wise. But the old Elector, in spite of many guarded words, was to discover at length that the jewel was being saved to grace not an electoral hat, but a crown.

In fact the House of Austria and Spain was soon to engross every crown in Europe. Charles's aunt, Katherine, was Queen of England; his sisters were, or were to become, Queens of Denmark, Norway and Sweden, of Bohemia and Hungary, of Portugal and France. On all sides his policy was clear; he intended not only to strengthen such alliances and bonds of peace, but to gain prospects of inheritance in the near or distant future.

A symbol of the policy underlying Charles's world-empire is to be seen in that magnificent series of painted windows in which, some years later, Charles had himself and his family represented in the Chapel of the Holy Sacrament at Sainte Gudule in Brussels. Here, in window after window, as though raised mid-way between heaven and earth, they stand, in brilliant colour and ceremonial pomp, royal brides and bridegrooms, two by two, kneeling in adoration before the most sacred mystery known to the medieval world. Who but Charles could have planned and ordered this? Who but he could have seen in this ostentatious display of power, no more than the outward sign of his own highest mission?

THE DIVISION OF THE INHERITANCE WITH FERDINAND. MARY IN HUNGARY. ISABELLA IN DENMARK

It was in accordance with this all-embracing theory of the dynasty that Charles now undertook to divide his inheritance with his aunt Margaret and his brother Ferdinand. The plan was not conceived without anxious forethought, nor carried through without inner hindrances; but it was conscientiously worked out and executed in the grand manner. The negotiations and correspondence which it entailed occupied the greater part of the years 1520 and 1521. Even against the will of the Cortes, Charles had insisted on Ferdinand's leaving Spain; he had moreover vigorously opposed all question of his candidature for the imperial throne. He had even refused to allow him to appear in Germany before the election. In all this Charles had been well advised. Soon after the election he began to busy himself once more with dynastic questions.

His chief adviser was Gattinara, and the first important note addressed by the Chancellor to the Emperor, immediately after the election, has survived. In this Gattinara began by exhorting Charles to fear God, to reverence the Queen-mother, to fulfil the testament of his forefathers and to act generously towards his royal brother. It is unreasonable in the circumstances to accuse Charles of political stupidity or of coldness in his treatment of his brother; there was undoubtedly a certain contradiction between the postulated ideal and the egoism and lust for power partly displayed by Charles, but this was no more than natural in a young and ruling prince. It is true that Charles sensibly modified the intentions of both his father and grandfather; he altered both the territorial extent and the financial burdens of the hereditary lands and tampered with rights of inheritance in certain single countries. Yet these actions were not dishonest attempts to rob Ferdinand of his just portion. Rather they were the essential and minimum precautions which could be taken by a responsible prince with new and very heavy tasks in front of him. The provision made for Ferdinand in the years immediately after Charles's coronation was bestowed on him both speedily and in full, without any outside pressure. The Viennese, it is true, broke into revolt, made their leader, Siebenburger, burgomaster, and with him as their spokesman, made a series of angry demands. But these riots cannot be supposed to have had any serious effect on Charles.

Let us once again take stock of the situation in the first months of the year 1521. Relations with France were extremely uneasy, reaching their worst moment with the departure of the French ambassador from Worms on May 22nd; negotiations with the Vatican were difficult and from Spain came news of a revolt, which, however stale, was nevertheless disturbing. Relations with England were still uncertain; meanwhile Charles was deep in argument with the German Electors and Estates, and last but not least, involved in the Lutheran problem, itself vitally connected with the demands of the Estates. It is thus more than comprehensible that he put off his brother's affairs at least until April. On April 2nd Ferdinand made his state entry into Worms.

Ferdinand was impatiently awaited by an embassy from Louis II of Hungary, the provost Hieronymus Balbi and Stephen Verböczy, sent specially to call to his mind the fact that the double marriage between the Hapsburg and the Hungarian dynasties must now be completed. In the meantime there had been a slight disturbance. Earlier on, Maximilian had over-excited the ambitions of the Hungarians by adopting Louis II and dropping hints about the imperial crown; for this reason Louis would sooner have bestowed the hand of his sister Anne on the Emperor than on the landless Ferdinand. But at last he had to yield to the inevitable. Rumours of the Turkish danger, like gigantic shadows, warned him to be discreet. On December 11th Anne of Hungary, who all this while had kept her Court with Mary of Austria at the secure and beautiful city of Innsbruck, exchanged rings with Ferdinand's plenipotentiary.

The next important move was to establish Ferdinand as a ruling prince in one or other of the Hapsburg lands. This was the least that could be done, seeing that he was to have as his bride the daughter of the King of Hungary and Bohemia. Ferdinand's apanage had to be found in Germany, for even his grandfather, Ferdinand of Aragon, much as he had cherished him, had never suggested that he should play a more important part in Spain than that of regent during Charles's absence. Neither could Ferdinand rule anywhere in the Netherlands, where he had meanwhile been completing his education, partly under the influence of Erasmus. Charles had been informed, probably by the province of Brabant, that division of inheritance was against the law in the Low Countries. This left only the Austrian lands, which Charles now made ready to divide, as they had so often been divided before. The acquisition of Württemberg had greatly enlarged their extent, but it had added a huge burden of debt. Over and above this the old debts of Maximilian hung heavy on dynastic finances. An attempt had been made to write off some of these against the bribes paid out at the election; others were still completely un-funded, such as the claim of Duke George of Saxony for the sale of Friesland by his father. Charles made himself responsible for this particular debt. The firm of Fugger, which had financed the election, was indemnified by grants in Tyrol. Charles asserted that he had used Aragonese money to acquire Württemberg — a statement which was only half true. In any case the burden of debt and mortage on the whole inheritance, both singly and as a whole, was hopelessly confused.

Many points were left undecided. The payment of many debts was postponed. The negotiations over a so-called 'honour-able' division dragged wearily on. Yet enough was decided at Worms for Ferdinand's Hungarian marriage to be solemnized at Whitsuntide at Linz on the Danube. Already on April 28th Charles ceded the five Austrian dukedoms to his brother — Upper and Lower Austria, Styria, Carinthia and Carniola, with

all their privileges. Carniola was, however, to be divided and
Charles was to have control of the Adriatic coast, the important
district between the Pustertal and Trieste, including the whole of
Istria, for fear of trouble with Naples or Venice.

In May, Ferdinand made his state entry into Linz and celebrated his marriage. In his train were many foreign ambassadors,
the Dukes Otto of Luneburg and Lewis of Bavaria and the three
Margraves of Brandenburg. After magnificent wedding festivities
the Austrian Estates acclaimed him at Ibbs on the Danube in
June and at Graz in Styria in July.

These independent and self-willed Estates had little sympathy
with a prince barely twenty years old and scarcely master of the
German language; faced by Ferdinand's immediate demand for
money it was hardly surprising that they made trouble. The
people still underestimated the necessities of the state and overestimated the proportion of their money which was spent on the
empty pomps of the sovereign. As early as the autumn Ferdinand
re-organized the personnel of the administration, set up his own
court of councillors, and began to raise a moderate army to help
his Hungarian brother-in-law against the Turks. This done, he
returned to the Netherlands to complete his negotiations with
Charles. December 1521 found him in Ghent and in January and
February 1522 the treaties were drawn up in their final form,
which far overstepped the limits previously indicated at Worms.
These Brussels agreements, which are in part doubly preserved,
both in the Spanish and in the Austrian archives, may be divided
into two groups, the public and the private treaties. At the first
glance they seem unfavourable to Ferdinand and, as I have
already shown, they have often been used to cast aspersions on
Charles's brotherly affection; yet I cannot but feel that they are
fundamentally straightforward. Not until he had been elected
and crowned, not until he had attended his first Diet, could
Charles regard his position in the Empire as definitely secure.
Ferdinand could do him good service in the imperial government
by acting as his regent and it was in Charles's own best interests
that his regent should not be without personal power. Charles
therefore enlarged his original grant by extending the boundaries
of the five Austrian duchies to include those districts which he
had withheld at Worms — the Pustertal, Ortemburg and Cilli,

Istria, the lands on the Carso, in Möttling, Mitterburg, Trieste, Sankt Veit, Gradisca, Tolmein and all the other parts of Friuli which Maximilian had won. He also named Ferdinand regent in all the adjoining lands, that is in the parts of Hither Austria from Tyrol and Vorarlberg to the Upper Rhine, including Württemberg. On the other hand the Emperor clearly saw that it would be unwise to renounce altogether and publicly his control over the Austrian lands. To satisfy his brother he did this only in the secret treaty of February 7th; Ferdinand in return renounced his claim on the heritable lands of Burgundy and Spain. In this treaty, too, Charles made over to Ferdinand his rights of inheritance throughout the Germanic lands of the Hapsburg dynasty. He even made over Alsace, Pfirt and Hagenau to Ferdinand for life, on condition that they should return to the Burgundian inheritance after his death. He thus as it were reverted to the policy of Charles the Bold, a reversion achieved at the expense of imperial unity. Later the same policy was to be developed by the Spanish Hapsburg in the Thirty Years War, when they seized the Palatinate in order to secure that line of communication between Milan and the Netherlands, which was of such immense strategic importance. For the rest, Charles and his advisers clearly revealed their intentions in these general treaties of 1522, when they added the clause that the treaty was to be kept secret for six years, or at least until the imperial coronation. Only after the formal coronation in Italy could Charles's legal position as Emperor be finally confirmed. After Charles's coronation, Ferdinand could be crowned King of the Romans. Thus Ferdinand too was to play his part in heightening the universal prestige of the dynasty; Charles himself was to attempt to increase that prestige even further by his later plans for the so-called Spanish succession.

Over and above the lands, Charles granted his brother the revenues which had been set aside for him by their grandfather from the Kingdom of Naples; these amounted to 50,000 ducats. In return for his renunciation of his other rights, Ferdinand received a further 10,000 ducats annually. The division of their grandfather's personal goods, as also of Maximilian's unfunded debts, was held over for a later agreement.

The division accomplished, Charles withdrew from Germany.

Over and above the fiefs in the Netherlands and the Burgundian circle,[1] he himself retained ultimate control over the Empire as well as the prestige which clung to the imperial title — little more in fact than had once been held by an Alfonso of Castile or a Richard of Cornwall. The actual German lands belonged henceforward to the Austrian line, and Maximilian's family alliances both with the northern and the southern powers, both with Denmark and Sweden, Bohemia and Hungary, was to affect the Austrian branch alone. Their relations with the Danubian powers alone were to become highly important to their future expansion — an expansion which was nevertheless very dearly bought. The Danish alliance, useless to Germany, became in the end merely an additional burden on the Netherlands.

A fortnight after the marriage of Anne to the Archduke Ferdinand, on July 8th, 1521, her Innsbruck playmate, Mary, was married in Bohemia to Anne's brother, Louis of Hungary. The thoughts of the youthful bride and bridegroom were troubled even during the wedding festivities with forewarnings of a disastrous future.

Their Court, no less than all Christendom, was filled with anxiety at news of a Turkish advance by land and sea; but a delay over the investment of Belgrade unexpectedly determined Suleiman to withdraw and when Rhodes fell on December 21st, 1522, the pressure on Hungary was temporarily relieved. Nevertheless the King and Queen returned from Bohemia to Ofen for a Turkish Diet in April 1523. Both were young and high-spirited; the King, cultured and chivalrous, charming, but light-hearted and extravagant. The Queen appeared to experienced statesmen both more intelligent and more energetic; her portrait at Munich, done in 1524, shows, beneath the delicate and attractive contours, a certain virile austerity; the quality was to develop as she grew older. But what could the princess do? Born in the autumn of 1505, she was not yet within sight of twenty. Among the great mass of spiritual and temporal magnates in Hungary and Bohemia who outdid even the nobility of Burgundy and Spain in self-interest and self-will, the royal pair found inadequate support from the Chancellor, the Bishop of Erlau, Ladislas

[1] The 'Circles' were the districts into which Maximilian had divided the Empire for fiscal purposes (TRANSLATOR'S note).

Szalkay, and the Archbishop and primate of Gran, George Szakmáry. All the more valuable were the services of the imperial ambassador Adrian da Burgo, and the statesman Sigismond von Herberstein, who had already proved his worth under Maximilian. Yet even in Hungary these two had to contend with the insidious and persistent opposition of a French ambassador. During the whole of this period Maximilian's policy in the Danube basin proved a more fruitful source of danger than of advantage.

Things were little better in the north, where Charles's second sister Isabella was married. Christian II of Denmark, Norway and Sweden was thirty-four years old and had already had experience as a ruler when, during his father's lifetime, he had been regent of Norway. But the circumstances of that regency, peculiar in themselves, had unhappily developed his rash and aggressive temperament. Moreover he brought with him to Copenhagen from Norway a companion whose presence augured no good to the young Queen. At Bergen the prince had been approached by the sly Dutch wife of an inn-keeper, Sigbritt Willems, and her handsome daughter, 'dat Düweken' — the little dove; he took both mother and daughter with him to Oslo and Copenhagen. At first it was said that the young Queen received this half-educated countrywoman of hers as a great consolation in her exile, but her husband's open favours to the girl, accompanied as they were by harshness and ill-manners towards herself, soon made the situation unbearable. The Captain of the Guard, Torben Oxe, was alleged once to have taken his pleasures with the 'little dove' somewhat too indiscreetly; after her death in 1517 he was tried for his life. The same fate befell a gentleman attending on the Queen herself. But even after the 'little dove's' death, her mother, Sigbritt, remained the King's right hand. He was unlucky, too, in the men whom he trusted. They urged him on in his struggles against the opposition of the nobility, of Sten Sture in Sweden for instance, to unblushing violations of justice and bloody executions.

When Christian, who had hitherto been respected and liked — for when he chose he could be very charming — suddenly demanded the remainder of his wife's dowry and military help against the Swedes, it was ill-received in the Netherlands. Christian had certainly chosen his moment badly, for the imperial election had left the Court deep in debt. Finding his demands unsatisfied he shamelessly applied to the French Court, and in fact received thence some very useful mercenaries. With a considerable army and six Dutch warships, he attacked Sweden and early in 1520 the three kingdoms seemed to be once again consolidated by the Union of Calmar. But instead of the amnesty which all expected, Christian fulminated indictments against both nobles and priests: two bishops, thirteen knights — among them the father of Gustavus Vasa — three burgomasters and twenty-six burghers were executed. Men reported shuddering that they had even been refused the sacraments.

That no attempt at Lutheran Reformation could flourish in the hands of so uncontrolled a prince is doubly comprehensible. The people received his measures with growing mistrust. Nevertheless he had the impertinence to seek out his imperial brother-in-law personally in the summer of 1521 in the Netherlands. Welcomed with all the splendour which became a knight of the Golden Fleece, he gave himself up for the time being to free enjoyment of all the pleasures which the wealthy provinces afforded him. At that time Dürer drew him; the painter was once even asked to sit at the high table when the King was entertaining his imperial brother-in-law. Christian was granted the fief of Holstein, but the possession of Lübeck and help against Sweden and the Hanse were refused. Margaret and her advisers had rightly emphasized the dangers to Netherlandish trade which must arise from participation in a northern war. True to his crude instincts, Christian worked off his anger at his disappointment on his young wife when he got home; time and again her piteous plaints assailed the Court in the Netherlands. But none of this in the least prevented her husband from relying on Charles's help and even increasing his vain expectations. We have not heard the last of his catastrophic career.

RISE AND COLLAPSE OF THE COMUNEROS
AND THE 'GERMANÍA'

Charles had been in the Netherlands since the summer of 1521. Here he was able for a short while to take his ease before returning to Spain. Here in spite of the signs of gathering storms and his own increasing worries, he was able to watch the gradual consolidation of his position and its effect on European powers.

Grave news from Spain had for long enough formed the background of all the decisions which he had taken. Charles had left the country on the eve of revolt. One cannot but admire the calm of a minister who, like Chièvres, allowed the young ruler, even with such prospects as the imperial crown before him, to travel by slow stages to the Netherlands and Germany, leaving the Spanish kingdoms without resources and in the charge of a weak prelate. Clearly Chièvres did not suffer from nerves. Yet he had exposed the Spanish kingdoms to far greater perils than he himself seems to have realized. The arrogance and self-advancement of the foreigners, the obvious haste of the Court to leave not only each kingdom, but the whole peninsula as soon as its demands were satisfied, had provoked an annoyance among the Spaniards — a proud people already conscious of their political and national entity — which led on July 29th, 1520, to the formation of the Holy Junta and its demands for a special government of the land. The revolt broke out the more rapidly because the Spaniards were long used to schisms and conflicts, both between the separate kingdoms and within them.

Social disagreement between Grandees and towns, the latter led for the most part by small nobility, sharpened the conflict. Yet this also to some extent lightened the task of the Crown, for the two parties neutralized each other. Moreover many important towns in Castile, and nearly all those in the South were free of the movement. Aragon too knew nothing of it; but here this was cold comfort since Aragon and the whole kingdom of Valencia was in the grip of another revolutionary movement, social rather than political in its significance — the *Germanía*. News of this second outbreak was already filtering through to Charles. Collusive action between the two centres of unrest was never achieved, as far-sighted organization is never the strong point of revolutions. Nor did alliances with foreign powers come to anything. The King of Portugal, it is true, did once send the poor, forsaken government a considerable sum of money, but that was all. On the other hand the French government would gladly have fanned the blaze. But neither the fleet which cruised round Majorca, nor the war which France managed to provoke in Navarre, gave any real help to the revolt. The Navarrese movement was too late in any case.

But we must not anticipate. Internal as well as external causes combined to strengthen the royalists in Castile. The rebels, like the peasants in Germany at a later date, were unable to conceive of government in any but the traditional form. They demanded the 'old law'; they used the royal seal. They appealed to the King against the King's government; they even appealed to Queen Joanna.

It was indeed a critical moment in the history of the Comuneros when their leader Padilla, after seizing the castle of Tordesillas, bowed the knee reverently before the old Queen and asked for her help. Since they began by expelling the Marquis of Denia, whose presence she had always resented, the wretched Queen may, in some twilit moment of half sanity, have felt that they had indeed come to release her from bad dreams and bring back again a long submerged reality. She nodded graciously to them and listened to the speeches of the leaders with apparent patience, but every effort to induce her to action, nay to gain so much as a signature from her, foundered on her mental condition. Soon she relapsed into the old hopeless darkness.

Like the attempts to win over Joanna, the practical demands of the rebels seemed calculated rather to strengthen the King's prestige than to further their own cause. 'It is not the custom of Castile to be without a King', they complained anxiously in the *Capitulos del Reyno* of October 20th, 1520, to the absent monarch. Since the rebels thus attacked the evils and errors of the government in the name of the King himself, the regents saw the way to restore quiet. 'If the King comes back', declared the rebels, 'he can govern the whole world from these kingdoms, as his forefathers did before him.' The very first article of their demands reflected their respect for the dynastic principle, for it was an entreaty to Charles to take a wife. He should choose her, they added, 'according to the desire of his kingdoms' — and everyone knew that they meant by that, neither a French nor an English bride, but the princess of Portugal.

They longed to see as his partner on the throne a native Queen only — such a Queen as they had known in the time of his 'glorious forefathers', Ferdinand and Isabella. Doubtless they hoped that with such a Queen the simplicity of previous times would come back to drive out the extravagant ostentation of the present. If the King's absence were truly necessary, they asked that they might at least have Spanish regents. They demanded that taxes be lowered, that administration and justice be reformed. There was nothing new here; these were the same demands that had already been made by the Cortes and in the memorials of Charles's leading councillors — even down to the appeal for better currency and the complaints of unjust government in the West Indies. They did not think that grants of royal land should be made to private people either in Spain or in the Indies; indeed these grants, the *Mercedes* as they were called, were more often the object of indignation than of greedy ambition. Actual practical questions of the day, there were few among their demands. Nevertheless they asked that the deputies to the Cortes might be chosen from each Estate and have their expenses paid, that meetings should be periodically fixed and freedom given to negotiate. They also asked that Antonio de Fonseca, the licenciate Ronquillo, and Gutierre Quijada, might receive condign punishment. They regarded them as responsible for the destruction of Medina del Campo, that great treasure house which had gone up in smoke when the Comuneros first came to blows with the government. Of the messengers dispatched to carry these terms to the Emperor, only one, Antonio Vasquez, reached Worms from Avila; he was arrested and although he was soon set free, his embassy was without success. The others did not dare to go farther than the Netherlands. Charles listened to their demands, even to those which had the sanction of the regent Adrian himself, with the utmost coldness.

And yet these complaints evinced nothing but the deepest reverence for the supreme, noble and righteous institution of royal authority. Although the deeds of the Comuneros were certainly less restrained than their words, their attitude at least was not unfavourable to Charles. After the manner of revolutionaries who are uncertain of their power, they suspected not only the royal officials but almost everyone, and they did not hesitate to act with singular brutality. On the other hand there were serious waverings and violent quarrels within their own camp between towns and individuals. Padilla himself was temporarily replaced by Pedro Giron; but this mood soon passed and the Grandee came back to his old place of leadership with Pedro Laso and others. It was Padilla who was received at Valladolid 'as if he were God himself come from Heaven'.

In the meantime on September 29th, Charles had appointed as regents, alongside Adrian, the constable of Castile, Don Iñigo Velasco, and the Admiral Don Fadrique Enriquez. The constable in particular soon gave proof of his remarkable energy. The troops of the Grandees and of the government gradually improved in order and discipline. The Constable made peace with Burgos in September and on December 5th reconquered Tordesillas. But the Junta moved to Valladolid and the worst time seemed yet to come. For at this moment there came to lead the rebels the ambitious Grandee and prelate Antonio de Acuña, Bishop of Zamora. His intention was to gain for himself at least the Archbishopric of Toledo, the see which had belonged to the great Ximenes himself and was now once again vacant since the death of the young Croy. Strange, unreal and fantastic scene — this spiritual dignitary, this aristocrat, led troops of begging friars and peasants to waste the land and plunder convents, himself solemnizing mass in the dismantled ruins. Yet fundamentally this was no more than a sign of that general disorder which gives an outlet to social criminals, of whatever rank and birth they be. At Adrian's complaints, the Vatican intervened and appointed certain ecclesiastical judges. Strangely misunderstanding the personalities of the two men, they spoke at Rome in horror of the Bishop of Zamora as the 'Spanish Luther'.

But the hostility of the Vatican declined when the Bishop, by means of his good friends, the French in particular, laid counter-mines against Adrian.

The decisive action took place not in Toledo but in the very birthplace of the movement itself. Gathering recruits from all sides the Constable soon had larger forces than Padilla. On April 23rd he was victorious at Villalar, not far from Toro on the Douro; he owed his triumph largely to his superior numbers of cavalry. Padilla was taken and tried on the following day. On April 27th the victors entered Valladolid. In the autumn Toledo fell. The Bishop had fled, but Padilla's valiant wife, a sister of

146

the great Mendoza, defended the town desperately until at last her strength failed and she took refuge, a wretched fugitive, across the Portuguese frontier. The Bishop of Zamora, seized on his way to France, was imprisoned at the castle of Simancas.

The victory was only just in time for the French troops in Navarre were gaining ground. Their leader was André de Foix, Lord of Esparre. With Lautrec and Lescun he was one of the three brothers of Françoise, Madame de Chateaubriand, who passed at the time for the reigning mistress of Francis I. Pushing his way across the Pyrenees, he took Pamplona on May 19th, Tudela on the Ebro on the 21st, and began the siege of Logroño. It was rumoured that the news of this advance completely cast down the distant Emperor. For if the French could stretch their dominion as far as the southern point of Navarre, they would drive a wedge between the Spanish kingdoms at their narrow end in the valley of the Ebro. But before Charles had further news from Navarre he must have heard of the victory at Villalar, which set free the Castilians and their troops against the French.

The Aragonese, too, determined to send immediate help. Esparre had to keep an eye on his own line of retreat; he raised the siege of Logroño, but was caught up as he withdrew, and a little south of Pamplona at Noain, forced to fight. Here in a very bloody engagement on June 29th, he was utterly defeated. All Navarre was once again assured to Spain. Nor was the position sensibly altered by the attack made shortly after by Admiral Bonnivet on the border town of Fuenterrabia at the mouth of the Bidassoa. Fuenterrabia was not unimportant and the French held it for some time, but Navarre as a whole remained a Spanish kingdom with its own Cortes and Viceroy. The regent Najera was succeeded by Count Miranda.

At the same time the movement in Valencia came to a stand. The postponement of the royal visit and the unpopular measures of the government had strengthened the rebels, but the fundamental differences of the various Estates were far more marked among them, than among the predominantly mercantile rebels in Castile. The Aragonese struggle is reminiscent of the conflicts between guilds and burghers in the Italian cities of the thirteenth century; in Valencia there were nearly fifty guilds. Royal permission had sanctioned the *Germanía*, which had appointed a council of thirteen, on the model of Christ and his twelve apostles. But the nobility, too, were organized and had received favours from the King: on the other hand they had had to stomach Charles's refusal to visit them personally and his appointment of Mendoza as Viceroy.

Mendoza spoke the guilds fair, but in the end agreed with the nobility in supporting the old order. The self-willed *Germanía* was not anxious to withdraw again into political impotence; it demanded a voice in the city council. In these circumstances neither Diego Mendoza, nor his brother Rodrigo, although this latter had lands in Valencia and was therefore more popular in the country, could maintain his authority. A singularly spectacular revolt forced the Viceroy to fly from Valencia, first south to Jativa, then to the coasts, to Denia and Gandia, while the *Germanía* overran the whole land. Jativa was taken by the troops of Vicente Periz. Under the title of Captain-General he pressed on into the interior, oppressing the wretched Moriscos, whom he found working on the estates of the nobility, as he went: with a mixture of religious and democratic fanaticism, his men baptized or killed. The constitution of the *Germanía* had been originally devised for defensive purposes; now it had become a challenge to the whole state. 'The ideas of the nobility and of the heathen', asserted the rebels, 'belong to the past. The whole Kingdom shall live in peace and justice, as one brotherhood under one King and one law.' This attitude finally revolted the Grandees who collected their strength to defend themselves. There was no lack of serious fighting; it went on until the spring of 1522. In March, Vicente Periz was finally arrested and sentenced.

Events not unlike these took place in the Balearic Islands, particularly in Majorca. Here the rigid class division between peasants, labourers and artisans on the one side, merchants and nobility on the other, seemed to be sharpest and led, time and again, to bloody clashes. Don Miguel de Gurrea, regent for the crown of Aragon, had to surrender to the landowner Don Pedro de Pachs, who himself fell a victim to the infuriated mob. Only the well defended town of Alcudia, open to the sea, remained true to the nobles and merchants, who were able repeatedly to harry their opponents by bold sallies from the city. Using Alcudia as a base, the governor, with four galleys and the necessary troops, won back the islands; but this was not until after Charles himself had returned to Spain.

So desperate had been the condition of the Spanish kingdoms, both internally and externally, at the time of Charles's departure, so forlorn had been Adrian's cries for help from his powerless position in Castile in the autumn and winter of 1520-1, such incalculable dangers would have arisen had the French armies been better led or acted in closer conjunction with the rebels, that it is easy to understand the sense of relief with which Charles turned again towards his Spanish kingdoms in the summer of 1522.

ALLIANCE OF CHARLES WITH LEO X

Meanwhile the balance of European politics had shifted in the Emperor's favour in two important centres — in Rome and in London. Both England and the Papacy stood between Charles and France, and both were gradually to be drawn into firm alliance with him.

The relations between Charles and Leo had been severely strained at the imperial election. The chief difficulty was that the Pope, a close friend of Francis I since the victory of Marignano, had so openly espoused his cause. Moreover Leo may well have hesitated to defy the tradition of several centuries, by sanctioning the union of the imperial and Neapolitan crowns, the more so since the Emperor in question controlled all Spain and the New World, together with richer possessions in the Low Countries than any of his predecessors. Nor had there been any real change in the attitude of France; here if anywhere the Pope could rely not only on ancient friendship, but could find the only really effective counterblast to the power of the Emperor.

Although it is impossible to unravel every detail of papal policy, the actions of Leo X are worthy of particular attention. Our knowledge will, however, only be complete when the whole correspondence of the Spanish ambassador in Rome, Don Juan Manuel, becomes available. We have already met this remarkable scion of the Castilian aristocracy. Unimpressive in his carriage and appearance, he was feared for his skill and determination.

Ferdinand of Aragon had hated him and he was obviously unpopular in the Netherlands. We do not know whether Chièvres sent him to Rome because he thought so important a position needed an exceptional man, or merely because he wanted to be rid of him. Whatever his reason Manuel had been continuously in Rome since his official entry on April 11th, 1520.

Prompted chiefly by fear of the new power, the Medici Pope had concluded the Concordat of Bologna with Francis I in 1516. Fear of Spain played its part, too, in his later actions. Nevertheless he could hardly forget that in 1512 Spanish help alone, in the teeth of French opposition, had restored his family to their rule in Florence. And the new French ruler of Milan was singularly unforthcoming in all territorial disputes — in the problems of Parma and Piacenza as much as over the papal claims to Ferrara. At the same time he did not cease to bombard the Vatican with demands, as if the Pope had to consider the convenience of Paris alone in all Europe. These demands almost overstepped the bounds of decency when Francis I doggedly opposed the elevation of Eberhard de la Mark, Bishop of Liège, to the dignity of a cardinal, because the latter, who acted sometimes in unison with, and sometimes in opposition to, his brother Robert, had withdrawn from the French party. Moreover, as ruler of the papal states, Leo naturally regarded the Turkish danger as extremely grave, and he could not but see that the King of Spain and Naples, whose own dearest interests dictated the same policy, offered him the surest safeguard and the best defence. Although it was true that the Neapolitan coasts had since been plundered, Hugh de Moncada had defeated the pirates in May 1520. And above all — little as this point has been emphasized in surviving contemporary accounts — it was the obvious policy for the Pope to unite as far as he could with an Emperor who was clearly willing to stand his friend against that powerful Lutheran movement in Germany, of which Aleander had painted so fearful a picture. Read in full, some of Manuel's dispatches give an unmistakable indication of the part which this chief cause actually played in Vatican politics; it played a no less important part in the shadier movements of diplomacy. Manuel added a damping comment to the flattering papal letter which greeted Charles's declaration against Luther on April 19th. The flattery, he hinted, would have to be paid for in other coin. Leo's apprehensions at the Emperor's great power may have been partially lessened by the apparent compliance of the young ruler; there is evidence to support the supposed saying of the Pope that the Emperor was a 'good boy'. Manuel even deemed it advisable to insist that the Pope treat the Emperor with greater respect.

Had the crafty Castilian exploited all the possibilities of the situation, it should not have been difficult for him to draw the Pope away from the French alliance and towards his master. Nevertheless the news from Spain was often very unfavourable and the Pope might well ask himself if it were wise to enter into an alliance with a disintegrating power. On the other hand the King of France had adopted so aggressive an attitude and spoken so often of his intention to invade Naples, that Leo would be forced to ask for a very emphatic guarantee from the Emperor before he could be induced openly to take his part. Neither Leo nor his representatives in the North had made head or tail of the interplay between France, England, and Burgundy since the spring of 1520 — since those incomprehensibly contradictory meetings before and after the Field of the Cloth of Gold. This bewilderment was an important element in determining, or failing to determine, Vatican policy. Unless we are very much mistaken, the cunning director of English affairs, Cardinal Wolsey, whose ambition to stand for the Papacy was later to become a millstone round his neck, took part in this deception. He was himself surrounded by members of the cardinals' college, just as other influential cardinals were surrounded by the competing powers. The hope of an English marriage led the conscientious Charles himself to make a bold request to the Pope for absolution in advance for a 'possible future sin' — namely the dissolution of his French betrothal; politically overanxious, he would not admit the actual reason for his request. All these possibilities and considerations had their effect on Manuel, and there were times when both his hopes and his demands sank very low indeed.

But gradually the Pope leaned towards the imperial side. In the end it was he who openly asked for an offensive alliance against France, while the imperial Court, particularly during the lifetime of Chièvres, still hung back in fear. Not that Leo did not waver; once at least he made as if to accept the offers of the French ambassadors, St. Marceau and Count Carpi — or so he let it appear. On the other hand the English were now definitely anxious to separate the Emperor from the French, and were pressing for a formal decision in favour of the English marriage — without however insisting on very drastic terms for the future. The true object of English policy was merely to unmask Charles's intentions to the French and thereby make a Franco-imperial alliance impossible.

It would be idle to deny that Leo's uncertainty, torn as he was between fear of France and fear of Charles, did much to inflame the desire for war on both sides. Leo himself needed war before he could grasp the true meaning of the situation. As the outlook for Charles both in Spain and in Germany brightened in the spring of 1521, so in Rome the hopes of the French King waned and those of the Emperor increased. Francis had signed treaties with the Swiss for the employment of mercenaries; in these the Swiss had refused to serve against the House of Austria and Naples. Francis on the other hand had expressly declared that they were not to be employed against Ferrara, a clause highly unpleasing to the Pope. Possibly it was this perseverance of France in the Ferrarese friendship which finally decided Leo. In any case Manuel was able to inform the Emperor on May 21st that the Pope had at length sent him the signed treaty, by the hand of Raffaelle de' Medici, while the secretary, Giovanni Matteo Giberti, had affixed the seal to it in his own presence. The original in the Vienna archives bears the date of May 28th and a note in the margin in the Pope's own hand — 'This do we promise'.

This month of May, whose clouds lowered so darkly over the Emperor at Worms, broke in a shower of triumphs at its close.

The alliance between Pope and Emperor, although apparently confined to the political world of Italy, was in fact very far-reaching. It included a guarantee that the rule of Francesco Sforza should be re-established in Milan and that of the Doge Antonio Adorno in Genoa; they in their turn were to find the money for the war. For the execution of their projects the Pope and Emperor proposed to employ sixteen thousand Switzers. Furthermore, Charles was to restore Parma and Piacenza to the Pope, to help him in the Ferrarese trouble, and — this with special regard to Leo's plans for Siena and Florence — to take the whole Medici family under his protection. Charles was also to make himself responsible for the Pope's spiritual welfare. In return the Pope promised to receive Charles and crown him in Italy, as also to give him help against the Venetians. The Swiss and the English were included by both participants in the treaty. A few days later Manuel announced that Leo had promised to invest Charles with Naples, in return for seven thousand ducats in interest and supplies of corn, should the papal states be in want. The act of investiture was drawn up on June 28th. We need not linger over the other provisions which included a grant of ten thousand ducats from the kingdom of Naples for Alessandro de' Medici, the son of Lorenzo, and ten thousand ducats for the Cardinal de' Medici from the revenues of the Archbishopric of Toledo.

Perhaps one should blush for a Pope who so avowedly showed himself to be no more than the head of the Medici dynasty and ruler of the papal states. But in the narrow limits of his interests he had made a movement which was to be decisive in European policy and which was in turn immensely to strengthen the imperial position. A life and death struggle between the Emperor and the King of France, or perhaps it would be truer to say between the Valois princes, Francis of France and Charles of Burgundy, was now about to begin in earnest; the moral support of the Pope for one or other of them was therefore of inestimable value. Even more important was papal support in Charles's struggle to control the Spanish Church. In centuries now long forgotten the soil of Italy had witnessed the struggle for the dominance of the western world. And even in the days of Ferdinand the Catholic, Louis XII and Maximilian, that con-glomerate of states, to which the Holy Father of Christendom in his right as a temporal prince belonged, had been rightly regarded as the keystone of European politics.

But if we look for the driving influences within Charles's cabinet, which forced his policy towards Italy, we find only the Chancellor Gattinara. A whole year before, the English ambassador Tunstal had remarked on Gattinara's pre-occupation with Italy. Until his death the Chancellor never wearied in his efforts to effect the proper settlement of Italian affairs and to bring about war with France, regardless of opposition from the Burgundian nobility and even from some of the Spanish Grandees. In the private archives of the Albano family at Vercelli there is the rough draft of a third important, but unfortunately undated, schedule, in which Gattinara discusses the number of troops necessary for the war. He began with words which echo earlier formulae: since God has called Charles to be the first prince of Christendom and even Emperor, nay to be greater than Charlemagne, in the flower of his youth, it is fitting that he should turn his attention above all to Italy. Be he who he may, he continued, 'who counsels you to turn away from Italy and pursue your interests elsewhere, he counsels you for your own ruin and will bring shame and blame upon himself'. The expense of the necessary Italian campaign, he went on, would not be excessive. Nevertheless 6000· light horsemen would be essential for such purposes as reconnoitring, transport and requisitions, 2000 heavy armed cavalry for fighting, and 30,000 foot to give a decisive superiority in numbers. Over and above this, there must be fifty cannon with gunners, powder and two hundred balls each, as well as the necessary pioneers.

The inner necessities of the powers had thus carried them beyond the game of diplomacy to the grim earnest of war. The first half of those great conflicts in which Charles's life was passed did indeed take place on Italian soil. We shall trace the course of each new crisis as it arises.

Meanwhile the borders of the Netherlands continued to be a bone of contention in Franco-Burgundian policy, with England playing here the part which the Pope played in Italy.

THE FIRST CLASH WITH FRANCIS I

Judging by his memoirs, Gattinara regarded the disturbances in the Netherlands, in Gelderland, and on the borders of Luxembourg, which at this time diverted imperial policy, as having direct connection with the Italian invasion and the papal alliance. England, he tells us, offered to mediate but the French refused for, with an eye on Spanish troubles, their government still hoped for success in Navarre. But the end was neither as one side had hoped nor as the other had feared. Spain was quieted, Navarre cleared of invaders, and on the borders of the Netherlands Henry of Nassau and the Count of Werdenberg took Mouzon and besieged Mezières.

Meanwhile the French had already opened fire on Charles through their partisans. The French spokesman, Barroys, was still in Worms when hostilities broke out. Acting on instructions from his master, on April 22nd, 1521, he informed the Emperor and the Electors that the imperial ambassador in Paris, Philibert Naturel, had complained that the French in flat contravention of all treaties, were supporting Robert de la Mark, lord of Sedan and Duke of Gelderland, and the Crown-prince of Navarre, now in arms against Charles. The French King wished, however, to emphasize the fact that peace was his dearest desire since he was Charles's kinsman and neighbour, and his country needed commercial intercourse with Flanders. He pointed out that he had renounced the conquest of Naples, easy though it would have been with all his Italian allies, solely because he wanted peace. Moreover he had fulfilled the terms of the treaty of Noyon and paid Charles the necessary contributions from Artois; Charles, he added, had failed in his obligations. He could not therefore be justly called the aggressor. Besides he was innocent of participation in the affair of Robert de la Mark; he had even decisively opposed it and had told the Swiss that he would have none of it. In any case Robert was merely fighting for his just rights against the Seigneur d'Aimeries. Furthermore Francis asserted that he had even less to do with Gelderland. As for the Crown-prince of Navarre, he was wholly justified in attempting to regain the lands of his parents, for the Emperor had broken his word to him. In conclusion he announced that he had no choice but to assume that Charles's representations were meant as a challenge. He would act accordingly.

These propositions found no ready listeners among the German princes; they admonished France to keep the peace. Francis was unlucky, too, in having one of his letters to Count Carpi intercepted a few months later by the imperialists. Its contents flatly contradicted all his previous denials, for here he shamelessly declared that he was helping Robert de la Mark so as to occupy Charles in the Netherlands and prevent his interference in Italy.

Further that he had an army in Navarre, two in Picardy and on the Meuse. All these things Carpi was to explain to the Pope. Francis was apparently still in ignorance of Leo's final agreement with Charles.

As King of Naples Charles thus found himself in the same position in which his grandfather, Ferdinand of Aragon, had been in the year of the Holy League. At that time Navarre had been for the first time conquered, and Spanish power in Italy, in opposition to French, had been definitely established. Now once again the two parties and their allies faced each other as they had done in 1511; fundamentally England too was with them and against France. But in 1511 Burgundy had been able to remain neutral; now it had to bear the impact of the initial blows in this struggle for the control of Italy. Charles's very power was thus in itself a source of weakness. Now that they were a part of a world-empire, the Netherlands could no longer remain neutral, and Charles found that he was vulnerable in all too many places.

The war, which Chièvres had spent his life striving to avoid, had come at last. When he died at Worms in May 1521, it had already broken out. True that at that time Charles had accepted the offer of English mediation. True that neither side actually wanted war. It had been conceived rather as a diversion to be carried out in relation to the struggle in Italy and Navarre; campaigning in the Netherlands was permanently accompanied by negotiations which hindered the direct course of arms. The conflict dragged out in a formless series of defensive movements and counter-attacks.

Things should have been different in Italy. Here at least there was a comprehensible goal: the expulsion of the French from the duchy of Milan, and the seizure of Piacenza, Parma and possibly Ferrara for the papal states. Here, too, active forces were at work. The Pope had been working at this plan for months; so had Francesco Sforza, whose hereditary dukedom of Milan was at stake and who had at his side that energetic statesman Morone. Charles could thus hope for support in Milan itself, for troops from Naples, for Swiss and German landsknechts. Certain hindrances occasionally arose because the Swiss were serving in both camps, and the Confederation attempted to prevent fighting between its subjects by sending embassies and restrictive commands.

But for all that, both sides were now armed and approximately equal in strength. Over against the French generals, Lautrec and his brother Lescun, Colonna commanded the papal armies, Leyva and Pescara the Spanish and Neapolitan forces, the latter taking over when the armies were already on the march.

The situation in the summer of 1521 was thus still undecided. Returning from the Rhineland, Charles was at Brussels at the beginning of July, then in Ghent and towards the middle of August at Bruges. Gattinara had already gone to Dunkirk in order to take part in the peace conference which Wolsey had called with great *éclat* at Calais at the beginning of August. During these last days of idleness the Chancellor prepared for the coming negotiations by opening his heart to his master in a curiously paradoxical memorandum. It was, he said, difficult to choose between peace, which many ardently desired, and war against the enemy on both sides of the Alps. Making use of an allegorical symbol he took for his example the conflict between the seven deadly sins and the ten commandments. First he discussed the seven causes for avoiding war. It was an uncertain method of solution and involved a very great stake on a single throw. It should not be undertaken until adequate means were in the imperial coffers, which was far from being the case as Naples and Spain could give no help and the Netherlands were exhausted. Negotiations with Milan and Genoa were on an uncertain footing. The Switzers, in whatever army they were, might at any moment declare themselves the friends of France. The Spaniards had already withdrawn their army from Navarre at the behest of the Archbishop of Toledo — an event which left Charles's honour unsmirched as Navarre was already conquered. Robert de la Mark had been quelled and the French had gained nothing by his rebellion, while the English were ready to make and guarantee a peace. Last of all, time was short, there was as yet no army on foot, and with September the winter would be already upon them and much cost and peril would have been undergone without hope of result.

On the other hand Gattinara raised these arguments in favour of war. The Emperor was bound in honour to the Pope. Furthermore Leo had shown real courage in declaring himself for Charles at a time when the French King had seized Navarre and was ready to make further conquest, while Naples had not even an army for its defence. If Charles were now to abandon Leo the disillusioned Pope might well withdraw the investiture of Naples and bring the whole Empire into jeopardy. A break with Leo would imperil all Charles's hopes of subsidies from the Empire, not to mention his revenue from tithes, benefices and the Cruzada. Moreover Leo would at once make friends of France and Venice, who in their turn would seduce the Swiss, and Charles would find that he had lost all his friends on both sides of the Alps. The army was already almost mobilized and no one would understand it if, at this eleventh hour, the Emperor let all his preparations drop. Besides which, Charles had a good cause; clearly God was on his side and to let the enemy escape would be to tempt providence. Once let the occasion slip, and those who had taken up arms for him would not be so ready to come a second time. His own subjects, who had shown themselves so ready to make sacrifices, would be disappointed if he weakened now and would think the less of him in future. Lastly it was the Emperor's duty to win honour and glory; now that Spain was quiet again, all the world was expectant. Italy was calling for his help, Germany feared and loved him, the Switzers were disinclined to oppose him and the enemy themselves were losing heart.

Naturally Gattinara saw to it that his ten commandments triumphed over the temptations of the seven deadly sins. He knew very well that his words would find no merely superficial echo in the mind of the young Emperor.

Very slowly Charles moved towards the assertion of his personal will in politics. As earlier he had, without himself realizing it, looked to Chièvres for guidance, so now he was guided by the no less fluent, methodical and expansive theories of Gattinara. He had not ceased to wear splendid clothes and take delight in knightly sports, but it was now as if the majesty of the Emperor sought and found expression in the trappings of a Burgundian nobleman. He still indulged in the pleasures of the table; it was a weakness for which his observant confessors were later to reproach him, thereby taking upon themselves the office of unofficial medical advisers. But already his chief interest in life was affairs of State. Daily now he sat from morning to evening in council. Henceforward he controlled everything personally. Once he even wrote to Wolsey that they would be able to do more in a day's personal conversation than their ambassadors in months. He was learning to be silent, to listen and to judge. He was anxious therefore about the war. He went personally to visit his troops and once apparently took part in their manœuvres. He listened carefully to the reports of Alva and Fonseca on the situation. This was in sharp contrast to the behaviour of his buoyant and gifted adversary in France. He, on the other hand, never tired of uttering splendid sentiments, but even in moments of crisis preferred the pleasures of hunting parties and masques to affairs of State. His mother, Louise of Savoy, was universally recognized as the real ruler of France.

Gattinara, too, never ceased to show his master the best way of keeping his friends, of striking terror into his enemies, of preserving the loyalty of his troops and sending help to his commanders. The French had no general equal to the Count of Nassau, Gattinara declared; it would therefore be easy to conquer Tournai, Guise and Thérouanne. Charles, he advised, should try to gain some minor victory while the situation in Italy gradually ripened of itself. He must watch England carefully until Wolsey revealed his true intentions. The Pope might have good reason to hope that by next summer England too would be ranged openly on his side.

Gattinara judged both the Emperor and the situation with amazing accuracy. His advice was bold and from the financial point of view, as some have pointed out, frankly irresponsible. Yet in criticizing Gattinara we should not forget that the State loans of our own time are often raised with an even greater optimism than he himself displayed, on the future hypothetical revenues of the country. As things then stood, particularly in Italy, withdrawal was a political impossibility. Such a retreat would have strengthened Francis so much that Charles would never again have been his equal.

All the same the spreading war brought with it fearful distress on Charles's frontiers, particularly in Hainault and Artois. The Netherlands, too, suffered from the disturbance to their French trade and were forced to find not only the money but the men for the war. They had to sacrifice their sons to the murderous perils of warfare and camp fever, so that Charles's generals might complete the necessary operations for the siege of Tournai.

There were two chief scenes of action on the frontiers. One of these was near the lands of Robert de la Mark, that is on the middle waters of the Meuse, round Sedan, Bouillon, Mouzon and Mezières. The second was in the angle of the Upper Scheldt, the region so often disturbed by the Burgundian wars of old, along the Somme to the north by Cambrai, Valenciennes, Tournai, Audenarde and Ghent. Here, if full use were made of the navigable river, was the gateway to the heart of Flanders. And Tournai was therefore not merely significant as a town and a district, but as a barrier across the passage of the Scheldt. Here therefore was the centre of operations, and here the two Kings each appeared to play his minor part in the campaign. It was a heavy blow to the Emperor when, the valiant defence of the Chevalier Bayard proving too strong for them, Sickingen and Nassau had to withdraw from Mezières on September 17th, 1521. On the other hand Francis failed to relieve Tournai; he was bogged by marshes and rain in the plain between the Scarpe and Scheldt. The town itself had been recently well-fortified by Henry VIII before its return to the French. Nevertheless it yielded to the imperialists on December 1st.

The lords of Nassau, Gavre, Wassenaer and Werdenberg, the flower of the Burgundian nobility, had all come with their troops to assist in the siege. Against this defeat, the French could claim a small but significant victory; in that ancient scene of battle, not far from the coast, where Crécy and Agincourt had been fought, the Connétable de Bourbon had surprised Hesdin in Lower Artois, a little south of the long-contested town of Thérouanne.

WOLSEY'S NEGOTIATIONS AT CALAIS AND BRUGES

During all these stirring military diversions Wolsey continued to negotiate at Calais and Bruges. Our knowledge of his strange attempts at mediation is the greater in that we have not only exhaustive dispatches but numerous attempts to interpret his actions. The participants were long doubtful of the actual object of English policy. Yet in spite of deceptive words and the haze of ceremony which blurred the outline of all that Wolsey did, it is comparatively clear to us to-day. Henry VIII had begun early by bestowing favours on his nephew, the young Emperor; by now he had finally decided to wean him from the French alliance and to bind him to England by marriage. In ecclesiastical matters he stood by Charles; he had but just completed his book against Luther, which won him the title of Defender of the Faith. In answer to Manuel's sneering comment that the title was nothing remarkable, since all princes were necessarily defenders of the faith, Gattinara had shrewdly answered that that was precisely what gave the title its value: it was a hint that all other rulers had fallen short in their duty. In spite of the inward sympathy between the English and Burgundian Courts and the generous help which Margaret offered, to further their understanding, Gattinara felt himself to be essentially opposed to Wolsey. It was only too clear that Wolsey was thinking chiefly of the honours and gifts which the Emperor might give him, and calculating that he would have a better chance of the Papacy if he appeared not as a pensionary of France, but with the imperial support. Yet in spite of this he took a great delight in playing his part of arbitrator, and it must be admitted that, in the interests of peace and English trade, he acted more honourably than he has been given credit for. His King had furnished him with extensive powers, in accordance with which on August 2nd, 1521, soon after his arrival in Calais, he asked Francis and Charles to submit themselves, in writing, to his judgment.

Naturally enough neither of them would agree to this. Yet since the negotiations might be the occasion of either losing or confirming English friendship for either party, both thought it good to enter into them. Wolsey thus became a witness to the showy play-acting of the two Chancellors, Duprat and Gattinara, who now appeared before him, each attended by a staff of advisers and diplomatists, in order to hold a royal battle of words. Wolsey had skill enough neither to unmask his intentions too soon, nor to bind himself to anything. He appeared to listen with equal indifference to the extravagant demands and insolent speeches of either party.

The chief question raised was that of the responsibility for the war. Duprat set his life on the blamelessness of his King. Gattinara produced the intercepted letter to Carpi and declared that Duprat's life was forfeit. Duprat made new objections and

Gattinara then magnanimously asserted that he would not insist on the sacrifice of his life: there were better men than he. Nor did either party omit any form of dialectical argument or historic casuistry in the discussion of actual facts. Next they discussed whether a full peace or an armistice was to be signed, and if the latter for how many years or months and on what terms. In the course of these disputes Wolsey repeatedly found occasion to call a halt, to hesitate or to demand a more exact definition of terms.

In the meantime he paid a ceremonial visit to Bruges, ostensibly to win over the Emperor to a settlement in France's interests, but in fact to discuss with him a project for a close alliance and a marriage treaty. He came with all the pomp of a Roman Cardinal, did not even dismount to greet the Emperor and kept the ambassadors and nuncios who visited him waiting for a considerable time. To avoid problems of etiquette he met the King of Denmark in a garden. He expected Margaret to visit him before he visited her.

Charles called several secret meetings of his inner council. From the minutes which have survived, we learn that his advisers thought it essential that these new marriage negotiations be concealed for fear of offending Spain and Portugal, both of which countries they hoped ultimately to include in a definite offensive alliance with England. On the whole Charles's ministers urged him to postpone a final decision until England came into the open; conclusions could thus be put off until the end of next May, which was as well since no subsidies from the Empire fell due until August 1522. So spoke La Roche and de Mesa. But the Bishop of Liège, Eberhard de la Mark, said that England must immediately make herself clear; much might happen before the end of May. Berghes wanted peace at all costs. La Chaulx calculated that as Charles could not return to Spain until the end of April and would probably stay there some time, it would be already too late to move in 1522; war ought therefore to be postponed until May 1523. Haneton and Lannoy voted with the majority. Antoine Lalaing wished Charles to take his decision at once, even if he kept it secret. He went on to speak in some detail of Sickingen's operations before Thérouanne and Tournai. When these were completed the Cardinal could arrange his armistice; on the whole he thought it best that Wolsey and Madame Margaret should continue their discussions. Gattinara summed up the situation with his usual brevity. The Cardinal, he averred, still feared that Charles was privately negotiating with Francis; if he were given a guarantee that this was not so, he might be trusted to go on 'amusing the French with fair words' — cheating them in fact. In the meantime Charles must act with force and decision.

His advice was taken. The Archduchess, always friendly to England, soon brought matters to a conclusion. Charles was to have Princess Mary to wife as soon as she was twelve years old and, as a guarantee of the betrothal, a close treaty was to be concluded. This treaty was to have as one of its clauses the demand that Francis should return to Charles all such land as the French crown had unjustly seized. Furthermore, Charles was to return to Spain by way of England and war was to be declared on France in May 1523. Wolsey received a substitute for his French pension, which now obviously lapsed, and a promise of imperial support at the next papal election.

The meaning of this demand for the return of Charles's rightful lands was still uncertain. Once again in Calais the imperial ambassadors discussed the matter hotly. Gattinara read out a catalogue of the Burgundian inheritance: Bourgogne and Auxonne, Mâconnais, Boulonnais, the towns of the Somme with Péronne, Montdidier and Roye. He demanded the fulfilment of the treaty of Arras and indemnification for losses suffered by Charles's grandmother, Mary. For Spain he demanded Narbonne, Montpelier, Toulouse and Languedoc; for Navarre nearly as much; for the Empire the kingdom of Arles, Provence, Dauphiné, Lyonnais, Beaujolais. To crown all, Milan, Genoa, Asti.

Duprat declared that this was not an offer of peace but a declaration of war. To this Gattinara replied that the Emperor was singularly modest in his demands. He might have asked for the whole of France, since Boniface VIII had promised it to the Emperor Albert. Duprat retorted that if the Emperor wished, by dragging in references to the Treaty of Arras, to dig up the murder of John the Fearless, he for his part would demand full retribution for the murder of the Duke of Orleans.

It is not absolutely true to say that these arguments were merely dialectical tricks and a waste of time. Each party raised questions which their opponents took seriously, and each party soon talked itself into believing in the justice of its own most extravagant demands. With Charles himself, this demand for all the hereditary land of Burgundy, gained a dangerous hold. Arguments grew more embittered, minutes and dispatches grew stronger in tone, as news came in intermittently from the battle fronts in the Netherlands, Italy and the Pyrenees. For all this while the war was raging. The Emperor's representatives were at last forced to lower their demands and to renounce even their claim for the return of Fuenterrabia. From time to time the Court gave way to despair. For a moment, even, Wolsey's negotiations for an armistice seemed to be the only straw left for them to clutch. Only Charles remained obdurate. To crown all Wolsey threatened to break off negotiations.

Margaret realized with horror that the achievement which had cost her such care and pains was drifting rapidly towards the abyss. In the middle of November she wrote with her own hand, in the greatest anxiety, to her confidant Berghes. 'Vous savez bien', she said, 'que j'ai toujours esté et suis bonne Englese; above everything in the world I desire the close friendship of these two princes. For long enough I had good hope, but now I am in despair. The Emperor has a will of his own and councillors who strengthen him in it. This very day he said openly: "I see that the Cardinal thinks he can treat me as he has advised my ambassadors to treat the French; he asks for things which are unreasonable and affect my honour. But he has met his match! I shall have no difficulty in finding a bride and he cannot sell me his princess so dearly." I entreat you, my lord of Berghes', Margaret continued, 'what can this mean? There is danger in delay but I would dearly love to have but two hours' talk with the Cardinal to set all right again, and show him where he has made a mistake. If I did not fear to make a false step I would long ago have written him a few lines with my own hand. I beg you to take action and to consult with Haneton what is best to be done.'

Often, although not always in his long career, Charles was to be justified in his obstinacy. This was such a time. Wolsey may have already wrought him to the pitch which the warlike King of England needed; or else the Cardinal was disgusted at so many months of useless argument. Possibly when the French helped to restore his old adversary John Stuart, Duke of Albany, to the regency over King James V of Scotland, Henry saw that he could hesitate no longer. In any case he, too, broke with France and on November 22nd — a Papal grant of plenary powers having already arrived — a secret treaty came into being between the Pope, the Emperor and Henry VIII. The original now in Lille is dated November 24th and the signatories extended a cordial welcome in their bond to the Kings of Portugal, Poland, Hungary and Denmark, and to the Duke of Savoy.

Amazing change of front! In the ensuing days Charles's self-confidence blazed forth beyond all expectation and relieved Wolsey of much anxiety. On November 25th, 1521, the Cardinal had news that Milan had fallen; French troops had withdrawn and the imperial and papal troops taken possession. Tournai surrendered soon after.

A great and comprehensible glow of self-satisfaction suffused the young Emperor, who had so firmly refused to yield to bad fortune. For the first time in his life the skies were unclouded by anxiety. This must have been the time when Barend van Orley painted the portrait which now hangs in Budapest — the only likeness of Charles which breathes a certain arrogance. Above the red doublet, under the olive green cloak trimmed with fur, the edge of a gold-embroidered shirt frames the Emperor's bare neck. The harsh-featured face is almost in profile, the blue-grey eyes with their green lights gaze into the distance. The prominent chin is raised in a gesture of challenge and the expression has grown firmer with the years. A jewelled black hat is pressed down over the thick hanks of his straight hair. The heavy chain of the Order of the Golden Fleece rests on the fur collar of his cloak. The left hand, bare of rings, is full of latent energy. The portrait shows the Emperor still scarcely more than a boy, still unscathed by the disillusionment of life.

In mid-December Charles returned to Brussels from Audenarde where he had lodged for six weeks. These weeks had also seen his brief liaison with Johanna van der Gheenst, of which was born the child, later to be Duchess of Parma. The incident was little enough in itself, a transitory flame which burnt neither long nor brightly. But the historian cannot afford to forget it when tracing the Emperor's gradual development towards maturity, his slow emergence from his natural reserve. From the beginning, he took the same care of his own child as his ancestors had done of the bastards of Burgundy, boys and girls alike. She was called after the Archduchess Margaret, and even in the smallest things the Archduchess saw to the welfare of her little namesake.

THE ELECTION OF ADRIAN VI. CHARLES RETURNS TO SPAIN

The unmistakable tendency of English policy had not been the least important factor in directing the development of the French war on the Flemish border to Charles's advantage. All the autumn and winter news from Italy had varied from good to bad, swaying the negotiations at Calais, now this way, now that. But now there came a message which, of all the events of that winter of 1521-2, was to reveal to Charles his true mission. His old tutor and present minister, Adrian of Utrecht, was elected Pope. With the death of Leo on December 1st, 1521, the essential driving force of his last enterprises, undertaken both as Pope and as master of Florence, was diffused and lost. Adrian was a very different man. He fitted as ill with the Rome of the Renaissance and the arts, as with the Italy of Macchiavelli and Guicciardini. But the choice of Charles's most trusted confidant, his viceroy and Grand Inquisitor in Spain, for the headship of Christendom, without any personal help from the Emperor, bordered on the miraculous.

Hitherto we have seen few of Adrian's written opinions in so far as they affected his relations with Charles; henceforward we shall be repaid fourfold for this lack. During the first months of his pontificate, both the spiritual teacher and the imperial pupil were inspired by a lofty conviction that they were the objects of God's special grace. This led them to the emphatic and mutual expression of their thoughts and feelings. The immense event gave rise to a flood of letters on both sides. The relations of Adrian and Charles were not exactly those of Gerbert of Rheims and Otto III, yet once again, as five centuries before, a time of great spiritual tension in the western world was marked by the miracle of a German Emperor and a German Pope,[1] each with theories for

[1] Pope Sylvester II, Gerbert of Aurillac, was born in Auvergne. He was 'German' in the sense that he belonged politically to the Germanic Empire of his time (TRANSLATOR'S note).

CHARLES V
aged 22

CHARLES V.

the government of the world. Charles sent a close friend of his youth, the lord of La Chaulx, to greet the new Pope, and he boldly put into the mouth of Don Lope Hurtado Mendoza, the ambassador extraordinary who preceded him, the words: 'We hold it for certain that God Himself has made this election.' The words came from his heart. With his own hand he wrote to Adrian that their community of thought would enable them to do great things together. Mendoza, too, was to tell the Pope how much Charles expected of his profound learning and natural goodness, and how happy it would make him to receive the imperial crown from the hand of a man who was not only his countryman but had 'educated and taught him from early childhood'.

The horizon was but slightly clouded by the behaviour of Juan Manuel. The pride of the Spanish grandee and the skilful man of affairs, had led Manuel to receive the Pope, whom he regarded as a bourgeois priest from the Netherlands, with a letter, devout enough it is true, but overfull of pretentious learning and uncalled-for advice. He advised him, contrary to the custom of other Popes, to keep his own name of Adrian; above all he emphasized the great help which he and his Emperor had given at the election. Adrian, who was prouder and more easily offended than men of coarser natures deemed possible in persons of his spiritual gifts, showed that he was hurt and refused to be soothed in spite of numerous apologies. He answered briefly and dryly that he knew from Cardinal Santa Croce that the Emperor had not helped at all to secure his election. When Charles himself intervened, although he continued to complain, he declared that he did not doubt Charles's good intentions; but he did very gravely doubt Manuel's honesty, and from what he said it was clear that Adrian had a surprising knowledge of Manuel's underlying political motives. He wrote to the Emperor with his own hand, that it was his chief delight to feel that he had been called to his high dignity for no ulterior motives; 'for the sake', as he beautifully phrased it, 'of that purity and sincerity which both God and man have a right to demand of such occasions'.

Sometimes Adrian and Charles would discuss the most important questions in this almost familiar manner. The Emperor reminded his teacher that when he was still his pupil, he had told him that the French might speak fair and friendly but would seek in action only to outwit and deceive everyone. Adrian admitted that he had so spoken, but added with that fine sense of justice which is a quality typical of the Netherlander, that this was itself a reason to conceal his feelings from the French King and not to act as his personal prejudices dictated — namely in the sole interest of the Emperor. Adrian's firmness and justice on this point was in the end to loosen the deep-rooted and almost inborn confidence between him and his pupil.

Adrian left Spain before Charles returned. Thus they were never again to meet. On August 7th, 1522, Adrian put to sea from Tarragona, landed in Ostia on August 28th and entered Rome on the 29th. Charles's departure from the Netherlands had been postponed in the usual manner and the visit of his Court to England contributed further to delay him. But now Pope and Emperor, native both of the Netherlands, stepped decisively forth to play each his part in world politics.

Before leaving the Netherlands Charles freed Flanders and Artois of all allegiance to the *Parlement* of Paris and made Malines their court of final appeal. Then, on April 15th, 1522, he appointed the Archduchess Margaret once again as regent and, as before, gave her a secret council, the *conseil privé*, and a financial advisory board. As president of the *conseil privé* he chose the experienced Jean Carondolet, lord of Chapuans, who had been born at Dôle in 1469. His father too had been in the service of Charles the Bold and had been Chancellor to Maximilian; the son held many rich benefices, including since 1520 the Archbishopric of Palermo. His portrait in the Pinacothek at Munich shows a man with strong features and a somewhat angular head; one guesses at an energetic and decided personality. His clothes were rich, his appearance well cared-for, and we know that he was a friend of Erasmus; this placed him at once, at least as to his outward person, in the courtly and intelligent world of the Archduchess Margaret. In the struggles with ministers and nobility which now began again, she was to find her chief support, besides Carondolet, in Josse Lauwereys, President of the Great Council at Malines.

After taking leave of the Estates General, Charles once again sailed for England. Here in the meantime the situation had at last cleared. Wolsey made one more vain attempt to evade war with France but at Lyons on May 28th the English herald delivered an ultimatum after which the English ambassador, Cheney, took his leave. Meanwhile in England Charles and Henry passed the time in jousting, the Chancellors in negotiating, and on June 16th the Treaty of Windsor was concluded, the secret articles following on the 19th. The terms were the same as those previously outlined at Bruges, saving only that the great joint invasion of France was now put off until 1524.

The Emperor had brought with him to England, for the amazed contemplation of his hosts, a certain singular object. This was a part of the almost legendary treasure of Montezuma. It had been sent first to Spain, thence on to the Netherlands, where Dürer himself had stood in wonder, contemplating the 'subtile ingenuity of men in strange lands'.

THE WEST INDIES. MAGELLAN SAILS ROUND THE WORLD. HERNANDO CORTES IN MEXICO

This carries our gaze beyond Europe, beyond the Atlantic, to the farthest provinces of Charles's world kingdom. Not for many years to come did these far countries influence either the politics or the finances of Europe, yet their remote distance and their seemingly inexhaustible riches added exotic glamour to the already glorious Empire of the first Spanish Hapsburg.

We cannot guess the exact date at which the Indies assumed a meaning to Charles's mind. As a boy in the Netherlands, he must surely have heard of them from his Spanish teachers. And certainly when the Portuguese seaman Magellan, after failing to interest his own government, sought Castilian help for his projected expedition, Charles must have had some part in the government's decision to finance him. The decision had been taken at Valladolid on March 22nd, 1518. Even if the material value of perfumes and spices alone tickled the financial greed of the government, the decision to help Magellan did not lack a loftier significance. Charles's cosmographers too were interested in the idea of reaching the spice islands by way of the west. This purely scientific element was no less marked than the political apprehension that the expedition might lead to ill-feeling with Portugal. As was only natural, the Portuguese government was not ready to share her recently acquired and immensely profitable spice monopoly. After extensive preparations Magellan sailed from Seville with five ships on August 10th, 1519.

Magellan set out to find the Moluccas not by way of the Cape and Africa but in the opposite direction. Should the venture succeed he would be the first man to circumnavigate the globe — and he would have done it in the name of Charles V. The venture was bold in conception, difficult and perilous in execution, vivid and terrible in its course. The mere reading of a catalogue of events, seen through the eyes of one of the few survivors, drags the reader even to-day into the full tide of adventure and sheds over the life of Charles himself the lurid reflection of a terrible and unique achievement.

The crew had been hastily scraped together and, even before he passed the straits which to-day bear his name, Magellan had to quell a dangerous mutiny; by exerting that virile determination so characteristic of him, he proved that he was master. In October 1520 they passed the straits in the teeth of terrific storms. One of the ships could go no farther and turned back, but four pushed on and by November reached the open sea which, in gratitude, they named Pacific. They crossed this ocean too, landed on the southern coast of one of the Philippines, hence to reach at length the longed for east Indian archipelago. Fearful indeed were the days through which they had lived — long months of mutiny, hunger, disease and despair lay behind them. Now fulfilment was theirs. The natives seemed more ready to make friends with the newcomers than with the Portuguese whom they already knew. It was a proud and joyous moment for Magellan when the King and Queen of Cebu agreed to be baptized under the names of Don Carlos and Doña Juana. The Spaniards set up a cross and held a thanksgiving service. With European chivalry they then offered their new friends help against hostile neighbours.

The casual undertaking ended in their leader's tragic death. Fighting in a native war, Magellan was killed, saving his men. All arrangements with the natives now collapsed. The anger of the Portuguese against interlopers in their sphere flared up. The return was almost more terrible than the journey out. Five ships had become four; four now became three, two, one only. After ghastly privations and hostile treatment on the coasts, the last ship

rounded Africa and returned again to Spain under Sebastian del
Cano. With him sailed Pigafetta, the chronicler of the journey.
On September 8th, 1522, the *Victoria*, with all that remained of the
crew and the booty, put into Seville. Received by Charles himself,
del Cano received the reward for the deathless service of Magellan.
Full of joy, Charles wrote on October 31st, 1522, to the Archduchess
Margaret, telling her the great news — how his ships had girdled
the earth and what treasure they had brought back from the
Moluccas — cloves, pepper, ginger, cinnamon, muscat and sandal
wood. In future, he said, he would make frequent use of this new
route. He carried out his intention with the help of German ship-
owners and merchants, who played as large a part in developing
the Spanish spice trade as they had previously done in the
Portuguese. On February 14th, 1523, for instance, Charles particularly asked the men of Lübeck to support the enterprise. Inevitably some embittered wrangling with the Portuguese ensued.
Finally a mixed commission of Spanish and Portuguese cosmographers and navigators was set up to determine whether the
spice islands lay to the north or the south of that line of 180 degrees,
which Pope Alexander VI had drawn in 1493 from the Cap Verde
Islands, to mark the boundary between the possessions of the
two crowns.

In the meantime the gigantic mainland of America with its
ancient riches was beginning to emerge into European consciousness. The Spanish Indies had comprised hitherto only the islands
which were ruled — if ruled at all — from San Domingo. On the
discovery of the New World, hordes of ruffians, relying on European superiority in arms and the impetus of attack, had flung
themselves mercilessly on the natives. Greedy for gain, contemptuous of all who were not Christians, they had already all
but stamped out the original inhabitants. This uncontrolled
plundering of a world, in which conquest and exploration were
one, threatened to annihilate not only the wretched natives but the
profits of the *Conquistadores* themselves. From sheer necessity the
rudest laws of property and justice had to be applied. The administration of these customs, which were only gradually beginning
to take their place as laws, lay economically with the *Casa de
Contratacion*, the 'board of trade' at Seville, politically with the
Council for India, the *Consejo de Indias*. Squabbles and complaints

had forced Ferdinand of Aragon, even, to limit the number of native families who might be seized as *Repartimiento*.[1] But the actions of the private owners, or *Encomiendas*, as they were called, defied both justice and humanity; everyone concerned in the business winked at the faults of his fellows and the *Letrados*, or government officials, whom the *Conquistadores* hated, had no real authority.

Complaints piled up. For the honour of Spain and her kings, it must be admitted that if they could not give justice in practice, they did at least promulgate every kind of restrictive law. But a King of Castile and Aragon, even when he was Holy Roman Emperor to boot, could hardly administer a continent so large that fugitives from justice might easily disappear for ever. Once again the very extent of Charles's power was a cause of his weakness.

In 1515 the lay-priest, Bartolome de las Casas, came back to Spain and publicly condemned conditions so appalling as to make a mock of all morality. The hideous truth stands out not merely from his complaints, but more horribly still in certain graphic pictures of a still earlier date. These were the work of a young Indian, Guaman Poma, and are now to be seen at Copenhagen. Like the composers of Italian allegorical pictures in the fourteenth century, he tried to represent ideas in visible form. The Indian is shown imploring mercy while about him prowl jaguars, dragons, pumas, rats, foxes and wild-cats. These represent the *Corregidores*, high dignitaries, travellers, priests and officials, against whom the despairing Indian has no defence. They take all — his land, his home, his possessions, his wife and daughters, his health and his life. Las Casas hoped to bring true Christianity and Christian principles into this hell, and to relieve the wretched natives by importing foreign slaves, but the Bishop of Burgos, Juan Fonseca, the chief director of Spanish policy in the Indies, worked against him. The problem remained unsolved. Ximenes himself set his strong hand to the plough in vain; he sent out three Hieronymite Fathers, but they achieved nothing. And so in 1517 the government intervened with its well-meant but fateful decision to replace the almost extinct native population by negro slaves. The idea was at once taken up. The earliest permit for the import of negroes was one of the many privileges granted to foreigners in

[1] i.e. as each man's fair share (TRANSLATOR'S note).

the early years of Burgundian rule in Spain. The recipient was Laurent Gorrevod, who at once resold his rights to the Genoese.

After Ximenes and Sauvage, Gattinara gave ear to the lamentations of Las Casas. But Las Casas himself lost heart; the plaints dragged on from year to year, they echoed even in the demands of the rebellious *Comuneros*; but all in vain. Las Casas ended his days among the Dominicans on Hispaniola. His life work, a book entitled *The Ruined Indian*, rang out the last despondent knell over the work which had been useless.

In the newly discovered parts of the mainland of Central America it should have been easier to make a new start, avoiding the old mistakes. The coasts of Honduras were the first to be settled; soon bold attacks were made on Mexico, which borders it to the north. These lands, to which their conqueror, Hernando Cortes, gave the name of New Spain, were the seat of an ancient and advanced civilization. Of the strange conditions in which this part of the world became fused with the general history of humanity, we have innumerable graphic accounts; these are in turn elaborated by acts of State. In all, the bold personality of Cortes himself is the dominating figure. Almost from the moment of their arrival in Spain, the reports which Cortes made to Charles V belonged to the literature of the world. They were everywhere circulated in copies and extracts. In their mixture of recklessness, nay of heroism, with unutterable barbarity and callousness, they make the blood run cold. Rarely does the voice of history strike so harshly on the ear.

Born in 1485, Hernando Cortes is the most famous of all those Hidalgos whose very nature made them love arms and bodily exercise above all things. His father had been a minor cavalry officer. In his lifetime the Moorish wars ended, and he decided that his son should study at Salamanca. The blood of the young Cortes revolted against this enforced fusion with the bourgeois group of the *Letrados*. After several scrapes, the boy escaped at nineteen on a boat for the West Indies. Here he was offered land. But he despised agricultural work, he gained first a small post, then a larger *Encomienda*, finally reputation and wealth. His restless nature was still unsatisfied. Diego Velasquez, the governor, had advanced the bold young man only to be repaid by defiant insubordination. Reprimanded, punished, imprisoned, Cortes escaped, all in the most daring and romantic fashion. He was chosen to lead an expedition, then at the last minute passed over. But he himself collected arms, men and ships, and on February 20th, 1519, he set out for the conquest of new worlds.

Now began an epic *Conquista*. The anger and jealousy of recognized rulers was at war with the inherited self-will of their offspring. The intoxication inherent in independent and rebellious action, personal amazement at the unexpected course of events, the hugeness of the land and the terror so immediately spread by so small a troop, combined to increase the determination of Cortes and his men. They grew ever bolder, more reckless and more enduring, and with these qualities they acquired also a boundless lust for violence. The ill-armed natives, terrified of fire-arms, fled before them, even though far superior in numbers. Terrified princes and peoples accorded them ceremonious embassies, received them with humility and fear, giving them presents of gold and precious stones, of provisions and female slaves. All this, with the tropical heat, made Cortes and his men drunk with power and ambition. The 'white gods' overpowered the unsuspecting children of nature.

Cortes ascended gradually from Vera Cruz on the coast to the Mexican highlands. Here were many towns and rulers at enmity with one another; it was no earthly paradise, yet it was an ordered civilization. The conquerors shattered it like an earthquake. The natives often told them wrongly which way to go and who would stand their friends: sometimes this was done to lead them astray, sometimes in good faith, often enough out of ill-will or fear. Disappointment, with Cortes and his men, bred resentment, anger and horrible vengeance. The rulers strove in vain to keep the uninvited guests out of the land. Cortes made answer that he came in the name of the greatest king in the world, of Don Carlos, and in the pursuance of his all-highest will. He had secretaries and notaries with him to take formal possession, to receive vassals, to make solemn treaties. He wrote to Charles himself as his vassal and obedient servant.

Cortes swept irresistibly on. By the way he sent an expedition to examine the columns of smoke which he saw rising from Popocatapetl, and he described with admiration the towns, temples, flower gardens and public institutions of the people. Yet whenever he met with the slightest resistance or misunderstanding he killed and burnt with complete disregard for human life or civilization. His men would convert a flourishing village into a shambles — and would boast of it.

At last they came to the capital; it was superbly situated in the midst of a great lake, reached by long bridges and fed by waters brought in pipes from distant springs, resplendent with towers, palaces and squares. There lived Montezuma. A strange and ceremonious meeting took place, at which, it was later alleged, that Montezuma had said that his people too had come as emigrants to the land, so that undoubtedly that distant and great Emperor was his true overlord. Cortes and Montezuma exchanged gifts; the Spaniard was splendidly entertained but remained on his guard. At every clash with the natives he had challenged them to accept Christianity and destroy their ancient objects of worship. Now he struck against irremovable difficulties. At length Cortes saw that he could put pressure on the people if he took the ruler himself prisoner. Accordingly he made overtures to Montezuma through his interpreter and led him off with all apparent honour to the Spanish headquarters. But the people were already openly suspicious. They were right, for Cortes used their sacred ruler partly as an adviser, but chiefly as a hostage.

Then suddenly a far greater danger threatened from the rear. News came from the coast that a second Spanish expedition had landed under Panfilo Narvaez. Narvaez came on the authority of Diego Velasquez, with more ships and men than Cortes, to demand an explanation from him. A rumour started and quickly spread that Cortes and his men were deceivers; their own lord was ready to abandon them. At this crisis the *Conquistador* showed his abilities at their best. With a handful of men he marched against the far superior forces of Narvaez, sent him a courteous embassy, stormed his stronghold with a few men, and took him prisoner as a rebel, without further ado. His troops he then took into his own service. With extraordinary dexterity he thus maintained his position between his own countrymen on the one side and the amazed inhabitants on the other. The superhuman strength of the invaders had already profoundly weakened their faith in their own gods.

In the meantime revolt broke out in the capital where Cortes had left Alvarado as his deputy, a man unequal to the task. When the Spaniards laid violent hands on holy images and attacked the defenceless worshippers, the priests aroused the multitude. The Mexicans now defended themselves with the courage of despair, and Cortes himself, even with his reinforcements, could not control the situation. He was cut off in the island city, the dams blocked, the people threatening on every side. Cortes brought out Montezuma. All in vain. He spoke but his people would not hear him; instead they greeted him with a hail of stones. He died soon after, either of these wounds or at the hands of the Spaniards, for he was now useless. Driven by necessity, Cortes decided to leave the town. He intended to concentrate on repairing a single dam and to retreat in the night with his treasure and his men. But the enemy were far too angry to let the plan succeed. The retreating Spaniards were harassed on all sides and many of them slaughtered; long after they were to tell of the *noche triste*. Nor was this all. At daybreak they found their retreat blocked by the assembled manpower of Mexico under a new leader, gorgeous in feathers, gold and silver. The battle lasted for hours and all seemed lost when Cortes once again saved the day. With a few determined volunteers he broke the enemy ranks and attacked the leader himself; his death ended the battle. With reduced forces and many wounded, Cortes and his men made their difficult way to Tlascalla, which had remained true to them. Using the coast as a base, he armed again and in the next months won back all that he had lost and more.

In the midst of these events Cortes wrote his report of October 20th, 1520. To precede it, with the King, he sent some of Montezuma's treasure: impressive proof of what he had done, and pledge of his own return.

We shall have more to say of its effect on Charles. To judge by certain occasional utterances, and by the amazement they evoked in the Netherlands, the treasures did not fail to make an impression on the Court. Some of them Charles presented to his brother Ferdinand. To this day a part of them may be seen in the *Museum für Volkerkunde* in Vienna — stupendous works of art and ingenuity, gold, precious stones and feathers. The Emperor was already on his way back to his Spanish kingdoms, where the *Conquista* was to keep him occupied for months to come. After some hesitation between the governor Velasquez and the rebel Cortes, he decided in favour of the bold, if insubordinate, conqueror of Mexico.

While he was still in the Netherlands, at Bruges on May 22nd, 1522, Charles drew up his first will, 'having regard to our coming perilous journey'. It was witnessed in England and completed, significantly enough, immediately before the continuation of his sea-voyage, on July 3rd, at the castle of Waltham, near Southampton. At this turning point of his life the Emperor stated once again his guiding principles. He surrendered himself to the protection and intercession of his patroness, gave order for religious services and foundations in his name after his death, and chose for executors to his will the lords whom he knew best, Nassau, Lannoy and Hoogstraeten, as well as his confessor Glapion and the treasurer of the Order of the Golden Fleece, de Blioul. Last of all he gave great thought to the place of his burial. Should he die in the Netherlands or near by, then he would rest with his grandmother, the Lady Mary, Duchess of Burgundy, in Nôtre Dame at Bruges. But should he at the time of his death have regained possession of the old French duchy of Burgundy, that duchy which he had claimed in his treaty with England, then he would rest in the Grande Chartreuse, near 'his' town of Dijon at the side of his forefathers, Philip the Bold, his son John, and Philip the Good. Should death overtake him on some distant voyage in Spain, then he would rest in Granada with his grandparents Ferdinand and Isabella, the Catholic sovereigns, and his father Don Philip.

Longingly Charles stretched out his hands towards the old duchy of Burgundy, which he yearned to win again. Yet his journey and his thoughts were alike fixed on the future — on Spain. Here in Spain, among a people grown skilful and loyal in long conflict, the dominance of the world awaited him. Here in Spain he was soon to find the home of his heart, and here in Spain, of which he had thought so tenderly in this his first provision for his death, his bones were at last to rest.

BOOK TWO

CHARLES MAINTAINS HIS
INHERITANCE: YEARS OF GROWTH

CHAPTER I

THE EMPIRE, THE STATES OF EUROPE AND THE STRUGGLE FOR ITALY

When Charles landed in Spain for the second time at Santander on July 16th, 1522, Europe was already at war.

All the treaties which had been signed seemed to serve no other purpose than the transitory exigencies of the situation and to perpetuate destructive tumult at the expense of the spiritual and material welfare of oppressed subjects. Yet this superficial view is but a moral dictum which brings us no nearer to understanding the actual truth. Such convenient generalizations on past happenings are dangerous to true historic knowledge. As many bewildering and contradictory features can be found in the wars of those days as in the diplomatic forms which preceded them. The inevitable follies and inconsistencies of peoples and rulers may be entertaining but can never be truly important in history. We need not emphasize the ephemeral nature of their treaties, their ingenuous underestimation of their opponents, or the finicking details of petty diplomacy. We need not trouble ourselves with the play-acting of ceremonial receptions and formal speeches, the grand and purposeless courtesies exchanged between Chancellors and Councillors on both sides, without the least evidence of any resultant effect. No less threadbare than these forms themselves were the ideologies with which they were stuffed — the theory of a united Christendom, of wars against the infidel and a general Crusade as the final objective of all their conflicts. All this assumes reality only because here and there a single man stands out in all sincerity for these ideas and thereby seems to break a way athwart the political system; because in these apparently useless wars men suffered and learnt by suffering; because words and ideas did occasionally win through again to their original meaning.

FORMS OF WARFARE

This period of transition was to see for the first time that whole peoples might, in terrible and logical sequence, become engulfed in the whirlpool of war. In spite of all, military forms remained old-fashioned and inadequate. Mercenaries were employed, while the growing resources of the State and the anticipation of future revenues made it impossible to shift or spread the conflict at will. Nevertheless the technical difficulties of raising and distributing money made all forms of warfare for long enough lumbering, broken and confused. Nothing was more obviously lacking than that 'second wind' of which Charles so often spoke. In full career a victorious army might suddenly come to a stand. Nay, in the greatest triumphs lurked a still greater danger — money might run out. For neither the subsidies of the Estates nor the loans of financiers came in fast enough or covered a long enough period.

Even if subjects could be induced to see that their own country stood in need of energetic defence, for which money must be forthcoming, the mistrust of the Estates kept pace with the princely tendency towards absolutism — a tendency itself the outcome of the State's most crying needs. The Estates of Hainault, Artois, Flanders and Luxembourg were as anxious for peace as those of Overyssel, Utrecht and Friesland, although these latter provinces were repeatedly provoked to discontent by the Duke of Gelderland. But the suppression of ancient independence and inherited demands for self-government could not anywhere be achieved without fighting. Margaret was even now in the midst of it. Vainly did statesmen strive for a final settlement of the frontier question between France and the Netherlands in the old Burgundian lands of Artois and Picardy, between France and Spain in Roussillon and Navarre, and above all in the confederation of Italy. As vainly did statesmen strive to defend Europe against the Turk in Spain's Mediterranean possessions, in Naples, Venice and Hungary.

Over and above all this, England and Scotland disquieted the North with their political and economic squabbles, while the Northern Union quarrelled with the German Hansa and threatened daily to plunge the Baltic lands into war; Europe was a mass of infectious sores which might at any moment spread to the whole body

Events both great and small combined to cause the outburst, while the strangest and most old-fashioned, though not always the most ineffective, methods of warfare persisted. Beside the

highly developed form of fighting typified by the Spanish infantry
or by the exclusive bands of German and Swiss landsknechts with
their special terms of war and their unchanging tactical tradition,
there were local militias and town guards. Beside generals skilled
in the highly developed art of war, there were leaders who belonged to the old world of feudalism. Now and again there would
be resounding encounters and ambushes, in which insignificant
fortresses and towns would assume an incomprehensible importance, while the fate of kingdoms hung in the balance, so that it is
difficult to judge the importance of each single event. Those am-
biguous powers which were at the same time less and more than
the State itself, the great lords, played a part which cannot be
overestimated. In all countries the nobles grew more powerful as
they entered the service of the State. They were at one and the
same time leaders of parties, financiers, officials, soldiers, diplomatists; they caused an exceptional fluidity of interests and
alliances, they altered the course of campaigns and were a constant
threat to the stability and durability of treaties. This period which
was to convert ancient and knightly virtue into patriotism, and
the corporate relationship of the landsknechts into a mere business
agreement, made possible the loosening of all bonds, by recognizing that 'breach of contract for lack of money' was a legal ground
for mutiny. Religious differences dragged men asunder, yet the
forms which their conflict assumed on European soil defied interpretation. The planned warfare of experienced soldiers goes
strangely hand in hand with crazy onslaughts, amateurish efforts
and fantastic plans.

And the centre of the kaleidoscope in which the general and the
particular, the significant and the meaningless, the purely personal
and essentially historic mingle so madly, is the Emperor's policy.
He alone was in a position to grasp the outline of changing events
and to modify it — had he but the eyes to see and the will to act.

The concentration of so many lands under Charles's single
authority, the long-expected contest with France on the much-
divided soil of Italy, where a confederation of states had so pre-
cociously developed, were both significant. Both furthered the
development of the European system out of the confused mass of
its component states. Both contributed to confirm the internal
solidarity and the external relations of these states. Yet they did

not then evolve, and have not since, a final and satisfactory conformation. For each state, individually, had to wrestle with its own problems, problems which, localized though they were, were yet of importance in the history of the world.

THE GERMAN ESTATES AND IMPERIAL ADMINISTRATION. SOCIAL CONFLICT. DANISH TROUBLES

In 1521 Charles had left the Empire to his brother Ferdinand and an imperial government under the presidency of Frederick, Count Palatine. He had bestowed on his brother the larger and more important part of the Austrian inheritance, and allowed him to rule as regent — in appearance at least — over the other half, including Württemberg. He himself kept nothing save his own debts to the Electors and to Ferdinand, to which were added the very considerable remnants of his grandfather Maximilian's debts. During these next years the imperial registers contain hardly more than a dozen wholly unimportant imperial orders in a month. These deal either with the disposal of temporal or spiritual fiefs, largely in favour of imperial and court officials, or with minor troubles in the imperial cities. Naturally it was always possible to appeal from the government to the Emperor in Spain, but in fact the government itself rarely received an answer thence, even to its most pressing demands. From the last mandates issued by Charles when he was in the country and from indications of what he was likely to do on his return, the date of which was not yet fixed, it was possible to make out a rough idea of imperial policy. On this, and more still on their country's own modest needs and ambitions, the policy of the German Estates was based.

Only in one particular does the action of the imperial government, and more especially of certain resolute imperial councillors, call for further comment. This was in a question of immeasurable importance in German history — the question of Martin Luther. In 1522 Pope Adrian sent the nuncio Chieregati to the Diet at Nuremberg, to demand the execution of the edict of Worms and to insist on prompt action against Luther; but as his instructions gave him warrant he coupled this with the promise of thorough reform throughout the Roman hierarchy and openly admitted the partial guilt of the Vatican in the decline of the Church. From all that we know of Adrian we cannot doubt but that this promise was made in all good faith. Bitterly as they spoke of him in Rome, he had nevertheless done a great service to the Church by making this significant admission. It was the first step towards the counter-reformation. Unhappily the Germans used this very confession as a reason for repudiating the Edict; they declared that they could not have it appear 'as though they wished to oppress evangelical truth and assist unchristian and evil abuses'. Both in the recess drafted on February 9th, 1523, and in the decisions of the Nuremberg Diet in 1524 they reiterated the same opinion. At this second Diet the Cardinal-legate Campeggio was present and did not attempt to conceal his disgust at the behaviour of the Estates. All his efforts did not prevent them from deciding on April 18th, to call not indeed the general Council so much dreaded by the cardinals, but a 'general gathering of the German nation'. This was to meet on Saint Martin's day next following at Speyer and was to decide what was to be done 'until the calling of a general Council'. Like the papal legate, the Emperor too refused to countenance this national gathering. Otherwise he took no part in these deliberations.

Although he got little thanks for his efforts, the Archduke Ferdinand was not lacking in zeal; but he was barely twenty years old, had little mastery over the German language and none over German affairs. He could as yet do very little. He was as ill at ease among the congested affairs of his hereditary lands as in the Empire. Worse than this, he entrusted finance largely to a Spaniard, Salamanca, who was unpopular both in the hereditary lands and in the Empire. Princes and councillors alike complained of this upstart from Burgos, and their hatred was only increased when he became a Freiherr and soon after celebrated his marriage at Innsbruck to a Countess Eberstein. 'While Innsbruck was Innsbruck', one report has it, 'never was such expense of gold, gold chains, and hangings, such a show of racing, lance-breaking and jousting.'

The longing for activity in war, or at least for greater freedom of action, was innate with Ferdinand. He pestered the imperial Court with demands for the revenues which had been promised to him, asking first for the publication of the secret treaty of February 1522, then later clamouring to be openly elected King of the Romans. He did not grasp that Charles's position was not yet so firmly established in the Empire as to allow, on personal or on purely material grounds, of so important a renunciation of his own title to power in Germany. Ferdinand's ambassadors, Henricourt and Salinas, of whom the latter was for years to come to send detailed reports from Spain, were instructed to explain his difficult position to the Emperor. They were to add that he had been forced to give up many of his finest jewels to Duke George of Saxony in order to cover certain old debts. For the satisfaction of immediate demands he needed at least 200,000 Gulden, which, unhappily, he did not possess. The Emperor's answer was brief and cold. Yet, although the Archduke had abundant cause for complaint, he never failed his brother either in loyalty or assistance. In 1524 he sent a free offer of help through Bredam.

Full and favourable were the reports which Charles and his councillors received from Germany. These reports were, however, partly falsified; even the most careful minutes were coloured with strong dynastic prejudice. For the earlier years, these minutes have survived in full, and they provide unrivalled evidence not only of conditions in Germany but of the unchanging and smooth relationship between the two brothers. In questions of universal policy during these years, Ferdinand was wholly in agreement with Charles. His lack of familiarity with Germany made it difficult for him to form independent opinions. As for Luther, he echoed the common opinion of good Catholics. Doubtless his words had some effect on Charles when he told him that Luther had a few very determined opponents among learned men of blameless life, but for the most part such men supported him while the people followed their lead because they wrote in German. The people, he added, scorned the sacraments and the celibacy of the clergy, doubted the divine nature of Christ, were contemptuous of those in authority, Pope, Emperor or princes, and, although they spoke of nothing but peace, they had already resorted to violence. Ferdinand was anxious to help his brother against France in the Italian war; he advised that the Duke of Milan be deposed, the duchy engrossed in the Empire and placed under his personal control. He wished also to have hereditary possession of Hagenau and Alsace, in return for which he was prepared to relinquish certain important border districts to satisfy the Venetians. Franche Comté would suit him very well too. Clearly enough, young Ferdinand was tormented as his grandfather Maximilian had been. He wanted to conquer far afield, not to stay at home like a good paterfamilias, and conscientiously build up what he had, little by little, as other German princes did.

The Nuremberg Diet was remarkable for an attempt — vain alas — on the part of the towns, to combat the economic projects of the government and to confirm their own position in the Empire. The towns raised two important problems, which were referred to the imperial Court in Spain. One of these arose out of the government's plan for covering the expenses of administration and of the *Reichskammergericht* out of a general tax; the cities were uncertain whether to fight this, and if they did, with what means. The other concerned trade: the cities were much exercised as to whether the dangers of unrestricted capitalism — monopolies and forestalling — should not be checked. Naturally enough the imperial Court handled both these complaints in a manner wholly pleasing to the towns. For who was to finance Charles's wars if not the cities and the great trading houses? A commission, consisting of Maximilian Transilvanus, La Roche, Hannart and the provost of Waldkirch, negotiated at Valladolid with the city delegates in August 1523. The provost finally gave a singularly favourable answer, in the Emperor's name. Thereupon the delegates, or rather the trading firms whose representatives were among them, while they admitted that they were not authorized to make any definite offers, declared that they would put their credit at the Emperor's service, and this in spite of the already gigantic debts of the Crown.

Charles's outlook even in the Empire was still predominantly Burgundian, for at the second Nuremberg Diet he chose as his representative, a nobleman of the Low Countries, Jean Hannart, Lord of Likerke, who from February until April 1524, sent regular and simultaneous reports to Charles and Margaret. His news was not always good; he noticed that the Electors, the Elector Palatine in particular, were discontented because Charles had failed to pay the money he had promised them. He noticed too that the

Estates, who had at last been allowed a voice in the imperial government, which they had greedily demanded since Maximilian's time, were far from pleased when they found that in return they were expected to bear some of the financial burden of government. Hannart had no authority from the Emperor, but he imagined he was acting in the dynasty's best interest, when he supported Ferdinand in making half the total cost of administration and of the *Reichskammergericht* an imperial responsibility. Yet he did not think that the Archduke Ferdinand had enough experience to be equal to the demands which the princes might make on a King of the Romans. Ferdinand for his part was annoyed at Hannart's attitude and behaviour; and, writing to his brother with his own hand on July 11th, 1524, he complained of the instructions which Hannart said he had received. Subsequently the Spanish Court denied their validity and agreed to make careful inquiry into the actions of their representative.

But foreign policy was Hannart's chief task. And in this Ferdinand, both before and after his complaints, did all he could to help him. Their chief object was to get a subsidy against the Turks in Hungary. At the end of August 1521, Belgrade and Semlin had fallen. The advance was only temporarily held up while Suleiman collected all his forces for the attack on Rhodes, the last Christian outpost in the Turkish world. And when, shortly before Christmas 1522, the fortress of the Knights of Saint John surrendered, the Turks, encouraged by a growing contempt for the Christians, saw no further barrier to their advance up the Danube. A solemn embassy from Hungary did not pass unheeded at Nuremberg. The affection of Ferdinand for his sister, the Queen of Hungary, the immediate threat to the last Christian kingdom between the Empire and the Turk, and the ensuing menace to Austria, should have roused all to energetic action. Yet only after much weary argument did the Estates at length declare themselves ready to pay half of the subsidy which they had already voted at Worms. The Elector of Saxony pettishly declared that the Emperor would probably forget about this later and demand the full subsidy. His attitude was typical of the kind of obstruction with which Ferdinand had to deal.

The Estates proved both the short-sightedness of their political outlook and a phenomenal lack of pride when they suggested sending simultaneous embassies to the Emperor and the King of France, asking them to make peace and to collect all the forces of Christendom against the Turk. They relied on the assistance of the Pope in carrying out this scheme. In vain Hannart and Ferdinand tried to persuade them that Christendom could only be united if they would agree to support their Emperor; the step which they contemplated would have an exactly opposite effect. Ferdinand went even further. Speaking in Latin he hinted to certain princes that his duty to the Emperor might force him to take steps which he would rather avoid. The indignant princes repeated this threat to the Estates, who entered a formal protest in writing. In writing, too, Ferdinand made answer. He was angry at the indiscretion of the princes and explained his words as best he could by asserting that, as the Emperor's deputy, he might have to forbid them, on their duty as vassals, to send any embassy to the King of France. In their present mood, the Estates were only the more incensed. To use Hannart's expression, they felt that they were being treated '*à la façon d'Espagne*'. It was a belief which was to be often and bitterly re-echoed in years to come.

Moreover, Hannart had the difficult and delicate task of informing the Elector of Saxony that he must give up all hope of the alliance which had been promised to him at Charles's election. The Infanta Katherine was not for the Electoral Prince. Although Ferdinand himself had instructed one of his delegates in Spain to ask that both sisters, Eleonore and Katherine, might be contracted to German princes, yet at the imperial Court the interests of Portugal and Spain loomed larger.

The marriage of the fourth sister Isabella, too, had some effect on the negotiations at Nuremberg. From the end of March until the beginning of April the unhappy Queen of Denmark and her three children were in the town; she had come not only to see her brother but to implore help for her husband.

Christian II had soon earned the hatred of all his subjects in the three united kingdoms of the north. First he alienated the Swedes and the city of Lübeck; then he quarrelled both with the Danish Estates and more violently with his uncle Frederick of Holstein, whom he had tried to deprive of his inheritance — or so Frederick said — by separating Holstein and Lübeck from the Empire. Realizing at last, when he tried in vain to calm the infuriated Estates of Jutland, that his situation was desperate, Christian made ready to defend himself in Copenhagen. On April 14th, 1523, he was forced to leave by sea with his wife and children, a fugitive from his own land. With little more than a dozen ships and four or five hundred men, he fled to Isabella's native land; here, after having to abandon his first plan of entering the Zuyder Zee, he landed at Veere on Walcheren with the permission of the admiral Adolph of Burgundy. Both to the people of the Netherlands and to his wife's family he was an unwelcome guest.

All his efforts to raise an army to go back to Denmark failed. The stadhouder of Holland, Hoogstraeten, refused him help almost rudely. And Margaret, tenderly as she treated the three children, Hans, Christina and Dorothea, was forced for political reasons to treat their father with the utmost reserve. The Baltic trade of the Netherlands was once again on its feet and she could not afford to endanger it by wantonly entering into alliance with a bankrupt king, against whom almost all the northern powers were united. Nevertheless, it is comprehensible enough that the city of Lübeck and its allies went for some time in deadly fear lest the Emperor and the Netherlands should help Christian. Should this occur the danger of Dutch competition in their trade would be very serious. But they overestimated Charles's resources and underestimated Margaret's intelligence. Her fundamental good sense was never seriously impaired by her occasional outbursts of temperament. Wood and corn from the Baltic were far too necessary to the life of the Netherlands for the government light-heartedly to espouse Christian's cause. Paul vom Felde, the delegate from Lübeck, found a readier welcome than the Danish King. A few ports in the Netherlands exacted reprisals because the Sound had been closed to strengthen the blockade of Copenhagen; but these did not last long.

Christian next opened negotiations with England, whence he got nothing but fair words. He got even less from France and Scotland when he tried to interest them in his cause. He still cherished hopes of North Germany, of his brother-in-law, the Elector of Brandenburg and his Lutheran co-religionists. He called a meeting at Hamburg, to which the Pope, the Emperor, the Archduke Ferdinand and his neighbours were to send delegates. Meanwhile Isabella tried to borrow 20,000 Gulden from her brother. Her efforts provoked sympathy but no help. Even her husband's request was refused. The Estates were prejudiced against him by the accusations of his uncle Frederick. On June 8th, 1523, the Danes had elected this latter king at Roskilde and he himself wrote to inform the German Estates on January 26th, 1524. Hannart records that when the Queen was questioned about her husband's shameful behaviour, she defended him nobly. But other people confirmed the stories of his misdeeds. Ferdinand was moreover horrified to hear that his sister received the sacrament in both kinds at Nuremberg, a fact which may perhaps have supplied the reason for Luther's attack on Christian's enemies. But Isabella's religion was not a strong enough argument to persuade the citizens of Nuremberg, or others of her faith in Germany, to advance money for her husband's cause. It was typical of Christian that he continued to boast about his financial resources. From time to time he even persuaded princes and mercenary leaders to raise large armaments on his behalf. On the borders of Holstein and in Lübeck his enemies were even forced to take steps to defend themselves. But all Christian's undertakings collapsed when the truth leaked out, that he was nothing but a bankrupt prince in sore need of help.

On January 6th, 1524, Copenhagen at last surrendered and with its fall Christian's part in Denmark was for the time being at an end. An emigrant, distrusted by everyone, he took up his residence with his family in the town of Lierre in the quarter since known as the Court of Denmark. Some of his servants, like Johann von Weeze, Archbishop-elect of Lund and himself a native of the lower Rhineland, and his secretary Cornelius Schepper, later entered imperial service. The long-suffering Isabella lived to see the liberation of the Sound and peace made between the Netherlanders and the Hanseatic League at the end of 1524, but not to return to Denmark. She died on January 18th, 1526. Once again her aunt, the Archduchess Margaret, took charge of a family of orphan children.

For some time to come Charles was troubled with the Danish question. Naturally enough he wished in one way or another to make good his family's dynastic claim; at the meeting of 1524 he had not failed to lay emphasis on the imperial overlordship of Denmark. This made no impression either on the Hanseatic League or on the northern kingdoms. In the interests of Flemish trade Margaret's delegates made peace with the Emperor's Danish opponents 'under the very eyes of the imperial representatives'. The incident was clear proof of the fact that the economic needs of the hereditary lands were incompatible with the interests of the imperial free cities and Hanseatic League.

Unrest grew throughout the Empire and the Estates felt ever more keenly that they needed a King of the Romans. Everywhere trouble was brewing: counts, lords and knights stormed the Diet with complaints. Among the knights Franz von Sickingen had perhaps the most modern outlook; a condottiere in the Italian tradition, he lacked nothing save wealthy employers and had once again withdrawn unsatisfied from imperial service. He gathered a swarm of discontented knights about him, not to mention the hordes of landsknechts who always crowded to his banners. With Ulrich von Hutten he envisaged a plan for secularizing Church lands and granting them to deserving knights. It was wholly superfluous to deck out this plan with fine words about the true interest of the German nation; it was wholly misleading to disguise this ruthless attack on wealthy prelates as an effort to 'forge a path for the Gospel'. Yet even this selfish war against ecclesiastical overlords ultimately played its part in determining the form of the Protestant Confession. In August 1522, Sickingen declared war on Richard von Greiffenklau, Archbishop of Treves; he opened his campaign in September. After the first shock the Archbishop's supporters stood firm. Help came from fellow princes in Hesse and the Palatinate. The imperial government condemned both parties for flying to arms, but the Emperor had already renounced Sickingen, and the princes, the better-organized power, gained the victory. The castles and houses of the knights were systematically attacked and destroyed, last of all the fortress of Kaiserslautern whither Sickingen himself had fled. When, on May 7th, 1523, the princes entered the battered and burning ruin, they found him dying in a cellar. With him died an age. Unable to find a place in the new world which was growing up about them, unfitted to be either the officials or the soldiers of the new government, the German knights perished. The wretched end of Sickingen must stand for a symbol of the passing of a whole generation, of a whole class, to its doom.

The simultaneous and widespread movements among burghers and peasants, caused by so many and such varied discontents, did not at the moment directly affect the Emperor. So far as he was concerned, their only effect was to force the government of the Netherlands and of Austria to proceed more sternly against heretics. In practical politics the risings hampered Ferdinand's freedom of movement in Tyrol, a fact which did not escape the Venetians. But there is no need to linger over them. The Peasants' War cannot be explained by any single formula, and all efforts to do so rest on prejudice. The causes were partly economic but social, emotional and political reasons underlay all. Sooner or later the people had to come to some understanding with the increasingly powerful territorial states in which they lived. The general will of the nation played its part in bringing to birth and in spreading the ideas which found expression in the outcry of the peasants. The general will of the nation created the Reformation, itself part cause and part result of the Peasants' War. An illuminating comparison can be drawn between the trouble in Germany and the older and more essentially political movement of the Castilian comuneros, or the even more violent *Germania* in Valencia, this latter embittered as it was by differences of race. Such a comparison throws into strong relief the predominantly agricultural and religious nature of the German movement. In Alsace as early as 1522 rumours had been rife that the 'motley shoe' would soon step out — that is, that peasants would revolt, for the rebels took this symbol of peasant dress for their device. In 1523 and 1524 several minor risings took place in south Germany and in the winter of 1524-5 widespread trouble broke out in south-western and central Germany. Experienced landsknechts joined the peasant hordes and lent them an additional danger. But the people had no leaders and their revolt collapsed when all the princes between the Danube and the middle waters of the Rhine united against them. The Swabian League, that ancient support of Bavarian and Hapsburg power, defended Württemberg and thus proved itself once again an effective political instrument. It was indeed far more effective than that coalition of Bavaria and the south German bishops, created in July 1524 and called the

Regensburg Convention, which Ferdinand so warmly praised in Charles's name in the ensuing autumn.

Neither the Peasants' Revolt nor the Danish war seriously affected North Germany. Even hostilities in the Netherlands, on the border of the bishopric of Münster, had no repercussions farther afield than East Friesland. Religious upheavals, both in the Netherlands and in the south, had even less effect on the north. Yet all this while internal war raged horribly in the northern provinces for very different reasons. In Friesland all that Duke Albert had done in Maximilian's time was to do again. Tireless in their efforts, Georg Schenk von Tautenburg and Josse von Cruningen at length mastered the situation and put an end to the repeated malevolent intervention of the nobility of Gelderland. In 1522 Overyssel was pacified, in 1524 Friesland, and both were included in the body-politic of the Netherlands. The older war on the French frontier in Artois went less well. This luckless borderland had been for more than a generation the scene of Anglo-French hostilities and a disputed part of the Burgundian inheritance.

This brings us back to the affairs of Europe.

A keen-sighted statesman, Wolsey had tried to keep England at peace. As we have seen, he had not succeeded. But war was to be postponed at least until 1523 or 1524; this too was the wish of the council in Bruges. Unhappily the two Kings, in their courtly festivities and personal conversations, had outrun their ministers. Irritated by the hostility of the Scottish regent, the Duke of Albany, towards their English allies, and encouraged by some measure of military success, the Flemings in the autumn of 1522 threw off the last vestige of disguise from their war on France in Artois and Picardy. English troops under the Earl of Surrey and Flemish under Buren, after the unsuccessful siege of Hesdin, pressed on into the defenceless country until winter, cold, hunger and lack of resources forced them to ignominious retreat. Of all the campaigns of these years, this was the most purposeless, ill-considered and therefore truly expensive. Margaret had her hands full, negotiating for money to wage war; worse was to come when she met the Estates General at Malines in the spring of 1523. Energetic, and indignant at delay, she tried to coerce them, in particular the obstinate cities of Brabant. Not pausing to consider her own position, she acted without consulting her councillors. This led, neither for the first nor the last time in her career, to embittered quarrels and explanations. Meanwhile Wolsey tried to evade his obligations, for as early as September 1522, he was threatened by what at first appeared to be a serious invasion from Scotland. Fortunately it soon came to an end. Henry VIII's lust for war, in the meantime, flared up when he had news that the first peer of France, the Connétable Charles de Bourbon, the conqueror of Hesdin, was ready to revolt against his King and give help to England and Spain in shattering the power of Francis.

THE EMPEROR IN SPAIN

In the meantime Charles was wholly absorbed in his Spanish kingdoms. He was to remain in Spain for seven long years, from the summer of 1522 until the autumn of 1529. During this time it has often been averred that he became a Spaniard at heart. The statement needs modification.

Spain, itself under the influence of Burgundian and Italian culture, was changing before men's eyes.

The historian Santa Cruz has left us a detailed description of Charles's outward person, of his stature, proportion, complexion and bearing, at the outset of these seven years. The writing of Santa Cruz is typical of that period which rediscovered 'the world and man'. It was an age which, to judge by Firenzuola's book, *Of the beauty of women*, took not the least of its pleasures in contemplating the classic shape of the human body. Not wholly emancipated from the Middle Ages, men still felt to some degree that the body was but the outward expression of the soul. When Charles first set foot in Spain on his return, the Venetian ambassador, Contarini, greeted him with the pious hope that he would one day carry his victorious arms as far as Constantinople. Contarini, too, was a typical Renaissance thinker; later he became a lay theologian and a cardinal and was one of those who inspired the Counter-Reformation. The culture of the Renaissance was now reaching its high-water mark, and an even better known representative of this civilization at its flood-tide was shortly to visit Charles's Court as papal nuncio. This was Baldassare

Castiglione, the author of *Il Cortegiano*, a friend of Contarini and of Firenzuola. Charles himself built among the frond-like arches of Granada, whose springing traceries reproduce the natural charm of growing trees, a palace in the ostentatious and man-made style of the High Renaissance.

Fate and circumstance turned this Burgundian nobleman into the herald of the Renaissance on Spanish soil. Charles may indeed have remained unaffected by the paganism of the period, but he was profoundly influenced by that heightening of human values which was typical of the thought of the late Renaissance. Strangely enough it was this outlook which led to the final and heroic expression of Renaissance thought, the Counter-Reformation. Charles introduced into Spain the hierarchy of rank and the myriad formalities of the Burgundian Court, but gradually the light-heartedness and colour of Burgundy yielded before the restrained solemnity natural to the Spaniard. In his *Cortegiano* Castiglione commends above all the black clothes of the Spaniard, because of the dignity which they bestow on their wearer. Charles was now something more than a knight and a duke, something more even than an Emperor in the formless and vaguely romantic manner of his grandfather Maximilian. His ministers addressed him as *Sacra Caesarea Majestatis* — Your Holy Imperial Majesty — and were thus in part responsible for the intensification of Charles's consciousness of his own sovereignty. Yet through it all they kept enough private freedom to complain to him and of him, and even to appeal to his conscience.

Much had changed in his personal surroundings, yet Court formalities remained substantially the same although the men were different. Nassau was still there and had replaced Chièvres as First Chamberlain. A widower for the second time, he married a Spanish lady of good family, Mencia Mendoza, Marquesa de Zenete, whose father we have already heard of in Valencia. The wedding was celebrated with Burgundian pomp, with feasts and jousting, but the union was nevertheless symbolic of the gradual metamorphosis of Charles's circle. His Court was slowly re-created to combine the features both of Burgundian and Spanish culture, of Renaissance thought and imperial tradition. With all these Spanish and Burgundian elements, there was yet a universal significance in the Court of Charles V. Perhaps the most outstanding and typical figure was that of the Chancellor Gattinara, who, himself educated in medieval traditions, was nevertheless profoundly imbued with the Italian theory of world monarchy. The Spaniards themselves basked in the reflected sunlight of imperial glory. To this day through the length and breadth of Spain, the great imperial coat of arms is to be seen, blazoned on monuments and buildings.

One last thing is worthy of notice. Charles's old jousting companion, Lannoy, was appointed Viceroy of Naples in April 1522, immediately after the death of Cardoñas on March 10th. Other leading Burgundians remained in their own land. After a thorough examination of genealogical claims, Charles limited the number of Spanish grandees, as the higher nobility were called. In Castile there were to be twenty families of that rank, with twenty-five separate noble titles; held in high honour socially, they were nevertheless excluded from the inner council of the State. Their once dominant place in the King's immediate surroundings was taken now by lesser nobility and high administrative officials. Less politically class-conscious, these two groups were far more suited to royal service in the growing modern state. At a sitting of the inner council, which we shall shortly have occasion to mention, those present included Nassau and Gattinara, Charles de Poupet, lord of La Chaulx, one of Charles's oldest servants, Gérard de Pleine, lord of La Roche, grandson of a man who had been chancellor of the old Duchy of Burgundy, Laurent Gorrevod, whom Margaret had brought with her from Franche Comté — and only one Spaniard, Hernando de Vega. No German was present: the representation of all Charles's different lands on the inner council would probably have been an error. The two most important secretaries were the Fleming Lalemand, lord of Bouclans, and the Spaniard Francisco de los Cobos, who married a Mendoza. Lalemand remained in his confidential position until the autumn of 1528 when he was suspected of having injured imperial interests, was arrested and disappeared from public life. Cobos, on the other hand, rose to be secretary of state in Spain and Charles's chief financial adviser.

The constitutions of Castile and Aragon differed substantially. The Cortes of Aragon, consisting of four Estates, were divided according to the separate kingdoms of which Aragon was made up: Aragon, Catalonia, Valencia. Charles made it his custom not to hold these Cortes separately at the respective capitals, but to call them simultaneously to Monzon on the Cinca, north-west of Lerida. His chief concern at these meetings was to gain subsidies and to deal with protests from the Estates. Negotiations, which were full of repetitions, are more complicated than illuminating even in their written residue. The Cortes of Castile, with which we have been already concerned, consisted merely of the delegates of the so-called eighteen Cortes towns — a form which entailed very uneven representation of the different districts. Frequent meetings, the voting of a daily salary to the representatives — a reform which had long been desired — and the presence of a *Deputacion* from the Cortes at the imperial Court during the intermission of sittings, brought the King into ever closer contact with his people. Their meetings gave Charles the opportunity to explain the point of view which governed his policy in external as well as internal affairs, and filled the Spaniards with a consciousness of their mission to the world. Technical details, such as the replacement of the old *Alcabala* by a poll-tax, the *Encabeziamento*, and all the varied regulations connected with it, were of far less importance. [1]

Separate local councils in Castile and Aragon controlled the administration. The *Contadores majores*, or paymasters in chief, and the *Consejo de la Hacienda*, the ministry of finance, had charge of money matters. The cabinet, that is the Chancellor and the inner council, directed foreign policy: in essence this meant that Charles himself had the last word. For the council was not a ministry for foreign affairs, but merely that circle of the Emperor's closest advisers who controlled between them the guiding threads of all his kingdoms. Moreover since Chièvres died, Charles was developing the custom of directing his own policy even in its smallest details. As he worked slowly and was painfully cautious in coming to decisions, his determination to govern himself often reduced his ministers to despair. Those who had his confidence, particularly his fellow-members of the Order of the Golden Fleece, often reproached him for his irresolution.

The Spaniards, meanwhile, had long been urgent in their demand for the Portuguese marriage. For years the secretary

[1] The *Alcabala* was a tax on commercial transactions (TRANSLATOR'S note).

Barrosos had been smoothing the way for it at Lisbon. His surviving letters are drearily repetitive: again and again he was forced to go over the same points. The King of Portugal, Don Manuel, he reiterated, was anxious for his daughter Isabella to marry the Emperor. At Barrosos's persuasion he had agreed to give her the splendid dowry of a million ducats, a portion to be paid even before her marriage. But, as Barrosos continued, the King of Portugal would not conclude matters until Charles confirmed the plenipotentiary powers of his agent and repudiated his French betrothal — later he had to add, his English betrothal as well. Last of all, the King of Portugal would do nothing until Charles returned to Castile.

The ambassador made a good report of Queen Eleonore. In June 1521, she had given birth to a daughter, but already on December 13th, she was left a widow. To Barrosos's troubles over the marriage of Charles and Isabella was now added another consideration; he had to negotiate for the marriage of the young King of Portugal to the Infanta Katherine. His pursuance of this plan did not prevent him from making the thrifty suggestion that much money and trouble would be saved if the widowed Queen Eleonore would marry her stepson, rather than leave him for her younger sister Katherine. We shall have more to say by and by of French intrigues and a projected alliance with Savoy. But now that the English friendship had been secured, how could Charles, except for the most urgent reasons, break off his contract with the Princess Mary? For the present he could only postpone his marriage to Isabella.

The important instructions which he gave to La Chaulx, on an embassy to Portugal in the spring of 1522, contained among other things an entreaty to the young King to put off the bestowal of his hand in marriage for the time being and to assist as far as possible in the grand alliance now in process of formation between England, Denmark and the Jagellon dynasty, against the Turk.

But in the excuse which he lamely urged for his own close alliance with England — it was necessary for the safety of his journey — we catch a hint of his own actual preference for the Portuguese alliance. At the same time Charles commended himself to his sister Queen Eleonore, as to the person whom he 'loved best in all the world'.

The next task before the Spanish government was to cleanse the country of all traces of those troubles which had at last been stilled. On November 2nd, 1522, in Valladolid, with the greatest pomp and solemnity, Charles pronounced sentence on the leaders of the Comuneros. Mercy, he said, should triumph, but nevertheless he named two hundred and ninety rebels whom he considered worthy of judgment. At about the same time seven members of the Holy Junta were executed in Palencia. Both earlier and later Charles was urged to act mercifully and he did not altogether neglect this advice. In the administration of justice, he showed that same painful conscientiousness which he had developed in the Netherlands while handling lesser matters.

For the rest, there was great talk of filling the State coffers with money raised on confiscations, for many of the condemned were wealthy and landed men. Yet strangely enough many of the sentences were never carried out. Some of the *Exceptuados* remained abroad; Barrosos negotiated with the Portuguese for their surrender and Gattinara sent a messenger to France to ask for Pedro Taxo, Hernando de Avalos and Juan de Mendoza. But after a year or more had gone by the government began to consider the possibility of letting them purchase pardon for their misdemeanours. Besides, such confiscations as were made were almost immediately swallowed up in covering the cost of the war and in repairing the damage.

In the district where the *Germania* had made its stand, the forcible baptism of the Moriscoes once again raised the problem of the relapsed heretic and infidel, and thereby opened up the question of a final conversion. In this district, therefore, not only the rebels but their victims were handed over to justice. After long hesitation, Charles allotted the appalling task of this double punishment to the widowed Queen, Germaine de Foix. Since the death of Ferdinand of Aragon she had married and buried the Margrave of Brandenburg and was now Vice-reine of Valencia with her third husband, Don Ferdinand of Aragon, Duke of Calabria. In January 1524, she ordered innumerable arrests and executions. This was not the end, for the settlement of scores with the rebellious Moriscoes, many of whom had gone back to a wild life in the woods, continued its bloody and eventful course for many years to come.

THE EMPIRE

Adrian of Utrecht had left Spain when he became Pope. From the moving and sincere letters which pupil and teacher had then exchanged, it seemed that as Emperor and Pope each was now more bound to the other than ever before. But since that time Adrian's conscience was making it increasingly difficult for him to justify his alliance with the Emperor against the other powers of Christendom. He was even less likely to follow out the policy of his Italian predecessor, Leo X, save in so far as he feared the Turk.

Soon the greater and lesser actors on the European stage had begun a remarkable game of cross-purposes. In the foreground, Pope and Emperor played heroic parts. Charles was no wit less convinced than Adrian of the moral justification for his actions. He had challenged Francis I in his Italian possessions with the sanction of the previous Pope, and he now demanded through La Chaulx that Adrian renew the treaty. Adrian could not feel justified in agreeing.

As a background to these actions, the weary struggle for Milan dragged on, not without reacting occasionally on the College of Cardinals and the papal states. The more important aspects of this war have hitherto eluded our attention. It is therefore all the more necessary to recall now that this contest for Milan was inextricably connected with the war for Naples, which had begun as long ago as 1494. Lodovico il Moro, usurping Duke of Milan, had helped Charles VIII to invade Italy and attack Naples, because his own nephew, the legitimate heir of Milan, was the son-in-law of Alfonso of Naples, and had counted on his help against the usurper. Since that time Ferdinand of Aragon had intervened in the Neapolitan struggle and snapped up the prize, while Louis XII, discovering some remote Visconti ancestors, had indemnified himself by seizing Milan. The latter duchy, as a fief of the Empire, played a continuous and important part in Maximilian's French policy; it had for instance been the object of that feudal grant made at Hagenau in 1505 for Louis XII, Charles and Princess Claude. Meanwhile the French invasion awakened the Italian states, collectively, to a consciousness of their political weakness and geographical unity. The Papacy, Venice and the lesser states, realized that the successful invasion of greater powers might cost each and all of them their existence. Several times they expelled the French from Italy, but never, unhappily, without Spanish help. At Florence for instance, in 1512, a democratic republic supported by the French, had been overthrown and the Medici restored by the Spaniards.

Thus it would have been almost against nature for Leo X, the Medici Pope, to ally himself with the victor of Marignano (1515). But it was only natural that he should snatch at the chance of a new alliance with Charles after the imperial election, so that the French might once again be driven out of Milan. The last joy which he lived to experience was the entry of the allied army under Colonna and Pescara into Milan on November 19th, 1521 — not that this was a great victory won by deeds of heroism, for the French troops were demoralized and the Milanese anxious to have back their hereditary lord, Francesco Sforza.

On Leo's death papal subsidies to the army ceased, the French commander, Lautrec, rallied, and the Swiss, perturbed by events in their own country, responded to skilful and magnanimous French diplomacy and set an army on foot to regain Milan. In Rome, too, and in other Italian states, fear of an over-powerful Spanish Emperor at Adrian's side, was widespread. Lautrec, at the head of Swiss and Venetian troops, reappeared before Milan. Meanwhile German landsknechts under Georg von Frundsberg were on their way and some critical manœuvring took place between Milan and Pavia. Colonna made himself fast in the park at Bicocca. The unruly Swiss, under Albrecht von Stein and Arnold Winkelreid, clamoured for battle. *'Wir wöllint dran!'* they shouted, 'We want to be up and at them!' And so, against Lautrec's better judgment, on April 27th, 1522, they stormed the stronghold of the German landsknechts and the Spaniards. At the crucial moment the troops in Milan made a sally and the French attack, caught between two fires, was beaten back with great slaughter. It was the first serious and bloody battle of these years, the first great victory of the German landsknechts — and that against the Swiss. Lautrec withdrew to France while Lescun attempted to hold one or two fortresses in the duchy of Milan. When on May 30th, 1522, Genoa surrendered to Colonna and Pescara it seemed no more than the natural outcome of Bicocca.

Pedro Navarro tried in vain to relieve it in French ships; he himself and the Doge Fregoso were taken prisoner. Antonio Adorno was made Doge under imperial protection.

Thus in the summer and autumn of 1522, Charles was at a loss to understand why his old friend Adrian should choose this particular moment to dissociate himself from his joys and sorrows. For his part Adrian was even more bitterly disillusioned when he admonished Charles to make peace in the most benevolent and pastoral manner, urging him to go half-way to meet the French in Navarre and Italy. In moving words, the Pope besought him to take to heart the menacing advance of the Turk by land and sea. He pleaded that Pedro Navarro be released, to act as a mediator between the Spanish and French, defended himself against the accusation of loving the King of France no less than the Emperor, and confessed himself amazed at the implacable hostility of the English towards Francis. When, in the New Year, he had news that Rhodes had fallen, his grief and anger at the lethargy of Christendom passed all bounds, and he thundered reproaches at the princes of Europe.

Charles's bewilderment only increased. He did not feel that it consorted with his dignity to make formal answer to Adrian's complaints, but instructed his ambassador, the Duke of Sessa, to reply by word of mouth alone. In the meantime, on January 10th, 1523, he had again summarized his own opinions in writing. Not he, he averred, but the King of France had caused the troubles of Christendom. The most that could be said for Francis was that at the beginning of the pontificate, when everyone expected the new Pope to take the Emperor's part, he had shown a certain tendency to lower his demands. No sooner had Adrian revealed his peace plans than Francis expected Charles to give him everything. His demands had then outsoared all limit. Unquestionably he meant to use the occasion for reopening the war in Italy on a far larger scale than ever before. This, if anything, would give the Turks the opportunity for which they were waiting to press farther into Christendom. Charles added that he could not but regret Adrian's innate goodness. For, he continued, 'it is clear that if Your Holiness would once openly declare to the King of France that no consideration will separate you from the Emperor, that in all circumstances the two highest powers in Christendom must stand together, and that Your Holiness will support us in the defence of Italy, then, and only then, would you be fulfilling your duty as Holy Father and Pastor, then, and only then, would the King of France show himself ready to accept honourable and reasonable terms. We beseech Your Holiness to apply your great intelligence to these things before it is too late.'

It was too late. Adrian was to drink his cup of disappointment to the dregs: discovering at last how vain were his hopes of Francis, he did not change his course until his opportunity was gone. Unlike Charles, Francis I loudly proclaimed his desire for peace. While the leader of the imperial party, Cardinal Medici, sulked in Florence, the leader of the French party, Cardinal Soderini, seemed to have the situation well in hand. But one day some of his letters fell into Cardinal Medici's possession: from these he learnt, without the least shadow of doubt, that Soderini was no better than a disguised agent for the French war policy. He was pressing Francis to intervene in arms in the north and was ready to help him himself by engineering a revolt in Sicily. Great was Adrian's grief to find a cardinal of the Roman Church thus treacherously and wantonly undermining his devoted work for peace, and, in spite of the neutrality he had been so scrupulous to maintain, deliberately representing him, the Pope, as Charles's partisan. He had Soderini immediately arrested and imprisoned in the Castle of Sant' Angelo. On April 30th he proclaimed a general armistice throughout Christendom for three years. In the meantime either in the hope of winning papal support, or in a truer knowledge of his own position, Charles had made offers of peace. The arrest of Soderini helped him; papal friendship was his once more. Adrian permitted him, along with other favours, to unite the three great knightly orders of Santiago, Alcantara and Calatrava under the Spanish Crown.

Nevertheless his position was far from safe. Disturbing news came from all his lands and he had no money. He insisted on looking after everything himself — finance, war, his personal revenues. As La Roche complained to Margaret in January 1523, he would not take advice from anyone, but acted 'as the spirit moved him'. Much was left undone and much was done with insufficient deliberation. The French still held the citadel of Milan, together with Fuenterrabia, Hesdin and Cremona. In

February Cremona seemed on the point of surrender. Should it yield, Colonna was ordered to keep it as far as possible under imperial control. Mercifully these instructions came too late, and Colonna did not hesitate to tell Charles that an imperial garrison at Cremona would have had a very bad effect on the Venetians, whom he was anxious at this critical moment to win over from the French. Still more would it have offended Francesco Sforza.

Soon after, the problem of the garrison for Milan provided an object-lesson to carry Charles's political education a stage further. Gattinara felt impelled to write the Emperor a note of astonishing freedom. This memorandum awoke Charles from his dreams and decided him to govern Italy not directly but through the recognition of already existing powers — and thereby the more securely. The Chancellor saw in Charles that inner lack of confidence, which La Roche had not dared to mention to Margaret, and which the Emperor himself concealed under a mantle of pride.

In his usual fashion Gattinara began his lesson with a quotation from the Psalmist. He was sick at heart, he lamented, for the troubles that were fallen upon his master's house. His greatest grief, he continued, was to see important matters perpetually postponed. Things might be decided but the decisions were rarely carried out. As far as he could see Charles was following in the footsteps of his grandfather Maximilian, who, for all his gifts, was called the 'bad gardener', because he would never harvest his fruit in the right season. Maximilian had been as pressed for money as Charles, Gattinara admitted, but this was in itself a reason for retrenchment. As Alonso Gutierrez had suggested years before, a proper budget of expenses and revenues ought to be drawn up. Finances should be centralized. The Cortes should be induced to disclose some new source of revenue and Charles should carefully exploit their every meeting in order to find the way to the hearts of his subjects. Gattinara added that he would gladly sketch out an opening speech for each meeting; this could be then translated into good Castilian and Charles could add a few personal words to it. The Emperor could conduct a policy of European significance with comparatively little expenditure, if he could only give the impression that he was preparing mighty armaments. Genoa and Milan would not be expensive to hold. On these depended the possession of Naples and Sicily, not to mention the friendship of Venice. Given so firm a base in Italy, Charles could easily direct a powerful attack on the Turks.

Almost passionately Gattinara went on: 'Only, Sire, I implore you in the name of God, that neither in the council nor elsewhere, neither in jest nor in earnest, do you make it known before your coming to Italy that you intend to take personal possession of Milan. Do not hand over the citadel to the Spaniards or take the town away from the Duke. Such things must not be spoken of, be it never so secretly, for walls have ears and servants tongues. Later, when you are in Italy and have considered well of everything, if then you still find it good to take the duchy of Milan for yourself — then, but not sooner, will I contrive a means for you to do it. In such things make no account of what Don Juan Manuel may say, for he understands nothing of Italian affairs.' After this entreaty Gattinara grew almost petulant. If Charles insisted on letting things go on as heretofore, he complained, daily expecting God to work miracles for him, then the Chancellor would beg leave to be excused from further concern either in war or finance. He could no longer bear even a part of the responsibility for mistakes which occurred daily and hourly. Otherwise, however, he only wished to continue in Charles's service until the happy day when he should see him crowned Emperor in Italy and sitting triumphant upon his throne. Then indeed he could say: 'Nunc dimittis servum tuum, domine.'

Gattinara worked with exemplary devotion. By far the greater number of the surviving documents relative to all affairs of State, lengthy though they may be, are written in his scholarly and delicate hand. Had he himself been a ruling prince, he might well have made mistakes, but as a minister he avoided many of the follies of his predecessors, both in his advice to Charles and in his handling of public affairs. Following his own suggestion in the foregoing memorandum, he drafted a speech for the opening of the Cortes which had been called to Valladolid in July 1523, and thereby helped to bring about the reconciliation of his master's policy with the desires of his Spanish kingdoms.

In the speech from the throne, Charles admitted the earlier mistakes of his government, attributing them to his youth, to his ignorance of the country and to the lack of statesmanlike insight among his ministers. In the true humanist style, Gattinara made Charles cite as his examples, Caesar, Trajan and Titus. He declared that peace was the greatest of all blessings, but did not omit to characterize his opponents in such a way as to suit Spanish prejudices. The French seizure of Fuenterrabia was an affront to imperial prestige and Spanish dignity. Francis I had crowned his misdeeds by showing friendship to the Turk, while the only true duty of every prince was to preserve the Christian faith in all its purity. Since God had called him to the highest honour in all the world, Charles declared that he would set his own life and all he had on the preservation of the Christian faith. Here, as every-where, religion and the true forms of worship were to be his first care. The Spanish kingdoms were the leading members of all his realms. The Cortes must therefore make it their chief task to reorganize the royal councils and reform the high courts of justice. They must wipe out the national debt, now nearly a million ducats, win back Fuenterrabia and take action against the Moors and Turks. They must sweep the plundering dogs off the seas and give freedom again to Christendom. 'The hand of God is upon His Majesty, to whom he hath given both lands and victories. The hand of God will be upon the Spanish people and will give them peace and honour beyond all other peoples in Christendom.'

The lesser nobility, who represented the towns at the Cortes, seemed to be deeply moved. They discussed fully the burning questions of the day: finance, justice and administration. From all the wearisome argument one fact emerged: the lesser nobility, warlike and ambitious, were being gradually brought into closer sympathy with this world-governing monarchy of Castile. Their identification with it gave them a renewed confidence in their own high mission.

Under the guidance of the Emperor and the Pope, the affairs of Europe in the high summer of 1523 seemed once again about to follow the course which both these potentates believed to be ordained by God. Soderini's arrest had provoked the French King to a grave indiscretion. He had issued a pamphlet against the Pope, the like of which had not been seen for many centuries. In this he threatened to chastise Adrian as his forefather Philip the Fair had chastised Boniface VII. He then counted up all the services which the French monarchy had rendered to the Papacy since the time of Pepin, showing how the Pope had always found support in France against the exorbitant demands of the Emperor. Francis boasted of his constant desire for peace and in the same breath claimed the Duchy of Milan, but he jeered at the Pope who proclaimed a three years' armistice and simultaneously made advances to the opponents of France. He accompanied his telling allusion to the fate of Boniface VIII by the sneer that, 'Your Holiness may apply your greater intelligence to considering what is now to be done'.

The pamphlet was one of those unconsidered outbursts which so often aggravate the dangers of a situation. Yet the Pope hesitated to answer for fear of driving Francis into the arms of Luther. Only when Francis stopped payments to the Vatican, and thereby reverted in all seriousness to the policy of Philippe le Bel, did the patience of even the over-conscientious Adrian come to an end. He had several decisive interviews with Charles de Lannoy, the Viceroy of Naples, at Rome.

He called, too, on Henry VIII for help. While Charles, Henry, the Archduke Ferdinand and the Venetian government secretly concluded a treaty on July 29th, the Pope entered into alliance on August 3rd, with Charles, Henry, Ferdinand, the Duke of Milan, with Cardinal Medici, for Florence, with Genoa, Siena and Lucca — all in order to defend himself against Francis. It was a new Holy League. The army which they raised between them and for which the Pope alone contributed 15,000 ducats a month was placed at his own request under the leadership of Charles de Lannoy. Adrian's pontificate, which had opened so hopefully, ended in spite of all his fruitless and idealistic negotiations, with Europe in exactly the same position in which it had been when Leo X died.

The alliance was the last political act performed by Adrian VI. Almost immediately afterwards he fell ill; his constitution had proved unequal to the excitements of the last half year. On September 1st he received Lille Adam, the Grand Master of the Knights of St. John whom the Turks had driven out of Rhodes. For Adrian the interview must have seemed like a farewell to all his dearest desires on earth. A fortnight later death released him.

THE EMPIRE

In the spring and summer of 1523 the imperial Court was the sport of high hopes and grave anxiety in rapid alternation. Into this variable atmosphere the news of a certain event detonated with as violent an impact as it had in England. Charles de Bourbon was planning a revolt against the French King. Adrian de Croy, lord of Beaurain, Charles's trusted adviser, had negotiated with him for the release of his mother, taken prisoner at Hesdin, when Bourbon had been commander-in-chief of the French troops. On that occasion Croy learnt of the profound discontent of the Connétable with the French government. Bourbon's reasons were personal: when his wife, Suzanne de Beaujeu, had died childless, certain of her fiefs had escheated, in theory to the Crown, in fact to the Queen-mother, Louise of Savoy. Hence the Connétable's indignation with his King. In the early sixteenth century political society in Europe was still balanced on the knife-edge between medieval and modern times. In spite of all the formalities of vassalage the great nobles still felt that they had equal rights to freedom of action with their over-lords; the time had not yet come when the conception of the state as an indivisible whole made such actions as this of Bourbon appear simply as high treason.

Yet Bourbon deceived himself and his friends for the modern theory was already gaining hold in France. His conduct was in no way comparable to that of the old dukes of Burgundy, which arose largely from their position as the owners of imperial fiefs. Nor yet had Bourbon's action much in common with the later alliance of Protestant imperial princes with the King of France. Bourbon's motives were frankly personal. Fundamentally he may have clung to that indestructible theory of uncontrolled power which is older than the emergence of the state and which cannot admit the control of any judicially established authority. His own hereditary title gave him additional power, yet the Courts which so readily fell in with his schemes were chiefly moved by the hope that the French monarchy, surrounded as it was by

enemies, could be finally destroyed by a revolt within. Clever as
were the advisers of these rulers, they do not seem to have taken
into account the fact that, obviously enough, the treacherous
Bourbon would lose what little influence he had as soon as he
was detached from the land in which his power was rooted.
Something more than a venture of the kind he planned would be
necessary to destroy a kingdom. Yet had the ministers of Charles
and Henry grasped these facts, it would have availed them
nothing against the tourney mood of their masters.

Negotiations with Bourbon dragged on for about six months
before reaching a conclusion; both the English and the Burgundian
Courts entertained the most exaggerated hopes and both took
surreptitious measures to ensure themselves against the treachery
of the other. Mutual distrust was ineradicable. At the beginning
of August Louis de Flandres, Seigneur de Praet, imperial ambassador to England, was able to announce that terms had been
concluded. By a contract of August 4th the Emperor bound
himself to King Henry, the Archduke Ferdinand and Bourbon.
Each promised to do nothing without the others. Henry's claim
to the French Crown, and thereby to Bourbon's allegiance, was
submitted to Charles for his decision. For the rest Bourbon was
to marry one of Charles's sisters, probably Eleonore. At the end of
August at the latest the Emperor was to march on Narbonne
with a large army. He was also to raise 10,000 German landsknechts exclusively for Bourbon's service; the King of England
with equally large forces was to land during August on the coast
of Normandy. Henry and Charles were to share the expense of
the troops, which amounted to 100,000 ducats. Bourbon was
apparently required to do no more than betray his King. The
agreement was settled informally between Beaurain and Bourbon
at first, then it was made binding on all the participants in the
scheme.

At the first glance the situation might seem extremely dangerous
for France and correspondingly hopeful for the allies, who were
still strong in the support of the double alliance recently signed
in Italy.

The noble rebel meanwhile remained quietly on his estates at
Forez on the upper Loire. No one imagined that he had any
following in the land itself. The King of France, who had for

long heard rumours of Bourbon's dark dealings, unsuccessfully tried to arrange a meeting. Bourbon said he was ill, gave out that he intended later to accompany the King to Italy and remained for the time being unmolested. Only when all doubt of his treason was dispelled was he removed from office. He himself escaped in disguise, a solitary fugitive. Nothing came of it: the ambitious plan for the destruction of the French monarchy was piteously mishandled in the execution. The German landsknechts were ready and marched down the Marne as far as Chaumont under the leadership of Count Felix Werdenberg and Wilhelm Furstenberg — it was a shot in the dark for, contrary to their hopes, no one appeared to support them. The same happened to the vaunted Anglo-Flemish advance on Paris. It got as far as Compiègne and then, as in the previous year, degenerated into a mere plundering venture. Scarcely more successful was Charles's planned invasion of France across the Spanish border. His troops set out too late, although as things then stood it mattered very little when or what they did. The Constable of Castile marched over the frontier of Navarre as far as Sauveterre, only to turn back to Fuenterrabia.

Perhaps shame at the wretchedness of this effort prompted Charles in October 1523 to write very graciously to his 'brother and friend' Bourbon and to send him, by way of Bissy, 100,000 crowns. Moreover as late as the end of December he was prepared to listen patiently while a servant of Bourbon, Jean de l'Hôpital, boasted in a manner worthy of his master, declaring that the French King had been so terrified that he had collected all his troops from every corner of the kingdom. He added that the people of Toulouse would joyously welcome a foreign master, and the German landsknechts should have continued their march on Paris, as they would have met with no opposition.

Yet a sense of defeat brooded all that winter over the imperial Court at Pamplona. The Court was very near to its own retreating army in the Pyrenees, Adrian was dead, and as yet no news had come of the new Pope's election or intentions. Gattinara profited by this moment of depression to continue his master's political education. He devoted himself particularly to the more important aspects of his internal and external policy. Charles asked his other confidential advisers for their reports on the situation. These were accordingly made and from them we learn the moral background of the recent political events and the want in which the executive stood. All the councillors, with the exception of Hernando de Vega who wrote in Spanish, delivered their reports in French. Charles wrote his comments in the margin, briefly for the most part.

Gattinara began with a compliment to the young ruler. 'If Your Majesty added to all your gifts even the wisdom of Solomon, you would still be unable to do everything yourself.' God Almighty, he said, had commanded even Moses to spare himself by taking helpers; how much more therefore should Charles seek for assistance, for unlike Moses he could not speak personally with God, and yet he was responsible for far greater kingdoms. Under the sub-heading, the 'Prince's good name', he next proceeded to discuss current events. Charles should undertake nothing, he said, unless he was sure he could carry it out. The royal resources should be exploited only to gain the possible. In order to keep his friends, at this particular moment, England and Bourbon above all, the Emperor should be meticulous in fulfilling all his obligations — a task in which he had just most signally failed. He reminded Charles that the army was still in hostile country, here it must be carefully looked after so that it could proceed to new conquests or withdraw in good order to undertake the reduction of Fuenterrabia. At this point La Roche had scribbled a comment in the margin, 'Since this was written the situation has altered'. La Chaulx added, 'Fuenterrabia will not prevent the King of France from marching on Italy'. Yet even La Chaulx went on to admit that a victory at this fortress would be very important. Gattinara continued with the advice that, as all the forces were drawn up so near Fuenterrabia, it would be wise to collect all possible troops and attack it at once.

Now as always Gattinara was chiefly concerned with financial administration and the government of Italy. Money, he declared, was the sinews of war and sooner or later a clear account would have to be made of revenues and expenditure. Some account, too, should be kept of debts, particularly of those which were daily increasing as the interest mounted. The running expenses of government ought to be clearly differentiated from extraordinary outlays. Further, since the Emperor, as his councillors well knew,

THE EMPIRE

was in constant straits for money, means must be found to make
an honourable armistice before worse happened. Before he died,
Adrian had dispatched the Bishop of Bari to France to establish
the projected three years' truce. Gattinara thought it possible that
he would return with reasonable terms for a peace.

The French had apparently evacuated Italy. But this would
not end the danger. Milan and Genoa alone were the keys by
which Charles could gain possession of the peninsula, and with the
retirement of the French, the Italian League ceased to pay the
army which Charles must still keep on foot. The impoverished
city of Milan could not support it. The new Pope must therefore
be asked not only to undertake Adrian's obligations but if possible
to do even more. An ambassador extraordinary should be sent to
Rome at once to promise allegiance for Naples. In return the
Pope was to renew the investiture, and the Italian League was to
promise subsidies for at least another three months so that, if
necessary, new troops could be immediately recruited. Further,
it was urgent that the Duke of Milan be properly invested with
his duchy to reassure his subjects and encourage them to defend
the land for their master. This act, Gattinara added, would relieve
Milan's neighbours of the fear that Charles intended to keep
the duchy for himself. La Roche and Gorrevod emphatically
agreed with Gattinara that the Emperor must on no account
keep Milan for himself; it would be a violation of his treaty with
Venice. Gattinara went further, he averred that Maximilian
had lost Milan by refusing to return it to his hereditary lord. The
Papacy was in constant terror lest Naples and Lombardy should
be united under one hand and the Pope had even specially
excepted Lombardy out of the dispensation for the Empire.
In short, Gattinara concluded he would continue, Cassandra-
like, to reiterate his warnings, whether Charles heeded him or
not.

Next he proceeded to practical details. The quarrels between
Lannoy, Colonna and Pescara, he said, must come to an end.
If each one proved unwilling to obey either of the others, all three
must be given a common commander-in-chief, say the Duke of
Milan, the Archduke Ferdinand, or Bourbon.

It was not essential, Gattinara repeated, that Charles should
be in actual possession of Milan or any other Italian principality;

but it was essential that the dukes, princes and rulers of these principalities should respect him. Once he controlled Italy he would have the key to world dominion. This led him to a long disquisition on the art of handling men. The love of his subjects — here the Chancellor quoted Seneca — was an impregnable fortress: they must be cherished, their complaints heeded, their friendship cultivated. Charles should leave unpopular actions to others — and here Gattinara was echoing a maxim of Macchiavelli — nor must he overwhelm his people with new laws. Extensive legislation indicated nothing but a tacit disapproval of the Sovereign's forebears. Here La Roche added a gloss: in Spain, he wrote, the grandees not only showed an unwarrantable appetite for digesting Crown lands, but were everywhere unpopular because they and their creatures had gained control of the leading ecclesiastical and administrative posts. Moreover the country cried out on the extravagance of the Court, asserting that it could not support it as well as its other burdens and debts.

The councillors entered in great detail into the question of administrative reform. It was, they said, absolutely necessary to relieve the Emperor of countless trivialities, which so often took precedence of important affairs of State. For mere formalities neither a royal contract nor a personal signature was needed. A seal or a name stamp in the charge of a trusty official would suffice. Affairs of State, of finance and of war, ought to come up for daily consideration and decision. The council ought to assemble in a room near the Emperor's, in the winter at seven in the morning, and in the summer at six. There they could go through everything and explain it to the Emperor so that he need not 'break his own head' over it. To ensure a proper arrangement of affairs, minutes of all their proceedings should be regularly kept.

Lastly Gattinara and the councillors stepped on to the shifting sands of Charles's personal prejudices. At the head of this section Gattinara wrote, 'Reverence towards God'. Under this title he dealt with all such matters as he knew lay near to the Emperor's conscience. Here he discussed whether the Moors and Infidels were to be tolerated in the land, whether the inhabitants of the West Indian islands and of the mainland were to be converted to Christianity, whether the Inquisition was to be reformed and the will of Charles's ancestors to be executed, whether tithes, indulgences and the Cruzada were to be repaid, or absolution for their misuse to be got from the Pope. La Roche, La Chaulx and Vega thought the Moorish question important but declared that it could not be solved without assistance from the Viceroys and the councils of Aragon and Valencia, since the welfare both of the land and the grandees largely depended on it.

Of the Indians, La Roche said with disarming frankness that they had been treated hitherto not as men but as beasts. La Chaulx suggested that not only Spaniards but some of the Emperor's other subjects should be sent to the Indies — this was, in fact, already happening. Laurent Gorrevod asked for the reform of the Indian council and Gattinara suggested that the Emperor's confessor, Don Garcia de Loaysa, Bishop of Osma, be made president. Charles at once confirmed this. The councillors further added that the judges of the Inquisition should have definite salaries and not be allowed to recoup themselves out of the confiscations inflicted on the condemned; they were no longer to feed on the 'life-blood of men', and they were to remember that their office was to save, not to destroy, the accused. La Roche raised his voice against this further burden on State finances, but Vega persisted in demanding a higher standard of justice. La Roche however carried the day, at least for the time being. As for the misused moneys of the Church, La Roche argued that as it had all come originally out of the pockets of Charles's subjects and had only been used for just wars, 'the Pope should readily sanction such use'.

No other surviving document of this period gives so deep an insight into the motives and anxieties of the rulers, as do these deliberations of the Emperor's chief ministers. The young prince in their midst had still much to learn. Yet high as they pitched their measures and demands, the youthful ruler could hardly have had a better training than through listening to their arguments. Nor did the councillors confine themselves to words, for one by one they now set themselves to carry out the measures which each had advocated.

The council's recommendations in internal policy could only gradually be brought to fulfilment. In foreign policy their advice bore fruit, partly as the outcome of the new Pope's policy, in the spring of 1524. On May 14th, Gérard de Pleine, lord of La Roche, who had played so large a part in the deliberations of the council, set out, armed with an instruction drawn up by Gattinara, to negotiate for peace at the Vatican. We learn from his subsequent reports that he did in fact take with him that declaration of allegiance which had been decided on at the council. Through the length and breadth of Italy his embassy was regarded as a magnanimous gesture on the Emperor's part.

The reign of Clement VII, the new Medici Pope, who had been elevated to the Papacy in November 1523, was to be a bitter disappointment to the imperialists who had furthered his election. He began by refusing to take over the obligations of his predecessor and in April and May he followed this up by dispatching the Dominican, Nicholas von Schomberg, Archbishop of Capua, on an embassy of peace to France, Spain and England. Gattinara took full cognizance of these facts in his instructions for La Roche.

Gattinara envisaged nine possibilities for settling the dispute between Charles and Francis with the mediation of England and the Pope. The pivot of these nine possibilities was the hypothetical exchange of the French duchy of Bourgogne for the Italian duchy of Milan. In the spring of 1524, the French, led by Bonnivet, were once again vainly attempting to recover this latter place; but when on April 30th Bonnivet was wounded and the chevalier Bayard killed, their efforts came to a stand. Gattinara was therefore sincere in offering Milan; in return, however, he wanted not only the old duchy of Bourgogne, but the lands which were supposed to belong legally to the Connétable de Bourbon and to the widowed Queen, Germaine de Foix. This demand was tantamount to an attempt to split up France from within. Besides, Gattinara added innumerable stipulations, not one of which was La Roche to abandon. France, for instance, was to renounce all claim on Flanders, Artois and Naples. When Charles at length agreed that Francis, in the event of his Queen's probable death, should have his sister Eleonore to wife with Milan for a dowry, this was a long step towards compromise.

Papal mediation, said Gattinara in his instructions, might be successful in pacifying Europe on somewhat these lines — Charles's bride, Mary of England, could marry the King of Scotland and thus unite these warring kingdoms. Charles could have in her place Charlotte, the daughter of Francis I, with Bourgogne as her dowry. Francesco Sforza was to be satisfied with Renée of France, the daughter of Louis XII, who had by this time been almost more offered than any other potential bride in Europe. Later she did in fact marry the Duke of Ferrara. Bourbon was to be quieted with a fixed income, guaranteed out of his estates. But above all, Gattinara insisted, the Pope was not to be allowed to make peace until the French were expelled from Italy. Further, he must be prepared to find the money for the Spanish garrisons in the north, so that the French would not be able to make a surprise counter-attack.

All through his reign Charles thought in terms of dynastic marriage and territorial exchange. But in this summer of 1524 nothing came of the plan. On August 20th La Roche described to the Emperor his progress through Italy, his ceremonial entrance into Rome and his first audience with the Pope. Eleven days later, on August 31st, he succumbed to the plague, then raging in the city. With him one more outstanding figure of the old Burgundian epoch disappeared from among the surroundings of the Emperor.

PROVENCE AND MILAN. CHARLES'S REFLECTIONS ON THE EVE OF PAVIA

The passage of events once again submerged the peace policy. On March 24th the Spaniards reconquered the fortress of Fuenterrabia, lost three years before. The struggle had wavered long, and once the garrison had been revictualled by La Palisse, in the teeth of Beltran de la Cueva. Meanwhile, in November 1523, and in April 1524, the French were repeatedly defeated in Lombardy. At these unexpected victories, all the lust for war and the reckless hopes of the various allies flamed up again; 1524 was indeed the year on which they fixed for their decisive coup. Was the young Emperor to fail them? Had not his own councillors firmly impressed upon him that he ought not to fail his friends? Yet it would have meant very little to Henry VIII or to Charles himself, had the experienced and victorious troops now in Lombardy invaded Provence. The only person to whom such a campaign would have been important was Charles de Bourbon. On the other hand Charles had been advised by his councillors to make use of all his means in one place and at one time. The time seemed opportune, and the territorial gain might be valuable. On August 9th Charles's troops entered Aix. The undertaking was seriously held up at Marseilles. From August 14th until the end of September the imperial troops laid siege to the port. Bold as was the attack the defence proved too strong for it, and in the end the Emperor's troops were forced to withdraw, baffled, to Italy. The youthful leader Montmorency pursued them, and although Pescara covered the retreat with such dexterity that the army regained Lombardy without disaster, its morale was sadly diminished.

The retreat was only just in time. Far more serious than the check in Provence was the danger of being cut off from their base in Lombardy. For, in spite of the checks which his generals had received, Francis I had at last found means and resolution to march into Italy in person. Through the valley of the Durance he hastened to make the passage of the Alps, whence he threatened the retreating imperialists. With his fresh troops, he rapidly won the upper hand. On October 26th he entered Milan.

In this altered situation, much depended on the Pope. Like Adrian, Clement VII felt that he must avoid all prejudice, but in him this righteous attitude was more than a little coloured by his own incorrigible irresolution. Clement's weakness, so different from Adrian's personal obstinacy, no less than the increasing danger of the situation, contributed to the sudden and bloody issue of the conflict. In the autumn Clement sent Schomberg once again to the belligerents. Gattinara was already prepared to receive him, and had jokingly declared to Lalemand that he intended to baffle him with hints of a possible cardinalate, when the military situation suddenly altered Clement's tone.

Apparently taken completely by surprise by the French victories, the Pope allowed himself to be won over on December 12th, 1524, to peace and alliance with Venice. The French, it was true, had failed in an assault on Pavia, magnificently defended by Leyva; the Duke of Albany, who had accompanied Francis I, was equally unlucky when he attacked Naples. But now as always the chief importance of such campaigns was to arouse unrest

in the country. In great mental agony Clement confessed to
Charles on January 5th, 1525, that 'unwillingly and under
pressure', he had agreed to submit to the French. In despair
at his own military position and at Clement's desertion, Charles
suffered from the additional torment of that 'mistrust of his own
judgement', which he had not yet overcome. As he told Contarini,
he no longer depended on his ministers as he had done when
Chièvres was alive. But his independence made him only the
more alone.

About this time, then, closeted with his own thoughts, he took
up a pen for inspiration and jotted down a few notes, which lay
for centuries unnoticed in the Vienna Archives. It was almost as
if he had some forewarning that the first great crisis of his career
was at hand. As far as we know this was the first time in his life
at which he took stock either of the troubles which lay so heavy
on him, or of the possibilities which were yet open to him.
Compared to the dialectical skill and stylistic perfection of
Gattinara's disquisitions, his musings were but a wretched scrawl.
Yet even through these disjointed lines, we can see the outlines of
the Chancellor's thought, reflected in that of Charles. Only
through such struggles as these towards self-expression was the
Emperor at length to achieve that which he most passionately
desired — the mastery and leadership of his own policy.

> When I sat down to think out my position [he began],
> I saw that the first thing at which I must aim and the best
> that God could send me, was peace. Peace is beautiful to talk
> of but difficult to have, for as everyone knows it cannot be
> had without the enemy's consent. I must therefore make
> great efforts — and that, too, is easier said than done. How-
> ever much I scrape and save it is often difficult for me to
> find the necessary means.
>
> A successful war may help me. But I cannot support my army
> let alone increase it, if that should be necessary. Naples
> did not provide the money I hoped for; that kingdom will
> have to manage for itself if it is attacked. All sources of
> revenue here in Spain are daily tapped without result; at this
> present moment it looks as if nothing whatever could be
> raised. The King of England does not help me as a true
> friend should; he does not even help me to the extent of his
> obligations. My friends have forsaken me in my evil hour;

all are equally determined to prevent me from growing more powerful and to keep me in my present distressed state.

Furthermore, the armies are now very close to one another. A battle in which I shall be either victorious or wholly defeated cannot be postponed for much longer. Perhaps it would be best if I were to send to the Viceroy [of Naples] with all speed, for a large sum of money in bills of exchange or some other form, to support and pay my army as otherwise it may melt away. If I can only keep my army on foot, it will surely force the King of France to fight to its own great advantage. Or else it must force him to withdraw from Italy, which would be a great disgrace to him. In either case, when the King and his army have retired to France without doing any harm and the duchy of Milan has been reconquered, it will be best to lower the taxes, to treat the soldiers whom I retain as well as possible and to treat those whom I intend to pay off even better, so that I can recall them if necessary. But I must not put too much faith in all these projects.

But when I consider this present situation, and realize, as I have said, that peace is not to be had without the enemy's consent, I see that it may be all up both with peace and with war because my prospects are bad now and will be worse if it starts again — all because I have not the wherewithal. Therefore I cannot but see and feel that time is passing, and I with it, and yet I would not like to go without performing some great action to serve as a monument to my name. What is lost to-day will not be found to-morrow and I have done nothing so far to cover myself with glory and cannot but blame myself for this long delay. For all these reasons therefore, and many more, I can see no cause why I should not now do something great. Nor yet do I see cause to put it off any longer, nor to doubt but that with God's grace I shall succeed in it. Perhaps it will please him to strengthen me so that I shall possess in peace and quietness all the lands that he has graciously bestowed on me. Taking all these things into account and considering well of them, I can think of no better way in which to improve my condition than by going myself to Italy.

Doubts may be raised because of the money needed, or because of the regency in Spain, or on other grounds. In order to overcome these difficulties I think the best way would be to hurry on my marriage to the Infanta of Portugal and to bring her here as soon as possible. For the money which is to be sent with her is a very large sum in actual bullion — possibly too this would be a good opportunity to settle the question of the spice trade — on the other hand there is the King of England to be satisfied, my treaties with him must remain in force and he must be prevented from marrying his daughter in France. But my marriage will be a good reason to demand a great sum of money from the Spanish kingdoms. I shall have to call and dissolve the Cortes to achieve this. The Infanta of Portugal, who by that time will be my wife, must be appointed regent of these kingdoms, to rule them well according to the good advice of those I shall leave with her.

In this way I ought to be able to set out for Italy with the greatest splendour and honour in this very autumn. I shall go first to Naples, on whose loyalty I can rely. Here I shall receive my crown and raise an army before winter falls. I shall thus be ready for an important undertaking by the following spring, and I shall ask the King of England to carry out his great plan at the same time. Yet if peace may be had on honourable terms I will accept it and I will not cease to work for it.

Plunged in the deepest gloom, Charles thus painfully committed these and other such opinions to paper, valiantly trying to reconcile in his own mind Gattinara's theory as to the political necessity of the Italian campaign, with his own more simple and vivid emotions of honour and fame. At this very time, on the plain between Milan and Pavia, his army was fighting as it had fought once before in the conflict at Bicocca. It is tempting to play with the dramatic idea that in those very moments, when Charles was marshalling his thoughts in his now almost native Spanish, his troops were fighting out the decisive conflict in Italy.

And now let us leave Charles in Spain, and join his troops in Italy.

As at Bicocca, German auxiliaries under Frundsberg were on their way. As soon as he had news that Milan had fallen, Ferdinand at once turned to the Venetians for help and urged his government at Innsbruck to hurry on the recruiting of 10,000 landsknechts. Bourbon himself came to lead some of these across the mountains. Ferdinand would gladly have gone too, but, as he wrote to his brother, he had, to his great grief, neither the means to intervene more firmly in the Milanese struggle, nor to make the planned diversion into Burgundy by way of Pfirt. But he was at great pains to counteract French intrigues in Poland and Bohemia and repeatedly urged the Emperor to send an embassy to Muscovy for the same purpose.

The best surviving account of events in Lombardy is that of the plenipotentiary who accompanied the army, the Abbot of Najera. Funds were exhausted, but Pescara persuaded first the Spaniards, then the Italians, last of all the Germans, to continue in his service a few days more without pay. Leyva was at Pavia, King Francis, acting on the military theory of his time, well entrenched before it. The imperialists, under Pescara, Bourbon and Frundsberg, appeared from the north. From February 6th onwards the two armies were very close to each other, as in a war of manœuvres, the leaders remaining always between the two armies. The time-limit to which Pescara's troops had agreed had run out and mutiny was imminent, when, after several well-timed sallies from Leyva, the imperialist generals decided not to attack the strong French position but to attempt a junction with Leyva himself in the park of Mirabello, to the north of the city.

This was the first move in the battle of Pavia.

Strangely enough, Francis I had also marked out this park as an advantageous position, difficult as it would be to make it ready for defence. Against the advice of his oldest officers, he abandoned his own strong position and attacked the imperialists in their still unfortified and disordered state. At first successful, Francis all too soon exhausted his ammunition. The battle wavered back and forth until, some of the Swiss having withdrawn, a determined sally of Leyva from the town caught the weakened French full on the flank and turned the indecisive day into a victory for the Emperor. Francis I had plunged into the mêlée; he fell, was pinned under his horse, and was only at length recognized as King by a servant of Bourbon. He surrendered to Lannoy. His fate was shared by almost all the French officers who escaped death — the flower of France's chivalry. The list of their high-sounding names covers many pages in the Chronicle of Santa Cruz.

THE FATEFUL ROAD TO THE PEACE OF MADRID.
THE TEMPTATION OF PESCARA

The war, which had started in 1524 with so much uncertainty, almost, as it were, with a divided purpose, had thus been brought to an unexpected and glorious end during two hours of a winter morning. The day of Pavia, February 24th, 1525, was also the Emperor's twenty-fifth birthday. The capture of the invincible French King overtopped all the good fortune which the young ruler had hitherto enjoyed. This was an act of God indeed, fit to resound through all the provinces of ancient Burgundy! Now once again, as before at Péronne, a King of France was a prisoner in the hands of a Burgundian duke. Yet fate had overwhelmed King Francis without loss of honour, only after long and knightly combat, in the very tumult of battle, at a moment when he was defenceless. Charles de Lannoy looked after him well and later he was awarded generous treatment in compliance with the old traditions of chivalry. The imperialists took up their quarters at first in the camp which had been the King's, and hence on the day after the battle Lannoy wrote a full account to Charles. At the same time he sent a special messenger, Peñalosa, with a safe-conduct from the King, to carry the miraculous news through France to Spain.

'God has given you your opportunity', wrote Lannoy, 'and never will you have a better occasion than now to take possession of your Crown. Neither this land nor Navarre will get more help from France, and the heir of Navarre himself is your prisoner. In my opinion, you should come to Italy at once.' In the meantime, Lannoy continued, the fleet should be made ready; the money could be found in Italy, in Naples anyway, and probably also in Spain. 'Sire', he entreated, 'you will remember that the lord of Bersele used to say that God gave every man one opportunity to reap a rich harvest. Should he fail to reap it, the occasion would not come again.' Charles should therefore grasp his moment. Lannoy then commended by name such officers as had particularly distinguished themselves: the lengthy catalogue reads almost like a modern Honours List. He declared that Pescara deserved more than any other man; in the battle itself he had been three times wounded. Next he praised Bourbon,

Alarçon, the Marquis del Vasto, Frundsberg, Marc Sittich of Hohenems and others, each in turn; Antonio Leyva, he added, deserved all honour for paving the way to victory by his heroic four months' defence of Pavia.

The news reached Madrid on March 10th, 1525. Charles was with Gattinara, Gorrevod and La Chaulx when he received Contarini's congratulations. All the ambassadors were amazed at his bearing: he forbade noisy rejoicings and arranged for thanksgiving services, himself seeking relief in prayer after the inner conflicts of the last months. In every way this young ruler was growing unlike all other European princes: more and more, men praised his kingly bearing.

But what was the political significance of Pavia?

A bulky document in the hand of the secretary Perrenin, covering more than twenty questions and laced with Charles's marginal comments, has survived. In this, innumerable problems are raised. What is to be done with Francis? What conditions are to be offered to him? How is Charles now to handle his ally Henry VIII? Beyond these points of European policy, the paper deals with the condition of the army and of Italy, with the effects of the battle on Germany and on all Christendom. As always these considerations are phrased with precision, insight and breadth of outlook, yet it is impossible to read them without realizing that even Gattinara had been partially swept off his feet by the intoxication of the moment. Among the many excellent suggestions, we search in vain for any discussion of immediate realities, for any attempt at a definite political decision. With all his industry and high sense of duty, with all his anxiety lest anything should be overlooked, Gattinara had not that serene indifference to events which had made of Chièvres, in his way, almost a great statesman. He was too circumspect, too prone to theory. But let us listen to his own words.

The King, he suggested, could be kept safe prisoner at Naples; were he to remain in Lombardy, then it must be in the citadel of Milan. In all negotiations the Emperor must show the magnanimity of the lion and the mercy of God the Father; he must add nothing to his demands but ask only for what was his by right of inheritance, and for the estates of Bourbon. Should the King of France now ask for the hand of the widowed Eleonore of

Portugal, Charles must refuse for he had already promised his sister to Bourbon. He could put forward Eleonore's daughter, Mary of Portugal, as a bride for the Dauphin instead, and ask in return that Dauphiné be restored to its old position as a fief of the Empire. Bourbon was to be treated with every consideration and his marriage hastened on. If the King of England were suddenly to demand that the whole original 'great plan' be carried out, in accordance with the first treaty, then the ambassador de Praet could be instructed to tell him that Charles had already carried out his own part in the joint scheme without Henry's help. He now felt that it would suit better with his imperial duties to collect the arms of Christendom against the Turk, for private interest must give place before the common weal. It would be a mistake, Gattinara added, to make Henry VIII more powerful than he already was.

Gattinara now proceeded to the crux of the whole matter. Charles was to claim the whole of the Burgundian inheritance, as it had been defined long ago in the treaty of Arras, together with Péronne and Conflans, while he was to ask for Provence for Bourbon as a fief of the Empire. This was to demand nothing but his just rights. Long prepared, the moment had come at last. The fatal catchword was uttered. Charles demanded, 'Burgundy, no more, no less'.

Gattinara next insinuated against Wolsey. He was continually injuring imperial interests, and should be brought into disrepute with his master. For the rest, France's allies, Milan for instance, could be made to bear the cost of the army in Lombardy. In other matters Charles would be well advised to be generous to the Italian states and to the Pope. Only in this way would he be able to unite Christendom against the common enemy, to root out the Lutheran heresy and to beat off the Turk. This brought Gattinara to another important point: a general Council of the Church must be called and the Emperor, as guardian of the Church, should look to it himself, for the Pope did nothing but invent excuses. Seeing how badly Clement had behaved, it would do no harm to enter into a secret agreement with the Duke of Milan, giving him a free hand to seize Parma and Piacenza. If the Pope raised objections he could be quieted by the promise of an inquiry into the extent of imperial rights in Italy. On the same principle, Charles would be justified in closing his eyes if the Duke of Ferrara took it into his head to seize Modena. Gattinara seemed to have developed a truly Macchiavellian vein of statesmanship.

In the meantime Charles could call off his war in France and demobilize the soldiers in Roussillon. Though, Gattinara mused, if there were means to keep on these troops they would be an effective threat to force the French to evacuate Languedoc, if only Charles could prove his claim to it from the documents in the archives at Barcelona. The land-route to Italy, by way of Languedoc, Provence and Dauphiné, would be safer than the sea route, if Charles could gain control over it. Still this might well prove too difficult. In any case, Charles must keep up his fleet and strengthen it against the Turk.

The Portuguese marriage, Gattinara went on, must be speedily concluded. Charles ought to hasten negotiations by sending a splendid embassy under La Chaulx to support Barrosos. While making all his preparations to go to Italy, Charles was to consult the Cortes. It was of the first importance that, before he set out for Italy, Charles should invest Francesco Sforza with the duchy of Milan. Although the new duke would be expected to pay for this very handsomely in money, the investiture in itself would do much to preserve Charles's reputation for keeping his treaties.

Gattinara went on to advise Charles to keep his brother Ferdinand fully informed of all he intended to do, and to thank him warmly for the timely help he had sent from Germany. This done, Charles could proceed to Rome for his coronation and afterwards take steps to have Ferdinand elected King of the Romans. He ought, for the general good of Christendom, to resume his old alliance with the Swiss. This brought him back once again to Francis. The King should be asked not only to return the Burgundian lands, but to renounce his claim on Naples and Milan and to refrain from helping Charles's enemies, the Dukes of Gelderland and Württemberg. The papers taken at Pavia gave all the proof that was needed of Francis's help to these rebels.

Last of all Gattinara discussed the question of negotiations with Francis: would it be best to leave these to Lannoy in Italy, or should the negotiations take place somewhere on the Franco-

Spanish frontier? It was always safer, he said, to deal with a free man than with a prisoner. The French King had only to name the Queen-regent his plenipotentiary, while the Emperor sent plenipotentiary ambassadors to meet hers. Since La Chaulx was already destined for Portugal, Adrian de Croy, lord of Roeulx, came highest in consideration among the noble servants of the Crown. Among the learned ministers and lawyers at Charles's disposal, Gattinara went on, there were many skilful men, but perhaps only one — and here the Chancellor was transparently recommending himself — who was truly fitted to deal with 'Maître Jehan de France', as he put it — with the slippery French froggies.

Almost everything happened otherwise.

Instead of acting quickly while the tide was at the flood, Charles surpassed himself in delay and obstinacy. While in England, France and Italy forces were rapidly gathering which were to rob him of the fruits of Pavia, he remained oblivious of their very existence.

The imprisoned King of France indignantly refused to listen to any suggestion that his country should be stripped of provinces. In order to give the French government a free hand, he empowered his mother, Louise of Savoy, to make all future decisions. Growing restive at his enforced inactivity at the little fortress of Pizzighettone on the Adda, where Alarçon kept watch on him, he persuaded Lannoy that it would be best not to take him either to Milan or Naples, but rather to the Emperor in Spain. An old friend of Charles's youth, Lannoy may have guessed how nearly this desire suited Charles's own mood, and he could not well conceal from himself that the arrangement would be very favourable for him personally. Accordingly he gave the captured Montmorency permission to go to France and make ready the necessary galleys and other guarantees. Without any definite order, but acting on an instinct which did not play him false, Lannoy conducted Francis in safety to Barcelona on June 19th.

The effect of Pavia in Italy was very significant. For a little while the imperial victory put everything out of joint for Charles's opponents. But soon the Emperor's demands for the citadel of Milan, together with other indications that the Spaniards intended to establish themselves by force, awakened the gravest anxiety. Those Italian powers which were favourable to France — the Venetians, for instance, who had but newly joined the imperial alliance, certain cliques at the Vatican, and other lesser rulers — began to form tentative alliances among themselves. The imperial generals who stayed in Italy were ill-armed to face the rising storm. They were themselves divided and although they had been entrusted with the care of the army, Charles did not send them the means to pay it. Leyva, Pescara and even Bourbon, were disgusted at the self-willed behaviour of the Viceroy, who, proud of his kingly prisoner, gave himself out for the victor of Pavia. In spite of their entreaties to the Emperor, no money came for months on end and they were forced to rely on their private resources. Charles had even disregarded Lannoy's mild request that Pescara should be rewarded with the gift of Carpi. The Duke of Milan was still waiting in vain for his investiture. While the army dwindled, the Italian states grew daily in unity and in fear of the Emperor. Wounded and worn out, Pescara lay sick at Novara for many weeks; he did not trouble to hide his disgust from his Milanese comrade in arms, Girolamo Morone. But Morone was an Italian, and anxiety at the increase of Spanish power in his native land weighed more heavily on him than on Pescara. He could not but regard Charles's demand for the citadel of Milan as an earnest of what was to come.

Should this Spanish Emperor reign undisputed in Naples and Milan, should he find — as men had feared he would when Adrian VI was Pope — a compliant ruler for the papal states, what would then become of the Italian princes? What power in Europe would then be able to hold the balance against him? Might it not be wise to take up arms against him while yet there was time? The last chapter of Macchiavelli's *Prince* makes it clear that ideas like these were warmly received by such Italians as were still conscious of their Roman ancestry. The expulsion of the barbarians from the garden of Italy had been a political catch-word since the French invasions of the last century. There were many in Italy who knew those lines of Petrarch in which Macchiavelli had himself recognized a prelude to the closing passages of his own yet unpublished book:

Virtù contra furore
prendera l'arme, e fia'l combatter corto;
che l'antico valore
negl'italici cor' non e ancor morto,[1]

— the antique valour of the Italian soul was living yet.

The Medici Pope indeed was still wavering. Belatedly, on April 1st, he entered into alliance with Henry VIII and Charles and offered to make Gattinara a cardinal. But his own anxious hesitation was counteracted by the zeal of his datary Giberti. This latter was in close sympathy with Morone; even though Charles had at last invested Francesco Sforza with Milan, his condescension came too late and the new Duke entered into an understanding with Giberti and Morone.

Florence was always predominantly francophile; the French party was not without support in Genoa. The French themselves were ready enough to fan the blaze everywhere. The same, astonishingly enough, was true of the English, although it was hard to prove it later. Apparently the conviction was general that France was too sorely wounded to be likely to step into the place of Spain, when Charles was overthrown in Italy.

The new allies had but one thing to fear — the experienced imperialist generals. What had not Leyva and, above all, Pescara, achieved since the days of Ravenna and Bicocca! Ferrante Pescara had been born at Naples, a member of the Spanish family of Avalos. His grandmother was heiress to the estates of Pescara and Vasto on the Adriatic — the titles which he and his nephews now carried. He was related to the last royal dynasty and also to Cardona. Much might happen if Pescara could but be won for the Italian cause.

Morone undertook the task. His technique revealed both the ingenuity and the psychological limitation of contemporary intrigue. Morone pointed out that the situation might well become very dangerous for the imperial armies if all the other powers were to unite against them in their present moneyless and unsupported state. Pescara knew this only too well. 'What then will become of Naples', Morone asked him, 'if no one in

---

[1] Let constancy take arms against the rage of the foreigner, and the conflict will be brief; the antique valour of the Italian soul is living yet.

this country can make himself master of it?' Later on he spoke even more plainly.

On July 30th, Pescara wrote a letter to the Emperor. The original can hardly be read without overpowering emotion. In this profoundly moving manifestation of his constancy, Pescara related that he had, at Morone's request, given him a promise of absolute secrecy.

> Then [Pescara proceeded] he spoke to me of the discontent in Italy and of the possibility of a new French alliance. He reminded me of all that had been said against me and of how my deserts had been passed over. He told me that I was born in Italy, that I might win great glory as the liberator of my fatherland, that it lay with me to put myself at the head of the movement, so that all might work together to win for me the kingdom of Naples.
>
> I hesitated for one moment [Pescara continued], whether I should not punish him in that very hour for saying such things to me. Then I yielded to the thought that in time I might learn more. So I made answer, saying that I had indeed good reason to be angry and that the prospect which he set before me was indeed very great; but, I added, that if I broke with the Emperor, it would be in a manner worthy of a nobleman. I would do it only to show the Emperor that I was worth more than all those for whom he had passed me over.

Morone, it appears, was disappointed but not discouraged. He came again. He wrote letters. But his letters did not stay with Pescara — they went to Spain with the dispatches of the loyal general, and they lie now in the archives in Vienna, eloquent proof of the 'temptation of Pescara'. When things became really serious Pescara arrested the tempter on October 15th, and his later confessions fill the gaps in our material. Next Pescara seized the chief places in the duchy; yet when he died on the night of December 2nd-3rd, 1525, he was still waiting in vain for any sign of recognition from the Emperor. His widow, the celebrated Vittoria Colonna, who was later the friend of Michelangelo, received the only reward Charles deigned to grant — an imperial letter of condolence.

'I do not believe what Pescara reports', said Gattinara to the Emperor, blindly trusting the Milanese. 'Morone is more trustworthy than the general, and we certainly ought not to suspect the Duke whom Pescara himself has always praised.' Consequently he advised Charles not to intervene in Italian affairs until he reached the country itself. Instead Charles sent Michael de Herrera with instructions to win over the Pope, if possible, for the investiture of Bourbon with Milan, in place of Francesco Sforza. With all their intrigues the Italians achieved nothing. Their conspiracy, hampered on every side by mutual mistrust, was no more than the palely glimmering background for the drama played out between the great powers. On the stage itself, the rulers still wore the traditional garb of medieval chivalry.

The King of France was at Jativa, south of Valencia; on July 20th he arrived in Madrid, impatient to see Charles and fully conscious of the heroic figure which he intended to cut. Among other things, Charles asked him to renounce Burgundy. Although he had subsequently sobered down, Henry VIII on receiving the news of Pavia had wished to proceed straight to Paris for his coronation, and then to divide France with his allies. If necessary he was even prepared to fight.

Henry and Charles both imagined that Pavia would mean the satisfaction of all their dearest wishes. Unhappily, their leading councillors, instead of advising them to stand together, each outlined a different policy. At Calais, Gattinara had advocated the most extravagant demands against France and had made a lengthy summary of all Charles's claims on Bourgogne. Now, justifiably suspicious of Wolsey and the French, he sought to strengthen his master's actual power — by setting his finances in order, by improving administration, by confirming Charles's position in Spain, and above all by urging the Emperor to behave magnanimously in Italy and to go to that country as soon as he could.

Wolsey for his part did not for one moment subscribe to the extravagantly chevaleresque ambitions of Charles or Henry. He sought now by means of fantastic overstatement to make Henry abandon them of his own will. If Gattinara was anxious that Henry should not grow more powerful, Wolsey was no less anxious that Charles, already master of Spain and the Netherlands, should not extend his dominions. For political and financial reasons he felt that the time had come to call in France to redress the balance. The moment was favourable since England could dictate the terms at which her renewed friendship was to be bought.

Each of these statesmen, therefore, strove to arouse his master's animosity against the other. Both knew that the old foundation of their alliance was broken in pieces. The plan for the Portuguese marriage was known in London just as the Anglo-Scottish alliance was known in Spain. So well did the clever imperial ambassador, de Praet, follow the questionable schemings of the English government, that Wolsey, after watching him with growing annoyance, at length surprised one of his messengers, faced the ambassador with his own intercepted letter, threatened him in the rudest fashion, and finally forbade him the Court. This incident took place even before Pavia, but then Charles had swallowed the insult, for he was in sore need of English friendship. When, after Pavia, Henry's wildest hopes soared up again, Wolsey instructed his ambassadors, Tunstal and Wingfield, to force the 'Great Project' upon Charles at Toledo in May 1525, with the craziest elaborations. At that moment, when the Portuguese marriage was all but determined, he chose to inform Charles that Princess Mary of England would bring with her as her dowry nothing less than the Crown of France if Charles would but join with Henry in the attack. At that moment when Charles's government, in the direst financial straits, was thinking of nothing but how best to make peace, he urged the necessity of war and reminded Charles of his old debts. The excuse which he needed to break off negotiations came at last when an imperial embassy arrived in England and Wolsey was able to convince his master that Charles had been the first to violate their common treaty. Wolsey grasped with his native English clarity how little was now to be had from Charles, how much from France.

Great indeed would be the relief of the French government if it could at this moment divide Henry from the Emperor. Wolsey easily contrived to present Charles's bewildered offers and demands in the most unfavourable light to his King. Thereafter he proceeded to come to a separate understanding with France, which paid the English government 170,000 soleils and added a personal present for Wolsey of 130,000. Armistice followed on August 14th, the treaty was signed by Sir Thomas More on the 30th and published on September 6th. England improved its relations with Scotland, abandoned its wild projects, pocketed a small but useful gain — and maintained its neutral position, wooed alike by both sides.

Thanks to Wolsey's hard-headed policy, England was the first to gain anything by the battle of Pavia.

The collapse of the English alliance freed Charles to conclude his Portuguese betrothal. For the rest his position was still sadly perplexed. He had bad news from Germany and the position in Italy was uncertain. Surrounded by her great nobles, at Lyons, the Queen-regent of France had received his first embassy proudly. Both this and all later embassies foundered on Charles's obstinate determination to make the French King renounce all the land which had of old belonged to the Dukes of Burgundy. The French were equally determined to resist the demand. The generous response of the French Estates to the sudden call now made upon them recalls the days of Philip the Fair.

Francis was disappointed if he had hoped anything of a personal meeting with Charles. Although he had never yet seen his opponent face to face, for months Charles took no notice of him. Only when a courier informed him, while he was out hunting, that the King who had fallen ill was lying at death's door, did Charles hasten to him, express his sympathy in a somewhat exaggerated form, and repeat the visit once again, only to leave the King afterwards more severely alone than before. In September the widowed Duchess of Alençon, the King's devoted and intelligent sister, arrived in Spain to open negotiations. Charles received her with such courtesy that men soon began to talk of it, yet the negotiations which followed at Toledo between October 4th and 13th were wholly without result. Nor did the lengthy conversations between the Queen-regent and de Praet, who had been sent to Lyons on his recall from England, lead to anything more. Margaret, who longed above all for peace, was no more successful. Yet her efforts have a certain interest for the historian because she employed a man who was later to be of the utmost importance to Charles — Nicholas Perronet, lord of Granvelle.

Once more let us listen to the voice of Gattinara before it is drowned in the din of these endless negotiations. His papers, which have hitherto been little used, take us far deeper into the secrets of the imperial council than the reports of foreign ambassadors, on which most previous accounts have been based. Before the Duchess of Alençon left and while Francis still lay sick, Gattinara summed up the situation. His final goal was still the inception of a policy which should be truly 'imperial' — which should lead to a general war on the infidel and the heretic. His first objective was the Emperor's voyage to Italy as soon as the fleet was ready. He concealed the reason for enlarging the fleet by reference to troubles in Mexico. In the meantime Charles should send some important person — the Viceroy Lannoy, for instance, whom Gattinara patently wanted removed from Spain — to the Pope to make a temporary settlement of Italian affairs. The Pope, Gattinara added, was not lightly to be approached on the question of a council: being a bastard himself and irregularly elected to the Chair of St. Peter, he would naturally be afraid of it. But he was to be asked for money to fight against the Lutherans and the Turks. Financial cares still weighed heavily on the Chancellor; he suggested that the Cortes be wooed for money, that the Portuguese marriage be concluded, that the resources of New Spain be united with those of the Church, and their management be put into the hands of Alonso Guttierez and Juan de Vozmediano. It was true, he reflected, that both of them were Jews, but in the present situation there was no other choice. In this way Charles would have the means to satisfy even the English — the document, it appears, must have been composed before Gattinara heard that the English had already made their peace with France.

Above all Gattinara urged that Charles should decide as soon as possible on the ministers who were to carry out the measures on which his policy rested. In vain. Charles clung to his demand for the whole Burgundian inheritance, waited only for the French King's word and was deaf and blind to every other consideration.

The latest offer from France included the total renunciation of Italy, Naples, Milan, Flanders, Artois, including Hesdin and Thérouanne, and a ransom of three million talers in gold.

Charles did not want money. He wanted his just rights — the Burgundian inheritance or nothing. Nine months of negotiation had not carried them an inch beyond their starting point. Francis failed in a rash plan to escape. He was sick of his imprisonment, the more so that his illness had exhausted him so that he could not indulge in his favourite pleasures of hunting and sport. At the end of November he declared that he was ready to hand over Bourgogne, but that he could only do so if he might return to France to make the necessary arrangements; it seemed that Charles had gained his point. As a pledge of his good faith, he offered to marry Queen Eleonore and to send his sons as hostages. Eleonore herself had been successfully wooed in the King's name by Lannoy, and Bourbon had retired defeated. He was to have Milan instead. Yet, by a legal protest on August 16th, Francis had insured himself against all subsequent troubles; at that time he had announced that if a long imprisonment should force him to make concessions contrary to his duty, these were to be regarded as of no validity.

At last in December the negotiations were taken out of the hands of the despairing Gattinara and entrusted to Moncada and Lannoy, with Lalemand for their official secretary. Gattinara jeered at Lannoy's blind faith in the King and foretold disaster. When Lannoy retaliated by calling him superstitious, he answered proudly that his superstition was rooted in historic knowledge and modern observation. From these alone, he read the future. Lannoy, however, went on negotiating in Madrid and on December 19th reached a conclusion. The enormous document summed up in fifty articles all the promises made by Francis, and all the pledges he had given for lands belonging to Charles's subjects in France, that is, the estates of Orange, Nassau, Croy, Fiennes and Vergy. He was to abandon his old allies, Navarre and Gelderland, Württemberg and Robert de la Mark, to provide a fleet with sailors and guns to take Charles to Italy, and to keep 200,000 soleils and 500 soldiers ready for imperial use. Last of all, he promised to join Charles in a Crusade. Strange reversion to the outworn beliefs of medieval France and Burgundy! The King was to be released as soon as his two eldest sons were exchanged for him as hostages. The treaty was to be ratified six weeks after his release and confirmed by the Paris *Parlement* and the Estates General four months later.

January 14th was the day assigned for the completion of the act.

On January 13th a strange preliminary took place. Francis, under vows of the strictest secrecy, repeated his protestation of August 16th before his own ambassador, the Bishop of Embrun, the president of the *Parlement*, de Selve, the Connétable Montmorency and others. The final scene, too, was played out in the King's room. At the back there was an altar with the Bible on it. Present were the imperial plenipotentiaries Lannoy, Moncada, and Lalemand, who wrote the minutes of the meeting. Opposite them was the King with his suite. Francis confirmed the treaty with a solemn oath and gave his hand to Lannoy with the promise, on his word as a nobleman, that if the treaty were not kept he would return to his imprisonment.

This was that Treaty of Madrid, accepted in all good faith by the Burgundian nobility, which was dead before ever it was born. When Gattinara was called upon to seal it he refused, appealing to his duty to the Emperor.

On January 19th Lannoy, representing Queen Eleonore, exchanged promises of marriage with King Francis. Not until February did Charles, accompanied this time by Eleonore herself, meet the King for a few days at Illescas. Again they exchanged the most solemn guarantees. Charles once more promised Francis, this time as brother to brother, that he would not cheat him, least of all in this matter of Eleonore. As brothers the two monarchs took leave one of another.

Lannoy and Alarçon, his guards and jailers from the first, accompanied the King to the frontier. On April 17th he was set at liberty at San Sebastian after guarantees had again been exchanged, with all the forms of law, and the young princes had been taken in place of their father. 'Your Highness is now free', said Lannoy, 'do not forget your promise.' 'I shall fail in nothing', replied the King, and stepped on to the soil of France.

CHAPTER II

EMPIRE AND PAPACY 1526 — 1530

HISTORY has one curious characteristic which verges upon comedy, although in truth the logic of the dramatist could make little of it. The retribution for a certain action will often fasten upon a person or a group of persons who previously knew nothing either of the action or of each other. Yet the impetus of this illogical and wholly unexpected juxtaposition brooks no resistance. Empire and Papacy sprang like twin stars from the same origin. Even in their contradictions they were complementary one to the other. This fact was never more clear than in the years which followed the fall of Rhodes, when the danger to the Catholic Apostolic King of Hungary was on all lips, when the western world was even more acutely conscious of the growth of heresy and rebellion, begotten in the womb of the Lutheran movement. The rich revenues of the Papacy in Germany were threatened; and at a time, moreover, when the Pope himself came of a family which owed its re-establishment in Florence to Spanish arms. Clement VII was an old supporter of the Emperor and had twice been his candidate for the Papacy. But in his lengthy and under-hand dealings with the English government, the Pope had piled upon himself a load of guilt for which there was to be neither atonement nor pardon. He was to feel its weight to the full in the coming quarrel with the Emperor. Heavier yet was the burden of guilt accumulated by Bourbon in his actions against the King of France; by the King of France in his dealings with Charles. Guilty consciences intensified the bitterness which was to work itself out at last in bloodshed and war.

ISABELLA

Yet the fateful year 1526 opened amid brilliant, joyous and courtly scenes. By the treaty of Madrid, the Emperor and King of Spain imagined that he had secured the Crown of France for his sister Eleonore: he had only to wait for the formal ratification of the terms. Now, in all the loveliness of an Andalusian spring, he himself celebrated his long looked-for wedding with the Infanta of Portugal. He had never before visited Andalusia. Early in February he sent a splendid embassy to meet the bride on the frontier. The princess, who was twenty-three years old, had an easier task before her than many of her rank, who had to go like her into a strange land, to meet an unknown husband. She at least had not to go far from her own home, had to live among a people closely allied to her own by race and culture. The festive, and almost exaggerated welcome which she received at Seville, the city chosen for the wedding, must have appeared to her as regal as it was friendly. Rich and spacious, Seville was like many a town in her own country; the river and its banks were bright with the many cargoes and motley flags of ships from far countries, they were alive with the coming and going of mariners and merchandise. In the Arab fashion, streams of clear water ran through the town, to feed and refresh gardens, courts and bathing pools. On March 10th the Emperor made his entry with even more splendour than she had done herself. On the same day they were betrothed and married. Charles was ready to lay both his young manhood and his royal dignity reverently at the feet of his chosen bride; but soon something more than duty directed his actions. Profound and tender was the love which he learnt to feel for his frail, feminine little Empress, Isabella. Later on Titian was to paint her, delicate and reserved, the very symbol of aristocratic womanhood. Charles could not have wished it better done.

As the heats of summer grew, the youthful pair moved from Seville by way of Cordova to Granada, and in the paradisal surroundings of the Alhambra, Charles may well have realized that life had much joy still in store for him. His quiet determination, his restraint, his mingled reverence and timidity towards her person seemed to the Infanta at once imperial and enchanting. In religion he was, like her, very devout. On the evening after their wedding they had heard Mass together. Both Cardinal Salviati who had betrothed them, and the papal nuncio Baldessare Castiglione remarked on the Emperor's marked devotion to the Catholic Church. Once, later on, in the course of justice, Charles had to execute a high prelate. It was the Bishop of

Zamora, one of the last surviving rebels of the revolt of the Comuneros, who completed his villainous career and put himself finally beyond the pale of the law by murdering one of his guards. In spite of the circumstances Charles learnt with dismay that by dealing justice to the bishop he had incurred excommunication. He took it bitterly to heart, for weeks he would not attend Mass and when later he gained absolution, he retired to the beautifully situated monastery of the Hieronymites at Seville, there to bask in peace in the sunshine of his atonement to the Church.

THE KING OF FRANCE BREAKS FAITH. NEW DEVELOPMENTS IN ITALY

Into the haven of peace in which the Emperor and his wife were living, news from the outer world broke harshly through. Queen Eleonore, and with her Lannoy, waited in vain for the fulfilment of French promises and the ratification of the treaty of Madrid. At Bayonne, Francis I had met his mother once again; thence the Court gradually proceeded farther into the land. The imperial ambassador, de Praet, reminded the King of his duty. Growing anxious, Lannoy sent one of his gentlemen after him. In April the King answered by way of Robertet, a member of his council, saying that he had indeed received the message which Peñalosa had brought, but the Treaty of Madrid, to which he had yet to persuade his subjects to consent, had, contrary to all agreements, been printed in the meantime in Antwerp, Florence and Rome. As a result of this his nobility, particularly in Bourgogne, were very restive, so that he must find means to calm them, which with God's help would be possible, before he did anything else.

Lannoy, who was at Vittoria with Queen Eleonore, wrote in bewilderment to the Emperor, saying that he wished to entrust Queen Eleonore and the French princes to the constable of Castile, and himself to serve the Emperor elsewhere. But Charles, on Gattinara's advice, forced Lannoy to take the consequences of his own actions. Had not the King given him his word of honour? Lannoy must go to France and speak personally with him.

Lannoy found the French Court at Cognac, where Francis had

been born. Here he witnessed the death struggle of the policy which he had himself advocated and pursued. On May 16th he informed Charles that he and the ambassador de Praet had been called before the royal council, and had there been curtly told that the treaty of Madrid was signed under pressure and was therefore not binding. Bourgogne could not be given up for any consideration, and for the rest, Francis would act as circumstances dictated. Once more Lannoy implored Charles to recall him.

But the Emperor was playing for time and commanded him to stay. For many weeks, therefore, Lannoy remained at the Court of the King who owed him so much. Small wonder that rumour and scandal were soon at work. Macqueray tells us that the King, realizing how unfriendly a welcome Lannoy was likely to have from Charles on his return, handed over to him with all formalities the honours and possessions of the Connétable Bourbon. Lannoy refused. Whatever the truth of this, Granvelle, who was at that time in Cognac with de Praet and Lannoy, noticed that the latter was treated with great consideration. In fact, Charles was far too chivalrous even to think of venting his disappointment on Lannoy, whatever his responsibility. When, in a letter of May 16th Lannoy hinted that he feared Gattinara's enmity in a particular personal matter, Charles hastened to assure him of his continued favour. When he came back, Charles not only received him kindly at Granada, but continued to treat him as his most trusted councillor, and sent him at once on an embassy to Italy with Hugo de Moncada and Francisco de los Angeles.

In Italy the situation was again very perilous. Charles's coming, which in February he had planned for midsummer, was again put off, to the great distress of Ferdinand who was hoping for help in Germany and Hungary, for the imperial coronation by the Pope and for his own election as King of the Romans. Gattinara urged, advised and entreated all in vain. One day, full of hope, he declared that Charles was 'as one awakened from a dream'. But still nothing happened.

Meanwhile at Cognac on May 22nd, 1526, almost under the eyes of Lannoy, King Francis concluded a League of alliance with the Pope, Francesco Sforza of Milan, Florence and Venice. This was partly the outcome of the Italian situation which we have already discussed, and partly the result of busy machinations engineered by the Venetian government and the Vatican. The most significant thing in this new League was that Clement had been won over to join with the Emperor's enemies. Moreover, although Henry VIII categorically denied this to Charles, the League was said to be favourably viewed in England. Furthermore the English government endorsed the French King's attitude to the treaty of Madrid, asked that Charles release the princes for a ransom, and set up Sforza again as Duke of Milan. They even appealed to Clement to limit the size of the following with which Charles was to come to Italy for his coronation. England's behaviour was a mockery indeed.

Gattinara realized that a conflict between spiritual and temporal authority was imminent, and rightly gauged how heavily such a conflict would weigh on the Spanish soul. He took his measures in advance, turned to the royal council in Castile and urged them to demand in so many words the confirmation of the King's right to defend the country in arms, even against the Pope. The council recommended that if force had to be used, it should be supported by the prayers of the Churches as in the days of Ferdinand and Isabella. The Emperor, they said, had no desire but to live and die as a good Catholic; could not the Pope be made to see that at this critical time he would act more justly and more wisely if he laid down his arms? The arch-heretic Luther was still at large and every division in Christendom ought most carefully to be avoided. The College of Cardinals, too, should be adjured to act as true pillars of the Church, and to withhold the Pope from fighting an Emperor who was himself the Church's truest friend. Last of all Gattinara added that the Cortes should be called, and not only the procurators of cities, but also prelates and grandees, so that their advice might be taken in the crisis. The Chancellor revealed his political shrewdness by advising the Emperor to take this occasion of repeating his Coronation Oath before the Cortes of Valencia. The coast was near and Charles could set out for Italy immediately afterwards.

Over and above all political fears, Charles felt the Pope's desertion as a heavy personal blow.

Castiglione tells us that when on August 17th a French embassy, in the presence of the Venetian ambassador, bluntly told Charles on what terms the League had been formed, anger overcame his usual restraint. 'Had your King kept his word', he said, 'we should have been spared this. I will take no money from him, not even for his children. He has cheated me; he has acted neither as a knight nor as a nobleman, but basely. I demand that if he cannot fulfil his treaty, the Most Christian King should keep his word and become my prisoner again. It would be better for us two to fight out this quarrel hand to hand than to shed so much Christian blood.' He spoke to deaf ears. The French government was confident both in the support of its own people and in that of the Holy League.

Gattinara was thus proved right in every prediction. But he did not boast of it. When he was asked for his opinion at a meeting of the inner council, 'I would rather say nothing', he replied. But since he was asked for an opinion, he added, he could not refuse it. The wound, he feared, was deadly, but perhaps those who had always put their trust in France to the neglect of Italy, had something to suggest. Like Susanna, he declared, he was 'straitened on every side'. The blame for wasting Italy must now fall on the Emperor. God might pardon those who repented their sins, but Charles would have to alter his policy thoroughly and fundamentally.

At the end of July Charles's journey to Italy again came up for discussion. Should Charles be unable to go, Ferdinand was to invade Italy from the north. To enable the Archduke to do this and to gain access to German resources for the enterprise, Charles's council suddenly and surprisingly hit upon the idea of a religious peace. It is true that they intended to yield only the absolute minimum, but this does not alter the curious fact that the idea of making concessions in Germany arose in the first place out of the Italian situation. Copying Gattinara's draft almost word for word, Charles wrote confidentially to Ferdinand on July 27th, 1526. The ideas expressed in this letter foreshadow the Emperor's subsequent policy. Here for the first time he declared himself ready to offer oblivion and indemnity to those who had defied the Edict of Worms by supporting the Lutherans, and had thereby laid themselves open to the imperial ban. In return they must agree to submit to the verdict of a general council, meanwhile placing themselves and their resources at the Emperor's disposal.

Charles added a suggestion that he should publish this decision in a new and carefully prepared proclamation. All this was meant in the first place as a threat to the Pope — a motive which Charles did not attempt to conceal. It was well known that the Pope feared nothing so much as a council and the well-timed threat might well frighten him back into his right senses.

But events in Italy itself moved too fast for the ingenious subtleties of this policy.

Neither the embassy of Herrera nor the later insinuations of the Emperor could divert the fateful course of Italian policy. Once again a war, produced only by the fatal conjunction of two destructive elements, French resentment and Italian weakness, was to overwhelm the peninsula. Once again the Spaniards were to be driven out of Milan and Genoa; once again the plains of northern Italy were to be the scene of 'plundering, robberies, exactions, and violence, the raping of women and maids, the burning of houses, horror and ruin, to the utter destruction of that most beautiful land'. And all this, as Gattinara cried out in the bitterness of his heart, as the outcome of Charles's ill-considered policy.

In those days Niccolo Macchiavelli was eking out the short measure of his remaining days at Florence. To the end he hoped for the liberation of Italy, believing that the spirit must at last awake. But the great historian did not live to report these last events of his life. This was left to his compatriot, Francesco Guicciardini. As papal governor, Guicciardini stood in the very centre of action; he was in fact one of the leaders of papal policy. His clear and cogent letters give a no less impressive picture of the clarity of his vision, than does his interpretation of those same events in his history of Italy. It is sad to find that even Guicciardini has little good to report of his countrymen. Courage, magnanimity, strength, and the indefinable quality of 'greatness', these we find in the imperial generals alone, in Leyva, even in Bourbon, magnificently exemplified in Frundsberg. Hesitation, timidity, irresolution, characterize the Pope and his allies. Once again the trivial territorial ambition of the Papacy plays its wretched part. Once again Reggio, Rubiera, Parma, Piacenza, and the old problem of Ferrara occupy the political foreground at the Vatican. In vain Lannoy and Moncada wore themselves out in an effort to mediate, carrying out Charles's restrained policy, seeking to avoid a clash. For at least a year after the apparently decisive conflict of Pavia, indescribable confusion reigned in Italy.

As if to expose to all the world the incoherence of Italian politics, a foul survival from the darkest period of the Middle Ages reared its rebellious head in the Roman Campagna. This was the private feud between the Colonna of Genzano and the Pope, led by Cardinal Pompeo Colonna. The days of Boniface VIII were come again. Colonna marched on Rome with a great following; on the frontiers of Naples, not far off, stood the imperial reserves. Clement chose the lesser of two evils and came to terms with Colonna.

Like Charles's earlier statements, his instructions to Hugo de Moncada on July 11th were astonishingly moderate. As a permanent rule of conduct he recommended that everything be done to preserve Clement's friendship. Only if this proved to be impossible was Moncada to seek the alliance of Colonna. But in fact Clement would have none of the imperialists. He was governed by minor selfish considerations and partly intimidated by those who had once again taken it upon themselves to free Italy from the barbarians. Vain hope, for with his release, Francis had grown so arrogant in his demands that it was clear to all that Italy's choice lay only between French and Spanish domination.

For the second time, therefore, Clement had broken with Charles without even waiting to hear his last offers. In a long letter written on June 23rd, 1526, he strove to justify himself. The letter, which was to have profound effect, was conceived in the usual style of the Vatican. In the frozen altitudes of European politics, the supposed pastor of Christ's Church still played the cooing notes of a shepherd piping to his peaceful flocks on sunny uplands. Submerged in meaningless contradictions, the melody emerged as no more than a hypocritical jangle. All the world knew what forces had buffeted and baffled Clement since the last French attack on Milan, yet he now declared that thoughts for the peace of Christendom had alone governed his actions. Peace, he insinuated, was disturbed by no other than the Emperor on whom he had showered so many favours. He must defend himself against enslavement by Charles's temporal might: Moncada's offers had come too late.

The trouble with Colonna had been checked, not ended, by the armistice of August 22nd. The clouds hung over Lombardy, big with storm.

THE DIET OF SPEYER (1526). FERDINAND IN BOHEMIA AND HUNGARY

In these August days of 1526 Charles himself was still at Granada, his army in Lombardy was making ready to resist an attack from the League, Lannoy was arming in Naples, and in Germany the Archduke Ferdinand had brought the Diet of Speyer to an end. He had feared the outcome from the beginning and the meeting did indeed end with a compromise settlement to which he was forced to pledge his word.

The Diet, opened under the imperial aegis on June 25th, bore witness to the rise of a new Germany. It used to be the fashion to argue over the supposedly important results of this meeting. In fact it produced only a compromise settlement, thus stabilizing various elements, all of which had been recognizable in Germany before it met, and some of which had even found expression at the Diet itself. Sickingen's revolt and the Peasants' War had strengthened the princes: they had realized how great a power they could exert by forming groups among themselves. After centuries of experiment and misuse, the policy of princely coalition was entering upon a new phase of greatness. For now the problems which the German princes faced were more important than those ancient subjects for argument — inheritance and territorial boundaries. Dimly the princes were beginning to feel that this Burgundian-Spanish Emperor had linked them up once more with the rest of the European world; dimly, too, they realized that the Lutheran problem was not merely a mental, but a political challenge. Complaints of the Pope had been much bruited abroad; now the German princes were beginning to grasp that this very Pope was a single-minded political power, which might so clash with the Emperor that chaos would ensue in Germany. And liberty might perhaps be born of this chaos. Princes and cities were impelled to face the Church problem not only to defend themselves against rebellion, riot and insubordination, but to purify the true gospel, both in the flesh and in the spirit, from the multiple abuses of Rome. The German rulers began to make alliances, with various different objects. Certain princes of central Germany, the Elector of Mainz, Duke George of Saxony and Henry the younger of Brunswick-Wolfen-büttel, met at Dessau in June 1525, and later sent Henry of Brunswick to the Emperor. This group was loyal to Charles, and to the ancient traditions of Germany. Not so the Elector of Saxony[1] and the Landgrave of Hesse who founded a League at Gotha, and concluded it at Torgau in February 1526. The allies who had banded themselves together against Sickingen, the Elector Palatine, the Elector of Treves and the Landgrave of Hesse again, formed the kernel of a neutral group into which the Dukes of Bavaria might easily be drawn, should they finally decide on a policy of separatism directed against the imperial dynasty. The occasion was soon to arise.

The propositions made by Charles, who was neither governing personally nor yet imposing taxes at this time, asked simply that the Edict of Worms be carried out, that heresy and rebellion be put down, and, in the last resort, that final decisions be postponed until a council could meet. But the Diet of Speyer conclusively proved that such inept tinkering with what was now a crucial question, no longer satisfied the majority of the German princes. In the recess which they ultimately sanctioned they admitted that they, like the Emperor, desired a general council. But with things as they now stood in Europe, such a council could not be called and they renewed their demands for an immediate national gathering. Until this met, each Estate demanded the right to treat the Edict of Worms in such a way as 'he would be ready to answer for, before God and His Imperial Majesty'. In the original draft the phrase read 'before God above all', but later 'above all' was crossed out and the rights of Charles and the Almighty established thus on an equal footing. No one could be blind to the meaning of this. Some of the princes felt that they were justified by ancient historic rights; others, more naturally revolutionary, appealed to the hitherto unexpressed right of choice which they

---

[1] Duke George of Saxony of the Albertine line (Meissen) was first cousin to the Electors Frederick the Wise (1525†) and John, of the Ernestine line (TRANSLATOR'S note).

believed to exist in their own consciences. The antithesis found expression in the Dietary declarations of August 27th. The two parties appeared to be about evenly matched.

Before they broke up Ferdinand drew their attention to the appalling news from Hungary and managed to extract a small subsidy for use against the Turks. In these circumstances Ferdinand might well have recruited his army at once and set out to defend the Austrian border, if not actually to intervene in Hungary. Instead he went to Innsbruck, and even when he had news of the catastrophe at Mohacz on August 29th he seemed to be more absorbed in the imperial struggle for Milan than interested in the fate of the Danube lands. Bred in the old imperial tradition, he felt, presumably, that Milan, as a fief of the Empire, was more his affair than Hungary. His action, extraordinary in itself, must nevertheless be accounted to him for a virtue. It proved once again his unswerving loyalty to his brother, so often severely tried, yet never broken.

He had turned his back on one of the most terrible and significant events of the century. The Hungarian monarchy had been shattered at Mohacz. The blow was utterly unexpected. The battle itself was so improvised and light-hearted an affair as hardly to deserve the name. Unwillingly, the young King himself had taken part. No leaders were chosen, no plans were made. In this haphazard fashion the few troops of the Christians rashly flung themselves against the overwhelming forces of Sultan Suleiman. The King was killed in the rout. He had no children; the whole of his country, neglected since the days of Hunyadi, was left defenceless and without an heir. Heirless, too, were Bohemia, Moravia, Silesia, Lusatia — a gigantic, disorganized, disunited conglomeration, destined by dynastic right to Poland, by political contract to Austria.

Everything broke down. When he signed his treaties of inheritance and marriage, Maximilian had cheerfully considered the unification of these scattered lands with Austria as an easy task. Now it seemed far beyond human compass. Only Ferdinand's obstinacy and the traditions of Austrian statecraft, gradually formed by experience, ultimately solved the problem.

The immediate question was Bohemia. The three Estates, lords, knights and towns, vehemently defended their privilege of freely electing the King, and sent for cart-loads of documents to prove it in the very midst of the negotiations. The chief burgrave wrote to the Estates proclaiming a free election. There was no lack of candidates. The King of France even presented himself. More serious were the efforts of William and Lewis of Bavaria, had not each of them hampered the other. The most probable claimant was the Archduke Ferdinand himself, not, however, on account of inheritance or treaty. His delegates, Siegmund von Pollheim, Hans von Starhemberg and Niklas Rabenhaupt, who were accompanied by the highest dignitaries of Austria and Styria, Georg von Buchheim and Siegmund von Dietrichstein, showed that mixture of bold cession and skilful compromise which is necessary in such cases. Ferdinand was proposed by a deputation of the three Estates on October 22nd and unanimously elected on October 23rd in the chapel of Saint Wenceslas in the Hradschin. This tremendous victory for the Hapsburg dynasty was all the more remarkable because of its present weakness and the ceaseless complaints which assailed Ferdinand's government. Possibly the hereditary rights of Ferdinand's wife Anne assisted him. Possibly, too, the idea of uniting all the eastern powers from the middle waters of the Oder to the Danube, for the defence of Christendom against Islam, may have had some imponderable effect on the choice, as it had undoubtedly had in the time of the Emperor Sigismund. On February 24th, 1527, Ferdinand was crowned in Prague and the Bavarian Wittelsbach were left to chew the bitter cud of their defeat.

Hungary proved more difficult. Unbowed by misfortune, the young widowed Queen Mary displayed extraordinary devotion in attempting to secure the throne for her brother. The Hungarians and Bohemians had always realized that she was far more intelligent than her husband, and now again she gave proof to the political insight common in her family. Later, and more effectively, she was to use her gifts in her other brother's service, as Charles's regent in the Netherlands. King Louis had not waited at Mohacz for the arrival of the first magnate in his lands, John Zapolya, Voivod of Transylvania. He had therefore escaped death, and he now used his unopposed power to stir up in nationalist circles a violent demand for his election. On

November 10th he had himself crowned at Stuhlweissenburg. The country seemed lost to the Hapsburg dynasty. Ferdinand was in a double quandary; faced by an accomplished fact, he yet had to deny the nobility's right of election. Should he once recognize this, all was lost. Taking his stand therefore on inheritance and Maximilian's treaty, he stigmatized Zapolya as a usurper. At the same time he did not altogether waive the formality of an election but arranged for a small group of the nobility, under Mary's presidency, to elect him at Pressburg. His prospects were not very hopeful, even though the Turks, after their astonishing victory, still more astonishingly evacuated the land as far as the Danube. John Zapolya was not only Ferdinand's rival in Hungary, he was a natural ally for all Ferdinand's enemies in Germany, Italy and France. Mediation, through the King of France for instance, for which the Emperor urgently pleaded, came to nothing. Only in the following year did Ferdinand, by a bold attack, at last gain ground on Hungarian soil.

COMPLAINTS OF THE POPE. THE SACK OF ROME

The great increase of Hapsburg power in the east brought new and heavy burdens in its train. The Chancellor of Bohemia took full account of this in a letter to Ferdinand's Chancellor, Count Harrach. 'My dear lord', he wrote, 'we have not yet taken all our fences... The war in Hungary will exhaust all our resources. It would be better to have Hungary for a friendly neighbour, rule it who may, than the Turk for an enemy.' But to Ferdinand the war in Hungary was a welcome excuse to withdraw from imperial affairs. He could hope to gain little from Germany as things were, and he was tired of participating in his brother's troubles in Italy. All the same, in the intervening months he gave himself an astonishing amount of trouble on Charles's behalf in Upper Italy. Once again in October, Frundsberg, that ever present help in time of trouble, set out for Milan to join his compatriots, among whom was his own son Caspar.

The outlook in Italy was black indeed. Overshadowing the

chaotic interests of the smaller states, loomed the growing menace of conflict between the spiritual and temporal powers. On September 23rd, 1526, the imperial garrison at Cremona capitulated; almost at the same time, on the 21st, Colonna's faction entered Rome, humbled the Pope, and forced him to grant them absolution for invading the city. Clement absolved them indeed, but in his heart nursed the hope of revenge.

Meanwhile in Granada Charles was composing an answer to that papal letter of June 23rd, which had so unjustly and so clumsily accused him. The archives of Simancas yield conclusive proof of a belief long held by historians that the answer was from the pen of the secretary Alonso Valdes. The document places him at once in the same rank as Gattinara as an ecclesiastico political polemist. In polished phrases he challenged the threadbare arguments of the Pope, mercilessly exposing the weakness and injustice of the papal accusation. It was, he said, totally untrue to pretend that all the Kings in Europe had put pressure on the Pope; the exact contrary was known for a fact about the Kings of Portugal, Hungary, Bohemia, Denmark, and Poland. As for the King of England, he, too, denied his part in the League. Next, Valdes proceeded to attack papal policy. He recalled Leo's behaviour at Charles's election, Clement's conduct on the eve of Pavia, his attempt to suborn Pescara, and many other sins of this Holy Father of Christendom. Well might Europe stand amazed at his unscrupulousness; well might the Emperor feel as one in a dream. As for Clement's assertion that he must defend himself, nobody was attacking him. On the contrary — thus spoke Charles by the pen of Valdes — this war could not but lead to the ruin of the Church and the destruction of Christian concord. Had not he, the Emperor, set himself up in Germany to defend the apostolic chair from attack? Did he not still want peace? If Clement would but lay down arms, all others would follow his example and the forces of Christendom could be turned against heretic and Turk. But should the Pope continue to play the part not of a father but of an enemy, not of a shepherd but of a wolf, then the Emperor would be forced to call a council.

This struck the authentic note of righteous indignation, and when after careful preparation it was later published, the note deepened into the menacing peal of a tocsin. Next the letter was solemnly handed over to the papal nuncio at the Chancellor's house and in the presence of Bartolomeo Gattinara, Chancellor of Aragon, Jean Lalemand, secretary to the imperial cabinet, the secretary Alonso Valdes and the lawyer Alexander Schweiss from the bishopric of Treves, who made a report of the occasion. Castiglione answered that he had in the meantime received a second letter from the Pope, dated June 25th, with which he was instructed to replace the first. At Rome, Clement had realized that he had acted too hastily. So, now, the nuncio argued that the Pope's second letter proved that Charles's answer was unnecessary and unrestrained. Yet since he would sooner be a messenger of peace than of war he would not refuse to accept even so challenging a letter.

Not content with making this formal protest at Gattinara's house, the nuncio next asked for an audience with Charles in order to complain of the bitterness of the imperial reply. After receiving him as always courteously and with dignity, Charles calmed him with a personal note which the nuncio kept; it ran something as follows: 'My lord nuncio, after you had accepted that paper for His Holiness in which I refuted several unjust accusations, I took occasion to express myself yet more fully to you by word of mouth, and I can but hope that hereafter the Pope will resume towards me the attitude of a good father towards a devoted son. I, the King.'

But although he thus smoothed over the occasion by personal intervention, Charles saw to it nevertheless that his answers to the letters of June 23rd and 25th were presented to the Pope before the whole consistory, in the hall adjoining the Parrot Court at the Vatican on December 12th. He also sent a letter to the consistory by the hand of Cardinal Orsini exhorting them, even if the Pope refused, to insist on calling a council. Alonso Cueva drew up the legal instruments necessary for these negotiations; the originals, dated September 17th and December 12th, are now at Simancas and Madrid. But the imperial government immediately printed and published the whole correspondence, including these two legal instruments. To this they added Gattinara's draft of the imperial answer to the ambassadors of the Holy League, that is of the Pope, the French and the Venetians, which was given some weeks later, on February 12th, 1527. A protocol relating to this transaction was also drawn up and witnessed by Henry of Nassau, Juan Manuel, Don Garcia Loaysa, Bishop of Osma, president of the India Board and the Emperor's confessor, de Praet and the whole inner council. For the opposition we find the papal nuncio, Baldassare Castiglione, the French ambassadors, Jean Colinot, President of Bordeaux, and Guilbert Bayard, as well as the Venetian ambassador, Andrea Navagero. On February 17th letters were sent to the Duke of Milan and the Doge of Genoa.

Although these letters circulated throughout Europe, even in Germany, the whole series was no more than a kind of diplomatic prologue.

In Italy the military situation was developing along unusual lines. Georg Frundsberg had once again crossed the Alps; thanks to the auxiliary artillery sent him by the Duke of Ferrara, who had been won over by the Emperor before he received a belated bribe from the Pope, Frundsberg had gained the passage of the Mincio at which engagement a cannon ball had carried off the papal commander, Giovanni de' Medici. This was at the end of November 1526. The Duke of Urbino, a born dawdler, became the military leader of the League. The Pope's opinions continued to veer this way and that with the news from France, England or his other allies. On New Year's Day, he appealed solemnly to Lannoy and Colonna, feeling sure at that time of rapid French intervention. But in return for the 'liberation of Italy', Francis now wanted the kingdom of Naples itself. Lannoy had several interviews with Clement. Meanwhile the driving force in Italy was no longer in Rome, nor yet in Naples, but in the imperial camp in Lombardy.

Now and again in history long-forgotten decisions and long-suppressed emotions, under the direction of some invisible impulse, generate elemental forces, which, like gigantic and slowly rolling dice, work out their horrible and destructive course, guided by chance alone. Such forces had the imperial army in their grip. Leaving Leyva in Milan, Bourbon and Frundsberg joined about the middle of February 1527. As always, money was lacking. Nevertheless the army pressed on into the papal states. Unpaid, the soldiers grew daily more uncontrollable. They began to recognize in the Pope not only the Emperor's bitterest foe but the true originator of all their own distress and privation. The German landsknechts invested him with the face and attributes of a grasping and war-like Antichrist, living in the Roman Babel. Imperial loyalty, Spanish pride, Protestant passion, hunger and want, the sense of guilt at their own insubordination, greed and the longing for plunder — all these contradictory emotions blazed up together into a frenzied hatred for the rich and vicious city of Rome. Held back by the Venetians, the Duke of Urbino did nothing to prevent their advance. The Duke of Ferrara sent them money, but not enough to satisfy the men. Mutiny could no longer be quelled. In the old German fashion, Frundsberg made the men form a circle, and himself with the Prince of Orange, the most distinguished of the leaders, stepped into the midst, there to reason with the troops as he had done at Pavia. In vain. They shouted him down with cries of 'Money!' They threatened him with raised lances. At that, his stout heart broke. They carried him to Ferrara, a dying man. Conrad Bemelberg, called the 'little Hessian', took over the command, if command it could be called. No one in the world could have led these unpaid hordes back to Lombardy. Frundsberg had hinted something about payment in Rome. The idea took hold, and the hordes swept forward, through Tuscany. Passing by Siena and Florence, they marched on Rome.

Lannoy and his ambassador Fieramosca attempted to hold them back in accordance with their promise to the Pope. They were as powerless as the generals. Only gradually did Clement grasp the danger in which he stood. Then he offered 150,000 ducats to calm the storm. The troops demanded 300,000. Long ago intelligent advisers had urged Clement to get himself some money by creating half a dozen cardinals. Wrestling with uncertainties, he had not let himself be persuaded. When he gave in, it was already too late.

On May 5th the army lay before the Eternal City. On the 6th they stormed the walls. Bourbon fell as he mounted the first scaling ladder, thereby atoning for his wasted life; the Prince of Orange was gravely wounded. Relieved at last of all control, the army swarmed in. They seized the Leonine city, besieged the Pope at Sant' Angelo, crossed the Tiber, poured across the whole Holy City, wreaking their will on gardens and palaces. It was an hour of dizzy triumph for the soldatesca, an hour of bitter realization and self-reproach for Clement and his advisers.

GATTINARA'S VOYAGE AND ADVICE.
SPANISH PROPAGANDA

The historian need not dwell on the horrors of the conquest: the *Sacco di Roma* lasted for months and its fame spread across Europe. The Emperor had not wanted it, had told his representative to spare no effort to prevent it. But as soon as the Pope was taken prisoner, imperial policy could not scorn to make use of so tremendous an event. All the same, months passed in negotiations which throw a strange light on the ideas and intrigues rife at Charles's Court. This time Charles's hesitation had a particular cause. At the very time when the Pope was his prisoner and his troops were swarming leaderless over Rome, the Emperor himself was without his chief adviser.

Gattinara's journey to north Italy is wrapped in mystery. In his memoirs he himself admits that Charles's Court, and foreign ambassadors accredited to it, made adverse comments on his departure. Some deep misunderstanding must have lain at the root of this for Gattinara, who had worn himself out with work and worry for no reward or thanks, was surely justified in asking for a rest. Once, it is true, in the autumn of 1524, he had been given a present of his entire revenues for two years and three months, and the money for his journey to Calais, a sum amounting to 14,628 ducats. But what was this in comparison to the princely income and honours of a Wolsey, with whom Gattinara might favourably compare himself? And with what problems was he not always expected to wrestle?

At the end of March 1527 Gattinara took a holiday, intending doubtless to pay a visit to his family and his estates in Piedmont at the same time, and, as he himself once hinted, to 'pave the way' for Charles's coming to Italy. He began his holiday at Montserrat, among those lofty peaks whose clear atmosphere disperses all dismal humours. He may have appreciated the invigorating effect of the mountain air for he travelled slowly, almost as if he hoped to be recalled, by way of Barcelona to Palamos, and set sail only at the beginning of May, apparently before hearing that Rome had fallen. Farther on his journey he wrote to Charles, saying that his friends at Court told him that many rumours were being circulated about the reasons for his going — as that he counted on being immediately recalled, that he was only leaving in the hope that his salary would be raised. He besought the Emperor to remember the actual words which he had spoken on leaving and not to believe any of these slanders. He would be back, he said, in three months, or at the very latest in September, by which time the Pope was expected at Barcelona. The answer, which Lalemand drafted for Charles, was friendly and gracious; he gave him permission to stay longer away and promised to tell him the latest political developments.

Gattinara's first letter of any length is dated at Monaco, an important post station and port of call in the imperial system of communications, on June 7th. In this he informed Charles that he had disembarked and been most splendidly received by the owner of the town, Agostino Grimaldi, Bishop of Grasse, a partisan of the Emperor. Above all he spoke of the fireworks and salvos which had been organized to celebrate the birth of a prince in Spain. On May 21st, at Valladolid, the Emperor's heir had been born. At his baptism, on July 5th, he had received the old Burgundian name of Philip, after his grandfather Philip the Handsome. His godparents were Iñigo Velasquez, constable of Castile, Juan Zuñiga and Queen Eleonore. This same year saw the birth of Ferdinand's eldest son, Maximilian, afterwards Emperor. The dynasty now had two lives to its credit for the coming generation. Among the letters of congratulation which Charles received was one from the imprisoned Pope in the castle of Sant' Angelo.

The temporal and spiritual organization of Christendom was indeed in a state of strange confusion. England and France now hastened to settle their old differences and form a common alliance to help the Pope against Charles. The Emperor's one time friends, the English, thus finally threw off the mask; and France, which had but just made peace, made ready, with the help of new allies, to gain better terms by a renewed war. This new war and Charles's negotiations with the Pope must now engage our attention.

In a separate note, enclosed with his letter, Gattinara expressed his opinions on the political situation. Judging by what he has to say in his autobiography, the news of the sack of Rome left him in some doubt as to how he should advise Charles to behave. Would it be wisest for the Emperor frankly to applaud all that had happened in Rome, justifying this action by declaring that he had no desire to injure the priesthood, but only to punish the enemies of Christendom? Or would it be best altogether to repudiate responsibility for the disaster? With certain modifications Gattinara decided in favour of the latter.

On June 7th therefore he wrote saying that so shattering an event could not but resound throughout the world. Charles would be blamed for it and he must find means to justify himself, without actually foregoing any advantages which might accrue to him from what had happened. So extraordinary a victory must be an act of God. Gattinara next named Valdes as the man best suited to draft a letter for the princes of Europe, setting forth Charles's grief at what had happened and drawing the appropriate moral that henceforward wars in Christendom must stop. Only a general council, called to extirpate heresy, to reform the Church and to reorganize the temporal powers, could achieve this end. Pope and cardinals, who had so often been implored in vain to call a council, must now agree to do so. After outlining this appeal, Gattinara turned to the immediate and vital question which Charles alone could decide: would he do as all the world advised and undertake a journey to Italy? If this was his sincere intention he must at once collect all his money, then obtain the consent of the Cortes of Aragon, and proceed thence to Valencia or Catalonia, at the same time preparing his fleet to defend Genoa against the French and to protect his own crossing. The Duke of Ferrara, who already carried the title of Captain-general, must be won over to take Bourbon's place; he must be requested to keep the popular Prince of Orange as his lieutenant. To prevent the Duke from exploiting the command for his own ends, Lannoy was to be set above both of them as the Emperor's representative. On the other hand, Gattinara concluded, if Charles did not seriously intend to come to Italy himself, King Ferdinand would be the man best suited to the chief command.

Milan, Gattinara continued, had been promised to Bourbon, should proof of Sforza's guilt be forthcoming; it was therefore free to be disposed of. For reasons which he had often stated before, Gattinara did not advise Charles to keep it himself. If he bestowed it on Ferdinand without more ado the infuriated Venetians would inevitably be driven into the arms of the Turks. If he returned it to Sforza, it would be a tacit admission that he had done him a wrong beforehand. It would be best to stage some sort of an inquiry before which Sforza could be called. All else could be decided when Charles himself was in Italy. If Sforza were found guilty, then Milan could safely be given to Ferdinand, or to the Infant Philip. This, several years later, was what Charles did. In the meantime Gattinara advised that Milan be ruled by an imperial governor, and its finances entrusted to a treasurer and a receiver. Parma and Piacenza must once again be united to Milan, Florence and Bologna be handled with tact so that they would remain loyal to Charles. The Venetians, who were undoubtedly much to blame for the last war, would in their anxiety be casting about for a Turkish alliance; it would be wise to prevent the conclusion of such a bond by nourishing them with hopes of favour at least until Charles himself should come. For the Emperor must not lose sight of the fact that once he had both a victorious army and a firm base in Italy he was well on the way to rule the world. Once establish his power in the peninsula, and all his other lands would be only too ready to do him service.

While Charles perused these suggestions in Madrid, Gattinara after being forced back by French galleys into the blockaded port of Genoa, escaped by way of Corsica and landed once more in Spain, safe and sound. There at Montserrat he fulfilled a vow made doubtless when the French ships attacked him, and appeared again at Court in October.

During his absence, in spite of the usual delays, much of importance had been done in Charles's immediate surroundings.

Underlying these actions, we guess at deeps of which we have hitherto suspected nothing. Already once before, at that important moment in German history when the young Emperor first met the princes at Cologne, the great figure of Erasmus of Rotterdam had passed swiftly by. Now, for the second time, his path crossed that of Charles, this time in Spain. His *Enchiridion Militis Christiani* had just been translated into Spanish and in fact dedicated to the Grand Inquisitor, Alonso Manrique de Lara, Archbishop of Seville and one of the Emperor's closest friends. Alonso de Fonseca, Archbishop of Toledo, who had baptized the Infant, and the Chancellor himself, as well as Alonso and Juan Valdes, were among the admirers of Erasmus. But the mendicant friars, so often mercilessly exposed in the biting satires of this great man, now launched an attack from the pulpit on his modern and secular theology. Under the presidency of Manrique, discussions were held at Valladolid and, in response to monkish indignation, the Archbishop obtained a brief from Clement VII by which all attacks on these 'warriors against Luther' — as the monks now proclaimed themselves — were prohibited on pain of censure.

Six months earlier Gattinara had written a letter to Erasmus, in which, in his usual graphic vein, he drew on examples of this kind to prove that Christendom was divided into three groups. Some stood blindly by papal authority, whether it governed well or ill. Others clung to Luther with equal obstinacy. Neither of these groups was capable of independent thought; their praise was an insult and their scorn an honour. The third group cared for God's word and the common weal, predilections which were not likely to preserve them from calumny. To this group belonged Erasmus and his admirers. He himself hoped to see the Emperor eradicate the Lutheran heresy and reform the Church.

This opinion was shared by Gattinara's secretaries, above all by Alonso Valdes. Deeply moved, this latter now set pen to paper. Like Ulrich von Hutten in a like hour of conflict, he wrote in his native tongue. This in itself was likely to secure him a wider hearing. His two Dialogues, *Mercurio y Caron* and the still more bitter *Lactancio y el arcediano*, were not only effective in spreading the spirit of Erasmus, but are to this day outstanding monuments to the beauty of the Spanish language. In Gattinara's letters, too, we cannot fail to recognize the weft of these political and ecclesiastical ideas running through the theories of his time.

In Gattinara's absence Alonso Valdes had thus again wielded the pen in the conflict between the secular and the non-secular Church. He was long to continue in the foremost ranks of battle, at his side his brother Juan, who was later in Naples to become the moving spirit of a circle of devoted reformers. In his Dialogues Valdes sketched the portrait of a Christian monarch, a ruler with a mind above the desire for great possessions, above ceremonies and above deceit, fixed only on the happiness of his people. Valdes drew his inspiration direct from Erasmus and Gattinara, nor did he show himself less their pupil when he elaborated his theories from the gospels and took Christ himself as the great example.

On June 5th, 1527, the Pope formally surrendered, handing over certain strong places and many hostages. From now on he was a prisoner. An imperial garrison occupied the castle of Sant' Angelo under the leadership of the experienced Alarçon, who had but recently been the jailer of Francis I. Such was the situation on which the Spanish councillors had to act.

On July 21st the Emperor designated Pierre de Veyre, lord of Mont St. Vincent, as his ambassador to Italy; but he did not send him until August 18th. His instructions, partly conceived in Gattinara's vein, handled the papal question with somewhat greater asperity, and showed throughout a certain independence of style and tone. The ambassador was instructed first to join Lannoy. The imperial council had decided that he was to express his regret for the Sack of Rome. But he was to flavour this apology with the addition that, since God had so brought it to pass, the Emperor was overjoyed to think that the last obstacles had been removed and the Pope would now have no difficulty in restoring peace to Christendom and in reforming the Church. The hint could be further embellished with the statement that Charles was himself on the point of setting out for Rome, to kiss the Pope's feet and set him at liberty; only unfortunately his preparations were not yet completed. Veyre was furthermore to inform the Viceroy Lannoy that Charles was constant to his plan of visiting Italy, not merely for the empty honour of Coronation, but so that he might fulfil his duties towards Holy Church, the Bride of Christ, and give thanks to God for the victories which he so persistently bestowed upon him. As Lannoy well knew, the Pope had often said that he would come to Spain to mediate a firm peace between Charles and Francis; if every possible precaution were taken, Charles felt that this might be tried. In this view, the Emperor showed how much he was still dominated by the recollection of that other great captive he had made at Pavia. But if it were impossible to arrange to bring the Pope to Spain, Veyre's instructions went on, Charles was prepared magnanimously to set him free, so long as he would give adequate security against treachery or bad faith. Once again Charles was thinking of Francis I and the treaty of Madrid. Lannoy was to decide what securities were adequate, Charles himself was thinking of several fortresses, of the city of Bologna, and the Pope's own kinsmen as hostages — all these to be held until Clement saw fit to carry out his duties towards Christendom.

From Lannoy at Naples the ambassador was to journey to the Pope himself. He was to tell him with what grief Charles had learnt of the horrible crimes which had been committed against his express will, and which he would gladly have prevented at the risk of his own life. Next he was to express the Emperor's sorrow at the divisions of Christendom, and above all at the schism in Germany, which, but for this, would be the only state in Europe able to withstand the Turk. Veyre was to explain that these were Charles's reasons for offering the Pope extremely mild terms, the details to be laid down by Lannoy. Furthermore Veyre must express the Emperor's delight at learning through the general of the Franciscans that Clement hoped to come to Spain to mediate a peace. Such an act would ensure to the Pope both honour in this world and eternal glory in the next. The Emperor must, however, postpone the discussion of temporal matters, such as the necessary payments to be made in Italy, the Ferraresse question, the problem of Milan — in which Clement had no right whatever to interfere — until the Pope was once more at liberty.

But Veyre arrived in Italy too late to carry out his instructions. In his first dispatch, on September 30th, 1527, he reported Lannoy's death. Like Pescara, Charles de Lannoy had worn himself out in the exertion and nervous excitement of the last years; his powers of resistance were so diminished that he succumbed, with hardly a struggle, to the plague which was then raging in Rome. He died at Aversa on September 23rd, nursed to the last by his devoted wife, who had hastened to his bedside. His death altered everything. The staggering news of Rome's fall and the Pope's capture gave to Charles's enemies the opportunity they had long sought. In Europe the whole situation changed. Hesitation and doubt were transformed into rage and the lust for war, and a bad cause found justification when it was disguised as a crusade for the 'liberation of the Pope'.

At the Spanish Court which had moved from Valladolid to Burgos in the winter months of 1527-8, these events were slow to produce action. The delay was partly caused by the time which news took to reach them and partly by the Emperor's temperament. During his long stay in the peaceful and pleasant Spanish kingdoms, Charles had withdrawn himself ever further from the world. His actions now lagged far behind the impetuous haste of politics. The young ruler's days slipped by beside his queenly wife in the dilatory pursuance of State affairs, in courtly amusements and diversions, with an occasional serious interval when he talked matters over with Gattinara, or with his confessor, Loaysa, or sought to quiet the many conflicting elements in his Court. His letters to his brother Ferdinand, to his aunt Margaret, and still more the reports of Ferdinand's representative, Martin de Salinas, draw a picture of an existence almost monastic in its calm.

Yet Charles's subsequent comments, and his correspondence with Loaysa, prove that under this smooth surface his inner life was far from stagnant. His character developed as he observed men and affairs, and studied the deepening problems of his own great dominions. He strove with himself, fought against his lusts and limitations, and if occasionally he failed, it was because the body was not always strong enough to bear up the wearied spirit. All that he undertook seemed to succeed, and soon he grew convinced that the Hand of God was on him, that his well-considered instructions and careful memoranda were alone sufficient justification for his rule. Even the Sack of Rome had not taught him that events will sometimes move of their own impetus. This appalling happening, even, was interpreted at Court, as we ourselves have seen, as a special providence of God.

The minutes of council meetings, from which we derive a limited but important knowledge of the forces at work in Charles's surroundings, are tedious to a degree. Even when Gattinara came back and Pierre de Veyre sent his first dispatch from Italy, the council decided almost nothing. Lalemand took the notes on that occasion. Present were de Praet, La Chaulx, the confessor Loaysa, Juan Manuel, Nassau, Gattinara and the Emperor. All of them spoke in Spanish. De Praet voted that the Pope be released in whatever circumstances, on the terms suggested by Veyre. If Charles did not set him free, he argued, others would step in; once he was at liberty he could be asked to confirm the misuse of the *Cruzada*. La Chaulx agreed. Loaysa urged Charles to ask for some securities in return for Clement's freedom, although not the Castle of Sant' Angelo. A ransom could be dispensed with once Clement confirmed the *Cruzada*. Manuel advised caution: he thought that Lannoy should be at once replaced by a suitable person, or else that Hugo de Moncada, whom Lannoy had always trusted implicity, should have plenipotentiary powers. When this had been done Clement's release could be made known throughout Europe. Nassau too favoured procedure in that order: first the guarantees, then the release, then the confirmation of the *Cruzada*. Gattinara indicated that the Emperor would have been well advised not to lay hands on the Pope, qua Pope; a case could always be made out to prove Clement's election invalid for it had undoubtedly been simoniacal. But if Charles could once gain the papal fortresses, the *Cruzada* and the control of the benefices, he could do without the ransom. He could then re-establish the Pope and make peace, stipulating for a council. To all this Charles answered that the council had already decided in Valladolid to accept Veyre's terms for Clement's release. For his own part, he went on, he was ready to let the Pope go, were it not for other considerations. There was Parma and Piacenza, Modena and the Colonna problem — all of them thorny questions; that very day for instance the nuncio had declared that Clement demanded the re-establishment of his own dynasty in Florence. Besides Charles declared that he must have some written security, lest the treaty be broken. His troops too must be paid out of the resources of the Pope or the Spanish Church. Above all God's will must be done in all things.

In this speech Charles was clearly thinking of recent events in Florence. The Florentines had been members of the League. But Clement's indecision, while the imperial army was fast descending upon them, drove them to despair and they had again driven out the Medici and proclaimed themselves a republic. Another event which had some bearing on Charles's arguments was that the imprisoned Pope and the once implacable Cardinal Pompeo Colonna had recently solemnized a touching reconciliation in the apartments of the Castle of Sant' Angelo.

In the meantime Clement sent as ambassadors to Charles, first the general of the Franciscans, Francisco Quiñones, and then Cardinal Farnese, who was later himself to be Pope. Farnese got no farther than Lombardy. But Hugo de Moncada, Veyre and the newly returned Quiñones at length concluded a long-desired agreement with Clement, as a result of which the Castle of Sant'

Angelo was evacuated. The treaty was signed on November 26th, the castle abandoned on December 6th. On the following night the Pope fled, not without the connivance of certain imperial officers, in the dress of his own major-domo, from Rome to Orvieto. After months of perilous argument, peace in Christendom seemed again established.

Events were soon to prove the vanity of all such hopes.

ENGLAND AND FRANCE DECLARE WAR. THE STRUGGLE FOR MILAN AND NAPLES

Event followed upon event, as if at the command of some unseen power. In the interim the alliances binding the European states to each other had dissolved and formed again. Once again the separate outline of the individual forces, so menacingly ranged on each side of the arena, become coherent.

Ever since Charles's victory at Pavia the governments of France and England had been negotiating. For a brief moment, it is true, Henry's romantic ambitions for the French Crown had flared up, but Wolsey had firmly guided his master out of his fool's paradise. After the unsatisfactory conversations between the Spanish and English governments in 1526, England and France were in close sympathy by the spring of 1527. Only a few days before the Sack of Rome, on April 30th, the powers reached agreement. The contract, impatiently desired by both parties, soon found expression in the renewed fervour of the Anglo-French friendship. On May 29th Henry VIII declared himself ready to subsidize a French campaign in Italy with the monthly sum of 32,000 crowns. Francis I entrusted the leadership of the expedition to a bold, if not always a fortunate, leader — Lautrec.

A new and surprising development completed the estrangement between Henry and the Emperor, and drove the English King into yet closer alliance with Francis. Even in earlier times English dislike of Spain had sometimes been vented in popular hostility towards Queen Katherine, and at this crucial moment Henry's troubled relations with his legal wife became a major cause for political unrest. Henry's reasons were peculiarly shameless. Not his alleged pricks of conscience at having contracted an incestuous marriage with his brother's widow, nor his desire for a male heir drove him ultimately to seek divorce from Katherine. He was dominated simply by the fact that Anne Boleyn could be obtained in no other way. The influential kinsmen of his desired bride strengthened him in his purpose towards Katherine, and Cardinal Wolsey himself was dragged into this new labyrinth, never again to find his way out.

On his visit to France in July and August 1527, Wolsey seemed to repeat his earlier diplomatic triumphs, for he brought with him to Amiens a singularly valuable offer — Henry's total renunciation of all claim on the French Crown. Nor were the arrangements to which he agreed on August 18th lacking in importance. True that Wolsey refused the hand of Francis himself for Henry's eldest daughter; but the princess was to be considered for the Duke of Orleans. The French and English governments were at one in feeling that the Pope must not be allowed, either through weakness or a revulsion of feeling, to carry out Charles's policy. Together, too, they repudiated the idea of a council, thus influencing the course of European politics for years to come. Among other remarkable arrangements, Wolsey had a plan for assembling at Avignon all those cardinals who had not been taken prisoner, in order to prevent the government of the Church from becoming wholly subservient to Charles. Wolsey was himself hoping to be made into a kind of Vicar of the Church during Clement's captivity. He had been won over to the King's divorce policy in the last few months, and had already taken various canonical measures towards its achievement. It was rumoured, therefore, not without justification, that he had decided to use this interval to pronounce the King's marriage null in the name of the Pope. The affair was not to be so easily settled: it dragged on for months to come.

The Emperor too was drawn into this divorce question and feelings grew sharper on both sides.

An embassy from the allied powers of France and England, although received at Valladolid with all due respect, had no more effective outcome than any other negotiations during that autumn and winter. Gattinara, as he himself tells us, had already decided, for incontrovertible reasons, to abandon all the negotiations which had been set on foot in the summer of 1527. Nevertheless he advised Charles to continue the appearance of treating while he armed secretly. The details of these negotiations are therefore of no consequence, for neither side meant them in earnest.

In the meantime Francis I had declared to his Estates that he would return to his imprisonment, if the ransom for the princes was too heavy a burden on his kingdom or the money needed for the coming war was too much for them to raise. The offer was enthusiastically refused. In Spain too a similar atmosphere of enthusiasm and heroism prevailed in face of the coming conflict.

And so at Burgos on January 22nd, 1528, the first of those scenes, in which the protagonists acted the prologue of their war, was played out with Homeric formality. The Kings of England and France formally handed over a declaration of war by the hand of their heralds. The Emperor answered cuttingly that he was astonished to find his own 'prisoner' thus formally declaring war on him, since he had previously shown no scruples in carrying out the lengthiest campaigns against him without pausing for any such formality. As for the Pope — his champions could set their minds at rest; he had long been released. He concluded with several further reflections on the Anglo-French challenge. We need not trouble ourselves with these wordy battles. Even in their modern printed form they cover many pages. It suffices to add that at the end of the ceremony Charles repeated in a strengthened form the words he had used at Granada in August 1526. He told the French ambassador that his King had acted the part of a coward and a varlet and had broken his word. In support of this accusation, he continued, he would be ready to risk his life in hand to hand conflict.

Charles's advisers attempted to restrain his ardour. The elder Diego Mendoza, Duke of Infantado, uttered the shrewd opinion that the duel as a means of discovering God's justice, could be used only when there was a gap in the law. Here there was no gap in the law: all was as clear as day.

The return declaration was uttered on March 28th before the assembled French Court and foreign ambassadors. As soon as the imperial ambassador, Nicholas Perronet, lord of Granvelle, had, in the Emperor's name, asked for his pass home, King Francis rose to speak. Trying to justify himself, he gave a paper to Granvelle asking him to read it aloud. When Granvelle refused, the King had it read by Robertet, and later, after some delay, on June 17th, handed it over by a herald at Monzon, the seat of the Cortes. A third time the empty ceremony took place. The French herald handed over the paper, the Emperor gave it to Lalemand to read. In this new declaration Francis vigorously repudiated all blame and added that if Charles wished to fight, he had only to name a place and time for the meeting.

But it never came to a duel. Embarrassed by this reply, Charles sought to enlarge his sphere of action. Impressed by these repeated and open declarations of war, he sent Balthasar Merklin, provost of Waldkirch, who had been elevated in the previous year to the Vice-chancellorship of the Empire left vacant by Nicholas Ziegler, to the German princes and Estates. His instructions, dated February 3rd, 1528, were to urge them to arm against France. This prelate, who had been first a servant of Maximilian, then coadjutor of Constance and later administrator of Hildesheim, had gone early to Spain where he had handled German affairs under the advice of Gattinara. But the diplomatic mission now entrusted to him seems to have been beyond his powers. Like the imperial ambassador of five years before, Hannart, he immediately struck the wrong note with Ferdinand. Ferdinand could not but fear that simultaneous demands for help against France would reduce the Empire's willingness to fight the Turk. Charles answered Ferdinand's complaints with the assertion that the Vice-chancellor had had clear instructions to do nothing save what was approved by Ferdinand himself. For the rest Waldkirch's passage through Germany from June onwards may be followed in various sources which give a clear enough picture of what he actually did. The greater number of the Estates could not be moved by such an embassy into giving any military help — which was the chief object of his mission; but he touched also on the Lutheran problem, the Turkish danger and the question of Ferdinand's election as King of the Romans.

An incident, trivial in itself, sharply emphasized the trust which Charles was placing, at this time, in the German princes. He added a postscript in his own hand to the letters of credit, given to Waldkirch on February 3rd, 1528, for the Elector Palatine. This reads: 'Do the best you can for me this time, I will do the same for you. Carolus.'[1] Rarely indeed did Charles write notes of this kind. He also besought his brother to renounce all friendship with the King of France. Yet it is clear that he counted on moral support above all from the German princes.

He postponed the Diet which had been fixed for April 16th at Regensburg, a town very well suited to Ferdinand. In his effort to strengthen his position in Europe, he was naturally anxious to avoid, for the time-being, the raising of such difficult questions as a Diet would bring forth.

Against this background the Italian war went on. And here, rather than at Court or among the ambassadors, do we find the most reliable powers over which Charles had control. Lannoy, Frundsberg and Pescara were gone, but one man still defended the imperial cause with honour unsmirched. The last of the elder generation of commanders, Antonio Leyva had been for years Charles's surest prop in Lombardy. He had something of that quality so much admired by his age, *virtù*, a virile resolution, to which he added a never-failing devotion to the Emperor. Yet all complaints, whether directed against the violence of the men or the greed of the generals, made him their target. However unfair these accusations were, Leyva could hardly have avoided them, for like the leaders of his time he stood or fell with his troops. The majority of the imperial army had swarmed on to Rome. Leyva held back the remnant in Lombardy, not without difficulty and sacrifice. In those times the alleged wealth of the generals served for a reserve, out of which the troops could be paid when the responsible authorities failed in their duty. His service in keeping these troops together is not lightly to be dismissed, for he seldom received answers to his entreaties and complaints, and yet more seldom money. His greatest title to fame is that even in these times he was able to win victories with his unpaid army. Bitter as is the outcry of the just, both among contemporaries and among posterity, against men of this bold type, they will always be the darlings of history.

At the beginning of August 1527, he informed Charles in detail of the behaviour of Francesco Sforza, against whom, in spite of the opinions of some more cautious persons, he had opened an inquiry. At the same time he told Charles how much he owed to

[1] Thut auf dissmal bey myr das best, das wyl ich bey Euch auch thun. Carolus.

the soldiers who poured in from all over Europe to serve under his banners. In an earlier letter he had spoken of the bad morale among the men, which was Bourbon's legacy; of Morone's departure from Milan with Bourbon. Leyva spoke too of the help which the protonotary Carracciolo had offered him in the administration of the duchy, and of the many other details relating to the military occupation of the land. Last of all he informed Charles that he had news of a coming military invasion from France.

For as long as he could, he occupied all the vital strategic positions with his small forces. Only in the last resort was he forced to concentrate on the most important of all, on Milan. In this, as in everything, he was successful. First the Venetians and the French under Pedro Navarro came against him, then Lautrec himself. But even this latter had to abandon the siege of Milan and at the beginning of 1528 turned southwards, ostensibly to 'liberate' the already long-released Pope — in fact to conquer Naples for France. At this juncture the Duke of Ferrara and the Marquis of Mantua espoused the French cause. Leyva had good reason to complain that all his labour had been lost: the most devoted servants, he lamented, sacrificed themselves in vain for an Emperor who neither knew nor cared what they did. Like Pescara, so Leyva: forgotten and unrewarded.

Yet if Charles were really so unresponsive a master what was it that inspired these Spaniards, these Neapolitans, these Burgundians and Germans to pile one deed of valour upon another, and to retain through five long years of conflict in Italy so unswerving a devotion to their Emperor? Those who saw him at Court and in public affairs despaired at his irresolution; those who fought in his armies found him niggard alike of money and gratitude. Yet all felt themselves uplifted by the consciousness of that imperial and royal theory which he so splendidly embodied. Faithfully and patiently, they awaited his coming to Italy; all that they had and all that they hoped found expression only in and through him. To the Spaniards in particular this conflict in the Emperor's service seemed like the height and climax of their nation's history.

How often had not Charles planned to visit Italy! Since the spring of 1525 he was seriously contemplating the journey; even in those disjointed jottings on the eve of Pavia he had spoken of it. After Pavia he regarded the Italian voyage as the next step in his triumphant progress. From the purely personal point of view, he regarded it first and foremost as essential to his honour and reputation, which he had hitherto done nothing to secure. The repeated postponement of the plan was no less opposed to what he took to be the direct line of his own fate, than to the plans of Gattinara. At every fresh opportunity the Chancellor was for taking time by the forelock and establishing the power of the Emperor in Italy without more delay as a permanent guarantee of peace, not only in the peninsula itself but in all Europe. Gattinara's views were still rooted in those of Dante. But always something had prevented a swift conclusion. Charles's own irresolution, the coming of the French King to Spain, the slothful course of negotiations, and later the menacing League of Cognac and the shortage of money.

Up to the very end there was deep-rooted opposition on the imperial council itself and at Court. Gattinara repeatedly averred that many were against his plan. We may hazard a guess that one of his opponents was in the very heart of the imperial family; Navagero tells us that on one occasion at least the Empress wept at the prospect of losing her husband. Gattinara, too, specifically states that Don Manuel did not appreciate the Italian project. Certain other Spaniards held back, notably the president of the council of Castile, the Archbishop, Juan Pardo de Tavera; Charles had to reckon later with this same man's determined opposition to his universal policy. All these years the Chancellor had been fighting a double battle: he had been fighting against France and for Italy, and, in so far as he advocated Charles's personal intervention in Italy, he had been fighting against Spain.

All the time important and stirring news poured in from every quarter to the Emperor and his Chancellor — reports, complaints, demands from the Empire and from Austria and Hungary, no less than from the Netherlands, and last of all from the much-vexed Indies. In spite of opposition, Charles received Hernando Cortes, the conqueror of Mexico, with every honour, created him Marquis de la Val de Oaxaca, knight of Santiago and Captain-general of New Spain. But scarcely was this done when Francisco Pizzarro suddenly appeared in the very midst of the South American continent, and demanded with the greatest eloquence, the Emperor's permission to conquer Peru. Unlike his deputies in Panama, Charles did not forbid him to proceed.

In the meantime the imperial troops had undergone their last and hardest test in the struggle for Naples. Lautrec, marching from Romagna along the Adriatic coast, was in the Abruzzi before Hugo de Moncada, Philibert of Orange and Pescara's nephew, the Marquis del Vasto, could hasten up for the defence of the kingdom. Apulia was soon in French hands, del Vasto managing to save Troja alone. On March 16th, 1528, a decisive battle ought to have been fought; in spite of his superiority in numbers Lautrec had hitherto postponed it and now, when he was ready, Orange skilfully evaded his encirclement. Yet the imperialists had little left to them beyond the city of Naples. Hugo de Moncada had made a bad beginning and Charles refused to honour him with the title of Viceroy although he entrusted him with full responsibility for the kingdom.

Greater dangers threatened. As early as the previous December they had had word in Spain that hostile galleys, Genoese above all, were approaching Naples; yet they could not raise help against them. The populous town and large garrison were in danger of starving, since the harbour was blockaded and the city besieged on the landward side. With the assistance of his best officers, Moncada risked a sea-battle in an effort to bring in Sicilian corn. The issue was disastrous. Moncada was killed, the Marquis del Vasto taken.

The youthful general, Philibert of Chalon, Prince of Orange, now bore the whole burden of defence, single-handed. At its last sitting in December 1527, the imperial council had decided to appoint the Duke of Ferrara himself as commander-in-chief of all the imperial troops, with Orange as his lieutenant. Since then the Duke of Ferrara had turned traitor, and Orange was left to find what support he could in the experienced Alarçon. He was still too young to be made Viceroy, said Charles.

Orange was in fact only twenty-five years old, but he had ripened young. His father had died a few weeks after his birth, and his mother, Philippine of Luxembourg, had permitted him to enter the social world of Paris at a very early age. He had been in Spain since 1520. His mother, too, administered his broad estates in Franche Comté, in Bresse, Bourgogne and Flanders.

His only sister was the second wife of Henry of Nassau. His power-ful relations, his kinship to the royal house of Burgundy, marked out the young and wealthy prince for early advancement. Very soon he became a Knight of the Golden Fleece and was given a command in the field. Already he had experienced much and proved his mettle; he had been wounded and taken when the un-controlled soldiery swept him with them on their march to Rome. He had been again gravely wounded before the Castle of Sant' Angelo and had sought in vain to check the plundering of Rome.

The struggle for Naples made him into a great leader. While the harbour was still blockaded, the garrison sought, as Leyva had done at Pavia, to gain breathing space by sharp sallies to the landward. These harassed the French army, now a prey to plague. Yet for weeks the position in Naples was desperate, the leader without money, the men without food, and the blockade impassable. Relief was impossible. Whence could it have come? All entreaties for help echoed into the void, as Leyva's had so often done before.

Then the beleaguered forces gained unexpected relief. Andrea Doria, whose nephew, Philippino, guarded the harbour, changed sides. The old Genoese had not been paid by the French; he placed himself therefore at the Emperor's disposal and on July 4th, 1528, he withdrew his ships. On the following day the sea lay, blank and empty, before the eyes of the besieged. Soon after Orange intercepted some letters from which he learnt more of the distress in the French camp. He attacked them more vigorously, was more successful and managed to revictual the city. Pedro Navarro was taken prisoner by his countrymen during one of these sallies. But only the unexpected death of Lautrec on August 16th, brought the siege to an end. The central point of the war shifted again to the north.

Here the situation of the imperialists, unlike that at Naples, grew ever darker. Hope had flared up when a German prince, Henry of Brunswick Luneburg, was won over for imperial service in Italy, and much was expected of the new troops with which he appeared in the neighbourhood of Trent as early as May. The rest of his career serves but to illustrate the importance of money, experience and knowledge of men to a commander in those times.

Having pushed forward into the country round Brescia, Duke Henry found himself threatened by his own troops and in July was forced to save his life by fleeing from them. All his trouble and expense had been for nothing.

On the other hand, as early as September, the Count of St. Pol re-entered Italy with a new French army of ten thousand men. Once again he challenged Leyva's weakening hold on Lombardy and threatened to prolong the war indefinitely in spite of the heavy losses sustained by the French at Naples. On the other hand Andrea Doria had reopened Genoa to imperial troops and resumed his own control over the town.

The circumstances for the Emperor's coming seemed therefore as favourable as they were ever likely to be. The war was not at an end, but Charles felt the call of honour. During the year 1528, as the news from Lombardy grew steadily worse, he seems to have become at last truly impatient for action. In April he wrote to his brother that he 'desired nothing in the world so much' as to go to Italy. He desired it, he said, as much for Ferdinand's sake as for his own, both so that he might 'reform' the Church in Germany, and so that he might be crowned — a ceremony from which both he and Ferdinand stood to gain. Only he lacked the chiefest thing of all — money. When at last in May 1528, he paid his long-postponed visit to Valencia in order to receive its homage, he had indeed satisfied the last demands which the Spaniards could justifiably make of him. Charles had now personally made up his mind to go to Italy. His personal letters to Balançon, which were to be privately given to him by the Prince of Orange, and those to Montfort in the autumn of 1528, betrayed in almost every sentence a frantic desire for the journey. He built on this more than on anything, he declared, and added specifically, 'I mean my journey'. He would go, so he told Montfort, writing from Toledo, 'should I have to sell this town'. At the same time he complained to him of the negotiations for money with the Portuguese — 'they are too mercantile for me'. During May and September at Valencia and Madrid, during November in Toledo, he dropped hints in the council, and sometimes even more openly. The last of these specific statements has been recorded in the Chronicle of Santa Cruz. Charles often spoke from notes, and so clearly does this last expression of his opinion reflect the ideas of

Gattinara, that it is safe to assume that he had drawn up its outline.

Charles's own growing self-confidence was revealed in the fact that he no longer asked his councillors *whether* — that was already settled — but *how* he was to undertake his journey. In an introductory paragraph he hit upon a triple *motif*, in the very manner of Gattinara. He declared that he would be prevented from carrying out his purpose neither by fear of the League, against whom God had repeatedly given him the victory, nor by fear of the Pope, who was far more profoundly disgusted by the behaviour of the French than he had ever been by the Sack of Rome, nor yet by any doubt as to the welfare of Spain. Things were not now as they had been in his first absence, for he could leave behind him both his Queen, as regent, and his heir. Furthermore, he continued, the question of cost no longer perplexed him; he had found the money for eight years of war and he could not therefore fail to find it for his coronation journey. Yet his journey was not merely for the coronation; that ceremony could have been performed as well by the Pope in Spain. Nor yet, he pursued, did he go to take vengeance on his enemies; he left that to God. Still less was it his intention to seize any land, for, as he had repeatedly asserted, he asked for nothing save what was his by inheritance. He was going rather to induce the Pope to call a council, both for the extermination of heresy and the reform of the Church. He was going to lay balm on the wounds which war had inflicted on the land. Last of all, he concluded, as it beseemed a shepherd to lead his flocks to pasture, so it beseemed him to visit his own lands, estates and vassals.

Gattinara hastened the final decision by a curious tactical ruse, of which he boasted in his autobiography. As often before, the Chancellor had taken to his bed, sick with annoyance. Charles came to visit him, and was soon talking of the fleet which was to be ready at Christmas and to put to sea in January 1529. Gattinara smiled; he did not believe in this fleet. To this Charles replied that the Chancellor was being inconsistent, because he had always been anxious for the journey. Gattinara agreed, but added that he had now given up all hope, for every necessary was lacking. Recently, even, he had expressed his disapproval of the whole business; it was not easy for him as many of the Spaniards suspected his motives and even threatened him because he was thought to have interests in Italy. And, he added slyly, it was absurd to pretend that the journey would not expose Charles to great danger. That old pirate, Andrea Doria, was not to be trusted and Italy itself was a morass of dangers and difficulties. In his opinion, therefore, the plan would be best dropped.

This speech had precisely the effect on which Gattinara was counting. Every word provoked Charles to contradict. As a noble animal is impatient of difficulties in his path, so Charles could now no longer be withheld.

Still the preparations for the journey dragged on for many months. As early as April 1528, Charles prepared his grant of plenipotentiary powers to the Empress and his instructions for the separate members of the council. Three years before, in June 1525, in a note to Doctor Lorenzo Galindez de Carvajal, there had been talk of these. Yet it was only on March 3rd, 1529, that with the help of Loaysa he composed his second will — this, too, was later superseded. On the same day he dated his last instruction to Isabella, with detailed advice on affairs of State and on her own bearing. On the following day he left Toledo for Saragossa by way of Aranjuez and Siguenza. At the end of April he was in Barcelona, after a year of hesitation and delay.

In the meantime the war in north Italy had unexpectedly ended. Spanish troops had landed at Genoa and put Leyva in a position not only to maintain his stand but to follow on the heels of St. Pol when the latter attempted to attack Genoa from the land. On June 21st Leyva smote the French at Landriano; St. Pol himself was taken. These last blows created a will to peace even in France. Thinking of the welfare of the Netherlands, the Archduchess Margaret had for the last months done all in her power to cherish it.

THE PEACE TREATIES OF BARCELONA AND CAMBRAI

During all these months the Pope at Orvieto and Viterbo was gradually regaining his balance between his old allies and the Emperor. The Venetians had taken possession of the age-old estates of the Church at Ravenna and Cervisa, and the League pestered the Pope to let the illustrious republic of St. Mark keep the towns. But Clement VII clung to them, as also to Parma and Piacenza, above all to his lost Florence. He was annoyed, too, that the cardinals had been held so long as hostages in Naples. The Venetian ambassador Contarini had a detailed and constructive interview with the Pope and discussed the necessity of abandoning earthly things when the weal of Christendom and the dignity of the Church hung in the balance. But the Pope was too restless a politician to be ready to conform unless he got something in return.

Clement VII had little resolution, but enough intelligence to perceive that his advantage lay now all on the imperial side. For months the general of the Franciscans, Francisco Quiñones, a member of the Count of Lerma's family and once for a while the Emperor's confessor, had acted as a mediator between Charles and the Pope. Clement VII made him Cardinal of Santa Croce, thus strengthening him in his neutrality towards the Emperor. Possibly for this reason Charles now sent another Spaniard to replace him, choosing a man who would attend rather to imperial interests than to mediation. This was the Aragonese Micer[1] Miguel Mai. His manner was justifiably compared to that of Juan Manuel. He staked everything on his understanding of Clement's personal character and drew him over surely to the imperial side by assiduously considering his personal caprices. But joining the Emperor meant abandoning the League, and the League for its part showed no sign of relaxing its pressure on Clement. On the other hand Clement might legitimately complain that not one member of the League, not England, France, Venice, not Florence even, had raised a finger to help him in the hour of his direst need when Charles's troops were marching on Rome. Now began an elaborate game at cross-purposes. The Pope announced repeatedly that he would come and visit the Emperor in Spain. Mai recognized this at once for a mere pretext to keep Charles out of Italy. Clement went on to say that he would confirm the *Cruzada* to Charles, but, as Mai added, 'in his mean way' the Holy Father wanted a share of 30,000 ducats for himself.

---

[1] A Spanish title of honour (TRANSLATOR'S note).

Another cause contributed to Charles's desire for peace. This was the Turkish danger. In Ferdinand's name and with the support of the imperial ambassador, Andrea da Burgo appealed for help from the Pope, when Suleiman, with new and enormous forces, once again began to march up the Danube.

Two things decided Clement. First he wanted the ambassadors to free him from his terror of a council. In this Mai and da Burgo acted very cautiously. Although even Gattinara had expressed the opinion that pressure could be put on the Pope by threatening a council, neither Mai nor da Burgo seem to have acted in accordance with their master's universal policy. The Pope's feelings were clear to all eyes when Andrea da Burgo informed him that he need not fear a council, for the Emperor set more store by peace in the world and in Italy than by the incalculable findings of a council: a friendly Emperor would be a great help to the Pope and the Lutherans could be dealt with by other means. In this speech da Burgo uttered the first hint of the coming policy of religious discussion. Barely had he spoken, when the Pope rose from his chair as if a burden had fallen from him and said: 'By my faith you speak truth and sense: if that were indeed so, concessions could easily be made.' The other infallible way of gaining Clement's support was through the fulfilment of his intentions with regard to Florence. Here the events of 1512 were to be repeated.

Thus all tended towards a separate peace with Clement. Castiglione died at Toledo, very suddenly, early in February, but Clement, as early as April 16th, replaced him by his own major-domo, the Bishop of Vaison, giving him plenipotentiary powers and arming him with the necessary sanctions for the *Cruzada* and the Spanish benefices. Gattinara, de Praet and Granvelle then drew up articles in Barcelona which led to the signing of peace on June 29th. In this peace of Barcelona, as the high-flown diplomatic language of the time expresses it, Pope and Emperor joined hands, 'out of grief at the divisions of Christendom, to beat off the Turks and to make way for a general peace'. The Pope was given Ravenna, Cervisa, Modena, Reggio and Rubiera; the Emperor was reinvested with Naples and received the right to dispose of benefices. King Ferdinand was included in the peace and both Emperor and King undertook to proceed against heretics, should these refuse to obey the shepherd of all Christendom and the mandates of the Emperor. The problem of Milan was reserved for further discussion. The Pope threatened to excommunicate any who helped the Turks and he absolved all those who had taken arms in Italy to fight against the papal states.

A few weeks after this treaty had been signed, on July 16th, Clement referred the English divorce to Rome. Since Pope and Emperor were now friends there could no longer be any doubt of his judgment. The Defender of the Faith was shortly to become the Faith's most dangerous enemy.

While tracing these events in Italy, we have temporarily lost sight of the political world about the Channel. Even after the declaration of war in 1528 there was no actual fighting in the Netherlands, although the evil effects of a state of war were sadly felt in the insecurity of roads on the frontiers and in the general economic depression. Margaret's serious anxieties in connection with Christian of Denmark, after the death of her niece Isabella, have nothing to do with Anglo-French affairs. In this painful business Margaret showed all her old vigour, repeatedly opposed the king in person, took over some of his debts — probably in memory of the queen — but absolutely refused to guarantee others. She also demanded full charge of the royal children when she could not prevent the uncontrolled adventurer from going his way with bag and baggage — more still when she heard with horror that he perpetually received the Communion in both kinds.

War in Gelderland was one bitter fruit of the enmity between Charles and the King of France. This disturbance had one curious effect: first the Utrecht districts, Overyssel in particular, and then all the neighbouring country, sought imperial help, each province acting of its own free will and with greater or less enthusiasm. Learning at last by bitter experience, even the usually stubborn estates of Brabant and Holland agreed to provide some of the money for their own defence. And thus, by the treaty of Schoonhoven in 1527, Charles's sovereignty over Utrecht in his right as Count of Holland was recognized; in the following year the treaty of Gorcum, on October 3rd, confirmed his supreme rights over Gelderland and Overyssel in his right as Duke of Brabant. His authority was thus finally recognized in accordance with the more or less spontaneous wishes of the estates in question.

The attack made by John of Cleves on Gelderland, armed with hereditary claims, as also the barbarous onslaught of the marshal of Gelderland, the unbridled Martin van Rossem, on March 6th, 1528, foreshadowed later conflicts. Yet these were but the trivial outward signs of a movement both more profound and more universal.

Margaret's government was that of the modern state, sufficient to itself, secret and closed; as such it stood out in sharp contrast to these remnants of feudalism. Such also was the government of the Catholic Church and of Charles in Spain. In the process of evolution, these new governments had absorbed the lesser rights and privileges which stood in their way, had brought into being an able bureaucracy, had oppressed the higher nobility and crushed out particularism. The Archduchess Margaret had no qualms in opposing the privileged cities of the Netherlands if her nephew's interests demanded it. Yet, when the nobility complained of her rule to Charles, he sent one of his most important advisers, de Praet, to reside in the Netherlands, an action which throws an illuminating light on his opinion of her proud and sometimes over-confident conduct. Margaret's personal attempts to justify her actions breathe a spirit of haughty independence, and it was typical of her royal attitude that, when the quarrels with the nobility became serious, she refused to accept any mediator other than the Empress herself. She would forgo not one imperial right, not one of her possessions or revenues. At the worst she would fall back on her own resources for the support of her government. In this she showed herself very different from the lords whose avarice she bitterly attacked. She was modern, too, in her grasp of the economic needs of her country, and thereby of the importance of English friendship.

The English war was profoundly unpopular for obvious reasons, both in the Netherlands and among the merchant and working classes of England. Wolsey's power was by this time tottering, and the imperial ambassadors in London cleverly emphasized the fact that his ambition had caused the war, against the proven will of king and people. On the other hand for a short while the imperial side nourished a hope that Charles might win the war by sea — thus ante-dating the threat of the Armada by half a century. Immediately after the declaration of war at Burgos, in

January 1528, for instance, Gattinara had drawn up a memorandum in which he suggested that, relying on an offer of help from Portugal, it would be possible to arm Portuguese, Castilian and Flemish ships for an attack on the English coast; Charles's troops could then land to avenge Queen Katherine's wrongs and protect the legal title of her daughter. A Scottish alliance, which could easily be made, would help in the general scheme. Guillaume de Montfort received permission to recruit 6000 German soldiers for the invasion as early as February 6th. Perhaps this was the first serious plan for an invasion of England in modern history. It came to nothing. Supported by the imperial ambassador, Iñigo Mendoza, Bishop of Burgos, Margaret strove for peace, and on June 15th, 1528, an armistice was signed at Hampton Court, which led in time to peace.

In the French war, on the other hand, the customs governing the little world of the Court, lightened Margaret's task of mediation. She had, for instance, social relations with the Duchess of Vendôme, who inherited at about this time the legacies of her brother-in-law, the lord of Ravestein. At an evening party given in Paris by the French King's mother — and Margaret's sister-in-law — Louise of Savoy, someone asked Margaret's ambassador, des Barres, whether his mistress and he himself would not agree to make peace, seeing how deep was the desire for it on all sides. This was the first step towards a settlement. Margaret ensured a rapid diplomatic victory by first holding back and then allowing herself to be over-argued. About this time she seems to have consulted very frequently with Guilbert Bayard, Bishop of Avranches. A fruitful correspondence, which has survived to our own time in several stout packets of documents, led at last to a personal meeting between the two princesses at Cambrai on July 5th, 1529. Here Margaret, intelligently exploiting every possible personal and practical opportunity, at length brought into being the so-called *Paix des Dames*. Signed on August 3rd, 1529, it was wholly favourable to Charles.

Louise of Savoy had suffered bitterly at the captivity first of her son, then of her grandsons, and later at the devastation of Italy. Margaret recognized and used to the full the advantages of her situation, showing throughout that knowledge of facts and power of decision which mark her out as a woman far above the ordinary.

As early as December 31st, 1528, she knew from her confidants, Rosimbos and des Barres, that the Emperor would consent to her chief points.

The *Paix des Dames* at Cambrai was in essence a confirmation of the Peace of Madrid, save only for the restitution of Bourgogne, which both parties now recognized as impossible. Nevertheless, Charles did not renounce his claim to it. The treaty is a fat document, for it deals with innumerable territorial questions, with the respective rights of the two rulers and the position of their subjects. The chief stipulations were that Francis I should recognize Charles as sovereign over Artois and Flanders and renounce all his claims on Milan, Genoa and Naples — and this in spite of the struggle which French kings had waged at so much sacrifice and with so much intermittent success for upwards of five and thirty years. Abandoned, too, were all the partisans of Francis, particularly in Italy — which was lucky for the Pope. Thus in the north the Duke of Gelderland and Robert de la Mark were at last put out of action. On the other hand, King Christian was included in the peace. The French princes were to be released on payment of a ransom of two million soleils, and the French were to make themselves responsible for payment of Charles's debt to the English government. This was to be a great relief to Charles, in internal administration as well as in European affairs. The widowed Queen Eleonore, whose formal betrothal to Francis had placed her for the last months in a most invidious position, was now in very truth to ascend the throne with him. Dynastically Charles could have asked for no more splendid alliance, and even politically the marriage was not wholly meaningless.

About this time the great Hall of Justice at Bruges was nearing completion. To celebrate the occasion medallions of Eleonore and her husband, supported by Cupids, were added to the main pillars of the gigantic and elaborately carved three-tiered chimney-piece. To the right and left the founders of the Hapsburg-Burgundian-Spanish dynasty were represented — life-size figures of the Emperor Maximilian, the Duchess Mary of Burgundy, King Ferdinand of Aragon and Queen Isabella of Castile. In the background, seated on a throne, were Philip the Handsome and Joanna; in front of them, their son, the youthful Emperor, in the robes of the Golden Fleece, the Sword of Justice drawn in his hand, and lifted as if to Heaven. Behind the figures, the arms of all his countries over which he ruled decorated the wall, and among them the busts of Lannoy and the Archduchess Margaret — his representatives in Naples and the Low Countries. The whole is a proud symbol of triumphant power, of the elation which all must have felt on thinking of the victory at Pavia and the peace at Cambrai.

Charles now dispatched de Praet to make a settlement in Italy. A private letter written by this latter to Granvelle is illuminating evidence of the opinions of an experienced minister of State on the peace at Cambrai. The treaty, he said, was so favourable that at first he thought it must be a trick. But on counting up the chances of its violation, he found that everything now pointed to its unconditional acceptance. At about the same time, in September 1529, Charles de Poupet, lord of La Chaulx, the second man in the close inner circle of Charles's council, wrote in the same tone to Charles himself.

Soon after, in October, La Chaulx and des Barres met in Paris, and on the 21st both reported that they had been splendidly welcomed. The King received them in the great hall of the Louvre, sitting in the midst of all his Court. This was a change indeed from the formal declarations of war and open challenges of the previous year! Now the King stepped down to greet the ambassadors in the middle of the room, and without waiting to hear what La Chaulx would say, burst out himself in praise of the noble ladies who had given them peace. Henceforward, he said, he would live and die as Charles's true brother and friend: the Emperor could dispose of him and of all he had — a spate of fair words. Later and privately he approached the Turkish question; expressing his lively desire to support King Ferdinand, he sketched out a plan of campaign using some 60,000 men, cavalry and artillery. The natural commander was of course the Emperor, while he, the King of France, would lead the vanguard. Unhappily he could provide no money since he already owed the English so much, but he would gladly hurry across Savoy and Piedmont to meet Charles in Italy and help to plan the campaign.

On October 20th, after Mass had been celebrated at the Cathedral of Nôtre Dame, peace was sworn in the presence of all the leading nobility, as well as of the English, Venetian, Milanese,

Florentine and Ferrarese ambassadors, who had come rather against their will. Afterwards the King entertained the ambassadors to breakfast in the episcopal palace. In the evening they visited the Grand Maître, who managed to put in a word for the Duke of Ferrara, the King's brother-in-law.[1] At the same time, and with the same ceremony, Charles had confirmed the peace at Piacenza in the presence of the Admiral of France.

THE EMPEROR IN ITALY. CORONATION AT BOLOGNA

In the meantime Charles had begun his Italian progress. The forty mules laden with gold from Portugal and Castile had arrived, after endless delay, at Barcelona. Here, too, the Court had news of St. Pol's defeat at Landriano. It was 'as though the Emperor's cause were miraculously guided by God Himself', Gattinara declared. All the omens pointed to a happy voyage. Only Margaret penned one last warning against the Italian journey. 'My master,' wrote the Emperor's aunt, 'your bold and exalted mind cries out for this journey to Italy; both I and all your servants here are well content to hear of this your care for your honour, your name, your safety and your lands. Yet the dangers to your person and the difficulties of the task cannot but awake at the same time our apprehension and anxiety.' The Emperor should not undertake the journey, she said, unless he had money, troops and provisions in plenty. Otherwise he might fare like Charles VIII of France, who marched successfully into the land, but had to withdraw from Rome for lack of money, leaving his honour behind him.

But all was now ready to start and Charles was already too familiar with Margaret's argument to be thus withheld at the eleventh hour. Besides, many of the points which she raised had now been satisfactorily settled. At the end of July Charles put to sea, on August 6th he was at Monaco, on the 9th at Savona, on the 12th at Genoa. From here he went by way of Tortona, Voghera and Piacenza towards Bologna. The young and warlike

---

[1] He had married Renée, daughter of Louis XII and sister of Claude, the first wife of Francis.

Emperor was almost disappointed to find that the land through which he passed was already at peace. On December 6th he entered Bologna.

Every resource of the Renaissance had been enlisted to do him honour. Every statue and facade in the wealthy town was hung and garlanded. Triumphal arches spanned the streets, enriched with symbolic sculptures, depicting with a wealth of classical allusions the whole history of the land and people. Gattinara, now sixty-four years old and recently elevated to the rank of cardinal, must have felt his heart beat high as he contemplated the portraits of the Roman emperors — Caesar, Augustus, Titus and Trajan — next to the arms of his own imperial master. He rode in the immediate suite of the Emperor, next to Henry of Nassau, Alessandro de' Medici and the Marquis of Montferrat. He was himself count and marquis of an imperial fief in Piedmont. News that the tide of Turkish advance had been stemmed at Vienna cast an additional radiance over these glorious days of fulfilment.

A little earlier Clement VII had reached the town, and the two heads of Christendom, who so short a time ago had seemed to be irreconcilably at war, now spent long weeks in confidential discourse. Their apartments in the Palazzo Publico communicated by means of private doors. The visit lasted for nearly four months, from December 1529 until towards the end of March 1530. It is difficult to understand the delay for Ferdinand was imploring Charles with increasing urgency to come to his help against the Turks.

What held Charles so long inactive in Barcelona? In Spain, he had made very different plans for his journey. But the rapid changes in the political situation mocked his laboriously planned decisions. Feeling the need to justify himself to his brother, he wrote, in January 1530, a full and confidential letter. In this letter the lines of the Emperor's thought follow very closely those of Gattinara, the Chancellor's ideas forming, as it were, a scaffolding on which Charles now constructed his own. As in 1525, but this time with riper and surer judgment, Charles tried to elucidate his own position in Europe.

He wished, he said, that his letter had wings so that he might have an answer at once. Ferdinand had asked whether he should not make a treaty with the Turks. To this, Charles sensibly replied that they two alone had not the means to make war on the Grand Vizir, while other princes were not at present likely to give them any help worthy of the name. Peace therefore, at whatever price, was not to be rejected. Naturally everyone would say afterwards that they would have been able to work wonders, had they fought, and would remind him of his frequent intention of fighting the infidel. The Sultan, too, might realize that Ferdinand was in dire need of peace and might therefore seek, by pressing him yet harder, to gain yet more. Or feeling himself safe from Ferdinand, he might turn his forces on Charles. But the need for a treaty outweighed these doubts. The Pope, indeed, was preparing at this very moment to send an appeal against the Turks to every prince in Europe. The answers would be slow to come, and the princes might possibly express annoyance at being asked to help in a war, when peace was actually being made. All the same it would be wisest to wait and see what developments next took place in Germany. He therefore advised Ferdinand to send a provisional answer to the Pope rather than an official embassy, expressing his regret at the delay and his willingness to oppose the Sultan, although rather by negotiation than by war.

As for his own future actions and his journey to Germany, Charles seemed disposed to employ the same formula which he had indicated to Ferdinand. He asked his advice for three possibilities. Either he could be crowned at once and proceed to Germany as soon as the ceremony was over; or he could be crowned in Rome and come to Germany in May or June; or finally, if this suited the Germans, he could go to Naples to see to his rights there and come to Germany only in the autumn. So that Ferdinand could judge each course fairly, Charles then proceeded once more to summarize the reasons for his journey, together with an account of all that had happened since.

His chief reasons for the Italian voyage, he said, were first, that although his resources were running out, peace had not been made. Secondly he felt that the terrible growth of heresy in Germany might lead to the election of an anti-king of the Romans; his own influence for Ferdinand's election as king depended, of course, on his having first been crowned Emperor by the Pope. Last of all he wanted to visit Naples and give peace to Italy. Here he added that he did not intend directly to control the whole peninsula;

such an action would inevitably lose him the Pope's friendship, which he desired above all. But he felt that, although many had advised him against it, it would be safer and wiser to arrange the settlement of Italy in person.

Since then, he went on, many unexpected changes had taken place. Owing to opposition to his journey, he had been obliged to wait for money from Portugal and his plans had been long delayed. On his way he had news that peace had already been made with France and he had to abandon his plan for a campaign in Italy. At about the same time he had Ferdinand's good news of the preliminary check to the Turkish advance. Both these events gave him the opportunity to devote himself more exclusively to the settlement of Italy, even though this would delay his meeting with his brother for longer than if he had stuck to his original plan of going straight to Venice. In Italy he had repeatedly declared his peaceful intentions, but, he lamented, 'it is usual to achieve the opposite if one shows very obviously that one desires a particular thing'. So it had fallen out in Italy. The Pope demanded that he fulfil his promise and restore Florence to the Medici. First he pretended that this would not take more than a fortnight or three weeks, then he wanted longer, and so the affair dragged on, heaven knew whether out of good faith or the opposite. In the meantime he had concluded treaties with the Venetians and the Duke of Milan. In this latter town he could hardly have retained the sovereignty either for himself or Ferdinand without provoking 'endless war'. It was still doubtful whether France would stand by the peace, too, for Francis was leaning towards England, and King Henry, it seemed, was absolutely determined to be rid of his wife, Charles's and Ferdinand's aunt, whether he could get the papal dispensation or no. But France and England, Charles concluded, would not fight him if they saw that order had been re-established in Italy. That opinion might have come straight from Gattinara. He had already firm command of Naples, Charles went on, and 21,000 men at his disposal. The problems of Florence and Ferrara were all that remained and the moment seemed opportune for trampling out the last hot ashes of war.

This then was his present situation. He wanted to keep his word to the Pope, even though there were those who told him that he would get nothing but shame from it. He wanted to wait and see what King Francis intended, for he had already begun to fulfil the terms of the peace in Naples, Stenay and Hesdin. In spite of this some people seemed to think that he was still intriguing in Italy, in Florence and Venice for instance, and that he would break the peace as soon as his sons were set free — if not before. As for Henry VIII, the Pope could not agree to his shameless demands, but he was naturally afraid of losing English allegiance altogether. Henry could of course be depended upon to commit some folly or other which would make an occasion for war. The treaty with Andrea Doria, Charles went on, ran out in May or June; he hoped nevertheless to keep him loyal. Out of all this, one question arose: did Ferdinand feel that Charles had time to be crowned in Rome, a ceremony which some of his advisers held to be very important, or would it be better to be crowned in Bologna and proceed straight to Germany? If Ferdinand decided for the latter he must outline some course to be taken in dealing with heresy in the Empire, and resolve firmly upon his own election as King of the Romans, an election which Charles was prepared to support.

The letter was long, full and confidential, yet as Charles put it, 'many things remained stuck in the pen'. These Charles hoped to discuss with his brother when he met him in the flesh.

Thus did the Emperor sum up the situation in mid-January. Rome and Naples had not yet been altogether evacuated. But Ferdinand's renewed insistence forced Charles to decide for himself. From the Netherlands, too, came Margaret's warning; she implored him to squander no more money but to satisfy the Pope and have done with it, for Ferdinand could wait no longer for help against the Turk. 'Ye heads of Christendom', she wrote to her nephews, 'will never gain so much honour there in Italy as you are losing by your sloth in defending Europe from the Turk.' There was no other means of getting money, she went on, than to sell a part of the Church lands throughout Christendom, as well as some of those belonging to the knightly orders — even in Prussia. The measure was all the more necessary because the German princes, the Lutherans in particular, were indiscriminately turning them into private domains. The Pope's help must be sought for this policy, she said. As for a general council of all Christendom, she went on, this would bring too many formalities in its train. Rather she suggested that three gatherings should be held: Charles should preside over one for Italy and Spain, herself over a second, for England, France and Scotland at Cambrai, Ferdinand over a third for Germany and the neighbouring lands. All these should deliberate how best to launch an expedition against the Turk. In this plan Margaret showed herself a true daughter of her family. Her father Maximilian would have applauded her desire for a Crusade, no less than the plan for three great international gatherings, each one under the presidency of a Hapsburg.

At Bologna they entertained no such thoughts. Clement was thinking of quite other things than sacrificing the resources of the Church. We know little of his negotiations with the Emperor, but in the archives of Simancas there is a paper on which Charles made a few sporadic notes. At the top is the phrase: 'Concerning the Queen of England.' That cause we have discussed already. Next comes, 'the confirmation of the Bull for extending the royal patronage and sanctioning the union of the three grand-master-ships'. A little lower down comes 'a brief giving power to dispose of their rents for nine years after my death for the salvation of my soul'. Even now in the prime of his life Charles was thinking of death. Lower still comes a request for an alteration in the brief granting the Emperor absolution for the Sack of Rome, and last of all a series of personal wishes and demands made in the name of the Spanish Crown or Church. Among these we find, 'that which concerns the Inquisition, of which I have a memorandum'; not to mention a reference to the revenues which the Pope drew from the archbishopric of Toledo.

In his memoirs Charles reports that he also discussed a council with Clement. Soon we shall have cause to mention this again.

But to both these illustrious rulers, Italian affairs seemed for the time-being far more important than any others. Francesco Sforza, after he had been given and had taken the opportunity of clearing himself of treachery, was granted the fief of Milan. Charles could hardly view Sforza with disfavour when the Pope, whose disloyalty had been far more rank, was reconciled to him. Venice, through its able ambassador Contarini, came half-way to meet the Emperor. The Ferrarese question led to acrimonious argument but to no serious quarrel.

The imperial coronation was fixed for Charles's birthday, February 24th, 1530. For the sake of Germany, the Emperor had decided not to go to Rome. Charles's wish to have some of the German princes round him for this solemnity foundered on the shortness of the time. Only the young Count Palatine, the Elector's nephew Philip, and the Count Palatine, Frederick, were able to be present. At the solemn entry into the Church, Frederick bore the orb before Charles; this at least was a symbol of the Elector Palatine's office and of the Holy Roman Empire of the German Nation. On February 22nd Charles received the iron crown of Lombardy from the hands of the Pope, on the 24th the imperial crown. The coronation was magnificently solemnized. For the last time in history the world saw the two highest dignitaries of Christendom, Emperor and Pope, in the full splendour of their ceremonial robes — a scene depicted a hundred times in fresco on the walls of churches and town halls over all Italy.

The only task now left to the imperial generals in Italy was the most painful. Clement VII insisted that Florence be reduced. The last and most unworthy offspring of the family of the elder Cosimo was chosen for Duke, and Charles decided that he would later bestow on him for his wife his own natural daughter, the eight-year-old Margaret.

Thus three years after the Sack of Rome the imperial soldiery appeared outside the walls of the noble city of Florence, to reduce it by force and subjugate it once again to the expelled Medici. In this last struggle the last flowering of its art, the last ripening of its civic virtues was trampled in the dust. For long enough they fought, both in the countryside and under the walls on which Michelangelo himself had worked as an engineer. Both sides suffered terribly. Charles lost his best and youngest commander. On August 3rd at Gavinana not far from Pistoia in a cavalry skirmish, Philibert of Châlons, Prince of Orange, was killed. His mother raised a monument to his memory, sculpted by the hand of Margaret's protégé Conrad Meit. His titles went to his nephew Réné, the son of Henry of Nassau by Philibert's sister Claude. So it was that Orange came to Nassau.

Meanwhile Charles had long left Italy. In April, May and June he went by way of Mantua, Peschiera, Rovereto, Trent and Innsbruck into Germany. He had now entered the land with which his fate was to be bound up. And at Innsbruck on June 5th, not wholly unexpectedly, his Chancellor Gattinara died. The life of the minister had been spent in unceasing labour for the imperial house, but with nightfall came fulfilment and he died when he had already reached his goal; Charles had been crowned Emperor by the Pope and peace had come to Italy. But for Charles a new stage of his life was beginning, and Gattinara's death was a symbol that his youth and all those connected with it, were passing before his eyes.

Gattinara's death marked the end of Charles's inner development. Henceforward no one had decisive influence on him again. For long enough no one had even thought of his appointing another First Chamberlain to play the part once played by Chièvres. For three more years, Charles was still able to depend on the written advice of his one-time confessor, Loaysa. Yet he had almost abruptly dismissed this man from the council, and although he continued to correspond with him, Loaysa never regarded himself as anything but an exile in Rome, although he had been elevated to the rank of cardinal. His letters breathe a tone of courtly devotion which proves that he would gladly have come back to Charles's service. 'If my absence from your Majesty', he wrote, 'is repaid by the knowledge that you stand always by what is right, then I will accept my punishment with joy.' Charles prized Loaysa's ability, and to judge by the confessor's letters frequently raised his hopes, yet he never recalled him. Nevertheless he followed Loaysa's advice as to the men between whom he should now divide Gattinara's responsibilities, Cobos and Granvelle. 'I have always held', wrote Loaysa, 'that you will find Cobos the best repository for your honour and your secrets; his character will make up for any lack in yours and he will be well able to relieve you of burdens. He does not waste his intelligence thinking of subtleties and epigrams as some do. He never complains of his master and he is very popular. The lord of Granvelle on the other hand is a skilful lawyer and a good Latinist, a good Christian, a man who understands affairs and withal — a personality. He is not so easy to deal with as the secretary of state, but when he holds office he will doubtless learn patience. I therefore suggest that your Majesty becomes your own Chancellor, but looks after affairs with the help of these two.'

Lalemand's successor in the secretaryship was Antoine Perrenin. As secretary and notary public he witnessed the codicil of 1532 after Cobos. But he was not politically the equal of the other, and for all affairs outside Spain he was overshadowed by Granvelle. This latter was never secretary, but rather a diplomatist and a statesman. He was born in 1486 at Ornans in Bourgogne, and, like Gattinara, had made his way to power through the *Parlement* at Dôle, the service of the Archduchess Margaret and an embassy to France. It was he who in future assisted Charles in his general policy. Cobos, on the other hand, had exceptional financial gifts; being a good man of business he was apt to forge his own profit. He had worked his way up from small beginnings. Making himself indispensable to Chièvres, he had little by little, with all his native Andalusian subtlety, combined the chief administrative offices in Castile in his hands. He derived no less advantage from his position than Chièvres, but his income was somewhat more skilfully combined with the chief sources of the revenues. As secretary of the India board for instance, he had control of smelting and casting precious metals, with a commission of 10 per cent; he had rights no less advantageous on the Salt tax, and on most of the American colonies — this secured him prodigious wealth.

Meanwhile Loaysa advised Charles not only about his ministers but about his private life. His harsh criticisms seem to have defeated their own ends. Yet they are illuminating for the light they throw on that profoundly serious yet commonplace approach to moral matters which was the stock-in-trade of the Church, and to which Charles most passionately subscribed. The Cardinal told him that it was in his power at any moment to raise himself out of the deepest pits of sin, to 'start a new book of conscience'. 'Your Majesty', he said, 'should be assured that God gives no man a kingdom without laying on him an even greater duty than on ordinary men to love Him and obey His commands.' Another time he wrote, 'In your royal person, indolence is at war with fame. I pray that God's grace will be on you in Germany and that you will be able to overcome your natural enemies, good living and waste of time.'

Such thoughts occupied the Emperor too. His expectation of earning fame by a war in Italy had been disappointed. But honour and fame were perhaps beckoning to him from some other sphere. Hitherto, in spite of all his troubles, his boldest dreams had ultimately come to fulfilment. With God's help he might yet restore the lapsed, and shatter the infidel. He had once told Loaysa that he would stake his life to win such a prize. Loaysa now reminded him of his words. 'The time', he wrote, 'is at hand.'

CHAPTER III

THE GERMAN PROTESTANTS

THE Emperor's devout piety and that passionate desire for salvation evinced by many of his German subjects could give no support to each other. The shower of rain which blesses a thirsty land means nothing to an already well-watered garden. Martin Luther had had horrible experience of that profound religious belief in supernatural powers of good and evil struggling for the human soul, before he found the way to his glad message of redemption. Both his interpretation of ancient theology and his grasp of the verbal meaning of the scriptures bear witness alike to the intense suffering through which he had passed and to his joy in the ultimate discovery of consolation. Personal peculiarities but lightly veiled the universal nature of his experience which served to heighten its vital effect on the German people, both his contemporaries and posterity. All religious belief implies a certain restraint, a submission to the traditions of man.

But the storm which he had raised shook the ecclesiastical structure to its foundations. Thereby in Germany he struck a heavy blow at the order of secular life itself. For centuries both the theory and the reality of the state had swayed unsteadily between the national and the universal. To Luther, bred to the belief that God's kingdom was worldwide and the Empire was its reflection, national theory was but a means to an end. It served, to a greater or a lesser degree, in solving the problem of the secularization of Church organization. But no sooner did Luther fully grasp the irreconcilable contradiction between traditional authority and his new unalterable convictions of faith, than he began to see the foreign and artificial elements of the Roman Church in the mirror of German history. At the same time he saw that the growing German territorial states, among which he lived, provided a basis for the new Christian congregation. Naturally he did not abandon his reverence for the 'Empire' in which the German people had for the first time found the true expression of their political unity. Unconsciously therefore he became a party to that fatal contradiction in German history. For centuries the theory of universal Empire had been exploited to imbue the German people with Christian culture, in readiness for a world-order based on God's eternal laws. In spite of the vigorous individuality of their various groups, so prone to division, coalescence or change, this idea had held them together. Furthermore Luther was falling rapidly under the spell of the German language — that language through the use of which he became the instrument of historic change — and as he did so he was able to appeal ever more directly to the hearts of his own beloved people. It was as if he had in his own person already anticipated the inner unity of the nation. And yet he had nothing to give them which could help them in forming a new political framework for themselves.

In the very moment in which Luther, the great lover of men's souls, became aware of his responsibility towards the whole Christian congregation, in the very moment in which he first gave loud expression to his fear and joy, his cause had already become political. Since the day when he had stood out fearlessly for his belief at Worms, his name had become a password in Germany by which men knew their friends.

THE GERMAN STATE, THE REFORMATION AND THE FORMULATION OF CREEDS

The Lutheran password was adopted by a number of princes and cities. Several of Germany's territorial states, and some of the towns which still at that time felt themselves to be the equals of the princely states, recognized, as Luther had done, the duty of Christian rulers to further the will of God. It was not difficult for them; contemporary political theory helped them, both because of the functions it attributed to the state, and to the so-called 'ordinary man'. This then lay behind those repeated assertions of the imperial cities that the Edict of 1521 could not be carried out. This was at the bottom of the first efforts made by the secular authorities to attack the already tottering principles of the Church, and to evolve instead their own princely or municipal formulae for spiritual truths.

Without losing its spiritual vigour, the Lutheran movement

fermented the development of the emerging German state. It lifted the ideas which governed that development from the sordid rut of private interest and selfish gain into the rarefied atmosphere of moral duty. The guiding principle itself was too diversely interpreted to escape defacement; it was soiled by empty and threadbare slogans, spattered with crude egoism. There arose about it all those crises and struggles in which we can recognize even to-day the outward expression of spiritual conflict. About the year 1529 this development was at its most confused and already there were signs of internal reactions which were later to take their places within the development of Germany as permanent forces.

The original danger which had imperilled the Lutheran movement was that the enthusiastic overstatement of individual religious needs might lead to the overthrow of all traditional ecclesiastical forms. This danger was already over in 1529. So also was the second and more serious danger — that which had cost Germany the most loss and disaster; social unrest among the lower middle classes and the peasantry in south and central Germany had endowed the movement with temporary frantic, but self-destructive life. That second and serious danger had left Luther himself and his friends with a profound mistrust of all individual, spiritual and revolutionary tendencies. Now a third danger was emerging: the theologies of the past had left a legacy which, taken in conjunction with the natural desire to express doctrinal distinctions with the utmost dogmatism, was threatening to make a rabbit-warren of the whole Protestant movement. Luther's speeches, and later on even single sentences in his writings, were quoted as dogmatic formulae. While his warm and vital words went straight to the hearts of men, the theologians were left arguing over points which would have been better suited to the limbo of legal terminology and were in any case totally incomprehensible. A thousand years earlier much the same thing had happened in the Christian Churches.

Gradually groups came into being. Some arose spontaneously, others were consciously formed as men felt the need to strengthen their own convictions by leaning on others, or to express them in the secular world. The groups varied infinitely in the nature and firmness of the relation between the spiritual idea and its practical organization.

Points of contact can be discovered, for instance, between the humanist Reformers, not one of whom had dared to attack the fundamental doctrines of the Church, and those spiritual enthusiasts the Anabaptists, who blew all doctrines against the skies. Luther stood about midway between the extremes. But even among his friends many different opinions flourished, from those of the Wittenberg group on the one hand down to Zwingli on the other — for although the Swiss Reformer rose independently in Zurich he was nevertheless under Luther's influence. And the closer the contact between men of even mildly differing opinions, the more acutely they felt them. To a lesser degree something of the same kind was to be found in the Roman Church; here too there were spiritual points of contact between old and new theories — a fact comprehensible enough since all had their origin in the same source. The gigantic flood of polemic literature on both sides, meanwhile, defined differences of doctrine and exacerbated the tempers of men.

By nature all the combatants were more or less uninterested in politics. But the necessities of the time made it essential for them to gain political support, and the burning question for each party was to discover its most probable and its strongest allies. The 'growth of faith and religious policy' are not merely to-day the object of constructive research; unless we examine the ideas then current in Germany we shall not be able to understand the political situation which confronted Charles in the summer of 1530.

The recess issued by the Diet at Nuremberg in 1524 gave the Germans their first impetus towards the exact formulation of the new doctrine. This recess decreed that all states which had control of one or more universities were to arrange for their 'learned, reverent, experienced and understanding doctors to prepare an extract of all the disputed points in all the new doctrines and books'. This pronouncement marked the abandonment of the old policy of exterminating the heretic, as expressed in the Edict of Worms, and substituted for it the examination and comparison of the new ideas, or 'confessions'. As far as we know the old Margrave Casimir of Ansbach was the first man to become really active in this new field. He was an old friend of the Hapsburg dynasty, and although from time to time powerfully influenced by the Lutheran movement, he nevertheless ended his life in their service. When he died in 1527 he was succeeded by his brother and heir, Mar-grave George, who was in need of Hapsburg friendship in order to maintain his claim to his Silesian fief of Jägerndorf; but in his heart Margrave George was more ardently concerned for the truth of the gospels than his brother had been. It was he who once, at the Hungarian Court, had exerted a powerful influence over the young Queen Mary, even in this crucial matter of religion. The political alliances of the princes in the Peasants' War had also drawn them together at least to some extent according to their religious beliefs: Saxony and Hesse stood together, so also did the various Brandenburg princes in Franconia. The Elector John of Brandenburg sent a decision, made in his council, to Wittenberg for examination, where it won the approval of Luther, Melanch-thon, Jonas and Bugenhagen, who were now recognized as the leaders of the new religious movement.

The fundamental conditions for the later development of the Protestant movement in Germany had thus been laid down. Afterwards politics and religion moved forward hand in hand, if not always without friction; alliances were made which, based on religious agreement, yet tended rather to the preservation of political freedom. It is only fair to add that political freedom was in some sort a condition for the establishment of religious freedom. Curious indeed were the developments which now followed: all these groups of allies sought to come to an understanding with the ancient Church while, among their opponents, other alliances came into being in which religious and political motives were no less confusingly mingled. The shrewd councillors of the Emperor were thus not far wrong when they foresaw that an almost infinite number of permutations and combinations could be made out of the political divisions of Germany. By playing on these they hoped to combat the dangers which threatened them. Yet the pursuance of such a policy brought with it moral problems and temptations which might prove difficult to resist. In judging imperial policy it must be remembered that the price which he thought it worth his while to pay for a temporary or a permanent peace was reckoned not by any fixed inner determination, but rather on an underestimate of his opponents' strength and a failure to understand surrounding circumstances.

In the meantime two events had hastened the growth of

doctrinal differences and of political alliances, while at the same time increasing civil disturbance and sharpening the bitterness of feelings. The first of these was the so-called affair of Pack in 1528; the second was the Diet of Speyer in 1529.

Otto von Pack, an adventurer who had got for himself a seat on the council of George of Saxony, forged a document purporting to be an alliance for war against the Protestants, signed by the chief Catholic powers. This aroused the Landgrave Philip of Hesse to defend himself, or more accurately, to strike out. Among his supporters were the Elector of Saxony, the new King of Denmark, Francis I and John Zapolya — all enemies of the Hapsburg dynasty. The Landgrave's too hasty attack on the neighbouring bishoprics of Mainz and Würzburg made an impression which was all the worse because his soldiers plundered ruthlessly, and Pack's document was proved to be a forgery almost immediately afterwards. The Elector of Saxony then withdrew, the Elector Palatine offered to mediate, and the whole incident petered out. It had been a danger signal to the Hapsburg dynasty, but a signal only. Nevertheless, it was an example, and the first which had so far been given, of the way in which political conflict between the German states might pile fuel on to the flames of the already existing conflict between the theologians, and inflame the minds of the people. This was the fatal and dangerous web into which all the greater and lesser territorial quarrels of Germany, nay of all Europe, were to be caught up, until the longest and bloodiest contest of all, the Thirty Years War, at length purged out the fatal poison.

More profound in its effect was the Diet of Speyer in 1529.

When it was called and opened on March 15th Charles was still wrestling with his Italian problems. Nevertheless, his position in Naples and Lombardy was mending and, after the business of Pack, he himself entertained the greatest hopes of the mission on which he had sent the provost of Waldkirch to Germany. The adherents of the Roman Church in the Empire had been for the first time seriously alarmed by the disturbance of the previous year; their anxiety to defend their own interests enabled Ferdinand, acting as Charles's deputy, to adopt a far bolder attitude towards the Protestants.

The representatives of the imperial Estates at the Diet of Speyer were still that generation of German princes who had elected Charles and welcomed him into Germany ten years before. There were the same three spiritual Electors — Albert of Brandenburg at Mainz, Richard von Greiffenklau at Treves, Hermann of Wied at Cologne. Among the secular Electors, John of Saxony had replaced his brother, Frederick the Wise; he was not much younger and his opinions, although more outspokenly Lutheran, were much the same. Lewis, the Elector Palatine, brother of Charles's friend the Count Palatine Frederick, expressed no opinion on religion and leaned towards mediation. The Elector of Brandenburg was emphatically Catholic, although his Danish wife, who was now living under the Elector of Saxony's protection, probably had other reasons for leaving his Court than the mere fact that she was a Lutheran. But he did not attend the Diet. It was said that his absence was occasioned by his equivocal relations with the wife of Wolf Hornung.

Of the other secular princes, Luther's most ardent opponent, George of Saxony, of the Albertine line,[1] was also absent. He was deeply interested in theology and very learned, but he was at the moment indignant with the Hapsburg dynasty. The Luneburg branch of the Welfs sent no representative either, Duke Francis appearing only at the end of the meeting. Their rivals, of the Wolfenbüttel branch,[2] however, sent a representative in Duke Henry of Wolfenbüttel. He it was who had offered to serve the Emperor in Spain but had achieved as little there as in his tragicomic intervention in Italy. Most important of all were Lewis and William of Bavaria. The political and religious interests of these princes were in diametrical opposition, for while both of them resented Ferdinand's victory over them at the Bohemian election, both were strong Catholics and anxious to preserve religious uniformity in their duchies. Thus, in spite of all their jealousy of the King, they wanted a Catholic League. The ruling dynasty of Württemberg was quiescent. Margrave Philip of Baden supported the old faith. But the younger branch of the Palatine dynasty leaned towards Luther. The Franconian branch of the House of Brandenburg was represented by Margrave George of Ansbach, whose opinions we have already discussed. Hesse, although one of

[1] The Albertine line were descended from Albert, Duke of Meissen and Friesland, who died in 1500. George was his eldest son. *See* note, p. 246 (TRANSLATOR's note).
[2] The inheritance had been divided between the two branches of the Welf family in the latter half of the fourteenth century (TRANSLATOR's note).

the newest of the German principalities, was rich enough to fit out a magnificent suite for its twenty-five-year-old Landgrave. Although Philip had not yet foregone his political connections with his Catholic neighbours, he had drawn closer to the Elector of Saxony both for religious and political reasons. The Hapsburg dynasty suspected him because he was known to have decisively Lutheran sympathies, he was constantly quarrelling with the rulers of Nassau, and he had played a leading part in the disgraceful business of Pack. Meeting him by chance as he rode into Speyer, Ferdinand received him with marked coolness.

The predominantly Catholic atmosphere of the Diet was not due merely to the number of Bishops present. Many prelates not only stayed away but did not even arrange to be represented, although others, roused by the events of the last year, made special efforts to be present. In spite of the demands which they had made at the last Diet the towns did not receive the position which they wished. The greatest among them — Strasbourg, Nuremberg, Augsburg, Ulm with its Swabian neighbours — had recently devoted themselves quite openly to the doctrines of reform and were thus gradually estranged from the imperial government.

Besides Charles's spokesman, the provost of Waldkirch, Ferdinand could also rely on the help of the imperial representative, Frederick Count Palatine, as well as on that of his own Chancellor, Bernard of Cles, Bishop of Trent, who was later sent to greet the Emperor at Bologna and received much praise.

Notwithstanding all this support, Ferdinand found that his position as King of Hungary and Bohemia prevented him from taking up an uncompromising stand on the religious question. The necessity of getting help against the Turks forced him to show favour to those very Estates whom, in other matters, he most wished to oppose. Although defence against the Turk was important to all Christendom and to the German nation, yet Ferdinand, as King of Hungary, could not but appear to be the first object of their attack, a situation which weakened his position very seriously in dealing with the German Estates. All the same he showed himself far more unbending in religious matters than his brother. Charles's councillors, partly under the influence of Erasmus and his worldly knowledge, partly under the effects of their unlucky experiences with the Pope, but above all out of a misunderstanding of German affairs, were extremely hesitant. The imperial propositions arrived late and, in their place, Ferdinand read out his own far less conciliatory suggestions in Charles's name. This error hampered the negotiations of the Diet.

First and foremost among Ferdinand's propositions was the condemnation of the way in which the recess issued at Speyer in 1526 had been interpreted. The Estates had taken it to mean that they had each the right to make what religious reforms they chose. Ferdinand now specifically denied them any such right. Moreover Ferdinand demanded that the old religion be tolerated in all states, a demand which ran directly counter to the growing need for spiritual uniformity felt in these lands. He forbade all innovations and threatened not only the Anabaptists, but the Zwinglians with total annihilation. This last attack aroused several of the powerful cities of south Germany, who felt themselves in sympathy with the doctrine of Zurich.

The answer of those affected was the Protestation of April 19th, 1529. By this the German princes and towns, openly and by name, ranged themselves on the defensive, basing their position on a principle formulated by the Saxon Chancellor, Brück. This was as follows: 'In matters concerning God's honour and the salvation of our souls, each man has the right to stand alone and present his true account before God. On the last day no man will be able to take shelter behind the power of another, be it small or great.' This was signed by the Elector of Saxony, by the Landgrave of Hesse, by Margrave George, by the Prince of Anhalt and the ambassador of the dukes of Luneburg, as also by the representatives of sixteen towns.

Those who protested, the *Protestantes* as they were afterwards to be called, placed themselves at once outside the protection of the majority in the Diet, which had hitherto been held together by many selfish or unselfish motives. Hitherto there had been scattered opposition to different elements in the constitution of the ancient Church and it had been possible to play off one section by appealing to another. Now everything was changed. One small group of just men, fully conscious of their own advanced and dangerous position, had separated themselves from the mass. As early as April 22nd, feeling the danger and the need for further consolidation, a number of these *Protestantes* formed themselves into a league, by which each bound himself to give help to the other should he be attacked on account of God's Holy Word. These allies were the Elector of Saxony, the Landgrave of Hesse, the towns of Strasbourg, Ulm and Nuremberg. The others held back. Although they bridged over all distinctions for the time being by an insistence on the Word of God, there were differences of doctrine even among these first allies. Had they but held fast to those things which all believed in common, they might have formed the nucleus of that great but still unformed union of 'Evangelicals' which was to be of universal significance. It could not rest, as did the Roman Church, on tradition, but rather on that other foundation of the Christian ethic — on conscience and the Holy Scriptures, the foundations on which Luther himself had built at Worms.

Yet these foundations were in themselves to be productive of the widest differences of opinion and the bitterest schisms. It is all the more comprehensible that the Protestants began at once to search for other and more definitely formulated principles on which to found their creed.

Here the danger lay in precisely the different direction. They were faced with the appallingly difficult task of finding general formulae which would cover not only whole systems of already established doctrine, but satisfy even those intense personal convictions which they had drawn from the Scriptures. It was amazing in itself that even the clear-sighted and energetic Landgrave succeeded in so far overriding personal doubts that he managed to collect a considerable convocation of theologians from all Germany at his castle at Marburg at Michaelmas 1529. He had representatives from Wittenberg as well as from Zurich, and by insistent pleading he overcame even Luther's unwillingness. Looking at his achievement in the light of modern research, it is even more astonishing to find that his labour was not altogether in vain. Their irreconcilable differences over sacramental doctrines did not prevent the deputies from growing more friendly in the course of debate and they left Marburg in almost brotherly good-humour. 'Our friendly talks at Marburg are at an end, and we are in agreement on almost every point,' wrote Luther to his wife on October 4th.

It is consoling to reflect, for those who have any belief in what can be achieved by good will, and it is important to remember in apportioning the blame for what happened later, that there was no breakdown in the Protestant group at the Landgrave's castle. The breakdown came later, in December, at Schmalkalde, where the allies had gathered for a political discussion. Here the deputies sent by the Elector of Saxony, by Margrave George of Ansbach, and by the city of Nuremberg, clung wantonly to their own older confession of faith. Words were spoken in anger. The Landgrave strove in vain to still the elements. Jacob Sturm, Burgomaster of Strasbourg, himself a man of deep theological knowledge, besought his temporal colleagues of Saxony and Brandenburg, at a special meeting, not to provoke fresh quarrels among the preachers. But the Elector himself was deaf to reason. 'The towns who think wrongly on sacramental doctrine', he announced, 'sin knowingly against God's word and therefore against the Holy Ghost; this is a crime to which no other sin, merely committed out of ignorance, can be compared.' And the Margrave's Chancellor, Vogler, who at an earlier date had issued warnings against 'confining our consciences to such narrow limits', now wrote 'that we cannot with clear consciences come to any understanding with those who are in ignorance, nor can we agree as to what embassy to send to the Emperor'.

On these two rocks — religious agreement and a common protest to the imperial government — they foundered.

'Greater Germany' and the European Protestantism of the Landgrave had to give place to the imperial policy of the Elector of Saxony. This policy, which was ever more sharply defined, had no object save to secure toleration for the straitest Lutheranism. It aimed at independence, but peace with the central government. The Elector John had not had his title confirmed by the Emperor although he had reigned since 1525. He was injured too because he had been allowed to play so small a part in the business of Otto von Pack. Even before the Diet of Speyer he had tried to draw imperial attention to himself by sending an ambassador to Charles at Barcelona. The result of this embassy was depressingly meagre; Charles said that he could decide nothing until he came back to Germany. In the meantime the Elector had been drawn into closer sympathy with the imperial Court by an alliance with the Count of Nassau-Dillenburg, brother of Charles's chamberlain, Henry of Nassau. Count William of Nassau-Dillenburg, the father of William the Silent, leaned towards the Reformation, but in his perennial conflict with Hesse he sought the help of Saxony. At a meeting at Arnstadt in February 1530 he pressed the Elector to inform Charles at the next Diet of all that was happening in the Protestant movement. His brother, he said, would further his cause with Charles. The imperial summons to a Diet on April 8th which the Elector had just received, seemed to bear out Count William's optimism. The Emperor, so it ran, was determined 'to hear the opinions, advice and point of view of each one of the princes in all charity and affection'.

So it happened that when Hans Dolzig, the Elector's representative, accompanied by the Counts of Nassau and Neuenahr, and armed with important instructions, set out to meet Charles, he came with the definite intention of abandoning the other Protestants. The Elector, who had set out early for Augsburg, thought of going on to meet Charles at Innsbruck in person. But the Emperor behaved with a greater show of tact than the meddlesome prince: it was highly unsuitable, he said, to enter into private engagements with single states before the Diet.

The division in the Protestant ranks was clear to every eye.

THE DIET OF AUGSBURG, 1530

Such was the situation when Charles, now fully crowned Holy Roman Emperor, reached Ausgburg by way of Innsbruck in June 1530. At Innsbruck he met his brother Ferdinand and his sister Mary of Hungary. Here, too, he met his brother-in-law Christian of Denmark. This latter now shamelessly declared that he had lived for the whole of his past life in falsehood and sin, and was received back into the bosom of the Roman Church in the presence of the Papal legate Campeggio — all in order to gain Charles's help for the reconquest of his northern kingdoms. On the previous February 8th, at the Treaty of Lierre, he had promised to hold his crown and kingdoms as the Emperor's vassal. He promised to submit himself in future to Charles, the Archduchess Margaret and King Ferdinand, to remain true to the Catholic faith and to restore his lands to the papal fold if he should be restored to them. He would prove himself moreover a true ally both on sea and land against all Charles's enemies and above all against the Turk. He would also guarantee freedom of trade to the Emperor's subjects throughout the north.

Even greater hopes now beckoned to Charles. How splendid it would be if England too lay at his feet! Henry VIII was so set on his divorce that he was sparing no pains to get theological and legal approbation for it. He sought Charles's agreement above all, for he knew that the Pope's decision depended on that. At Christmas 1529 he had informed the imperial ambassador Chapuys that he would admit imperial suzerainty over England if Charles would but remove his objections to the dissolution of the marriage. Charles accepted the humiliation of the Danish King because it was in the direct line of his policy. With England it was different: he felt the injury to his own family far too deeply to agree, even for a moment, to Henry's suggestions. On the contrary he wrote at once to the Empress in Spain — his first letter since his arrival in Germany — bidding her summon with all possible 'care and activity' the theologians, lawyers and men of learning from the universities to defend the cause of his aunt, the English Queen.

In Germany itself, however, he was to face a much more serious test. His attitude towards heresy and heretics had not sensibly altered since the Diet of Worms. But this time he did not face a single heretic, but a group of states who had entered into what was virtually open revolt, not so much by their dogmatic attacks, as by the innovations they had introduced in the outward forms of religion within their lands and in their refusal to obey either the Edict of Worms or the decisions of the Diet. Even for the Emperor the problem had thus entered the political sphere. And in politics there was room for negotiation, restraint and the exploitation of opportunity. Even earlier Charles had made strange suggestions — as that the Edict should be suspended, or that indemnity should be offered as a reward for political help. Even now opinions as to the best way of dealing with the problem hung in the balance.

Charles might either negotiate or proceed at once to force. Or he could combine both forms of action, as Loaysa suggested; he could attack those who were in arms while at the same time winning over princes and theologians with gifts and fair words.

'Force alone', said Loaysa, 'suppressed the revolt against the King in Spain; force alone will put an end to Germany's revolt against God.' There was however yet a third alternative: a council might be summoned. But this last alternative was in the Pope's hands to decide and his hatred and fear of a council was no secret. At the height of Charles's struggle with Clement, his advisers had therefore been most insistent in their demands for a council. Charles himself had wanted it, because as guardian of the Church he foresaw that he would play an important part. When he informed the Pope in July 1524 that he had forbidden a national gathering in Germany, he advised him to forestall such a meeting by himself calling an international council. At that time he had gone so far as to add that 'since the Germans asked that the council might be called in Germany, His Holiness could fix on Trent for the place of meeting as the Germans held this to be a German town although it was over the Italian border'. Later, he added, the place could be altered. When the Diet of Speyer had been called in 1526, an understanding between Pope and Emperor for the calling of a council had been announced, There was talk at the imperial Court from time to time of a national council in Germany. But on December 23rd, 1528, when Charles sent his propositions for the second Diet of Speyer to his brother, he added a letter in which he declared that he had given up all idea of a national council, 'for the more the German nation is together, the more will it increase in its errors'.

The signing of the Peace of Barcelona with the Pope had certainly been made no easier by Charles's reserve in dealing with this question. The Pope declared that he would be ready to 'meet' the Germans in some other way — this declaration was to become an important catchword. Charles stated in his memoirs that he did not again mention a council until he met Clement at Bologna; his correspondence with Loaysa and the Pope confirm this statement. In general the Emperor and his advisers now openly felt that a general council must be called to satisfy the Germans; but in the meantime they expected those who had 'fallen off' to return to the usages of the ancient Church and to agree to submit to episcopal jurisdiction. As far as the German Protestants were concerned, this was of course out of the question.

All now depended on the personal impression which Charles made at the Diet.

At Innsbruck the Hapsburg brothers and their ministers completed their preparations for the meeting. Besides Granvelle, Charles had the two secretaries of state, Cobos and Perrenin, with him. Ferdinand had his Chancellor Cles, and Mary was accompanied by her own advisers. The papal legate, Cardinal Campeggio, handed over a highly challenging memorandum to the Emperor, but on the whole opinions in his surroundings were fairly unanimous.

From Innsbruck the Court proceeded by way of Munich to Augsburg, where the princes were expectantly waiting. This time the eloquent Elector, Joachim of Brandenburg, as well as Duke George of Saxony had come. The imperial summons of January 21st had briefly outlined the purpose of the meeting. They were met to 'settle disputes, to commit previous errors to the mercy of our Saviour, to hear, understand and weigh the opinion of each man with love and charity, and thus come to live again in one Church and one State'. It sounded hopeful enough, since Charles admitted his intention of stretching out his hand to 'unite all opinions into one undivided Christian truth and to put an end to all such things as had been enacted unjustly towards *either* side'.

Yet Charles's first active measures hardly bore out this declaration. On July 8th he wrote to his wife: 'I came through Bavaria, where the Dukes, my true friends and servants, received me well. I entered Augsburg on the vigil of Corpus Christi (June 16th) and was solemnly received by Electors, princes and ambassadors. On the following day they held the procession which had been discontinued for some years. I took part in it as usual. And, although some of the Lutherans refused to take part, I was well accompanied for those who stand firm in the faith outnumber by many those who do not. We have already started on the religious question and are tearing out heresy by the roots. Far the most dangerous people in this town are the chaplains of the Lutheran princes. Therefore I have proclaimed that, under penalty, no one shall preach who has not been selected by me. This proclamation was unanimously accepted. This is a good beginning. The Diet opened on June 20th, and the propositions were divided into three heads. The first and most important is the religious question. The second deals with Hungary and the Turkish trouble. The third concerns the government of Germany. I pray God that all will fall out according to his Holy Will.'

In these words Charles gave a superficial summary of what had in fact taken place during his first days in Augsburg.

Under the surface a cautious desire for mutual friendship, a defiant spirit of independence, and an honourable desire to preserve ecclesiastical unity and imperial peace, struggled one with the other. The adherents of the old faith were better armed and more emphatic in their demands. This was not only true of the legate; the German theologians and bishops had been roused by Ferdinand's vigorous challenge in the previous January to take stock of the heresy and of its evil results. As a result of these activities, a Professor of Ingolstadt, Doctor Johannes Eck, handed over to the Emperor a paper, dated March 14th, 1530, and containing four hundred and four articles of primary importance to the Catholic Church. At Augsburg Melanchthon too saw these articles, and they probably had some effect on his thoughts when, at the command of his Elector, he sat down to formulate the celebrated Confession of Augsburg.

Both parties, therefore, stepped fully armed into the lists. On June 25th the Elector John of Saxony, the Margrave George of Brandenburg, Dukes Ernest and Francis of Luneburg, the Landgrave Philip of Hesse and Prince Wolfgang of Anhalt, together with Count Albert of Mansfeld and deputies from the towns of Nuremberg, and Reutlingen handed over the Confession in the form in which Melanchthon had drawn it up. The Landgrave was somewhat doubtful in his support. The cities of south Germany had withdrawn; only a little later did they, too, come into the open with the Confession of the Four Towns, the so-called *Tetrapolitana*. Charles did not personally receive this Confession of faith, no more than he did that drawn up by Zwingli, the *Ratio Fidei*.

All the same it was a great moment. To the political group of *Protestantes*, formed in 1529, was now added the religious group of those who subscribed to the dogma of the Augsburg Confession. True to the character of this confessional movement, which we have now traced from its source, the Diet slid from the political back into the religious sphere, and developed into a national meeting for the settlement of the religious problem. Only Charles reserved to himself all final decisions, strong in the support of a Catholic majority.

The Confession was specifically addressed to the Emperor, to whom the signatories offered all due reverence. Its twenty-one articles laid down the fundamental points of the new doctrine and repudiated all rival and opposing dogmas. The doctrines relating to the position of the Church and to sacramental beliefs were here clearly expressed, along with articles relating to free-will, justification, good works, and the worship of the saints. The new Church recognized itself as a form of temporal government under God's will and decisively denounced the Anabaptists. It declared that it most warmly supported the idea of the vocational mission of the clergy towards self-discipline and the more arduous good works. Other articles were added to the main body of the Confession dealing with subjects over which 'there is some difference of opinion'. These justified the alterations which had been introduced 'so that His imperial Majesty might see that we have not acted unchristianly and blasphemously in this, but only as being forced thereto by God's commandment'. Among these articles we find the administration of the sacraments in both kinds, marriage of priests, the mass, the confessional, the doctrine of the lesser good works, fasting and the monastic vows. Last of all the Confession discusses episcopal power — in reality the most important question of all. For in this the Papacy was included, although it was never named. The Confession declared emphatically for the separation of temporal and spiritual power. In this context it is fair to remember the political nature of the onslaught on the spiritual princes. The Confession admitted the key power of the Church but only in the spiritual sphere.

In spite of this we must not underestimate the theological kernel of the whole business; for indeed the Lutheran movement would not have been in vain had it had no other effect than to force the ancient Church to recognize doctrines and usages in which the peculiar qualities of Lutheranism might have found expression. Judging from the purely oecumenical standpoint, Melanchthon's far-reaching desire for compromise is not to be undervalued; it was paralleled by the mediatory offices of the Emperor's learned advisers and by renewed efforts on the part of

Erasmus. Once again both sides had appealed to the great scholar of Rotterdam. And at Court Mary, the widowed Queen of Hungary, was not unsympathetic to the advocates of moderate reform. There was room to hope for some alleviation of old wrongs, and above all for the renewed unity of Germany.

But the development which was to prove so important in the history of the world fell out otherwise. The universal rule of the Church was shattered and the German state sanctified and unified only through conflict with the ancient universal idea. As far as men, individually, were concerned, the religious and ethical principles of the Reformation were only saved and put into practice through the creation of a new ecclesiastical structure. Luther was in so far superior to Melanchthon that he recognized the impossibility of reconciling his fundamental doctrines with the continuance of the old authority. His clear insight found its warmest and most impassioned expression in the letters which he wrote from Coburg during these weeks when the theologians assembled at Augsburg were trying, by means of discussion, suppression of inessentials and compromise to patch up an understanding with the Roman Church.

After receiving the Confession at the end of June, Charles called a council of his advisers and presented three alternatives to them. The first was that the Confessors should be asked to submit themselves to the imperial judgment. If they refused, the second alternative was to offer a council, asking them in the meantime to desist from innovations. Should this alternative succeed, it was to be hoped that the Pope would begin by condemning the abuses within the Church. If both these alternatives failed, then the third way was — to use force. But first Charles attempted to get his way in peaceful fashion.

The Emperor and his councillors were anxious to reach an understanding with the Protestants because they were most keenly aware of the internal and external difficulties in the way of a general council. They were no less aware that with the Turkish menace on the border and the problems of Europe but indifferently solved, an appeal to arms would be no less risky. Thus Charles himself mitigated the tone of the answer which the Catholic theologians, Faber, Cochlaeus and Eck, had prepared to the articles laid down in the Confession. Only after it had been repeatedly re-drafted did the Emperor, on August 3rd, hand over to the Estates the completed result, the so-called *Confutation*. The efforts at mediation continued until August 30th; they had lasted for two months in all, being committed first to a select group of fourteen, four princes or councillors, and three theologians from each side, later to a smaller group of six. Charles himself took an active part. The climax was reached when Melanchthon had a personal conversation with the papal legate — naturally in vain. As early as June 28th, however, the Protestant princes asked Melanchthon to thank the legate for favouring peaceful discussions rather than war — so deeply indeed was the need for peace felt on both sides. Melanchthon's answer to the *Confutation*, however, the *Apologia*, resumed the freer tone of definite opposition. Very gradually the two parties began to drift apart once more.

Charles did not fail to exploit all the possibilities of the council. His correspondence with Loaysa is full of such considerations. On July 14th he appealed personally to the Pope, with a pointed reference to 'those things which I arranged with Your Holiness at Bologna'. This letter exists to-day only in a copy of a draft but the style, with its numerous repetitions and the emphasis laid on one ruling principle, proves that the original must have come from Charles's pen. The assumption is strengthened by Campeggio's reference in a note to Salvati to a letter written by the Emperor.

Charles wrote that he found some of the German princes in great fear, others on the contrary, very stiff in their determination. But, he went on, all were alike in desiring a new and better order than the present, and in thinking that it would be wisest to offer a council, at a time and place to be generally decided on, to satisfy those who had fallen into error. In the meantime, these latter would of course have to abandon their practices. The worser sort wanted the council, he thought, chiefly in the hope of making something out of it. The good, however, felt that it would prevent worse developments and stop the Church's more doubtful opponents from drifting away because of its undue postponement. The good were losing courage, the bad growing ever bolder. The chief blame for the failure to call a council would be laid to his charge and to the Pope's. But if they were to call it they would gain great advantages over the heretics, who 'in the intervening

time will have to live according to the old faith and to submit
to a council held in accordance with it'. 'Something good',
Charles went on, 'is certain to be decided. If the heretics refuse
so generous an offer they will have everyone against them. But if
there were to be no council,' — here Charles became prophetic —
'Germany, the strongest and most warlike nation in Christendom,
would fall into the gravest peril. At present the world is at peace
so that a council can easily be called to prevent the further
breeding of schism. If it should again come to war, then at the very
worst we could dissolve the council. We then, Your Holiness and
I, would have done what we could and others would have to bear
the blame. God, I hope, would then punish those who were
answerable for the evils which would fall on Christendom.
Therefore I entreat and beseech you to consent to the council,
so that we may avoid the burden of blame and win the approbation of all good men. It would be best if Your Holiness would in
the meantime do your own part and get rid of such abuses as
can readily be stopped. As the situation now stands, that would be
a great help.'

On July 31st Clement answered Charles's letter with the
greatest reserve. In spite of admonition and entreaty he was
wholly opposed to a council. In the second half of August, when
the prospects of settlement in Augsburg seemed at their most
hopeful, Charles plied him again, with hints rather than with an
open demand. But he did not complete the final draft of his
answers to Clement's letter until October 30th. He, too, remained
steadfast in his opinions.

About this time Christoph Amberger painted his portrait of
Charles. Looking at this picture, one feels almost as if one were
spying on the Emperor during one of those theological or politico-
ecclesiastical discussions. He sits there as if intently listening,
the index finger of his right hand inserted between the pages of a
book which he is about to open. His dress is simple yet rich; in
the left hand, on one finger of which he wears a costly ring, he
holds a glove. The face is pale, crowned with blond hair, the
blue eyes gaze as if into the distance. The mouth, with its unhealthy lip, thrust out unbecomingly, is eloquent of pride. But
there is seriousness and depth of feeling in the attitude and
features.

By this time Charles had begun to despair of the peace policy which he had so honourably attempted.

In fact the quarrels of Germany were not now to be reconciled. Feebly indeed, in the midst of this deafening clamour, sound the words of Erasmus. With the layman's piety natural to him, with his native common sense, he still preached the doctrine of peace at any price and repeatedly besought the warring factions not to take the occasion so seriously: heresies had disappeared before and would disappear again. His intellectual cleverness, which found a natural resting place in the wide humanity of the Christian faith, strengthened the already existent tendency of the Court towards mediation and discussion. But as each party, with deadly earnestness, approached the main issue of the conflict, the split between them widened. How could John of Saxony, who had shown himself so unreasonable even to his co-religionists at Schmalkalde, yield now to the Catholics on any question of fundamental importance? How could the Pope and the alliance of Catholic princes give in an inch, after defending their position with such vigour for so long? How could Charles abandon a position he had once taken up? Granvelle was cynic enough to think that the request which Charles made to the Protestants, that they should desist from their innovations until the council met, was like that command of Solon to the Athenians, that they should not alter his laws until he returned — when he well knew that he would never return. In this Granvelle showed himself out of sympathy with Charles's deeper motives.

It is unfair to label Charles 'Roman' or 'Spanish', unfair to represent him as cool or calculating. His worldly and spiritual duties were to him alike sacred: what he owed to his ancestors and to his own position as a ruler was inextricably connected in his mind with the idea of religious orthodoxy throughout the world and of universal empire. But he had furthered the council which the Pope abhorred and asked time and again for reform: in this he showed himself a true disciple of Ximenes, Adrian and Gattinara. This time, however, his pride was injured because his active efforts to win over theologians and princes came to so little He forgot that he had had sound political reasons for starting the discussions and could think of nothing but his failure. Since the way of peace had led to nothing, he saw but one other

CHARLES V
aged 32

alternative. The Protestants had refused his mediation and made light of his council. Nothing was left but force.

The demands of the Catholic Estates finally loosened his tongue. He dismissed them on September 8th in a document which, in the original French, was certainly of his own composing. He even superintended its translation into German under the care of Ferdinand and the Count Palatine.

The Elector of Saxony and his supporters, he declared, had been willing enough to take advantage of his generous efforts at mediation, but they had not abandoned a single one of their articles, appealing always to conscience. He had not expected so serious a rebuff: his opponents would now have to remember that 'His Majesty was their Sovereign and immediate overlord and moreover Vicar of all Christendom'. He also had a conscience; he also had duties, both to his own honour and to his position as a ruler. His conscience would not let him abandon the ancient Christian faith, hallowed by long usage. He also had his soul's salvation to think of, and a greater responsibility towards Almighty God than any of them, the Estates, could boast. It did not sort with his honour to grant any more concessions on the fundamental points of religion, or to agree to independent innovations. Their conduct, he added, was all the more distressing to him, since it seemed that his very presence emboldened them to make demands more extensive than any which they had dared to make while the wars, now so happily concluded, had kept him far from Germany.

'But if His Majesty's goodness and mercy availed nothing', Charles pursued, then as a Christian Emperor and Catholic prince he would set his life and all he had on the vindication of his own cause and of the ancient and holy Catholic faith. In this he would call on the Electors, Princes and Estates, on the Pope himself, and on all Christian potentates to help him. Should the heretics agree to his proposition of a council, their case would be justly heard; otherwise they would have to answer his challenge. As for the lands which they had seized from the Church, he, the Emperor, as their liege lord and rightful owner of all that they had, demanded that it should be incontinently restored or handed over to imperial custody until such time as a council should meet. On all these points Charles sought the opinions of the Catholic Estates.

They answered him emphatically if briefly on September 12th. Baldly they declared that the recreant and obstinate were to be treated like notorious heretics, and deprived of all rights and privileges. But when Charles asked for a further elaboration of this view, they very cautiously modified their opinions. Negotiations, they said, ought not to be abandoned, and for the rest they agreed with the Emperor in everything. As for what active help they intended to offer, this was not touched upon in a single syllable. Only the clergy decisively opposed Ferdinand's plan for disposing of some of their property to pay for the Turkish war: warmly agreeing that the Empire must be defended, they showed little inclination to help in the work.

Comprehensibly enough Charles thought the Catholic princes chicken-hearted.

The rude intervention of the Elector Joachim of Brandenburg in the sessions of September 22nd and 23rd merely increased the timidity of the Catholics and the determination of the Protestants. Later, when the Estates drafted a recess providing for the calling of a council, the Protestants appealed to the gospels and refused to have anything to do with it. Meanwhile they had an answer to the *Confutation* ready to hand over, but neither the Emperor, nor Ferdinand, nor the Count Palatine Frederick would agree to accept it. The moment for negotiation, they were told, was now past. The time for action had come. Charles himself rose up in anger to answer their appeal to the Gospels. 'Did they mean by that', he asked, 'that he and the other Estates were enemies of God's word?' In spite of this attack the Protestants refused to budge. On September 22nd the Catholic Estates met alone. On the 23rd the whole Diet met, and the Elector Joachim, in the Emperor's name and that of the whole Empire, once again reproached the Protestants with their pride, with their arrogance in taking the Gospel as *their* justification alone, against all other peoples in the world. Emperor and Empire, he went on, were at a loss to conceive which of the Gospels had given them a right to seize the property of other people. As for the recess, it was far milder and more generous than they deserved, and had been designed to spare the German nation the worst consequences of their divisions. The Emperor, Joachim concluded, was indignant at the mere suggestion that the Protestants had an *Apologia* to offer him. As Vicar of the Church he had already pronounced his final judgment: he had allied himself with the Catholic Estates for the preservation of the truth.

These were unmistakable threats. They had been uttered in so uncompromising a tone as to provoke some trepidation as to their consequences even at Court; several of the Catholic Estates, the Electors in particular, thought it wisest to offer an apology to the Elector of Saxony! But their timorousness altered nothing.

Called in such high hope, the Diet broke up in shrill discord. The Landgrave of Hesse had indeed withdrawn as soon as the Catholic party produced its *Confutation*. He, too, felt that the hour for action was at hand. The Elector of Saxony, a man of very different temperament, took formal leave of the Emperor, although still in open disagreement with him. Only some of the princes' councillors and the deputies of the cities remained. The Catholics assiduously sought the favour of the towns, but even Augsburg, under the Emperor's very eyes, stood by its opinions — a bold action. All such Estates as had introduced the condemned 'innovations' repudiated the recess which was issued on October 13th. As a result on November 19th a final recess was drawn up in a yet harsher form. It was no more than a manifesto of the Emperor and the Catholic party — the only group 'who accepted this recess'. Their opponents were given until April 15th, 1531, to think over what they had done.

Stuffed with theology, the Augsburg recess of 1530 embodied the bitterest elements in Catholic opinion, much as they had come to the surface during the session. 'This doctrine,' they declared, 'which has been already condemned, has given rise to much misleading error among the common people. They have lost all true reverence, all Christian honour; discipline, the fear of God and charity to their neighbour — these are utterly forgotten.' This was the reason, they continued, that the Emperor had sought the help of the Catholic princes to restore the old faith and its traditional forms of worship. This statement was followed by a list of all such articles of faith and customs of worship as were to be respected, under pain of punishment. The imperial ban and edict of outlawry were invoked to protect the ancient Church in its entirety.

These provisions were to be executed by a mandate issued from the *Reichskammergericht*. One power only could give reality to this formality — naked force.

And after all these preparations nothing whatever happened. The Emperor and the Catholic princes, having uttered these blood-curdling threats, sank into peaceful inactivity. No more even was heard of that Catholic League which had been so vociferously advertised. At the height of his war fever, the most that Charles had done was to send orders at the end of September to his ambassador Muxetula in Italy, to see that the five or six thousand Spanish and Italian troops who had completed the reduction of Florence, be transported to Hungary and there kept in readiness for use in Germany. This action, received with delight by Campeggio and the Pope, had had no consequences. Clement's own hesitative efforts to raise money for the war had been even less successful. The Venetians commented maliciously on his failure and even Loaysa revised his opinions of the advisability of war. It was undoubtedly Charles's duty, he wrote to the Emperor, to eradicate heresy, but at the moment the obstacles in his path seemed to be insuperable. A council was the best way out, but the Pope and Cardinals would sooner see it in Hell. The Catholics were faint-hearted and the French appeared as usual disinclined to keep the peace. The King of England, meanwhile, would gladly make an alliance with the Devil to combat the Emperor. And so, he concluded, 'I dare ask Your Majesty, since you may quiet your conscience by thinking of these things, to make a settlement, be it good or bad, with these heretics, even as your brother has with his subjects in Bohemia'. For long after this Charles toyed with the idea of a compromise, even over sacramental doctrine, such as had pacified Bohemia.

Even had Charles acted with the violence which he threatened, it must for ever be a doubtful point, whether he could have defeated the Protestants. He could, however, have prevented them from making preparations for war both at home and abroad. They had now a formal Confession of Faith on which to build. They were not slow to act on the warnings which had been all too freely showered upon them at the Diet. Circumstances, too, played into their hands.

TRIUMPHS AND TROUBLES OF THE HAPSBURG DYNASTY

Ever since 1519, and more seriously ever since Charles undertook to go to Italy, there had been talk of Ferdinand's election as King of the Romans. By the ancient law of the Holy Roman Empire, such an election could only be held after the formal Coronation of the Emperor. This Coronation had now taken place. But the Golden Bull gave no warrant for the choice of a brother during the lifetime of an Emperor. Opposition, therefore, was rife and had to be stilled with bribes and favours. The religious opinions of the Saxon Elector presented yet another difficulty, for his colleagues refused to countenance his exclusion from the Election. The Elector of Mainz sent him an invitation. Charles forestalled all difficulties by sending to the Pope, with his usual formality, and gravely asking for two bulls of exactly opposite meanings. The first of these was to give the Saxon Elector permission to vote in spite of his heterodoxy. The second, to be dated a little later, was to forbid him to vote. This latter bull was, of course, only to be produced if the Elector voted against Ferdinand. Judging by the letter in which Charles asked for these documents, he was not altogether easy in his conscience about the business. In Rome they took it far more light-heartedly. Loaysa disadvised the second bull as probably unnecessary. But the Pope, on the persuasion of two richly bribed Cardinals, Pucci and Accolti, cheerfully conceded both. Besides its blatant dishonesty, the whole matter was a criminal surrender of Germany's hard-won imperial rights to the Papacy.

Cologne was fixed on for the place of election — men said because Frankfort had refused to sign the recess. But in his memoirs Charles gave another reason: plague was raging in Frankfort. On the receipt of the papal dispensation, the Elector of Saxony was again pressed to come, but he refused. Instead he protested formally against the election through his eldest son, John Frederick. Nobody mentioned the Golden Bull. They concentrated rather on Ferdinand's election oath, and when the main points of this had been settled, they chose him King of the Romans on January 5th, 1531. He undertook to protect religion and preserve it in its present form. This promise was far more serious now than it had been when Charles made it in 1520. In view of the Saxon protest, Charles once again laid the question before the Electors; this time he asked them whether they believed that, since the conciliar idea had failed, and the Protestants seemed likely to proceed to an offensive, a preventive war ought to be risked. In answer, the Electors repudiated the idea of war, but again demanded a council.

On January 11th Ferdinand was crowned at Aachen with traditional splendour. On March 12th Charles outlined the future policy for imperial government.

The Elector of Saxony continued to protest against the election and in general against the kingship of Ferdinand. He was strengthened in his indignation by events within the Catholic camp itself. Lewis and William of Bavaria, with whom their defeat in Bohemia still rankled, now joined the opponents of the imperial dynasty. Already in Augsburg Charles had had a painful scene with Duke William. Following this up the Landgrave of Hesse sent Schenk von Schweinsberg to Bavaria, while the Bavarian dukes sent Weissenfelder to the Elector of Saxony. In August 1531 the Bavarian Chancellor, Leonhard von Eck, met the Landgrave at Giessen, and on October 24th the two dukes entered into formal alliance with the Protestants at Saalfeld. Earlier in the year, Henry of Brunswick had secretly informed Charles of what was afoot.

Ferdinand's election had even more astonishing consequences in other directions. The tone of the recess, together with the threats uttered by the Elector of Brandenburg, caused the Protestants to think better of those minor doctrinal differences which had hitherto prevented their union. The Elector of Saxony first suggested that they should form a general alliance; then he grew nervous and dropped the project. But when he received his invitation to Ferdinand's election he scented a constitutional conflict in the wind and felt that he had best not be left alone to fight it out. Accordingly on the very next day, November 29th, he renewed the invitation to the Protestants of the Hessian and Saxon lands to meet at Schmalkalde.

In the meantime Bucer's much discussed negotiations with Luther had been crowned at least with political success. They had decided on a firm theological basis, common to them both, and had thus bridged the division between north and south, between towns and princes, which had so long prevented all progress. A new *activismus* submerged the old ecclesiastical and political belief in implicit obedience. In 1529 most thinkers had held approximately the same views on the right of subjects to rebel. Lazarus Spengler of Nuremberg denied that they had any right of resistance 'since the Emperor is our liege lord and master, ordained by God'. Even Luther held this view, in spite of his piteous outburst — 'Ah God, I am a child in such worldly matters.' But when the recess of 1530 was issued, he wrote very different advice in his *'Warning'*. 'Proceed then joyfully,' he advised, 'come what may, be it war or revolt, as the wrath of God shall decide.'

But the councillors laid even more solid foundations on which to build their new conception of the state; they put such words into the mouths of the princes, as that it was their duty, when faced by the Emperor's violent actions, 'to stand by our subjects and to defend our own against all comers'. While they spoke and acted thus, they naturally lost sight of the subtle distinction between purely defensive action and very different forms of procedure. On February 27th, 1531, after long negotiations, the *'Compact'* of Schmalkalde was signed. Those who subscribed to it were the Elector John of Saxony, the Landgrave Philip of Hesse, Duke Ernest of Luneburg, Philip of Grubenhagen, the count of Mansfeld, the prince of Anhalt and the deputies of Magdeburg, Bremen, Strasbourg, Ulm, Constance, Reutlingen, Memmingen, Isny, Biberach and Lindau. The *Protestantes* of 1529 had become the Schmalkaldians of 1531, and included the adherents both of the Augsburg Confession and the Tetrapolitana. Only the Zwinglians, in the true sense of the word, were left out.

Until that moment Switzerland had been the scene of the most violent political activity, but now events in that country moved swiftly to a close. Ill-feeling between Berne and Zurich weakened the position of both, and when the *Alte Orte*,[1] irritated at last beyond bearing by economic interference, struck out at the

[1] The *Alte Orte* were the three original cantons, Uri, Schwyz and Unterwalden, with the five other cantons which had joined the Confederation before 1353 — Lucerne, Zurich, Glarus, Zug and Berne. The *Alte Orte* which retained the Catholic faith were Uri, Schwyz, Unterwalden, Lucerne and Zug (TRANSLATOR'S note).

reformers, they found Zurich insufficiently prepared with either allies or troops. Without the help of the Hapsburg dynasty, which had seriously considered coming to their help, the Catholics won the victory. The battle of Kappel on October 11th, 1531, ended the soaring hopes of the Zwinglians; the Reformer himself was killed, his party defeated.

For the first time in history the towns of south Germany sorely needed the support of the princes. The Swabian League which had been for more than a generation their most important safeguard, broke down through religious cleavage. When the time came for it to be renewed, it had already split up beyond recall.

But this is to anticipate the future. We must return to those autumn days of 1530 to find Charles travelling from Augsburg, by way of the Rhineland, back to his own Netherlands. On his way he had news at Speyer that his aunt, the Archduchess Margaret, Governess of the Netherlands, had died on November 30th, 1530. Six months after the death of Gattinara, Charles lost this other prop of his youth. It is unnecessary to sum up her life; these pages are sufficient proof of that feminine sensibility and virile energy which were so well mingled in her. The daughter of an Emperor and a Princess of Burgundy, she closed her eyes for ever to the world in that same proud and fearless spirit in which she had lived. On the very day of her death she had written to Charles. 'At this hour', she dictated, 'I cannot write to you with my own hand for my conscience is now at rest and I am ready to accept all that is yet to come from God's hand. My only sorrow is that I shall not see you before I die. This is my last letter. To you, as my only heir, I leave the lands which were entrusted to me. You will find them not only unspoiled but greatly increased, after a government for which I hope to receive God's reward, your contentment and the gratitude of posterity. I commend to you above all the policy of peace, with England and France in particular, and I beseech you not to forget my servants. With these words I bid you my last farewell.'

Once again Charles entered the ancient realm of Burgundy, the home of his early years, now so sadly empty of those whom he had loved. On December 5th, 1531, he held a solemn Chapter of the Golden Fleece, the first for many years. The last had been in Barcelona in 1518. Twenty knights had died since then, and new elections were urgent. He chose Tournai for the meeting place because the Church of St. André was large enough, and besides there was the abbey next to it. The deeds of all the knights, even of the sovereign, were as usual examined at this meeting. After the preliminary compliments the Chancellor of the Order declared that the Chapter were unanimous in thinking the Emperor too slow to act in affairs of state; he cared too much for trivialities and let greater matters pass; he consulted his council too little and had allowed it to dwindle too much; he had not appointed enough suitable men for the administration of justice; he paid his servants badly. Faced by the same accusations fifteen years later, Charles answered humbly, as he did now, that hitherto his sloth had brought him nothing but advantages.

The new knights now created included the Kings of Portugal and Scotland, the three-year-old prince Philip of Spain, the electors of the Palatinate and Brandenburg, the dukes of Julich and Saxony, the Count Palatine Philip, the Viceroy of Valencia, the dukes of Frias and Albuquerque, Francisco de Zuñiga, Count of Miranda; three Italians were also included, Ferrante Gonzaga, the Marquis del Vasto and Andrea Doria, prince of Melfi. To represent the Low Countries among the new knights, Charles selected Schenk von Tautenburg who had long since proved his merit, and Louis de Praet, of whose services to the Emperor we need no reminder; to these he added Antoine Berghes, Philippe Lannoy, Charles Lalaing and various other members of the younger generation.

Of more essential importance in these lands was the choice of a successor for Margaret. Charles decided on his sister Mary, the widowed Queen of Hungary, a young woman of twenty-six years old. Early put to the test, the Queen was already a self-reliant woman, not altogether free at that time from a leaning towards Protestantism in her Court, for which she was prepared to justify herself. Charles nevertheless proved his full confidence in her in the formal intimation of her new office, which he sent to her by the hand of Boussu. 'If I had doubts of your religious integrity', he said, 'rest assured that I should neither give you this place nor accord you the love of a brother.' He went on to say that such laxity was not for a moment to be tolerated in the

Netherlands, although it might have to be tolerated, whether he would or no, in the Empire. Charles felt that he could not exempt her from the necessity of making alterations in her already suspect household. On her side the Queen made conditions. She was not to be forced into any new marriage, she said, thinking no doubt of the questionable fortunes of her sister Eleonore, twice bestowed on an elderly widower, and her sister Isabella, the wretched wife of Christian II. In this respect she took Margaret for her model. She was indeed the equal of her great predecessor in industry and political sense, her superior in handling Charles. She took up her residence at first not at Malines but at Brussels; later on she spent much of her time at her castle at Binche.

On March 2nd, 1531, Charles opened the Estates General of the Netherlands with a speech written by Carondolet. The Estates answered him through Laurent de Beioul. Afterwards Charles spoke separately to the representatives of the different provinces. As usual they made every possible difficulty about raising money. Soon after, on March 4th, the Emperor met his sister at Louvain, and after spending weeks and even months discussing with her the problems of government in the Netherlands, inducted her into her new office on July 1st before the reassembled Estates General. He took Mary into his particular confidence, as he had done his aunt. On January 14th, 1532, for instance, he added a codicil to his will of 1529, in which he granted to Mary, in the event of his death, all those rights of regency and guardianship which he had originally guaranteed for Margaret. In this codicil, too, he spoke of uniting Pfirt and Hagenau with Burgundy, should his own daughter Mary marry a son of Ferdinand; this couple were then to inherit the Netherlands.

The nobility of the Netherlands were no less jealous of their influence than were the Estates of their privileges, and since Charles habitually demanded more of the Netherlands than he was able or willing to give them in return, Mary's task of government was to be no sinecure. Charles tried to lighten her task by altering the council of state, the *conseil privé* and the financial committee. He thought that the conflicts which had so often arisen under Margaret could be avoided if the *conseil privé* were able to meet without being specially called. But time soon brought new troubles to replace the old ones.

When Charles once more bade farewell to the Netherlands, Mary was left to face these alone. As the years went on they grew only more acute.

One of Margaret's heaviest burdens was her unwelcome Danish guest. His recklessness and its results cast a shadow over Mary's opening years. With five or six thousand soldiers, which he quartered in Overyssel and Holland, regardless of the people, Christian was now storming for the remaining portion of his dead wife's dowry, and asking Charles to provide him with 50,000 gulden and twelve warships for the re-conquest of his kingdoms. After gaining a little help from Norway, Christian at length put to sea on October 26th, 1531, and landed — whether according to plan or driven by a storm is not clear — a little south of Arendal on the Norwegian coast. In this country he easily regained the mastery, but he failed to reduce either the citadel of Bergen or the strong fortress of Akershus which overlooks Oslo. These remained permanent bases for his Danish opponents. Abandoning the contest he now took to negotiations.

There was no limit to the base deceptions to which Christian was prepared to stoop. Eighteen months before, he had done penance in Innsbruck and been received back into the Catholic Church. Now he wrote unctuous letters to his nephew Fredericke depicting himself as the champion of the Gospels.

Small wonder that the Lübeckers took him for a partisan of the Dutch to whom they immediately closed the Sound. They did not realize that threats alone had induced the Netherlands to help Christian, while Charles himself was far more interested in the return of the north to the Church, and in the inheritance of his sister's children than in the fate of Christian himself. The Lübeckers preferred their own interpretation of events, as it gave them the opportunity to keep their rivals out of the Baltic. This enmity of the Danes and the people of Lübeck drove the Dutch, willy-nilly, into Christian's arms. They were not averse to a royal alliance if it promised them any commercial advantage. Amsterdam, and the stadhouder of Holland, Count Hoogstraeten, were in favour of open war. Trouble in the Sound, together with a long drought, had caused a great shortage of bread; ships lay idle and there was serious unemployment. These facts hastened the intervention of the Netherlands. A preliminary discussion, fixed originally at Hamburg, was put off to June 24th and moved to Copenhagen; in the meantime the government of the Netherlands had prepared forty warships, so as to be able to support its negotiation with armed force.

All these preparations were brought to nothing by Christian himself. With incomparable folly and his usual thoughtlessness he accepted an invitation of the Danish government and its Hanseatic allies, to sail to Denmark and have a personal conversation with his nephew. His opponents guaranteed his personal safety. On July 24th he was at Copenhagen. In the capital, the Danes were already discussing with the representative of the Hanseatic towns, whether it would not be best to seize the deposed King. Almost at once they began to deceive him. They lured him to the strong castle of Sonderburg, saying that King Frederick was awaiting him there; he found no King Frederick, but he remained within that castle for twenty-seven years, almost until the day of his death.

At about the same time his son and heir Hans, a boy of twelve, died at Charles's house in Regensburg. Charles had as yet no reliable news from his brother-in-law, but his nephew's death touched him profoundly, drawing from him words of the deepest grief. Seldom indeed at any other time did Charles express so touching a sorrow. 'He was the nicest child I knew', he wrote to Mary. 'I feel his death like that of my own son, for I held him as such. He was already growing up, and we were very good friends. It must be God's will but I cannot help regretting that he should be taken from us. I could better have spared his father, God forgive me. Still, the little lad will be better off where he is. He died with so little sin to his account, that had he had all mine to bear as well as his own, he could not have missed eternal salvation. His last word was: Jesus.'

THE RELIGIOUS PEACE AND THE TURKISH MENACE. GROWTH OF PROTESTANTISM

Having gained nothing but the most mediocre subsidies, Charles now hurried back to Germany, in response to an urgent need.

324

He took with him a hundred and fifty cavalry. In his letters to the Empress he explained his reasons for going.[1] Not that these letters betray very much either of his conjugal relations or of his political opinions. The Empress seems to have exerted almost no political influence and her place in the Spanish government, where she had been given the clever, taciturn Archbishop Juan de Tavera, with his narrow Castilian outlook, for her chief adviser, seems to have been nominal only. Perhaps for that very reason Charles felt that he could give her exhaustive and highly confidential accounts of the events actually taking place in Germany, though it must always remain something of a mystery that he could keep his letters to so charming and so beloved a wife on this prosaic level.

Isabella had by this time given the Emperor two more children besides Philip, the heir to the throne. These were a daughter, the Infanta Mary, and a son who died almost immediately. She yearned for Charles's return, and implied it, although she dared not say it, in her letters. In an attempt to comfort her, he had written to her as early as July 13th, 1531, from Ghent telling her his plans for the future. He used the usual highly formalized style and dictated the letter to Cobos. 'Illustrious and all-powerful Empress!' he wrote, 'I have had to postpone some of my plans for this year, for I had hoped that some decision about a council might be reached, since the weal of Christendom hangs on it. But the Pope and the Most Christian King are still making difficulties which imperil the whole business. The postponement of the Council has had the worst effect in Germany. The Turkish menace has increased so much that I have even considered coming to an agreement with the Lutherans in order to prevent worse disaster, and coming home this year. It is my dearest wish to see you again and to be once more in my own home, not to mention the needs of my Spanish kingdoms. I have allied myself with my brother, the illustrious King of the Romans, and he has told me of the evil effects arising from the postponement of the council, and of how Saxony has refused to elect or crown him. All are agreed that I cannot for the moment be spared, and that I must stay and take control of German affairs. I have consented there-

[1] Hitherto almost unknown, these letters will shortly be available in a complete edition.

fore to make one more effort and have put off my return to Spain, although I hope not beyond **next March**.'

Ferdinand's urgent entreaty to Charles to stay longer in Germany was hardly surprising in the circumstances. The council had been indefinitely postponed, the Pope was unreliable, the King of France unfriendly, the King of England indignant; with the siege of Vienna two years before the Turkish danger had swept into the very heart of the Hapsburg lands; the Protestants had taken up a determined stand and were courting foreign alliances, a fact which the imperial Court cannot have ignored; the Catholics were faint-hearted if not actually hostile to the dynasty. In such a situation Charles's temporary wavering in favour of a religious compromise is no less comprehensible than Ferdinand's cry for help. The Emperor's representatives in Rome, Loaysa and Miguel Mai, strengthened Charles in his new attitude.

The imperial Estates, however many Protestants there might be among them, were indispensable in dealing with German affairs and, above all, with the Turkish danger; moreover they were willing to help. Luther himself still wrote of the Emperor as 'our dear Emperor Carolus', and declared that he had behaved so far, even at the Diet, 'so as to win the favour and love of all'. Luther, too, was in favour of united action against the Turk; nay, his great war-hymn — 'A strong fortress is our God' — had but recently been interpreted as a topical song directed at the ancient and evil enemy, the Turk. Besides, the Lutheran theologians had come half-way to meet the Catholics at the Diet.

The situation was indeed altered when Charles, instead of standing out for religious unity, sought their help in his distress. This was what now happened.

Schweinfurt, which had been the scene of the formation of the Schmalkaldic League in 1532, was also the scene of the mediatory efforts now made by the Elector Palatine and the Elector of Mainz. News from the Danube urged them to make haste. The Protestants knew their adversaries' peril and did not scruple to exploit it. The Elector of Saxony pitched his demands higher than ever before. He asked that Ferdinand's election be withdrawn, that all Church land which had been secularized be confirmed to its owners, that trials in the *Reichskammergericht* cease, that Lutherans be everywhere tolerated and that a free council of the German nation be convened. Neither side had ever before even so much as thought of some of these demands.

Worst of all, the adherents of the old faith, who were prepared to sacrifice nothing to help Charles, now effectively hampered even his mildest efforts at conciliation by an open statement issued on June 22nd. The Bavarian dukes were at this very moment concluding an alliance with the French King at the monastery of Scheyern; they had even opened negotiations with Ferdinand's rival in Hungary, John Zapolya, although this latter was known to be the Sultan's vassal, to have close relations with the Turks and to be under a Papal ban. At Regensburg, where the Diet had met in the meantime, the Catholics were in the majority; negotiations, even for a temporary religious peace, went on both here and at Schweinfurt and were later moved to Nuremberg. But the discussions proved as useless as they were lengthy. The Estates allowed themselves to become a party to the gravest injustice, by voting that an imperial mandate for the withdrawal of cases from the *Reichskammergericht* could only be issued to such Electors as were actually present, and could only be passed on by them to the Emperor by word of mouth. When, on July 27th, the Diet at length issued its recess, it was in flat contradiction to the detailed and highly modified religious mandates which were issued on August 2nd and 3rd.

In spite of all, a religious peace was patched up and an army against the Turks was set on foot. On August 9th Charles was able to tell the Empress that all the Estates, even the Protestants, had acted with equal zeal. Charles could now add to Ferdinand's troops under Katzianer and the German troops under the Count Palatine Frederick, his own soldiers from the Netherlands under Nassau and Roeulx, and his Italians under Leyva and the Marquis del Vasto. These last two were, of course, by far his most experienced and best commanders. The great moment was now at hand. All was ready for an attack on the Turk. After so many years it seemed that the oath made by his forefather at the *Fête des Faisans*, and the purpose for which the Order of the Golden Fleece had been founded, was at last to be fulfilled.

But while the Emperor was held up by the negotiations at

Regensburg and Nuremberg, the die had already been cast. The little fortress of Güns in western Hungary held out against the Turkish assault from August 7th until August 28th. This seems to have decided Suleiman to turn back. He may also have had disturbing news from the coasts of Greece, for Andrea Doria and his fleet were active there, and had seized Patras and Castelnuovo. In Styria, on September 13th, at Fernitz, German troops defeated the Turkish rearguard, and they had to withdraw from Graz with nothing achieved. But neither the complaints of the German generals at the slothful leadership of the Elector Palatine, nor the entreaties of Ferdinand, persuaded the imperial troops, or even his own Bohemians, to march farther into Hungary and contest his own cause against the usurper Zapolya. Winter was at hand and there was, as always, no money.

On September 23rd, just as the last military engagement was over, Charles entered Vienna. His troops had maintained their reputation in the few skirmishes in which they had been engaged and had brought in some Turkish standards: crowned with laurels, therefore, Charles entered the city to receive the acclamations of his people. He deserved this recognition, in part at least, because he was certainly the only ruling prince in Europe, besides Ferdinand, who had taken the Turkish danger seriously. At the beginning of October he went back to Italy by way of Styria and Carinthia, thence to return to his Spanish kingdoms, which he had not seen for four years.

He was not free of anxiety for his other dominions. He was a prey above all to worry about the council, which he now saw to be an absolute necessity if Germany were ever to be won back again. The council could not be called until Italy was satisfied, until the Pope agreed to prefer the interests of the Church to those of his family, until the King of France could be depended on to keep his treaties. All these postulates were doubtful.

THE LOSS OF WÜRTTEMBERG

Charles was hedged about by delay, withdrawal, indecision. Even in Germany the settlement was temporary, the outcome of immediate circumstance. Yet in spite of this, Charles now left the Netherlands for years to come in the sole care of his sister Mary, the Empire to Ferdinand. The administrative ordinance of 1531, with all its important economic and social measures, was issued in Charles's name; in his name too went forth the *Carolina*, the universal criminal code, based on the ancient traditions of German law. But Charles had no personal part in either of these measures. The true government of Germany was controlled by the Estates, the administration, the King.

Ferdinand was thus forced to meet the coming onslaught of the Protestants unaided. The German Reformation was already undergoing transformation into a European attack on the Hapsburg dynasty. The Catholic princes, the Bavarian dukes above all, had little inclination, either now, or later in the Thirty Years War, to minister to the omnipotence of the Hapsburg by intervening on their side in the religious conflict. They had no less a share of the blame than the Protestant rulers for the dismemberment of the Empire. Both parties were alike guilty of that worst crime of all, the making of European alliances.

All too soon the ill-effects of these were to be felt in Germany.

Assisted by the King of France, the princes now proceeded to their first successful attack on the imperial dynasty, and robbed them of Württemberg. Although it had but recently been won, Württemberg was of the greatest strategic importance. This importance might have been more obvious to the Emperor had his councillors in 1520 insisted more firmly on the significance of Württemberg as a bastion against the democratic ideas of the Switzers and the cities of south Germany. They had emphasized its importance in itself and they had hinted that it might be useful if France grew stronger, but this latter opinion would have gained a greater credence if it had been supported by the former contention. And as things now stood, these forgotten councillors, had they come back, could hardly have failed to hint that the Catholic Estates of south Germany were likely to need the support of some greater power. The Hapsburg had missed one excellent opportunity when they had failed to support the *alte Orte* of the Swiss Confederation against the Zurich reformers. Whatever the extent or importance of their help, it would have immeasurably strengthened their position in the very heart of the dynastic lands.

The opposing side now initiated an attack on the Hapsburg

position which was not only enormously to strengthen the Protestant position, but to mark the beginning of French intervention on the Upper Rhine. This French advance began with the demand for Mömpelgard in Württemberg in return for help in re-establishing Duke Ulrich, and ended with the engrossment of all Alsace. In the intervening years the Hapsburg dynasty had planted their standards in many lands, in Burgundy, Hungary, Spain and Italy; but they had forgotten and neglected their old hereditary lands and their cradle on the Upper Rhine.

The business of Württemberg was carried out openly. When in 1533 the Hapsburg dynasty attempted to renew the Swabian League, which had long been their ally and which they felt could be used as a support to the Catholic Church, they found that, after many long and wordy sessions, the sense of the meeting was — a refusal. The French ambassador, du Bellay, was present at the last of these sessions at Augsburg in 1533. He took an active part in all discussions of the Württemberg question. He behaved as though it was perfectly natural for him to intervene, and nobody apparently protested. It is true that Charles subsequently complained to France of this very unfriendly behaviour, but by that time it was too late to amend it. The French for their part judged the situation with unerring skill when they realized that, after fourteen years, the time had now come to restore the Duke. As early as March, Charles was forced to face the unpleasant fact that the King of France and the two Bavarian dukes had espoused the cause of young Duke Christopher of Württemberg.

In spite of the use of Christopher's name, both his supporters were well content that their efforts should ultimately be used for the restoration of the old duke, Ulrich, who, by religion and politics, was the natural ally of the Landgrave of Hesse. King Francis saw the Landgrave Philip at Bar-le-Duc at the end of January 1534, and, as Charles wrote in horror to Ferdinand, paid him his subsidies and gave him his orders. Troops were immediately raised, and after a slight clash at Lauffen on the Neckar, on May 12th-13th, the rebels were in possession of the duchy before the summer was well advanced. Ferdinand had too many other troubles to risk anything to regain Württemberg. Charles's help, first 50,000 and then 100,000 Gulden, came too late. It is difficult to understand why the imperial dynasty, which was prepared to fight a whole generation for Milan, accepted the loss of Württemberg so philosophically. In Germany it was a key position: it was the connecting link between Tyrol, Alsace and Franche Comté, the very heart of the ancient Hapsburg lands. But at the time of its loss both Charles and Ferdinand had too many troubles on their hands; Charles was absorbed in his plan for sending an expedition against Tunis, and he had, moreover, been long mentally estranged from any true understanding of German affairs.

Ferdinand made peace with the German princes at Kaaden, near Eger, on June 29th, and accepted in return for the loss of Württemberg his formal recognition as King of the Romans by the Elector of Saxony and his friends. This was an advantage which, at that time, he rated very highly. He also gained subsidies against the Turk. In the following year both the Landgrave of Hesse and the eldest son of the Elector of Brandenburg fought for him in Hungary. Besides these petty concessions, Ferdinand also retained a remote right over Württemberg, as a fief which might ultimately escheat to the House of Austria. In his letters to Ferdinand, Charles seems to have feared the continued alliance between the princes and the King of France more than any other danger, and he took the cession of Württemberg in good part. The 100,000 Gulden which he had set in motion with the help of the firm of Welser, for Ferdinand's assistance, was held back in case it should be needed for some other purpose.

The history of political Protestantism began at the Diet of Speyer. In the first ten years of its existence the movement, in spite of all its internal divisions, had increased enormously in strength. The Diet at Augsburg in 1530, to which they had looked forward with such trepidation, was now but a milestone on their path to power. No one had dared to put into execution the threats vainly uttered against them by the Elector Joachim of Brandenburg. Nothing had come of Christian's plan to restore Denmark by force to the Catholic Church. His successors, both in Denmark and Sweden, were consolidating the forces of Protestantism in the north. Unpalatable as were the accompaniments of the declaration of independence recently made by Henry VIII of England, that too tended only to strengthen the Protestant movement. In such circumstances the princes might well be emboldened to take up the offensive against the Hapsburg dynasty. They grew stronger as they waited, while the Catholic powers — Pope, Emperor, princes and the King of France — hindered and neutralized each other.

CHAPTER IV

UNIVERSAL POLICY

FOREIGN as were German politics to Charles's understanding, they were ultimately to become the dominating force in the shaping of his destiny. Within the Empire those elements which were to be his undoing gradually assumed shape and strength, while throughout Europe the gigantic changes, which were so soon to come, remained yet hidden. The political landscape was bathed in that brilliant yet unreal sunlight which foretells the gathering storm.

During all these years the Emperor's will-power had been slowly forming; he had emerged very gradually into the full mental strength of manhood. In the autumn of 1532 he had behind him a long series of victories, yet he had hitherto achieved no definite, final and altogether satisfying triumph. Solving the immediate problems in his path, he had but postponed the final issue.

He now owned the whole of Italy from Naples to Milan and Mantua. But the Florentines burned with vengeful anger against the Spaniards, and not the Florentines alone. Over all Italy the Spanish victory had served but to strengthen Italian sympathies for France. The Vatican, Florence, Venice, Milan, even the lesser states — all now looked towards the French. Trouble was brewing, too, in Montferrat, for the present Marquis was very old, and the hopes of all his neighbours, Savoy, Saluzzo, King Ferdinand, and the reigning family of Mantua, were fixed on his lands. They could not all be satisfied.

In Spain the years of revolution were over and the monarchy was firmly established. But the remote glories of the Germanic Empire satisfied the vanity rather than the immediate needs of the Spaniards, and the higher officials grew restive at Charles's long absence.

Germany enjoyed for the time being a religious peace which was the outcome of an idle compromise. No one was satisfied; some thought it not favourable enough to themselves, others too favourable to their opponents. The Turks had withdrawn: but the single valour of isolated fortresses, like Güns and Graz, had been more decisive in their defeat than the general mobilization which came too late. No decisive victory had been won, such as would hold the Turks in check for any length of time, and neither Ferdinand's negotiations nor his campaigning met with further success in Hungary.

The apparent peace was, over all Europe, but a thin veil for unfulfilled hopes and threatening dangers. During the ensuing years the web of European diplomacy was but a tangled mesh, deceptively concealing the tension beneath. There was no dominant power nor group of powers to give it strength and unity.

The immense size of his empire was at the same time the source of Charles's strength and of his weakness. That conglomerate of states, so far-spread and of such fabulous wealth as seemed a figment of dreams, rather than a reality, had a definite political existence as a corporate state and was, in its own time, as it is for posterity, the object of boundless speculations. The dominating power seemed to radiate from the Emperor himself to the remotest corners of his dominions, and, unrecognized by Charles himself, the intoxicating scent of Indian spices, the magic glint of Peruvian silver filled his surroundings and fired the imaginations of himself and his courtiers. The more confusing the relations of his lands and kingdoms, on this side or on that of the Atlantic, the more numerous the antagonisms and complicated the purposes in which his policy seemed to be submerged, the more necessary was it for him to maintain his own self-control, to stand fast by those maxims of conduct which he had laid down for himself. We have now reached the middle period of his life. Looking back and looking forward along that great career, we can see to what different forces he was a prey: inspired though his life and actions might be by a universal theory, he lay open nevertheless in the political sphere to the ceaseless onslaughts and insidious undermining of separatist elements; and in the personal sphere he had to fight against the anarchic power of individual self-will.

Let us therefore consider what the lands and ideas were for which he fought, and what were the theories on which he built the organization of his dominions, both old and new.

In the conquest of Mexico we have already witnessed one of those bold, ruthless and destructive movements, by which nevertheless a new world came into being — a *Conquista*. While Cortes was yet at work, Charles and his council had been troubled by the moral problems of the New World. They had played their part, too, in those problems of cosmography and commerce which arose from the first circumnavigation of the globe. In 1529 Charles had received at his Court in Toledo both Hernando Cortes and Francisco Pizarro. This latter was at the moment on the point of following the example of Cortes, with even less preparation and even more success. This second *Conquista* went on for many years, Charles's West Indian Empire growing ever larger. In deeds of valour and endurance, in alternating peril and success, defeat and victory, Pizarro's achievement was equal to that of Cortes. The men, by whom these two *Conquistas* were made, were for the most part Spaniards of that middle class which was composed of soldiers and uprooted landowners, men who had all to gain and nothing to lose. Yet from the first members of other social groups played their part, *Letrados* and clergy. There was that Bishop Bastidas, for instance, son of the first governor of Santa Marta, who was murdered; there was the lawyer Quesada who combined, strangely enough, the courage of the *Conquistador* with a true sense of justice. These two were borne along in the wake of the new movement. And, even at the beginning, Portuguese, Italians, Germans were to be found fighting alongside the Spaniards.

The *Conquistadores* advanced in the name of the all-powerful Emperor Don Carlos. In his name they demanded submission and the acceptance of Christianity. Like Cortes, the later *Conquistadores*, too, laid the vainglorious yet impressive records of their actions at his feet, many of them to be popularized throughout Europe in print, almost as soon as they were received. In Charles's name these restless, insubordinate governors of provinces, Captains-general and leaders of free-booting gangs, fought out their endless and eventful disputes with the royal officials in the Indies. Apart even from incidents arising out of the open defiance of orders, two adventurers setting out simultaneously from different points would often meet at the same supposed hiding place of fabulous treasure; then would be let loose the greedy passions common to men of all ages. Then would be enacted scenes worthy of nineteenth-century gold-diggers and twentieth-century diamond hunters. And yet, in the last resort these self-willed and violent men bowed before the will of the King of Castile, that King whom they now so proudly hailed as Emperor.

In 1526 the first royal *Audiencia* had been held at San Domingo. Since then Spanish exploration and Spanish conquest had spread out over the whole of the west Indian basin. At first they spread westwards; the idea of a trade route from east to west was for many years the chief directing force in the development of a whole continent. From Panama, in 1513, the *Conquistadores* saw for the first time that farther ocean which Magellan had not yet named the Pacific. But long before the isthmus had been subjected to rudimentary organization and Panama and Guatemala chosen as the seats of government (1532-43), New Spain or Mexico had been given a firm political framework; Nuño de Guzman held the first *Audiencia* on December 13th, 1527, and in 1528 Antonio de Guzman was appointed Viceroy. Cortes himself soon sank to a position of lesser importance beside him. All the lands forming the northern shore of the Gulf of Mexico, from Florida to the region of the first advance of Cortes, were now reckoned to the possessions of this latter government. Here, in the vast marshes of the Mississippi basin, in Alabama and Colorado, all efforts to make new settlements had hitherto come to nothing. That very Narvaez, whom Cortes had once so callously taken prisoner, had here attempted to penetrate in vain. Last remnant of his attempt, Alvaro Nuñez Cabeza de Vaca, with two companions, had wandered about the lands, living 'naked among the Indians, like one of them'. After six years he made his way back to Mexico, not without appalling hardships, in 1534, there to find how difficult it was to accustom himself once again to the dress of an ordinary Christian. In 1493 Alexander VI had granted a monopoly of power to the Kings of Castile and Portugal on the farther side of the Atlantic, and they themselves had confirmed the situation by their treaty of Tordesillas in 1494. But the North American continent had been invaded first by the

Venetian Cabot, in English pay, and later by the French following in the footsteps of their first explorer, Jacques Cartier. Thus Charles's first tentative efforts to press northward were an attempt to preserve his own monopoly.

The ports on the north coast of South America and the Pacific coast with Panama, now became the centres for expansion to the south. The nucleus state on the north coast was already known as Venezuela or little Venice, from the pile-supported buildings on the north shore of the lagoon of Maracaibo; it was subject to San Domingo. After several inadequately prepared attempts, the *Conquista* of this district was at last successful. Trivial as are the details of the achievement, they are interesting because of the part played by the Germans. The fact that Germans, too, were active in Spanish America is in itself a proof of the essential unity of Charles's Empire. As we have already seen, Charles depended on the capital supplied by the firms of Fugger and Welser in his military undertakings, no less than he did at elections. Both his own and Ferdinand's had been financed by one or other of these families. The sums of money needed to supply the men, ships and arms for a *Conquista* had to be very considerable and very heavily insured, but the firm of Welser of Augsburg was prepared nevertheless to finance one. No actual partner of the firm went to America, but they had agents and factors in Spain and at San Domingo, and these, with the help of the Ehingers of Constance, signed a contract with the help, and for the benefit of, certain German adventurers and settlers, among whom there were some women.

The Welser money found its way to Venezuela through the contract which their two agents, Heinrich Ehinger and Hieronymus Seiler, signed in the spring of 1528. The first clause dealt with the recruiting of German miners, and in fact twenty-four miners from Joachimstal did go to San Domingo. The next clause covered the importation of 4000 negro slaves by licence, — like that which had been granted to Laurent Gorrevod in 1518. Slave hunting within the land itself had already been proved inadequate. The next clause traced out the rough limits of the land itself; its eastern boundary was to be Cape 'Maracapana', of whose position they could be moderately certain, its western boundary the well-known pearl fishery of Cabo de la Vela.

The ancient nucleus of the province was the lagoon of Maracaibo with the wretched little port of Coro to the north-east, and a chain of mountains to the south; crossing these mountains to the south-eastwards, one came down into the valley of the Orinoco, which is Venezuela to-day, while crossing them to the south-west one reached the civilized lands of the Chibchas in Bogota. To get the best possible advantage from the commercial products of this new land, the Welser arranged that one harbour in the Atarazanas at Seville was to be kept clear for them. Heinrich Ehinger and Hieronymus Seiler entered into an agreement with the secretary of state, Francisco de los Cobos, at the same time, by which he took them into partnership with him, and promised them a due share of the percentage which he had been granted on each bar of gold and silver imported. This Heinrich Ehinger, factor of the firm of Welser at Saragossa, was the same man who in 1523 had bought up the largest proportion of the spices brought back from Magellan's ill-starred expedition. In 1530 he was *Argentier* and *Tesorero* to Charles V and he followed the Court as a knight of Sant' Iago. His brother, Ambrose, factor of the Welser at San Domingo, was the first governor of Venezuela. The new colonists set off almost as soon as the contract was signed, crossing the sea with Garcia de Lerma of Burgos, who was to be made responsible for Santa Marta on the western frontier.

Ambrose Ehinger at once devoted all his energies to his task. His object was to open up the hinterland and if possible to discover unknown gold-mines. His search did not prove altogether in vain, although in the end it came to nothing. He himself died early, wounded by a poisoned arrow.

But before he died an energetic competitor and successor had appeared at his side, in his lieutenant, Nicholas Federmann of Ulm, whose reports were printed twenty years later. Federmann had all the bold and unscrupulous spirit of the *Conquistadores*. Being incensed with the royal agent, Hernando de Naveros, who had been sent with him, he had him put in irons — an act which was not without consequences. To his justification be it said that the difficulties he faced were indescribable. He had to cross a pathless land, exposed throughout to the harassing attacks of the natives and of wild beasts, and hampered rather than helped by the fantastic geographical errors mapped out for him by the originators of the expedition. Terrible were the losses which the German colonists suffered. Moreover, Federmann quarrelled violently with Ehinger, broke off the relationship and returned to the Welser at Augsburg in 1532. Later, under their protection, he became governor.

But the colonists complained of his nomination and the home government displaced him for George Hohermut of Speyer. Nevertheless, Federmann ultimately succeeded Hohermut as governor. He then made the difficult journey across the mountains to Bogota; successful in itself, the voyage led to nothing, for two other suitors had reached that land before him. The most he could do was to appeal to the Spanish government to decide between them. Pedro Heredia of Cartagena on the north coast demanded the land; so did the Welser, who claimed that their governor, Federmann, had undertaken to conquer it; so did Sebastian de Belalcazar of Quito who had sent Pascual de Andagoya to conquer it; so did Hernando de Luga, governor of Santa Marta. It was in the service of this latter that Gonsalo Ximenes de Quesada had pushed his way up the river Magdalena, facing unutterable and uninterrupted peril from natives and alligators, hunger and exhaustion. The province, which is now Colombia, and was then New Granada, was in fact granted to the governor of Santa Marta, but the seat of the *Audiencia* was transferred to Bogota.

But the government exercised by Belalcazar at Quito extended only over a small district in the midst of the ancient Inca kingdom of Peru. And in the meantime, Pizarro, with amazing tenacity and heroism, had conquered that kingdom itself. On July 26th, 1529, the Empress Isabella had issued a mandate giving Pizarro power to effect the *Conquista*; Peru was to be the last addition to Charles's Empire made under an imperial mandate of this kind. Dominated by the heights of the Cordilleras, the ancient kingdom of Peru spread out to the east into the plain of the Gran Chaco, to the west as far as the gulf of Guayaquil, and as far north as Chile. It was on the west coast of the gulf that Pizarro first set foot. In spite of the road-system which united this gigantic country, the distances which the Inca government, no less than Pizarro, had to dominate, almost defy the understanding. How so vast an expanse could have been organized and controlled under a

339

comparatively well-administered and uniform law remains inexplicable. Yet this vast kingdom was a despotism, and proved true to Macchiavelli's theory of despotism, for it fell when its leader went.

Man for man, Pizarro was not the equal of Cortes, and in his handling of the ruler of Peru, he did no more than copy the horrible crime which had been committed by Cortes against Montezuma. Yet Pizarro's impudence was in itself heroic. Although he seems to have been tolerably well-informed of the size and power of the Peruvian kingdom, he set out from Panama in January 1531, with only 180 men and 27 horses. Such reinforcements as he received were in just proportion to his original strength. For the rest, everything was against him — the Spanish colonial officials, his own companions, naturally the natives. But he overcame all opposition by his dogged determination and his bold decision in moments of crisis. Within a few months he had conquered the kingdom. It would be tempting to attribute to these men something of the crude nobility of beasts of prey seizing on their natural victims, were it not that their cold-blooded and calculating wickedness forces one to recoil in horror at a vileness peculiar to mankind.

Pizarro had already led one or two unsuccessful attacks on the coast, and had for years previously attempted to penetrate into the interior. During this time he had found interpreters and gained a knowledge of the country. His companions, Almagro and Luque, were named with him in the imperial charter, but they brought him more trouble than help. On the other hand he had brought with him from Spain several of his half-brothers, some of whom were bastards like himself, and these were his staunch supporters. Pizarro seized the occasion of an internal dispute within the Inca kingdom to launch his attack. Huescar, by the tradition of his country the only legitimate son of the last despot, by a marriage with his own sister — a custom sanctioned by local law — had been deposed and imprisoned by a rival claimant, his half-brother Atahualpa. Yet in spite of this internal broil, Pizarro's action smacked of madness, when he rode up from the hot and richly vegetated coast-lands to the frozen heights of the interior, intent on the conquest of the land, with only 62 cavalry and 102 infantry in all. On November 15th he entered the town of

Cajamarca, whence he sent an embassy to Atahualpa. Here, too, he received messages in return. He had expressed the demands for allegiance now usual among the *Conquistadores*, and Atahualpa himself came out to meet him, magnificently apparelled and borne high in a litter among a following of many thousand.

Pizarro next, by an act of treachery, made the ruler of the land indebted to his power. He ordered his men to set on Atahualpa's followers, with drawn swords and fire-arms, while he himself protected their leader from bodily harm. Faced with this outburst of hideous force in his peaceful land, the despot of the Incas accepted it as an inevitable destiny. He declared himself ready to buy his freedom for a great sum of money, and when he was set at liberty to raise this ransom, he used his freedom to make away with his half-brother Huescar, so that Pizarro would have no opportunity of setting himself up as a judge between them. Pizarro was too clever for him; seeing that there might now be a serious rising among the people, he fanned the flame and Atahualpa was arraigned for his crimes, and sentenced to be burnt alive. Pizarro had just mercy enough, when the wretched despot agreed to be converted to Christianity, to have him strangled first and burnt only after he was dead.

This was in the spring of 1533. The conquerors now pushed on, and arrived at the capital, Cuzco, about the middle of November. Almagro stayed there. Pizarro returned to the coast and on January 18th founded the new capital, Lima. A younger brother of the murdered ruler, Manco, was set up as Inca, a kind of symbolic survival of the old government of the kingdom. But in fact all control was now in Spanish hands, and remained so even when those in power quarrelled so violently among themselves that the whole country became the scene of violent civil war between the conquerors. Almagro perished in the conflict. His men nourished thoughts of revenge, and years later on June 26th, 1541, Pizarro, too, was murdered. Only in the following year was the royal *Audiencia* finally established at Lima. The period of *Conquista* had ended, that of colonization had begun.

Pizarro's conquests came to their climax in the spring of 1533. It was then that Charles received the first, highly-coloured report of what had happened, of the successful 'campaign' in which Pizarro had defeated the Caciques and amassed a booty of more than 50,000 ducats. In this report Pizarro told how the Inca had come to see him, in a golden litter, his robes ablaze with gold and gems. Horribly and unconsciously accusing himself, he went on to describe how he had been surrounded by his trustful and peaceful followers, with music and dance. Later on, he added, the Inca had collected and given them his great treasure of gold dishes and ornaments, and had been astonished when the Spaniards fell upon them and smashed them to pieces. He did not understand that all they wanted was gold — just gold!

Later Charles received Pizarro's brother, Hernando, bringing with him more detailed dispatches and a part of the treasure itself. This meeting took place, with mutual contentment to both parties, on January 20th, 1535, at Catalayud in Old Castile. Charles cannot have had the faintest conception of the horrors which had been committed in his name. The charter issued by the Empress reflected the demands so often made by the council in Spain; it had enjoined on Pizarro the duty of upright administration and justice towards the natives.

GUIDING IDEAS

The immense expansion of Charles's power had little effect on the politics of Europe. But who can tell what effect it had on Charles's mind, and on the things which men now believed of him and his kingdoms?

His Empire was not united. Unlike the Imperium Romanum or the British Empire, it was not based on the strength of a single people. It had been brought together by the chances of political inheritance and bundled up regardless into a political whole. It included Burgundy and Spain, with all their component parts and their colonies, Italy and the German Empire. The Emperor and his family provided the only guarantee for the unity of all these lands. There was no united constitution and since Gattinara died there had been no single Chancellor: each land had its own. The council which advised Charles was his own council in a very personal sense, not a politically approved body, such as each of his kingdoms separately possessed.

Yet in each individual land, and throughout the whole extent of this great Empire, the idea of the dynasty was a force which made for unity.

The dynastic theory of rulership by inheritance had been accepted over all Europe. In so far, all states were alike. Even among the city states of Italy, only Venice, that strange hybrid of classical and byzantine tradition, and the tiny republican states of Siena and Lucca, had managed to combat the principle. Thus all Europe might be conveniently drawn into a great web, bound together by brothers, sisters, children, nephews, nieces of the Emperor. And this structure, in its completed form, had an essential value which was not to be reckoned merely in terms of generations and personalities. The conception might weaken national ties, but it had all the features of an international civilization. Trade and commerce, capital and labour, arts and sciences all pulled together, turning up many a fruitful furrow in the great expanse of the Hapsburg Empire.

Charles was now to follow the teaching of Gattinara to its logical conclusion, and in so doing he was to use the dynasty as his tool for the pacification of Italy. He intended his natural daughter Margaret for the new Duke of Florence. He determined to pin down the irresolute Duke of Milan by marrying him to his niece, the twelve-year-old Christina of Denmark. Only here he met with opposition. Queen Mary was beside herself. 'It is against nature and God's laws', she stormed, 'to marry off a little girl who cannot yet in any sense be called a woman, and to expose her, herself a child, to all the dangers of child-bed. I pray you will excuse me, but my conscience and my love towards my niece prompt me to speak plainly.' Charles's answer was curt and cold: he was in lieu of father to the Danish princess — since the King was as good as dead — and he had the interests of his Empire to consider. She was woman enough to do very well for the slippery Duke. Sacrificing himself for his kingdoms, Charles demanded a like sacrifice from his sisters and his nieces. The marriage contract of June 10th, 1533, was ratified in December, and de Praet accompanied the royal child, decked in cloth of gold and silver, almost buried under silks, furs, pearls and jewels of every kind, on her bridal journey to Milan.

In Milan's neighbour state, Savoy, Charles's sister-in-law Beatrix of Portugal ruled, as the wife of Duke Charles III. Her husband cherished hopes of acquiring Montferrat, but he had had the misfortune to fall foul of Berne and Geneva, while the French government harassed him perpetually with claims for the inheritance of the late Queen-mother, Louise of Savoy. On April 30th, 1533, Gian Giorgio, the aged Duke of Montferrat, died. Charles refused to allow any of the claimants to take possession. Instead he set up a court of justice which bestowed the fief on Federigo Gonzaga of Mantua. This latter immediately divorced his wife, Giulia of Aragon, and married the sister of the last Marquis of Montferrat.

But the King of France and the Pope could play at Charles's dynastic marriage game, and Francis, at least, with more splendid effect, since he had royal children of his own to give away, not bastards and nieces. His sister-in-law, Renée of France, daughter of Louis XII, and more celebrated later as the protectress of Calvin, after being offered on paper to more bridegrooms than any other European princess, had been used at last to cement an alliance with the Duke of Ferrara. But a far more significant marriage than this had taken place within the French royal family. The most vexed political question in Europe was reflected in the splendid alliance found for the Pope's niece, Catherine de' Medici. She had been given to the second son of the French King, the Duke of Orleans. His elder brother's death made him Dauphin and later King Henry II of France; this was a marriage which was to have European consequences.

The dynastic idea was thus not only a guiding principle but a powerful weapon in the hands of statesmen. Charles used his family to supply his own place: it was the most natural thing in the world to him, that the Empress should be his regent in Spain, his aunt and then his sister in the Netherlands, his brother in Germany. The dynastic weapon was now to be used to settle some of Charles's European problems. About this time he seems to have been considering a Bavaro-Austrian marriage, and such a marriage was indeed twelve years later to lead to a sharp change in Bavarian policy. The two Wittelsbach dukes had played their part in depriving the Hapsburg dynasty of Württemberg, yet in spite of the resentment which Charles naturally felt, it was in the years immediately succeeding that incident that he first contemplated a Bavarian marriage alliance. On August 18th, 1534, he wrote to his brother saying that although he felt such a plan to be a 'hard morsel to swallow', yet when he considered the wealth, importance and policy of the Wittelsbach dynasty he could not but realize how important such an alliance might be for the 'interests of Christendom'. The Archbishop of Lund, he added, might approach the subject. A little later, on September 11th, by the treaty of Linz, the Bavarian dukes did in fact agree to recognize Ferdinand as King of the Romans.

The unsuccessful marriage negotiations between the Hapsburg and Valois dynasties, all of them tending to that one end, the settlement of their rival claims to land, are a typical example of the use made of this, the most common political weapon of the time. Disputed inheritance had given rise to the quarrel between France and Burgundy: marriage might bring it to an end.

The Connétable, Anne de Montmorency, was the most determined advocate of this view at the French Court. He had approached the imperial ambassador de Praet with hints of this kind as early as the spring of 1530, and, at Charles's Court, in accordance with his own guiding principles, every occasion for peaceful negotiations was joyfully welcomed. Charles's sister Eleonore had entered Paris as Queen in the summer of 1530; since that time plans for the settlement of all land disputes, or Milan and Burgundy alike, by marriages between the children of Francis and those of Ferdinand or Charles, followed hot upon each other. These engrossed an ever larger portion of Charles's diplomatic activities, reaching their climax about the middle forties of the century. Ambassadors at both Courts corresponded at great length on the perennial topic, and insignificant as these unrealized plans, these detailed and unfulfilled conditions, now seem to us, they played an important part in the European politics of the time.

Eminent representatives crossed between the French and imperial Courts intent on furthering these projects. In the autumn of 1534 Charles sent the most important member of all his personal household, Henry of Nassau, to Paris. His instructions, his reports and the secret information of which he was in possession, supply one of the clearest pictures which we have of the objects and instruments of this dynastic policy. Particularly notable was Charles's repeated assurance to Francis — for both Nassau and Noircarmes were instructed to make it — that he was prepared to give up his claim on Bourgogne out of his great love for peace and friendship for the King, although Bourgogne was certainly more important to him than was Milan to Francis. In the course of negotiations it was even suggested that the two sovereigns or their ladies should meet to discuss the matter personally. The peace of Cambrai bore recent witness to the success of such personal meetings. Yet deeply as Eleonore of France and Mary of Hungary longed to see each other again — the sisters had not met since their childhood — Charles could not agree to let the governess of the Netherlands go to France in the winter of 1532-3. He seems to have feared that she would let herself be out-argued.

Like all political instruments, the dynastic alliance could be blunted by misuse. The negotiations were for the most part exploited rather as a means for concealing and softening ill-humours and for veiling the discussion of more problematical questions, than with any more permanent intention. The King of France exploited these hypothetical marriage contracts as an excuse to reopen the question of Milan and Naples, settled long ago by treaty.

The dynastic idea was not, however, the only principle of any force in Europe. Already the individuality of the separate kingdoms foreshadowed that feeling which, in the nineteenth century, came to be called 'nationalism'. Such principles were old and deep-rooted in France, strong too in Spain; in Germany they were growing, but in deadly peril. In Spain the national characteristic was a love for fighting, orthodox in itself and as it were natural to the people, although it owed something of its power to the tradition of the *Reconquista*. With this Charles had little natural sympathy. His chivalrous soul found more to move it in that curious figure which recurs so often in Spanish national literature, the poor nobleman whose ideas are bounded by his God, his King and his honour. But even here Charles cannot have been altogether sympathetic, for his Burgundian inheritance had taught him to care more for the good things of this world than was the custom among the lean and hungry knights of the Spanish popular ideal.

Very different, indeed, was the outlook of the Netherlands.

'These lands are rooted above all in commerce,' wrote Charles to Henry of Nassau in his highly confidential instructions in 1534. 'We must not lose sight of this.' He himself showed how profoundly he appreciated it, for when he told his ambassador in Rome, Cifuentes, to apply to the Pope to punish Henry VIII for his treatment of his legal wife and Queen, Katherine of Aragon, he added the request that the censure or interdict might affect the King alone, not the whole of England. Any serious penalization of England, he well knew, might have disastrous effects on the trade of the Low Countries. More curious still, he had actually agreed to protect the merchants of Antwerp from any attack on their property for religion's sake; they had helped him in his financial difficulties, and whatever the expense to his pride, he could not do without them.

But the protection of commerce was not merely a private concern. General welfare and national wealth were rooted in it, and Charles might find himself forced into war with Lübeck or Denmark in order to protect it. Other plants flourished no less in that soil. The idea of liberty first took root among the merchants of the Netherlands when they contested the monopoly so long established by the Hanseatic League in the northern seas. The merchants of the Low Countries stood out for the freedom of the seas. They were very different in this from Charles's other subjects, the Portuguese and Spaniards, who stood fiercely by their treaties and privileges, and would tolerate no one but themselves in the ocean about the West Indies.

The Venezuelan venture was proof in itself that commerce and colonial enterprise cannot be confined to single peoples, and that the life blood of Charles's Empire was not always pumped from Spain. Yet in spite of this the theory of commercial peace, nourished in the Netherlands, was never in any sense one of the guiding principles of Charles's Empire. It was merely an idea which might, with other such ideas, serve its purpose now and again in Charles's wider schemes. It was important, for instance, in governing his relations with England and Scotland.

Beneath all these theories and developments, medieval conceptions still had strong hold both on the governing classes and on the people. The Emperor himself was deemed to hold an office midway between temporal and spiritual; he was the defender and patron of the Roman Church, to whom alone men looked to drive back the infidel, root out the heretic and convert the heathen of the New World. This idea was not without a curious effect in strengthening the Spanish belief in their monopoly of the New World. At Salamanca in 1532 Francisco Vittoria had taught that neither Emperor nor Pope could give the Spaniards a right to govern the natives of the Indies, who were protected by the laws of nature; but the Pope could and did give them the right to convert the people and this carried with it an equal right to exclude other nations, so that the conversion might proceed in peace and uniformity.

Since the time of Sigismund, the Emperor's highest duty to the Church itself had been expressed in his right to call a council; this was the last resort in times of such grave danger as might arise from the growth of heresy, schism or the power of the Turk. The conciliar idea was indeed a main current in imperial policy, against which certain cross-currents perpetually strove, for as to the Emperor's supreme rights at such a council there was always dispute. Conciliar thought had many facets. The democratic principle, and the representative principle which is its natural corollary, had been fully established in the fourteenth and fifteenth centuries, when the idea of such general gatherings of the Church had gained fast hold. But these principles had been wholly submerged at Constance and Basel by the ancient oecumenical trust in the *charisma* of the council itself. Meanwhile a possible difference of opinion between the council and the Pope had made it politically possible to use the threat of a council to put pressure on the Holy See. In 1532-3 matters had come to such a pass that Germany and the Emperor wanted a council, but the Pope, who was a bastard born and a temporal sovereign as well, stood in terror of it. The King of France supported him; for very different reasons, so did the King of England. And so the conciliar, like the dynastic, principle became the occasion for endless broken promises and elaborate agreements, formal invitations, evasions, refusals and postponements.

True to the imperial idea, Charles regarded the Pope as the leading power in Christendom, next to himself. For more than twelve years now we have followed the ups and downs of their relationship. Many harsh words had been uttered against the Pope both at Court and in the chancelleries, and although Charles had often taken the edge off these, he had never altogether repudiated them. In spite of all his bitter experiences, he spoke of the Papacy in his memoirs with the most admirable restraint. Never does he express an opinion with greater asperity than to say an occasional, 'God knows why the Pope acted thus'. And these words should be taken at their face value; Charles meant merely to appeal to God for an explanation of something which he could not understand but did not presume to condemn. Charles was nearly always patient, always reverent. He had moments of dismay and agitation, but no more.

From December 1532 until February 1533 he was again with Clement at Bologna. On his way from Vienna, by way of Carinthia and Friuli, he had stopped at Mantua where he had been magnificently entertained by the Duke, Ferrante Gonzaga. This latter, who was soon to be Viceroy of Naples, was one of the youngest knights of the Golden Fleece. Besides which, he owed the acquisition of Montferrat to the Emperor. Both here, and at Bologna, Charles was brought into contact once again with the culture of the Italian Renaissance, yet he seems to have derived little real pleasure from it. Nevertheless, he was pleased to accept the dedication of Ariosto's latest work, *Orlando Furioso*; and he found in Titian the greatest of all his painters. Charles took his chief pleasure in music, and perhaps for this reason he singled out Titian, who, after Giorgione, understood better than any other Venetian master the subtle harmonies of colour. About this time Titian painted the portrait of Charles now in the Prado. It shows him full-length, standing with his hand resting on the neck of a mastiff of the Ulm breed. It is a princely picture, rich and sumptuous to its last detail; so must Charles have often appeared to his contemporaries at this time. He still loved hunting, feasts, banquets and knightly sports. Not until later did Titian gain insight into the deeps of his soul.

Speaking of the negotiations at Bologna, Charles wrote sadly in his memoirs 'that he had met his Holiness, but had not had the success for which he hoped'. It is not clear whether Charles was thinking of the council, which had once again been promised to

349

the Germans at Regensburg, or of the French alliance planned by Clement. Perhaps of both. The contract which he himself concluded with the Pope on February 24th, 1533, bore witness to the predominantly French sympathies of the Holy Father. By this agreement, Charles and Clement each undertook to send embassies to the King of France and to the German Protestants, advocating a council. Should the Protestants refuse, then some other means to an understanding was to be attempted, although without sacrificing any fundamental point. If all these efforts failed, then some new means must be thought of. As for the Turks, Charles agreed to prepare eleven galleys, the Pope three; but if the Turkish danger increased more seriously, then each of them would summon his whole power to fend it off. In this extremity Clement promised to give all the help he could from fourths, tithes and the money raised on indulgences. The German Estates and the Order of St. John were also to be called in to help. The next clause dealt with Clement's French plan: if he succeeded in marrying his niece to the Duke of Orleans, he promised to use his influence with the French King to further the council, to get assistance against the Turk and to enforce the execution of the treaties of Madrid and Cambrai. Clement also agreed that he would use his power to secure a general recognition for his judgment in the case of the English King's marriage.

As always Charles's chief object was the pacification of Italy. This he once again attempted to achieve by a grand alliance of all the Italian states, even including Venice. Emperor and Pope were thus in alliance with one another, the Pope representing also in his own person the city of Florence and the whole Medici dynasty, with the Dukes of Milan, Mantua and Ferrara, with the towns of Genoa, Siena and Lucca. They bound themselves together to defend the present territorial subdivision of Italy and to help each other in case of attack. Certain special provisions were also added for the recognition of the treaties of Madrid and Cambrai. The quota which each ally had to pay for the support of the army was clearly laid down and Antonio Leyva was appointed Captain-general of the forces. The whole alliance could only be interpreted as a veiled threat to France. The same held good of the agreement reached between Charles and his sister-in-law, the Duchess of Savoy; this too was signed at Bologna. It was

CHARLES V
aged 33

at this time that the Duke and Duchess of Savoy entrusted their son to Charles, to go to Spain for his education.

And so Clement's reign closed with European affairs in much the same posture as when Leo X and Adrian VI died. By standing doggedly to his single purpose, and employing generals and ambassadors who did likewise, Charles had achieved at least this measure of outward success.

Yet the treaty between Clement and Francis, specifically recognized even in the imperial agreement, no less than the Pope's notorious aversion to the council, made all Charles's arrangements but a hollow show. Both Charles and Clement sent out their ambassadors to enlist support for the council, but it is significant that Charles thought it necessary to warn his envoy to the German princes, Lambert de Briarde, president of the council in Malines, that he must keep watch on the papal nuncio lest this latter should be secretly intriguing against the council.

Soon after Clement went to Marseilles, to attend his niece's gorgeous wedding on October 27th, 1533. This was no less than an open declaration of his friendship to the French Court. The Pope thought that the young couple should be given Urbino. But Francis had a mind to Milan, Montferrat, Parma and Piacenza for their satisfaction. From Marseilles, too, Clement wrote to inform Charles that the French King had an alliance with the Sultan. His action may have been prompted by some belated prick of conscience as to his duty as the Holy Father of Christendom; it may equally have been a thinly-veiled boast of his new French ally's growing power. It was a strange boast if this were so, for the Turks were at that very time making ready to descend on Italy, on the coasts of the papal states themselves, and to carry off thousands of Christians to slavery. Accurately viewing the situation, Charles realized that an alliance with the deluded Pope had inordinately increased the French King's insolence; unsatisfied with his illegal possession of Charles's Burgundian inheritance, undeterred by his repeated failures, Francis was again making ready to descend on Italy. On April 24th Charles wrote to Ferdinand declaring that he would have to speak plainly to the Pope: since his visit to Marseilles disturbances were breaking out afresh in Italy and Germany and it was growing increasingly difficult to do anything to help the Church.

351

In spite of all Charles's efforts, the most important event of this year 1533 remained the unorthodox alliance of a Christian King with the Turk, of Francis I with the Porte and with his new vassal, Chaireddin Barbarossa, Lord of Algiers and Tlemcen. This alliance forced Charles once again to take up a Mediterranean policy, so long neglected. In this new direction he was to win, of his own volition and by his own actions, a new claim to fame — in Tunis.

But before passing on to his Tunisian venture, let us once more take stock of the European background.

THE LANDS ABOUT THE NORTH SEA

Many years had gone by since Cardinal Wolsey held the balance of European politics, and the personal meetings of Kings on the borders of the Channel were the focal centre of the political world. For many years now Charles himself had been the dominating figure on the European stage. Others might stir up discord, might attack his power at its most vulnerable points, might act independently of his authority, but in the end everything turned on the Emperor.

England was for the time being wholly absorbed in her own internal troubles. Those two years 1533 and 1534 were marked by Clement's long-delayed pronunciation on the royal marriage, by his excommunication of King Henry on July 12th, 1533, by the decisive defiance of his authority both by the King and Convocation on May 23rd, 1533, and later by the confirmation of Parliament in March 1534. Henry VIII needed the support which he found in the King of France, and Charles could not but apprehend the worst from such an alliance. On February 5th, 1535, while his aunt, the divorced Queen of England, was still alive, Charles actually went so far as to give certain confidential instructions to his ambassador in Paris, Hannart. So great were the dangers now threatening Christendom, that the Emperor felt he would be justified in coming half-way to meet not only King Francis but even King Henry — although naturally the Emperor's honour and conscience could not be sacrificed. Hannart was to ask the English King to hold up the question of his marriage at least until a council should meet, and to use the Queen and her daughter with all possible honour in the meantime; he was also to ask Henry to desist from giving help to the enemies of the Emperor and of the King of the Romans in Germany, Denmark or Lübeck. Charles would have been justified in adding Italy and France to this list — and he probably meant Hannart to add them of his own discretion.

The death of King Frederick on April 10th, 1533, had ushered in a new phase in the Danish struggle. The Danish council postponed the election of a new King and thus provided the Lübeckers, who were still indignant with the Netherlanders, with an excellent excuse for re-entering the fray.

Trade between the Netherlands, England and Scotland at this period was mutually advantageous; that in the Baltic, on the other hand, was highly competitive. Lübeck, the Queen of the Baltic, now saw fit to behave in a way totally out of tune with her actual power. Her government, a radical democracy since 1529, was weak and divided, yet she suddenly set up a demand for all her old privileges, claimed that she could nominate the candidate for the Danish throne and had the right to close the Sound. The situation was very delicate, and called for more skill and tact than Jurgen Wullenweber[1] of Lübeck and his confederates were able to bring to it. Gustavus Vasa of Sweden had a better right to intervene, while the still unsolved ecclesiastical problems of Denmark played their part in complicating the position. Frederick had left two sons. Of these the younger, John, was a minor. His father had attempted to win one of the deposed King's daughters as a bride for him, but although the plan in itself was a good one, the imperial government had at length decided against allying with a usurper. John, in spite of his youth, was generally thought to be a Catholic. The elder brother, Christian Duke of Holstein, was like his father in sympathy with the Reformers. He was supported by the nobility of Holstein, who were on the worst of terms with Lübeck. Jutland too supported him, and by the Treaty of Ghent on September 9th, 1553, he bought the support of the Netherlands, in return for a promise to keep the Sound open. This treaty placed him in emphatic opposition to the Lübeckers, who had been molesting

---

[1] The democratic burgomaster; he resigned in 1535 and was executed in 1537 (TRANSLATOR'S note).

Dutch ships in the Sound ever since the last war. The Netherlands had chosen the wiser path, and great were the commercial prospects which now opened before them. For the age of the great territorial powers had begun, and the individual cities of the Hanseatic League sank into decline.

The government of Lübeck had no coherent policy and was thus ill-advised enough to take up the cause of its old enemy Christian II, although even at the height of its success, it never found means to set him free. Copenhagen and Malmo, the two cities of the Sound, sided with Lübeck; in Christopher of Oldenburg the three ports found an active leader, while Marcus Meyer of Lübeck canvassed foreign powers for help. He received that of Henry VIII in a formal treaty, the first clause of which was, significantly enough, the recognition of his legal divorce and of his marriage to Anne Boleyn. So high a value did the King set on moral support! The towns fought bravely but they lacked both caution in their councillors and loyalty in their subjects. A fourth candidate for the throne was easily found in the Duke of Mecklenburg, and he and his men were able to wreak serious damage on the Oldenburg party. The Duke's personal feelings were more in sympathy with the nobility than with the towns.

The government of the Netherlands was doubly interested in these events. Dynastically Charles wished to defend, if not the rights of Christian II, at least those of his daughters. Nor could he forgo the hope of a religious restoration. Projects were thrust upon him on all sides. One of his cleverest servants, Johann von Weeze, Archbishop of Lund, who was at this time acting as ambassador to Ferdinand and mediator in the Hungarian quarrel, deluged Charles with memoranda and reports, in which he even suggested that he would himself re-conquer Denmark if Charles would not. Another project also engaged Charles's attention: this was the marriage of his elder niece Dorothea. Charles had first thought of giving her to Lewis of Bavaria, in spite of the recent ill-feeling over Württemberg; but the Bavarian dynasty were at that time more interested in their prospects of gaining the ducal coronet of Milan than the royal crown of Denmark. Of the other possible suitors Charles preferred the elderly Count Palatine Frederick — he who twenty years before had wooed that other Hapsburg princess, Eleonore, in vain — before the younger Count

Palatine, his nephew Philip, or the King of Scotland. In September 1535, the fourteen-year-old Dorothea was married to Frederick, now fifty-three. In spite of the supposed claim which this gave Frederick to the Danish throne, he pursued it, both now and later, only on paper, in letters and manifestos. Even to attain the Crown of Denmark, he mounted no war-horse and set foot on board no ship.

In the Netherlands, Mary concentrated on the commercial aspect of the problem. She played an active part in the meetings, which were held for the most part at Hamburg, for the settlement of these disputes. The most important of these was the session of March 1534. This was attended by George of Austria, Bishop of Brixen, Gerhard Mulert, Maximilian Transilvanus and Cornelius Benninck, for the Netherlands. The discussion was acrimonious. The Emperor's Dutch and imperial subjects found themselves in conflict, while the medieval principle of privilege contested with the modern theory of free trade. Hieronymus Schorf defended the people of Lübeck against the attack of the Dutch; he declared that the Netherlands were to blame for Lübeck's rebellion, since they had expected the city to forgo all indemnity for the last war. The city was, however, prepared to renounce this indemnity if the Netherlanders would agree to interfere no more in Baltic trade. 'The sea', answered the representatives of the Netherlands, 'is open to everyone.' Lübeck remained stubborn. Only the utter shipwreck of its policy, only the triumph of Christian III in Denmark and the fall and execution of Jurgen Wullenweber within the city itself, at length opened the way for a settlement. The people of the Netherlands received full rights of trade and passage in the Baltic.

But much had happened before this, and the Danish question was for many years the cause of disturbances in the north.

Both now and later the Netherlands possessed great strength in their religious and moral susceptibilities. At the very beginning of his reign, Charles had noticed with anxiety the various movements towards reform in the Netherlands. His harsh measures had driven them downwards into the concealed recesses of political life. Persecution forced the young Church to become dangerously radical, to adopt with ease the most exaggerated ethical and moral doctrines. Deprived of any objective or visible organization, the

355

Protestants were drawn ever closer together by the secrecy of their meetings, by their terror of informers. There was no room for the half-hearted in their number; instead the influence of single personalities was the more deeply felt and the deliberate character of their strenuous faith was made the more clear to them. The experience of cruel executions, the example of heroic sacrifice, strengthened enormously among all of them the sense of being a chosen people, of being indeed the children of God. In this way, for instance, Melchior Hofmann of Schwäbisch Hall had abandoned his earlier enthusiasm and become an Anabaptist, because this creed seemed to him to embody the essence of true spiritual and religious experience. In 1530 the baker, John Mathis of Haarlem, had himself given out for a prophet and edified the people with the visible propaganda of his extraordinary actions. Ideas, such as those later to be found in the *Book of Vengeance* at Münster, were now rife among the people. 'God will smite the ungodly and take away their strength. He will confirm the hand of David and teach his fingers how to wield the sword. He will furnish his chosen with iron claws and horns of brass. They shall fashion swords and pikes from ploughshares and reaping hooks. They shall find a leader; they shall unfurl their standard and blow a blast on their trumpets.'

Disastrous floods in Holland and Zeeland, bad harvests, lack of imports because of the Danish war, unemployment and the lessened output of industry, aggravated the distress of the people, and brought hunger, distress and revolt in their train. The procession of three thousand 'children of Israel' over the Zuyder Zee was, for instance, an entirely spontaneous movement; but although officials and judges let many of these poor devils go free, there were enough bloody executions in other places to increase the uncontrolled passions of fanatical believers, whose spiritual exaltation was already at boiling point and who believed themselves to be bound by Apocalyptic commands. When the governor of the episcopal city of Münster was forced to surrender to the 'children of God', there were many who took it for the outward sign of a fulfilment for which they had been waiting. The event was first hailed with awe-struck wonder, which was followed by an outburst of wild enthusiasm, which lasted for all its course. But when in the summer of 1534 the Anabaptists had to defend their city against armed besiegers, the bitter fanaticism, induced in them by long persecution, drove them to perpetrate unutterable excesses. When Münster fell, nothing was left of Anabaptism but a burnt-out crater, sulphurous and dead.

The raging fervour lasted for yet longer in the Netherlands. To the historian this continued ardour seems but the shadow of things yet to come, the forewarning of those glorious times when freedom and faith were to carry all before them. But even in this second quarter of the sixteenth century a deeper sense of unrest stirred within this Spanish Hapsburg Empire than could be accounted for by the demands of the nobility, the selfishness of the towns or by recurrent slumps and alternating periods of prosperity in trade.

THE MEDITERRANEAN. ASIA AND AFRICA. THE TURKS AND THE FRENCH

The struggle between East and West, between Christendom and Islam, a struggle which may have altered but has not disappeared from the world to-day, came to an issue both in the eighth and in the twelfth centuries. In both these times of crisis, Burgundian and Flemish noblemen had stood forth as the leaders of Christendom. The early Hapsburg Emperors, Albert II and Leopold I, had inherited the struggle and had pursued the long and bloody contest with the Turks along the valley of the Danube. As heirs to the Catholic sovereigns, and to Ximenes, the Hapsburg family now in Spain, too, took up the ancient quarrel with Islam. The persecution of the Moriscoes could not fail to awaken sympathy among those of their race and faith in North Africa, whither many had fled. The Moriscoes still left in Spain were said to give help and guidance to the pirates who plundered the coasts, in Cadiz, Malaga, Murcia and Valencia, not to mention Sicily and Naples.

The Spaniards on the other hand had certain strongholds on the African coasts whence to keep the marauders in check. From these vantage points, they pursued the criminals, took them prisoners and shut them up in their well-garrisoned castles. Occasionally, too, they engaged them in sea-battle, but rarely with that success for which they hoped. They held Santa Cruz de Mar pequeña on the west coast of Morocco, and Velez de la Gomera on the north coast at least until 1522. They had once held, but had recently lost, Tenes, Algiers, Peñon d'Angel, Dellys and Bugia. Chaireddin Barbarossa, of whom we have heard before, had taken the citadel of Algiers in May 1529. In the spring of 1530 Charles sent Andrea Doria to carry out a successful attack on the pirates' nest at Cherchel to the west of Algiers. But even Doria dared not attack Barbarossa himself. Still less did the knights of Saint John dare to do so; since the spring of 1530 they had settled finally at Malta. In the next year, 1531, Alvaro de Bazan took the port belonging to Tlemcen, a city which lay itself a little inland — the small harbour of Honeine, just to the north. We have already had occasion to mention Doria's attacks on the Turkish ports in the Adriatic. Coron in the Pelepponesus fell to the Christians not long after, but in April 1534 surrendered once more.

The aged Barbarossa, whose vigour still seemed undiminished, was chiefly dangerous for the services which he rendered the Sultan, who had in return given him command over a large part of the Turkish fleet. He devoted himself almost exclusively to piracy, plundered the coasts and carried off thousands of Christians into slavery. It was rumoured that in the course of a raid on the Neapolitan coast he had very nearly carried off the most beautiful woman in Italy, Giulia Gonzaga, wife of Vespasiano Colonna, to give her as a present to the Sultan for his harem.

These continual irritations exacerbated the hatred between Christendom and Islam, and Charles was forced not merely by imperial theory but by more primitive necessities, by his duty to his own subjects and by common humanity, to act in his own defence. But Turkish attack, both in the Mediterranean and on the Danube, was directed against the Hapsburg dynasty; it was thus a sore temptation to the French King to make common cause with the Turk. He even entertained a faint hope that he might gain control of Genoa if he could make use of the Turkish fleet. As Francis I trod ever deeper and deeper in the quagmire of his Turkish policy a new element emerged in European history; henceforward the Turk, hitherto the abhorrence of the western world, would have to be recognized as an equal by the powers of Europe.

In Transylvania, as in France, the same process was visible.

The Voivod, who was brother-in-law to the King of Poland, was also vassal to the Sultan. Thus on the Danube, too, a new policy was coming into being. After the double attacks of 1529 and 1532 Ferdinand himself entered into negotiations with the Porte and showed himself ready to come to a settlement of the Hungarian frontier and to make peace. In a solemn audience of June 22nd, 1533, Ferdinand's ambassadors received the assurance of a perpetual and honourable peace.

Charles, too, had wished to have his part in these embassies, and had actually sent Cornelius Schepper, although he was to pass officially for Ferdinand's ambassador. Admirable spies and agents kept the Turkish government well informed of everything which went on in Europe, and the ambassadors of Ferdinand revealed in their detailed dispatches the full extent of the Sultan,s pretensions. He was ready, he declared, to make peace wit h Ferdinand but not with Charles. He was openly scornful of the Emperor's impotence against the Protestants on one side and the Pope on the other.

The French Court had been in touch with the Porte since 1528 at the latest for it was then that the Spanish emigrant Rincon began his nefarious activities. Count Nogarola, who was with Ferdinand's ambassadors to the Sultan, found Rincon already in a position of high confidence. In 1532 the first definite agreement was signed, not without the help of Marillac and la Foret. In 1535 the French government sent a formal embassy to Constantinople and the long-prepared treaty was concluded in 1536. Although even in his own country King Francis had to make allowance for a determined opposition to his policy, he was nevertheless able to receive Turkish ambassadors in 1537.

On the other hand the Hapsburg dynasty had lost no opportunity of attempting to stab its opponents in the back. The Spaniards, and the Portuguese settled in the nearer Indies, had for instance made overtures to the Shah of Persia, himself in constant if intermittent warfare with the Sultan. In May 1530, however, Jean de Balbi had found a singularly unfavourable situation in Persia as the Shah had just made peace with the Turks in order to have his hands free against his enemies in Khorasan. Portugal, on the other hand, both as a colonial power and as a dynastic ally, remained true to Charles. The French government, it is true, made overtures to the Portuguese but, thinking primarily of their own interests, the Portuguese sought to steer a neutral course.

Towards 1535, therefore, the groups of powers in Africa, Asia and central Europe were fairly well balanced.

Charles had returned to Spain at the end of April 1533. The Empress had been lucky in her dealings with the Cortes of Castile, but in the summer of 1533 Charles had all his old difficulties in dealing with the Cortes of Aragon at Monzon. For months he argued over the usual complaints and his own subsidies. When he had to be absent for a short time because the Empress was ill, this was again made an excuse for endless delaying formalities. Afterwards the Court moved back to Castile. In the spring they were at Segovia, then at Toledo, in the autumn in the north again, at Palencia, and from mid-October 1534 until mid-March 1535 at Madrid.

All this time Charles's desire to take part in an expedition against the Turks on the African coast grew more determined. When, in August 1534, Barbarossa drove out the hereditary lord, Muley Hassan, and made himself master of Tunis, Charles's ambition took definite shape. Preparations went forward with the utmost secrecy; only at the last moment did Charles publish his own intention of taking part.

Apart from his negotiations with the Cortes and his participation in the endless series of hunting parties and entertainments at Court, Charles spent the greater part of these months making ready, both by diplomacy and arms, for the attack on Tunis.

He was anxious to make certain that no entanglement in the north, above all with France, should hamper his action in the Mediterranean. This, for instance, was what led him to accept the settlement of the Württemberg question in the summer of 1534; his chief immediate need was to prevent the German princes from allying themselves with the French King, and he was prepared to stomach the loss of Württemberg rather than take so great a risk. This, too, was the reason behind his warm advocacy of a Bavarian alliance to Ferdinand on the following August 14th. He urged his brother to realize the necessity of forgetting such injuries as the Bavarian dukes had done him, to further the common weal. 'We must take things as they are', he repeated in his letter of September 4th. The same attitude characterized his dealings with the French and English governments, from whose present friendship he knew that he had much to fear. Much as he desired justice for Queen Katherine of England and her daughter, he found it best to give nothing but fair words to both these governments, and instructed his ambassadors to be as pliant as his honour would stand.

The death of Clement VII on September 25th was a great relief to him. The Pope's last actions had been nothing if not disturbing. His visit to Marseilles was an insult to Charles, and his policy was at the same time infuriating the King of England and shamelessly encouraging the King of France.

In spite of temporary weaknesses and internal changes, the French government had a strength which it could not fail to appreciate in the single and united monarchy; Charles's immense and sprawling conglomerate of sovereignties was a clumsy weapon against it. Fearlessly, therefore, Francis continued to make the most exorbitant claims. Declaring that he would gladly see marriage alliances between his own children and Charles's, he announced that his children had rights of inheritance to Milan, Genoa, Asti and Montferrat. If Charles should protest that he could not depose the Sforza duke, Francis went on, he had but to give the French a free hand to take their own. Or at the very least he might guarantee them the duchy on Sforza's death.

Charles found it necessary to arrive at some clear definition of his position. Granvelle now stepped forward to fill Gattinara's place in this: his minutes were not so all-embracing as those of the late chancellor, but they were clear and distinct. In November 1534 he summarized briefly the arguments for and against an understanding with France, and came down finally in favour of refusing the French demands. 'Past experience has taught us that it is a French custom to break all treaties; therefore there is nothing to be gained either from their offers or from any agreement with them. The Emperor's best policy would be to show the utmost punctiliousness in fulfilling his own obligations to all states, to that of Milan for instance, so that peace should be maintained throughout Italy. He must do nothing which could possibly give a handle to the most shameless and unreliable of all opponents.'

The more firmly did Charles share this opinion, the more difficult it became to restrain Francis. The solemn embassies of

Nassau and Noircarmes were dispatched solely for this purpose. Yet Charles was so anxious that he gave Nassau secret instructions telling Mary to make ready in the Netherlands for a defensive war, should it be necessary. His letters to Ferdinand in the autumn of 1534 show that he was convinced that Francis would fly to arms 'should Nassau have no success'. At the eleventh hour in April 1535, he told the Count Palatine Frederick, then on a journey from Spain to the Netherlands, to assure King Francis of his continued goodwill, of his readiness for peace, of his free renunciation of Bourgogne, and of his desire to have nothing but what was justly his. Charles wanted no more than the fulfilment of the last treaty; Frederick was to counter the King's objections by pointing out that by intervening in Gelderland and Württemberg he had already broken his own part of the terms. 'If the King of France has any good in him', said Charles, 'he must realize that the Emperor has come to meet him as far as he can. In writing to the Electors, princes and Estates of Germany as he has done, asserting that the Emperor has been preventing a council, the King has been guilty of deliberate falsehood.' Charles's negotiations were wholly unsuccessful.

On February 1st, 1535, Francis I had indeed issued a manifesto to the Germans which was intended to strengthen the relations he already had with them. The Emperor declined to issue an answer in the same form as he felt it would be undignified. But at Barcelona on April 19th he gave instructions to Adrian de Croy, Count of Roeulx, before dispatching him to the German princes and Estates. These instructions are important for the light they throw on Charles's policy towards the Empire. They were drafted by Granvelle and annotated throughout by Charles himself.

The Emperor began by declaring that the French King must think the German princes foolish indeed if he imagined he could deceive them with such patent lies. The King's attitude to the council and to the Turkish war was clear as daylight; he had said to the Pope himself at Marseilles that he not only took the Sultan's part but would actually encourage a Turkish attack, while he would not attend the council unless he might first have Milan. The Sultan's people themselves had confirmed this to the imperial ambassadors when they were negotiating their peace treaty. The Emperor, so the draft continued, would not submit to this mediation of the Turk in the affairs of Christian princes. He did not at present intend to enter further into the question of Barbarossa; Gritti, the Sultan's agent had frankly told that trustworthy man Cornelius Schepper, that the Turkish fleet had been placed at Barbarossa's disposal only at the express wish of the French government. The Turks themselves were bound by definite promises to the French not to continue their wars on the Shah of Persia but rather to assist in the reduction of Genoa and other Italian strongholds.

As for the French King's slanderous attribution of tyranny and aggression to the Emperor, the draft went on, there was hardly any need to refute such things. It was common knowledge that all the wars of these late years had been the outcome of the French demands on Milan. Francis had often enough tempted the Emperor with honeyed words, saying that he would make him ruler over all the earth if he would but give him Milan. But Charles had remained steadfast to his three great objects, the peace of Christendom, defence against the Turks and the great council. He called to witness for him the words he had himself spoken at all the German Diets, at Augsburg, Regensburg and Nuremberg. When he had considered alliances between his children and those of the French King, he had been thinking only of defence against the Turks, and of the council. For the rest he had promised the King's son a large revenue from Milan. But Francis, still unsatisfied, was demanding Milan, Genoa, Asti, Montferrat, nay Florence even! Who then was guilty of aggression? The King's assertion that he had furthered the council more zealously than the Emperor could be disproved from the statement of a nuncio who was still living. The Pope had tried in vain to persuade the King to support the council or to help against the Turk. If the King persisted in saying that he had made the calling of a council a condition at the last papal election, this was as good as to boast that he had infringed the dignity of the College of Cardinals and usurped imperial rights. Meanwhile he need not worry as to where a council could meet, for his presence there would be quite unnecessary. On the commercial side, the Emperor had only to add that all precious metals for coining came from his own and Ferdinand's land, while, to the general distress, they were merely debased in the French mints. Last of all Roeulx was to lay special emphasis on the fact that both Ferdinand and Charles were Germans born.

By such embassies as these Charles tried to free himself for his operations against the Turk. Yet even in Spain and among his closest followers he found hindrances no less irksome to his purpose. Don Juan de Tavera, the Cardinal Archbishop of Toledo, was the most trusted among all Charles's ministers in Spain, but he had long represented the narrowest interests of Castile and refused to countenance Charles's universal and imperial policy. In January 1535 he took pen in hand and committed to paper a series of cogent arguments against the Emperor's campaigns in either Italy or Africa. In the meantime Charles had revealed his plans to his councillors. He had then declared that he must undertake the expedition against Tunis because God's honour, the weal of Christendom, the distress of his kingdoms and his own honour and reputation gave him no other choice. These were the very points which the Cardinal-Archbishop most strenuously opposed. The enterprise, he said, was dangerous and would have little practical significance. Warned by France, Barbarossa would manage to evade an issue. If Charles insisted on allowing the plan to proceed then he must at least take no personal part. Greater still were Tavera's misgivings on the subject of further intervention in Italy: Charles, he said, would be able to do nothing without provoking another general war.

The most distinguished minister of the Spanish Crown thus represented a point of view which was the exact opposite of that of Gattinara. Now for the first time the persistent strength of the dead Chancellor's influence was to make itself felt. Tavera's arguments, although we have not space here to follow them in detail, were not only weighty in themselves, but were supported by many forces in the Spanish government, in all probability by the Empress herself. Yet Charles was not to be misled. It was his belief that he could issue forth out of Italy, crowned with victorious laurels, to wage war on the infidel, and thereafter to force peace upon the King of France. And from this belief he would not budge.

Now, at last, the Emperor had grown to full manhood, to reliance on his own judgment. He had even outgrown his teacher Gattinara, as action is the outcome of thought. Tavera had boldly argued that it would be dangerous to put Spanish loyalty to so hard a test as Charles's renewed absence must impose. He had frankly characterized the Emperor's exalted ambition as the adventure-lust of a 'young nobleman'. These quiet and serious-minded councillors of Charles's had in their own way a fair share of haughtiness. Even as late as 1543 we find Granvelle boldly writing to Queen Mary of her brother, the Emperor, in much the same tone. The expression which Granvelle used was even stronger; Charles, he said, ought to avoid 'enterprises fit only for young lordlings'. Yet what would Charles have been without this passion for honour and fame, without this bold readiness for action? And what quality could in fact have endeared him more to the adventurous souls of the Spaniards?

TUNIS. SICILY. NAPLES

Very different were the feelings with which Charles now took the field against the Turks from those with which he had done so before in Styria and Hungary. After his many disappointments in Germany, he had set out on his campaign with a sinking heart and almost too late to be of any use; his thoughts had been all the while in Italy and Spain. But this second time he was himself the architect and champion of his own plans; it was his own cause and that of all Christendom in which he was to fight. For ten long years he had wanted nothing so much as to visit his kingdoms of Sicily and Naples; now he planned to do it as a victorious warrior.

And this time the Turks did not elude him as they had done in Austria. An attempt to seduce Barbarossa from his allegiance to the Sultan came to nothing. Arms were now the only argument. On March 1st, Charles had already issued his credentials to the Empress-Regent in the customary forms.

At Barcelona the Portuguese and Spanish galleys joined forces. Joyfully the Emperor welcomed his brother-in-law, the Infant Luis of Portugal, who was to fight at his side throughout the campaign. The flower of the Spanish nobility flocked to join the enterprise and on June 10th Andrea Doria sailed up with his fleet. In the meantime the German contingents had assembled, with the other Italian and papal troops and the Maltese at Cagliari on Sardinia;

they had a hundred warships and three hundred transports. On Monday, June 10th, the whole fleet, the greatest which had been seen for years, put out for Africa. In good weather the crossing was but a matter of twenty-four hours. On the 15th they rode at anchor before the ruins of Carthage.

To the south of this north-easterly point of Africa the round bay of Tunis was outspread, closed by two moles, at the narrow passage of which the strong fortress of La Goletta stood. This was the first objective of Charles's attack. The disembarkation and necessary preparations followed in good order. Barbarossa's best troops, a thousand Turks and many Moors, were within the fortress. He himself was in Tunis, whence, issuing out by way of an olive wood, he repeatedly harassed the besieging forces. In spite of Charles's extensive use of artillery the siege lasted for three weeks. The lack of food and water made it a severe test of discipline for the Emperor's troops. Illness broke out. Yet in spite of all, every nation in the army vied with every other in deeds of valour and endurance. Charles himself set a good example. He had made the Marquis del Vasto commander of Doria's fleet and of the operations on land; he was proud to submit personally to that leadership.

The storming of La Goletta on July 14th saw his baptism of blood. He took it for a special grace of God and indeed the day was fortunate. The troops of all contingents attacked the fortress simultaneously. The Germans and Spaniards were in the north and east; the Emperor himself with the artillery. The Italians had the west. The knights of St. John attacked from the sea. The cannon on the warships, acting in conjunction with the batteries on the land, fired all together, three volleys in succession. Before the fortress itself, the troops advanced in the usual fashion along saps, until they were close enough to scale the bastions under the leadership of the experienced Alvaro. After a short resistance the Turks fled, only a few of them making good their escape to Tunis. In the enormous booty left within the fortress, many French cannon were identified by the lilies embossed on the barrel. And all of Barbarossa's fleet, eighty-two sail, fell into the hands of the victors.

But tests of endurance yet more serious awaited Charles and his men. At first many in the Emperor's following thought it best to content themselves with this morsel of victory and the great spoils it had afforded them. Charles, after yielding at first, then hardened in his determination to take Tunis itself. During the siege of La Goletta the exiled ruler of Tunis, Muley Hassan, had appeared with a contingent of troops — only three hundred when he had promised more. But his soldiers knew the country. They could guide Charles and his men to the springs of sweet water for which they so longed. But the way to Tunis lay across shelterless country, with dry scrub underfoot and the blazing sky above. 'We die of thirst and heat', Charles wrote in his own hand to his sister Mary. The soldiers had to harness themselves to the cannon, for the horses perished. Water became ever more essential. This was exactly what Barbarossa had expected; he not only contested their way to the springs, but fell unexpectedly on those who had had the good fortune to find their way thither. The Christian leaders proved themselves his equals, for they managed to keep order among their startled and unprepared men. Yet the battle so suddenly forced upon them was an ill-conditioned mêlée. Charles himself was in the thick of it; later it was said that his horse was killed under him and one of his pages at his side. But he himself never boasted of these things.

Barbarossa withdrew to Tunis. Here in the meantime an extra-ordinary revolt had broken out. In his wrath the corsair had threatened to blow up several thousand Christian slaves in the citadel. During his absence some renegades had given them arms, and they had seized the town in Charles's name. Barbarossa was defeated. Yet he gained one slight advantage. Charles had promised his soldiers the plundering of Tunis and he did not feel justified in withdrawing his word even in the altered circum-stances. Profiting by the disorder, Barbarossa was able to make his way to Bona on the north coast, whence, with what remained of his fleet, he sailed to Algiers. Charles had not the means to follow him thither.

His escape left the coasts still exposed to his attacks, nay more, to his revenge.

In spite of this the enterprise could not be regarded as anything but successful. By converting his favourite game, the tourney, into bitter earnest, Charles had regained his own self-respect; his victory did the same for his subjects. Both at Vienna and at Tunis the Emperor had acted with all his heart in the business. Turks and Moors knew once again that they had to reckon with a serious opponent.

The poet Garcilaso de la Vega accompanied Charles; so also did the Dutch painter Vermeyen, from whose sketches the celebrated tapestries in the *Kunsthistorisches Museum* at Vienna were later made. This magnificent series of pictures shows the seavoyage, the marches and the assault, with all the privations and suffering, the heat and thirst which Charles and his men endured.

After the sieges of Tunis and La Goletta Charles stayed for another three weeks in the country with his troops. On August 17th he put to sea again and landed on the 22nd at Trapani in Sicily. He spent September between Monreale and Palermo, where his statue in the Piazza Bologni commemorates his visit to this day. After centuries of neglect the Sicilians rejoiced once more in the presence of their ruler, of whose personal care both for their internal welfare and external prosperity they now had evidence. Messina, above all, greeted him with joy. The Chronicle of Santa Cruz tells of his triumphal entry to that city, of the gorgeous arches, trophies and inscriptions which greeted the eyes of the victorious Emperor in unending sequence as he rode along the shouting streets. One streamer bore the legend: 'Champion of Europe in Asia and Africa!' One of the city gates was enriched with two columns, between which hung garlands of trophies, inscribed with a device which seemed to endow Charles's own symbol, the pillars of Hercules, with a new meaning. 'From sunrise to sunset', ran the proud words. Here then is the origin of that resounding phrase since adopted by another people, here the first boast of an Empire on which the sun could never set. Past and future united to glorify the name of Charles; Jupiter's eagle, Rome and Carthage, Scipio and Hannibal. And as he rode under each successive arch the cry echoed before and behind him down the thronging streets, 'Long live our victorious Emperor, father of the fatherland, conqueror of Africa, peace-maker of Italy'.

When he crossed to the mainland and made his first progress through his kingdom of Naples the same welcome awaited him. At Naples the Porta Capuana through which he entered the city bears to this day the splendid sculpture which was made in the winter of 1535 in readiness for his coming. He stayed in the city for Christmas and remained until March 1536; here he celebrated Carnival tide and gave great feasts and joustings. Later he told Coligny that at Naples he had first found white hairs on his head, and had them plucked out.

The cares of Europe found their way even through his rejoicings. Charles had confided the administration of Spain to the energetic Viceroy, Don Pedro Alvarez de Toledo. But he continued himself to direct unbroken negotiations with France and to control his own Church policy. On his journey he received momentous news, which altered his attitude to the French demands and forced on him the necessity of taking an important and immediate decision. On November 1st Francesco Sforza, Duke of Milan, had died. The child-princess of Denmark had not borne the Hapsburg heir for whom Charles had hoped. Louder than ever did Francis clamour for his hereditary rights.

In a lengthy memorandum Granvelle took stock of the situation. The theory governing his advice contrasted strongly with Gattinara's old belief in the imperial government of Italy as an organic whole. Moreover he had apparently forgotten that he had but very recently strongly urged Charles neither to trust Francis nor to increase his power. Not that an increase in the French King's power was exactly what he now advocated. Granvelle suggested rather that Francis might be robbed of one of his chief causes for complaint if Milan could be bestowed as a fief on his third son, the Duke of Angoulême. In this way alone is it possible to explain the growth of minor arguments with which Granvelle qualified his main theme; some of these were doubtless mere quibbles, to be used only to gain time during the negotiations, but others were an organic part of his propositions. He suggested that Francis and all his family should again confirm the Treaties of Cambrai and Madrid; that Charles should bestow Milan on the Duke of Angoulême and his heirs, specifically disallowing all other hereditary rights in the French royal family, and demanding in return that the French King support the council, give him help against Henry VIII, John Zapolya and the Sultan, and assist in the effort to win the Danish Crown for Princess Dorothea of Denmark and her husband, the Count Palatine. Francis was also to renounce all his intrigues in Italy and Germany, all commerce in the Indies, all attempts to unsettle the Duke of Savoy; he was on the contrary to give Charles his support in combating the pretensions of Geneva.[1]

While the chief of the imperial councillors drew up these conditions, Francis himself had made a blatant error of policy; he had formulated and issued two totally different claims to Milan. He had instructed his ambassador de Vely to press his demands for Milan for the Duke of Orleans, a candidate whom Charles declined to consider, partly because he stood too near to the French throne, and partly because of his Medici wife. But Queen Eleonore had already made it known that her husband would in reality be prepared to accept Milan for his younger son the Duke of Angoulême. In spite of Granvelle's recommendations, it is doubtful whether Charles ever seriously contemplated giving up Milan to a French prince. The negotiation never even went so far as an exchange of terms. The Milanese ambassadors themselves only asked Charles not to give the duchy to the Infant Don Philip; they would prefer him to keep it for himself. When, by way of persuading Charles, they pretended to raise doubts as to the various forms of disposing of fiefs, the Emperor gave vent to such an outburst of laughter that the whole Court took notice of it.

On March 22nd Charles left Naples. At the Pope's invitation he proceeded next to Rome. He went by Capua and Gaeta, and then from Terracina along the Appian Way. On April 7th he made his entry into the Eternal City from San Paolo Fuori. He was dressed as befitted the occasion and accompanied by every circumstance of military pomp. In the days following this sumptuous entry he resumed the plainer dress of a rich nobleman and visited the great ladies of Rome, of the Colonna, Pescara and Farnese families. Needless to add that Rome, the ancient seat of Empire and still the artistic centre of the European world, prepared for Charles a welcome worthy of the occasion. Christopher Scheuerl of Nuremberg, who had been Professor of Wittenberg when he was young and had known all the reformers, Melanchthon above all, but who had later gone back whole-heartedly to the Catholic side, prepared a printed account of Charles's entry into

---

[1] The Dukes of Savoy had long tried to reduce Geneva to dependence on their dynasty. During the last decade the town had first joined the *Combourgeoisie* of Fribourg and was now gradually adopting the Reformation (TRANSLATOR'S note).

the imperial capital. He was in correspondence with learned men the world over, and he was able to combine in his report news from 'every variety of foreign and German source'. On the title-page, under the Emperor's portrait he wrote the biblical words: 'Thou mayest reign over all that thine heart desireth.'

IN ROME WITH POPE AND CARDINALS

To Charles indeed this journey was like a home-coming; it was the culmination of all his desires. He had now set foot in each one of his lands, discovered its needs and fulfilled his duty. He had made a personal contact with each one of the states over which he ruled. Naturally enough he could not do more than gain a very partial knowledge of each, for his visits were short and the demands made on him many. Nevertheless he had summoned and attended the Estates General of the Netherlands, the Cortes of Castile and Aragon, the Electors, Princes and Estates of the German Empire both in local sessions, and at the general Diet, and last of all the Estates of Sicily and Naples. He had included some of the leading men of each of these lands in his Order of the Golden Fleece.

Gattinara had intended Charles not to govern northern Italy directly, but rather as a confederation of subservient dynasties, owing their position to him. The Emperor was therefore the equal of the Pope as guardian of the Universal Church, his superior in the confederation of Italy. Since October 13th, 1534, the papal throne had been occupied by Paul III, Farnese.

The eldest of the cardinals, Alessandro Farnese, like the princely, and titled Medici, was the product of an earlier epoch. His outlook was still that of the Renaissance Papacy of the later fifteenth century. Paul III did not blush to recognize his sons and grandsons, nor to bestow on them, in their right as *nepotes*, great positions in the Curia and in the State. But unlike Clement VII he had for long enough realized the necessity of bowing to the exigencies of the time. The last pontificate had been a crying example to all the world of how *not* to behave. In the fifteenth century the desire for Reform had been submerged in mere constitutional quibbles; but now the whole of Christendom had united to demand a thorough revision of Church policy and a change in the morality of the clergy. For even among the lower ranks of the clergy the medieval idea of privilege had done untold harm. The popular literature of every country in Europe, not excepting even Spain, made a mock of the canonical laws which had grown up, like a thickly blossoming hedge, to screen the immorality of the clergy. The north had already seceded, England too, and half of Germany. Clement VII had been in terror lest the faintest opposition should send the French King the way which the English King had already taken. Melanchthon, it was said, had been invited to the French Court. In 1526 sharp reproaches came from the Spanish Court, and even here vernacular literature had grown vehemently hostile to the priesthood.

A general council was, after all, no more than a reasonable disciplinary measure. It might be used to furnish an impressive example of the fundamental unity of much-divided Christendom. Paul III was by common consent a man of great ability; he was in sympathy, too, with that group of cardinals who were not only convinced of the efficacy of a council, but felt that the Pope's initiative in calling it was likely to be in itself a salve to the wounds of the Church.

At his first consistory on October 17th, 1534, Paul himself had already declared that a council was necessary and recalled to Rome all those whom he felt best understood the problem — Aleander, now nuncio to Venice, and Pietro Paolo Vergerio, nuncio at the Court of King Ferdinand. Strengthened and confirmed in his ideas by consultation with these better-informed men, Paul repeated his opinion that a council was necessary at a later consistory on January 15th, 1535. He next dispatched nuncios with special missions to the leading princes of Christendom: Guidiccione to the Emperor, Vergerio to King Ferdinand, and Ridolfo Pio de Carpi to the King of France. Yet, although his intentions were far more serious than those of Clement VII, his embassies brought in no better results.

Of more immediate importance was Paul's encouragement of reform within the body of the Church; in the sunlight of his favour a whole growth of serious and admonitory books had already sprung up. Naturally resolute, Paul did not hesitate to act. On June 9th, 1535, he formed a commission for the reform of the Curia itself, and judging by those of whom it was composed this body and its activities were to be taken seriously. But neither the nature of reforms in themselves nor yet the intentions of those who initiate them can alone be decisive in the life of a Church or a State; the character of the men who execute them is the fundamental cause of their success or failure. Adrian VI had been defeated by personal opposition. Nothing, therefore, could be done until the College of Cardinals had been completely reorganized. At the very first creation of cardinals Paul III elevated two very young *nepotes* — this time they were real nephews — Alessandro Farnese and Guido Ascanio Sforza of Santafiore. But on May 21st, 1535, men of a very different calibre were brought into the college. Paul conferred the cardinalate on the German Nicholas of Schomberg, who had lived long in Rome, the Englishman John Fisher, the Frenchman Jean du Bellay — against whom Charles protested in vain — the Venetian Contarini, the Milanese Simonetta, the Sienese Ghinucci. The creation, with its deliberate concession to all possible national and political claims, was in the main a political move. Nevertheless, Gasparo Contiarni, once ambassador from Venice to the Court of the young Emperor, overtopped all others in importance. Contarini was exactly of an age with Luther; he belonged to that generation of devout men who were nevertheless not lacking in their duty to the State. Laymen of his kind were familiar with the scriptures and with the writings of the fathers; in Venice theological arguments were read, canvassed and discussed in cultured society with intense interest and even passion.

It seemed inevitable that such a Pope as Paul III must cleave to Charles, if only for political reasons. Yet this was to be the problem of the next twelve years. Where an Adrian VI had disappointed the hopes placed in him, a Paul III could not be altogether trusted.

When Charles was in Naples Paul III had sent his son, Pier Luigi Farnese to him, bearing an invitation to Rome. Doubtless the Pope had chosen the messenger with the intention of giving him a valuable introduction to the imperial Court. But in this Paul failed. Moreover it soon grew apparent that papal and imperial policy were not in sympathy. Charles would not listen to whispers about giving Siena to the papal states, and later on he was to turn an equally deaf ear to other suggestions. The answer which he sent back by the hand of Pier Luigi was nothing if not masterful; the successful expedition to Tunis had enormously increased his self-confidence, since he now truly felt himself to be the protector of the Church. It was the Pope's duty, he said, to force the King of France, by canonical pressure if it should be necessary, to appear at the council on which the general consensus of Christendom was now agreed. Charles went on to lay it to Paul's conscience, that he must make it his duty to separate the sheep from the goats. By this of course he meant that it was Paul's duty to support him against Francis. To his brother, however, Charles confessed his anxiety lest this conduct should lead to a schism in the Catholic Church; he hoped that the council, together with his own appearance at it, would prevent any such division.

His somewhat peculiar views of the spiritual duties of the Emperor prompted him to make yet another suggestion. Paul, he said, ought to join in a League with him and the King of the Romans, for the defence of Italy as well as for 'the cause of the faith and the council, for defence against the Turk, for an attack on the infidel and the disturbers of European peace, for the preservation of the Apostolic See in power and dignity and the person of the Pope and his illustrious house'. This last sentence may have been the outcome of advice given by Cifuentes and others who knew the politics of the Vatican. It was wise, they pointed out, to yield to the personal wishes of the Pope, as Miguel Mai had been careful to do with Clement VII.

Yet Paul III was predominantly interested in the wider politics of Europe.

Although the European situation had not sensibly altered during the Emperor's absence in Africa, it had to some extent grown clearer. The German princes stopped their ears to the siren notes of the French King. The Bavarians were contemplating a marriage alliance with the widowed Duchess Christina of Milan, by which they hoped to gain possession of the duchy. The death of Queen Katherine of England on January 8th, 1536, had materially eased Charles's relations with Henry VIII. Although he still thought it his duty to uphold the rights of his cousin, Princess Mary, and to work for Henry's return to the Roman allegiance, the Queen's death shelved the problem of the divorce. As early as February 29th he told his ambassador in England, Chapuys, to urge Henry, as if of his own accord, to abandon the galling alliance with France, a source of constant irritation, and to renew his original friendship with Charles. Emperor and King together could then devote themselves to finding a husband for the princess. To these instructions Charles added the cautious admonition that Chapuys was not to act as though 'I set any particular value on the friendship for its own sake, but merely to damp the shameless arrogance of France'. Henry's chief minister, Cromwell, expressed great pleasure in Chapuys's suggestions; the King himself, on the other hand, cold shouldered the offer.

King Francis meanwhile had thrown off the mask. He had long been evolving a plan to make himself master of the key-passes to Italy by seizing Piedmont and Savoy. He was strengthened in this design by the open friendship between Charles and the Duke of Savoy, by his own claim on the duchy through his mother, Louise, and by the recent weakening of the Savoyard state owing to the Reformation at Geneva and the officious interference of Berne. In February, Francis seized Bourg en Bresse; in March 1536, without more ado, he marched into the amazed duke's country and took the fortress of Montmeliano, ceded to him by treachery. His advance was bloody, for the people flew to arms and valiantly defended themselves, but still the French pushed on. On April 3rd the army entered Turin. The Duke fled to Vercelli.

Ambition for Milan, that city whose conquest had been the glory of his now long-forgotten youth, was at the root of the King's action. He had seen to it that Charles's forces should be mostly occupied in the Mediterranean, and he hoped for an easy conquest. Several months before he had appealed to the Venetian ambassadors to help him make good his rights on Milan, and had on that occasion indiscreetly revealed his intention of using force if diplomacy failed. But although he insinuated that Charles's power was a threat to Venice, the republic of St. Mark refused his offers. They did not have long to wait for evidence as to which was their greatest danger — the Emperor or the Turks, newly stirred up to mischief by French encouragement. Yet in spite of all, there was still a peace party at the French Court and the possibility of a settlement had not yet altogether vanished.

Charles had long been prepared for something of the kind, but the King's invasion of Savoy was a far more blatant violation of the peace than any which had hitherto taken place. The Emperor did as the occasion demanded; he listened to the French ambassador's insolent demands and 'temporized' without ceasing to arm himself. He even kept the fruitless negotiations still on foot by agreeing to consider — although for form's sake only — the cession of Milan to the Duke of Orleans. For the rest his letters have more to say of military activity in the Netherlands, Germany, Italy and Spain. The chief purpose of the negotiations was, at best, to deprive the French King of moral support.

Great was Charles's indignation at these renewed obstacles in his path. He had done all that years of campaigning and solemn treaties could, to allay the internal conflicts of Christendom, and yet at this very moment when he saw himself as a Crusader with a united Europe behind him, the old troubles had broken out afresh. He raged inwardly to find his victories thus suddenly put to scorn and he, who had seemed so near the goal, thus forced back to the starting post.

The French King's demand for Milan cannot, with the best will in the world, be represented as an effort to give geographical frontiers to the French national state. His was a policy of naked prestige, undisguised and unexcused by any theoretical national-ism. Far from being the policy of the future, the King's actions recall rather the more primitive ideas of the Frankish Empire. The desire to gain power in Italy owed far more to the imperial policy of the Middle Ages than to any more modern conception of a European balance of power. Charles's Italian policy was at least based on a theory of universal responsibility and of duty to the Catholic Church. Francis had not even any true conception of carrying out his aggression in Italy to a logical conclusion.

In so far as Charles believed in his duty to the Church, he had a right to expect the Pope to support him. Yet his negotiations hitherto had lamentably failed to produce any such result. Like his predecessors, Paul was horrified at the secession of northern Christendom and indignant at what he took to be Charles's mild-ness to the German heretics; like his predecessors, he did not wish to become Charles's subordinate, wished rather to remain neutral, to prevent schism in central Europe, and if possible to maintain his position independently of the Emperor, and be the arbiter of Christendom.

Charles therefore could not achieve any results by negotiating in the usual way. Yet, as he wrote to his brother, it was absolutely essential for him to get some support for his policy in the face of French intrigue. He therefore decided on a step as unusual as it was impressive, a step which although it but partly served his turn, yet undoubtedly altered the course of events. On April 2nd, 1536, the second day of Easter week, he invited the Venetian and French ambassadors to accompany him to the Pope before Mass. The whole College of Cardinals, the imperial suite and several other high dignitaries whom Charles had invited, were assembled in the *Sala dei Paramenti* of the Vatican. When all had taken their places the Pope himself appeared. Charles then, taking up his station next to the Holy Father, delivered an impressive speech which lasted for more than an hour.

He developed, as he spoke, those ideas which he had so often discussed with his ministers and with which he was familiar in every detail. By this act he laid bare the true meaning of his policy more solemnly and more effectively than he could have done in any written document. Strangely enough, he spoke in Spanish, and we know both what he said and how he said it, for the many witnesses made their various reports on it, he himself recorded it, and there has moreover recently come to light the reply which he composed to a French answer to it.

He began by thanking the Pope and the cardinals for their work on behalf of a council, and declared himself ready to second them in this. Proceeding next to the question of peace, he had meant, he said, merely to visit his kingdoms, to pay his respects to the Pope and to collect forces for an attack on Algiers, the chief stronghold of Barbarossa. But now the French King barred his path. He then gave a detailed account of his relations with the French Crown ever since Maximilian's death. Here and there he strengthened his story with personal recollections; when the peace of Madrid was being signed, he told them, he had chanced to pass by a cross-road with King Francis, where a crucifix stood: Francis had then solemnly sworn by the body of the Crucified Saviour that he would keep peace in Europe. Sometimes he accentuated his speech with dramatic gestures; speaking of the guarantees he had wanted when he offered Milan to the Duke of Angoulême he held up a finger; speaking of those he wanted to make the same offer to the Duke of Orleans, he stretched out his whole arm.

From his earliest years, he said, he had striven to live in peace with the French King. He called to witness a long series of treaties. He had settled their quarrels both on the field and by agreement, but the King never tired of infringing even the most solemn settlements by renewed demands and surreptitious attack. For his part, Charles protested, he had come as far to meet Francis as was humanly possible, and far farther than he had any obligation to. The King had rejected all offers of friendship; he had deliberately invaded the Duchy of Savoy, which was a part of the Empire and was specifically protected by the Treaty of Cambrai. By renewing his claim on Milan he had threatened Christendom with yet another war, when Turks and heretics were already a menace to its security without and within. Charles added that he desired peace with all his heart and would make one last bid for it; but, he went on, he was not afraid to fight. To spare the blood of his subjects, he would be willing even to engage in personal combat, either on land or sea. The prizes of this combat were to be Bourgogne for himself should he win, Milan for the King of France should he lose.

Thinking that this was the end, Paul III broke in with warm words of praise for Charles's generous and peace-loving mind.

But Charles, who had meanwhile been scanning his notes, now cut him short with a final sentence. He had forgotten to add, he said, that he looked above all for the Pope's decision in this great quarrel. Should Paul be truly of opinion that he was in the wrong, then let him support the French King. But if not, then before God, His Holiness and all the world, Charles called down judgment on the King of France.

Paul suggested mildly that Francis, too, had made offers of peace. He could not himself see any reason, therefore, why peace should not be maintained. He could not permit a single combat. For the time being he and the cardinals must preserve their neutrality or their mediation would be useless. But should either of the princes set himself up to oppose a reasonable peace, then indeed, Paul declared, he would pronounce against him.

Charles seized upon this sentence. Clasping the Pope's hand he exclaimed passionately: 'I kiss your Holiness's hand for that answer.'

A short epilogue to this dramatic scene followed on April 18th, when Charles parted from the Pope. In the interim one of the

French ambassadors had made an answer to the speech; now they both, through the medium of the Pope, asked for an explanation of Charles's accusations.

Charles was ready to offer it at once. He had not, he said, wished to attack the French King, but rather to defend himself. He desired peace above all things, but should he be attacked, then he would summon all his resources to defend himself, and he would not even allow himself to be deterred by the Turkish danger. He had not, he explained, actually challenged Francis to single combat, but merely suggested it as a possible solution. He was well aware that he took a risk in so doing for the personal courage of the French King was well known to him. But should there be war within Christendom he had yet more to fear, for it might well cause the destruction of the Church and of religion and bring down upon them all the bitter wrath of God.

Thus although Charles had not forced the Pope into openly espousing his cause, he had bound him to strict neutrality and made him promise to use his influence seriously for peace. Charles's actions soon bore fruit. On April 8th the Cardinals' College had already, under his pressure, agreed that a general council should meet at Mantua in May of the following year. In contrast to the political shilly-shallying of Clement VII and his refusal to call a council, this was in itself a great advance, in Charles's favour.

Besides, he had established his own position in the public mind. All those who had been at the meeting in the *Sala dei Paramenti* carried away a profound impression of Charles's sincerity. Pasquino, the convenient mouthpiece of Roman opinion, summed up the general view in an imaginary dialogue with a cardinal. Christoph Scheuerl translated and circulated this to Germany within a month of its appearance in Rome. It ran as follows:

CARDINAL Well, you old truth-lover, what do you think of the Emperor?

PASQUINO I think that he will come again to judge the quick and the dead.

CARDINAL That's a strange thing to say, Pasquino! Have we not a Pope to make friends of the parties?

PASQUINO Ah, ye mighty ones, take heed how you walk, for you have to do with a strong man and the day of reckoning is at hand.

The words of Pasquino ring like an echo of 1527.

But now Charles committed a serious error. Francis had not yet dared to attack the Duchy of Milan which was therefore still at peace. Was the Emperor therefore justified in trying to win back Savoy for the Duke by an appeal to arms? Leyva, the master of Charles's defence plans, thought that he was. But an attack on Savoy alone was not bold enough to please Charles's still venturesome spirit. He determined to carry the counter-attack into France itself. He determined to revive the plan which had failed so dismally at the time of Bourbon's treachery. This was to invade Provence, while at the same time occupying the French armies in the rear by a simultaneous attack from the Netherlands, on Paris. Possibly Charles thought that his attack on Provence could be seconded by his fleet, as his attack on Tunis had been. But in this he miscalculated utterly. The fleet was too far away to be any use in re-provisioning the army, and there was almost no resemblance between the little fortress of La Goletta, exposed both by sea and land, and the great port of Marseilles, in its difficult country.

On July 25th, 1536, the imperial army crossed the border. Almost at once they found themselves in a wasted country. The last and most drastic measure of defence is to evacuate and lay waste the land. And this, driven by harsh necessity, Montmorency had done. The larger the imperial army, the more appalling would be the consequence of his action. The French troops had fallen back as far as Avignon and entrenched themselves firmly behind the Durance. They could not be attacked where they were and they would not let themselves be drawn out. The walled cities defended themselves and in the open country Charles's men suffered great hardship; illness decimated the ranks, and on September 3rd, after a campaign of barely six weeks, the imperial forces beat a retreat. Leyva did not survive the campaign, yet his great fame cast a final glory over his last hours, for the French commander-in-chief sent his own litter to transport the dying general. It was a last courtesy, a last mark of respect to his great opponent of so many years standing.

The attack on the rear of the French position in Savoy had thus failed. The attack on the Flemish frontier was no more successful. Nassau, who was in command, was successful at first, but soon his operations came to a stand. He suffered minor reverses and even lost ground. Queen Mary urged him on, but like Margaret before her, she was easily moved to impatience and weariness of government.

Among the French, too, money ran short, hunger and plague raged, and the commanders disagreed. Following Leyva in the supreme command, the Marquis del Vasto pressed forward into Piedmont and won it back as far as Turin.

All this while negotiations for peace had not ceased. Both sides were to seek it for a long time to come — usually in vain.

ARMISTICE. NICE AND AIGUES MORTES

By this time the deliberations of Charles's council had ceased to be as important as they had been in his youth. Nevertheless the minutes of the meeting which discussed the failure of the campaign in Provence throw some light on the ideas which still influenced the Emperor.

The Emperor's advisers agreed that, should King Francis cross the mountains himself or send a strong army, Charles would have to meet him with a force no less powerful. With the French, they said, 'c'est le premier pas qui coute'. Otherwise Charles would do best to return at once to Spain, leaving the Netherlands to Queen Mary and Nassau. He would not need more than another fortnight in Italy to complete all arrangements.

Next they discussed whether peace, armistice or war were the most advisable. Peace could only be had by yielding Milan, and if Charles would not surrender it then the peace plan became automatically useless. The King of France might be willing to make an armistice, but it would be with no better intention than to fool the Emperor and carry on his own evil practices unhindered. Francis was more heavily pledged than Charles over Turin and Savoy. And yet, they went on trying to still their consciences, a continuation of the war would be the ruin of both parties, would create an irrevocable hatred between the two dynasties and bring untold misery on Christendom.

Perhaps Charles would say: rather war than the cession of Milan. This was right. If he went still further, and pointed out that his offer of Milan for the Duke of Angoulemê, made when in Rome, had been refused, that too was relevant. But if Charles had been serious in making this offer, he could make it again in the present circumstances. The death of the Dauphin on August 10th, 1536, altered the situation to some extent, as the Duke of Orleans had now taken his place as the heir and was therefore ineligible for Milan. If Charles could bring himself to make this offer inestimable advantages would accrue from it: the Council and the Church would benefit, Christendom would be united against the Turks, the religious question in Germany might be dealt with, Hungary and Denmark might be recovered, England be restored to the Church and Princess Mary suitably married; Gelderland and the Low Countries would be secured against attack, and Charles's prospects in Algiers would be far more favourable.

The councillors were thus more than sanguine in their anticipation of the results of peace. Yet the sum total of their arguments was gaseous and feeble. Even if the King of France failed to carry out his obligations, they tentatively suggested as a parting shot, peace would have other effects almost equally desirable. The Pope, the Italian states, the Germans and the Swiss could be included in the general treaty, they rather vaguely added. Besides, should the King of France again break the treaty surely God would intervene against him and smite him according to his deserts. Honour would be saved and the Emperor could return to Spain, the Duke to Savoy, with all honour and satisfaction.

Charles had remarked in his reflections before Pavia, and he now repeated it to his brother: 'One cannot have peace unless the enemy will agree to it.' And so in fact it was. The French government was not thinking of peace. Nor yet was it contemplating the dispatch of a great army under the King. In so far, at least, Charles might have gone quietly back to Spain as his councillors told him. The campaign in Provence remained an irrelevant episode, leading neither to peace nor yet to general war.

Political news from all over Europe assailed Charles continually; yet it had little effect on his policy, which was deep-rooted in the realm of thought. At the moment the very pulse of European politics seemed to keep the same slow time as his own. His attitude to religion, and his belief in Italy as the key to imperial power, made the Pope's friendship still the most important object in view. Pier Luigi Farnese visited Charles's Court at Genoa, but he derived no more profit from this visit than from his journey to Naples in the previous year. Charles had not yet grasped the importance of entering into the Pope's family ambition, and the Pope on his side had further disappointed the Emperor's expectations. Apart from this disillusionment, everything seemed calm in Italy, and Charles arranged to return to Spain under the charge of Andrea Doria. The crossing was stormy, and the dangers of the passage were increased when the weather drove them to take shelter for some time off the French coast among the islands of Hyères and not far from Marseilles. But all went well in the end, and at the beginning of December 1536 they safely reached the harbour of Palmos, north of Barcelona.

After staying for a short while in Barcelona, Charles travelled in state and slowly to rejoin the Empress at Valladolid. He was there by February and remained there until the summer was far advanced. Santa Cruz has much to say of bull-fights and tourneys and silver prizes for the winners. From his own knowledge Santa Cruz adds another detail. 'Being troubled by gout, the Emperor amused himself by discussing astrology and astronomy with his first cosmographer, Alonso de Santa Cruz; he wished to know all the particularities of the philosophy of nature and of the stars. He grasped things much more quickly than most men. He wanted to understand every kind of mechanical device and clock, both arabic and western, and how they were made.'

From April onwards Charles held the Cortes of Castile. On August 11th he opened the Cortes of Aragon at Monzon, where they dragged on until November 1537. As always the representatives asked him to stay in the country and use his people's money only for their own good; but they voted the *Servicio* just the same. Negotiations with France had now begun in earnest and after a brief visit to Valladolid, Charles removed again to Barcelona, to be near the seat of diplomatic action. The Empress, who had borne a second son during the last few years, but lost him again almost immediately, took these partings from her husband very hard, and usually with tears. But 'she consoled herself', as Santa Cruz tells us, 'with the consideration that the absence of the husband whom she so dearly loved was for the service of God, the weal of Christendom and the faith'.

Let us turn once more to the other parts of Charles's dominions, to Germany in particular. During this Spanish year, 1537, the chief object of the Emperor's policy was to secure peace with France so that he should be free to attack the Turks and the heretics. His dealings with the Pope had had this for sole end. The murder of Duke Alessandro de' Medici of Florence opened up new possibilities for Charles in Italy. He was now able not only to make his successor, Cosimo, wholly dependent on him but further bribed him by promising him his natural daughter, Margaret, to wife. But meanwhile Cifuentes, Charles's ambassador in Rome, had been recalled to be the Empress's major-domo. His successor, the Marquis of Aguilar, arrived in Rome in February 1537. He was now instructed to find out the wishes of the Pope. As a result of his inquiries another marriage for Margaret was soon in the air: she was to be given to the Pope's grandson, Ottavio Farnese; while his son, Pier Luigi, was to be given a principality. Yet Charles was not yet altogether satisfied of the wisdom of this advice. Dynastic considerations still played a dominant part in European politics. The marriage of a niece of Clement VII to the Duke of Orleans had seriously hampered imperial policy: now the suggested marriage of an imperial lady, if only a bastard, to a grandson of the Pope was to have a marked effect.

At first the French Court felt nothing but irritation, and the war on the Flemish frontier grew suddenly more virulent, through the personal presence first of the King and then of the Dauphin in the French army. On January 15th, 1537, Francis enacted another dramatic scene before the Paris *Parlement*. He had the procurator-general read out a formal accusation against Charles for breaking the Treaties of Madrid and Cambrai by his present hostilities. In accordance with this accusation, Francis then formally resumed possession of Flanders, Artois and Charolais. This was the opening passage of an attack which was to increase in violence.

The Netherlands were ready to defend themselves. On March 24th Queen Mary opened the Estates General, entrusting the eloquent Louis de Schore with the task of explaining Charles's point of view. She herself also spoke, and, under the pressure of events on the border, received the exceptionally high grant of 200,000 Gulden a month. It was notable that although Brabant led the way, the city of Ghent refused to contribute. A considerable force was raised under Nassau and Roeulx, assisted by the lords of Arschot, Buren and Philippe Lannoy. They soon took St. Pol in Artois, between Arras and Hesdin; but in a bloody battle on April 13th they lost Hesdin. The cockpit of Europe, from Lens and Arras in the east to Crécy and Hesdin in the west, was once again the scene of disastrous conflict. The wild forward push of the French army, the appalling massacre at St. Venant, contrasted strangely with that document read out in the Paris *Parlement*, which had spoken of the 'protection' of these lands by the French crown.

The disasters and the charge of this terrible war induced Mary to strain every diplomatic and financial resource to maintain her own in the field, and to make terms with the aggressor. Her letters to her sister, Queen Eleonore, and her entreaty for imperial confirmation, led at last to a formal meeting between Buren and the Dauphin at the little village of Bomy south of Thérouanne, where an armistice was signed, for ten months, from June 30th. The reasons underlying this armistice were to be found rather in the European situation than in Mary's diplomacy or her passionate desire for peace. The French were glad enough to call off hostilities on their northern frontier, in order to have their hands free for the Mediterranean and their nefarious dealings with the Turk.

But the truce of Bomy brought more with it. In September the papal nuncio sought out Charles at Monzon with a plan for peace. This the Emperor could not accept, but soon after a councillor from the Netherlands, Cornelius Schepper, made his appearance to ask for the ratification of the Treaty of Bomy. He had already made certain of the general desire for peace at the French Court. Queen Eleonore had given him hopes of a truce of two or three years at the very least. Charles sent back a friendly answer. On September 15th he told his brother Ferdinand in a letter that Schepper had found the French Court more disposed to friendship than they had been for many years. They could no longer carry the expense of a war themselves, and the Turks were in fact the only hope now left to them.

Yet this very hope of Turkish help was of no advantage to French policy. It was an alliance which weakened as much as it strengthened them, for the Sultan was an exacting ally and not always ready to give in return. Moreover the Turkish onslaught on Venetian ships, and last of all on Corfu itself, had driven the Republic of St. Mark and with it the Pope into the arms of the Emperor.

Last of all the French advance in Piedmont had been partly neutralized by an armed demonstration of the Emperor's in Languedoc. On October 26th Montmorency had taken the pass of Susa — the road to Turin — forcing the imperialists to abandon Pinerolo, the southern outpost of Mont Genevre; but at the same time Don Francisco de Viamonte had advanced from Rousillon in the direction of Narbonne. It was but one of those destructive and pointless invasions such as had taken place before, but the general situation gave it its peculiar importance. All the same it would have been more significant from the military point of view had Charles timed it to coincide with the invasion of Provence in the previous year. Not until 1543 did Charles hit upon this plan.

Schepper's second embassy was followed by the coming of the new French ambassador de Vely, who had been accredited to Charles's Court before. He was at Monzon on October 15th, got his answer soon after and was back in France by November 16th. As Charles told his brother Ferdinand during those days, he was not only hoping to see French diplomatists, but even the King himself. Nevertheless, he added in a postscript that he was sending his generals to Italy to see to the raising of troops!

The King of France did not come in person. He sent the Cardinal of Lorraine, and Montmorency to Narbonne, while Charles sent Granvelle and Cobos to meet them at Perpignan. Half-way between these towns, at Salses on the lagoon of Leucate, a little village of fishermen's hovels, the delegates met. Both groups were filled with the gravest suspicion of the other. At first they did not advance a step. The French began by asking for Milan. Words were bandied to and fro; no decision was made. But the truce was prolonged for another three months, from January 18th. When, early in February 1538, Charles met the Sieur de Presseu at Barcelona, their long conversation, the innumerable details of which have survived in several contemporary accounts, brought very little to light save the Emperor's desire for a personal discussion. Each side expressed his faith in the other in the warmest terms but nothing came of it.

Meanwhile on February 8th, 1538, Charles concluded an anti-Turkish alliance with King Ferdinand, the Pope and Venice, thus immeasurably increasing his strength on the Italian front. Great was the agitation at the French Court when this became known, and it looked at first as though the Pope's offer of mediation would be refused: he was, after all, now no longer a neutral. From very different motives, both the monarchs now wished for a personal meeting. The King of France hoped that he might still separate the Emperor and the Pope; the Emperor hoped that he could persuade the King of France to submit to the Pope's judgment. The Pope's emphatic intervention brought the deadlock to an end. On March 23rd he left Rome, in accordance with an old arrangement, to meet the Emperor and the King of France at Nice. The castle of Nice had been chosen for his residence, but at the last minute the Duke of Savoy made difficulties. His obstructionism did him neither credit nor good, for the Pope went instead to the Franciscan monastery outside the town.

With undiscouraged optimism Charles still thought that the affair must end well for him. He still fancied that he could quiet, if not actually solve, the German problem, by showing his willingness to a council and a religious peace — and this in spite of the disturbing reports which he had from the Empire. In other respects things were certainly easier. With the help of the Archbishop of Lund, Ferdinand had entered into friendly relations with the Voivod of Transylvania, and had been able to conclude on February 24th, 1538, the Treaty of Grosswardein: by this Ferdinand recognized the Voivod as the ruler of Hungary, and was in return recognized as the eventual heir. Peace had been re-established in Denmark and the Netherlands. Relations with England were mending. Rudely awakened from his vision of a Crusade and a Turkish war, by the attack on Savoy and the wars in Provence and the Netherlands, Charles was once again relapsing into his happy dreams. To hasten their realization, he now set out for Nice: so, at least, he interpreted his own action in a letter to his brother on March 25th. Helped by his allies, the Pope and the Venetians, he intended to launch a terrific attack on the Turks in the following year. He added that he loved his brother no less than himself, and fully realized how deep must be Ferdinand's own desire to take a personal part in the conflict: between them, he hoped they would achieve something truly great, did God but give them grace to serve him. Although he had no definite prospect of peace with France, yet his optimistic thoughts were already soaring up into the free air of universal ideas.

He had reached Barcelona with a great following and a more sumptuous train than usual. On April 24th he embarked, once again trusting himself to Andrea Doria; after a few adventures, he landed at Villafranca, not far from Nice, on May 9th, in the best of health and spirits. The Pope had come by way of Savona but Charles avoided a personal meeting, for fear that any unworthy suspicion of his motives should be aroused.

Pope and Emperor now waited, expectantly and singly, for the coming of the French King. Francis had argued for a long time that the chief points to be discussed ought to be decided by their ministers before the two sovereigns met. But since Pope and Emperor thought otherwise, he had to waive this argument and agree to come forthwith. Much as he feared the consequences of this personal interview, Francis was not the man who could easily have borne to stay away from this momentous meeting of the great powers of Christendom. Curiously enough the three great ones never met simultaneously, during all their stay in Nice. Charles and Francis each met and talked separately with the Pope. The only connection between King and Emperor was provided by Queen Eleonore, who paid repeated and lengthy visits to her brother.

The conference bore meagre fruit. In the agreement reached on the eve of June 18th, 1538, they compromised on a truce for ten years and the continuance of all possessions in the hands in which they now were. Nothing more constructive than that. All the chief problems, that of Milan above all, were left unsolved. War might break out afresh at any moment, for not one of its causes had been removed.

Yet the personal negotiations of the two Kings gave this truce of Nice a heightened importance. Its terms were, so to speak, under the protection of Christendom. When the Pope had gone the inner emptiness of the truce was endowed with some semblance of substance by the personal meeting of the two sovereigns, first on shipboard, and later in the castle of Aigues Mortes on the Lagoons west of the Rhone. Francis issued the invitation which was enthusiastically received by Charles. He welcomed his brother-in-law first on his galley and then returned the visit on land, on July 15th. Besides which, he saw his sister Eleonore once more alone. He himself, and even his councillors, hoped that a personal conversation might yet win something from the French King. Long ago in Madrid, Francis himself had relied on his youth and charm to soften the heart of Charles — all in vain. The positions were now reversed. Now it was Charles who longed for the meeting and imagined that he would soften Francis's heart. His brother-in-law's invitation filled him with fantastic hopes, as did his meetings with his sister, and the accumulated courtesies of the French Court. In Rome they were but half justified in acclaiming the Pope as the peace-maker of Christendom; and Charles, like the Roman populace, expected too much of these days at Nice and Aigues Mortes. He believed that he was already on the way to settling his account with the German Protestants and the Turks. The two sovereigns spoke much of family alliances. Charles still trusted in the feminine influence of his beloved sister; he was strengthened in that trust by the recent and moving meeting between Eleonore and his other sister, Mary of Hungary, at Cambrai, as also between Mary and the King at la Fère in the previous October. At this last meeting certain vexed legal points had been happily settled. But this time there was no new *Paix des Dames*.

Yet something of permanent value was gained at Nice, better than the delusive gains made at Madrid and Cambrai. Those other treaties had misrepresented the true relationship of the rival powers and had thus failed of their purpose. But this time, when the intoxication of the actual meeting had worn off, Charles could be mistaken no longer: permanent peace between himself and Francis there could never be. He could never achieve that perpetual and unalterable settlement, which would guarantee to him all that he possessed and all the resources of his power, and in the shelter of which he could proceed, without fear of interruption, to the solution of the German problem and to war on the Turk. He was forced at last to realize the fundamental imperfection of man and all his systems. He saw at last that he must carry out the great objects of his life, without ever being free from the fear which had oppressed him ever since he began to rule. Nature may from time to time create perfection, but the life of man in history is never perfect. Its course is transitory, torrential and full of strife. Ultimate solution, there is none.

Whence then does man still gather new courage to seek the unattainable, to solve the insoluble? On what foundations could Charles now rebuild his shattered hopes? Would his opponents, whom he now knew to want no peace, stand even by their armistice? How was he now to attain his ultimate goal? Must he be satisfied with restricting, not with crushing, heresy in Germany? Must he sanction temporary peace, knowing in his heart that his enemies would use it only to prepare a new war?

The incomprehensible condition of human existence, in which each single man is but an atom, and which we call fate, drove him restlessly onward to the unattainable goal. He was borne forward not only by the might of his own ideas, but by a necessity to which all humanity is alike enslaved.

BOOK THREE

THE STRUGGLE FOR GERMANY: CLIMAX AND DECLINE

CHAPTER I

THE SETTLEMENT BREAKS DOWN

NEVER in his life did Charles forget his duty to pass on the inheritance of his forebears to his descendants, without the least diminution of ecclesiastical or political rights, and without lessening it by so much as a rood of land. He felt the necessity of preserving not only the boundaries of his land but its public laws and institutions; in his youth he had even felt it a duty to restore all that was lost, the ancient inheritance of Burgundy. But hardly one of these laws and privileges, hardly one of these territorial rights was not, at some time or other in his reign, the object of attack. He was thus condemned to pass his life in a tangle of negotiations, to which he saw neither end nor solution. It was his fate to keep his head above water in this struggle. He was for ever involved, and always under different conditions, in the oldest of all political choices, that between diplomacy and force. Sometimes he felt that one method would serve his turn, sometimes the other. Usually he seemed to be using both at once. In this autumn of 1538 the idea of fighting the Turk so filled his mind that he set to work in almost frenzied haste to free himself simultaneously of all his chief problems. At first it almost looked as if he would be successful. Only in Germany opposing tendencies, which he had not yet had time to notice, suddenly traversed the straight line of his desires with intolerable perversity.

Charles V was himself neither a diplomatist nor a commander. By birth and education he was a knight and a nobleman, taking delight in arms and very brave, but he had not the experience of a youth spent in armies, nor the education which might have made him into a military leader. His education in geography and strategy was not sufficient to enable him to trace out a campaign or to direct operations, often as he attempted to learn the art. He inherited an interest in artillery from his grandfather, Maximilian. And he was intelligent in grasping the importance of camp-followers and baggage, especially after the disaster in Provence. He preferred since then to conduct what he called a sea-war, with provisions in the ships, so that he would not be forced to depend on what could be got 'in the enemy's country', as he wrote to Ferdinand on November 30th.

His diplomacy was equally limited. He was a good judge of men, but his reserved character, the inheritance of all his family, had been trained too soon on the open stage of a Court, to enable him to move among men with any natural ease. His private notes and reflections, like his letters, are deliberate, earnest, and questioning. His strength was in the regal virtues of sureness of purpose and a high sense of honour; with these his growing self-confidence now went hand in hand, not always for his good. Delicate, unhealthy, slow in his movements and on the whole ugly in his person, Charles nevertheless expressed in his outward manners something of these inner forces: undeniably there was about him something impressive, something of the leader. It would not be fair to compare him to the great men of other ages, but certainly in his own he stood head and shoulders above any other prince in Europe.

He chose and made use of the men in whom he trusted, with critical insight. Unwilling to abandon them, he nevertheless did so when he found them really incapable of their office. In the field he first trusted Lannoy, the friend of his youth, then the prince of Orange, in the thirties Andrea Doria. This latter predilection may have been unfortunate, for Andrea Doria's influence and the successful expedition to Tunis gave Charles a preference for sea-fighting which was not always wise. His Spanish kingdoms were most vulnerable by sea; by sea he wished to defend them, and by sea he had been victorious. The prejudice in favour of such warfare was comprehensible. Charles placed his trust in Ferrante Gonzaga and the Duke of Alva, next only to Doria. He thought rather less of his old friend Nassau, who was seldom successful, and placed more confidence in the two Burens, father and son.

The administration of his dominions had become remarkably decentralized. Charles never ceased to need the cleverest men at his disposal in his immediate surroundings, to give him advice and to undertake foreign negotiations. The Grand Chancellor of Leon, as Francisco de los Cobos was called, owed his position as much to his lack of any very decisive personality, which enabled him to think and feel as the Emperor thought and felt, as to his indefatigable industry. Nicholas Perronet, Lord of Granvelle, on the other hand, was expert in all the arts of observation, formulation and negotiation. In spite of his great abilities he was not capable, as Gattinara had been, of initiating a policy. Yet he was critical enough of Charles's judgment to cultivate and cherish the importance of the imperial council. He addressed his memoranda to 'His Majesty and these Lords'. For all this, the ancient constitutional theory of government does not seem to have resumed its old force. In the earlier part of the reign Chièvres, Gattinara, La Chaulx, La Roche, Gorrevod and many of Spain's greatest prelates, had exercised a real influence on policy; but that time had gone never to return. For his Confessors even Charles now chose men of religious distinction only, and avoided politicians like Loaysa, whom he had dismissed from that office although he still valued his advice in other fields.

Charles concentrated his energy and ability on the problems of foreign policy, on observing and handling the Courts of Europe. Granvelle, too, had diplomatic gifts, and although the Emperor could ill afford to spare him from his central councils, he entrusted him with foreign missions of special importance. Granvelle's brothers-in-law, Bonvalot and St. Mauris, were given the most important ambassadorial offices. One of them, for instance, was sent to France, where Charles had made use in turn of a long series of Burgundians — de Praet, des Barres, Noircarmes, Hannart, and later Marnol. In England Charles employed both his Burgundian and his Spanish subjects; he sent Le Sauch, Eustache Chapuys, the Bishop of Badajoz and later Iñigo and Diego Mendoza. His representatives at the Vatican were always Spaniards, both Castilians and Aragonese, Juan Manuel, Duke of Sessa, Miguel Mai, Cifuentes and Aguilar. In Venice and Genoa he also used Spaniards, Diego Mendoza and Figuerroa fulfilling the office at this time. In northern Europe he trusted his diplomatic affairs entirely to the court and government of the Netherlands. And in the Empire, when Maximilian's councillors gradually disappeared, he replaced them, too, by men from the Netherlands; it is true that the Vice-chancellor, Sebastian Merklin, and later on Seld were north Germans, but they were exceptions to the general rule. All the rest had the culture and background of the Low Countries for their heritage: Matthias Held came from

395

Arlon in Luxembourg, from Luxembourg, too, came Johann de
Naves; the Bishop of Lund came from Weeze near Cleves, and
Cornelius Schepper was lord of the Dutch estate of Eeke. Even
Gerhard Veltwyk, a baptized Jew, a clever theologian with the
active interests of the convert, was a native of the Netherlands.
During the next years the importance of these appointments was
to be gradually revealed by the course of events.

NEGOTIATIONS WITH THE GERMAN ESTATES. HELD'S MISSION 1537

All this time Germany was partly governed by Ferdinand, who
had acquired the right to formulate his own policy when he became
King of the Romans, and partly by Charles himself through the
medium of ambassadors extraordinary. Ferdinand's good nature
and natural generosity, no less than the perpetual diversion of his
interests to Hungary, made this arrangement possible without
friction.

Charles meanwhile revealed his own intentions for Germany in
a series of detailed letters to his brother, the greater part of which
have never been printed. His guiding consideration, more particularly since the loss of Württemberg in 1534, was fear of French
intervention. Next only in importance to this was his fear of
alienating the princes of north Germany from the dynasty, and
thus throwing open one of the most fertile recruiting grounds in
Europe to his enemies. Third in importance Charles placed
Ferdinand's claim to Hungary; repeatedly since 1526 he had been
urging him to make friends with John Zapolya, even at the price
of concessions. This advice sorted well with Charles's guiding
principles, for it was well known that Zapolya was in communication with the Bavarian dukes and the King of France as well as
with other opponents or doubtful allies of the Hapsburg dynasty.
The Emperor's persistent efforts to win over the Bavarian dukes
were an essential part of his policy: he saw clearly enough that
the political danger of their enmity no less than the fundamental
unity of their religious interests dictated an alliance. The Danish
question had been almost dropped: Charles's interest in it now was
very indirect. He wanted the friendship of the Palatine Wittels-

bach, and he entrusted to Ferdinand the task of keeping the loyalty of the Count Palatine Frederick by marrying him to the little Princess Dorothea of Denmark. Neither he nor Ferdinand made any serious preparations for regaining the Crown of Denmark for its rightful owners. Charles also expressed himself at some length as to the proper government for the small county of Pfirt. This district played an important part in his schemes of foreign policy because it served as a bastion for the protection of Franche Comté, from hostile troops and from heresy.

The internal problems of Germany seemed less important to Charles than any of these. The Landgrave of Hesse, who had so easily deprived them of Württemberg, considered that Ferdinand and Charles were lamentably weak. Both joyfully accepted his offers of help, although neither of them can have failed to realize that his continued support depended on the preservation of that religious peace which had favoured the growth of heresy. The Elector of Saxony acted with less good sense and more pettiness in opposing Ferdinand's election as King of the Romans. His conduct was to have a sad outcome for his heirs. Besides which the Elector had come to an agreement with his brother-in-law of Cleves-Jülich as to their common inheritance. The still unsolved problem of Gelderland brought any agreement between Saxony and Cleves-Jülich into immediate contact with the problems of the Netherlands and France.

But leaving all such questions aside, the most important problem for Germany in the thirties was the settlement of the religious peace which had been arranged at Nuremberg in 1532. The settlement was the fruit of the Turkish danger and affected religion alone. But irreconcilable enmity had now broken out between the spiritual and the temporal powers, and, while the heretics continued to engross the lands of the Church, the *Reichskammergericht*, which was still predominantly Catholic, decided every case that was brought before it in the interests of the ancient faith. At this very time cases against five princes and fifteen towns were in process of being heard, and two of these had already led to the pronunciation of an imperial ban. Moreover, there was some question as to whether the adherents of the Augsburg Confession had any right to enjoy the privileges of the religious peace since the more recent imperial recesses had all forbidden the practice of further innovations. The Protestants themselves regarded this limitation as only natural. As early as the Augsburg Diet of 1530, they had discussed the possibility of force. And when during 1535 and 1536 the Emperor seemed to be increasing in strength, he had officious adherents enough, and the Protestants had distrustful and far-sighted politicians, to foretell the worst with the utmost certainty. Possibly it would be wisest to give in. The imperial concessions had, at best, only been made until such time as a council should meet. No illusions now remained as to which way the council would decide the question, and the execution of its decisions would in all probability rest on force in any case.

With an eye to these probabilities, the Schmalkaldic League had recruited further strength. In December 1535 it had extended its existence not merely to 1537, but for another ten years beyond that date. As its membership grew, among princes and towns alike, its constitution gained substance and its prestige mounted. England and France had sent ambassadors to its last meeting. In October 1536 King Christian III of Denmark made a treaty with them which he renewed in April 1538. Nevertheless, with the Turkish danger still threatening, the Schmalkaldic League carefully preserved an appearance of loyalty to the Emperor. To the irritation of King Francis and the relief of the Emperor, they rejected the overtures of the French government. But the imperial government and the other Estates of Germany could not fail to notice that the Schmalkaldic League was gaining in self-reliance. In 1536 rumours that Charles was about to turn his victorious arms against the Protestants were rife. Great was the relief when, writing from Savigliano south of Turin on July 7th, the Emperor informed the Elector of Saxony that he had no such intention. At Nice he received an embassy from the Schmalkaldic League, in the person of Count Pappenheim, who came to explain their grievances and to complain of the injustice of the *Reichskammergericht*. Charles replied cautiously and promised to send a special ambassador to inquire into the business.

The remaining Estates of the Empire were far from united in the Catholic faith. Certain adherents of the Augsburg Confession were in sympathy with the Schmalkaldic League without actually belonging to it. Many were undecided. The bishops were all equally afraid, not only of the Protestants but of the Catholic territorial princes. The Elector of Treves gloomily drew attention to the fact that the Emperor himself had secularized the bishopric of Utrecht. The Catholic lay princes were divided: some were loyal to the Emperor, but others were jealous. The first group was, naturally enough, the weaker. Its leaders were Duke Henry the younger of Brunswick-Wolfenbüttel and Duke George of Saxony. The soul of princely opposition to the Hapsburg dynasty was, as always, in the Bavarian Wittelsbach. But these same Bavarian Wittelsbach were also the most ardent supporters of the ancient Church; political and religious interests were thus thrust into a dangerous and complicated opposition. Even the historian of Bavaria[1] admits that in the winter of 1534-5 Bavarian policy 'can rarely have been surpassed for deceit and double-dealing'. A thousand fears and hopes dragged the two Bavarian Dukes in every direction at once. They hated Duke Ulrich of Württemberg, but they recognized in the Landgrave of Hesse an active champion of princely rights; they resented the election of Ferdinand to the Bohemian Crown and his title as King of the Romans, but they needed his neighbourly support and were in sympathy with his religious policy; they sought the alliance of those who opposed the Hapsburg dynasty in Europe, and asserted vigorously that they had no evil intentions; they greedily hoped to acquire Milan by arranging for the widowed Duchess Christina to marry Duke Lewis, and they were indignant when Charles expressed himself somewhat sceptical as to the reason for their sudden desire to help him in his campaign in Provence. All these conflicting ideas and events had the worst effect on Bavarian policy. The two Dukes wavered from side to side without deciding on any guiding principle by which to control their actions.

Thus, Duke William made overtures to the Landgrave of Hesse and to the Schmalkaldic princes, but at the same time, under the erratic guidance of his chief adviser, Leonhard von Eck, he reproached Charles for his criminal weakness to the Protestants and urged an appeal to force. His brother Lewis followed him in the same course, and his minister Weissenfelder, although more subtle than Eck, did not stand far behind him in this. When, in February 1536, Weissenfelder had to go to the imperial Court

[1] SIEGMUND RIEZLER, whose *Geschichte Baierns*, Gotha, 1878-1905, is the standard work (TRANSLATOR'S note).

on some dynastic business, he did not scruple to suggest that Charles should make a pretence of recruiting for his north Italian wars, and at the last minute turn his arms against the German Protestants. The suggestion was perhaps genuine in itself, but its purpose may partly have been to make trouble for the Hapsburg dynasty.

At Augsburg in 1530, and earlier than that in 1526, Charles had given clear proof of his own desire to make a religious settlement. The German princes themselves were in the first place responsible for that transverse pressure which ended in religious cleavage, and left the decision to force of arms.

All against his will, Charles now perpetrated an act which further sharpened the bitterness of parties. On returning from Provence at the end of October 1536, he carried out the promise he had made to Pappenheim at Nice, and sent the Vice-chancellor, Held, to talk personally with the discontented princes. Held was the last man for the appointment: he had himself been a member of the *Reichskammergericht*, was an ardent adherent of the old Church, an unbending jurist, and above all a man whose unimpressive personal appearance led him to make the most exaggerated claims to social precedence. The instructions with which he was armed, and which he had probably drawn up himself on hints from Charles, merely stated once again the terms of the Nuremberg settlement. The princes were asked to support the *Reichskammergericht*, to appear at the council, to give their help against the Turks and to dissociate themselves from France. When he showed his credentials to the Archbishop of Lund, this latter was dismayed at the manner in which the purpose of his mission was expressed, and very doubtful as to the wisdom of his coming.

More important than Held's general instructions were the secret clauses relating to France alone. These were Charles's own work and revealed with startling clarity what his personal views on the religious problem now were. The Emperor wished Held to discuss these clauses secretly and carefully with King Ferdinand and his chief minister, the Cardinal of Trent. Ferdinand was presumably expected to use them as the basis for his own religious policy in future.

Charles began by stating that he could not yet be certain

whether the King of France truly wanted peace and would accept the proposed arrangements for Milan, or whether he was determined to fight on. Should King Francis fight, the actions of the Pope and the Venetian republic would be more than doubtful. It was important therefore to canvass the German princes and Electors for their opinions on the war. So long as Germany remained disunited both in religious opinion and in loyalty to the Emperor, the King of France would be ready to continue the war and naturally to oppose the council. It was always possible that the Pope, intimidated by the French King or afraid that France too would secede, might refuse to come to the council, or else that he might declare when war broke out that he was the Father of Christendom and must remain neutral. Charles left it to Ferdinand and Held to discover what the reactions of the German princes would be to either of these contingencies. He himself would of course do nothing to oppose either the Apostolic See or the fundamental tenets of the Church. But if the Pope persistently refused to give him his whole-hearted support, he had no choice but to take his own measures for the prevention of further disturbance in Germany. He could not afford to risk an attack on his power, either from within Germany or from the Turks, who were being once again encouraged to attack him by the French.

He went on to say that the council was the first problem to be considered. Neither the Pope nor the King of France was likely to attend, but there would always be the representatives of Portugal, the Italian states, and probably Poland. England of course would send no one. Was it therefore advisable to hold the council? With so little probable support, it might be wisest to forgo the council. In that case Charles asked his brother, whether he thought that any permanent peace could be made in Germany if the Protestants were guaranteed in the present exercise of their religion. This was tantamount to asking Ferdinand whether the settlement of Nuremberg could be indefinitely prolonged. Yet another alternative would be to hold that long projected council of the German Nation, at which Charles felt he might be justified in coming some way to meet the heretics, on points which did not affect the fundamental doctrines of the Church. A last solution would be to leave the religious problem to look after itself, and to concentrate on regulating the relations between the princes and the imperial or kingly authority. God would doubtless provide them in his own time with the means to do his work, for he could not be doubtful of the sincerity with which both Charles and Ferdinand strove for his glory.

Held's instructions next passed from such general questions of policy to the immediate needs of the day. The King of France, Charles pursued, cared neither for God nor for honour, but honour was all in all to him and Ferdinand; this being so, every other consideration, even the interests of Hungary, must yield before it. He himself had to return at once to Spain where he was badly needed. All the more closely did he hope that Ferdinand would follow his advice during his absence. He must understand the reasons which made Charles hesitate to confirm the Treaty of Vienna recently signed with the Elector of Saxony, and he must realize that he could not for the time being make any serious attempt to conquer Denmark for the Count Palatine. Ferdinand must do his best to make some kind of a provisional settlement of these two points.

When we come to consider the underlying purpose of these exhaustive and complicated instructions, it is clear that Charles was extremely anxious for peace. That alone could explain his anxiety to secure not only the sympathy of Vienna and Prague but of the Protestant rulers. Charles wanted to know the opinions and projects of all parties, so that he could govern his behaviour according to their respective strength.

But what did Held do? He began well enough by going to Ferdinand in the winter of 1536-7, and talking everything over with him and the Archbishop of Lund. Next he proceeded to the Protestant Courts, and as ill luck would have it he was met at each one of them by the same answer: he must come to the next general meeting at Schmalkalde. At the general gathering, his opportunities of sounding each prince individually and working on the private fears or ambitions of each were considerably lessened. Not that this mattered very much, for Held seems to have had no idea of doing any such thing. He contented himself merely with putting forward the two main points in the first part of his instructions. He denied emphatically all the charges of injustice brought against the *Reichskammergericht* — omitting, however, any reference to the Court of Justice set up by the Estates themselves — he denounced French interference, and he emphatically advocated a council, although the Schmalkaldic League had already declared themselves unwilling to participate. Small wonder that the representatives of the League, who found themselves united in opposition to him on every point, met his demands with a storm of indignation.

A report which he wrote to the Emperor later in that same year has recently come to light. This proves, if proof were still needed, that he had a phenomenal lack of insight into German affairs. He described in general terms the enormities of the Lutherans, declared that they were supplying France with men and arms, and lamented that French pamphlets were sown broadcast, while all news favourable to Charles was suppressed. 'Turks, Voivods, Frenchmen and Lutherans are all alike in the goodwill with which they serve the Emperor,' he jeered.

Having sketched in this lurid background, Held then proceeded to give, in a few bold and dashing strokes, his idea of an infallible remedy. This was the foundation of a Catholic League, of whose structure and constitution, down to the last detail, Held boasted that he was the unaided author. God, he went on boldly, had so furthered this plan that no obstacle now stood in its way. 'Without this League', he prophesied, 'all is lost. The heretics are ready to attack the Catholics once again even as they did in Württemberg.' Only, he went on rather more encouragingly, they had not yet strength enough; the following spring was the time he assigned to their action. The Pope, he added, was quite unreliable. But — and he returned to his own vaunted scheme — 'once the League is made all disturbances in Germany and all French interference will come to an end'. It was a mistake to believe, as Charles had done, that the promise of a Diet would restrain the Lutherans. A Diet held before the settlement of the religious problem would be worse than useless: it could only be called with safety after the formation of the Catholic League.

It is difficult to say which was the more offensive, the Vice-chancellor's diplomatic bungling or his unctuous self-conceit. Both alike made him in the end unbearable to his colleagues Granvelle, Lund and Naves. Held was not even original in his ideas, for the theory of an imperial union had been canvassed some years before, although it had come to nothing, and the constitution of the League suggested by the Vice-chancellor was based on that of the Schmalkaldic League, and was partly in any case the work of others. It seemed that Held either would not or could not understand those clear indications of imperial policy, which Charles had given in the last and secret clauses of his instructions: the upshot of his mission was that he neither did what he was told nor achieved what had been hoped.

Held's mission, and the effect which it had on the Schmalkaldic League, led to the final abandonment of the conciliar plan. Looking back on Charles's policy up to this time, it is clear that since the days of Gattinara he had systematically stood out for a council, and in that had been in agreement with the German Estates, both Lutheran and Catholic. The hostility of Clement VII had served but to draw the advocates of the council closer to each other, and a genuine desire for it had for many years been the one safeguard of peace in Germany. As early as 1526 the Emperor had been willing to give a specific guarantee of peace, in order to have his hands free for Italy. So that he might be able to defend his lands against the Turk, he had agreed to the Nuremberg settlement in 1532. Although Clement VII had been against the council, he had yet made certain concessions to the idea, and these confirmed Charles in his policy. From the personal point of view, too, the belief in the ultimate decision of a council lightened the burden on Charles's conscience. But now the ostensible willingness of Paul III that a council should be called immediately, made German politics infinitely more difficult. So long as the Pope was against the council such ticklish problems as, where the council was to meet, who was to preside, what offers were to be made to the Protestants, could all be left open. But no sooner did the issue of formal invitations make the council an immediate reality, than all these questions had to be decided.

The first nuncio sent by Paul III was Pietro Paolo Vergerio, who ended his life as a Protestant theologian at Württemberg. He was with the Schmalkaldic League at Christmas 1535, and was there informed that they had always hoped for a general council of all Christendom, as being the best means of settling the bitter quarrels of the time. But they objected to Mantua as the place for the assembly; they asked that it should meet on German soil.

They went on to say that the Pope, being himself all too personally concerned, should not act as judge or president. Later on, after notice had been given of the council itself by the Bull of June 2nd, 1536, the Pope sent yet another ambassador, Peter Vorst, the auditor of the Rota, to canvass all the princes of Germany. He came first to Vienna, where he was warmly welcomed, went thence across Franconia by way of Nuremberg, Bamberg and Würzburg, and farther to Schmalkalde itself. Held had preceded him here, had already exhorted the Protestants with misplaced ardour to submit to a council, and had been sent away with the bad impressions which we have already noticed. The reason advanced by the members of the Schmalkaldic League for rejecting the proposed council was that they had been promised at the Diet a free Christian Council to be held on German soil. But Paul III had not only already condemned their beliefs before he called the council, but had actually spoken in the Bull of June 2nd in opprobrious terms of the Lutheran heresy. He was therefore a partisan whom they could not accept as a judge.

When Held tried to answer this, the League rejoined with a still more pointed repetition of the argument. Thus when the papal nuncio made his appearance, he found that they were unwilling even to hear him. They would not receive the letters which he had brought from the Pope, and referred him to the answer which they had already given to Held. In March both Held and Vorst visited the meeting which the related dynasties of Brandenburg, Saxony and Hesse, together with Duke Henry the younger of Brunswick-Wolfenbüttel, were holding at Zeitz. Here again they were unsuccessful. The only result of their visit was to increase their sympathy with the Catholic participants at the meeting, since the Protestants had treated their offers with such coldness. Such at least is the impression given by the nuncio in his account of March 23rd.

The cause of the council seemed utterly lost. Had he had the support of Germany, Charles had hoped, to judge at least by the instructions which he gave to Held, to take upon himself the chief responsibility for the council. Faced by the blunt refusal of the Schmalkaldic League, he had no further object in pursuing the council. Emperor and Pope immediately drew their own conclusions. On April 20th, 1537, the council was prorogued, for the first and not for the last time; the excuse advanced was that the Duke of Mantua was making difficulties. On October 8th the council was again prorogued; the excuse this time was the Turkish danger and the alleged reticence of certain Christian princes. The council was now to meet, with the agreement of the Venetian Republic, at Vicenza in a year's time. At Genoa, on June 28th, 1538, the Pope again prorogued the council for a year. The sun of peace was by that time high over Europe, but the Pope had other reasons for not wanting a council.

At this time, June 1538, Charles was still ignorant of the Catholic League which Held was preparing. He had just received news from King Ferdinand of the proposals for mediation recently made by the Elector Joachim II of Brandenburg, which were in close sympathy with his own. Faced by the happier prospect of a settlement in Germany Pope and Emperor could dispense for the time being with the council, whose prospects were so clouded, and devote themselves to the more urgent problem of the Turk.

But while Charles was with the Pope, Held's Catholic League had already come into being at Nuremberg on June 10th. Ferdinand had cleared the way for it at a thinly attended meeting at Speyer in the previous March, but although the negotiations which led to its formation had been long, very little had been gained. No Elector had agreed to subscribe to it, or at least not under his title as an Elector, and no bishops save the Archbishops of Salzburg and Magdeburg. This in itself was proof of how far Held had misunderstood the situation in Germany. Even among the League's most enthusiastic supporters — Brunswick, Bavaria and the Duke of Saxony — there was no unanimity as to its ultimate object. The wavering policy of the Bavarian dukes was another source of weakness. The Pope, acting on the advice of the nuncio Morone, refused his support. Yet in spite of this wretched beginning, the mere effect of the League's formation was significant enough within Germany itself.

Charles, although very far from allowing himself to be influenced by his self-willed Vice-chancellor, could not but trust Held's reports of the German situation, which were confirmed in the main by Ferdinand; he showed at first a favourable interest in the new League. All the same, as early as March 31st, he had earnestly entreated Ferdinand not to desist from his policy of mediation, merely because Held said that the Lutherans were 'shameless'. It was Ferdinand's first duty to prevent the members of the Schmalkaldic League from flying to arms. Even in the question of Church land, Charles urged his brother to make concessions, if he could. He suggested that he should promise the members of the Schmalkaldic League a Diet, which could later be postponed. Above all things, Charles insistently repeated, civil war in Germany must be prevented, for the Turks and the French were still menacing. Charles's attitude was made up of two contrary elements: relief at finding a firmness of purpose, whose existence he had not suspected, among the Catholic princes, and anxiety lest, by openly favouring an offensive alliance against the Protestants, he should force the Schmalkaldic League into war. He allowed the Catholic League to take shape, but he withheld his own final judgment. Hesitating long before he gave his consent, he hesitated yet longer before giving his support. This was hardly surprising, for Held's mission had not furthered his own policy; the Vice-chancellor had put the Emperor's name and credentials to a very different use than that originally intended. Yet, to judge by Charles's letters on the subject, this misinterpretation of his original intentions did not blind him to the fact that a weapon was being forged for his use, of which he might one day stand in need. Such hopes as he had were however prone to disappointment. From the very beginning the League was an offence to his opponents without being a strength to his own cause; Catholic determination seemed exhausted by the mere effort of bringing it into being, while the members of the Schmalkaldic League were confirmed in their darkest suspicions and strengthened in their purpose.

The leaders of the Catholic League, Henry of Brunswick and Lewis of Bavaria, naturally described their efforts to Charles in the most favourable light; and Held, the proud father of the misbegotten thing, conspired to support them for his own interests. But Leonhard von Eck, the Bavarian minister, had the courage to say that the League had been formed 'against his will'. The Hessians had meanwhile ingenuously admitted to the Bavarians that they had had a plan for a surprise attack on the Duke of Brunswick. The Bavarians in fact had the advantage of knowing something of the plans of both sides. For several years to come their allegiance was still in doubt, a constant source of unrest.

THE STRUGGLE FOR GERMANY

While an uneasy calm still brooded over European affairs, disturbed only by the machinations of Held and the rumours to which these gave rise, a curious change had taken place in the alignment of the powers.

The members of the Schmalkaldic League were at heart as little united as the members of the Catholic union. If all were agreed in doubting whether they could justly eliminate the rights of Emperor and Empire from their deliberations, the towns were gradually growing more restive at the thought of a French alliance; the knowledge that the French government had relations with the Sultan was probably at the bottom of this. In February 1538 the municipal council of Ulm first spoke plainly on this point to the delegates of Strasbourg. They declared flatly that they did not wish to have any dealings with a King who 'persecuted, tormented and hunted his own subjects out of house and home for the sake of God's word, and appalling to relate, had actually entered into alliance with the common foe of all good Christians, the Turk'. Nay, they pursued, he had given the Sultan both occasion and encouragement for his ill-doing. Before allying with such a King, 'whose shamelessness and levity are so blatant that there is not a drop of true Christian blood to be traced in all his actions', the councillors of Ulm besought their fellow-Protestants to consider well, lest 'God Almighty should once again withdraw the true light of his mercy and bring us to eternal damnation both of body and soul'.

Yet in this very spring of 1538 the Elector of Saxony, irritated now past bearing and urged on by the Danish King, sent repeated embassies to France. He failed to achieve anything, for much as his fears forced him into sympathy with the French King, he could not reconcile a definite alliance with what he took to be his duty as a prince of the Empire.

Another result of Held's mission and of Protestant fears was the alliance made between Queen Mary in the Netherlands and the Landgrave of Hesse. This union was more important than it at first appeared, for the Landgrave of Hesse was the virtual leader of the Schmalkaldic League and his importance in imperial policy was rapidly increasing. The secretary Naves opened a brilliant career by guiding these negotiations to a happy conclusion. The first overtures came apparently from the Hessian side. Naves visited the Landgrave in response to them, came back to Queen Mary and returned later to Hesse with credentials and instructions.

At the first visit from Naves, Philip hastened to deny the truth of various unfavourable rumours: he had not, he said, been opposed to the voting of subsidies against the Turk, he had never sought to make an alliance against the Emperor or to help France either with troops or moral support. Both he and all those who were with him in the Schmalkaldic League regarded it as their first duty to help the Emperor against the Turks. But, he added, if the Emperor really intended to overwhelm them by force of arms, as Doctor Matthias Held had not scrupled to tell everyone, they could hardly be expected to divest themselves of all their weapons and resources. If they might have some guarantee that no such plan was indeed being formed against them, the Emperor would find no more loyal supporters of his Turkish policy. But the guarantee would have to be more effective than any which had been given them at Nuremberg, 'for in direct contravention to this latter, the *Reichskammergericht* had proceeded against them, and had even gone so far as to publish the imperial ban'. When they complained to the Emperor, Philip reminded Naves, he had promised to send one of his ministers to inquire into the matter. But the only person who came was Doctor Held, and his discourse was such that the members of the Schmalkaldic League could not have been more astonished had the Emperor dealt them each severally a stunning blow on the head. Subsidies against the Turk, the Landgrave added, ought by rights to be voted in a Diet, not sued for by special ambassadors. The Schmalkaldic League was purely defensive. Now it was being rumoured that the Emperor was allying himself with the French King to annihilate them, and it was said that he had every intention of absorbing the bishoprics of Munster, Osnabruck and Bremen into the Netherlands.

Mary answered that she was sure Held had gone beyond his

instructions in speaking as he did: she was convinced that the Emperor had no intention of making war in Germany. Such rumours were doubtless the work of the French or other ill-wishers who sought to sow tares among the wheat. The Emperor cared for all Christendom, and she would be very willing to propose to him that he should let the religious question rest until a council, or some other general assembly, could meet to decide it. She knew that the Emperor was very anxious for a council and was indeed hurrying his return to Germany to expedite it. As for the bishoprics, he had no intention whatever of infringing their boundaries. She furnished Naves with particular instructions for the problems of Gelderland and Cleves; that ancient disturber of the peace, Charles of Gelder-land, had drawn up his will in such a way that his heir William of Cleves was bound to be involved in difficulties and disputes.

William's brother-in-law, the young Elector of Saxony, had grown so nervous of Charles's intentions, that he actually asked the Landgrave of Hesse whether it would not be wise to fore-stall an imperial attack. But the Landgrave, contrary to his expectation, curtly answered that it would be foolhardy to act on mere suspicion when they had not even the money they needed. Inevitably a great part of Germany would be exposed to attack, were they to move, and a reasonable plan of campaign would be difficult to evolve. The best scheme would probably be an invasion of the lands belonging to Duke Henry of Brunswick and Duke George of Saxony. But on the whole an honourable peace treaty was much to be preferred.

On both sides the seeds of peace were striking root.

In a letter to Ferdinand on July 28th Charles revealed his pre-occupation with the news from Hesse. He asked his brother to bestir himself in accordance with the agreement made with the French King and the Pope. By this he meant the various arrange-ments agreed on at Aigues Mortes, and which he had himself published in a somewhat undefined form. This was that same agreement which the members of the Schmalkaldic League had quite mistakenly thought to be a plan for a war on the Protestants. In fact not even the most highly confidential letters between Charles and Ferdinand so much as hint of any such plan. Their one desire was to separate the German princes from the French

King and thereby to remove one obstacle in the way of a settlement. Mary herself most urgently pleaded for peace in Germany; emphatically she dissuaded Charles from any project of war by sea, and urged him if he intended to fight the Turk, to win over the hearts of his German subjects and make them into his supporters by peaceful means. He must in fact cajole and tempt the German princes away from the French King.

All the surviving documents relating to Charles's policy in Germany in these years 1538-9 bear out the indications contained in the secret part of Held's instructions, that part which he had so signally neglected. On September 22nd Charles wrote to his brother: 'Our intention is to meet them on certain individual points which do not affect the fundamentals of our faith, and to avoid stirring up irritation by refusing things, either for a time or for ever.'

Once again Charles's political thoughts soared up to embrace the whole world. The situation in England was calm again. In January Henry VIII let the Emperor know that although he would not countenance a papal council, he would agree to an imperial assembly. Astonishing to relate, Charles now, conveniently forgetting the dismal career of his own aunt, not to mention the execution of Anne Boleyn, agreed in all seriousness to a plan outlined by Chapuys and Henry VIII. By this the English King was to marry the still adolescent widow of the Duke of Milan, and gain with her a claim on the Danish throne. As a preliminary condition for this marriage, Henry demanded that the Count Palatine Frederick, and his wife Dorothea, should renounce their rights. In May and June 1538, Charles discussed the details of these remarkable dynastic projects yet more fully in his letters to his brother. Lund was to approach the Count Palatine and his wife, either of whom had the personal resources necessary to make good their claim on Denmark, and persuade them to withdraw. But in spite of the emptiness of their pretensions, the prince and princess at once made difficulties. Dorothea had never ceased to sign all official documents with the formula: 'Princess and rightful heiress of the Danish kingdoms.' The Palatine family had other reasons, too, for opposing the English marriage.

But once again the complaints of the Low Countries sobered down Charles's all too wild ambitions. The first memorandum issued by Queen Mary bears no date, but in this she laid down minimum demands for the English negotiations. In 1506, driven by storms to make a forced landing on the English coast, Philip the Handsome had consented to that unfavourable commercial agreement the *Intercursus Malus*. This contract had been laid down for perpetuity and all efforts to improve its terms had failed: the agreements of 1515 and 1520 had both been based on it. Mary herself had been equally unsuccessful in trying to have it altered, and she laid down its modification now as an essential provision of any treaty to be made with England. If a perpetual treaty could not actually be abolished, Charles might at least refuse to give it explicit confirmation.

She asked also that in return for the renunciation of all Hapsburg claims on Denmark, the people of the Netherlands should be given freedom of trade and transit in all the provinces of the Danish kingdoms, in salt water and fresh, in the Belts and the Sound, together with rights of passage to Prussia, Riga, Reval and Danzig, without the payment of any new imposts. Their ships were also to be guaranteed against piracy and other nuisances to commerce. Should Henry leave more than one son the eldest was to succeed him in England, the second in Denmark; this would prevent the permanent union of the Danish and English crowns, a fusion as dangerous to the Netherlands as that between Gelderland, Cleves, Jülich and Berg, of which they now went in fear. In all treaties signed with the Duke of Holstein, the Netherlands were to receive special consideration.

In a second and yet more explicit memorandum addressed to Charles, Mary adjured him to promise no active help in the Danish question, and once again emphasized her extreme distaste for the whole scheme. All that eastern trade, of which Holland, Zeeland, Brabant and Flanders were now the repository, would be diverted to England, should Henry be established on the Danish throne, she argued. And, she continued, the Baltic cities would be extremely unwilling to have so powerful a monarch in the north: had Charles adequately considered what opposition he might have to contend with in that quarter? Besides which, Charles could not make war in Denmark without violating the recent and favourable treaty of Ghent. And if he did in fact proceed to such an extremity, had he conceived how serious would be his danger should Henry then withdraw, leaving him alone to face the danger? Henry ran no risk for he was unassailable in his island kingdom: the same could not be said of Charles. He was vulnerable both by land and sea, while the commerce of the Netherlands lay open to every attack. All these things, Mary added significantly, Charles might already have learnt by bitter experience.

As brave as she was intelligent, Mary went even further.

Happily for her, the English problem solved itself. The King proved as fickle to his purpose as Charles himself had half suspected. One care but gave place to another yet more serious. Queen Mary and King Ferdinand realized only too clearly from the Emperor's letters during the summer and autumn of 1539 that he was living in a mist of enthusiasm, borne up by the delusive hope of a successful campaign against the Turk, a campaign which was to outdo all previous efforts and which he was himself to lead. He felt that the temporary friendship of France gave him an opportunity, which he ought not to miss, to carry out an action in which he could not but succeed. During those happy days at Aigues Mortes he had written fully and frankly to Mary, telling her of his informal and friendly meetings with Queen Eleonore and her royal husband, and joyfully adding that they had now referred all their disputes to their respective ministers, and had themselves agreed to keep the truce, nay to regard it as a peace in itself, whatever decision their ministers should ultimately reach. Acting together, in peace and friendship, Charles had already agreed with the King of France to bring back those who had relapsed from the Church. The Pope approved their joint intentions, and all their arguments tended ultimately only to one and the same end — a joint attack on the Turk. In later letters Charles proceeded to outline his plans in detail, as he evolved them in conjunction with King Francis.

In the intoxicating atmosphere of Aigues Mortes, where life was one joyous and solemn festival, Francis seems to have embraced the idea of a Crusade with the same exaggerated enthusiasm which he had once before evinced for it, at Paris in October 1529. With the French King, such expressions of religious ardour evaporated almost as soon as they were made; with the Emperor they sank deep into his more serious mind and long left their mark.

The Venetian Republic, that member of the anti-Turkish League which was most immediately affected by such plans, was already pushing forward into Greek waters, attacking Turkish ports at the outlet of the Adriatic, and occasionally carrying her arms even farther to the east. Charles warmly acclaimed Venetian ardour. On November 30th, 1538, he wrote to King Ferdinand that he had already received letters from Rome and Venice, who were both agreed as to the size of the army to be employed, and the divisions in which it was to operate. He went on to explain that he had himself made all necessary arrangements for commissariat, artillery, munitions, and other necessaries. He was in agreement over details with Ferrante Gonzaga and Andrea Doria. By this time the talk no longer centred on coastal waters and the defence of the home shores. Once or twice the word 'Constantinople' had been mentioned.

Charles was as little hindered in the pursuance of these immense plans by the tactful hints of his nearest advisers than he had been in the time preceding his descent on Tunis.

And while Charles was thus bemused among his lofty aspirations, Queen Mary sent him the greatest of all her letters. Style and orthography both betray it as her own personal work: a document as impassioned as it is weighty, remarkable at once for its sincerity and its intelligence. Certain disturbances in the Low Countries, of which more must be said later, had doubtless inspired her to lay the case thus firmly before her brother's dazzled eyes. Her opening passage rings with the authoritative note of a Gattinara or an Archduchess Margaret. 'Your Majesty', wrote Queen Mary, 'is the greatest prince in Christendom, but you cannot undertake a war in the name of all Christendom until such time as you have means to carry it through to certain victory.' The east was far away, she went on, and great indeed would Charles's resources have to be, were he to undertake so distant a conquest: Tunis was but a day's passage from the ports of Sicily. Barbarossa had fought; but the Turks might prefer to withdraw, laying waste the land. What then could Charles achieve? One rapid campaign would be meaningless: the enterprise which Charles now had in mind could not be carried out, save in many long years. Such an undertaking as he intended must cost inexhaustible wealth. And whence, she asked, was this to come? What hope of support had Charles from his allies, from the Pope, from the Venetians, from the King of France? What reliance, she demanded, could be placed on so new and unproved a friendship? That which King Francis most desired, she pointed out, the duchy of Milan, was still in Charles's hands. Moreover, she pursued implacably, the finances of all the Hapsburg dominions were unequal to the strain. Naples, the Netherlands, Spain, all alike needed time to rest and gather their spent forces. With the Emperor absent, she pleaded, what was to become of the Netherlands? The Duke of Cleves, for instance, would undoubtedly take possession of Gelderland. 'Before God', she told him, 'nothing is so certain as that Your Majesty's first duty is to your own subjects.'

Let him consider, she went on, what the risk of his own person might not mean. Was he to go, and leave unprotected 'The Empress, your children, your lands and all of us, last but not least, the Christian Church which leans for its support on you alone? How will you answer for this before God?' The Turks could not be destroyed unless their whole empire fell, she reiterated. 'This cannot be done but in a very long time. And in what straits should we be if you were defeated, or never came home again? In the name of God, I implore you, bethink you of your duty to God Himself. So great a prince as you *must* only conquer. Defeat is the ultimate crime. Wait but for a year or two. Set your lands in order against a long absence. Win the love of the German princes, so that they may help you in this great enterprise, and have France for a friend, not an enemy, in that land. March from Spain across France, settle your last accounts with that King, then visit your Netherlands, so to Germany and at last to Italy. This is the advice, which in all humility, I offer to you.'

Before Charles could read this passionate appeal to his sense of duty, his ships under Doria and Ferrante Gonzaga, were already at Corfu, where they had joined the Venetian fleet under Capello and the papal fleet under Grimani. Over against them was the Turkish fleet, under Barbarossa's command. Smaller in numbers, it had the advantage of them in experienced seamanship and unity of command. Yet for long enough the decisive conflict, sought by both parties, did not come to pass. Before the two fleets finally engaged, Barbarossa sent Alonso Alarçon, who had been taken prisoner some days before, to Corfu to negotiate with the imperial admirals and generals. Apparently he was seriously considering whether he should come over to the imperial side, a change which might well have been as significant as that of Andrea Doria himself had been some years before. His condition was that he should be reinstated at Tunis, and this, because they could gain no guarantee of his future conduct, the imperialists thought too high a price. And so, on September 27th, the sea-battle of Prevesa took place, at the outlet of the bay of Arta, not far from the island of Leukas. It was a botched affair. The imperialists failed to shut in the Turkish fleet, and retired ingloriously. Soon after they sought to efface this bad impression by seizing Castelnuovo, a little to the north, on the bay of Cattaro. But as at Prevesa, the commanders disagreed, the Venetians opposing the plans of the Spaniards under Doria. When at length they agreed as to how the place was to be garrisoned, they failed to send it help in time, and Barbarossa returning, besieged and took it.

The depressing news of these events may well have damped the Emperor's crusading zeal. The valuable and uninterrupted series of dispatches from the Venetian ambassadors at the imperial Court, which cover the whole of this period, give a vivid picture of the rise and decline of Charles's great plan. In the spring, Mocenigo informed the Doge that the Emperor was planning to set himself at the head of a great enterprise in the following year. On May 24th all the ambassadors wrote together to the Venetian government, explaining that Charles had called them together and delivered a lengthy, interesting and impressive dissertation on the coming war. He had explained how difficult it was to withhold the Turks on land, because their nimble cavalry could evade serious engagements, while splitting up and reassembling at will, for plundering expeditions or ambushes. He had himself, he said, experienced this in Austria. And moreover, although he was not easily moved, he had wept when his brother told him, on the same occasion, that the Christian troops, because of their great numbers, did more harm to the inhabitants than the Turks. Hence he had realized that the only sure defence against the infidel by land was a series of strong border fortresses. This year, therefore, he intended to devote wholly to securing his defences. In the following year he would attack — but by sea. He had gone on to speak of his Tunisian venture. His experience there led him to believe that he would need 200 ships and 60,000 men for this greater enterprise; above all he wanted German troops for they were like a rock in defensive action. He would also need 2000 horses for the artillery, and these could best be transported in the big Flemish ships, 100 in each. As soon as his preparations were completed, he intended to sail straight for Constantinople, a city which he understood could be blockaded from three sides by sea.

To this height then did Charles lift his hopes. For months he thought of nothing but these preparations; or if he thought of anything else, it was only how best to meet the objections raised against them in Spain. The Castilians agreed to an attack on Algiers, but would hear of nothing more. When, on October 27th, they heard of the battle of Prevesa, they discussed at great length the refusal of the Venetians to submit to Doria's direction. The Venetian ambassadors naturally defended Capello. In December there was much dispute as to the best winter quarters for the fleet. By January 1529, although preparations for the great attack had not yet been abandoned, they figured much less largely in the Venetian dispatches from Spain than did Charles's quarrels with the Cortes. Meanwhile, in spite of continued negotiation for several dynastic marriages, the jarring discords between Charles and the French King were once more to be heard. The troubled issues of Charles's international policy resumed full dominance when the English Cardinal, Reginald Pole, made his appearance in Spain, with the suggestion of a descent on England, to enforce the papal sentence pronounced against that country. The King of France would have to be won over to this plan. And on March 12th, Mocenigo for the first time mentioned a projected truce with the Turks to be won by French mediation. For the time being Charles's dream of a great campaign was at an end.

All this while King Ferdinand and the Elector of Brandenburg had been busy trying to quiet Germany. King Ferdinand, in sore need of subsidies against the Turks, was particularly anxious for peace. The German princes, who had been responsible for deepening the religious cleavage, were now no less responsible for bridging it. Charles himself was anxious for conciliation. The papal nuncio, Morone, on the other hand, was ardently opposed to it. On July 4th, 1538, a new legate arrived, in the person of Aleander, now Bishop of Brindisi. He had been sent as a result of Charles's earlier discussions with the Pope; but as things now stood, the instructions which he brought were not very conciliatory. Remembering the Diet of Worms seventeen years before, Ferdinand feared that they might hinder rather than advance a settlement. Fabio Mignanello, Morone's successor at the Austrian Court, was subordinated to the legate, but neither of them played any part in the negotiations with the Protestants.

There were difficulties enough and to spare. The Schmalkaldic League was slow to formulate its demands. It asked that Ferdinand be given plenipotentiary powers by the Emperor, which he could delegate to the Electors of Brandenburg and the Palatinate, and that Frankfort be chosen for a meeting place. Ferdinand would have preferred a town more conveniently situated from his point of view, and suspected an intended slight. He suggested that Lund and Held act as imperial plenipotentiaries, the Electors merely as mediators. In spite of his desire for a settlement, Charles proceeded with exaggerated caution, and insisted on having detailed and confidential reports from Ferdinand of every step in the business. On October 28th he at length announced that he would send the Archbishop of Lund, and the instructions with which this latter eventually left Toledo were dated November 30th. They were couched in general terms, and to judge by their contents Charles seemed still to be counting on the help of the Pope and the French King. He was prepared only to make very limited concessions for bringing the Protestants back into the fold of the Church: they might have some licence in their dealings with the papal legate, but he would grant them no doctrinal deviation from the fundamentals of the Catholic faith. In return for such minor concessions, he wished both parties to keep the peace in Germany and give him their help against the Turk. Lund was with Ferdinand at Linz by the end of December. At the beginning of January 1539, they were deep in consultation. When the first Protestant demands were laid before him, Aleander was indignant: they seemed to him wholly unacceptable. And indeed while the Catholic party had expected a request that the settlement of Nuremberg be respected and trials in the *Reichskammergericht* cease, had perhaps even been ready for a demand for parity between the parties, they were taken by surprise by the demand for freedom of religion for all the imperial estates. This, later, was to be known as the *Freistellung*. Even more disturbing and unexpected was the request that subjects might have the right to choose their own religion and emigrate if they chose. The Protestant demands were based on the belief in a now inevitable and permanent separation of the two religions. The point was to be disputed for the whole of the coming century.

The outlook grew darker still when the members of the Schmalkaldic League, who had gathered at Frankfort, began to make serious preparations to defend their cause and spoke openly of a preventive war. Charles counted in vain on help from King Francis; he was far too clever to commit himself openly to either party. All the same, when William von Fuerstenberg, a well-known mercenary leader who had long been in French service, offered his sword to the Schmalkaldic League, it was at least probable that the King of France was behind him. The English King proved himself more openly favourable to the Protestants: he was negotiating for a marriage, either for himself or his daughter, with a member of the dynasty now ruling in Cleves-Jülich, and he was planning a general alliance with the Protestants and Denmark. His policy coincided with the abortive plan of the Catholic powers to make a descent on England. The young Duke of Cleves, too, was willing to ally himself with the Schmalkaldic League, whom he imagined would help him to make good his claim on Gelderland. But the Schmalkaldic League fought shy of an entanglement with a prince who so obviously wished to exploit them for political ends, and who had not yet openly declared himself in favour of the Augsburg Confession. In other fields, too, the peace party was still strong. Many members of the League were profoundly loyal to the Emperor and suspicious of French interference. The Landgrave of Hesse was strongly in favour of peace, although his influence was weakened by repeated illness and absence.

On the Catholic side the Archbishop of Lund seemed to be no

less obstinate than the Schmalkaldic League were exacting. The two mediators were in despair, yet they did not cease in their efforts to persuade the disputants to see reason, and they were for ever taking up and trying to knit together again threads which seemed irretrievably broken. Lund, in the meantime, showed that he, too, was equal to his task. He was remarkable for those very qualities in which Held was lacking. Obstinate in principle, he was nevertheless skilful in negotiation and easy of access. He would willingly accept invitations from the Landgrave or the Elector and would sit with them for hours, discussing in the friendliest possible way all the possibilities of solving their problems. A religious discussion began gradually to emerge as the best probable solution. Once both parties agreed to this, their mutual relationship could be more clearly defined and the points at issue narrowed down to essentials.

And so at last, on April 19th, 1539, these interminable discussions did lead to a settlement, which, astonishingly enough, went far beyond that of Nuremberg in 1532. By this 'Frankfurter Anstand' or 'Agreement of Frankfort' all the adherents of the Augsburg Confession were to be guaranteed against force, and the trials in the Reichskammergericht were to be held up for six months. Charles even promised to extend the truce for fifteen months if the Schmalkaldic League would undertake to seize no more Church land and to widen their scope no further: the Catholic Union would give an equivalent guarantee. Over and above this they agreed to meet at Worms on May 18th for a full discussion of the Turkish problem, and at Nuremberg on August 1st to thresh out their religious differences. The arrangement was in full accordance with the idea recently fathered upon the Protestant world by the Concordat of Wittenberg;[1] it was to play a prominent part in solving the relations between the Augustana and the old Church. From Charles's point of view, the new arrangement was the next step forward towards that agreement which he had so earnestly sought at Augsburg.

The great Erasmus had closed his eyes for ever on the world at Basel on July 11th, 1536. Yet in many ways the times still

[1] Signed at Wittenberg on May 29th, 1536, this represented a further effort of the north and south German Protestants to reach doctrinal agreement (TRANSLATOR's note).

seemed to reflect his own temper of compromise and good sense. On June 1st, 1540, Beatus Rhenanus dedicated his edition of the complete works of the scholar to the Emperor Charles V. There was a fitness in the act.

THE FIRST REGENCY OF PHILIP IN SPAIN. CHARLES'S JOURNEY THROUGH FRANCE

While the Protestant disputes were being settled in Germany, heavy sorrow brooded over the Emperor's household at Toledo. On April 20th the Empress gave birth to her seventh child. It died almost at once: of living children she had only Philip, Mary and Joanna. The Empress had been ailing for months and for her sake Charles remained in Toledo. In spite of her enfeebled state, it seemed at first that she would survive the strain of a premature confinement, but the fever suddenly resumed its hold, and on May 1st she died. Writing to Ferdinand, Charles declared that in his great sorrow he had no other comfort but the thought of her virtuous and devout life and her saintly death. He himself had nothing left to do but to submit himself in all patience to God's will, and pray him to take Isabella to him in Paradise.

For some days Charles withdrew altogether, to the Hieronymite monastery of La Sisla near Toledo.

In his memoirs, he speaks movingly of his wife's death, and of the sorrow which it caused to everyone. Then he proceeds to public business. 'After the meeting at Aigues Mortes and the continuation of negotiations for a solid and lasting peace with the King of France, disturbing news began to come from the Netherlands, from which country the Emperor had been absent since 1531. He judged that further absence would but increase this evil. He felt himself to be alone, and knew that his deepest wish was to preserve peace. He could not but think the prince, his son, still too young to govern in place of the Empress, and many other doubts were thrust upon him, yet he listened only to his own inner and sincere intention of doing what was best for his subjects so that they might not fall into greater distress. He wished, too, to see the conclusion of certain problems which he had left unsettled in Germany. He first thought of taking ship at Barcelona and going by way of Italy. But at this moment the French King urged him most cordially to travel by way of France, where he promised him every security and welcome. The Emperor felt that by refusing such an invitation he might well provoke serious trouble and awaken a feeling of mistrust Taking all these things into account, he therefore decided to leave Spain and to entrust its government to his son, young as he was.'

Tentatively as Charles embarked on the experiment of making the twelve-year-old Philip regent in his absence, he nevertheless used the occasion for the compilation of the first of those great political testaments which are to this day the best source of our knowledge of his character and intentions. Here, far more than in his letters to his wife, Charles set down the thoughts nearest his heart, and this with such emphasis and detail as would guarantee their execution even in his absence, even after his death.

As in his memoirs, so in the testament, he justified his renewed absence from Spain by his desire to make a permanent peace between his family, the King of the Romans and the King of France. The opening phrases of the great document recall the spirit of Gattinara. He admonished the prince to fear God and honour the holy Church, to fulfil his duties towards Christendom, his lands and his people.

Without intermission, he next proceeded to that thought which, since the temporary collapse of his crusading scheme, had entirely filled his mind, and for the realization of which he was anxious to have some security beyond his own life. He wished to see Europe dynastically organized for generations to come, under the leadership of the two great families of France and Burgundy, with the support of England and Portugal. The imperial office remained for the time being outside the ring of hereditary dynastic power, but he earmarked it naturally enough for the head of the House of Hapsburg. The breakdown of the negotiations at Nice, followed by the friendly meeting at Aigues Mortes, had given Charles another idea for the solution of his endless quarrel with the French King. Both lines of the Hapsburg dynasty might be allied by marriage to the Valois, and the disputed lands could be held alternately by members of each family. In this Charles was under the influence of the French theory for the solution of the European problem. He had abandoned Gattinara's idea of a free confederation of Italian states, with the papal states as an equal member, in favour of the dominance of Milan under a member of one or other of the two great dynasties. There were three possible solutions for the other great problem, that of the Burgundian inheritance. Either Charles's daughter, the Infanta Mary, could be recognized as heiress to the Netherlands and married to Ferdinand's son, thus bringing the Low Countries and the great claims of the Burgundian dynasty into the hands of the German branch of the family, or the Infanta could marry the Duke of Orleans, and make Burgundy what it had originally been in the remote days of its origin — the appanage of the second son of the French King. Thirdly and lastly the problem might be solved in Spain's favour.

In general Charles seems to have counted on leaving the Spanish and transatlantic kingdoms to Philip, and the Netherlands if the Provinces could be induced to receive him. Otherwise they were to go to the Infanta. The government of the Netherlands by the noble ladies of the Hapsburg family was gradually becoming a tradition. In compliance with the family compact, the Austrian lands were guaranteed to Ferdinand and his heirs. To satisfy Ferdinand's repeated demands for Milan, it was to be given to one of his daughters as a dowry on her marriage to the Duke of Orleans. Charles was reserving his younger daughter for the heir of Portugal, and he had planned to complete the circle of alliances by marrying the other prince of Portugal to his cousin, Princess Mary of England.

Charles and Ferdinand were occupied for several months in the discussion of these problems. The alternative solutions were variously canvassed. Was Philip or his sister to rule in the Netherlands? Was the Duke of Orleans to have Mary of Spain and the Netherlands for dowry, or Mary of Austria and Milan? The letters of the two brothers for some time were filled with nothing else; their ambassadors hurried busily to and fro. Now and again the family correspondence betrayed a human touch. Queen Mary advised Ferdinand to remember how difficult Charles could be in accepting propositions of which he was not himself the author, and urged him to act cautiously. Eleonore was not backward in furthering the good fortune of her stepson, the Duke of Orleans, or of her own daughter, the Infanta of Portugal.

Charles had settled on the heiress of Navarre or the princess of France for Philip. In later political testaments he was to revert again to this question of Navarre, for Ferdinand of Aragon's claim to it had been indefinite, and Charles himself had weakened his rights there by the treaty of Noyon. On the other hand, if Philip did not marry Margaret of France, she would be free for Ferdinand's second son or for the Infant of Portugal. Even this couple, Charles thought, might at a pinch be given Milan.

All these plans, Charles protested, were intended to make a firm peace in Christendom and to regain those lost to the Church. They aimed at securing Gelderland and Hungary and preventing the French King from allying himself to princes hostile to the Hapsburg dynasty. Ingenuous and transparent as was this dynastic scheme, it cannot be denied that the immense number of alternative solutions which Charles here outlined, gave it a certain flexibility and even skill.

True to his custom before a long journey, Charles once again drew up his own personal will, this time in the form of a codicil to the will of 1535. In this will he mentioned his whole system of political marriages. He also left a legacy for the saying of 30,000 masses for his soul, and asked that the Pope grant plenary indulgence to those who attended them. For his last resting place, he now chose Granada, where he would lie at the side of his wife.

He issued plenary powers to the regency council, on whom, as in the Empress's time, the actual weight of government during his absence continued to lie. Cardinal Tavera remained as always the minister chiefly responsible. And once again, as always before a long journey, he bade farewell to his mother at Tordesillas.

From Tordesillas he went by way of Burgos, San Sebastian, Bayonne, Bordeaux, to Poitiers and thence northwards into the Loire district. Either from Amboise or Blois, Francis set out to meet him, coming up with him at Loches on the Indre. Surrounded by a magnificent following, Francis himself was carried in a litter; he could no longer ride. In spite of the King's weakness, Charles averred that they did not loiter on the journey. He was delighted, too, to find that he was not at once to be overwhelmed with political business. On the contrary he was almost sated with hunting parties and joustings. The question of the family alliances was doubtless among the political business which was thus postponed. In spite of much persuasion from the French royal family, Charles refused even to consider his own second marriage. This was a sad disappointment to Francis; in his youth it had been his ambition to have the Emperor for a son-in-law, and he had been dreaming of that possibility once again. His Margaret, he insinuated to Charles, was a rose without a thorn, an angel beside whom all other women were fiends. But joyfully as he received Francis's other signs of affection, the Emperor turned a deaf ear to these particular praises. He prided himself on his own courage, and wrote to tell Ferdinand how delighted the King of France had been to find that his one-time enemy now travelled with such confidence through the land.

One evening, as they were entering a castle, an unpleasant incident occurred. Too many torches had been lighted and the horses took fright at the glare and smoke. But, as Charles added in his account of it, suspicion of foul play was groundless. Another story, from the *Zimmern Chronicle*, recounts the chivalrous way in which the Emperor behaved when his hosts provided him with a young girl for his private pleasures. The tale is probably an invention, but it serves well to show the high reputation which Charles enjoyed. The royal party was at Fontainebleau for Christmas, in Paris early in January. Thence they went by way of Chantilly, Soissons, St. Quentin, to Valenciennes and Cambrai, the whole Court following them. By the end of January Charles was in Brussels.

The letters which Charles wrote to Ferdinand, whom he had asked to meet him in Brussels, were more spritely than usual and give a good picture of the journey. A family council was now to meet and discuss all those dynastic questions which were of such importance not only to Ferdinand but to Mary, who was still at intervals reiterating a claim for parts of her dowry and for her widow's portion out of Hungary.

Queen Mary met Charles at Valenciennes. She had other and even more serious problems to lay before him.

THE STRUGGLE FOR GERMANY

THE EMPEROR IN GHENT. THE FRENCH
FRIENDSHIP BREAKS DOWN

Ghent had now been for more than two years in open conflict
with the government. Certain very radical alterations, partly the
outcome of the conflict itself, partly the signs of its deeper causes,
had taken place in the city during that time. General conclusions
can be drawn from the revolt of Ghent and wide comparisons
made. In its essence the struggle was not unlike the long-forgotten
contest between Frederick Barbarossa and Milan: economic
unrest and the growing idea of the dynastic state, as opposed
to these lesser states with their petty privileges, played parts of
almost equal importance. Ghent, indeed, was not, like Milan, a
rising town, but like Lübeck, a declining one. The economic
centre of the Netherlands had shifted from Flanders to Antwerp,
the industry of Ghent fell on evil days; unemployment and financial troubles ensued. Such things feed political and social unrest.
The constitution of the town was unusually democratic, for the
three Estates included, besides burghers and members of guilds,
the woollen weavers. Only a scattering of woollen weavers were
left, but the gaps in their ranks were filled by other manual
labourers, particularly from the transport industry. Representatives of these three Estates sat together in the general council, the
Collace.

Twenty-six justices controlled the administration of the town,
thirteen on each side. The burghers elected three of these, the
guilds and weavers five each.

Added to the commercial distress of Ghent, the last French
war in Artois had been particularly destructive, and the Queen's
government had been in great financial straits. The Estates had
granted her permission to take what measures she thought fit for
the defence of the country, but the town of Ghent had refused to
be included in these provisions. Only with the truce of Bomy in
June 1537 was the Queen able to breathe again. Her financial
troubles did not end with the war, and Queen Mary still depended
largely on the help which Ghent, alone in Flanders, refused to
give her. The city itself, no less ardent in the affair than the
indignant Mary, refused to pay any subsidy for which its delegates

426

had not voted, and sharpened the issue by appealing to general principles. The situation was not improved when Ghent offered to send men rather than money; Mary explained to its representatives that a hastily raised militia was hardly what was needed to wage a war in which money, horses, waggons and munition, were as important as soldiers. Ghent, she said, must pay, like other cities. When all her explanations failed to move the deputies, Mary, like Margaret before her, lost patience and appealed to arms.

The burghers took refuge behind ancient, but long disused privileges. The justices and their representatives showed a tendency to meet the Queen's demands, whereupon the quarrel rapidly developed into a civil war within the city, between the radical party and the bureaucracy. The usual mistrust of the lesser men for their betters, who were alleged to turn public funds to their own advantage, took on a peculiarly virulent form. The quarrel spread to the smaller towns and villages of the province, who followed the example of Ghent, and arrogated to themselves the same privileges, without being in any position to make good their claims.

Mary dispatched her cleverest advisers to Ghent. In April 1538 she sent Louis de Schore, later Lambert de Briarde and Adolphe of Burgundy, lord of Bevern. She sent Count Lalaing to Audenarde. All in vain. Her ambassadors themselves were threatened. The quarrel drove the people of Ghent at last to open revolution and betrayal of their country. They sought help from the French King. Unhappily for them they chose a moment when he was not interested, and he refused their offers. Yet in spite of this treachery, the movement had some elements in common with that of the Comuneros. The people thought that the Emperor was ignorant of what was going on. They decided to appeal to him. They were determined to settle nothing until he came.

The new elections to the magistracies brought the first serious internal war within Ghent itself. The external struggle was changed into an ugly internal conflict of personal hatreds. Some burghers fled in terror before the wrath of the mob, and the mob in turn avenged itself on those who stayed. Filthy and ungrounded slanders brought the most respected members of the community into contempt. Terrible scenes were enacted in the great hall of the Gravesteen: here Lieven Pyn, a reputable burgher, seventy-five years old, was cruelly insulted; his beard and hair were shaved off to exclude all possibility of demoniac assistance,[1] and he was dragged ruthlessly to the rack. He confessed nothing, and was condemned to death. With heroic courage, the old man forgave the people as he was dragged out to execution. He was but one of many, for in the passion of the moment any evidence was good enough to condemn a suspect, and informers sprang up like mushrooms after rain. The judges, even, showed less constancy than the accused. There was grotesque bathos as well as nauseating horror in the revolt. As Duke of Burgundy in 1515 Charles had granted the people a charter of privileges called the Calfskin. This the people now destroyed with shouts of joy, and for days after young ruffians walked the streets with its fragments stuck in their hats like ladies' favours. Queen Mary, they shouted, could shut herself up in a nunnery. They would not be governed by women.

Mary meanwhile defended her own rights with unswerving obstinacy and harshness. Yet in her favour it must be admitted that, in a time of national emergency, she more truly represented the needs of the state, whose defence and protection were the essential condition for the prosperity of each single town within it. Besides the revolutionary leaders showed no less obstinacy and far more harshness, without having any definite end in view, and without contributing to anything save the probable ruin of the town. Trade and industry suffered badly. For a long time there was no work, and a law made against the export of foodstuffs was of little use when provisions ran short in the town itself. The infection spread, meanwhile, to the whole country, and by the autumn of 1538 all Flanders was in a state of latent revolt. This was one of the considerations which had made Charles say, while he was still in Spain, that he must go to the Netherlands for the good of his people.

He expressed himself much the same, dryly and coldly, to the first deputation which he received from the people of Ghent at Valen-

---

[1] It was commonly believed that evil spirits hid in the hair and assisted a victim to bear torture. Witches were almost invariably shaved before being put to the question (TRANSLATOR's note).

ciennes. On February 14th, accompanied by Queen Mary, by the papal legate, by ambassadors, princes and nobles from the Netherlands, he entered Ghent in state. He was followed by a force of cavalry and five thousand landsknechts. With all his baggage and train, his entry lasted five hours. He took up his residence at his own birthplace, the Prinsenhof, quartering his troops in the different parts of the town. The people dared not stir.

Scenes of mob violence were now followed by scenes, no less horrible, of princely tyranny and military excess.

On February 17th Charles called on the leaders of the revolt to surrender. Some had fled; rewards were offered for their capture. On the 18th other prominent rebels were arrested. On his birthday, February 24th, Charles called the municipal council to the Prinsenhof, and in their presence the procurator-general of Malines read out the accusation against Ghent. The town was guilty of revolt, disobedience and treason.

While the city attempted to formulate a defence, Charles went to Brussels to meet Ferdinand; the rest of the sordid drama was played out in the presence of both of them. Charles harshly over-ruled Ghent's bewildered justifications. On March 3rd the trials of the leaders began, and the executions were carried out on the same spot where Lieven Pyn and many others had suffered. In its despair the city implored even Mary to intercede for it. The Queen replied, with cool cynicism, that it was a little late to pay humble respects to her: she had been present in their city for at least a month. But, she added, softening, she could forgive them and would do all in her power to restore peace. More disastrous than individual executions was the quartering of the undisciplined troops. Worst of all Charles pulled down a whole district of the town to set up a fortress. He did, however, make provision in his next codicil for a legacy of 30,000 Gulden out of his Spanish revenues as an indemnity.

On April 29th he pronounced his final verdict on the city. Ghent had forfeited all rights and privileges by its revolt against its hereditary sovereign and lord. Its whole public treasure was confiscated, its arms were taken away, its artillery and store of ammunition, last of all its great and famous bell, its Roland. Charles insisted on a solemn apology, and on May 3rd he received it, delivered in the same heart-breaking form as that in which defeated Milan had apologized to Barbarossa. The justices and their servants, thirty of the leading burghers, all in black, bare-headed and bare-footed, six representatives of every guild, fifty weavers and fifty representatives of the populace, who were known as *Creesers*, in their shirts and with halters round their necks, made a sad procession from the court of justice to the castle, and there, on their knees, asked pardon. On the following day Charles issued the new constitution of Ghent, the *Karolinische Concessie*. Medieval Ghent was dead.

Acutely sensitive to his position as a sovereign, Charles had felt that in acting so harshly towards the city he was acting but justly. While his cruel judgment took its course, other negotiations were discussed in the apartments of the Prinsenhof. Charles was equally busied about the dynastic alliances of his family, about German affairs and about the administration of the Netherlands.

From Ghent on March 24th the Emperor sent word to the French Court, through his ambassador Bonvalot, Abbot of St. Vincent. It was a curious message which Charles now sent, for he seemed to have forgotten all those interesting alternative alliances, and instead exposed Francis to the bitterest disappointment by suddenly demanding the most colossal concessions. Instead of attempting to solve the still vexed question of Milan, Charles actually dug up the old problem of the Burgundian inheritance. He suggested that the Duke of Orleans should marry his daughter Mary, to whom he would give as a dowry the Netherlands and the whole of Bourgogne. The King, he said optimistically, could not but admit that this inheritance was a great deal more splendid than Milan. In fact, Charles added, he would not be prepared to make such sacrifices of his own interest were he not determined to further an understanding with France. If Gelderland and Zutphen could be added to the Netherlands, the promised lands would be one of the finest inheritances in all Christendom. He was even willing to let the Duke of Orleans and his wife rule over the Netherlands during his lifetime. If the Infanta were to die childless, he went on, the land must, of course, revert to him. And, he added, it was only reasonable that Francis should now renounce Milan, since he had shown himself thus ready to renounce even Bourgogne. He hoped that he might count on the King's help in winning back Gelderland, while the return of Charolais, St. Pol and Hesdin must follow as a matter of course. Special provisions would have to be made for the possibility of the Duke of Orleans becoming the heir of France, or the Infanta the heiress of Spain. Furthermore, Charles blandly pursued, his brother Ferdinand must be indemnified, for he had first been promised the Infanta for his own eldest son. Charles now suggested that Francis should supply this young Archduke with a bride, in his daughter Madame Marguerite. The princess would in course of time become a mighty Queen, a prospect which would be materially assisted if Francis would immediately give help to King Ferdinand in Hungary. For his own son, Charles now wanted the heiress of Navarre, 'so that these claims too may be settled at last'. Eleonore's daughter must, of course, be provided for, and Francis was also requested to return the lands he had recently seized from the Duke of Savoy. As for himself, Charles went on with amazing tactlessness, he was too old to marry again: to the vain and ageing Francis, his senior by several years, this sentence must have sounded almost insulting. For the common weal of Christendom, Charles concluded, they must both conclude a general peace, with each other and with the Pope, the Empire, Portugal, Poland, England, Scotland, the Italian states, and the Swiss Confederation.

Did Charles really imagine that he could thus cheaply and easily settle all the problems and buy back the lands which had been so bloodily disputed for so long? Did he think that he had the least chance of thus obtaining a formal recognition of his rights in Milan as well as in Bourgogne, together with the restoration of the lost parts of Artois, of St. Pol, Hesdin, Gelderland and Zutphen? Nay, of Savoy and Hungary? Yet apparently he did think that such dreams could still be realized, for he was amazed when Francis made answer in terms whose arrogance far surpassed even his own. He imparted this answer to Ferdinand with the quiet comment that they must both act with more reserve in future, and trust in the meantime to the renewed personal assurance of King Francis that he was their best and truest friend. Yet one wonders whether even Charles believed these assurances on a more careful perusal of the French counter-claim.

Francis demanded that the Duke of Orleans should have an unqualified right of inheritance in the Netherlands. Should Charles grant this, Francis would withdraw his claim to Milan. But if the Duke of Orleans were then to die childless, Francis would resume his right to Milan. If the Infanta died before the Duke of Orleans he was either to be her heir, or Milan was to be restored. Francis went on to refuse to renew the treaties of Madrid and Cambrai. As for Savoy, he felt that he must hold the land in the interests of the French monarchy. He would be willing to indemnify the Duke.

Charles answered in the same unbending tone. He could not, he said, give Francis rights both in Italy and in the Netherlands. Francis retaliated with a request to hold Milan as a fief, as Louis XII had done. Gradually it became apparent that the two brothers-in-law had been working at cross purposes for the last months. Neither of them had the least inclination to concede anything. King Francis meanwhile had joined once more with Charles's enemies. In the traditional manner he had always kept one ally ready to strike Charles in the back. This was the Duke of Gelderland. Now Francis offered help to the even more powerful Duke of Cleves, and by so doing conjured up a storm worse than any other which the government of the Netherlands had yet had to meet.

Cleves was Charles's third great problem. It had brought him to the Netherlands; he knew that it lay very close to the roots of the German problem. By the Treaty of Grave in December 1536 the Duke of Gelderland had renounced his claim on Drenthe and Groningen and recognized Charles's hereditary rights. But in October 1537 he announced to his Estates that he had found a very powerful protector in the King of France. This caused general excitement, more particularly in the towns of Nymwegen, Zutphen, Roermond and Venloo. In the meantime Martin van Rossem, marshal of Gelderland, had already paid allegiance to the French King. The Duke now opened negotiations with the towns at Arnhem. The legitimate heir was his nephew, Anthony, son of the Duke of Lorraine by Philippine of Egmont. But the Estates of Gelderland, regardless of any obligations to the real master of the Netherlands, loudly adopted the son of the Duke of Cleves for their heir. Immediately the

father reverted to his own ancient claims on the duchy of Gelderland, which had in fact been sold by Gerard of Jülich to Charles
the Bold. As soon as Queen Mary heard of this she wished to
take action, but Charles had his hands full with other matters,
and preferred to let things drift. On June 30th, 1538, after a
reign of fifty years, the Duke of Gelderland died. In the next
winter, on February 6th, 1539, John of Cleves-Jülich followed
him to the grave. His son William was now lord of Jülich,
Cleves, Berg, Mark, and Ravensberg, and pretender to Zutphen
and Gelderland. He it was whom King Francis now drew into
the web of his policy, and through him began to take up points of
vantage for his attack on Charles, both on the Flemish frontier
and on the Spanish. On June 15th, 1540, Francis arranged for
the young Duke of Cleves to be married, at least as far as forms
went, to Jeanne d'Albret, the twelve-year-old heiress of Navarre.
The little princess protested vehemently, both through her
mother and her governess, and repeated her protests on June 14th,
1541, in the presence of witnesses. In spite of this Francis insisted
not only on celebrating the ecclesiastical ceremony of the wedding,
but had the young couple solemnly put to bed in the presence of
witnesses.

Charles was still ignorant of these things, but he nevertheless
painted the situation in gloomy colours when he wrote to King
Ferdinand on June 17th. 'As things now stand in the Netherlands,
in France and in Germany', he lamented, 'I am in no position to
use force. It is to be hoped that a discussion with the Duke's
representatives and those of the Estates may be arranged, if
possible in Holland, whither I am going. This would enable me
to explain my own clear right to Gelderland and to assure the
people that I shall leave them in undisturbed enjoyment of their
privileges.' He went on to recommend the establishment of good
relations with Lorraine, suggesting that the heir to that duchy
be married to a Hapsburg princess, either to the widowed
Christina of Milan, or failing her to one of Ferdinand's daughters.
'The French will make every effort to prevent his joining us,' he
concluded gloomily.

On July 2nd, in another letter, Charles closed enthusiastically
with Ferdinand's idea for dividing the Elector of Saxony and the
Landgrave of Hesse. Saxony was to be bribed by the confirmation

of his partial claim to the Cleves-Jülich inheritance and was to be offered one of Ferdinand's daughters for his eldest son. Charles went even further, for he suggested that the Elector's help in Gelderland should be bought by offering him the possession of the very fiefs in that country which were at present claimed by the Duke of Cleves-Jülich. This plan was to be used later and more effectively in the opposite direction — in winning over Duke Maurice of Saxony against this same old Elector.

For many months Charles played for time, raising one diplomatic point after another and evading the issue. The situation was growing more dangerous. The King of England married Anne of Cleves on January 6th, 1540, and was therefore to be counted at the moment among Charles's opponents, and several German princes at the same time espoused the cause of the young Duke of Cleves. This in itself was a reason for proceeding in Germany with the utmost caution.

Lund had promised the German Protestants that the Emperor would settle every problem when he came; in this hope the truce between the two parties had been lengthened to fifteen months. But although Charles neither denied his intention of settling the quarrel, nor yet broke the existent truce, nothing constructive was done. This did not prevent the Vatican and the extremist party among the German Catholics from slanderously asserting that Lund had been bribed by the Protestants at Frankfort. Held, his rival in both the political and personal sphere, took part in spreading these malicious slanders, and in a letter to Ferdinand Charles himself related an almost violent scene between these two learned councillors actually in his own presence. All the same the Emperor was soon convinced that the hot-headed Held was the last person he could safely employ in the present juncture; without undue regret therefore he gradually removed the aged Vice-chancellor from his various offices. Held was succeeded, as early as the following May, by Johann von Naves.

The meeting called at Worms to discuss the Turkish problem was a failure — the first disappointment to the hopes which the temporary religious truce at Frankfort had raised. True to his arrangement with the French King, Charles was now in favour of a Concordat. But the Pope was again pressing for a council and Charles found himself exposed to attack on all sides. On February

24th, 1540, the very day on which he pronounced sentence on the town of Ghent, he had given audience both to Cardinal Farnese from the Pope, and to a representative of the Schmalkaldic League. At the beginning of March, Duke Henry of Brunswick arrived at his Court, pressing, as always, for war on the Schmalkaldic League. Farnese and the Bavarian delegates complained bitterly of the Emperor's weakness. Charles in his turn begged leave to doubt the extent to which he might depend on the Pope's help if it should in fact come to war. Duke Henry of Brunswick, he knew or guessed, had good private motives behind his public-spirited zeal. He wanted to gain possession of Goslar. His own knowledge, therefore, forced Charles to proceed with caution.

THE RELIGIOUS DISCUSSIONS OF 1540 AND THE STRANGE CASE OF THE LANDGRAVE OF HESSE

The religious talks, which intermittently occupied the next two years, form part of the connected chain of imperial policy. They were neither intended to mislead the Protestants, nor were they merely a subterfuge to gain time. Like the discussion at Augsburg in 1530, they were genuine attempts at conciliation. But if they began seriously, Charles must at some point have realized how unlikely they were to succeed. Only gradually did he grasp the irreconcilable differences which now divided the two creeds, for he had been partly deceived of recent years by the vociferous political loyalty of the Protestant princes. During the greater part of those months during which the negotiations continued, Charles was genuinely convinced not merely of their necessity, but even of their efficacy.

There were others, however, who did not agree with Charles. The nuntius at Ferdinand's Court, Morone, himself a learned theologian and a politician of some insight into German affairs, held that the discussions were useless in themselves and degrading to the dignity of the Catholic Church. His opinion was shared by many of the more important personages at the Vatican, like Cardinal Aleander. This party did everything possible to prevent the discussions and to hinder their progress. They had their parallels among the Protestants, for here too there was a party

which felt that the differences between the creeds were too fundamental to be settled. It is clear to us to-day that the extremists
were right. But at the time there were many serious theologians
who felt that the common Christianity, even the common patristic
fundamentals of the two beliefs, need not be sacrificed merely for
a few differences in dogma. In the lifetime of Duke George, in
1539, Carlowitz had held a religious discussion between Bucer and
Wicel at Leipzig, where a doctrine of the sacrament, acceptable
both to Lutherans and Catholics, had been evolved. Nevertheless,
a settlement by discussion could only be successful if many other
points of doctrine were altogether passed over. The belief in
Transubstantiation, for instance, entailed the most complicated
consequences. It reached far back into the very fundamentals of
Christian dogma and into the meaning and office of the priesthood. It affected the nature of worship, the arrangement of the
Church itself and the preservation of the sacred wafer.

The advocates of the talks did not altogether deceive themselves
as to the difficulties they were likely to encounter. But they
felt that it would be best to see by experience how near to a
settlement they could get, and then, by carefully comparing
insoluble difficulties, they could more easily determine what each
side ought to tolerate from the other. In the Vatican itself there
were men who felt that, as to mere ritual, it should not be impossible to allow the laity to receive the sacrament in both kinds,
while the marriage of priests might well be tolerated. The
politicians were naturally prepared to go further than the theologians. They were as much or more interested in the men who
held the opinions than in the opinions themselves; they were as
much concerned with averting the present danger by winning over
some of the political leaders and separating the rest by exposing
their doctrinal differences, as they were with mere theological
argument. These elements made the religious talks so intrinsic
and so significant a part in the development of Charles's imperial
policy.

Nobody expected the Pope to give his consent to the talks,
although some of the dignitaries at the Vatican had attempted to
persuade him. He did, however, yield, not for any desire for peace
with the Protestants, but because Charles had wisely gratified the
claims of the Farnese dynasty on the lordship of Camerino.

Nevertheless, the assistance given by the Vatican was of no serious importance. Morone's instruction, dated May 15th, 1540, was not helpful. 'If they say to you that the settlement of this dispute is urgent', it ran, 'you are to say to them that the salvation of men's souls is yet more urgent.' The Pope himself, either with the help of a council or as the representative of the universal Church, was alone capable of approving the necessary means for a settlement. 'If', the instruction went on, 'they say that without a religious peace there can be no peace in this nation, you are to answer that other means will have to be found.' This sentence admitted of no two interpretations. Added to this, the nuncio was strictly commanded to keep aloof from the discussions. He might receive the Catholic delegates in his own house and give them advice, but even for this advice he was to stick to the letter of his very limited instructions.

Charles himself had been preparing for the decision which lay in front of him for almost as long as Ferdinand and the opposing German parties. He too had written letters, taken advice and listened to suggestions on the most important points. In long conversations with his confessor he busied himself with the distinctions between divine and man-made law, *droit divin* and *droit positif*; faced by the decisive refusals of one side or the other, he explored the boundaries of the possible. Plague caused the removal of the conference from Speyer to Hagenau, where it was opened on June 12th by King Ferdinand. Here the Emperor emphatically stated that no definite decision could be taken without the consent of the Pope. But in spite of this statement, Charles firmly opposed the efforts of Morone and the Bavarians to wreck the conference. As a starting point he commended the articles which had already been settled between Campeggio and Melanchthon at Augsburg. The Protestants began badly by objecting to this. They declared that they could not recollect the terms of those articles. It was an inauspicious omen for the conference.

The most celebrated theologians of both persuasions were assembled. Luther himself could not be present; he had not been present at Augsburg. Melanchthon was prevented from coming by illness. The Protestants included Cruciger, Myconius, Bucer, Osiander, Link and Blarer. From Strasbourg came another group among whom one man was outstanding, John Calvin. Owing to

Ferdinand's position, his own theologians dominated the Catholic group. These included Faber, Nausea and Cochlaeus. Next in importance was Eck of Ingolstadt. All the same, the serious work had not even begun when propositions were made for the postponement of the meeting. These were agreed to, and the conference dissolved, not without having found some friendly basis for discussion, until it should meet again at Worms on October 20th.

Urgent news had recalled Ferdinand to his lands. He returned in the nick of time, for on July 21st John Zapolya had died, and by the Treaty of Grosswardein Ferdinand was now his heir. In Ferdinand's absence the directors of the discussion were the Elector Palatine, the Duke of Bavaria and the Bishop of Strasbourg; the Elector of Mainz came to replace the Elector of Treves. The princes were represented by their councillors and chancellors. Charles gave particular proof of his personal interest in the conference by sending his first minister, Nicholas Perrenet, lord of Granvelle. This statesman, whose services had been hitherto confined to the diplomatic field, stepped with this employment into the forefront of imperial policy. Always a diplomatist at heart, his skilful management and refusal to accept defeat gave a certain superficial appearance of success to the discussions at Worms. The situation in which Charles found himself, and the chance circumstances surrounding the conference, confirmed the Emperor in his belief that it was expedient to handle the whole business as though it were predominantly political.

With the French friendship so rapidly waning, Charles had taken two important steps at the beginning of October. Although these were in a sense merely preventive measures, they made him all the more anxious to have new alliances and securities. Following out the schemes outlined in his recent political testament, he approached the nobles of the Netherlands on October 2nd with an important question. He asked them whether they would prefer to have Prince Philip as their ruler, with the hope that he would leave male heirs, or, with Philip's consent, the Infanta Mary, who should be married to the second son of King Ferdinand. The nobles apparently expressed no very strong opinion for either alternative.

Independent of happenings in the Netherlands, Charles had already bestowed the fief of Milan on Philip on October 11th,

1540. He may have done this because he remembered what Gattinara had once said of the disposal of Milan, yet he was not so much pursuing Gattinara's policy as his own dynastic plan. Even without the co-operation of Francis he was determined to put some of it at least into execution. A little later, on October 28th, 'considering the mutability of things', he cancelled the codicil which he had added to his will in 1539. The French King, he averred, had made such unreasonable conditions for the projected marriages, that his acceptance of them would only breed fresh problems. With the agreement of the nobility he had therefore postponed further arrangements for the future of the Netherlands. He could not, however, postpone a definite decision for Milan; it had cost all his kingdoms, particularly Castile and Aragon, heavy sacrifices to win and retain the duchy, which he could not now lightly bestow on some perhaps unreliable ruler. Prince Philip was therefore invested with Milan. By this action Charles had cut himself loose from the problems of the past and made way for the future. Surely and fatefully the centre of gravity of the Hapsburg power shifted towards Spain.

In the immediate present another event seemed more important. For the last year the Landgrave of Hesse had been officiously pressing his services upon the Hapsburg dynasty. More than twelve months before he had intimated his readiness to help Queen Mary through Naves, next he had approached Charles through the Bishop of Lund, later, in March, he had sent his own emissary, Siebert von Löwenberg, to Ghent, and finally he sent yet more pressing offers of friendship through Granvelle himself. On his way to Worms, Granvelle had stopped for a short time at his native town of Ornans, and Cornelius Schepper was the man whom Charles entrusted with the delicate task of negotiating with the Landgrave. The details of the transaction have survived in Schepper's reports to Granvelle and the papers which he enclosed with them. The acts preserved at Marburg confirm their general outline.

On March 4th of this very year 1540 the Landgrave had contracted his celebrated bigamous marriage.[1] Since that time he felt

---

[1] Philip's first wife was Christina of Saxony; he could not divorce her, but conceived instead the ingenious idea of contracting a double marriage, like the Patriarchs. His second wife was Margarete von der Saal (TRANSLATOR'S note).

that his position was very insecure, for his own co-religionists, the Elector of Saxony in particular, were threatening to desert him. Thus at the very moment when his conduct was, from the moral and religious point of view, most equivocal, he turned to the Emperor for help. The Emperor, for his part, was as we know only waiting for the opportunity of separating Saxony from Hesse. The Landgrave offered to assist Charles against the opposition which was collecting against him; to justify his conduct he explained that Charles's willingness to have a religious conference at Worms, followed by a Diet, was proof of his genuine desire to bring peace to Germany. The Landgrave went on to say that the opposition had used the Elector of Saxony's negotiations in July as a cover to make overtures to the French King, with no better end in view than to forestall Charles's efforts at reunion. For his part, continued the Landgrave, he had always worked against these people, and if the Emperor would let bygones be bygones and take him again into favour, he would continue to thwart the malcontents. He would support the Emperor, he went on, against French, Danes, Turks and English — against everyone in fact, except Germans. He would moreover dispatch his most trusted ministers to plan the terms of an agreement and to make further revelations of Protestant policy. He went further: he would not only hinder all the machinations of France, but he would speak in favour of religious concessions at the Diet and give his support to the Emperor and the King of the Romans, the future Emperor. He would be willing to give help against enemies in the Low Countries, in Gelderland first and foremost.

No offer could have been made more appositely for Charles.

Schepper noted down in his papers: 'On October 28th at 2 o'clock the Emperor entrusted me with the following answer to give to the Hessian Doctor by word of mouth.' The Emperor, Schepper was to indicate, would think over the Landgrave's offer, and would carefully consider whether he could confirm the existing high-school at Marburg.[1] Touching the Landgrave's other suggestions, the Emperor had never given grounds for the supposition that he intended to use force against any Christian prince, nor had he now any such intention. He had in fact but

---

[1] The University of to-day. It was founded in 1527, independently of the Catholic Church (TRANSLATOR'S note).

recently dispatched the lord of Granvelle to Worms with plenipotentiary powers to effect a peace between the Germans. If the
Landgrave was serious in his offer to enter into close alliance with
the Emperor, he had only to communicate with the lord of
Granvelle, who had full powers to act in his name.

Writing from Ornans, Granvelle thanked Schepper for his
detailed report, in a letter conceived in the elegant language of
humanism. He next proceeded to Worms to take part in the discussions, whose opening had already been somewhat delayed.
His letters to the Emperor were frequent and full, recording the
acts and bearing of the German princes and their ministers, of the
Hessians in particular, in detail, as they passed before his observant eyes. The papal nuncio, Thomas Campeggio, brother of the
Cardinal who had since died, was not present when Granvelle
opened the Worms conference on November 25th. But to the
astonishment of everyone he appeared on December 8th, and,
speaking in a friendly and conciliatory manner, deplored the
schism and admonished them to find a point of common union.
The Protestants had expected a very different attitude, and the
careful answer which Melanchthon had prepared, rejecting the
papal demands, was wholly out of place. After this misfire,
the two parties decided to communicate by writing. This method
soon revealed a deplorable lack of matter on the side of the
ancient Church. The eleven Protestant representatives stood
unanimously by their Confession. But of the eleven Catholics, the
representatives of Brandenburg, of the Palatinate, of Cleves-
Jülich, were sharply divided from the others. It seemed that the
Emperor was not to find clearly defined parties but small and
mutually exclusive groups. The desertion of the Protestants by
the Landgrave of Hesse began slowly to have its effect on the
debates. Through his councillors and theologians, Granvelle
maintained unbroken communication with him throughout the
meeting.

The situation, as interpreted by Granvelle, was characterized by
the gradual winning over of individual Protestants to the imperial
side. It was among the Catholics that he met a sequence of
increasing difficulties. The Chancellor of the Elector of Mainz
was said to be unable to stir an inch without the consent of Held,
while the Bavarians confronted Granvelle with a policy of shame-

less postponement. Another impression borne in upon Granvelle was that the Protestant party was itself growing. There were signs of it in the Elector Palatine's surroundings and in all his family. The Duke of Cleves too seemed to tend in that direction. Then there was the clever and active Elector of Brandenburg, a good Latinist, who was said to have some influence on Luther, and through whom contact with the great Reformer could perhaps be established. In short Granvelle was realizing that, at least from his master's point of view, the roles of the German princes were not at all what might have been expected. In spite of certain practical difficulties, the Protestants were friendly and the Emperor's immediate political future seemed to lie in an alliance with them. The Catholics, on the other hand, displayed a desire for war which was highly undesirable at the present moment, and were coolly indifferent to all attempts at mediation.

It was something of an achievement when Granvelle, in spite of so much opposition, managed to bring about some important private conferences. These, in which he was helped by the Landgrave, took place both before the public discussion began and during its course. Bucer and Capito for the Protestants, Veltwyk and Gropper for the Catholics, met for personal conversations, which at first looked almost as though they might bring forth great results. Bucer was the Landgrave's chief confidant in ecclesiastical matters and Capito, who came from Strasbourg, seemed inclined to work seriously for the furtherance of an understanding. Gropper and Gerard Veltwyk here make their first appearance in these pages. The former was a protégé of the Elector of Cologne, a man of a highly analytical brain, sympathetic, as was his master, to the idea of reform within the Church. The latter was a Jewish convert, native of Ravestein; as a young man he had written a book in the Hebrew language, the *Schwile tohu*, or *The Wanderings in the Wilderness*, in which, making use of the ancient vocabulary of the Old Testament, he had sought to convert his Jewish fellows to that Christianity of whose truth he was himself profoundly convinced. He was accounted the best Hebrew scholar of his time, and as such aroused the greatest interest among the Protestant theologians at Worms. Here both parties could tread the neutral ground of learning. Veltwyk, as a theologian, belonged to the same school of thought as his fellow-

Rhinelander, Gropper. The discussions held between these four men, which were in their turn doubtless based on the results of the Leipzig conversations, were carried on with the greatest good-will and with every possibility of a practical decision.

The central conference, meanwhile, was hedged about with formalities. The speakers added to the trouble by failing to comply with the time limit set down for them. Yet even here there was no lack of fundamental goodwill and mutual understanding. Taking advantage of this, Granvelle would not let matters proceed to any dangerous issue, but urged the representatives, in view of the approaching Diet, to rest contented with what they could easily achieve.

While the theological controversy dragged out its endless course, Granvelle and the Hessian chancellor continued their negotiations, not always uninfluenced by the religious discussion. The chief question was that of the guarantees which Charles was to give to the Landgrave in return for his support. The Landgrave did not want to be altogether cut off from his co-religionists and Granvelle was firm in his contention that if no religious concessions were to be made, then there would have to be other and more rigid conditions. By the middle of January Granvelle had nevertheless promised the Landgrave his pardon for his part in the Württem-berg incident, and for other secular transgressions. Charles was in Heidelberg for a short visit early in February; here Granvelle joined him and here received the news that the Landgrave had agreed to all the terms decided on, in the discussions which Gran-velle and de Praet had had with the Hessian chancellor. In the main this amounted to a guarantee of the Emperor's favour in return for his services at the coming Diet. Granvelle had made use of the intervening time, not without success, to persuade several of the other princes to come to the Diet in person.

The situation at the imperial Court itself seemed better. For instance, the Cardinal-legate, Marcellino Cervino, who had been sent to Germany not to take part in the religious discussion but to exert his influence in conjunction with Alessandro Farnese, against it, had found himself unable to resist the Emperor's obvious sincerity of manner and intention. Cervino was the governor and chief adviser of the Cardinal-nephew, who was himself later to be the Pope's legate at the Council of Trent, and later still to be

Pope himself. When Cervino was soon after recalled, his successor, whom he himself had chosen, was instrumental in furthering the religious conference for which papal support had now been gained. The Emperor himself had earlier singled out this new papal emissary as a man most likely to assist him. He was Gasparo Contarini, once Venetian ambassador in Madrid.

REGENSBURG, 1541

All seemed to develop according to the plans of the Emperor and Granvelle, and great were the hopes fixed on the Diet of Regensburg. The day for its opening was January 6th, 1541. The noblest and finest intellects in Germany were once again summoned to help in making a religious peace. Events, too, contributed to the probability of a settlement, for the conference at Worms had shown that such a thing was still possible, while Charles himself saw that the establishment of peace would be a step towards the confirmation of his own authority. Added to this, neither he nor Ferdinand were in any position to use force. A new and serious Turkish invasion threatened Hungary, where the King had vainly besieged the fortress of Ofen, terrified lest a relieving force should take him unawares. Charles was oppressed by the return of all his ancient fear of France, and harassed by his own gnawing desire to launch another attack on Turkish sea-power in the Mediterranean, if only for the defence of his own coasts.

Yet with all these prospects of religious peace, delay after delay postponed the issue.

Charles travelled from the Netherlands to Regensburg by way of Speyer. Here he suspended the ban on Goslar and Minden, and put off the trials against the Protestants which were at that moment pending in the *Reichskammergericht*. The news of his action resounded throughout Germany like a peal of joy-bells rung in rehearsal on the eve of some festal day. He was joyously received in Heidelberg and he also cheered the Protestant city of Schwäbisch Hall by a gracious visit. His entries to Nuremberg, and on February 23rd, to Regensburg, were splendid in the extreme. Yet, contrary to the practice of his youth, he himself was clad only in sober black. He no longer felt that need for personal splendour which had dominated his early years.

In Regensburg itself there was as yet little sign of a Diet. Duke Lewis of Bavaria and Duke Henry of Brunswick had alone reached it in time to greet the Emperor. A few days later Duke William of Bavaria arrived with his wife. Charles was uncertain of the social and legal forms which he ought to employ and wrote to Ferdinand for advice. He sent de Praet to speak his welcome to the Bavarian dukes, not wishing to reveal his own ignorance. Duke William approached him almost at once with friendly offers of help. Many things in the course of that Diet recalled what had happened in 1530. Duke William's liveliest desire, both in 1530 and in 1541, was that his thirteen-year-old son should marry Charles's niece, Ferdinand's daughter, a little girl of about his own age. Another of Charles's nieces also played her part in the Diet. This was the widowed Duchess Christina of Milan, offered and wooed so often before, who was now married, through the efforts of Queen Mary, to the heir-presumptive of Lorraine. A generation later Christina's daughter, Renate, was to marry into the Bavarian dynasty. In this summer of 1541 those great dynastic marriages, whose effect was to be felt far into the Counter-Reformation, were already partly arranged.

The political attitude of the Bavarians revealed their self-confidence. The so-called Protestants, they declared, were abusing the Emperor's goodness. Had the Edict of Worms been properly executed Germany would not now be in this divided state. The Bishop of Lund had acted very dishonestly both at Frankfort and later in his dealings with the city of Augsburg. The conferences at Hagenau and Worms, they complained, had shown them nothing except the feebleness of some of their fellow-Catholic rulers. The first essential was to stiffen the Catholic League. There were, of course, three other alternatives. They might negotiate, but that usually led nowhere; one argued for ever, but some Christian princes would never be convinced. Besides, the Bavarians unctuously concluded, they themselves had always entertained the belief that the decisions of the ancient councils and the traditions which had governed the Church since the time of the Apostles were above question. The second alternative was to call in the other Kings and rulers of Christendom to

445

help uphold the true faith by force of arms. The third was to proclaim a general council of the German nation within eighteen months, using the intervening period to strengthen the Catholic League and hold its opponents in check. All this, even to the suggestion of calling in foreign allies, foreshadowed the programme of the Counter-Reformation.

The Emperor's answer, which was given both by word of mouth and in writing, was no more than a general expression of gratitude, to which Charles added some hint of his fear of the Turks and other enemies. He went on to say that all his efforts to hold a council had been hindered by the Christian princes themselves, in Europe and within Germany. Such things could not seriously be discussed until the other Estates had sent their representatives to the Diet. A more secretive answer could hardly have been evolved.

Not until April 7th was the Diet formally opened. The Emperor had been forced to waste more than a month waiting for the delegates, and his hunting parties at Straubing had been, this time, a pastime in the fullest sense of the word. After the usual exchange of opinions, the Estates proceeded to discuss the religious question and a conference was at once fixed, at which it was hoped that the experience already gained by both parties would be turned to good account. The Emperor himself nominated three protagonists on each side: Gropper, Julius Pflug and Eck for the Catholics; Melanchthon, Bucer and Pistorius for the opposition. The two laymen appointed to preside were Granvelle, and the Count Palatine, Frederick; other laymen with a voice in the proceedings were the Chancellors of Saxony and Hesse and Jakob Sturm of Strasbourg. The religious policy which Charles was now pursuing was imperial in every sense of the word.

The talks went on for a month, from the end of April until the end of May. They formed by far the most important part of the Diet, and their details are full of interest. Sometimes the participants genuinely tried to reach unanimity, sometimes they acted from mere political necessity, sometimes they actively attempted to force a breach. A secret document, dating apparently from the conference at Worms and sparsely published, formed the basis of their discussions. Granvelle brought it with him, sealed up, on the first morning, and took it home with him, sealed again, in the evenings. The principles on which the disputants arrived at conclusions were later known as the *Book of Regensburg*. Before each meeting the Catholic delegates consulted with Contarini, who thus played an important part in the proceedings. Charles, too, took part. During these weeks there were many happy moments in which agreement seemed possible; Contarini even wrote his celebrated letter to Rome rejoicing in the fact that the disputants had come to an agreement over the important question of the doctrine of justification. In contrast to Eck's rude manner, Contarini's urbane suavity seemed highly persuasive. He openly blamed the theologians of Ingolstadt for busily trying to break up the conference, by introducing the most highly controversial points, such as the primacy of the Pope, as early and as persistently as they could. Once he entered personally into the discourse, by sending a written speech, and he let it be generally known that he was delighted with every new sign of approaching unity. On May 1st, that is at the very beginning of the discussions, Veltwyk actually brought Bucer to see him. The legate's conversation had but one general drift and chorus — 'How great will be the fruit of unity, and how profound the gratitude of all mankind!' Bucer replied suitably: 'Both sides have failed', he said. 'Some of us have over-emphasized unimportant points, and others have not adequately reformed obvious abuses. With God's will, we shall ultimately find the truth.'

Melanchthon played an even larger part than Bucer. He too adopted a wholly conciliatory attitude. But underneath it he remained as immovable as at Augsburg. When the question of the Blessed Sacrament came up for discussion, he declared, without waiting for the support of his fellow-Protestants, that no compromise could be reached on this point. Such things happened all too often and were so bitter a disappointment to Granvelle that once at least he lost patience, and attempted to gain his end by threats — an action which only made matters worse. These efforts to reach agreement, serious as they were in intention, were sometimes very ingenuous in execution. The Elector of Brandenburg, for instance, asked the Landgrave, the Elector Palatine, Granvelle, de Praet and the Saxon councillors to a dinner party, where the imperialist group attempted 'to prove to the prince in the course of friendly conversation the true doctrine of the Holy Sacrament'. 'The

447

evening', reported Sanzio to Cardinal Farnese on May 13th, 'was not wholly useless.'

Melanchthon assured the imperial councillors and his own co-religionists that there could be no unity as to dogma. The same statements were repeatedly made to the Emperor by Contarini and Morone. These assurances forced Charles himself to intervene in the discussions, not always with the happiest results. Yet he clung so passionately to the hope of ultimate reconciliation, that he once spoke almost with violence to the legate. He was no theologian, he said, but he understood that while the Protestants had shown themselves willing to yield even on the question of auricular confession, the Catholics were making trouble over the mere word 'Transubstantiation'. In the name of God, he protested, why could they not take up all their points of agreement with the Protestants first, and revert to the more arguable questions only when the basis of the conciliation was arrived at? The Catholic party had no cause to pride themselves on wrecking the whole conference.

Charles's indignation when Amsdorf inveighed against the agreement from the pulpit can well be imagined. His anger may have been increased by the rumour at Court that French intervention was confirming the theologians in their obstinacy. Melanchthon had certainly been seen one day in conversation with the French orator. For these reasons Charles reluctantly turned from the theologians to the princes and their ministers, and first of all to Philip of Hesse. This latter had fulfilled all his promises to support imperial policy. He also followed the conference with the keenest sympathy. His personal copy of the *Book of Regensburg*, with his notes, has survived, as also some minutes of his talks with the Emperor and his ministers.

From these sources we learn that Charles approached the prince with the greatest friendliness. He declared that the whole purpose of the religious conference was to bridge the gap between the two parties and complained bitterly of Amsdorf's sermon. It was cruel, he said, to characterize the talks as 'vain delusions', when everyone must know that they were the 'nearest thing to his heart'. Philip answered that they must not expect to overcome all difficulties immediately. After all the theologians differed very widely in their opinion of the possible Concordat. Eck, for instance, had gone about openly boasting of the concessions granted by the Protestants which had made a very bad impression. He went on to say that he would himself be prepared to do anything that was not contrary to God's word and his own conscience, to further the agreement. The Emperor interrupted him when he came to the question of French intervention. But the Landgrave protested that Melanchthon was quite innocent in this respect. Amsdorf, he admitted, was a firebrand. He himself felt that such points as had yet to be proved from Holy Writ, like the marriage of priests and the administering of the Communion in both kinds, ought to be conceded for the time being.

The Count Palatine and Naves also had private conversations with the Landgrave. But both parties continued to appeal, in the last instance, to the same gospels to support their differing theses; when they had not themselves come to any provisional agreement, it was useless for the Emperor to intervene with suggestions. The Landgrave had another hope. 'It would be a good thing', he said, 'if we could get Luther here himself; he is more peaceably inclined than the others.' Veltwyk too had private talks with the Landgrave. Meanwhile nothing happened to break down the understanding between Philip and the Emperor: Charles was prepared to favour him if he in his turn would use all his influence to solve the religious problem. Still full of delusive hopes, the Emperor next sought to appeal from the theologians to the Estates.

He was to be disappointed in the result.

On May 31st the conference of the theologians ended with the formulation of the twenty-three articles contained in the *Book of Regensburg*. On June 8th the completed book was handed over to the Estates. On July 5th the Catholic Estates sent in their answer, on July 12th the Protestants. Both sides rejected it.

Luther himself, as is well known, was at first hopeful of the news he had from Regensburg, but later he too repudiated the formulae of the Book, more especially the doctrine of justification. Contarini found the Vatican no less obstinate. On May 27th, the Consistory rejected that very formula of which he had himself approved. On July 15th, Paul III decided to inform the legate that he intended to call a council immediately. Charles received the news graciously. But Ferdinand, who was desperate for subsidies against the Turk, expressed himself more vehemently. As long as the Pope made no serious effort to reform the Church, he said, people would comment unfavourably on the fact that he never talked more glibly of calling a council, than when it seemed most impossible to do so. To do Ferdinand justice, it was certainly clear enough that the Vatican was set on wrecking the policy of conciliation.

This then was the situation. The theologians at Regensburg, Luther at Wittenberg, the Pope at Rome, the Catholic and the Protestant Estates of Germany, were unanimous in one thing — in repudiating Charles's policy of reconciliation. That Charles himself acted in good faith allows of no doubt. He had once expressed himself to the Saxon ministers in terms which bore no two meanings. 'We are breaking up an old house of which the stones and other parts are still good for use in another building', he had said. 'Even if decay has crept in and the whole structure is affected, you must not for that reason contemn each separate part.' He had even gone so far as to say that he would initiate reforms without waiting for the action of the Curia. Had he been sure of support in Germany he would have called the council himself. But he could neither institute reforms nor call a council, when the Catholics of Germany would do nothing but reject mediation as useless and clamour for force. Until this moment force had never been the object of his policy.

At Regensburg a profound change seems to have come over Charles's own opinions. This was the second time that he had been bitterly disappointed and the mortification he had suffered eleven years earlier at Augsburg increased his present disillusion. Faced now by the collapse of a conference which had opened under even more hopeful auspices than that at Augsburg, and which had broken down even more significantly, Charles grew ever more secretive. The outspoken and passionate Joachim I of Brandenburg, who had thrust Catholic policy into the open at Augsburg, had given place to his sober-minded son; with this prince Charles entered into a close bond for the defence of religion. Acting apparently on a careful plan, he began to tempt over to his side all the important or wavering Protestant princes. He began by concluding his alliance with the Landgrave of Hesse. Of his inmost thoughts we know nothing, but it is probable that this time it was not, as it had been eleven years before at Augsburg, personal disappointment and wounded dignity which made him despair of settlement by arbitration, but rather the deeper insight into German affairs which he had acquired with age. Moreover, he did not abandon all hope until he had tried every means to bring about his end. It was only when every effort had failed that he moved gradually over to the point of view so long and so vociferously held by the Dukes of Bavaria and Brunswick, and began to make preparations for action as soon as the occasion should be ripe.

He first gave clear expression to this new policy in the final form of his treaty with the Landgrave of Hesse, on June 13th. The Landgrave undertook to enter into no alliance with the King of France or other foreign ruler, to make clear exceptions in favour of imperial authority in each renewal of the Schmalkaldic League and to prevent the inclusion of the Duke of Cleves among its members. He agreed also 'to enter into no private treaty with the said Duke of Cleves'; rather he would support the imperial claims in Zutphen and Gelderland if the other Estates would undertake to do the same. In any case he swore to stand by the Emperor in a war against France, both he himself and his son-in-law Maurice of Saxony. In return for all these promises Charles declared that 'out of particular grace and favour we have taken His Excellency into our especial protection and friendship and have forgotten and forgiven everything, of whatsoever kind, which he may previously have attempted or done, openly or secretly, against ourselves and our brother, against imperial law and justice and the laws of the Empire'. To this treaty a significant stipulation was added. The Landgrave was to stand by the Emperor in the event of a war against the Protestants in the name of religion.

Reassured by the conference, the Protestants might still for the time being believe in Charles's peaceable intentions. They were daily witnesses to his efforts to restrain the representatives of the Vatican and the Catholic princes. They did not realize that Ferdinand's distress in Hungary now alone drove the Emperor to adopt this conciliatory attitude. At the end of June, the Court had definite information that the Sultan was himself about to invade Hungary, which with Zapolya's death had fallen to King Ferdinand, and to seize the royal fortress of Ofen. Recollecting his victories in the year 1529, the Court could not but be doubtful whether

Suleiman would rest content with Ofen alone. Immediate and extensive help must be found at once. Austria and its neighbouring lands themselves hung in the balance. Ferdinand and his representatives set all in motion: their speeches before the Estates were both impressive and convincing. But, convinced though they might be of the necessity of giving help, the Protestants insisted first on a guarantee of their religion. Nine years before in much the same circumstances the two negotiations — for help against the Turk and for religious settlement — had been carried out separately at Regensburg and Nuremberg. In 1541 they were combined into a single transaction. The two parties faced each other, armed and without intermediary. The members of the Schmalkaldic League demanded the recognition of the terms given at Nuremberg, the Catholics insisted that the anti-Protestant recess of 1530 should be specifically reissued with the recess of the present Diet. Who now could bridge so great a gulf?

The old Elector of Brandenburg had precipitated the crisis at Augsburg in 1530: the young Elector of Brandenburg strained every nerve to prevent a crisis at Regensburg in 1541. The Emperor pressed for a decision. He wanted to get back to Italy and Spain. He was planning to attack the Turks in Algiers, and had already taken one or two into his confidence on this matter. July 26th was the very latest date at which he could leave Regensburg. In his dealings with the Protestants he grew noticeably harsher. But to his deep chagrin he found after a few days that he must yield. On July 28th the final, angry negotiations took place at his lodging, Charles dealing separately with the Catholic and Protestant Estates. Princes and their ministers worked night and day to bring some sort of order out of the chaos. And in the end they found a way out of the labyrinth, although only by a devious path, marked out by highly complicated imperial proclamations. These proclamations were drawn up in haste and teemed with ambiguities. In return for such concessions as Charles had agreed to make, the Diet drew up a recess and granted the immediate help of 10,000 infantry and 2000 cavalry for three months.

At four in the morning on July 29th the Schmalkaldic League began their final consultation, for they had to give in their answer by six. Afterwards the negotiations were bandied about from group to group. The Count Palatine, the Elector of Brandenburg and the new imperial Chancellor strove hard to reconcile the parties. At midnight the previous day the Schmalkaldic League had heard for the first time of the probable publication of the imperial proclamation. They opposed its terms and the alterations which they proposed to the Diet were drawn up in haste and fear. When Charles received them he too was in haste to be gone. The minister of the Elector of Brandenburg, Eustace von Schlieben, made a short speech, and Charles then set his hand to the proclamation. He had not grasped that it was not the same which he had himself drawn up earlier in the proceedings.

The new declaration provided for the protection of pastors and adherents of the Augsburg Confession, even in the lands of Catholic princes, for the liquidation of the *Reichskammergericht*, the reform of monasteries and convents on secularized land. In fact it was far in advance of the Nuremberg agreement. Charles had no choice but to approve a second and secret declaration which guaranteed to the Catholics not only their rents and revenues, but, in so far as they still possessed them, their rights and privileges.

At ten o'clock the last session of the Diet was opened. Even at this last minute many delegates spoke with the utmost violence, but by two in the afternoon a decision had been reached.

Charles left immediately afterwards. His policy seemed to have broken down at every point.

The peace with France at Nice had come to nothing; the family agreement at Aigues Mortes had been fruitless, in spite of all the great results which Charles had foreseen. Months of conference had produced no peaceful solution in Germany. With unwilling steps the Emperor turned towards his other kingdoms.

THE ATTACK ON ALGIERS

Almost without a halt, Charles went by way of Freising, Munich and Mittelwald to Innsbruck. Here he rested for two days, in order to dispatch some important letters on August 6th. Among these was a re-draft of the declaration for the spiritual princes, an emphatic confirmation of his membership of the Catholic League, and nominations for the *Reichskammergericht*. Not least important were the credentials which he drew up for de Praet, together with instructions in which he told Queen Mary all that had taken place at Nuremberg, and all that he now intended to do. His instructions call up a vivid picture of the whole political world, of the Danish and Palatine problems, the affair of the Landgrave, the Diet, the *Reichskammergericht*, and above all the disputes over Gelderland and Cleves.

These instructions, too, give the clearest reasons for Charles's projected attack on Algiers. Queen Mary cannot have been unaware that lack of funds was the cause of Charles's return to Spain. He confessed to her that this alone prevented him from marching against Suleiman in person, a task which his honour demanded now that he had definite news that the Sultan was coming in person. In the eyes of the world, therefore, he could best justify himself by an attack on the Turks in Africa. He would need a war-fleet in any case for his return to Spain, as the French and Turks between them made the Mediterranean unsafe, and the costs could be borne by Naples and Sicily. Besides which, the Spaniards had always wanted him to attack Algiers and might therefore be the more willing to grant him subsidies. At this very moment the undertaking was still just possible, but it must be at once set on foot. The French King was indignant because some of Charles's people had murdered his emissaries, Rincon and Fregoso, on the way home from Turkey, near Pavia. He might fly to arms at any minute, but if Charles began the campaign against Algiers immediately he would have to postpone hostilities, for he could not face the moral opprobrium of attacking Charles while he was actually at war with the infidel.

Over the Brenner, through Lombardy by way of Milan and Pavia, the Emperor reached Genoa and here took to his ships. In the meantime he had bad news from Hungary: Ofen had fallen and the Turks were now in possession. On this intelligence Charles made a detour by way of Lucca to visit the Pope, and entreat his help for a council to be held in Germany, through which he might gain effective help against the Turks and protection against France. Charles achieved nothing; Paul III even warned him against attacking Algiers. From Hungary came the bad news that the Germans under Roggendorf had been defeated. And then came the surprising and relieving news that Suleiman had unexpectedly withdrawn. Possibly he did not want to risk a new siege of Vienna; possibly his resources ran out; possibly he had heard of the preparations which the Emperor was making against his outposts in Africa.

But meanwhile Charles's plans had come to nothing. Nature herself seemed to be in league with his enemies.

Landing in Corsica and Sardinia, Charles had arranged for his fleet to collect at Majorca under Andrea Doria, his troops under the Viceroy of Naples, Ferrante Gonzaga. To gain time, he sent the Duke of Alva with the Spanish galleons straight to Algiers. Along the coast of Africa his fleet gradually assembled from every quarter of the compass. But the sea was already stormy and the most experienced seamen warned the Emperor that the time of year was unpropitious. Charles was obstinate in his determination; he trusted in his habitual good fortune. Although there had been endless delay, partly, as Charles thought, through the fault of the seamen themselves, he was unwilling to see all his preparations made for nothing.

On Friday and Saturday, October 21st and 22nd, landing was out of the question. But on Sunday morning the Emperor re-assembled his fleet to the east of Algiers and began to disembark at a half-submerged spit of land, where the troops, with all their baggage, had to wade breast deep through the water for some distance. In the afternoon the sea grew rougher, and it became impossible to land either horses or provisions. In the evening the Emperor made a camp near to a spring. During the disembarkation the leaders tried to win their object by the quicker means of negotiating with Barbarossa's governor of Algiers, the renegade, Hassan Aga. After a moment's wavering, the governor decided to remain loyal to Barbarossa.

The Christians next armed themselves for the assault on the city which did not seem to be very well defended. At first their operations were successful. They drew very close to the city and gained possession of the hills which overlooked it, almost without serious fighting. But in the night of October 24th-25th a gale arose which made piece-meal of the fleet, with all its store of provisions, munitions and reserves. Terrible was the plight of the army on land, for the troops had brought provisions for two days only. The rain streamed down in torrents and there were very few tents to shelter the men. The Italian troops, unused to war, collapsed before a surprise attack in the morning. The enemy broke through and advanced to within a short way of the Emperor's own tent before his German troops eventually stopped them. The fighting now became general, and here and there Charles's troops were not unsuccessful. At one point they all but entered the town. It should have been exposed at the same time to a bombardment from the sea, but the fleet was destroyed or dispersed. Some of the crews had thrown cannon and munitions overboard, others lowered their masts and battened down the hatches to preserve the guns. Much of the imperial chancellery, which Charles had brought with him, had been lost in the storm. Only by the Wednesday was the sea calm enough for the remains of the fleet to reassemble. But hardly had the army regained some of its confidence than the storm blew up again, and this time Charles decided to abandon the contest, if not for ever, at least until the army could be properly reprovisioned and the communication with the ships re-established. He thought that by shifting his camp westwards he could best achieve this end. But all renewed efforts to disembark the provisions were in vain. The soldiers lived by gathering what fruit they could and by slaughtering their horses for meat. For two days, harassed by repeated attacks from the enemy, they marched almost without sustenance, and at last managed to re-establish communication with the ships.

Many eminent Spaniards, and among them Hernando Cortes the Conqueror of Mexico, were in the army. Cortes told Charles that if he would turn back, he could conquer Algiers in spite of all. Charles would not give his consent. Inglorious retreat was now the only way out, and both in the army at the time and later among contemporaries, many voices were loudly raised against those who had embarked on so ill-considered a campaign. Yet Charles's decision to go was not itself at fault. Had it not been for the storm, Algiers might easily have been taken, in despite of the general incompetence of the chief command.

In a long letter to Ferdinand, written on November 2nd, Charles gave his own account of all that had happened. He himself realized that he must justify his conduct. Meanwhile he was held up for many days at Bugia, west of Algiers, before the sea was calm enough for him to return home. Only early in December did he land at last at Cartagena. Going by way of Ocana, Toledo and Madrid, he reached Valladolid by the end of January 1542.

For the whole of the next year he gave himself up to Spanish affairs. Once again he busied himself over the condition of the natives in the Indies, once again he gave ear to the voice of Las Casas. In the political heavens of Europe, the powers marched with planetary precision back into their old formation.

THE GREAT PROJECT OF 1543

THE story of a man's life is simplified by his own recollections as it is by the mind of a biographer, but the process of selection is different. In both cases, hours and days of lesser importance are forgotten, taking second place behind certain outstanding events. But personal recollections arrange the facts according to their significance in the individual life itself: the biographer can only arrange them according to a standard of universal significance. The spontaneous impression of past events, before they can be selected and stylized, develops gradually into a traditional knowledge, and fixes the multitudinous happenings of the past in coherent lines. In a life of such political importance as that of Charles V, these outlines gain in meaning and clarity as the years go by and produce at length, as it were without external aid, a clear and coherent picture.

Charles was by nature reserved and his surroundings developed that characteristic: thus in his youth the outlines of his thought and the meaning of his actions were indistinct. Only as he grew older did the results of his personal opinions, the effects of his own actions, begin to take recognizable shape. In nature, too, we often notice that approaching age reveals the structure and characteristics of a face, which were hidden by the bloom of youth; there may be no beauty, but there will be character and meaning. Neither prejudice nor ingenious selection can make a convincing picture of a man, but only the strictest devotion to historic truth. Our knowledge must rest on the accumulated tradition and observation of centuries. Only by unfolding the material gradually and carefully, only by conscientiously recognizing its peculiarities and its limitations, can we draw valid conclusions. These are not to be made by rashly overestimating, and then as rashly decrying. Only in the utmost caution and observation lies the true scientific value of historical work, and only in that way can we arrive at a truer knowledge of things as they were and as they are.

The materials out of which Charles's life is to be constructed are of an oppressive vastness. So many and so various are the surviving papers, that the process of his development, of the growth of individual will and character through his youth and early manhood, can be followed almost from document to document. We do not need to watch him objectively, through the eyes of those who saw him. We can study him from within, from his own workroom. Year by year the material mounts up. After 1540 he entrusted Cobos with keeping and arranging all his documents in what is now the archive at Simancas. But his government grew increasingly personal, and as the years went by his writings become ever more important, for the light they throw on his character. In the messages which he drew up for his only son and heir he laid bare the furthest recesses of his very soul. These, revealing as they do his passionate leaning on God and his unconscious knowledge of his own personality, are as valuable as personal confessions.

Although he was tormented with gout, his mental, as opposed to his physical, constitution seems to have grown stronger under the influence of his recent misfortunes. He did not acquire 'self-confidence', in the modern sense, but he acquired a firmness of purpose which was based ultimately on his trust in God. On December 28th, 1541, he had written to Granvelle of the Algerian catastrophe in terms which were far from despondent. He repeated much the same opinions a little later to his brother. 'We must thank God for all', he wrote, 'and hope that after this disaster He will grant us of His great goodness, some great good fortune.' Men might blame him, he went on, for hesitating in Regensburg, 'but he had only realized too late that he ought to have waited at least another month to be sure of good weather. Nobody could have guessed that beforehand. It was essential not so much to rise early, as to rise at the right time, and God alone could judge what that time should be'.

Thus by his early forties Charles's political personality was fully developed, and in spite of that slowness in decision which he never quite overcame, he had achieved an amazing sureness of purpose. In the instructions, which he had given to de Praet for Queen Mary, on August 6th, 1541, he declared that it would take him two years to settle everything in his other dominions, and then she might expect him back to deal with the business of Gelderland and the Netherlands. He kept his word almost to the month. In the meantime he added to his instructions a slip of paper written in his own hand and covered with sketches of cannon. He told the Queen to have sixteen large guns and twenty-four small field-pieces cast, and added a note on the amount of ammunition for each. These cannon were to stay for the time being at Malines, although they were intended to complete the quota of the forty-eight large and thirty-six small guns which he had already had cast at Augsburg. While waiting for him to return, he urged Mary to proceed with great caution. She, in her turn, took his hint and set out as soon as she could to make a tour of her frontiers and fortresses, to reorganize the administration of the provinces, and to separate the Duke of Cleves from the Rhenish princes and the Landgrave of Hesse by diplomatic means if she could.

In the second half of 1541 Charles had already begun to lay the plans for his military campaign and hints of it in his correspondence grow more frequent.

Totally unforeseen accidents may hinder or precipitate the best-laid schemes and it is the politician's hardest task to be ready for every untoward circumstance. So Charles, although harassed by dangers which he had not prepared for, or driven forward by sudden opportunities and sudden flashes of insight, yet contrived to do no violence to the main line of his policy.

SPAIN AND THE IMPERIAL FINANCES

Charles had been hankering to get back to Spain ever since he reached the Netherlands and certainly for the whole summer of 1541. His reasons were financial. He had made the diversion to Algiers partly because he needed the fleet to cross the Mediterranean in any case, and it had seemed a pity not to make serious use of it, and partly to demonstrate his activity in protecting the Spanish coasts from Turkish molestation. Naples and Sicily, not Spain, paid for the expedition. During these last months Charles's finances were in even greater disorder than usual.

He had to postpone both the Turkish and the Hungarian war, simply for lack of means. In the last year he had even lamented to Queen Mary that he had not money to pay his courtiers their salaries. Although the flourishing Netherlands passed for the richest state in Europe, the continuous wars of the last years had squeezed them dry. The Estates had been repeatedly called upon to meet the costs of war — in Gelderland, Friesland and Utrecht, in Luxembourg, Hainault and Artois. The revolt of Ghent had shown what dangers were inherent in this policy of pressing the Estates, and Queen Mary's rule was beset with the difficulties which had surrounded that of Margaret. Over and above the wars, the state kept up by the noble governors of provinces and by the Court itself, cost the land great sums of money. Charles's revenues from German sources had never at any period amounted to anything. He had used the money sent him from Rome exclusively for the purpose of keeping the Turks at bay. The Austrian hereditary lands could barely afford to cover the charges of their own government. The Netherlands had to pay many of the costs of imperial policy — old debts, embassies, pensions, like the annual 5000 Gulden to the Count Palatine, and even the salary of the Vice-chancellor Naves.

Naples and Sicily brought in considerable sums from their trade in corn, Milan from its salt monopoly, apart from special votes and taxes. But all these revenues were rapidly absorbed in the cost of administration and in the payment of interest, even if they were not already earmarked to cover the cost of those unceasing wars, themselves the cause of economic decline in the Emperor's Italian dominions.

Spain alone had been at peace since the troubles of the Comuneros and the brief war in Navarre had come to an end. Here, therefore, the revenues of the Crown, in spite of all the wasting of Crown lands, remained extremely high. The chief sources of royal income in Castile were the direct taxes, the periodical vote of a *Servicio*, the revenues of the three great knightly orders, the grants of the Vatican on Church lands, the *Cruzada* and the money obtained for indulgences. The yield of the West Indies, which was now noticeably increasing, became a larger and larger additional element. Aragon, too, voted a *Servicio* at intervals.

In Castile the direct tax was known as the *Alcabala*. Originally assessed as a capital levy of 10 per cent, it had been altered by a calculation based on its usual yield, to a tax on each parish, raised by local assessment, and called the *Encabezamiento*.

The list of 140 odd municipalities, districts, estates, and bishoprics reveals interesting contrasts from year to year. In the last period of Isabella's reign the whole country was expected to yield 284,000,000 Maravedi. Of this sum, Seville accounted for more than 30,000,000, that is rather more than a tenth; Burgos, Valladolid and the Marquisate of Villena paid 5,000,000 each; the industrial town of Medina del Campo, as well as Cuenca and the bishopric of Salamanca paid between 7,000,000 and 8,000,000 each, Santiago and Toledo 10,000,000, Cordova 11,000,000, Xeres de la Frontera 12,000,000, Madrid only 2,000,000. Since the beginning of Charles's reign the yield of the *Encabezamiento*, in which not only the old *Alcabala* but the *tercios* of the ecclesiastical tithes were now included, had risen from 300,000,000 to 327,000,000 Maravedi. But the coin had itself depreciated, and the revenues were therefore more or less static. This can be converted with approximate accuracy into our currency by calculating that 150,000,000 Maravedi was about equal in buying power to 400,000 ducats; 300,000,000 Maravedi were thus about 800,000 ducats, or a round 10,000,000 gold marks. If we calculate that the buying power of money was about five times what it is now, the total revenue was thus about 50,000,000 gold marks at our present rate of currency.

The kingdoms of Aragon had no such taxes. Instead they paid for their own administration. But like Castile they voted a periodical *Servicio* in their Cortes. Until 1526 the sum voted in Castile was usually 50 Cuentos, or 50,000,000 Maravedi; it rose later to 100 Cuentos, and later still, after 1539, to 200 Cuentos. In Aragon and Valencia, as in Catalonia, it had remained static at 66 Cuentos, a large enough sum for the resources of the country. To these sums of money must be added the revenues of the three knightly orders, the *Maestrazgos*, which yielded between 40 and 66 Cuentos, an average of 50 Cuentos each. In the thirties the continuous levy of an extraordinary *Servicio*, together with the *Maestrazgos*, brought in another 300 Cuentos yearly, that is a sum equal to the yield of the ordinary taxes for Castile alone.

The extent of Charles's income from the Indies has been much disputed. It was at first, naturally enough, subject to terrific fluctuation. We learn from the accounts of the *Casa de Contratacion* that it was about 20 Cuentos at the beginning of the reign; in the late thirties it had risen to 100 Cuentos; by 1550 it had touched the 500 mark. It is perhaps safe to assume that during the thirties and forties it averaged 90 Cuentos net; that is about 240,000 ducats, or 15,000,000 gold marks in the buying power of our own time.

By making periodical special grants out of Church land, the Pope from time to time gave Charles an additional source of revenue. The yield of these grants was very uneven but they were usually rather more than 100 Cuentos. Besides these, several taxes had been taken over as they stood from the Arabic administration: such were the silk tax at Granada and the special tax on the district of Alpujerra south of the Sierra Nevada. There was also the not inconsiderable income from islands and ports. Altogether these may have accounted for another 150 Cuentos. Inclusive of the Church grants, this made another 400,000 ducats or 25,000,000 gold marks at the present valuation.

Charles thus enjoyed an income of about 2,250,000 ducats. Several exceptional revenues were from time to time added to it. The King of Portugal had paid a dowry of 370 Cuentos in Spanish money — 1,000,000 ducats — with the Infanta. He had paid a sum of 350,000 ducats for the Moluccas. The King of France had paid 1,000,000 ducats for the ransom of his two sons.

Yet the size of these revenues and the apparent clearness with which the Spanish accounts were kept, gives no true picture of Charles's finances. Although Charles himself exonerated Cobos, his chief treasurer, from responsibility, he does indeed seem to have been partly to blame for the deplorable state in which the Emperor perpetually found himself.

Gattinara had repeatedly urged Charles to keep some reasonable relationship between income and expenditure. But as the royal revenues increased in the later twenties, the royal extravagance more than kept pace with them. Perpetual war brought financial chaos. Rarely was there enough treasure actually in hand at the beginning of a war. Bankers were at once called in and loans were raised at high rates of interest; Crown lands and some of the more important sources of revenue would be instantly mortgaged, and the future income of the Crown was thus progressively crippled. Charles did not incur debts on any constructive principle, nor with any idea of ultimately bettering the financial condition of the State. He made them haphazard, as the need arose. Moreover, the money he thus raised for his wars was not used in Spain but outside it. And thus, in spite of the influx of bullion from the Indies, Spain grew poorer rather than richer during the glorious sixteenth century.

The covering of these accumulated debts was the chief object of all financial reform during the reign of Charles V. Its second object was the just distribution of the burden of taxation. In Castile in 1538 a serious attempt was made to achieve both ends. Its failure was a proof of the faults inherent in the whole financial system.

On October 15th, 1538, Charles had sent not only for the procurators of the towns, but for all the nobility and clergy, as was the custom in Aragon. He explained to the delegates that the total revenue of the land — from the taxes presumably — was 1,074,000 ducats, but that more than half of this was mortgaged in advance. Besides which the unfunded debt amounted to more than 1,000,000 ducats and would have to be covered by some exceptional means. The royal government, he proceeded, had therefore decided to levy a new tax, the *Sisa*. This would affect all members of the community, like the old *Alcabala*, and promised a far higher yield than anything hitherto imposed. The idea was not in itself new. Taxes on capital as well as income had been enforced to raise the money for the *Servicio* and sometimes even for the *Encabezamiento*. But the nobility felt that this was an attack on their privileges, and the towns followed their example and indignantly repudiated any attempt to raise the yield of the taxes. The Duke of Bejar introduced supplementary propositions. He knew the position because of his activity on the finance council, but the best he could do was to suggest that the rate of interest be lowered and certain minor tolls be imposed. He could not introduce the *Sisa* in any form whatsoever. The clergy wavered in the Emperor's favour but this did not mend matters, and although the negotiations dragged on until the spring of 1539, Charles did not care to force his will on his subjects, and nothing came of it all.

He made a second effort, to induce the Cortes of Castile, like Aragon, to shoulder the burden of their own administration, of the Court, of judicature and general order, not to mention garrisons and defence. This plan, which was falsely interpreted as an attempt to make Castile autonomous, was of course merely a plan to relieve the government of unnecessary expense, so that the *Servicio* and any other extraordinary levies could be used to meet internal debts. It too came to nothing.

The Emperor's balance sheets in the following year told a disastrous tale. Like the over-generous father of a family, he planned what was best for all his dominions without counting the cost, and then tried to raise the means after he had begun on the policy. This procedure, however fatal it may be, is in fact extremely usual in the political world.

The revenues for the year 1543 — over 2,000,000 ducats — were disposed of something in this fashion. About a tenth went to the upkeep of the Court, of the households of the aged Queen Joanna and of the young Prince Philip. Another tenth was consumed in the payment of debts incurred by these households in the previous years. Another tenth went on the fleet, both Doria's ships and the Spanish galleons. A fifth was set aside for the defence of the coasts against attack from Africa. All the rest, about half the total revenue of the State, went on armaments or bills of exchange for the Emperor in other countries, which were clearly being used for military preparations.

Such a disposition of the royal revenues might have been justifiable in time of exceptional danger or war. But the most unnerving aspect of the case was the inadequacy of the revenues to cover so many different calls. The so-called *Rentas reales* brought in 150,000 ducats of regular state income, but the yield from the *Maestrazgos*, that is from the mastership of the knightly orders, was mortgaged to the extent of 50,000 ducats to the Fuggers. Besides this, 150,000 ducats from the revenues of the coming year were anticipated, and a further 120,000 ducats from the year after that were already heavily pledged. Very heavy too were the burdens laid to the charge of the ecclesiastical revenues, the *Cruzada* and the *medios frutas*, nearly 350,000 ducats. The revenue from the Indies was estimated with the utmost casualness. With all these anticipations and sales, the money which Charles could raise covered about two-thirds of his expenses. It was indeed a forlorn hope to think that he could cover the remaining third by exchanging or selling *Juros* and letters of credit.

In Charles's favour it must be admitted that he had enormous estates to consider, and it was unusual in his time to give personal attention, as he undoubtedly did, to the Spanish revenues and their expenditure. In the second half of the century, when princes grew more careful in such matters, it is hardly surprising to find that petty little German potentates, in Saxony and Hesse for instance, were far more successful in setting their finances to rights than Charles was. The Emperor had to face a far more difficult problem, had to combat the resistance of the Grandees, and to find his way about the labyrinthine complexities of Spanish finance. More important to us than Charles's efforts to set the finances in order, as befitted a ruler who was also a father to his people, was his complete failure to achieve this end. In spite of all he never had much difficulty in getting credit and it would be an error to see in his financial troubles a dominant motive for the alterations in his policy. All the same the financial substructure must not be altogether forgotten. His difficulties hampered the execution, if they did not seriously modify the outline, of his policy, and they held back his generals, ministers and viceroys. Queen Mary was constantly at a loss for lack of financial support.

All the troubles of Charles's great kingdoms were to come to a head in the Netherlands. To understand them it is necessary to follow the widespread activities of the Emperor, both in their ecclesiastical and political aspects.

EMPEROR, POPE, FRANCE AND THE TURKS

Charles had left the Vice-chancellor Naves behind in Germany to attend to any problems which might arise out of the Diet of Regensburg, and to prepare for a new meeting which was to be held at Speyer in 1542.

At Speyer the chief question under discussion was the very same which had brought the Estates to that place many years before — help against the Turks. The Protestants made counter-claims. They felt that it was more expedient for them to use the present favourable situation to ensure themselves against the *Reichskammergericht* and the use of force in future, than to give freely out of any feeling of duty against the Turk. The Emperor's enemies were ready enough to tempt them from their allegiance. Charles had therefore instructed his delegates to get what help they could against the Turk by making as few concessions as was humanly possible. The Catholic princes were bound to contest the concessions, whatever they were. The delegates were also to defend the Emperor against insidious attacks from France, Denmark and the Duke of Cleves. The Diet of Speyer, fixed for January, did not in fact last very long. It sat from February 19th until April 11th. The division between the two parties showed no signs of healing, and a suggestion was even submitted that the Protestants should furnish out a contingent of their own to take part in the defence of the Empire against the Turk. As at Regensburg, they had to fall back in the end on the lame expedient of issuing two separate recesses. Many problems were merely shelved and when the meeting dispersed, the delegates had every intention of reassembling at Nuremberg during the summer.

In Italy meanwhile Granvelle and Aguilar were busy. Charles had had a brief conference with the Pope at Lucca in the previous September at which they had discussed the calling of a council the need for help against the Turk, and the position of the Pope in relation to both Spain and France. At Regensburg Charles had promised the Estates that they should have 'a general Christian Council of the German nation', or else a national council; only if both these failed would he fall back on another Diet. His delegates now pressed the Pope to agree to call a council at Trent; the Pope preferred Mantua, Vicenza or Cambrai. Charles further had it intimated that he was himself prepared to give an example to all Christendom by risking his own person against the Turk. He hoped for a defensive alliance with the Pope against the infidel, and if possible against any ruler who tried to disturb the peace of Italy. But Paul III felt it to be his duty to reject this offer, lest it should give King Francis grounds for mistrust.

The French King once again controlled the situation. He needed no council: his government burnt its native heretics and preferred the unpopular but serviceable alliance with Turkey to the cost and danger of a Crusade. Moreover the material and moral losses which Charles had suffered at Algiers, provoked King Francis to believe that he might now resume the struggle for Naples and Milan with good prospect of success. The King's temperament had not grown less mercurial with the passing of time. The negotiations at Nice and Aigues Mortes had led nowhere; the dynastic settlement had not even been tried. The truce which had been arranged with the help of the Pope was, of course, still in force, and Charles was anxious that Paul should guarantee it effectively. But the Pope turned a deaf ear to any hint that the Church stood in danger from France.

An unfortunate incident in July 1541 increased the tensity of the atmosphere. The French ambassadors to the Porte, Rinçon and his companion, Cesare Fregoso, were attacked and murdered by imperial soldiers on the Po near Pavia. The French governor of Turin, du Bellay, lord of Langay, sent an indignant protest, which was answered with as good a grace as possible by the imperial regent of Milan. This latter suggested that a French delegate should take part in the inquiry to be made into the matter, and sent the Count of Landriano to explain the disaster to the King of France. Du Bellay rejected all explanations, declaring tartly that he hardly presumed the Marquis to be so simple, as to think that he could really deceive the King of France and his councillors by his specious excuses. Francis himself saw in the incident the very excuse for which he had been waiting.

He immediately took reprisals. A natural son of the Emperor Maximilian, George of Austria, who, a little while before had become Bishop of Valencia, was now on his way across France towards Liège, of which see he was to become coadjutor, with a good prospect of ultimately succeeding to the large and wealthy prince-bishopric itself. Charles was anxious that the new coadjutor should arrive as soon as possible at his destination, for the present Archbishop, Cornelius de Berghes, lord of Zevenbergen, who had succeeded the energetic Eberhard de la Mark, was a weak and ailing man wholly unequal to his task. George of Austria on the other hand was about thirty-four years old, active and loyal. When Francis pounced upon him on his journey across France and placed him under arrest, this was a serious blow at Charles's defensive measures, for it crippled the resistance of the Bishopric of Liège, just at the moment when war was again likely to break out, here and in Luxembourg.

Charles guessed at once what the King's intentions were. His own plans were thrown back to the position of 1538: Ferdinand was making no progress in Hungary and any united help against the Turks seemed out of the question. His plan for a religious settlement had come to nothing, and his reputation in Germany was waning for he had signally failed to persuade the Pope to call either a general or a national council. The projected Catholic League, too, did not seem likely to prove strong enough to help him. The position of the Netherlands was gravely weakened by the machinations of the Duke of Cleves in Gelderland, as well as by the weakness of Liège, in the direct line of his frontier defences. Yet Charles still hoped that by exerting his influence on the Pope he might evade the worst of the danger. As soon as the French King violated the truce of Nice, Charles felt that he would be able to gain Paul's help in securing the release of his uncle, the co-adjutor of Liège, if not actually to win the Pope altogether to his side.

Granvelle was spending the winter of 1541-2 in Italy, and Charles corresponded fully with him. Their letters are not merely interesting for the light they throw on the complicated events of the time, but for the way in which they illuminate the guiding principles of imperial policy. Devious in its course and details, Charles's policy was yet coherent and homogeneous. In the instructions which he issued to Ferdinand and Mary, Charles followed Granvelle's advice, and a single document thus provides an outline of the whole scope of imperial policy. Towards the end of November, Granvelle gave Charles his advice at some length on all the urgent problems of the time. Written in Siena, the paper comprises forty-eight articles under such different headings as: the religious question in Germany, the Turkish war, relations with France. Like many others of its kind, Granvelle's memorandum was sent to the Netherlands, too, in code, so that it is to be found in duplicate, both in Spain and in the Low Countries, bearing the marginal comments of Charles and of Mary. Charles's comments together with the original were laid before the Council of State for their advice.

Here and there Charles disagreed with Granvelle, although the latter clearly thought out his advice to suit the Emperor's own opinions. The points on which they disagreed, and the aspects which they emphasized, reveal very clearly the main objects to imperial policy at this time. Granvelle assumed that the next

German Diet would be concerned, like the last, with the religious question and with the problem of raising money against the Turk. The Protestants, he calculated, would want an extension of the religious peace for at least another twenty years. He suggested that this latter demand should be countered by pointing to the extreme annoyance of the Pope at the last decisions which had been reached at Regensburg. The Emperor rejected this suggestion outright. He declared that he was not prepared to give any more guarantees in any circumstances, although of course an immediate breach must be avoided. Those responsible for the Diet could play for time by referring all decisions back to him. Charles was here relying on his usual method of postponement in a crisis. It was a method which distracted his advisers but had the advantage of leaving his own hands free.

As for help against the Turks, Granvelle admitted that he had had no more success with the Pope, than had the Emperor at Lucca. The Pope, he said, treated money as though it were as dear to him as life; he could not be persuaded to part with it. The Spanish Council, too, were unwilling to offer help unless they could be sure of something in return. If they gave support to Ferdinand in Hungary, then the Empire must in its turn support them in the hereditary dominions of the Spanish Crown. The Emperor's personal presence was everywhere in demand. The Netherlands wanted him most of all, for here matters were growing very serious. King Francis was much under the influence of the ladies of the houses of Étampes and Albret, who were in a fever to begin a war; the danger to the Netherlands was therefore imminent. The peril, in which the Empire and Italy stood, was only relatively less. But if France made war, and there was no doubt that France would, Spain too would need Charles's presence, and how could he then get back from Hungary or Italy? This was a point on which the Spanish Council lingered long. Granvelle suggested that Charles should enter into negotiations with the schismatic King of England. All other Christian princes had already done so, and seeing that Henry's views were in no wise so extreme as those of many of the German princes, with whom Charles did not scorn to negotiate, he need have no apprehensions on that score. To this Charles willingly agreed. But when Granvelle proceeded to advise that French public opinion should be worked up against the King's policy, Charles was not so enthusiastic. He distrusted this form of action, and said that it would have no effect.

Meanwhile relations with the Vatican had improved, and Granvelle was able to announce, in a letter which is now partly illegible with damp, that Paul intended to send a special ambassador, Montepulciano, to the Emperor. This intelligence permitted Charles to hope that Paul at least valued his friendship, and might, in the event of a French attack on Naples, range himself openly on his side. Yet the results of papal intervention were sadly disappointing. Paul did not even secure the release of George of Austria, and Charles felt that he had been cruelly deceived, both in the Pope's private intentions and in his universal policy.

Granvelle regarded the German situation with the gloomiest forebodings. The heretics, he asserted, were not only in a fair way of winning over the remaining Catholic Estates, but were even converting the peoples of the hereditary lands. He went on to speak yet more earnestly of the French danger. Should Francis make war, he might tamper with Navarre and England. A marriage between the Duke of Orleans and the English princess had been mooted. The document ended with several rash proposals from different quarters, intended rather to emphasize the danger of the situation than to form a serious part of Charles's policy. Queen Mary, for instance, had made as if she intended to seize the Duke of Cleves on his way back from France. She had not succeeded, and excused herself by explaining that there were too many roads out of France! Ferdinand had had an offer from some bold spirit to blow up the Turkish arsenal for 500 ducats. Charles set the sum aside in case the plot should mature, but not unnaturally added the comment that the explosion of the Turkish arsenal could hardly be effected with ease.

He too was uncertain as to where he should begin. During December and January 1542 the situation improved slightly, for England and France became estranged. But on November 19th, 1541, Christian III of Denmark, instead of lengthening the treaty of Ghent, entered into a formal alliance with the French at Fontainebleau. Sweden soon offered to join them, for the Count Palatine, husband of Princess Dorothea of Denmark, was now claiming both crowns. The King of Scotland, and the Duke of Cleves, both already allies of the French Crown, were automatically included.

THE WARCLOUDS GATHER IN FRANCE AND CLEVES

At this juncture King Francis took possession of Stenay, the crossing of the Meuse a little to the north of Verdun. His reason was that he was annoyed by the friendly attitude of the Duke of Lorraine to the Emperor, and his excuse that he claimed the place as a fief of Bar. Charles, on the other hand, held that Stenay was a fief of Luxembourg, and regarded the French King's action as one of open hostility. Rightly, therefore, did Charles command Queen Mary to make certain of the two chief border fortresses of Luxembourg, Yvoy, the Carignan of to-day, and Damvillers. King Francis revealed his sinister intentions yet more blatantly by giving help to the unbridled Marshal of Gelderland, Martin van Rossem, whose ruthlessness far out-distanced that of his dead master. Well provisioned and supplied from France, he was soon boasting that he would so waste the Netherlands that men should talk of his deeds a hundred years after.

Mary acted with undiscouraged energy. She had never shown herself greater than in these terrible years when war flamed up on every side, even in her straight path. From town to town, from fortress to fortress, from meetings of the Estates to gatherings of the council, from one military conference to another with each of her provincial governors, Roeulx, Arschot, Buren, Orange, and many others, Queen Mary went tirelessly on. And always she came back to her writing-room to send her brother full accounts of what was happening. She was obedient to him in everything, even submissive, but she did not spare to offer him advice.

At the end of January Charles sent orders for 50,000 ducats apiece to Germany, Antwerp and Genoa. He was determined to be armed against the worst. From Germany he hoped for 6000 infantry for use in Navarre and for the rest he wished his bills of exchange to be employed as the needs of the moment might direct. He had gone to Tordesillas to visit his ailing mother, and hence he wrote to Mary. He accompanied his exhaustive political instruc-

tions with a personal document written first by himself in long-
hand and subsequently coded. It throws a valuable light on his
personal views during this crisis.

From all that he could hear, he wrote, it seemed that the French
King would attack Navarre and the Netherlands at the same
moment. This intelligence had forced him to take measures for
his own defence. All the same he did not wish Mary to forget his
ultimate plans. 'Be mindful of my intention to win back Gelderland within these two years', he wrote, 'and to punish the Duke of
Cleves. I shall need the intervening time to set these kingdoms in
order and to raise money. But if this war is forced upon me it may
alter my plans, for I shall have to spend all that I had hoped to
save, on defending my lands. As my enemies threaten to be beforehand with me, I have myself been wondering if it might not be
better to turn this defensive action immediately into an offensive.
You may recollect that when I came back from my Provençal
campaign I had a scheme for sailing unexpectedly to the Netherlands with five or six thousand Spaniards, there to take the King
by surprise. But that time he seized Hesdin, as this time he has
seized Stenay, and so forced me back on to the defensive. That
time, it is true, he did not attack me in Navarre, which this time
he may well do. Should it come to that it would be wrong in me
to leave that kingdom unprotected in order to defend others — and
with their own money, to boot, which would deprive them of the
means to look after themselves. I have therefore decided to call
the Cortes of Castile and then those of Aragon, even though the
King of France may take action beforehand.' He went on to say
that he intended to proceed to Germany as usual by way of Italy,
and so into Gelderland. The objection to this was that it took so
long. But a sea-journey was beset with dangers. He asked her for
her personal opinion. Did she think it essential that he should
come to the Netherlands, either to defend the frontiers, to attack
the King of France or to march against Gelderland? Perhaps, he
suggested, she would talk it over with de Praet and let him know,
for Granvelle was away, and he had no one with whom he could
discuss the question. 'In this council', he explained, 'as you will
readily believe, there is not a soul who imagines that I have any
intention of leaving the kingdoms. If they knew, they would try
to prevent me.' He went on to consider possibilities of defeating

the French King. The winter, he admitted, was a very favourable time for making attacks across the ice; or at least preparations could be made for a campaign in the following spring. If his presence was desirable, he would like to know how many troops he had better bring with him and how much help he could expect in the Netherlands, when the people realized that he was coming to their defence in person.

Mary answered by increasing her activities. She hoped that Charles would come in person and said so plainly. She would have liked him, if this could not be, to appoint a commander-in-chief so that there should be unity in the councils of war. Failing this, she interpreted her own imperial commission as giving her power to keep the peace between her rival generals. This meant that the supreme command was in reality entrusted to her youthful but muscular hands.

The French King meanwhile intermittently masked his preparations for war by resuming the old negotiations for Charles's marriage to Princess Margaret, as if the Emperor had not already clearly stated that he would not consider this alliance. Undeterred, the King, Madame d'Étampes and the Admiral continued to fill the ears of Charles's ambassador, Marnol, with sweet nothings about the princess. On June 10th Charles felt it necessary to remind his ambassador of his personal disinclination for the match, and to urge him at the same time to report faithfully all the offers made by the French Court, so that the odium of breaking off negotiations might be shouldered on to them if possible. The papal ambassador, Montepulciano, offered him the Pope's mediation in his troubles with France, but Charles treated the suggestion with coolness.

In the meantime, while peace with France still hung in the balance, Charles had once again, apparently in all seriousness, brought up the question of going personally to Hungary with Spanish and Italian troops. Perhaps this was a recrudescence of his old idea of gaining honour in a war with the infidel, and so returning, laurel-crowned, to combat his other foes. Perhaps he was more directly affected by the alliance between the French and Turks, which had now become a serious factor in the political situation, and whose effect he may possibly have seen in the recent seizure of Marano.

The fortress, lying on a lagoon to the east of Venice and occupied by an Austrian garrison since the time of Maximilian, had been surprised by a condottiere from Friuli in the winter of 1541-2; he in his turn had betrayed it to the French under Blaise de Monluc, who had massacred the garrison. The French justified themselves for this shameless conduct by asserting that they had been seeking to preserve the place from the Turks. But the Venetians regarded their action as a barely concealed threat to the Republic. It looked much more to them as though the Turks and French were together finding vantage points on the Mediterranean, whence they could intimidate the Venetian government from its alliance with the Emperor.

And so Charles was apparently serious in suggesting that he should march across Italy to Hungary. After his own experience at Algiers, he showered advice on Ferdinand, telling him what baggage and munitions he should take, how he should bring ships with him down the Danube and what measures should be taken to make sure of Pest. On May 10th, 1542, he told him, secretly but with great conviction, that he was coming himself to take part in the campaign. Earlier on, he had refused to agree to a plan of imperial help for the Netherlands, except for Utrecht and Overyssel; but now he told Queen Mary that he intended to send a substantial sum in the hope that the Empire and the Netherlands would act in unison. This hint doubtless veiled some much more profound plan. In his heart Charles was once again building up his European policy to centre on the Netherlands.

It was about July 20th when Charles at last realized that Francis, 'in spite of every sacred and holy oath that he would resume arms only in self-defence', had in very truth reopened hostilities by an attack on two fronts.

All this time Charles's plans were repeatedly held up by severe gout. In ten weeks he had two grievous attacks, affecting his foot, his right side, his neck and his right hand. He was not yet in the hands of that great physician Vesalius, who later became his personal doctor, nor did he know Vesalius's sovereign remedy — the root of a Chinese herb. Now as later he would not listen to those who advised him to moderate his diet. He gave a graphic description of his hideous appearance to Queen Mary by comparing himself with various well-known dignitaries of his Court.

He made a fine picture of a knight-errant, he added with bitter merriment, hobbling about on a stick.

On his way to Monzon he stopped at Logroño to make a detour through Navarre. He wanted to make certain that it was in a state of defence. He arrived in Aragon late for the Cortes. 'Time will show what I have to do', he wrote to Queen Mary. 'God give me guidance!' During all July, August and September he was engaged by the Cortes.

In July the storm broke over the Netherlands.

STORM OVER THE NETHERLANDS

'Since the time of our grandfather, the Emperor Maximilian, the Netherlands were never in such danger', lamented Mary. But this was as early as June 30th, before the storm burst. The coast was exposed to Danish attack, for the counter-attack which had been planned to defend the Low Countries against Denmark and to throw open the Sound was now out of the question. The Dutch might think themselves lucky if they managed, with the help of the elements, to fight off their attackers. Coming from Picardy, the Duke of Vendôme headed for Artois and Flanders. The King's younger son, the Duke of Orleans, under the care of the Duke of Guise, was threatening Luxembourg along the line of the Meuse. The mists had risen at last, and before the eyes of Mary and her advisers, the threatening approach of their enemies was at last clear.

Yet more terrible was the threat from Martin van Rossem in Gelderland. The Prince of Orange feared that Rossem's rabble of Germans, Danes and Swedes, stiffened by a few emigrants from the Netherlands, would make a surprise attack on The Hague. They did worse. Making across north Brabant from the middle waters of the Meuse to the Scheldt, they marched for Antwerp and Ghent. If these troops from Gelderland could join those of the Duke of Vendôme in Flanders, the Netherlands would be rent in two. Nor was the enterprise unlikely to succeed, for the invaders counted much on malcontents of every sort, above all in the wealthy towns, where there were thought to be many Protestants.

The Queen was as unsparing of herself as of others. She redoubled her energy, arrested all suspects, and after extracting confessions, sometimes with the help of torture, had the culprits executed. She strained every resource to defend the country, called up the militia of both town and country as well as the retainers of the great lords, and set to work recruiting infantry and light cavalry. Her resolution encouraged others. She sent the Prince of Orange to Antwerp, a city inadequately defended, to see to its fortification. She told him to go by way of Bergen op Zoom, which was the surest, but he disobeyed her, and coming up with the enemy at Hoogstraeten, suffered a sharp reverse. Yet he was not altogether deterred, for he saved more of his troops than was at first supposed, and managed to race the enemy into Antwerp. The whole population had long since set to work to complete the fortifications of the town, following the example of an Italian merchant who had shown the way by urging all the foreign merchants in the city to work on its defences. Women and children had even hastened to help, and the municipal authorities directed their voluntary defenders with astonishing efficiency. When Martin van Rossem appeared, the city withstood his first assault and beat him off with great honour to themselves, even though he had taken the precaution of breaking the dykes in order to cover his flank. He was not prepared for a long siege, and when he found the city so well-manned he marched on.

All about him he spread terror and destruction. Burning, he declared, was the Magnificat of war, and he swore by his honour that his very spurs drew columns of smoke and fire out of the land. Close to Malines and Brussels, under the eyes of the Queen, he thundered over the land. His next objective was Louvain, to which city he intended to send a herald, asking for all their artillery and a great sum of money. But here, too, the infuriated people, led by the students, rushed to their own defence and the besiegers were forced to withdraw. The Duke of Orleans meanwhile had sent his outriders from the Meuse as far as the suburbs of Metz, and promised his protection to the Protestants of that town. He had taken and razed Damvillers, but Yvoy held out until Martin van Rossem joined the Duke, when the handful of defenders capitulated, on August 16th. Luxembourg lay open to the invaders. On August 31st the capital fell.

But suddenly the French advance, hitherto so swift and successful, came to an end. Was the Duke of Orleans weary? Had funds run out, or was the chief command at odds with itself? Had the defence suddenly grown stronger? The mystery is unsolved, but the French advance stopped as suddenly as it had begun both in Luxembourg and in Artois. On September 9th the French withdrew from the chief city.

In the third battle-area, where the French government had thought to be most successful, where the Dauphin himself was leading, in Rousillon, they failed altogether. In Navarre they made no more than a demonstration. But they had thought to win Perpignan and the district north of the Pyrenees with ease. Charles, however, had had the capital so splendidly fortified by the Duke of Alva, that it was able to sustain a terrific siege. On August 31st the huge army of besiegers appeared before it. On September 2nd they began to make saps and breastworks, but they were harassed by determined and bloody sallies from the town. Before the end of the month the Dauphin was constrained to give orders to withdraw, not only from the town but from the land. The army halted once more on Spanish soil, and remained for some time encamped. Charles realized that this was merely a subterfuge, so that they could call on papal intervention and appear to be withdrawing of their own free will.

The Emperor could breathe again. So, too, could Queen Mary in the Netherlands.

But in the Low Countries Queen Mary's military commanders were pressing for a punitive expedition against the Duke of Cleves, whom they regarded as the source of all their trouble. Mary, too, felt that it would rejoice her suffering people to see the fury of war unleashed against the lands of their tormentors. De Boussu forced his way forward to Jülich in October, and the Prince of Orange took Sittard, on the frontier of Limburg, over against Jülich. Several fortresses were slighted, imperial garrisons were put in others. After this exploit such of the troops as were not demobilized moved into winter quarters.

Almost at once the Duke of Cleves put a fresh army into the field. Duren and Sittard were taken yet again, and Meinhardt von Ham, the best known companion in arms of the 'Black Martin', was placed in command. De Boussu himself was surprised in his camp near Aachen. Mary attempted to set her armies once again in motion, but a bitter winter put a stop to all further operations, and she had to accept the situation as it was until the following spring.

She used the pause to carry out certain financial and political negotiations. The Pope had made her a grant of the *medios frutas*, half of the annual income of the clergy, but it was to be paid at two intervals, and Mary now sought to shorten the time. Undeterred by the wearisome delays of the Estates, Mary approached them once again for money. And, in spite of indignation and resentment in many quarters, she seized on the lands and goods of all the French Knights of Malta.

But the financial problem was far less serious than the lack of unity in the government of the land and in the direction of the war. Mary was to experience all the bitter and anxious hours which her predecessor Margaret had lived through. The gentry were no less resentful of the nobility than were the townsfolk. They demanded that they, too, be made governors, and be entrusted with the recruiting and leading of armies — tasks to which they were in every way unfitted.

Since October the Queen was in continuous correspondence with Charles about these problems. She was not contented with letters alone. She sent confidential ambassadors; her first emissary was the lord of Falaix, and she followed him on December 22nd with Philip von Stavele, lord of Glajon. He carried a letter which she had herself composed and written with her own hand, before it was put into code. In this letter she gave her brother the exact details of the use she had made of her money, the division of the command and the occupation of the various strong places. She went on to complain bitterly of the lords. She had no true supporter except de Praet. She was in desperate need of a commander-in-chief; yet the only men whom she could think of for the position were Roeulx and Arschot, neither of whom were exactly what she wanted. The intentions of the Prince of Orange were well enough, but he was young and inexperienced. De Boussu, the master of the Horse, whom the Emperor had recommended for the place, made difficulties by demanding so large a share of the indemnification money for towns. His greed gave rise to interminable questions in the council. 'I cannot speak separately to every one of them,' Mary's lamentation continued, 'nor can I be present everywhere at once.' Nothing would help her more, she concluded, than that Charles should come in person.

In this difficult position the Queen herself seems to have been responsible for the suggestion that the Landgrave of Hesse should be appointed commander-in-chief. This was a singularly happy idea and one not lightly to be dismissed. Among Schepper's papers there is a document giving the conditions in which the Landgrave was prepared to lead an army against the King of France. He did not want money for a reward; he wanted land. His army, he stipulated, must be strong and well-armed, with enough money and adequate organization.

For his part Charles conceded that the idea was not without merit, but added cogently that although the Landgrave had some experience, he had never come into contact with a very serious adversary. He went on to ask his sister to do what she could for herself in the Netherlands. He had, he said, sent the lord of Granvelle to the Queen and to King Ferdinand on October 31st, to impart to them certain very secret intentions of his. He knew, he added, that he could trust her in everything. Charles's statement was true: Granvelle was already in south Germany with Lierre, busily engaged in recruiting troops. The occupation brought him into close touch with the younger generation of German princes.

The Queen's position was still very precarious. From Lorraine she paid a visit to Longwy, the castle which guards the southern gate of Luxembourg. She wished to fortify it as the French had fortified Stenay, but in vain. She tried to interest England in her case. As early as the beginning of June she had attempted to form an alliance for defence and offence. Unhappily too great difficulties hampered her efforts. The English wished their obligations to be confined to the Netherlands only, that is, they would not agree to give Charles any help in Spain itself. He was prepared to accept this. But when Henry demanded that his titles as *Defensor Fidei* and head of the English Church should both be recognized, Charles was in a quandary. He observed cunningly that, as he had himself no right to bestow such titles, he was not in a position either to acknowledge Henry's right to them, or to deprive him of them. The King could call himself what he wished;

the Emperor would rest contented with addressing him as 'King of England etc.' With this compromise he hoped that His Majesty would be pleased to content himself. Agreement was at last reached on this and on all other points, but the final treaty in which the two monarchs agreed to forget the past and help each other in future was not concluded until February 11th, 1543. By this treaty the allies agreed that they would force Francis to relinquish his Turkish alliance, while themselves making claims to large stretches of French territory. The Emperor's dynastic sensibilities were soothed by Henry's recognition of Princess Mary's right to inherit the throne.

Behind all this the dominating motive was the re-establishment of commercial relations between England and the Netherlands. Drought and bad harvests in Spain had proved how indispensable to the prosperity of Charles's dominions were the efficient and far-reaching markets of the Low Countries. Charles had to appeal to Queen Mary for a great supply of corn, and she at once set to work to raise it.

Meanwhile innumerable efforts made in the German Diet or by individual princes had utterly failed to settle the affair of Cleves. Thanks to the importance of his allies, and the great success of his arms, apart from one setback, the young Duke had grown inordinately proud. Soon Martin van Rossem burst again into the Netherlands at the head of a large army subsidized from France. In the Netherlands they anticipated the worst in the coming spring.

But in spite of bitter cold and deep snow, the Captain-general, the Duke of Arschot, raised the siege of Heinsberg on March 21st. His attack on Sittard three days later failed altogether. The cavalry were successful and Arschot himself led them in pursuit of the scattered enemy, but when he returned he found that the infantry had withdrawn leaving his artillery unprotected. Although he lost few men in the engagement, the total loss of his guns was a very serious check.

Losing all faith in her generals, Queen Mary fell back on the defensive. In this way she hoped at least to preserve the fortresses and munitions for her brother. Martin van Rossem besieged Heinsberg during May and June 1543 — in vain. The town was relieved by the Prince of Orange on June 22nd. His appearance led to a second battle of Sittard, at which he took most of the enemy's artillery and recaptured eight cannon which had been lost in the previous fight. Mary heard of these victories with joy, but neither such minor successes as these on her side, nor the foraging expeditions of the French in the summer of 1543 made any material difference to the situation.

Everything really depended on Charles's decision to act.

SECOND REGENCY OF PRINCE PHILIP IN SPAIN. THE POLITICAL TESTAMENTS OF 1543

Singleness of purpose was typical of Charles's character, and outside pressure had but to be lessened, for his thoughts to revert immediately to their old line.

The events of the last years had shown him how closely every event in Europe was connected with others. He had learnt what were the best moments for him to intervene. The Duke of Cleves had seized Gelderland, on which Charles had a claim substantiated by many treaties. Now that he had already engrossed Utrecht, Overyssel and Friesland, Gelderland was all that he needed to round off the Netherlands. Gelderland, too, was the hot-bed of French intrigue and the base of French attack. France was in alliance with the Turks, they too the hereditary enemies of Christendom. Thus the feudal quarrel for the small province of Gelderland became a part of a far larger, of a universal, struggle. Charles saw it in this light. In an exhaustive letter to the Pope, dated August 28th, 1542, he explained this aspect of the matter. In this he once again expatiated on his own great services to Christendom, and on the failings of the French King. He besought Paul to do as God had done, to turn away from Cain's offering and accept Abel's. He gave the same message to the Cardinal-legate Viseu, Contarini's successor, to take back to the Vatican. Paul had sent Viseu to Charles while at the same time sending Sadolet to Francis: the Pope's continued treatment of the two monarchs, as though both were equal in their services to the Church, was a source of constant irritation to Charles.

Furthermore, Charles declared that Francis breathed life into the resistance of Germany, as he had done in 1534. If only the

Pope would take the imperial side against the 'most Christian King' — writing to Ferdinand, Charles thus mockingly emphasized the French King's title — the troubles of Christendom would be lightened. For if only the Germans would submit, either unconditionally or else to a compromise, the Turkish problem would soon be solved. What then could be more natural than that Charles should try to break through the net which had been drawn round him, by cutting or gnawing it through at its weakest point? Cleves was its weakest point.

By entering into alliance with Hesse and Brandenburg, Charles had partly split up the German princes. They were themselves busily completing his work, for their personal feuds made them quite oblivious to their own best interests. The quarrels between the two Dukes of Brunswick and the two Dukes of Saxony, for instance, played straight into Charles's hands. The heads of the Schmalkaldic League informed the Emperor on July 14th in a solemn *apologia*, that they had been driven to take action against Duke Henry the younger of Brunswick. This prince, regardless of the suspension of the ban against Goslar, had, contrary to all law, violently attacked the city, its subjects, possessions and lands. Charles was not sorry to hear of an attack on Henry of Brunswick. He had known for long enough that the Schmalkaldic League were only looking for an excuse to make war, and, as he wrote to his brother on August 11th, he was angry with Henry of Brunswick, whose attitude for some time past had been highly offensive, and who was now deliberately trying to start a Protestant war at a very inconvenient moment. He required reasonable behaviour from both parties, as far as they could manage it without doing violence to religion. The Turks were still menacing, and a religious war in Germany at such a time could bring with it only the destruction of the Empire and the collapse of the Church. When letters were found among the booty taken from the Duke of Brunswick which proved Charles's peaceful intentions, the Landgrave Philip felt justified in his friendly attitude towards the Emperor. He was thus rocked in a false security at that very time when Charles's intentions were gradually turning in another direction.

While continuing as always in his patient and unceasing courtship of the Pope, Charles decided also to strengthen his position with the King of England. If he was secure in this quarter he would be able to attack France and Cleves from two sides at once.

But the first essential at this time was to plan his departure from Spain. He owed the means with which he waged his wars to this country, and in this country too he built the future of his dynasty, yet he had no choice but to go. Conscious of the cruel injustice of this action towards his Spanish subjects, he strove to make amends and quiet his own conscience by fulfilling two of the wishes nearest his own and his people's heart. He determined once again to make a dynastic alliance with Portugal, and to appoint in his stead as regent a Prince of the Blood.

He was able now to achieve both these objects. The sixteen-year-old Prince Philip was appointed regent, and married in that same year to the Infanta of Portugal, herself the same age as the bridegroom. He supported this bold act by writing out for his son instructions so conclusive, so frank and yet so full of anxious care for the prince, as surely never monarch and father did before. With these instructions of Charles to Philip begins that long series of political testaments left by royal fathers to their sons. The spiritual god-fathers of Charles's own work were his own political teacher, Gattinara and his confessor Antonio de Guevara. This latter had himself written much and was the compiler of the *Horologium Principum*. Until the sixties of the last century the testament which Charles drew up for Philip was still to be seen, written in the Emperor's own hand and with fragments of the seal still attached, in the archives of the Ministry for Foreign Affairs at Madrid. Since then the document has been heard of from time to time in the catalogues of antique dealers, but to-day all trace of it has been lost. The textual substance has survived in copies of whose authenticity there is no doubt.

At the time at which Charles sat down to write, he had gathered all his determination to face the worst of dangers and take the greatest of risks. The experience of years went to the formulation of those desires and intentions which he now committed to paper, and against which he could brook no further opposition, either from other men or from his own doubts. When he set out from Spain in that year, he well knew that he would be risking all that he had on a single throw. This decision, the fruit of so great an inward struggle, secures Charles his place among the heroic figures of history. The Pope was a luke-warm friend, the King of England was not to be trusted, the King of France was a bitter and unrelenting enemy; as to any other allies of the Duke of Cleves, Charles had no information on which he could rely. The means with which he intended to make war had been scraped together through a financial policy of the utmost instability. The French and Turkish fleets, which soon after collected at Toulon, were a constant threat even to his safe passage across the sea. The Emperor did not know how soon the Turks might again march on Austria, nor whether the German princes would stand his friends.

Yet in the face of so much uncertainty he took his decision.

The Cortes of the three kingdoms of Aragon and the Cortes of Castile solemnly acknowledged the prince as his heir and regent. Next he selected for his son a council consisting of all the most experienced ministers in his service; but he gave to Philip full rights of sovereignty, placing him only under the moral super-vision of his god-father and one-time confessor, Don Juan de Zuñiga. He copied in nothing the arrangements which had been made for his own government when, at Philip's age, he too had become a ruling prince. Unlike Chièvres, Zuñiga, although he fulfilled somewhat the office of a Grand Chamberlain, was to have no part in the government. The Duke of Alva, as commander-in-chief of the army, was also excluded from the political direction of the country. All officers and ministers were in the last resort under Philip's own control, and behind Philip there was the imperial authority of his distant father. The members of the inner council were the experienced Cardinal-archbishop of Toledo, Don Juan Pardo de Tavera, the president of the Council of Castile, Don Hernando de Valdes, and Francisco de los Cobos.

My son, [thus did the Emperor begin his testament] my departure from these kingdoms draws near. I have daily proof that I must go for you have already sustained much wrong through my fault in this inheritance which God has entrusted to me, and worse can only be prevented by my going. Therefore I have resolved upon this experiment of leaving you to govern in my stead.

You are still young to bear so great a burden. I therefore commend you to the mercy of God and pray that you may take as examples all those who have made good their want in age and experience by their courage and zeal in the pursuit of honour. Then I shall have cause to thank God for giving me such a son. I for my part will do all I can to help you, and I am therefore writing to you, my son, in the faith that God will inspire my words. Be devout, fear God and love him above all else.

Be a friend to justice, my son. Command your servants that they be moved neither by passion, nor by prejudice, nor yet by gifts. Let no man think that your decisions in anything, least of all in the administration of justice, are the fruit of passion, prejudice or anger. After the manner of our Lord, temper justice with mercy. In your bearing, be calm and reserved. Say nothing in anger. Be easy of approach and pleasant of manner; listen to good advice and take heed of flatterers as you would of fire.

To enable you the better to fulfil your part I have left you here in Spain all the members of my royal council, and given special instructions to them, which I send to you by Cobos. I beseech you to act in accordance with what I tell you. The royal council will see to the administration of justice and will care for the welfare of the land. Support them in their endeavours. Do not permit the publication of interdicts and the prohibition of worship except on the most urgent grounds, or unless the commands proceed from the Holy See itself, when you must religiously respect them, for in these times many men no longer respect the Holy See. Trust in the Duke of Alva as commander-in-chief of the army. Obey my instructions in your dealings with the Council of State, the Council for the Indies, for finance, for the Order of the Golden Fleece, and in your relations with the Inquisition. Have a special care to finance which is to-day the most important department of the state; the treasury has a clear knowledge of the means which are at your disposal.

I have left you full instructions as to when and where you are to give your signature. The Cardinal of Toledo seemed to think that he should always witness it, but I do not feel that that is necessary. There must of course always be a second signature as well as yours. Cobos will read everything through carefully before you sign it, but you must be ready to take the final responsibility. If you are ever in doubt, ask advice from Don Juan de Zuñiga or some other. Never meddle in private matters and give no promises either in writing or by word of mouth.

You must behave to the council of Aragon exactly as I have instructed you, or even more cautiously. The Aragonese are more passionate and more easily roused than any other people.

I need hardly commend to your care the Queen, our mother. Nor need I ask you to care for your sisters, for I know how much you love them. Let them continue still in the retired life to which they are accustomed, and when you and your Queen exchange visits with them, see that everything is arranged in a seemly manner and do not let more gentlemen enter the room than is necessary.

And now my son, one word more — for your own behaviour. I entreat you to take my advice to heart. You must know that this your early marriage and your calling to the regency make you a man long before your time. But do not on that account falsely presume that study is an occupation fit only for a child. On the contrary, it is the only means by which you will gain honour and reputation. You cannot grow early to manhood merely by imagining and wishing; you must gain the knowledge and judgment which will enable you to do a man's work. Study and good company will alone help you to this. Remember how many lands you will be called upon to govern, how far apart they are, how many different languages they speak, how necessary it will be for you to know them all so that you may understand and be understood by your subjects, and you will see how needful it is for you to learn languages. Latin is indispensable, French very important. Until this time you have had boys for companions and amused yourself with the pleasures of childhood. From now on you are master of yourself and must seek the company of experienced men. You must not altogether abandon such pleasures as suit your age, but you must not neglect your work for them. Don Juan will be able to advise you for the best in this. He will know how best to deal with those flatterers who try to become your boon companions by splintering lances with you, riding at the ring, jousting and hunting, or who try to tempt you to more unworthy pleasures. You would do wisely to show no pleasure in the company of those who are for ever making unseemly jokes.

With God's will, my son, you are soon to marry. May God be pleased to give you grace to live soberly in this state, and to get sons. I am convinced that you have not deceived me as to your chastity until this time, and I am sure that you will continue so until your marriage. But you are still young and you are the only son that I now have or shall have, so that much depends on you; therefore let me entreat you to keep a watch on yourself and not to give yourself over too much to the pleasures of marriage. An undue indulgence may not only injure your own health but that of your heirs; it may even cut short your life as it did that of your uncle Don John, through whose death I succeeded to all these lands. Think what troubles might not ensue if your sisters and their husbands came to inherit what was yours. And so I advise you, shortly after your marriage, to find some excuse for leaving your wife, and do not come back to her very soon, nor yet stay with her long. But in this, above all, seek the advice of Don Juan de Zuñiga. Do not be angered with him but remember always that he acts in my best interests. I have also told the attendants of your wife, the Duke and Duchess of Gandia, to be mindful of this matter. I have no doubt that many people will be ready to fill your ears with hints of evil. But I beseech you to be strong and remember always what I have told you. And if, as you have assured me, you have touched no women before your marriage, so do not let yourself be tempted into any follies afterwards; such things are a sin towards God and a scandal in the eyes of your wife and the world. Therefore be strong in face of suggestions and temptations. My son, have a care too that there be good relations between your courtiers and those of your wife.

It is impossible to think of everything, for there are more exceptions than rules in politics. The chief is that you should pursue the straight path, have a good judgment and do good works. Even older men than you need someone to keep them constantly alive to their duty and to remind them of what has to be done. Every man needs advice, and so I ask you to make Don Juan de Zuñiga your watch and your alarum in all things. I too have commanded him to do his own part therein and to speak sharply if he must. Sleep is often sweet and an alarum is commonly a nuisance; therefore remember that he acts only out of devotion and duty to me, and be grateful to him.

Then there is the Bishop of Cartagena, a very virtuous man. You can read over and discuss this letter with him too. May

God grant, my son, that you may so live and act with His help that He will be rightly served, and that He will receive you at last in Paradise after your days on earth. This is the constant prayer of your loving father.

I, THE KING

Charles did not feel that even this confidential and personal admonition was enough for the occasion. He wished his son to have not only moral freedom from his surroundings but political independence so that he might have some insight into his father's wider plans. But he asked that the prince show this second letter to no one, not even to his wife. He was to keep it jealously under his own personal seal.

The second letter which Charles composed for his son reveals him not merely as father, but as King and Emperor. Here he shows all the self-confidence of the autocrat, tempered only by his religious sense of duty. Here he sharply characterizes all his ministers, describing them with perception, psychological exactitude and generosity. Here, intermittently, we catch the echo of his earlier letters.

It is my great sorrow and regret, [he wrote on May 6th] that I must leave you my kingdoms in such distress and inner weakness as they now are. I do not myself know how we shall weather the storm. All things are in God's hands; trusting not to my own merits but only to His mercy, I call for His help. The journey which I am about to undertake is beset with danger, to my honour, to my good name, to my fortune and my life. Yet if I were not to go, I should be in no position to ensure your inheritance. Nor would my abstention preserve you from having in your turn to meet these same perils. I owe it to my honour and my good name to go, although none can tell how it will end. The hour is late, our resources are few and the enemy is at the door. My life and fortune are both in danger, but with things as they now stand I must risk both. As for my life, God will do with it as He thinks best. It is my comfort that I shall at least have lost it in doing what had to be done. You will be troubled enough for money, for you will soon learn how slender are your revenues and how heavily mortgaged. But for your immortal soul, God of His Mercy will care for that.

In case I should die or be taken prisoner, I leave you yet

a third instruction. You are only to open it in one of these contingencies, and at the Cortes which will then be called, you are to read it out as my justification for what I have done.[1] But we are all mortal, you no less than I, so that I have put another paper with it, ordering that it shall not be opened unless I order it.

If God spares my life and gives me the chance to proceed with my projects, then I give you this advice. Some of the wishes which I express here may not be feasible. The King of France may attack me first and thus force me to deliver a decisive conflict in my own defence. Or he may leave my hands free to attack him either from Germany or the Netherlands. In either event, my opinion is that the Duke of Alva should invade Languedoc from Perpignan, with an army of Germans and Italians; Provence can be harassed from the sea and Dauphiné invaded from Italy. At the present time I know this is impossible. We have no money, no resources and very few arms. I have not troops enough and the united fleets of the French and Turks are on the seas. But should it come to a decisive conflict, there must at least be a simultaneous attack on the French position both from Spain and from wherever I shall myself be at the time. The Cortes must be called if money cannot be raised otherwise, but the *Sisa* must not at first be mentioned for I have promised to let it rest. Yet there is no better means than the *Sisa* to raise money both for you and me, and thus to get us out of our troubles in peace and war. If things come to such a pitch I will send you a personal note, and you must show me what you can do to help both your father and yourself. You must try every means to get this *Sisa*. If we were sure of this and of the revenues from the Indies, we could easily overthrow our opponents, and all other troubles could be set right in time of peace.

Let me once again rehearse to you all that I said to you in Madrid, concerning the personalities and the private rivalries of those about my Court and in the government. Make it clear to everyone that you hold yourself aloof from all parties and quarrels. In order to emphasise your impartiality I have included the heads of both parties in your ministry. This will prevent you from falling under the influence of either or becoming the instrument of their feuds.

The Cardinal of Toledo is a good man and in all serious

[1] This paper seems to have been subsequently destroyed.

questions you can rely on his honesty. Only do not subject yourself wholly to his influence, lest men should say, on account of your youth, you were but a tool in his hand. The Duke of Alva can be counted on to support whichever party best suits his private interest; I have therefore excluded him, together with all other grandees from the inner circle of the government. He is ambitious, bear himself with as much seeming humility as he may. He will do his best to make himself agreeable to you, probably with the help of feminine influence. Take heed of him, therefore; yet trust him implicitly in all military matters.

Cobos is growing older and easier to manage, but he is true. The danger with him is his ambitious wife. No one knows so much of all my affairs as he, and you will always have reason to be glad of his service. But do not give him more influence than I have sanctioned in my instructions. And above all do not yield to any temptations he may throw in your path; he is an old libertine, and he may try to arouse the same tastes in you. Cobos is a very rich man, for he draws a great deal from the dues for smelting bullion from the Indies, as also from the salt-mines and other sources. He looks on these things as his own particular privilege, but do not let them become heritable in his family. When I die, perhaps, it would be a good moment to resume these rights to the Crown. He has great gifts in the management of finances; circumstances, not he, are to blame for the deplorable condition of our revenues. Originally he was controller of the treasury during my absence only; it would offend him to take that office from him. But it is a good thing to have two men in that place of trust, and in your position I should bestow the other place sooner or later on Don Juan de Zuñiga. Do not give it to the Duke of Alva, who will probably ask for it. And do not give it to a son of Cobos or of Zuñiga, for it is an office in which great experience is needed. Cobos has a daughter married to the Viceroy of Aragon, but the Viceroy was only given the place because, of all the possible candidates, he was the least bad. The Vice-chancellor of Aragon, Miguel Mai, is an old man and wholly dependent on Cobos. For the moment you had better leave these men in their places, but you must be considering how best you can replace them later.

Don Juan de Zuñiga may appear rough and harsh, but do not forget that he is a devoted servant who thinks only of your good. You must show him as much gratitude as you can for all that he has already done for you; he is very different from many others, who have striven merely to have control over you for their own sakes. Zuñiga is jealous of Cobos and the Duke of Alva; he belongs rather to the party of the Archbishop of Toledo and the Duke of Osorno. Zuñiga and Cobos, you must remember, come of rather a different social stratum from the others, and Zuñiga, like Cobos, would be glad to see his children insured of a better income. Yet these two, each in his own way, will prove your best servants. Persuade them to get on with each other. In everything which concerns you personally, you will find no better guide than Don Juan. Do not think of him any more as your governor, but consider him rather as your and my devoted servant. Do not give way to impatience. If you can conquer yourself in this respect it will be the highest proof of your virtue.

You already know the Bishop of Cartagena as a man of extraordinary distinction. He may not have been the best instructor who could have been found for you, as he yielded too much to your desires. Now he is no longer your teacher but your Court chaplain and your confessor. I hope that he is not so mild with you over your conscience as he was over your books. Hitherto such gentleness may not have been dangerous, but in future it may. Take heed of this, for nothing is more important than your own soul, and it is important to take your duties seriously from the very threshold of your manhood, so that you may become early used to leading a good and well-ordered life. When you are away from your wife, you must be careful to follow his advice. Possibly it would be more salutary for you to make the Bishop into your Court chaplain only, and to take some young and austere friar for your confessor.

I shall say nothing of the Cardinal of Seville,[1] and president of the India board. He would do better to go back to his clerical duties, rather than to live at Court. If his health were not so bad he would have been outstanding in politics. He has always advised me very well. But his feeble health and his inability to get on with the Cardinal of Toledo are two great drawbacks. If he shows any inclination to withdraw from Court life, you will do well to encourage it. But do so without appearing to disfavour him.

[1] Loaysa.

The president of Castile is a good man, even if he is not quite so able as one could wish. I know of no one better at this present time. The fact that he gets on with Cobos is much in his favour, yet it is a qualified advantage, for Cobos would rather support him in his weaknesses than point them out to him. It would be as well to see that he is supported by able advisers. The Duke of Osorno is sly and deceitful, but he speaks so little that it is very hard to see through him. In his office as president of the council of the Golden Fleece, he is thought to be masterful and haughty; see to it therefore that he has good advisers to assist him.

I will give you no special instructions in regard to your kingdoms and the disposition of their inheritance. I myself am in doubt as to what had best be done for Naples and Milan. You will learn my wishes in my will and codicils.

Granvelle will be your best guide in international policy. He too has some private interests in Burgundy and several sons to provide for, yet I think him to be honest. You may make use of him in one of two ways. Either you can keep him with you, and that is what I should recommend at least at first, for he can instruct you in many things; or you can use him in the council for the Netherlands. If he is absent, his brother-in-law, the Abbot of St. Vincent, is the best substitute. Moreover Granvelle has carefully educated his son, the Bishop of Arras, in the hope that we will employ him. He is young but he has been well-grounded.

I would say much more to you, my son. But those other important matters on which I would gladly advise you are so dark and full of doubt, that I myself am still uncertain on many points and cannot therefore give you definite advice. One of the chief objects of my journey is to discover how I am to act in some of these problems. Keep to the ways of God, and trust wholly in Him. I also shall strive to perform my duty and to commend myself into His hands. I pray that He may send His blessing on you when you have fulfilled all your days in His service.

I, THE KING

Significant in themselves, these outpourings of Charles to his son are yet more significant as the fruit of his own lifetime of experience. How clearly here does he reveal the profound reaction from his own youth! How clearly does he express the religious conviction which was the very fount and origin of all his actions!

Like the *Confessions* of Saint Augustine, Charles's testaments to his son are in a sense personal confessions conceived in the form of prayers. The irresolution of Charles's character had as it were found the steadying influence which he needed: feeling his own limitations, he withdrew to the fortress of his faith.

These then were the principles on which his dynastic theory of the state rested. The Emperor was convinced that his family had a sacred call to perform the duty of worldly pastors, and that they must subject all human considerations to this task. As a ruler his only duty was to his subjects. He kept even the Grandees out of the inner government, although he was willing to use them for diplomacy and war. For this reason he made this complex attempt to gather together, in the regency of his son, the moral and intellectual forces of men of very differing characters and interests. Some of his advice — the uses, for instance, for which he designated Granvelle — was to take effect long after his death. His plan of campaign against France was crude enough, and was based on the same rather simple principles which had guided his earlier attacks on that kingdom; yet even here experience had taught him something, for he did not forget the necessity of provisions, baggage and money.

But what were those dark problems to which he referred? They had nothing to do with France or Cleves, nor yet with the division of the inheritance which he had explicitly referred to his son. Nor yet did he mean finances. On all these subjects he had clearly spoken his mind. He can have meant nothing but the religious question. His relations with the Pope and with the German Protestants were still indecisive; his mind was not yet made up. From all that we have learnt of Charles, I think it is reasonable to suppose that he was still hoping for a peaceful settlement. Yet he heard the whisper of God's voice guiding his action, and he was ready to strike, if it was God's will, sword in hand.

Half in hope, half in apprehension, he looked towards the future, strong only in his faith.

BUSSETO AND NUREMBERG

At Christmas 1542 Charles took leave of his daughters at Alcala de Henares. From the roads of Palamos he sailed with a heavy heart, leaving Spain for Genoa, on the way to Germany. He had said good-bye to his beloved kingdoms for many long years. Never again was he to set foot in Spain as a reigning King. He cannot yet have realized this possibility, for he was more certain of the duty which called him forth, than of the situation which he would have to meet.

He had made great preparations. Spanish soldiers had sailed round to the Netherlands, by way of the Atlantic, and permits for recruiting infantry and cavalry had been dispatched to Germany. During the last months he had fortunately managed to increase his revenues substantially from another source. The King of Portugal paid his daughter's dowry to the tune of 150,000 ducats in Spain itself, and an equivalent sum in bills of exchange on Antwerp. This was the money which was to finance his coming enterprise. He was moving more freely since its payment. Ferrante Gonzaga, whom he had appointed commander-in-chief, accompanied him from Genoa, as also the Marquis del Vasto and his wife, with a splendid train of 3000 Spaniards, 4000 Italians, and 500 light horsemen. A further 16,000 infantry and 2000 cavalry was to await him at Speyer on July 20th, with the artillery under Marignano, provisions, sappers, ships and munitions.

France was his objective.

Before he could strike at France, he must break down the bulwark of Cleves. He must also make a last attempt to win over the Pope to support his policy against the heretic and infidel. Against oppressive difficulties he had managed to achieve this end with Leo X, with Adrian VI and with Clement VII. He still hoped that he might repeat those triumphs. But of all the successors of St. Peter with whom he was fated to deal, Paul III was by far the most obstinate.

Alessandro Farnese had now occupied the chair of St. Peter for close on nine years. He was a scion of an old family, with a seat near Bolsena. His lovely sister Giulia had been the cause of his rise to favour at the Court of Alexander VI, and he had himself enjoyed to the full the life of a Renaissance prelate. By this time he was seventy-five years old. Titian painted a magnificent portrait of him at about this time; it hangs in Naples and shows, without any concealment, the Pope in the midst of his family. Near to the aged Pope, in attitudes expressive of filial devotion, kneel the two grandsons of his body, Cardinal Alessandro Farnese and Ottavio Farnese, Duke of Camerino. The picture is built up into a colour harmony of exquisite and expressive beauty, from the centre of which the aged Pope and grandfather gazes upon the world. Titian has delineated his character with truth and conviction, and in the features of the old man the impregnable obstinacy, which was his chief characteristic, seems to be mellowed by the gifts and experience developed in a long and full life. His attitude towards the necessary reforms of the Church was both shrewd and thorough, but his dynastic ambition, nourished by the political opportunities of the time, gradually came to dominate his policy. His grandson, Ottavio, had married Margaret, the natural daughter of Charles's youth. For the Pope's grand-daughter, Vittoria, there was repeatedly talk of the Duke of Orleans. Intermittently the richest prize in Italy, the duchy of Milan, had been hinted at for one or other of these young couples.

The Pope was surrounded by his own family and by French cardinals. After wearisome negotiations, Charles at length persuaded him to agree to another personal meeting. Parma as a rendezvous had to be avoided on account of technical difficulties, and the neighbouring small town of Busseto was decided on. The Pope arrived on July 21st with fourteen imperialist cardinals; the nineteen cardinals whose sympathies were with France remained behind. In the previous autumn the Spanish government had issued a *Pragmatica* forbidding any foreigner to hold a benefice in Spain. This annoyed the Pope scarcely less than the rumoured alliance between Charles and the relapsed King of England.

Such were the obstacles to an understanding between Charles and Paul at Busseto. On the other hand, the Emperor could dispose of Milan, Ottavio Farnese was his son-in-law, and the King of France was undoubtedly in alliance with the Turk. It is true that the Pope, alone in all Europe, refused to believe this fact. But on the other hand he must have known that the religious trouble in Germany could only be settled through the Emperor's agency.

Granvelle, who had been preceded by Veltwyk, rejoined Charles on June 13th, coming from Germany. Talks were organized between Charles's ministers and the cardinals, between himself and the Pope. Charles wrote to Mary and Ferdinand, in letters which are almost identical, explaining all that had passed.

The Vatican, it seems, began by making peace proposals. Charles answered almost bluntly that this was mere waste of time unless they took him for a fool. Did they not realize that the French and Turkish fleets were already acting together? The Pope declared that he doubted the truth of this report, and would hear nothing to the disfavour of France. All the same he was willing to send 4000 Italians to Hungary against the Turks. He postponed any definite decision for the holding of a council, in spite of Charles's urgent plea that Trent be immediately chosen for its place of assembly. But what most interested Paul was the acquirement of the duchy of Milan for his family. Negotiations even on this question were far from smooth. The Farnese family declared that Charles's request for a price of 2,000,000 ducats was exorbitant. But Cardinals Farnese and Cervino informed Granvelle, who passed it on to Charles, that they would come halfway to meet him in the appointment of imperialist cardinals, a subject hitherto canvassed in vain, if he would find some new solution to the problems of France and Milan. By this they meant that the marriage between Vittoria Farnese and the Duke of Orleans could be dropped, and she could be married to Ascanio Colonna. They added the covering proviso that the question of Milan was not to be regarded as having anything whatever to do with the settlement of Christendom's outstanding troubles.

At this juncture a man who is often to engage our attention hereafter makes his first appearance. This is Don Diego Mendoza, the ambassador to the Venetian government, in whom the spirit of Gattinara seemed to live again. He warned Charles very frankly against any renunciation of Milan.

> The whole world, [he wrote] knows that the Pope is answerable for all your past and present troubles. What prince has done you more hurt than he? The blind themselves can see that all your distresses are traceable to him, both the attacks of the French and through them the misdeeds of the Turks. Sire, keep what you have, and strengthen your own power and reputation. Milan is a fit inheritance for your only son and rightful heir. It is contrary to sense and reason to bestow it on a natural daughter.

Mendoza then appealed to the evidence of history to rescue Charles from that moment of weakness in which he had sought to give away Milan, a place itself unconquerable except by arms.

> Julius Caesar [he wrote], used to say that Sulla only resigned the dictatorship because he knew no history. Your Majesty will show an even greater ignorance if you resign Milan, for you have more right to it as Emperor than ever Sulla had to the dictatorship. I ask Your Majesty what right had the Romans to power over all the world, the Goths to Spain, the Franks to Gaul, the Vandals to Africa, the Magyars to Hungary, the Angles to England, save only their valour and their arms? If your conscience pricks you for Milan, why not give up Spain as well? There is but one distinction between the rights by which you hold these two lands — the one is a more ancient conquest than the other. Milan is the gateway to Italy. Let it but once fall into the hands of the French and all your friends in the peninsula will desert you.

Mendoza's anxiety was a little exaggerated, but it is worth noticing that Charles's ministers felt that they had to combat the extreme scrupulousness of his conscience. Perhaps it is more significant still to notice that Charles had already entrusted his representation at the council, if it met, to this determined and frank advocate of power politics.

The interview at Busseto ended like so many other interviews with assurances of the utmost friendship on both sides. The Emperor's chief impression, however, was that the Pope 'was very much concerned for the advancement of his house, and that his relations were extremely grasping'. Charles entrusted all further dealings with the Vatican to his new imperial envoy, Juan de Vega. Vega was to have many stormy scenes with the Farnese family. Charles's own daughter Margaret, forced to live in the bosom of a family which she heartily detested, was to develop in course of time into an impassioned admirer of her imperial father and an observant spy in his interests. Juan de Vega saw her first soon after his initial audience with the Pope, when he was asked to meet her and her husband, Ottavio Farnese, by Paul III. At this meeting, he urged Paul in vain to remember the promise he had made to take the imperial side, as soon as he had proof that the French and Turkish fleets were indeed acting in con-

498

junction in the Mediterranean. After the Turkish fleet had visited Toulon and seized Nice, there could be room for no further doubt.

Granvelle cannot have failed to make use of the intervals in the talks at Busseto to give Charles his opinions on German affairs.

The atmosphere had been cleared by the Diets held at Nuremberg in the autumn of 1542 and the spring of 1543. Both of these meetings had been very discouraging for King Ferdinand. At the latter he had given up negotiating with the Estates in general and had tried instead to deal separately, not indeed with each of the Estates, but merely with the Schmalkaldic League or the Catholic party. After countless painful discussions the Catholics at length offered him subsidies against the Turk. The Schmalkaldic League were not disposed to make a grant on terms which either Ferdinand, the Catholics, or the imperial representative felt they could accept. On April 23rd they issued a recess in which the Protestants took no part. When they attempted to register a formal protest, through the Saxon Chancellor Burkhardt, the King cut them short. The Chancellor had barely uttered the words, 'Most High and Mighty King', when Ferdinand rose to his feet and hurried out of the hall.

Over this Diet hung that same air of sultry and menacing distrust, which brooded sixty years later over the fateful Diet of 1608. Then indeed, for the first time in German history, the Estates separated without drawing up any recess at all, in order to take up their stance as hostile parties in the Protestant Union and the Catholic League. That was the prologue to the Thirty Years War. But this Diet, too, was a prologue to war, for after so much vain effort Ferdinand and Granvelle saw no way out of the impasse except by force of arms.

Granvelle was already preparing the field for this final issue. The recruiting campaign had been entrusted to him among others. The new activity brought him into contact with the rising generation of German princes. He expressed himself about this in a constructive report to the Emperor. He explained that he had had particular talk with the Count Palatine, Wolfgang of Zweibrücken, who was later the son-in-law of Philip of Hesse. He was even more pleased with Albert Alcibiades, the twenty-one-year-old Margrave of Brandenburg-Kulmbach. He found this prince very much improved since he had last seen him, when he was altogether under the influence of his uncle George. The Margrave did in fact enter imperial service as a cavalry commander. This was reported to his cousin, the twenty-nine-year-old brother of the Elector Joachim. Although he was a son-in-law of Duke Henry of Brunswick he was an open Protestant, ambitious and determined to make famous conquests. At the moment he was, with his father-in-law's assistance, arranging to serve the Emperor. This was to stand him in good stead later.

Far the most important of these young rulers, whose lives were later to interact so much upon the Emperor, was Maurice, Duke of Saxony, who had succeeded his feeble father, Duke George, in the rich duchy which borders Bohemia. It was said that as a statesman he learnt all his cleverness from watching the Emperor. But from his earliest years his own life had made him into an observant politician. Lively, intelligent, consumed with ambition, the young prince at twenty-two was controlled at home by his energetic mother, Katherine of Mecklenburg. This had sufficed to throw him all the more into the arms of his father-in-law, the Landgrave Philip. Two years ago he had insisted, against the will of his parents, on marrying the fourteen-year-old daughter of the Landgrave, Princess Agnes. Although he was so much younger than Philip of Hesse, his father-in-law put great confidence in him, and Maurice was proud of it. He was deeply flattered when Philip actually confided in him the details, partly political and partly more intimate, of his bigamous marriage. Treated as a person of account at his father-in-law's court, and relying on the Landgrave's support, he had for years defied his parents and their ministers, although he allowed himself to be drawn into their treaty of Regensburg.

Maurice had not come to Nuremberg in person. He sent his councillor, Christoph von Carlowitz. Carlowitz was completely won over by Granvelle's tempting bait. Never fully counting the consequences Granvelle dropped one startling hint: Maurice, he indicated, need have no fear of the Elector John Frederick of Saxony, for the Emperor could dispose of the Electorate some other way if he chose. For the first time the voice of the tempter sounded in Maurice's susceptible ear. All the same, negotiations with the Emperor dragged, for Maurice would not be content with a small command in the cavalry, and his own demands on the bishoprics of the Upper Saxon Circle seemed exorbitant to Charles. Yet the discussions had their uses, for Granvelle learnt from them the price for which Maurice of Saxony could be bought when the occasion arose. In the meantime, Maurice offered the King of the Romans 300 horse and 1000 foot for that very autumn, against the Turks. He promised to leave these in imperial service until the Turks withdrew from Komorn in Hungary.

The leaders of the Schmalkaldic League somehow came to hear of these transactions, but they were too much occupied with private troubles. The Landgrave, who was more alert, gave it as his opinion, to the Elector of Saxony, 'If Your Grace, Duke Maurice and I were as devoted to the Protestant cause as we give ourselves out to be, we should not quarrel so much among ourselves but should take heed to the teaching of Christ and St. Paul. We ought to take account of the speed with which matters are now likely to develop. Indeed, to judge by our quarrelling it is like to go with us as it went with the mouse and the frog when they fought each other, for the kite came by and gobbled them both up'. He lamented that 'our league is villainously built and full of holes, so that we are forced to go on chanting for as long as we possibly can: "Give peace in our time, O Lord" '.

The Landgrave spoke truly, and it had not escaped Charles's notice that every member of the Schmalkaldic League was thinking chiefly of his own interests and of the land he wanted to seize. The results of the Nuremberg Diet may have been meagre indeed for Hapsburg policy, but the report which Granvelle was able to give of his reconnoitring expedition among the German princes made up for a great deal.

THE DUKE OF CLEVES DEFEATED. LANDRECY AND CAMBRAI

The trouble in Cleves and Gelderland had come to a head. In the spring Duke William of Cleves received the sacrament in both kinds and his brother-in-law, the Elector John Frederick of Saxony, applied for admission to the Schmalkaldic League.

Landgrave Philip prevented it, as he had promised the Emperor. An armistice was suggested by several friendly princes, but rejected. And on April 12th Granvelle dismissed a last embassy from the Saxon Chancellor with an indication that an appeal to arms was now the only way out.

Charles entered Germany in a very different fashion in 1543 from that which he had favoured in 1530 and 1541. The impression he made was almost sinister, or so it appears in the description which the impartial observer Martin Bucer sketched for the Zurich reformer Bullinger.

> The Emperor is a man equally clear-sighted and determined in the pursuance of his plans. He talks over some, but not all, of his affairs with Granvelle and the Spaniards. In 1541 it seems he was half persuaded to yield to the articles of faith, the revised doctrine of justification, of marriage for priests and of the chalice for the laity. But finding he could not achieve his ends in this way he appealed to arms to make him master in Germany. He is very versatile, can do anything; he speaks German fluently and is himself recruiting his army. He is imperial in word and deed, in look and gesture, even in the greatness of his gifts. Even those who have long been in attendance on him are astonished at his present youthfulness, independence, energy, severity and dignity. This Emperor could do much, if he would but be an Emperor of the German Nation and a servant of Christ.

On August 17th Charles entered Bonn, where he requested the Elector of Cologne to get rid of Bucer and Hedio. Then he marched to Düren which was held to be impregnable because of its walls and towers, and which coolly refused a demand to surrender. The lord of Vlaten defended it boldly. But the imperial artillery made wide breaches in its walls, and the fifth assault on August 25th carried the town. The destruction of the place was appalling and Charles's gift of money to help rebuild the town can have been small comfort. The fortress of Jülich dared make no resistance. By the end of the month the Emperor was before Roermond, the first city across the frontier of Gelderland. On September 2nd it capitulated.

Charles marched on to Venloo. The young Duke, helpless and deserted by all his friends, here sought out Charles, hastening up from Düsseldorf, and fell on his knees before him. Somewhat ungallantly, he put the blame for his actions on his ministers. Charles agreed to pardon him if he would give up Zutphen and Gelderland, abandon his allies and return as a penitent to the Catholic fold.

The defeat of the Duke marked the eclipse of great hopes for the German Protestants. Had the Duke remained one of them he might have exerted some influence on the Elector of Cologne, Hermann of Wied, who was inclined to favour the Reformation. The collapse of Cleves could not fail of an effect on the whole of the Lower Rhenish and Westphalian provinces, on the bishoprics from Liège to Munster and Paderborn. The religion of the Netherlands themselves in part depended on it.

The Emperor had conquered.

By concentrating all his forces on a single object, he had succeeded in carrying out the first part of his great project with incredible speed and efficiency. Next he ensured the results by acting with moderation. The Duke of Cleves kept all his rightful lands and was rewarded a few years later for his necessary divorce from his French wife, Jeanne d'Albret, by being given a daughter of King Ferdinand. Looking back on his campaign in his memoirs, Charles wrote a few significant words. 'This experience opened the Emperor's eyes to the fact that ambitions such as these could be overthrown without difficulty by force, provided it was used at the right moment and with sufficient means behind it.' We shall have cause to remember this dictum later.

If caution and care are essential to human success, Charles had fully deserved his victory. There was something heroic in the deliberate manner in which he had come to his decision and the courage with which he had carried it out. He had left Spain regardless of opposition, he had defied the dangers of crossing the sea, of sailing along a hostile coast and passing close under the French fortresses of Piedmont, he had risked the disasters which an apparently powerful coalition of enemies might have brought upon him. He could not but remember the way in which the Netherlands had been wasted of recent years. But objectively the most important reason for his success was the shameful desertion of the Duke of Cleves by all his allies — France, Denmark and the German princes.

Charles saw at once that by this desertion all those princes had made a political blunder and injured their personal credit. He too, now, determined to form his own coalition. On September 12th he sent Granvelle's second son, the young Chatonnay, from his camp at Venloo to England, to announce his success. He stressed the fact that by sacrificing Cleves the French King had forfeited his credit in Germany. Now he wished either to launch an immediate campaign against him, or to prepare one for the following year. Unhappily, Charles explained, he had not the money and he suggested that the King of England lend him 150,000 ducats, the cost of the army for another month. Should the King be unwilling to give the money outright, he would guarantee its repayment in four or five months out of the revenues of Spain and the Indies. The need was urgent.

The old difficulties crowded upon Charles once again. The Duke of Cleves was gone, but there remained the King of France, a great opponent in place of a lesser one. In his political testament for his son, Charles had left the question of his military policy open: he had not decided whether to let Francis force him into a defensive position or whether to initiate the attack himself. He had launched the attack on Cleves, but Francis now launched a counter-attack on him. The French invaded Luxembourg. Charles pushed on through Hainault by way of Mons and Le Quesnay, but his advance was brought to an abrupt stand at Landrecy on the Sambre, where a strong French relieving force compelled him to offer battle. Thinking that the French had a great advantage of numbers, Queen Mary and Granvelle were filled with apprehension at Charles's rash advance. The situation was indeed very critical. Charles himself realized it and made ready in his own way. On October 28th he confessed and partook of the sacrament. On November 2nd he marched with his troops to meet the enemy. The Venetian ambassador foretold that the coming battle would be the turning-point of the century. He was disappointed. King Francis withdrew during the night.

The pursuit which started too late was not very successful. But the siege of Landrecy had been abandoned, and the French had contrived to re-provision the town. They were still holding Luxembourg, Yvoy, Landrecy and Guise.

In spite of recurrent attacks of gout, Charles, surprisingly enough, managed to support the hardship of life in camp in mid-winter, and very bad weather. According to his own statement, it was the continuous rain which made the roads impassable, and the shortage of money — 'in spite of new bills of exchange sent from Spain' — alone which forced him to withdraw to the Scheldt.

The military deadlock was outweighed by a political success of the greatest importance. Charles's reputation and the number of his troops enabled him to take possession of Cambrai, whose bishop was favourable to France, and set up a citadel with a garrison. This was the last step in the unification of the Netherlands. At his accession they had been split up by the encroaching territories of Gelderland, Utrecht and Cambrai; all were now under Charles's control. On November 19th the Emperor stated in a letter to his brother that the new position of Cambrai would not in any way affect the boundaries or prestige of the Empire. But in order to protect the imperial bishopric against France, which stretched out a greedy hand in its direction, Charles would have to give further attention to his hereditary lands. There was still talk of an attempt on Liège.

Charles pursued his policy of attack yet further. Luxembourg was partly occupied by the French; it was therefore all the more essential to protect the hereditary lands of the Hapsburg and above all the key-point of Diedenhofen. He determined to take steps to preserve the imperial city of Metz. This brought him up once more against that ticklish problem which was to give so much trouble to his dynasty: what was the precise distinction between hereditary and imperial lands? The engrossment of Metz in a national state in 1871 was no more effective protection against France than would have been the establishment of its incontrovertible position as an imperial city. But Charles failed to gain any such definite admission. Mary sent an agent, Charles Boisot, who managed to induce the city to make an impressive gesture in the Emperor's favour. Boisot said that the patrician families of the town were far more French than Burgundian in sympathy, but they were ready to ensure their neutrality by describing themselves as good imperialists. Boisot expelled a Protestant preacher who had found a large following in the city. He even managed to call a meeting of the burghers, against the will of the patrician families, the Paraiges, as they were called, and warned them vehemently against the danger of supplying the French with materials or provisions. Charles joyfully described these successes to his brother.

The Emperor's policy continued to be distinguished by caution and alertness. He had had to give in before the power of winter, but he did not on that account hold up his preparations for the coming year. Many things conspired to help him. The German princes in his army approved his action at Cambrai. Prince Maurice, too, was impressed and on that account the more annoyed at the break-down of his own negotiations for an imperial alliance. Impelled by mingled ambition and curiosity, the twin roots of so many human actions and human crimes, Maurice had come in person to Charles's Court. It was his first visit and he was open to innumerable different impressions. He found that here, too, as in Hesse, he commanded personal respect; he played his part in the campaign as far as Cambrai and then returned home. He carried back with him to the German princes an offer from the Emperor: Charles suggested that he should mediate in person between the Duke of Brunswick — then at the imperial Court — and the Schmalkaldic League. It was a Trojan gift. No more effective means could have been found to prevent Maurice from joining with his fellow-protestants, and to secure his good offices to the Emperor.

Meanwhile Ferrante Gonzaga crossed the Channel to prepare a further war-plan with the English, who had so far contented themselves with a few timid sallies from Calais.

POPE AND EMPEROR. THE DIET OF SPEYER,
1544

Early in January Charles resumed his journey, by way of Aachen and the Rhine, in order to keep his promise and attend the long-projected Diet at Speyer. He would have preferred the gathering to take place at Cologne, but he set aside his own desire in order to meet the wishes of Ferdinand and the Estates. His immediate objective, fairly openly expressed, was to win over the German princes against France. Since 1541 Charles had been thinking more and more seriously of using force against the heretics. This knowledge brings up a new problem: how far was Charles's present sharp attack on the Vatican and generous agreement to the Protestant demands the result of his real feelings? How far was it merely a means to mislead and tempt the members of the Schmalkaldic League? Both his attack on the Pope and his yielding to the heretics were sufficiently noticeable. To understand his underlying motives it is essential to follow events in great detail, keeping both possibilities in mind.

The imperial ambassador in Rome, with all his efforts to get the Pope to declare openly for Charles, had achieved no success: Paul sent the Cardinal-legate, Alessandro Farnese, simultaneously to both the imperial and the French Courts. In Germany he was to be supported by the nuncio Sfondrato, a widower from Cremona, whose son was later to be Pope as Gregory XIV. He, too, had once been in imperial service at Siena and the Emperor remembered this when Farnese presented him. 'You used to be a good servant of mine', he said, 'unless your cassock has altered your heart.' This suspicion offended Sfondrato, but it was more just than he himself knew. The mission on which he had come was hardly in Charles's best interest.

His instruction for the personal visits he was to make to the German princes has survived. We know from it that the mission had no other purpose, than to persuade them to restrain the Emperor, and to stand forth themselves as mediators between him and the King of France, as they had done twenty years before. The Bavarians were the most likely to agree to such a policy, but even they, when faced by the nuncio, remembered their duty to the head of the Germanic Empire and refused. The Elector of Brandenburg went further, and turned the tables on the Pope by demanding that the notorious ally of the Turk be deprived of his title of 'Most Christian King'.

Farnese had the thankless task of trying to make peace by outworn means. He suggested that Charles cede Milan, or at the least Savoy. In return the King of France was to make some other provision for the Duke of Orleans, and to relieve Charles of his persistent claim on Navarre. Yet this could hardly be done, for the French Court had already mooted a marriage between the Duke and Jeanne d'Albret, the heiress of Navarre. As Charles remarked the first step in this direction was a divorce. Possibly the whole negotiation was merely a feeler, put out by Paul III, for the marriage of the Duke of Orleans to Vittoria Farnese. This marriage was the dearest desire of the papal dynasty and in a confidential letter of Cardinal Gonzaga, he admitted that the mission to France had no other end in view save the furtherance of this alliance.

Granvelle's brother-in-law, Bonvalot, whose diplomatic gifts Charles valued very highly, had confidential information from the French Court — some of it from Queen Eleonore herself — and knew that feeling ran high in France against another royal mesalliance with a Pope's niece. The people said that the kingly blood had already been enough debased by a Medici. Yet what an abyss of foul dynastic greed was the policy of this aged Pope, who could pervert an important political mission at a critical time to so base an end! This representative of Christ on earth was ready to offer his loving services to the French royal dynasty against the attack of England and the Empire, by using his authority to make peace at Charles's expense. When the cardinal-nephew appeared before the Emperor uneasy indeed must have been his conscience, for he knew all!

Charles was indignant. He had received the legate at Kreuznach on January 20th, through Granvelle and his Spanish secretary Idiaquez. On the following day he gave him audience. He showed the greatest self-control. He made answer to all the demands in a long conversation. He explained that he had intended to hand over Milan or the Netherlands to the King of France's son, as the dowry of an Infanta or an Archduchess. This was not to be interpreted as any admission of a French claim; it was an indication of his own profound desire for peace. He expressed a deep sense of injury at finding that the Pope made no difference between him and the ally of the Turk. He declared that he could not possibly discuss the session of Siena, and various other points. And all the time he hinted that he did not think any purpose was served by further talk, as it was only too well known that the Pope would not budge from any of his opinions.

Angry and disappointed, or feigning to be so, the cardinal assured Charles that both he and the Pope had the greatest sympathy and respect for him. The Emperor cut him short with a sharp reminder of all that the Farnese dynasty owed to him. 'Monsignore', he said, 'you have had from us the Archbishoprics of Monreale, your father has had Novara, Ottavio our daughter, with a dowry of 20,000 ducats. I have sacrificed two of my friends, the Duke of Urbino and Colonna, to make room for the Pope. In return for all this the representative of Christ on earth makes alliances with the King of France, or rather with the Turks!' Charles went on to say that he would take up the question of Reform at the Diet, and put an end to all abuses. Echoes of things which Gattinara had once said now proceeded from Charles's own lips. And although he had couched his words in more respectful terms, he had expressed himself much the same in his Testament for Philip.

The written answer which Charles then prepared, although Farnese was not excluded from assisting at its formulation, was so sharp that Paul III did not read it out in the consistory. Instead Juan de Vega, who had been sent a full report of all that had happened by the Emperor himself, broadcast copies of it. Even in Germany the disfavour with which the papal legate had been dismissed was soon generally known. Granvelle had detailed to him yet again all the King of France's several crimes, his innumerable breaches of treaties, his invasion of Savoy, his open encouragement of the German Lutherans, his alliance with the Turks, his seizure of the Archbishop of Valencia — who had been able to buy his freedom merely by the loathsome expedient of bribing the King's mistress, Madame d'Étampes — his intrigues in Italy. All these crimes, Granvelle pointed out, the Pope was prepared to disregard, rather than to enter into alliance with the Emperor as his duty must obviously dictate.

The Pope thought of nothing less than joining forces with Charles. This knowledge soon outweighed the rooted mistrust and the political discretion of the Germans, strengthening their trust in the Emperor. On March 8th, 1544, Luther himself wrote to Amsdorf: 'The latest news is that the Pope, French and Turks have allied against the Emperor.'

Charles wished the legate to take his leave before the Diet met. He declared this opinion to his brother and spoke it openly to Farnese's face, adding that papal legates at Diets invariably caused trouble. Naturally Charles would not have the French ambassador present at the Diet either. The English King, Charles's ally, sent his envoy, Wotton, but Charles would give no passes for a French representative. Their government had to do the best it could by sending a written message; even this was chiefly taken up with empty words, expatiating on the ancient family connections between Charles and Francis, and speciously explaining away the Turkish bond. Abraham, David, Solomon, the French declared, and even the Emperor Frederick II, had had understandings with the unbelievers. The French King would be ready to drop this friendship, and help the Emperor against the common foe, as soon as Charles disgorged the lands which belonged by rights to France. Of course, the French message went on, Charles must do nothing to annoy the Turks in the intervening time: his seizure of Tunis had been highly irritating to the Sultan. To judge by the French attitude, one might have supposed that the Barbary pirates visited the coasts of Sicily, Naples, Spain and Majorca with no other intention than to catch butterflies. At that very time Barbarossa had carried off another 1500 Christians into slavery. An eloquent comment on French policy!

The German princes were not impressed. Still less the King of Denmark. His natural interest in shipping and commerce soon turned him away from his futile alliance with France and Cleves, and made him once more the friend of the Netherlandish government. While the legate's companion, Sfondrato, was busily inciting the Count Palatine to make good his claims on Denmark, Christian II was formally recognized by Charles in a treaty signed at Speyer. The Schmalkaldic League was fully disillusioned when the imperial Vice-chancellor, Naves, showed them some letters from the French King in which, in return for Milan, he shamelessly promised to help the Emperor against the Protestants.

The Diet of Speyer had begun well, but it soon degenerated into a formidable trial of patience.

Weeks went by before all the Estates were assembled. The leaders of the Schmalkaldic League drifted in separately, the Landgrave on February 8th, the Elector of Saxony on the 18th. Charles awaited their coming on tenterhooks of anxiety. Once again it seemed that, as at Regensburg, he would have to waste valuable months. When at last the chief of them had come, he issued his propositions demanding a subsidy against the Turk and their support against the French King. Surprisingly enough the first answer which he got was not unfavourable.

The Protestants naturally stipulated for a guarantee of continued 'peace and justice' in return. The Catholics were not prepared to give it. Charles next asked that he might preside over the council for raising the subsidy. This led to more troubles, and ended in his suggesting that they should begin to discuss methods of raising the money without entering into any definite obligation as to the sum. The Protestants now rejected this, knowing full well that the towns would support them because of the old jealousies between towns and princes. But soon after the Protestant leaders themselves, Hesse and Saxony, began to waver. They were affected in their course partly by the question of Brunswick, which was very much their own affair, partly because they were bound by treaty to the Emperor, partly because of the recent defeat of Cleves and partly by Maurice's jealousy. The towns, anxious for their trade, and the Rhenish Electors, who did not want to have a war on the Rhine held back; all were hoping that they would be able to escape with a declaration against France and a very small subsidy vote. Gradually the Electors yielded and the Landgrave, at a meeting of the princes, was borne forward to the most vehement expression of opinion against France. He advocated the war on the Turk, the ancient enemy of God and Christendom, with such violence that the young and very devout Catholic Bishop of Augsburg, Otto Truchsess von Waldburg, declared that he seemed to be inspired of the Holy Ghost.

The negotiations went on from the end of February until April 4th. After some difficulty Charles did at length gain considerable help. He was to have 24,000 infantry and 4000 cavalry for six months. It is hard to say which was the more valuable to him, the grant itself, or this open severance of the princes from the French friendship. The English and Venetian ambassadors were profoundly impressed. Granvelle was deeply gratified.

But Charles's real difficulties were only just beginning. There was some trouble as to the method to be used for raising the money, whether by the *matrikel* or the *Gemeinpfennig*. But this was nothing compared to the problem of the concessions which the

Protestants now demanded in return for their help. Charles had forbidden Protestant services in the Church of the Dominicans, but he gave the Landgrave permission to use the choir as he wished, and the Landgrave took him at his word. Charles was therefore showing an inclination to meet his subjects half-way, at least as far as he felt himself justified.

Once again the Protestants tried to persuade him to extend his imperial declaration to cover recent converts to the Confession of Augsburg. Granvelle opposed this with vehemence and passion. The original gains of the Protestants seemed once more to be called in question, for Charles had made all his grants only on conditions. But on May 1st the Emperor essayed a new method of dealing with the problem. He named the Elector Joachim of Brandenburg, whom he knew to be favourable to him, the Elector Palatine—Frederick had succeeded his brother Lewis in this title on March 16th — as well as the Vice-chancellor and the Cardinal-bishop of Trent, Christopher Madruzzo, as mediators.

In the meantime the Catholics were being even more troublesome than the Protestant Estates. These latter were fairly amenable, so long as the Emperor did not again try to palm off on them an invalid imperial declaration. Charles for his part could make concessions with a clear conscience, since he always set a time-limit — the meeting of the council. Important, too, was the nomination of members for the *Reichskammergericht*, since the course of justice depended on its personnel. The opposing demands, made by both sides, could not easily be reconciled.

The Emperor was in haste and on May 24th he made his last appeal. Granvelle abandoned persuasion for threats. On May 28th the Diet at last came to a conclusion. The imperial guarantee for the Protestants had to be included in the recess, to satisfy them. The Catholics agreed to this on the understanding that the guarantee was conceived as a proclamation on imperial authority alone, not as a formal decision of the joint Estates. They did not give in: they merely evaded the issue.

On June 10th the dietary recess was issued. The Estates promised to help the Emperor against the French King, and to raise reliable forces for a firm defence of the imperial circles, so that 'oppressed Christians, lands and peoples, should be saved from the bestial power of the Turks'. The Estates bitterly lamented the religious division and appealed for help to a 'Christian Reformation' and a new Diet, until such time as 'a general free Christian Council of the German Nation could meet'. Until that time Charles declared that 'of our own imperial power, no man shall persecute, attack, or invade any other, either for religion's sake or for any other cause, but all shall live together in good friendship and Christian love'. 'No Estate shall have the right to tempt away the subjects of any other', the document continued, 'nor to take them under its protection, even if the subjects in question are not the direct subjects of the Emperor; the revenues, rents and interests of the clergy are not to be stopped but are to remain the same as they were at the Regensburg recess; the ministers of churches, parishes, schools, alms-house, and hospitals are to stay as they are, regardless of religion.' The recess concluded with the ruling that trials in the *Reichskammergericht* against adherents of the Augsburg Confession were to stop. The composition of that court, and the appointment of worthy men to perform its offices, was to be reconsidered in time for the next Diet, once again 'regardless of the party in religion to which they belong'.

Charles had in reality abandoned his Catholic standpoint. Not, it is true, by the concessions which he had made to the Protestants pending the coming council, but rather by agreeing to a 'reformation' at the next Diet, and admitting the Protestants to parity in the Empire. Yet perhaps he had not, even in these concessions, strayed very far from the lines of policy which he had laid down during the past years. In 1524 his government had thought it wisest to postpone the national meeting of the Germans, but in other circumstances he had himself suggested it as a solution. In the instructions which he had once given to Held, in the threats which he had but recently uttered to Farnese, he had gone nearly as far as in the concessions he made at the Diet.

Small wonder that the Pope was incensed. On August 24th he issued his famous condemnation of the Dietary recess, censuring the plan of a national meeting in Germany, the interim rulings of the Emperor, and the sacrifice of Church lands. He characterized all these as attacks on spiritual privileges. With righteous complacency, the papal letter next held up Charlemagne and Constantine as worthy models for Charles to follow — and who else indeed had he tried to follow? -- and exhorted him not to be tempted from the straight path by the godless examples of Nero, Domitian and Frederick II. If he did not take heed, the Pope unctuously concluded, he would share the fate of the Jews and Greeks, on whose devoted heads the wrath of God had broken with a vengeance.

The atmosphere, the very actions, are those of the years 1526 and 1527. That time Gattinara had taken up the cudgels against the Pope. This time Luther and Calvin charged into the lists to defend the Emperor. Holding up a mirror to the Pope's actions, Calvin's dialectics ruthlessly exposed the historical and moral fallacies of the papal letter. The Chancellor Brück tried to hold Luther back, but the intrepid reformer, more violent even than Calvin, was determined to 'lay the axe to the root of the tree'. Charles was often lucky, never more so than now; he had found champions where he had least expected, where he was indeed shocked to find them! For his own part, he answered the Pope by word of mouth only. The contents and form of the letter were themselves too insulting for him to feel that a formal answer would have been anything but a lowering of his own dignity.

THE CAMPAIGN ON THE MARNE AND THE PEACE OF CRÉPY

It is possible that, going through Lombardy in the previous year, Charles had planned with Andrea Doria and the Marquis del Vasto, how they should support him from the sea and from Piedmont when he made his attack on France. This would have been in accordance with the great design he had in view. But we have no evidence for the actual fact. Whatever his plans, here too Charles was forced back on to the defensive. With Barbarossa's help the Duke of Enghien conquered Nice and crossed the Alps. He advanced rapidly into the land, marching on Carignano, just south of Turin. The Marquis del Vasto attempted to come to the rescue of the brave Pirro Colonna, but as he approached from the east, making towards Sommariva, he clashed with Enghien's troops on April 14th near the little village of Ceresole, and suffered a bloody defeat.

The French unhappily could not follow up this victory because they lacked the money to pay their Swiss mercenaries. Piero Strozzi attacked Milan but without success and was later crushingly defeated at Serravalle, south of Tortona on the river Scrivia. The 350,000 ducats which the French government had recently extracted from Venice as the price for disgorging Marano, had been wasted in these unsuccessful struggles. Enghien made a truce with del Vasto, and the imperialist position grew yet more secure in the summer when the French were forced to withdraw all their troops to the north. King Francis was, however, already boasting that he would pay the Emperor for fifty such checks as he had had at Landrecy.

Yet before the Diet of Speyer came to an end, Charles's operations for the regaining of Luxembourg had already begun; his commanders were Wilhelm von Fuerstenberg, who had deserted French for imperial service, and Ferrante Gonzaga. On June 6th they entered the city of Luxembourg. The Emperor next collected the main body of his army at Metz, intending to advance across Lorraine, where on June 14th the aged Duke had just died, to Ligny and Commercy on the Meuse, and on towards the Marne. The troops which he had collected at Metz made a gallant show. There were Italian and Spanish generals, German princes and mercenaries; the army consisted of 3000 Italian and 4000 German cavalry, much of it under the command of German princes; Fuerstenberg and Bemelberg had 8000 infantry each and there were between 6000 and 7000 troops from Spain and from the Netherlands, besides 62 cannon, 3500 horses, 1400 pioneers, 200 wagons with 8 horses apiece, 70 ships carried on wagons with all their crews; over 40,000 men in all.

Charles stayed in Metz from June 17th until July 6th. Here he received his niece Christina, once Duchess of Milan and now Duchess of Lorraine. Here he drew up a curious codicil which has but recently come to light. It was written in Spanish and sealed by his secretaries Idiaquez and Bave. It begins with an abrupt repudiation of all those marriage plans with the French house, which the King's faithlessness and his alliance with the Turk had brought to nothing. He sought, as he expressed it, not the salvation of the French but of his own dynasty, and therefore wished to strengthen the connection between the two branches by marrying his daughter, the Infanta Mary, to Ferdinand's eldest son. On the other hand if Philip were to make over the Netherlands to his sister, she was to marry the second son of Ferdinand, rather than the elder, because if Philip died childless the Infanta would have Castile and Aragon too. But if the elder Infanta married the elder Archduke, then the younger Infanta should marry the younger Archduke and the lands be divided between the two families, as they were now between Charles and Ferdinand. But there was to be one curious difference: the younger line was to have the Netherlands as well as the Austrian lands, for Charles held that the uniting of Spain and the Low Countries under a woman ruler would be impracticable. Once again Charles amused himself with the possible combinations of family marriages, building up plans which he was to alter, or at least to postpone indefinitely, only a few months later.

Setting out on this, his final and greatest war with King Francis, Charles occupied himself once again with plans for his possible death, as he had done in the Testament he drew up for Philip. Should he die, he wished not only the youthful Philip, but his even more youthful and still unmarried sister Mary, to be declared capable of inheriting and governing.

In the meantime his troops had pressed on to the Marne. Charles followed in their wake, by way of Pont à Mousson, Toul and Pagny on the Meuse. He took Commercy, the key to the Meuse valley and proceeded, over Ligny on Ornain, south of Bar-le-Duc, to St. Dizier on the Marne. He had gone at least sixty miles before he came up against any serious resistance. Then he heard that a French army of uncertain size was waiting for him a little farther down the Marne at Jaalons between Chalons and Epernay.

After he had laid mines, erected batteries, and sapped the walls, he gave the assault to St. Dizier. On the very first day of the siege, while digging in an advanced sap, the young René of Chalon, Prince of Orange, was wounded in the shoulder by an enemy bullet: he died on July 21st. St. Dizier was surrounded and sallies from within were easily beaten off, but the garrison of Vitry, farther up the Marne, attacked and harried the besiegers until Charles dispatched Maurice of Saxony, the Margrave Albert, the Duke of Este and Fuerstenberg to take it. It was stormed and fell on June 23rd-24th, not without a sharp cavalry engagement before the walls. Within Este found and seized the standard of the commander, Brissac.

On August 9th the garrison of St. Dizier offered to surrender if they were not relieved within eight days. No help came, and on August 17th the town capitulated on condition that the garrison and artillery were spared. The Emperor was now master of the middle waters of the Marne and Meuse.

Yet he was still barely half-way to Paris, the city which was now more or less openly recognized as his main objective. The whole French army was entrenched in his path and his own provisions were running short. Moreover he was anxious to have news of the English King, who had undertaken to attack at the same time. The distance from the English base at Calais to Paris was about the same as that from the imperial base at Metz. But King Henry was still loitering somewhere near Boulogne. Charles knew nothing of this. The word in his camp was: On to Paris! In the interval he was contemplating attacks on Troyes, Rheims or St. Ménéhould on the upper Aisne. He reconnoitred Chalons, carefully prospecting for a serious siege, but decided that it would be a long and dangerous business. It seemed better to march on into the heart of the land, thus solving if possible his difficulties in finding provisions and pay for his men.

In a long forced march at night, the army safely passed Cahors on September 2nd-3rd, going by way of La Chaussée, and so down the Marne towards the capital city, past Ay and Epernay. But when Charles attempted to cross the Marne and attack the new position of the French army, he failed. Nevertheless he hastened on, his light cavalry skirmishing as far in advance as Meaux.

Panic reigned in Paris. Many fled and the King, who could no longer fight but was still popular, needed all his authority to restore calm among the people.

In the meantime negotiations between the combatants had already begun, and were to lead within a fortnight to that peace of Crépy whose terms were long to remain secret.

The last weeks had been a time of great anxiety for the Emperor. His military operations had been conceived all too boldly, and the decisions which he was called upon to make in the field were often in sharp contradiction to the course of his diplomatic negotiations. Gonzaga and Granvelle served him with equal tenacity and circumspection, both in the delicate approaches to the negotiations and in their lengthy course. The transactions may be clearly traced in the terms of the peace itself, and yet more fully in the long and frank reports which Charles gave of them to Mary, and in the *Chronicle* of Busto, which supports them in the main.

On July 20th Charles reported that the Cardinal of Lorraine had mentioned the possibility of negotiating. This initial suggestion came to nothing, but instigated Charles to work out his exact financial position, and to calculate that he could not support his army beyond September 25th. This proved to him that it would be as well to make a truce, with English mediation, as soon as possible. Profoundly resigned to the perennial hostility of France, he did not believe in the possibility of a final peace. But his incredulity was founded on those very facts which this time, for once, led to peace. The confidential reports which he received from the French Court made him fully aware that the King got on badly with his two sons, and that the two sons, the Dauphin who had originally been Duke of Orleans, and the Duke of Orleans who had originally been Duke of Angoulême, got on even worse among themselves. The Dauphin belonged to that large party which wanted to marry off the Duke of Orleans to Jeanne d'Albret. But the Duke loudly declared that he would not always be treated as the second string to France's bow. He wanted an independent principality somewhere else. This made him the obvious candidate for Milan in the Farnese policy, as also the willing object of the Hapsburg marriage policy. Queen Eleonore strengthened him in this latter hope.

On July 30th the Duke's Grand Chamberlain, a lord of Villers who was also the *bailli* of Dijon, came to Granvelle with the suggestion that the Duke should marry the elder Infanta and have Milan. Granvelle refused, but he did not let go of this valuable thread of French policy, especially when he learnt that Villers had acted with the connivance of the King. Villers tried to intimidate the imperialists with tales of the huge reinforcements which the King expected in August, but they refused to be deceived. Later, when he told them that the Duke of Orleans might perhaps be married to Jeanne d'Albret, they perplexed him completely by agreeing that this was an excellent plan. All the same, Charles saw that the horizon was clearing, and gave Mary permission to continue her efforts to engineer a truce. Gradually the imperial party grew surer of the ground. When the Count of Brienne came to reconnoitre the diplomatic position, he was reminded of the very perilous situation in Europe now occupied by the French monarchy.

The next to send an envoy was the French admiral, Annebault, but his first effort was ineffective and he reinforced his embassy by sending the Dominican monk Guzman. Then came the King's secretary, Aubépine; he returned to the charge on August 31st. Meanwhile, on the 29th at the latest, Charles had issued passes for Annebault and one of the presidents of the French council. On the same day he drew up the plenipotentiary powers of Granvelle and Gonzaga. The conference took place at St. Amand, a little to the north of the Marne, between Vitry and Chalons. Propositions were discussed for the marriage of the Duke of Orleans to a Hapsburg princess and for Charles to Princess Margaret. But this was not a mere dynastic dream, such as had occupied the Emperor at Aigues Mortes. This at last was a serious attempt to make terms for peace, to exchange conquests, renounce the objects of the quarrel and swear a firm friendship. The terms seemed to combine the virtues of Cambrai and Aigues Mortes. Both sides promised to collect further information and to meet again on September 8th.

Meanwhile Queen Eleonore wrote to her brother, the Emperor, from Amboise on September 1st. The letter had no political importance but it summed up the feelings of the French Court. She could not express her joy, she said, to learn that at last a serious peace was to be made between her dear brother, the Emperor, and her lord, the King of France. She would ask the King for permission to go to see her brother, and in the meantime gratefully thank God for having at last heard her prayers. She was convinced that the greatness of the moment would not be lost on Charles: it was wonderful to think that at last the two greatest princes in Christendom were to unite in the service of God. She hoped indeed that this new peace would be firm and lasting, and she particularly commended the Admiral, Annebault, as a man of loyalty and honour.

Between September 6th and September 10th the actual terms were at length decided on. On the 10th the Emperor left the valley of the Marne and turned north towards Soissons. On the 7th he had sent the Bishop of Arras to the English King. He pretended to allow his ally freedom of action, but in fact Arras was to present Henry with a sharp alternative: either he must immediately march on Paris, or he must give Charles freedom to negotiate peace. The imperial Court waited long, almost in despair, for the return of their messenger. When he came, on September 19th, they had risked the King of England's displeasure and the terms were already settled.

The negotiations had not been all plain sailing. Now and again there were perilous moments. As Charles confided to Mary, the transactions were all but suspended no less than three times. Little details, such as the cession of Hesdin, caused bitter argument. The French said that the Dauphin could not be expected to make so many sacrifices. Charles soon realized that the crux of the problem lay in the French royal family and its complicated private relations. Was it possible to make peace with the King, the Dauphin and the Duke of Orleans? All the fruits of the treaty were for the Duke of Orleans. The King needed peace too much to reject it, but could the Dauphin be brought to agree? Francis had to consider his eldest son as much as possible. Nevertheless, although the Dauphin was left to make his individual protest later on, peace was signed.

The treaty was in two forms. In the open instrument of peace, the terms of Madrid and Cambrai were re-stated with only a few additional points. These points were that France should send help against the Turk, 10,000 men and 600 heavy cavalry; that both sides should restore all conquests made since the truce of Nice in 1538; Stenay was to be given back and the fortress slighted; the Duke of Orleans was to marry the Infanta and was to inherit the Netherlands on the Emperor's death. Alternatively he could marry the Archduchess Anna, who was already sixteen, and have Milan. After consulting Philip and Ferdinand, Charles was to have the last word in deciding which bride and which country was to go to the Duke.

Many days had gone to the formulation of these terms and it is surprising that a mere week sufficed to draw them up on paper. The speed of the final conclusion is the more astonishing since we know, on respectable authority, that quite a new cause of dispute had come between the two Crowns. In the past French pirates had once at least seized a treasure fleet sent by Hernando Cortes, and now the Spaniards complained that their colonial monopoly had been infringed by the attempt of the French explorer Jacques Cartier and the governor Roberval to settle in Canada. The French explicitly declared that they would abandon this policy, and in yet another document assured Charles that they would henceforward respect 'the rights of the Spaniards and the Portuguese in all the Indian lands'.

But far more important than the published document was the secret treaty of Crépy. The terms which contemporaries sought in vain to discover are known to us through the recent discovery of a draft. By this the French King agreed to help the Emperor in reforming the abuses of the Church, to further the meeting of a council, at Trent, Cambrai or Metz, and to bring back the German heretics to the Catholic fold. If the German Protestants could not be reduced except by force, then Francis agreed to give Charles exactly the same measure of help as he had already undertaken to give against the Turk. Furthermore he promised to help Charles to regain Marano, and to restore the imperial town of Geneva to the Duke of Savoy. This latter transaction was partly also intended for the restoration of religion. Calvin had already set up his state at Geneva. Lastly he promised to make no peace with England from which Charles should be excluded, and if by any misfortune Charles were to find himself at war with Henry VIII, Francis agreed to fight on his side.

On September 18th news came that Boulogne had fallen on the 14th. It needed only this to force the French to sign the treaty. The instrument drawn up by King Francis for the second treaty was dated at Meudon on September 19th. On the same day Charles wrote to Mary from Crépy near Laon saying that the Duke of Orleans had just handed over to him the instrument of peace, containing the King of France's obligations to him, clearly set down. September 14th is the official date of the secret treaty. At that time Charles was still at Soissons, and the text of the public treaty, to be found in the papers of Viglius van Zwichem at Göttingen, does in fact bear the comment 'written in the abbey of St. Nicholas, in the vineyards by Soissons, but signed at Crépy on September 18th'. Charles confirmed the treaty on September 19th. Both parties had agreed on this date for its confirmation.

On June 20th Charles had written to his sister saying that his means would not last beyond September 25th. He had reached his goal almost exactly a week before they gave out. This was a very different triumph from that at Tunis or Venloo. This time he had enforced the terms of Cambrai and Madrid — all but the cession of Bourgogne — at the sword's point. He had made the French agree to terms which covered not only Europe but his colonies abroad, not only political but religious matters. He had asserted his dominance over France as soldier, leader, diplomatist and Emperor. By the secret treaty, Francis had sworn to bring back the heretic and reform the Church because 'it was necessary to the dignity and imperial majesty of the Emperor'. The French King was ready to play his part, either immediately or when he was called upon, in arms if necessary, 'at the Emperor's command'.

CHAPTER III

THE SCHMALKALDIC WAR, THE EMPIRE AND THE COUNCIL OF TRENT

So profound was the fundamental opposition between Charles V and the Protestants that the consciousness of it has coloured the historic conception of the Emperor. Regarded from the universal rather than from the particular point of view, it is right to recognize this intense contradiction which governed the affairs of Church and State. Catholicism, both of thought, action and belief, was so highly developed in Charles that there is scarcely another figure in history whose career so well illustrates the piety and religious convictions of the layman in the period preceding the Reformation. His thoughts, his method of expression, his trials of conscience, his good works, are all alike typical of the devout life of his period.

Yet this emphasis on his personal belief underlines too violently his opposition to the Reformation; the unprejudiced observer cannot fail to realize that, within limits, Charles could show many different faces. Sometimes he belongs to that group of mighty figures in our past history who have set themselves up to champion the layman against the ecclesiastical hierarchy: he is of the same mould as Charlemagne, Henry IV, the Hohenstaufen Emperors, even Luther. A natural timidity in the face of religious authority prevented Charles from ever fully carrying out this aspect of his policy; he was, unlike Gattinara and Mendoza, always unsure of himself. Yet it is impossible to doubt what his opinions were. His councillors, even, were far from basing their hostility to the Roman hierarchy on power politics alone: they had higher motives. But with Charles these higher motives dominated; like many of the princes, both Protestant and Catholic, who lived in this opening epoch in which rulership became more definitely secularized, he had a high sense of his calling.

In spite of their errors in dogma and forms of worship, the German Estates were thus his natural allies against the Italian

Church-state of the Papacy. Since the beginning of his reign he had often enough used them as such. They, like him, had repeatedly asked for the council to stop abuses and perhaps even to recognize the Empire as one great ecclesiastical unity. He was often enough in far closer sympathy with the German Protestants than with the King of France for instance: this monarch mercilessly persecuted his own heretics, but allied himself with the German Protestants and the Turks, while throwing obstacles in the way of the council, and encouraging all those Catholic powers most hostile to the Hapsburg. Such contradictions as these caused Charles's perpetual hesitations, his desire for compromise, his shifting alliances and variable policy. Not since the beginning of time has there been a political programme whose supporters were all alike in their reasons and motives: policy must coincide only with some line of common sympathy between them, and it will be carried out in accordance with the individual and different enthusiasms of each executant. 'Mistrust' is perhaps too strong a word, with its suggestion of moral condemnation: yet we must apply something of mistrust, of caution, to the examination of all political action.

Charles in a sense embodied the theory of the Empire, almost that of the modern state, and this, bringing him as it did into collision with the Pope, endowed him sometimes with an almost national outlook. Luther had instinctively grasped at the fundamental truth: the loose and divided 'Empire' was far nearer to being the expression of the German nation's unity, than any individual state could ever be. The territorial principalities were to show themselves, in the course of the next century, as dynastic and as international as the Hapsburg imperial house; they were to tear German unity into shreds. Only after this did the territorial states become the generators of a German unity still undreamt of, which was to include within itself a 'Protestantism' both religious and political.

Charles's life-struggle thus grew more complex with the years. He had to solve not only European problems, but he had to fight for religious unity against a group within Germany, and for the unification of the Empire and the confirmation of imperial authority against the divided and private interests of all. It was his fate to win, not once but repeatedly, a victory in one single sphere, and to turn thence to combat with renewed, but delusive hope, those other troubles whose outline he could but vaguely distinguish, but of whose presence he was so acutely conscious.

WAR WITH THE PROTESTANTS, DIET OR COUNCIL?

Peace with France was Charles's first condition for the comprehensive reorganization of Germany. But the peace was marred by the continuance of the English war and by Charles's own inability to decide whether to part with Milan or the Netherlands. He was passionately fond of his native land, the Low Countries, yet he had but recently had clear proof of the importance of Milan to his European policy: that he found the decision painful is hardly to be wondered at. For the time being state visits and festivities drowned all anxiety. About a month after Crépy, Queen Eleonore entered Brussels on October 22nd, 1544, over-joyed to re-visit her native town. She brought with her her step-son, the Duke of Orleans, whom Charles already treated as a son or nephew, and who, feeling himself the centre of European political speculation, was uncommonly pleased with himself. Queen Eleonore brought a great train with her, among them Madame d'Étampes, the King's mistress. The Emperor was supported by Queen Mary, by his nephews the Archdukes Maximilian and Ferdinand, by his son-in-law Ottavio Farnese, the Viceroy of Sicily, by generals, secretaries of state, knights of the Golden Fleece, cardinals and prelates. Tournaments, games and balls followed fast — 'even at the reception it seemed they would never have done with kissing and embracing each other'. Could any man now doubt the solidity of the peace? To conclude all, the two monarchs exchanged letters of the most exaggerated affection, and the Viceroy of Sicily paid a state visit to France.

Charles was barely forty-five years old, but directly after these festivities he was again plagued by terrible attacks of gout. Wrapped in warm rugs, out of humour with himself and public affairs, he sat and brooded over the alternative marriages of the Duke of Orleans. Very late in February 1545 he at length came to a decision, embodied in a document thick with stipulations.

The Duke of Orleans was to have Milan with Ferdinand's daughter. But at Court they were whispering that 'there's many a slip 'twixt cup and lip'. The execution of the peace was indeed a constant source of trouble. What, for instance, was to happen if the Duke of Orleans did not live to consummate the marriage? Then the whole structure of the treaty would fall to the ground. Then there would be no one left but the King's one surviving son, the Dauphin Henry. This was the prince who had spent four years, with his elder brother since dead, as Charles's prisoner, and who had entered a formal protest to the treaty of Crépy. The French treaty hung by a single thread. Queen Eleonore foresaw endless troubles, and Granvelle and his circle feared a new Franco-English understanding.

The Emperor, it is true, was using French as well as Portuguese support, in an embassy to the Turks, on which he had sent Gerhard Veltwyk, to negotiate for peace or truce in Hungary. And the French government asked for Charles's help in preventing Flemish or German nobles, like Maurice of Saxony, from entering into the service of the English.

In the meantime Charles's increased strength had altered the Pope's attitude. The imperial councillors added their efforts in exploiting the favourable situation. They were ready to meet the desires of the Farnese dynasty with the utmost sympathy. They worked even for the imperial consent to bestow the fiefs of Parma and Piacenza on Pier Luigi Farnese, a proposition which the French King watched with the greatest annoyance as he felt that both these districts really belonged to Milan. Nothing had yet been decided when the King of France, in accordance with the obligation he had undertaken at Crépy, sent to the Pope asking for a council. Paul III hastened to carry out the request. On November 19th, 1544, he fixed the day for the council to assemble: March 15th, 1545, the Sunday of *Laetare*, at Trent. Unhappily the council, for which Charles had worked so long in vain, came into being just when it was most inconvenient for him. At Speyer in the previous year, he had promised the German Estates that he would regulate the religious problem at the next Diet. This was to meet very shortly at Worms, but there was the usual delay and it did not open until December 14th, 1544. Even so no propositions were offered and no serious business discussed until March 24th, after the coming of Ferdinand.

Tormented by gout and, as he humorously put it, unable to 'hope for any truce with it', Charles had first thought of letting Queen Mary represent him. Ferdinand dissuaded him, saying it was unsuitable. In consequence he chose, as well as his usual representatives, Granvelle with his son the Bishop of Arras, and the imperial Vice-chancellor Naves. On May 16th he arrived in person. Twenty-four years before the world had looked to Charles, in that same city of Worms, for a final decision: now once again the world waited for him to speak.

Soon after Charles's arrival the papal legate, Farnese, made his entrance. The Emperor had not directly asked for him, but had got Madruzzo to hint that he ought to come. Farnese's pretext for coming was that he brought subsidies against the Turk. He did in fact bring with him, to everyone's amazement, 100,000 ducats which were to be bestowed at Augsburg for the time being. For what purpose the money was intended was still in doubt. But the immense subsidy ensured him a favourable reception. As the Emperor jestingly told him, they would 'destroy the old score and start a new ledger'. From this beginning, both Charles and Farnese seem to have been carried much further than they intended. The Diet had yet to settle the religious problems of Germany, and the council which was to reform the Catholic Church was already in session at Trent. Farnese's instructions and Charles's original intentions seem to have been in accordance with these public events. Yet almost before either had taken account of the situation, they found themselves discussing the advisability of a Protestant war.

No one knows in which of these two minds the idea first sprang. Our sources, rich in every other respect, supply no answer here. Charles had suggested a war in rather different circumstances as early as 1530. In 1541, when the religious conference at Regensburg failed, he had it yet more clearly in mind. But in May 1543, when he drew up his testament for Philip, the idea had receded. In his memoirs, he seems to suggest that his triumph over Cleves gave him the final impetus. Yet the memoirs simplify the events which followed Cleves, so that the subtleties cannot be traced in them. When, a little before the Diet of Worms, Charles asked for papal support through his ambassador to the Vatican,

Juan de Vega, he had apparently not yet decided on his course of action, nor fully determined when and against whom he intended to fight. Besides which his policy of breaking up the Protestants among themselves had placed him under complicated obligations to some of them. But in his first interview with Farnese it appears that Charles, after first complaining of Protestant obstinacy, then confessed that he feared an attack, next recollected the onslaught on Württemberg and Brunswick, and so by degrees worked up both the cardinal and himself into a war fever, in which his original propositions for defensive action were totally submerged.

Judging by the letter, which Charles wrote to Queen Mary afterwards, Farnese was surprised by the revelations which he heard. Yet the legate certainly received Charles's opinions with the greatest sympathy, for within a very few days, from May 22nd to May 27th, they were planning decisive action. Tension was acute. Rumours filled the air. A Sicilian monk provoked an outburst by preaching a sermon before the legate in which he challenged the Emperor to make war on the heretic. On the night of May 27th-28th the cardinal disappeared, dramatically, during a thunderstorm. This did nothing to quiet feeling at Worms. Disguised and travelling in hot haste, Farnese had gone to Rome. He was there by June 8th.

By June 17th the Vatican came to its decision. Farnese's grandfather, the aged Pope, offered yet another 100,000 ducats for immediate use and an army of 12,000 infantry and 500 cavalry within four months. He made Charles a grant of 500,000 ducats on Church lands in Spain together with an equivalent sum from their revenues. After so many years, the flint and steel of the chain of the Order of the Golden Fleece had struck a mighty blaze out of the tinder in the Vatican.

The nuncio, Mignanello, confirmed the verbal message of the legate in a written declaration which ruled out all suspicion of the Emperor's political ambition. The case before the Vatican could hardly have been simpler. The Pope could afford to risk some danger for the great advantages which Charles's policy now offered him. An immediate Protestant war would sweep away the council which the ecclesiastical hierarchy feared so much. There would be no more talk of hateful reforms. The Emperor's attention would be occupied outside Italy and the Farnese dynasty would have a free hand.

But Charles approached the crisis with less optimism and calculation. For some weeks he did indeed seriously contemplate war, for the temporary peace with France and the Turks gave him an exceptionally favourable opportunity. Besides the Pope's burning desire to help him was unusual enough not lightly to be disregarded. It was convenient, too, to have at this moment in the council a second means of bringing pressure to bear on the Protestants. To use the old pun, canons might be enforced by cannon.

But the immediate inception of a war would be highly inconvenient. Charles wanted the agreement of Bavaria to let him use Regensburg as a base; but Bavaria's friendship was not to be had all in a minute. King Ferdinand and Queen Mary were full of apprehension. The Queen reminded Charles of the Emperor Sigismund, who, with all Hungary behind him and few enemies against him, failed signally to subdue the Czechs. She warned him to rely neither on the French King nor the Pope, who had betrayed him so often. England and Denmark, by helping the Protestants, might well make them more dangerous than ever the Huns or Vandals had been, who had once sprung from the same part of the world and had laid waste all the provinces of the Roman Empire.

Besides, a careful survey of the situation shows that Charles was not prepared for war, and the season was already far gone. Later the Emperor complained that the Pope had spoiled everything by banging on the big drum, mobilizing everyone he could, creating Ottavio Farnese Gonfalonier of the Church, and in fact advertising the plan to the whole world. Charles added that not only he and his brother, but Cardinal Farnese, had been sworn to secrecy. Excusing his change of mind as best he could to himself and the world, he decided at the beginning of July to postpone the plan for a year. On July 8th Granvelle privately informed Queen Mary that Charles had sent the chevalier Andelot to Rome to greet his daughter, taking this excuse to request the Pope to postpone his plans and draft a formal treaty. In Germany, meanwhile, the imperial party tried to efface the impression which it had been betrayed into making.

Charles was of far too cautious a nature not to feel uncomfortable in the company of hot-heads and war-mongers. He had undoubtedly made his position far worse by casually advertising his warlike project and then suddenly withdrawing it. The Protestants could now no longer be taken by surprise, as the Farnese family had hoped, while new suspicions among the Catholic party, particularly in the papal dynasty, might easily quench the crusading fire. The anger and resentment of the Protestants was now no longer to be stilled, either at Worms during the rest of the religious conference, nor yet at Regensburg when the meetings moved thither for the Diet. Meanwhile the ancient question had been raised, as to what possible significance a religious discussion could have, once the general council had met. If the Pope had agreed to such a discussion, he was acting either in sheer duplicity, or else for a comprehensible political motive — to ensure the Emperor's friendship to the Farnese dynasty. Contemporaries and historians have thought either motive possible. Charles's own motives have been called in question.

Let us consider the situation.

At Speyer the Emperor had promised to discuss the religious problem at the next Diet, and Melanchthon had awaited the conference in anxious hope. Charles had then deceived the Protestants by an apparent desire for peace. In his favour be it admitted, that the Protestants had never thought twice about throwing dust in Charles's eyes. Judging by past experience neither side can have had very high hopes of the outcome of a new conference. Charles made use of the subterfuge rather to restrain the Protestants from preparing for war, than to obtain a peaceful settlement.

But on the other side, too, Charles overstepped the line of reasonable demands in order to further his tactical needs. It was impossible to have both a council and a religious conference in Germany. The two meetings could only be held so long as the council was not yet formally opened and the conference confined itself to necessary reforms, keeping off dogma and disciplinary points. Such a conference would have suited Charles. He counted on the half-hearted, unfinished nature of German Protestantism and forgot the half-religious, half-political, but vital elements which were concealed under the surface. He imagined that he would be able to win over some of them, to put others in the wrong by forcing them to refuse the rulings of the conference or the council, or that he would be able to divide them among themselves. He was no longer thinking, above all, of keeping the peace. He did not realize how far he had miscalculated the parties, nor how unfavourable the atmosphere would be to a council, if it had to dance precisely to his tune.

It was hardly remarkable that posterity took Charles's all too complicated calculations for deliberate deceit. It was hardly remarkable that the delegates to the council, above all the secretary Massarelli, should be indignant at endless delays. Imperial policy seemed to take a pleasure in making fools of these impotent representatives of the Church. If they suggested that the council should be prorogued, Madruzzo or Diego Mendoza told them that, if the council were prorogued, it could only be called again in Germany. If they demanded that the council be formally opened, then they were told that the Emperor thought it better to wait.

To still Protestant anxiety, Charles wished to represent the religious conference in Germany as an important concession, and to leave all mention of the Pope and council out of the dietary recess. But his policy had only one result: the Catholic party in Germany whose support he urgently needed, grew even colder towards him. Charles only managed to include the calling of a new religious conference, this time at Regensburg, on November 20th, in the dietary recess issued on August 4th, 1544, by stating it on his own authority. The Elector Palatine had found the way out, that of offering the Protestants a national council, on whose decisions the general council should pronounce a final dictum. This proposition, although it dwarfed the importance of the religious conference within Germany, was nevertheless accepted. Charles, like many other rulers, deceived himself if he thought that his subjects were likely to make any concessions to him which were of greater real value than those he himself made.

Although the dietary recess made at Worms was in reality far more unfavourable than that made two years before at Speyer, the Pope did not this time condemn it. With war all but decided on, the new fear of a peaceful settlement might have been expected to provoke the Vatican to activity, but nothing happened. The Farnese dynasty had already got what it wanted out of the situation, and Charles had acquiesced: Pier Luigi Farnese, the Pope's son, had 'exchanged' the little states of Camerino and Nepi for the principality of Parma and Piacenza. Soon after, on August 27th, 1545, the Emperor's daughter Margaret gave birth to twins, who were called after their two grandfathers. One of them, Alessandro, was to become an outstanding figure in the history of Europe. The dynasties of Burgundy and Farnese seemed to be bound together by the closest ties.

The late summer of 1545 brought new hopes and fears, and new prospects for the future. On June 8th Prince Philip of Spain became the father of his eldest son, Don Carlos. The prince's birth gave the Bishop of Bitonto in Trent the opportunity for an exaggerated sermon in praise of the Hapsburg dynasty. But Philip's Portuguese wife died in child-bed. At eighteen he was a widower for the first time. On September 9th the Duke of Orleans died. The Emperor was honest enough with himself to add in his memoirs the comment, 'just in time'. The Duke's death freed him from making any decision as to his alternative marriages. He had no longer any need to give the King of France anything in return for the obligations he had undertaken. All the same, he felt that it would be wisest to keep Francis in a good humour, and as early as September 15th he instructed his ambassador, St. Mauris, to talk to the Queen about a possible marriage between Prince Philip and Princess Margaret. Eleonore, in the meantime, had made the counter-offer of her own daughter for Philip. Negotiations dragged on indefinitely.

French policy gained a new lease of life. The King at once gave voice to his old claims on Milan, and Charles was thrown back on to the defensive. At a council meeting, called to discuss the probable effects of the Duke of Orleans's death on the peace terms of Crépy, Granvelle made a brief summary of the situation. The two Kings, he declared, had signed the terms with no other intention than to make a perpetual peace. They could not now let the whole treaty fall because contrary to their hopes God had made a different arrangement, for which no one was to blame. If a town which had capitulated were suddenly to be swallowed up by an earthquake, he said, nobody would regard its disappearance as a valid reason for breaking the terms of the treaty.

But the French saw no reason to leave Charles in possession of what he had won on such easy terms. Soon the old feeling of restraint marred the relations between the two sovereigns. It drove them back to their old threadbare subterfuges. Mary of England, Jeanne d'Albret, and Margaret of France were still unmarried. The Prince of Spain, the sons and daughters of Ferdinand, offered unlimited possibilities. The Farnese dynasty were not fully satisfied even with Parma and Piacenza, which the Emperor would in any case sooner have bestowed on his son-in-law Ottavio than on Pier Luigi. The question of Savoy was still unsettled, the English problem unsolved. Towards November, the imperial government began slowly to realize that it was being inveigled into submitting to an Anglo-French mediation, the dearest desire of all the Protestant powers. As usual the best policy was to reconnoitre all the paths of diplomacy and pick out the best way.

Although the Council of Trent had not yet been formally opened, the Pope was restive. He was ready to make large concessions to have it postponed or prevented. Yet Charles made as if to disregard these efforts, and stood by the council. Juan de Vega, the Emperor's ambassador at Rome, a man of more than usual diplomatic sensibility, felt himself impelled to draw up a memorandum which showed unexpected sympathy with Vatican policy. On the other hand, he suggested that, with papal help, the Empire could be converted into an hereditary Hapsburg monarchy; furthermore he implied that Pope, Emperor and King of France between them would be able to establish a new order in England, Hungary and the German lands.

Dispatches and audiences were wasted in such idle dreams, or in stumbling and useless negotiations. Events marched on: the Council of Trent met and the Protestant war drew near.

CHURCH AND STATE TAKE ARMS

'The world must realize, that it is not in my power,' said Paul III to his adviser, Luigi Beccadello, on the evening of October 30th, as he made ready to have the council formally opened. He had proposed that council ten years before, and postponed it three times. He now fixed its opening date more than six months after the original time arranged for its calling. The true friends of the Church had at length forced his hand. The third Sunday in Advent, *Gaudete*, was selected for the formal opening, since it seemed a good substitute for the Sunday of *Laetare*, originally chosen. The assembled delegates, who heard the news only a few days before, on December 13th, breathed again.

The council could now begin to work. It was supposed to be made up of the Bishops of Christendom, under the chairmanship of the papal legates. Paul III had appointed Cardinals Giovanni Maria del Monte, Marcello Cervino and the Englishman, Reginald Pole, for this task. Del Monte was the active president, Cervino the particular confidant of the Farnese. In a draft of instructions to the representatives, Del Monte suggested that the four nations, the Spaniards, French, Germans, and Italians, should lodge in different quarters of the town. All the northern and eastern countries were counted as forming part of the German nation. Del Monte need not have worried about the quartering of the delegates for some time to come. A certain number of Neapolitans and Spaniards, led by the distinguished Bishop of Jaen, Don Pedro Pacheco, had reached Trent. About four French delegates had arrived, but of all the German nation, who were to be the chief participants in the council, only one had come. This was the consecrated Bishop of Mainz, Michael Helding, and no sooner did he appear than he decided to go back to Regensburg to take part in the rival conference within Germany itself. He was only with difficulty dissuaded from this course. One or two prelates from the papal states and Upper Italy had come. So also had a few abbots and generals of various orders, to whom, after some deliberations, seats and votes were allotted on the council. A few leading theologians accompanied these prelates.

The temporal powers were very scantily represented. The only outstanding person was the Emperor's representative, the imperial orator, Don Diego Hurtado Mendoza. He combined his duties at the council with being ambassador to Venice. Like most of his predecessors in the Vatican embassy, he was a Castilian of noble birth. He had seen service in arms, like most men of his rank, but he had also studied under Peter Martyr d'Anghiera, and was a humanist, a litterateur and a man of learning. He is usually thought to have been the author of the earliest of the Spanish Picaresque novels, *Lazarillo de Tornes*, the autobiography of a simpleton. As a young man he had watched the world about him with observant eyes, and he drew it with pitiless clarity: the dead-alive country town with the one poor hidalgo, who lived in a house without furniture and could not afford the rent, but went out walking in his one fine suit and paid courtly visits; the stupid but kindly ladies of piety; the fat archpriests with their rich benefices; the busy notary — all those figures of everyday life in Spain. Mendoza had spent his visit in Venice buying books for his remarkable library, for which he cared more than for jewellery or clothes. We have already noticed with what fluency, at an earlier period, he had summoned historical arguments from Suetonius to support his theories, giving them the particular flavour of meaning which his own independent judgment and Spanish ambition directed. The republic of Venice, cosmopolitan in outlook and independent of the Church, was friendly soil for the development of this outspoken servant of a universal Emperor.

At Trent Mendoza developed his ancient policy of opposition to the Vatican. It was essential to the moral strength of the Emperor's case: either the Church must embark on a determined reform, or else it must wait for such time as the Emperor chose, to hold its council. Unhappily Don Diego was intermittently ill and was often absent from Trent. It would be idle to pretend that the imperial cabinet treated the council with the respect it deserved, either as a part of imperial policy, or as a gathering of distinguished churchmen. The imperialist bishops were often not furnished with instructions. But at least Charles had appointed at the same time as Mendoza one other man whose personality should have made him useful in Italian politics. This was another noble Castilian, whose personal character and priestly office caused him to play a far milder part than Mendoza. Don Francisco Alvarez de Toledo came of the same family as the Duke of Alva. He was a nephew of the Viceroy of Naples, and a cousin of the Duchess of Florence. His kinsman, Don Enrique de Toledo, was one of Charles's most trusted chamberlains, but this does not prove that Alvarez, in contrast to Mendoza, was the real representative of imperial policy. Charles was surrounded by men of very differing outlook. His greatness was to bear with them all and control them all. Toledo and Juan de Vega represented the party favourable to the Vatican.

In the meanwhile Charles's confessor, Pedro de Soto, tried to put pressure on the Emperor. Although he was one of the most ardent advocates of an active policy, the Vatican did not regard him with a wholly uncritical eye. The nuncio, in his reports, often spoke of him and reported his zeal for war on the heretics. But we know that Charles still opposed him. He was afraid of the war for various reasons. Should his last, this time his very last, efforts at a peaceful settlement by compromise and concession, fail, then the Emperor wished to go to war only when he was more fully prepared than he had been in the previous summer. He wanted if possible to take the enemy by surprise, and he wanted a favourable treaty with the Pope.

It took him a whole year to secure this treaty, with countless embassies, letters and council meetings. The Pope consulted with his advisers as well as with Charles's pious ambassador de Vega, whose devout wife, a lady of the Osorio family, was one of the earliest supporters of Saint Ignatius. Now and later de Vega proved himself a mild man, willing to make concessions. His secretary, Pedro Marquina, who later became the agent of negotiations between Charles and the Pope, was bred in this atmosphere. Like his master, he was to fail.

Charles found great fault with the original draft of the treaty. He repudiated the manner in which the first clauses passed over the council, and discussed only the readiness of the two leaders to fight. He was far from wishing to give the Pope this opportunity to free himself from the council. He resented, too, any papal attempt to limit his powers of negotiation with the Protestants, and he defended the religious conference at Regensburg against papal attack. Both sides argued hotly about the more material clauses. Was the Pope to supply 200,000 ducats to help, or an even larger sum? Were monastic lands in Spain to be sold? Could the Pope be induced to keep on his troops for six months instead of merely four? On both sides there was delay and ill-feeling. In May 1545, Farnese had secured the consent of the Pope to help the Emperor, with lightning speed. The whole business had been concluded in a fortnight. This time it was very different. The Pope kept the imperial Court waiting for the return of Andelot and the coming of Marquina until October 3rd. Although Charles dispatched the messengers again with the utmost haste, they did not return to the imperial Court for another ten weeks, not until December 27th. It was now Charles's turn for delay, and he did not confirm the treaty for the next six months. He explained to his brother Ferdinand on January 30th, and told the nuncio, that he had to postpone matters so as not to go behind the backs of the Catholic princes.

All this time the elements of which we have often spoken, were wrestling for his soul. Pedro de Soto drew up a famous memorandum, urging him to break away from his fear of war and accept the treaty. The confessor argued that it was a sin to doubt whether the enterprise could be carried through. The Protestant princes and theologians, he pointed out, were quarrelling among themselves; the Schmalkaldic League was weaker than was generally supposed; the princes and the cities were estranged, and the towns depended for their prosperity on the Emperor. The only possible leader for the Protestants was the Landgrave of Hesse, and means could surely be found to remove him. Even if he remained, his past success against Brunswick had been exaggerated; the Duke would never have been taken prisoner but for his own stupidity. God, declared the confessor, was on Charles's side, and he could greet the Protestants as Abias greeted the forces of Jereboam, saying, 'Strive not against the Lord God your father, for it is in vain'. As for the chains with which the Pope sought to bind the Emperor in the treaty, they were not heavy and could easily be shaken off. Should the Protestants concede the chief points, and the Pope then refuse to give a dispensation for inessentials, that would be an obvious breach of the spirit of the treaty. If such a thing were to happen, Charles could call in learned theologians to combat the decisions of the Pope. The confessor even went so far as to admit that Charles had reasons for mistrusting the Pope, who did indeed appear to care more for his dynasty than for anything else. But, he concluded, he could not 'hold him for so devilish, that he would wish to destroy the Catholic faith, by forcing the Emperor into a great enterprise only to desert him'.

Yet this, precisely, was what Paul did. Pedro de Soto showed a considerable knowledge of the world and politics in the advice he gave the Emperor, but he proved himself a very poor prophet. Charles was far from following his advice without more thought. Instead he replaced the mild Vega in Rome by the harsher Mendoza, and two years later he dismissed Pedro de Soto himself, although it is not impossible that he took his advice during the course of the war.

Soto had referred in his memorandum more than once to the situation in Germany. This brings us back to the Protestants, and their preparations for war.

The restless Duke of Brunswick, always full of new plans, had, in October 1545, made an effort, which was at first successful, to win back his lands. But the Schmalkaldic League sent an army under the Landgrave to relieve the town of Wolfenbüttel, and Duke Henry had to give battle. The Elector of Saxony had placed his contingent under the Duke of Luneburg. Maurice of Saxony, on the other hand, did not belong to the League, but a private treaty bound him to give help to his father-in-law, the Landgrave of Hesse. He therefore followed the main army with his own troops, ready to assist where and when he could. The two forces met between Kalefeld and Northeim, the League army far outnumbering that of the Duke of Brunswick. Maurice in vain asked the Landgrave for permission to mediate a settlement. Undeterred, he set about doing it on his own responsibility. On October 19th he met Henry of Brunswick at the neighbouring monastery of Wiebrechtshausen, and made offers to him which his father-in-law had not approved. Not that that mattered, for the Duke of Brunswick rejected them, and a battle seemed inevitable. The situation was extremely black for the Duke; his unpaid troops grew mutinous and seemed more likely to attack him than the enemy. Maurice took advantage of the worsening situation to make a second appeal. This time Henry yielded. In vain: the Landgrave refused to accept the terms. Maurice's first attempt to mediate was a dismal failure. Henry and his son were taken prisoners to Ziegenhain in Hessian custody, and Maurice found that he had made enemies of both parties.

The time seemed ripe for the Catholic League to act, but Duke Lewis of Bavaria had died in the early spring, and Duke Henry of

Brunswick's capture in the autumn of 1545 deprived it of its two leaders. The Schmalkaldic League was mistress of the situation. Its members made ready for a new meeting at Frankfort, to take stock of their prospects and to remedy their internal weaknesses. Maurice was in religious sympathy, if not actually in alliance with his fellow-Protestants. He took this occasion to give his father-in-law a memorandum concerning the settlement of the religious problem. The document reads like a supplement to the Catholic plan. Maurice wanted renewed efforts at conciliation, a council on German soil, and, if all else failed, a discussion among certain chosen princes under the chairmanship of the Emperor. The Landgrave was hardly in a position to agree to these principles, but the fact that such ideas were even suggested may in part explain the still hesitant policy of the Emperor himself.

Just at this critical moment Maurice and his brother, the representatives of the Ernestine branch of the Wettin family, chose to bring up a whole series of minor territorial claims against the Elector John Frederick. It was the outward expression of that bitter jealousy between the two branches of the family which centred on the possession of the rich bishoprics of Magdeburg and Halberstadt. Such disputes as these led some of the younger Protestant princes to abandon their co-religionists for the Emperor. Margrave Hans of Brandenburg-Küstrin, the son-in-law of the captured Duke of Brunswick, was one of these, and Albert Alcibiades of Brandenburg-Kulmbach had been lured over to the other camp long since by Granvelle.

Nevertheless, the Schmalkaldic League had high hopes. Its sessions went on until February 6th, 1546, the members busying themselves with the constitution of their league and with the possible alliance of two princes on the Rhine. One of these was Hermann of Wied, Elector of Cologne, who, with the permission of his temporal Estates, had cautiously entered, some years since, on the path of ecclesiastical reform. His Cathedral Chapter and University had complained to the Emperor and even to Rome, so that proceedings were likely to be taken against him. He had already been admonished. The bishopric of Cologne was on the borders of Charles's own hereditary lands. He felt himself particularly vulnerable in such a quarter. The Elector of Cologne, for his part, turned to the Schmalkaldic League and to his fellow-electors for help.

Frederick, Elector Palatine, was the other prince on the Rhine who now turned to the Schmalkaldic League. On January 17th, 1546, he and his Danish wife Dorothea had received the sacrament in both kinds, and he was making in his own peculiar way as if to join the Protestants. He had not the political flair which was the making and the undoing of Maurice. Otherwise he would hardly have contemplated this step at the very moment when the Emperor's intentions were gradually becoming fixed. The Elector did not succeed in becoming a member of the League. The excuse given was an inability to decide on the terms on which he should be admitted. But it is conceivable that the Landgrave Philip did not want an Elector in the League who might challenge the unquestioned leadership which he, with the help of his adviser, Jacob Stürm of Strasbourg, undoubtedly enjoyed. In spite of this rebuff, the Elector Palatine, no less than the Elector of Brandenburg, undertook to follow the lead of the Schmalkaldic League in religion.

The Landgrave admonished the members to make ready for war. His view was remarkably confirmed by an intercepted letter written from the Emperor to the King of Poland, in which Charles asked for help against the Protestants, should they refuse to listen to reason. There was nothing new in an appeal of this kind. Its importance lay in the fact that the Emperor's position was now strong enough to give substance to his threats. In spite of this, many Protestants refused to believe the danger, and evaded their obligations in other ways. The Schmalkaldic League met again at Worms, but was prorogued on April 22nd to Regensburg. Its sessions did not present a very hopeful picture; they were marked by petty jealousy, by ill-feeling between towns and princes, cowardice and folly.

Yet this miserable handful of quarrelling Protestants managed, when the call came, to raise an army which was equal, and even dangerous, to that of the Emperor, who not only had greater resources, but could choose his moment to strike. This in itself was proof of the inner strength of the German movement. In spite of its wavering policy, in spite of its lack of discipline, it was to be a dominating force in the history of Europe.

All this time Charles had been traversing the Netherlands, his journey held up intermittently by attacks of illness. At Utrecht in January 1546 he held a Chapter of the Golden Fleece, and took the opportunity of appealing to the conscience of the Elector Palatine. By way of Zutphen and Nymwegen, he reached Maestricht on February 19th, and stayed there until March 2nd. Here he bade farewell to his sister Mary, saying 'that he would try every means to give order and peace to Germany without resorting to arms'. A few weeks later Granvelle wrote to the Queen from Luxembourg, declaring that he too would exert all his energies towards this end.

By way of Liège, Luxembourg, Wallerfangen, and Saarbrucken, Charles proceeded down the Rhine, to reach Regensburg during Lent. He felt, not wholly without justification, that the journey was perilous, and amused himself by comparing it to his bold voyage across an inimical France in 1539-40. But it was worth the risk as it gave him new opportunities to gauge the situation. His inquiries made him more angry, more anxious, more alert than before, but also more cautious and circumspect. He was magnificently entertained by one prince after another, and accepted their welcome with an outer show of friendship, beneath which his inner determination was growing only the stronger.

At Maestricht he met an embassy from the Electors and princes, appealing to him on behalf of the Elector of Cologne, and requesting him to bring no troops into Germany. They explained that Farnese's mission in the previous year had given rise to disturbing rumours, which the arrival of a new messenger from Rome, Marquina, had re-awakened. Charles referred the business of Cologne to the Diet and made a general answer to the princes of which he speaks with some complacency in his memoirs. He told them that he had decided against sending an ambassador to Rome for the time being, and added that they had only to use their eyes to see that he was not bringing more than his usual train of attendants with him into Germany. He reassured them that he desired nothing more than peace and order, and would not appeal to arms unless he was driven to it. In a sense he was speaking the truth.

But it was not the whole truth. On February 16th he had openly admitted in a letter to Prince Philip that he hoped to mislead the princes by adopting this attitude. For the moment he wanted to be able to answer them freely. His decision to fight remained firm. It was his duty to God, he declared, and to the high office to which he had been called. The moment, too, was favourable for the Turks were ready to sign a truce, France and England were fully engaged with each other, the Pope was offering adequate help and the Protestants were quarrelling among themselves. Moreover he hoped that the support of Bavaria and Austria would enable him to use Regensburg as a base.

At Wallerfangen Count Vaudémont, the brother-in-law and regent of Charles's niece Christina, came to meet him. The interview was satisfactory and Charles learnt with relief that he could rely on the good order and solidarity of Lorraine. This was important to him because of the geographical juxtaposition of that duchy to France and the Low Countries.

Between March 24th and 29th Charles was in Speyer, where he held some conversations of even greater importance. He met the new Elector of Mainz, Sebastian von Heusenstamm, who showed himself ready to deceive his Protestant neighbours and seek for imperial confirmation. Philip von Flersheim, the Bishop of Speyer, came with him. Charles also received the Elector Palatine and his wife who came to visit him unasked. He greeted them courteously, if not effusively. He was far more gracious to the Landgrave, making a special detour to see him and greeting him with marked friendliness and lack of formality. He was anxious to lull his suspicions to rest. Yet both princes felt that their meeting was a bold step. The Landgrave too adopted a free and outspoken style. He greeted Charles at the head of 200 horsemen, with a falcon perched on his wrist. They hunted and feasted together. A part of what they said has survived in considerable detail.

Charles was only strengthened in his hostile intentions by what passed between them. He had apparently counted on a milder attitude from the Landgrave. Instead he found him obstinate, rigid, almost blunt in his opinions. He asked point blank for an imperial confirmation of the concessions which had been granted at Speyer, and refused to discuss the Duke of Brunswick's business. He even took it upon himself to read a lecture to the Emperor on what the Empire was worth. At this Granvelle could not resist intervening. 'Not a penny,' he said, 'nothing but anxiety and vexation.' Once again, as at Augsburg in 1530, the Landgrave urged Charles to study the scriptures, an admonition which the Emperor regarded as tactless, to say the least of it.

Charles had now gained his first important advantage. He had crossed the Rhine, without attack on either side. But the various interviews at Speyer had a deeper meaning. They confirmed him in opinions which had been partly submerged by fear and uncertainty. On March 29th he assured Ferdinand that he was coming to join him without delay. He would stake his all on the game.

REGENSBURG, 1546

On April 10th, a fortnight before Easter, he entered Regensburg. The religious conference, whose participants he had taken the trouble to visit personally, had been wrecked by the opposing party. Even the theologians seemed to have become more bitter and impertinent. They could not again be brought together.

Heated and angry opinions were exchanged. A ghastly murder had been committed in the last few days, which appeared almost symbolic of the breach between the parties. Men talked of Cain and Abel. Juan Diaz, a young Spanish theologian, once a student at Wittenberg, had accompanied Bucer to the conference, at which, by a fatal chance, his elder and Catholic brother, Alfonso, was also present. Juan had a printing press at Neuburg on the Danube, to which he shortly after returned: Alfonso followed him thither and on March 26th had him murdered in his bed. Charles turned a deaf ear to the indignation of the Protestants. It was a proof that in matters of ordinary justice and morality the two parties were fundamentally divided.

A misty spring hung over the city, in which the bustling activity of the delegates did not conceal the sense of doubt and tension. Charles waited in vain, as he had done five years before, for the coming of the Electors. He was treated successfully for gout, and once again went out to pass his time hunting at Straubing until the princes assembled. He seemed to have taken a new lease of life. On his return to Regensburg he entered fully into the free and easy enjoyments of the Court, the temptations of whose splendour and pleasures were too strong even for some of the respectable burghers' daughters of Regensburg. Very little is known of Barbara Blomberg save that during these weeks she conceived the Emperor's child, the son who, under the name of Don John of Austria, was to rank with Alessandro Farnese among the heroes of the coming generation. Charles's son and grandson were both to show themselves men of exceptional gifts in war and the leadership of men.

The imperial councillors, meanwhile, were deeply engaged with negotiations. The outlook was hopeful — but not for peace.

It was essential to gain a firm understanding with Bavaria, an end to which Cardinal Otto Truchsess of Augsburg had already been working. The plan for a dynastic alliance between Wittelsbach and Hapsburg was an old one and many were the obstacles which had hitherto impeded it. For the last generation the two families had gone different ways. Now at last they came together to form a united front against the Protestants. The Wittelsbach were on the point of making that historic move to the Hapsburg side, which governed their part in international politics for years to come, and profoundly affected the course of the Counter-Reformation. The Bavarian dynasty were nothing if not proud, and great was their satisfaction when the heir-apparent, Albert, received, with the hand of Ferdinand's eldest daughter, a definite if a distant prospect of ascending the Bohemian throne. Their other great ambition was to acquire the Electorate held by their kinsman the Elector Palatine. That prince's present conduct filled them with hopes of gratifying even that desire. It would be a change indeed in German history if the Emperor, by redistributing Electorates, could convert the Electoral College, hitherto a check on his actions, into a weapon for the confirmation of his power! The Bavarians were even given hopes of acquiring Pfalz-Neuburg as well. The Bavarian alliance had been settled to the satisfaction of both parties before the chief participants arrived in Regensburg. King Ferdinand and the old Duke William of Bavaria arrived on May 30th. But the Bavarians still refused to support imperial policy actually in arms. They would not offer more than munitions, food and a base in their country. This stipulation was partly the outcome of natural caution, partly the last echo of their old friendship with Hesse. We have yet to learn whether Charles was likely to gain more advantage from Bavaria's actual alliance, than disadvantage from its supposed neutrality. On June 11th the treaty was formally ratified.

This gave the signal for the confirmation of the agreement with the Pope. On May 21st Cardinal Madruzzo, to whom Charles intended to entrust this important mission, arrived in Regensburg. The treaty was drawn by the secretary Vargas on June 6th and signed on the following day. Madruzzo left immediately afterwards and was in Rome on the evening of the 19th. The Pope received him on the following day, and the treaty was submitted to the cardinals on the 22nd. Madruzzo himself took a leading part in the heated discussion of its terms. His conduct was so skilful that even the Romans were forced to admit that the Germans were the equals of the Italians in diplomacy. After a few modifications had been introduced the treaty as a whole was confirmed and signed by the Pope on the 26th.

Charles had instructed Madruzzo to see that the papal forces were immediately recruited, that the promised money was paid on the spot, and the sum increased if possible. Besides which, Charles hoped for a grant of half the revenues of the Church in the Netherlands. He would have liked the treaty itself extended and the promise of troops continued at least until the autumn of 1547. Charles seems to have reverted to that dream of the early years of his reign — a permanent alliance with the Pope which could be used against France if need be. Madruzzo was to tell the Pope how successful Charles had hitherto been in Germany, and was to ask for the deposition of the Archbishop of Cologne and the Bishop of Munster.

Some of these demands were fulfilled. Paul granted Charles the revenues of the Church in the Netherlands. He pronounced sentence on Hermann of Wied on April 16th, and published it in a bull on July 3rd. Although he would not agree to keep the army on foot any longer than was set down, he began recruiting at once, and set the money in motion at the same time. The next weeks were given over to raising the men, buying the arms, appointing the leaders and making arrangements for commissariat and communications.

While Rome was active, Regensburg was not idle. They could not afford to lose any time. On June 6th the English and French Kings concluded the treaty of Guines. This set them both free, and gave Charles reason to fear that one or the other, if not both, would help the German Protestants. He instructed his ambassador in France, St. Mauris, to remind the King of his obligations. All in vain. His fears were to be justified.

In Germany events moved steadily towards war. On June 5th the Diet was opened. After an opening speech by the Cardinal of Augsburg, the imperial secretary Obernburger read the propositions. They sounded peaceful enough. But recruiting was in progress all over Germany. The Landgrave of Hesse feared that the troops which had been released by the treaty between England and France would now join the Emperor. As at Worms, so at Regensburg, electors, princes and towns were divided among themselves. Protestants and Catholics faced each other like two entrenched armies. On June 12th the Catholics answered the imperial propositions by referring everything to the council. The Protestants, on the other hand, said that this no longer offered a way out; they demanded serious offers of reformation in the Church, such as had been made at Speyer. They declared that they had not caused the conference to fail. At this Charles merely laughed.

Already speculation was rife as to whom Charles intended to attack. Cologne or Munster, Hesse or even Saxony? The Protestants decided to ask him. They tried to persuade the Catholics to come in with them, but after a day's argument the Protestants were left to ask their question alone. This was on June 16th. The Emperor answered through Naves that, in accordance with his supreme duty, he must take arms against disobedient states. This got them no further.

The Protestants still hesitated to put themselves in the wrong by quitting the Diet, and, while they wavered, the Emperor threw off the mask. On the 16th he once again approached the spiritual lords, using the Cardinal of Augsburg as his spokesman, and urged them to melt down their plate to help him in war on Saxony. Soon after an imperial herald appeared in the town of Ravensburg, which had just joined the Schmalkaldic League, and threatened it with appalling consequences if it did not abandon the Protestant religion. The imperial government denied its participation in this clumsy action, but events had already made it clear that a religious war had been planned.

The Diet was dead long before Charles formally dissolved it on July 24th.

In the meantime the imperial diplomatists had been busy making sure of their private understandings with the German princes. On June 19th Maurice of Saxony entered into a pact with the Emperor: he had long been sorely tempted to do so, but had at first struggled against it. Imperial diplomacy was a match for his obstinacy, and he soon found that he had gone too far to withdraw. Yet he had himself too little to offer to gain any very favourable conditions. He undertook to respect the decisions made by the council, and Charles in return agreed to keep the council under control. Furthermore, Maurice was promised that he might have any of the lands belonging to the Ernestine branch of the Wettin family, if he should conquer them in the course of the war. This was to indemnify him for his expenses. On the other hand, Charles refused to consider allowing him to have the Saxon fiefs in Bohemia. The prospect of patronage over the rich sees of Magdeburg and Halberstadt was held out as a bait, and he was told that he might make use of Church lands for 'peaceful purposes'. Charles's councillors went so far as to dangle the Electoral hat before Maurice's expectant eyes, but in the final interview with the Emperor on June 20th, Maurice could not persuade him to make any definite promise. When he pressed the point Charles answered evasively. 'If it comes to that', he said, 'each man must fend for himself. As soon as a ban or a like indictment has been issued, the man who has conquered anything may keep it.'

These minor agreements seemed far less important to Charles than his alliances with Bavaria and the Pope. He wrote a letter to his sister Mary, on June 9th, which gives the clearest and most emphatic summary of his own opinions during those critical days.

All my efforts on my journey here, and the Regensburg conference itself, have come to nothing. The heretic princes and Electors have decided not to attend the Diet in person; indeed they are determined to rise in revolt immediately the Diet is over, to the utter destruction of the spiritual lords and to the great peril of the King of the Romans and ourself. If we hesitate now we shall lose all. Thus we have determined, my brother and the Duke of Bavaria, that force alone will

drive them to accept reasonable terms. The time is opportune
for they have been weakened by their recent wars; their subjects, the nobility in particular, are discontented and there is
general indignation at the capture of the Duke of Brunswick
and his son. Added to this, they are divided into several
different sects, and we have hopes that Maurice and Albert,
for instance, will submit to the rulings of the council. Over
and above this we have good hope of papal help, of an offer
of 800,000 ducats or more. Unless we take immediate action
all the Estates of Germany may lose their faith, and the
Netherlands may follow. After fully considering all these
points, I decided to begin by levying war on Hesse and Saxony
as disturbers of the peace, and to open the campaign in the
lands of the Duke of Brunswick. This pretext will not long
conceal the true purpose of this war of religion, but it will
serve to divide the Protestants from the beginning. We shall
be able to work out the rest as we go along. Be assured, I shall
do nothing without careful thought: if our enemies outside
Germany intervene, they will be too late. The Netherlands,
too, will hold them up, by the way.

For the defence of the Low Countries, Buren must recruit
another fourteen companies, besides the ten which I
have already commanded. He must have 10,000 men in
all, 3000 horse and 200 arquebusiers. The nobility can
give their help by strengthening my body-guard with
another 300 men-at-arms. Buren's troops can be paid immediately out of the levy of half the revenues of the Church
in the Low Countries. The money from Spain is not yet to
hand, but you can raise 300,000 Gulden on bills of exchange.
As for the suggestion that Buren should undertake some
reputable feat against Cologne or the Landgrave on his way
hither, I think it best that he should march direct. Guard my
secret and have me informed of everything.

This was the order of mobilization for the Netherlands.

In the interim the political marriages were concluded and
solemnized. On July 4th Anne of Austria married Albert of
Bavaria. This was followed by a sop to the Duke of Cleves, who
had been so cruelly humbled three years earlier. He arrived on
July 16th and on the 18th he married Anne's fifteen-year-old sister
Mary, whom he had been wooing since the Duke of Orleans died.
Less to do him honour than to injure his brother-in-law, the

Elector of Saxony, Charles declared that Cleves could be inherited even by his daughters. This nullified the settlement which Charles had made in 1544 between the Duke and the Elector.

But during these wedding weeks the same confidence did not reign in Charles's Court in Regensburg, as had done during June. The reports of the Venetian ambassador bear witness to a growing anxiety. Things were not turning out as had been hoped. The towns of upper Germany would not obey Charles's orders for recruiting. Instead they began to take arms against him. That same July 4th which saw the celebration of the Austro-Bavarian marriage at Regensburg, and the proclamation of Ottavio Farnese as Captain-general of the papal auxiliaries at Rome, saw also a meeting of the Schmalkaldic League at Ichtershausen, a little to the south of Erfurt. The Landgrave and the Elector here bound themselves to raise an army of 8000 infantry and 2500 cavalry each. On the same day they completed their credentials and instructions for ambassadors to France and England. Later on they were to send pressing and detailed letters to reinforce their instructions, but all to no purpose. The following night the army raised by the Swabian towns marched from Augsburg, to break up the rendezvous of the imperial troops at Nesselwang and Füssen.

On both sides, war had begun.

THE CAMPAIGN ON THE DANUBE

For the first time in the history of Germany a war had broken out in which each side fought consciously for the issues most vital to national life and public order. On the one side was the Catholic Emperor representing a universal power, on the other a group of Protestant Estates, who, taken as a whole, represented a national principle. This was the first time that a European war was fought on German soil, the first time that a war was waged in Germany, which contemporaries followed breathlessly, down to the last detail.

Intelligence was of more importance than mere ferocity in the military practice of the time. The lengthy imperial wars, the ancient traditions of the German mercenaries and their leaders, their collective experience of recruiting centres, quarters, commissariat, marches, roads, passes, good and bad situations, reconnoitring, scouting, of the use and combination of the different weapons, of the protection and emplacement of guns, had combined to develop war in the manner in which it was conceived by the Italian condottieri and the humanist writers; that is into an art with a highly important economic and technical side. At the same time the importance of the protagonists, the concentration of so many forces in the control of two powerful rivals, and the personal leadership of the princes turned this war into a series of manœuvres rather than an immediate struggle for an issue. For four months there was no serious battle and few engagements of any description at all. In this elaborate game of military chess the characteristics of the leaders found graphic expression. Charles was naturally hesitant and thoughtful. This was partly true of some individual leaders on the Schmalkaldic side, like Schertlin of Burtenbach or the Landgrave, but profounder causes governed the character of their policy. The cumbrous constitution of the League, the delays caused by the war councils of the towns condemned them to caution, cunning and the avoidance of rash decisions. The mutual dependence of each side on the behaviour of the other led to a sort of mutual assistance. But the thinking man is always apt to attribute more clarity and consistency to the dealings of others, than they themselves are aware of, under the pressure of changing circumstances. Even among contemporaries, advice and criticism, disputes as to the real or apparent faults of the leaders, were rife.

One contemporary, the intelligent bishop and historian Paulus Jovius, wrote letters to the imperialists and their adversaries immediately afterwards, in which he commented on their actions, both good or bad. These letters were printed soon after. In his memoirs Charles summarized, not without some amusement, the mistakes of his opponents. Yet he did not thus divert the curious eye of posterity from his own. His historiographer, Luis d'Avila, interprets his leadership as though he had followed a carefully considered plan of action. The comparison to Quintus Fabius Cunctator, which he copies from Jovius, was barefaced flattery, not rooted in conviction.

This scholastic treatment of the facts makes them exceptionally vivid and easy to apprehend. The early interpretation of the events, by those who took part in them, or lived through them, makes it easier to distinguish the crucial points in politics and warfare.

Yet the most important question of all has rarely been asked. What was Charles's original plan of campaign? He wanted, naturally enough, to proceed against Hesse and Saxony and to attack them in their own lands. But this plan, no details of which have survived, was forestalled by the Protestants. Intervening in his path, Schertlin thrust him back on to Bavaria. Well informed by his excellent scouts, he judged that Charles's auxiliaries would advance by way of Innsbruck and the Fern pass from Italy. He therefore determined to make certain of Lermoos and the gorge of Ehrenberg, the road to the upper Lech valley and to Füssen, before he marched any farther. He seized the gorge, but the council of war recalled him so that all the troops at their disposal could collect in the upper Danube valley and defend the lands of the south German towns. In spite of this short-sighted command, which prevented him from carrying out his plan in full, Schertlin was nevertheless able to prevent the Italian troops from crossing the Fern pass. They were forced instead to go by the far more difficult river route, by Küfstein.

The defenceless Emperor was still waiting for his troops. He himself described the failure of the Schmalkaldic League to attack Regensburg as a serious mistake; he did not admit that Schertlin could hardly in any case have undertaken so difficult a task as an unprepared attack on the great city. When the army of the princes reached the Danube and seemed in a position to cut him off from Tyrol, Charles decided provisionally on July 26th, and finally on August 3rd, to march for the Inn, making a detour by way of Landshut on the Isar. He felt that this movement was hardly worthy of him, but prided himself that he had not let mere vanity interfere with his decision in a moment of crisis. At Landshut, on August 13th, he made a junction with the papal troops.

Now the Emperor himself was ready to attack. Yet he was taken aback when, on August 14th, the Schmalkaldic League formally challenged him, sending out a trumpeter in the traditional manner. He had drawn up a ban against the leaders of the League as early as July 20th, but he hesitated to issue it, and he was acutely sensitive to the fact that he was still unable to meet them with manifestly superior forces. He had left small garrisons at Innsbruck and Regensburg; with him he had not more than 30,000 infantry and 5000 cavalry. The League army had gathered at Donau-wörth; counting the detachments from the cities, from Württemberg, Hesse and Saxony, it must have been almost exactly the same size as Charles's. Added to this, the troops were elated with hopes of victory; this was likely to make them far more effective troops than the less enthusiastic soldiers of the Emperor.

In this quandary, Bavaria's neutrality rescued Charles. Afraid of penetrating farther into his country, the leaders of the Schmalkaldic League were held up for a week, while they negotiated with the Duke. During this time Charles drew off, scatheless, to the Danube.

His next move was to join with the army of Buren, which had assembled at Aachen on July 31st. This army was supposed to be 10,000 strong. The Schmalkaldic League had left 15,000 infantry under Oldenburg, Reiffenberg and Beichlingen to defend the Rhine. But Buren, with 5000 cavalry, had an immense advantage. All the same, his task was not easy for he had to cross the Rhine in hostile country. By elaborate manœuvres and skilful tactics, he managed to evade a clash and make the passage of the Rhine without fighting. In the night of August 20th to 21st he set his vanguard over the Rhine at Bingen; they seized the fortress of Walluf, and defended the crossing of their comrades. Next Buren turned up the Main to Würzburg, making a wide detour to meet the Emperor, without ever losing touch with headquarters. On September 4th, he passed through Miltenberg on the middle waters of the Main. He had with him not only reinforcements, but money for the Emperor's army.

His movements were not unknown to the Schmalkaldic League. But the generals had been taken aback by Buren's sudden crossing of the Rhine, and they failed to check him elsewhere because of a difference of opinion between the Elector and the Landgrave. The Elector, seeing that there was no immediate hurry about the Danube, had been at first in favour of marching to the Main. He felt that Buren could still be cut off. The Landgrave wanted to attack Charles himself. Thus the days passed in dispute, until Buren was already in the district between Regensburg and Ingolstadt. Only then did the League troops attempt to prevent the junction of his army with the imperial forces. Neither party could afford to sacrifice their communication with the Danube. Charles needed it to keep in touch with Bavaria, the League with the Swabian cities. Thus both armies were in curiously close contact with each other.

A little to the east of Ingolstadt, at Neustadt, the Emperor crossed the Danube. The troops of the Schmalkaldic League slipped past his camp unobserved in an effort to head off Buren's advance, falling back again on Ingolstadt. Horrified, the Emperor set off in pursuit. His position was the more favourable since Ingolstadt was at least friendly to him. A little to the west of the town both armies encamped. The troops of the League had the advantage of the ground.

On August 31st the first clash took place. The Protestants bombarded the imperial camp, thinking to wreak untold damage with their artillery. The effect was more important on the morale than on the material well-being of the troops, and Charles's own personal courage stood his army in good stead. During the next weeks the soldiers were soon singing a song invented in his praise, and not wholly undeserved.

> The Emperor is a man of honour.
> He marches in the foremost rank
> On horse or on foot.
> Take heart, all ye bold landsknechts,
> For the Emperor himself has said:
> 'We will not yield!'[1]

As a form of warfare, defence is technically superior to attack, but attack is morally more effective than defence, if it can be carried out with resolution and enthusiasm. Schertlin and the Landgrave carried this belief to the point of recklessness. The Elector, all too hesitative, would not agree. Thus they waited too long and missed their best moment. Had they but timed their onslaught when the effect of their bombardment was still fresh, when the thick dust and heavy smoke of the gunpowder would have covered their

[1] Der Kaiser ist ein ehrlich Mann
allzeit ist er der vorderst dran,
zu Ross und auch zu Fussen.
Seint wolgemut Ihr Lantzknecht gut,
da sprach der edle Kaiser gut:
'Wir wölln uns nit ergeben'.

advance, they might well have been successful. So Jovius thought. But after bombarding the Emperor's camp they withdrew. When they returned to the attack on September 2nd, the imperial troops had long since dug themselves in. 'We would be glad enough to exchange a cannonade with our good friends', wrote Charles in an unusually confident mood to his brother, 'if they would but come near enough to our trenches to give us a chance!' But the troops of the League kept their distance and once again suffered a moral defeat. It was more serious to the temper of their soldiers than a physical check, for the unspent rage of the troops was left to ferment within.

The army of the League next marched up the Danube to Neuburg and back again to Donauwörth. The Landgrave would not listen to the Elector's suggestion that they should attack Buren. A useless demonstration in the direction of Wending served no purpose save that of tiring the troops. On September 15th Buren came up with Charles, from the east, in the neighbourhood of Ingolstadt. The Emperor went out to meet him in person: the new and refreshed troops were joyfully welcomed in the camp. With Buren's coming not only new strength, but a new lust for attack filled Charles's men. There was also intense rivalry between Buren, the daring, hard-drinking Dutchman, and the sober, Spanish Duke of Alva, with his preference for night attacks and skilful manœuvres. He had had the ear of the Emperor, uncontested, before Buren came, and he always remained his more favoured adviser. All the same the imperial army could gain no advantage over the League. The commanders of the latter were alert, well acquainted with the country, and able to move their troops extremely fast. On September 13th they too had been reinforced, when they were joined by the Rhenish troops under Oldenburg, Reiffenberg and Beichlingen, reinforcements almost as large as those which had joined the Emperor under Buren. Both armies were now between Ingolstadt and Ulm, most of them in the neighbouring territories of Pfalz-Neuburg and Oettingen. Contemporaries felt that the Landgrave was much to blame for thus sacrificing the lands of his own ally, the Count Palatine of Neuberg. He was by far the greatest sufferer in the whole campaign.

The troops were spoiling for battle. Marching on Nördlingen, their routes almost parallel, they nearly clashed early in October. It so happened that on the morning of October 4th, St. Francis's Day, the imperialists, marching along the upper Wornitz, crashed on to the flank of the League army near Allerheim, as it marched westwards on its way to Donauwörth. Buren at once gave the order to attack, but the fog, which lasted the whole morning, robbed his troops of their advantage and gave the Schmalkaldic League the opportunity to withdraw. Buren had to be ordered to fall back, since it was impossible to gain any further advantage over the enemy who were well-defended by marshy ground. The action was an answer to the Schmalkaldic check at Ingolstadt, a sharp reverse to the imperialists.

Ten days later at Giengen, the troops of the League stumbled into the flank of the imperialists as they marched for Ulm. Charles himself was completely at a loss and for a moment his presence of mind utterly deserted him, so that, by failing to pursue their advantage the League commanders lost a double opportunity. This was on October 14th. The armies were now both equally discontented. On the 18th Cardinal Farnese took his leave. It was said that thousands of the Italians went with him. This was not for fear of the battle, for which all were longing, but for fear of the rain and cold of the fast approaching winter, which caused untold suffering to the southern troops. From October 24th onwards the roads became very bad, the camps cold and dank, both intolerably muddy. Disease soon broke out. The imperial army was alleged to have dwindled to half its size. Alva's petty little subterfuges were of no avail in drawing out the enemy. But Charles had one advantage: his staying power was greater than that of the Schmalkaldic League.

By October 30th the Landgrave was ready to come to terms. His personal intervention and a very discouraging letter to the council of war forced the towns of upper Germany to disburse another 130,000 Gulden for the troops. But the morale of the League forces weakened under the double pressure of weariness and lack of funds. On the night between November 8th and 9th Charles, on the other hand, had news which caused him to fire off a salvo. He had persuaded Duke Maurice and King Ferdinand to join in an invasion of the Elector of Saxony's land. In spite of this rear attack the Elector did not, as Charles expected, immediately hasten away from the Danube. Nevertheless, the Emperor felt justified in refusing to treat any longer with the Landgrave.

We need hardly linger over the last anxious struggles of the Schmalkaldic League. They tried to get subsidies from the French, to get credit from Lyons, and were not wholly unsuccessful. They received a little aid from Charles's old enemy, Piero Strozzi, who had once given del Vasto so much trouble in Lombardy. But the shortage of funds induced the League at last to end the campaign. The last sum of money, extracted from south Germany, was only just enough to ensure the orderly evacuation of the troops, who marched away on November 21st, by way of Heidenheim, to the north. Charles himself participated in an attack on the rearguard. But the retreat of the main body was skilfully covered, and the rearguard managed to detach itself under cover of darkness, without serious damage.

Charles was master of the field. He was now undisputed lord of south Germany, a thing which could hardly have been said of him when he opened the campaign. The real clash of arms between him and the Schmalkaldic League was yet to come. His first campaign had been purely defensive. But it had been a successful defensive.

THE EMPEROR VICTORIOUS. WAR IN SAXONY. TENSION WITH THE VATICAN

Ill-attended as it was, the Council of Trent had already made a contribution to history. The widespread need for reform found expression at its deliberations, although sometimes only in the deep mistrust of everyone for everyone else. This was increased by the highly political interpretation often superimposed on the conciliar idea. A purely formal and administrative problem, that of the manner in which the meetings were to be held, became a mask for far deeper antagonisms. Which were to be considered first, the doctrines of the Church, or the reform of abuses? Or could both be discussed together? The legates, with great cunning, stood for the combination of the two. 'Because', they said, 'you can get more done by saying "yes" than by saying "no".' At least this was the ingenuous explanation which they offered for their conduct in Rome. But the Vatican, following the methods of constitutional reform in use in the fifteenth century, wanted the doctrinal points settled first, and the legates were thus forced to withdraw a definite agreement of the council, made on January 22nd, 1546. The Pope allowed the legates to use a second line of defence. They contrived to prolong the negotiations for the formal arrangement of discussions. In this way they took the wind out of the sails of the opposition, without allowing themselves to be involved in dangerous arguments or confined to the difficult ground of reform alone.

Charles was fully occupied all this time with preparations for his war and with its initial unnerving developments. This led to his neglecting the council, so that his representative, Toledo, had a free hand for expressing his own rigidly ecclesiastical views. One day he even offered the legate, of his own initiative, the right to confirm the appointments of imperial bishops; this was little less than to destroy the only weapon with which Charles hoped to control the council. It was small wonder that when he at last received the actual demands of the Emperor to lay before the legate, Toledo did little good. As in May, when his negotiations at Regensburg with Maurice and others induced him to caution, Charles was still anxious that the council should not yet attempt to define fundamental doctrines, such as the heredity of sins. Yet the decree of April 8th, from the purely historical point of view, was to provide a far more significant and immovable standard by which to judge Lutheran and Roman theology, than the supposedly inspired writings of the scriptures or the fathers. Contemporaries were less conscious of this: to them the essential matter was the formulation of elementary doctrine. In April and May the Vatican lost faith in Charles's war project, and consequently allowed discussions of dogma to proceed unchecked. On May 13th Farnese emphatically confirmed the legates in this procedure.

Then came the war and with it a renewed and a far closer association of Emperor and Pope. The delegates at the council, on the other hand, soon began to feel the discomforts of war: troops marched through, food prices rose, and life in Trent grew expensive. Moreover the Vatican now declared that the outbreak of war made the council unnecessary. But Charles felt his policy to be endangered by a threat of dissolution to the council, for he rightly judged that the tepid and doubtful adherents of the Augsburg Confession were more likely to submit to a conciliar than to a purely papal decision. Besides he was personally anxious for necessary reform in the Church as well as for a moderate policy towards such of the heretics as had displayed no evil intentions. Yet as things now stood it was improbable that the Protestants would ever be persuaded to attend the council: it was already on its way to formulating a definite doctrine on the most complex of all problems — Justification. The door to conciliation was to be slammed in the faces of the heretics by the promulgation of an irrevocable formula.

Charles, for his part, was suddenly forced to take notice of yet another vulnerable point in his policy. He hoped to make war not only in arms, but also in the economic sphere, on the rebellious towns. But when he ordered their wares to be stopped in the Netherlands, he found himself face to face with that difficulty which he had experienced years before, when he was forced to yield to the merchants of Antwerp. He could not stop the influx of German wares to the Netherlands without endangering his own most valuable sources of revenue. At the mere threat of this, Queen Mary was so much distressed that she threatened to resign. She sent Cornelius Schepper to impress on the Emperor the gravity of the measure which he wished to enforce — and the Emperor yielded.

The international situation remained unexpectedly favourable to Charles. But there was no guarantee that it would long continue so. No one realized, naturally enough, that Francis of France and Henry of England were by now both played out; neither of them was to live much longer. Even had they realized this, Charles's ministers had no certainty that the change of government might not in itself be dangerous. The King of Denmark, too, after standing firmly to his obligations by the Treaty of Speyer, at length shifted his position and suggested that he should mediate for the Schmalkaldic League. He might always shift a little further, and take sides.

In the midst of these uncertainties, Charles had to face the fact that his main problem was still unsolved. The Danube campaign was merely a prelude, even if a lucky one. The Emperor could not relax his efforts to win new friends and pacify old enemies.

Towards the end of December he entered at length into negotiations with the Elector Palatine, an expedient he had long sought to avoid. For a short time in his youth, Charles had made Frederick, now Elector, and then Count, Palatine, his regent; from the time of his election onwards, this prince had done him many a good service. Had Charles forgotten this? Or worse still, did he permit the memory of it to sharpen his present anger? Since his meeting with the Emperor at Speyer, certain political and moral influences had been brought to bear on the Elector. Visiting the Duke of Württemberg, he had let himself be persuaded to furnish out a troop of auxiliaries, whose obligations, it is true, ended in October 1546. All the same his troops had been in arms against the Emperor. On the other hand Frederick had not been driven to submit by force. The decisive element in their relations was the imperial agreement with the Elector's kinsman, the Duke of Bavaria. According to the notes made by Eck, the Duke had demanded the Electorate in whatever circumstances. Charles promised him the reward only if the Elector was reduced by force of arms, not if he submitted of his own will.

Such was the situation in the winter of 1546-7, and Frederick might therefore consider that he had almost won a diplomatic victory, when he made his peace with the Emperor without the loss of his Electorate. He bought safety only by submitting to deep humiliation. For long enough his entreaties for imperial favour echoed against the stone wall of Charles's obstinacy, and his requests for an audience went unanswered. At last, when Charles was staying at Schwäbisch Hall in the middle of December, the Elector was allowed to visit him. His reception was offensively cold. Charles read out a list of his offences from a sheaf of notes, in the French language, and then worked himself up into such a rage that the old friend of his youth was put out of countenance and could not collect his wits. When he bowed the knee before the imperial throne and offered his excuses, Charles did not even give him his hand to kiss. The imperial suite noticed this with amazement and horror. But on the following day, in the course of a confidential talk, Charles at last came to a working agreement with him.

For us, who have followed the whole of Charles's career, his face in such a scene as this, assumes an almost brutal harshness, a bitterness alien and unreal. But from his earliest years his inherited belief in his own sovereignty had made him resent rebellion and contradiction with extraordinary vehemence. The outward expression of his indignation grew both more violent and more cold as the years went by. Time had made him more susceptible to offence, and his own gigantic efforts, the profound passions raised within him by his conduct in politics and in arms, were wearing out his natural forces. His health, too, suffered from his refusal to alter his habits; he liked to eat all the things which suited him least, and he would not be prevented from indulging his weakness. He sat down to huge dishes of meat at midday, and at the most unseasonable hours would indulge himself with great tankards of iced beer. His illnesses therefore grew more frequent and more painful, adding to the bitterness of his temper. His pride may in itself have been no more than the outward expression of some finer inward quality, but he went in danger of misunderstanding from the world. The more successful he was, the more unequal to success did his temperament reveal him. Yet the outward expression did him wrong, for he was not in himself so unworthy of, or so unequal to, his good fortune. Yet more and more in his spoken words, and above all in his laughter, men traced the note of scorn, the ugliest of all human forms of arrogance.

These ugly characteristics were clearly shown in his present dealings. The Elector Palatine attempted to plead the Duke of Württemberg's cause. Charles apparently listened. Duke Ulrich then entreated that he might be allowed to see the Emperor himself. Charles, who was spending Christmas at Heilbronn, conceded this. But when the defeated Duke appeared, he humiliated him even more brutally than he had done the Elector Palatine, forced him not only to apologize but to pay a fine of 300,000 Gulden. The aged and gouty Duke was unable to kneel in front of the Emperor when he made his apology. Charles excused him, but insisted that his councillors read out the apology, kneeling. There was little mercy in that.

Naturally enough Charles could not afford to let the Bavarians grow too powerful, and therefore made peace with the Elector Palatine. But it is strange that he did not behave in a more politic manner to Württemberg. He might even have reverted to

Zevenbergen's policy, and taken this occasion to stretch out the arms of Hapsburg power into Swabia, so as to strengthen the geographical boundaries of Austria. In fact he did toy with the idea of taking Württemberg himself, and bestowing it on the Archduke Maximilian. But these ideas soon yielded to the more immediate necessity of pacifying south Germany, and using it as a base for his troops. He had always looked on German affairs from the universal rather than the territorial standpoint. It was more important to him, therefore, to break the Schmalkaldic League, to re-establish imperial authority and to give unity to the Church, than to acquire land for the Hapsburg dynasty.

In the Netherlands alone his views were those of the purely territorial landowner. Here he had launched his first attack on the Protestants, on Cleves, in order to regain possession of Gelderland. Here, too, he had pushed on the ecclesiastical proceedings against the Bishops of Cologne and Munster. Farther to the east, towards Minden and Bremen, he had set a second army on foot under Josse van Cruningen, his governor of Zeeland. His struggle to gain control of Bremen and Verden will engage our attention later.

Charles's methods of pacification in south Germany varied with his military prospects. His letters to King Ferdinand during January and February 1547 supply the details of his policy. The letters themselves are in the nature of soliloquies. Asking for advice both by word and by letter, Charles decided and worked alone. He used his letters more as a means of arriving at certainty in his own opinions, than as a method of communication.

He explained to Ferdinand that he had pardoned the Duke of Württemberg because the Schmalkaldic League was still in arms; the duchy would have been expensive and difficult to conquer as it had so many strong places, and moreover, it was essential to avoid the appearance of pursuing the war for dynastic reasons. His chief task, he went on, was still in front of him. He had yet to make his authority paramount in Germany, and thereby to make the Empire more capable of resistance to the outer world. For the time being he intended to take his ease for a little at Ulm. Here he was in the midst of allies — Bavaria, Austria, Italy and Switzerland — so that he could exert pressure on Ulm and Augsburg while quietly thinking out his next step. He was thinking, he explained, of issuing a proclamation commanding everyone to return to the old faith: as things now stood, the rebels could not fail to realize that this was his ultimate aim. On the other hand, he mused, it might be wiser to carry the war further, to punish the rebels, and only when they had been eradicated to proceed to the settlement of Germany. Another alternative which had presented itself to him, he went on, was that of negotiating, either individually or at a general meeting, with all his friends and subjects, keeping a future Diet in view; this would involve no violation of the German constitution, it would mean that the administration of justice would be the first to be reorganized, and he would gain for himself the right to nominate the members of the *Reichskammergericht*. Having thus achieved the general submission of his subjects, Charles continued, he could probably form an Imperial League, on the lines of the old Swabian League, to act against those who were under the ban. In this way he could best counteract the intrigues of the French King, who was conspiring with the Protestants through the agency of the Saxon Chancellor, a Hessian, and Sturm, in order to form a league in which England was also to be included. Thus wrote the Emperor on January 9th.

By this time Charles was worn out with the efforts of the last year and anxious only for a rest. Since August 2nd he had slept in forty different places and often under canvas. He felt that he could leave the war in Saxony to Ferdinand and Maurice, while he occupied himself for a little with problems, old and new, in his other lands. The conspiracy of Fiesco in Genoa, against the Doria, and his own growing irritation with the Farnese, drew his attention once more to north Italy, to Parma and Piacenza, even to Siena. He had made Juan de Vega Viceroy of Sicily, and had appointed the enterprising Ferrante Gonzaga to succeed the dead Marchese del Vasto at Milan. Other plans were to follow. But for the moment the horizon was clouded.

By February 2nd the position had cleared sufficiently for Charles to listen to the appeals which poured in from Ferdinand and Maurice in Saxony, and to set out himself for the scene of war, leaving garrisons at Augsburg and Frankfort. First of all he thought of sending effective troops ahead of him. But again he hesitated and only on March 10th and 11th, at length let Ferdinand and Mary know that he was going to his brother's help.

Charles had now transferred the issue of the war to the Saxon battlefield. After months of negotiation Maurice had at last decided to take part in the reduction of his cousin's land. Many people have judged this aspect of Charles's career as an example of egotistic Hapsburg policy in which the Emperor and his brother played their cards together. But critics of the two brothers should not forget that Maurice was a very tempting object for the exercise of their statecraft and judgment, while he himself acted his own part with amazing skill, in a situation which was none the less difficult because he had voluntarily accepted it. Thinking of his subjects and of the rights of the German princes, Maurice was staunch to the Reformation; but he did not want to lose prestige with either side and he did want to draw what personal advantage he could from the situation. His obstinacy was a match even for the Hapsburg brothers. Once he told Ferdinand that he would break off negotiations and leave him to fend for himself.

Maurice had two weak points: his councillors were overwhelmingly in the Emperor's favour and tried to put pressure on him, and he could not himself keep his greed for other people's land within reasonable limits. This bold and enigmatic character was to become a decisive influence in German history. In spite of his crimes, in spite of his misgivings — among which those of his conscience were not the least — Maurice of Saxony remains an outstanding figure in the history of Europe. But at this moment his greed betrayed him into Charles's hands. Maurice had been in Prague from the end of September until October 5th; the lengthy arguments of the imperial ministers all but induced him to yield. The pleas of his fellow-Protestants, the solemn embassy from Duke Ernest of Luneburg, even the impression which their armed forces made on his councillors, failed to move Maurice. The entreaties of the princesses of Hesse, and the sharp and virile arguments of his aunt, the Duchess of Rochlitz, a sister of the Landgrave Philip, were alike in vain.

Yet the war in Saxony did not pass off altogether to the imperial satisfaction. Charles and Ferdinand began gradually to learn that their adversaries had unused forces yet in reserve.

At first the surprise attack on the undefended fiefs of the Saxon Elector in Bohemia was wholly successful. Maurice managed to preserve Plauen and Zwickau from the entry of foreign troops: the cities accepted his personal protection. His own attack on the lands of Electoral Saxony was equally successful. But he failed to win over the western part, Gotha, Eisenach and Coburg. Halle he seized on an imperial mandate. He gave religious concessions in every district which he occupied. Last of all he made ready to besiege Wittenberg.

In the meantime the Elector John Frederick had returned. Cautious and skilful, the Elector made no immediate attempt to win back his own lands. Instead he attacked those of Maurice. He invaded his adversary's country on December 23rd. The garrisons of Weimar, Jena and his other towns instantly abandoned their posts; the Elector was jubilantly received at Halle. Next he besieged Maurice's city of Leipzig, but it defended itself with great valour, and he had to withdraw on the night of January 26th-27th. For him, too, the decisive factor was lack of funds. But the crisis had not yet come. Maurice was appealing for help. Prague refused it him; he had complained too often and too grossly of the quality of the Bohemian troops. Besides the imperial party took it very ill, that, although he had had the electoral title bestowed on him in October, he was still too cautious to assume it openly. He was postponing his final acceptance of the honour, until the Emperor agreed to include his brother Augustus in the new arrangement.

Charles tried to calm Maurice by informing him that the Margrave Albert Alcibiades was hastening to his help. This was true. On January 24th and 25th the Margrave was at Zwickau. Maurice lay in Chemnitz, the Elector at Altenburg. Between the opponents the Mulde valley lay outspread, the river spanned at intervals by important bridges. Both parties eyed these watchfully. On February 25th the Margrave seized the city and castle of Rochlitz on the Mulde. But his forces were insufficient or illdisposed. The Elector had news of his march and may even have been encouraged by the Duchess, who had her seat there, to march on the town. Coming up unexpectedly by night, he attacked the Margrave early in the morning of March 2nd and made him prisoner. The road to Bohemia was now open, and thence the Elector, as leader of the Protestants, received messages of warm sympathy. But he did not use his opportunities. He should have continued his offensive campaign, and carried the war into the heart of Ferdinand's far from loyal country. He did not dare to go farther, a cowardice which may have had reasonable causes, and remained for the whole of March in Geithain between Altenburg and Rochlitz.

The Elector's fate was sealed by the different negotiations which were now taking place all over Germany. The Elector Joachim of Brandenburg had approached the Emperor for a truce in all humility. Charles refused to listen. But now the Estates on both sides began to take a hand in the game. The nobility both in Maurice's and the Elector's country grew active. The councillors and the Estates in Maurice's country combined in the dishonourable business of playing for time. They postponed a decision until the Emperor himself appeared in the field and the military position became suddenly far more serious for the Elector. John Frederick marched straight into the trap, which chance and the machinations of Maurice had together laid for him. He neither withdrew to his own land nor made sure of his defences.

Charles was already on the way. He stayed in Ulm until March 4th, then for a fortnight at Nördlingen and so came by way of Oettingen into Franconia.

All this while he had written an unceasing stream of letters to Spain, Italy and the Netherlands. From these, were it necessary, one might form a faint idea of the political anxieties which engulfed him. Dangers threatened to entangle him on every side, and he deserves all the more credit for managing, at such a time, to keep a calm enough head and a free enough hand to act decisively in Germany. His worst care in these last months had been the policy of Paul III, because that reacted on the military help which he was likely to get. In the previous year Charles and the Pope had disagreed over the moment of declaring war, since Paul felt the need of it in his own policy sooner than Charles was ready to risk it. They had also disagreed before over the bulls issued to the Swiss. Now their feelings over the council grew more embittered: Charles wanted his own presidency assured, the Pope wanted the whole meeting put off. The papal nuncio, Verallo, was quite unequal to the situation, and permitted Granvelle to use very emphatic language to him. The Pope had asked that he should be allowed to have a say in every concession granted to the Protestants. Verallo claimed this right. But Charles was now in favour of postponing the religious decision, and would not agree to anything.

When the difficulties at the council itself became insurmountable, Mendoza and Madruzzo proposed that it be prorogued for six months; they did not wish it to be altogether removed from Trent. Mendoza next left Trent on December 3rd to take up his position as ambassador to the Vatican. On his way thither he wrote a letter full of indignation and distress, declaring that the tyranny of the papal legates was such that the council was doing more harm to the Church than ever Luther had done. The fathers thought of nothing whatever except the private interests of the Vatican, or their own. The articles which they were preparing on the doctrine of Justification, he declared, were absolutely irresponsible. How could anyone believe — he demanded — that this wretched assembly was under the guidance of the Holy Ghost? And yet it seemed that once the council had pronounced a dictum, there could be no retreat. The Church would be firmly established with all its abuses strong upon it.

The Emperor, as his letters to Mendoza reveal, expressed himself with more reserve, but he could not feel anything but deeply injured that, in spite of his representations, on January 13th, the doctrine of Justification was generally accepted in the council. On January 22nd, the Pope, in a letter expressing the most unctuous devotion to the imperial cause, withdrew his troops. The action was a blatant violation of the spirit of their treaty, for everyone knew that the purpose for which they had jointly undertaken the war was yet unachieved, and Charles poured out the vials of his wrath on the nuncio. He had always thought, he raged, that the Pope was only tempting him into this war to desert him. And then maliciously giving voice to a common saying against Paul, he added, that the French pox was a disease which young people might be excused for contracting, but there was no excuse for the old. When the nuncio opened his mouth to answer, Charles cut him short by sweeping out of the room.

There is something almost symbolic in this desertion of the Emperor by the Pope, on the eve of his decisive conflict with the leader of the Protestant party.

MÜHLBERG. WITTENBERG. HALLE

On March 28th the Emperor left Nuremberg. On April 8th he reached Weiden and in the next days joined the troops of Maurice and Ferdinand at their rendezvous at Tirschenreuth on the edge of the Bohemian Forest. They were anxious to make a demonstration which would prevent the Bohemians from rising to join the Elector. John Frederick, for his part, it is true, was glad enough not to have to bother with them. By way of Eger, the imperial troops crossed the Elstertal, reached Plauen, and so on up the Mulde, straight for the Elector's headquarters.

The Elector had divided his army, so that they might harass the advancing troops, and forage more successfully. He made no attempt to prevent the opposing armies from joining, but stayed inactive at Meissen on the Elbe. He knew that Charles was approaching but had no idea of his further intentions. On April 12th, ingenuously thinking that he would be safe on the other side of the river, he crossed the Elbe. Marching on the right bank, he made for Wittenberg or Magdeburg. His way lay northwards, through Mühlberg. As the Elector again drew near to the Elbe on April 23rd, going through Colditz and Leisnig, the Emperor took him suddenly in the left flank. The imperialists had information unknown to the Electoral troops: from the neighbouring village of Schirmenitz, the Elbe was fordable to Mühlberg on the opposite bank. The ford was important, for they had not with them the materials to build a bridge.

Untired by the long march, the imperial army moved forward in fighting order. On April 24th they set out in the small hours, in a thick mist. The Emperor rode in the vanguard, accompanied by Maurice and his brother Augustus. Ferdinand and his son, the Archduke Maximilian, were in the second line. The imperial dynasty was thus boldly fighting for its own cause, with a great following. The cavalry marched first, then the infantry. The mist hung low over the Elbe all the forenoon. It was Sunday and the Elector was in church. When, between ten and eleven o'clock, both sides became aware of the presence of the enemy across the river, the Elector still thought he was safe on the far bank of the Elbe, and continued his march. The Emperor decided to lead the attack. Still the Elector, unaware of his danger, made no effort to fortify his bank of the Elbe, but sent all his artillery on ahead. His only precaution was to lower some of the boats for making bridges into the water and to put a few troops on them. Charles determined to seize these ships for himself, and soon a violent battle was raging about them. The Emperor himself was present in person, encouraging his Spanish soldiers to incredible deeds of valour. The gunners advanced, up to the armpits in water, to reply to the enemy's fire and if possible to silence it. The most determined threw themselves into the water, stripped, with knives between their teeth, to attack the ships at close quarters. Horsemen swam across the river. At length the defensive fire ceased and a peasant showed the Emperor where the ford actually was, so that he could cross. But in the meantime the Elector of Saxony's captured ships had been put to use, and the greater part of Charles's baggage and infantry went over dry-shod.

As soon as the infinitely superior forces of the Emperor had collected on the farther bank, there was no battle, only a hot pursuit. The Elector hoped that he might reach the protecting woods of the Lochau hunting reserve before nightfall. But already the forces were so close, that Maurice, who could never bear to lose a chance of mediating, sent the bold Lersner straight under the Elector's guns to ask him to surrender on terms. Angrily John Frederick asked whether Maurice took him for the Duke of Brunswick. But it was too late to do anything; the Electoral troops attempted to make a last stand in the wood, but some of the cavalry began the defensive attack too soon, and a general engagement followed. The infantry were not yet properly drawn up, could make no efficient resistance, and scattered, throwing the whole army into confusion. In the general conflict the Elector himself was slightly wounded and taken prisoner. He gave his sword to Thilo von Trotha. But it was the Duke of Alva who took charge of him and brought him, as Lannoy had done the King of France, to Charles himself.

Emperor and Elector were each mounted and fully armed. The Elector took off the hat which he wore in place of the helmet he had lost, but when Charles did not answer the salutation, he covered himself again. He opened his mouth to speak and had just uttered the words, 'All-merciful Emperor', when Charles cut him short. 'You would have done better', he said, 'to have thought of us in those terms some time ago.' What else he said was equally discouraging, and he concluded his cold speech with the words, 'I shall treat you as my affairs and your deserts dictate. Go.' Spaniards were set to guard him.

Charles's scornful words are sufficient proof of the triumph which warmed his heart. This April 24th, 1547, was one of the most glorious days in all his life. He had striven for this victory with all that he had, ardently and obstinately, sacrificing to it his health and his repose, his safety and, if need be, his life. He had taken part in the crossing of the Elbe, and joined in the battle at evening. To please his allies, he commissioned Titian to paint the great portrait of him as the victor of Mühlberg. He is shown, mounted on his charger, in full armour, his general's scarf over one shoulder, his lance in his hand, the insignia of the Golden Fleece glinting against his breastplate.

Charles slept that night at Schirmenitz on the left bank. Hence he set out on the following day on his march to Torgau, crossing the Elbe again only when he reached the neighbourhood of Wittenberg.

He expected a determined resistance from Wittenberg. Here undoubtedly immense spiritual forces would be up in arms to meet him, even though the Reformer himself had closed his weary eyes on the world a full year before. Charles feared a siege, for his artillery was inadequate. The situation was critical. The Elector's son, John Frederick II, was determined to defend himself at Grimmenstein, near Gotha. The restive Bohemians were still in Charles's rear, and during the last months Charles had been forced to consider what elements might not be aroused in Germany against himself or against Maurice, by their long continuance in arms.

But the Emperor and his councillors precipitated the issue by a brutal act which defied every constitutional right, and which was not soon to be forgotten. Charles had already humiliated the towns and princes of the south. He sought to bring the Wettin dynasty to book by a death sentence. A court of justice, which was a mockery of its name, condemned the Elector. The Emperor first confirmed the sentence, and then opened negotiations with his enemies. The old Elector, all this while, acted with such dignity and self-possession as to gain the respect of all beholders. He would not let himself be dictated to, but acted with firmness and calm. He made no effort to save either his Electoral title or his own lands, but strove to rescue something for his sons. He hoped, even, that they might one day have the Electorate again, by a complicated arrangement of inheritance between the two branches of the family. But chiefly he protested against the recognition of the Council of Trent. In the end Charles had to let him off with a promise to submit to the *Reichskammergericht* and the subsequent rulings of the Diet. The Emperor cherished a hope that he would be able to persuade the Diet into accepting some of the dictates of the Council of Trent, while the Elector imagined that he would himself have some mild influence on the drafting of later dietary recesses. The Elector challenged the justice of the ban which had been pronounced against him. Joachim of Brandendurg, meanwhile, stretched out a helping hand to him in these negotiations.

Hard as the conditions were, John Frederick had his own life to save, the princely dignity and honour of his sons to think of, and the possible services which he might later do to the Protestant religion. On May 19th, 1547, he set his hand to the Wittenberg Capitulation. On the 23rd, the town surrendered on honourable terms. On June 4th, Maurice, who had refused the earlier offer, was solemnly invested with the Electorate and the Electoral lands. His treachery had served Charles's turn.

But neither the collapse of the south nor the shattering defeat on the Elbe had brought the German Empire altogether to its knees. Still less had it been pacified. Magdeburg was in revolt, and Bremen, the other archbishopric of northern Germany, had put up a valiant defence.

Until February 12th Josse von Cruningen had been everywhere victorious, occupying in turn Tecklenburg, Osnabrück, Lippe, Hoya, Schaumburg and Minden. On the 27th he was about a mile from Bremen, whose archbishop, cathedral chapter and gentry came out to meet him. The town itself refused to negotiate. On March 19th he was still without its walls, waiting in vain. He was short of munitions, and by the 30th the troops were mutinous because money, too, had run out. From Eger, Charles wrote to him commanding him to march on to Hamburg, but in the mean-

CHARLES V
aged 47

time Cruningen had fallen before Bremen. On March 14th the young prince Erich von Calenberg had concluded a treaty with the Emperor, and he it was who now took command. He had to leave the town unsubdued, and on May 23rd at Drakenburg on the Weser a little to the north of Nienburg, he suffered a bloody defeat at the hands of the relieving forces under Christopher of Oldenburg and Albrecht von Mansfeld. After praying and singing psalms, the Protestants and their two leaders, accompanied by their preachers, attacked and seized Calenberg's position. He himself escaped only by swimming the Weser and his people were drowned, killed or taken. The news of the disaster reached Charles at Wittenberg, and caused him some anxiety, for he still had many plans in Germany to carry out, and the Landgrave of Hesse left to subdue.

But Charles's anxiety was relieved by the constant interference of the new Elector, Maurice, and by the evident cowardice of the Landgrave who had hitherto taken no part in the action, which was being played out so near to his own country. Without the least resistance, Philip gave in to the blandishments of Maurice, and let himself be deluded with thoughts of negotiations and mercy. It was now too late to retract. The Landgrave, who had taken so haughty a stand at the beginning of the Schmalkaldic war, slid gradually downhill to his humiliating end. Maurice was partly responsible, for Philip could not but be tempted by the evident success with which Maurice had played his part, and could not but reflect that he, too, in the past, had given his son-in-law the example by himself toying with an imperial alliance.

In the initial negotiations with Maurice, Philip gave in little by little. At first he refused to consider a separate peace from the other members of the League. But soon, frightened by Charles's success, he became more tractable. When Maurice made cautious inquiries from King Ferdinand, this latter left him in no doubt that the Emperor would yield to a reconciliation with the Landgrave, if at all, then only on the harshest of terms. Until April, the Landgrave consoled himself with the hope that his help would be needed against the Elector; he even prided himself on his loyalty to the Protestant cause, because he decided to refuse to fight the Elector, before anyone had so much as suggested that he should. Maurice was ultimately shameless enough to suggest it.

Even after Philip's refusal, they continued to correspond without ceasing.

Charles approached the situation with very different ideas. Nevertheless, he gave Maurice his head because such negotiations were a sure guarantee against the Landgrave's further efforts in the field. At Wittenberg, Joachim of Brandendurg, the Landgrave's contemporary and brother-in-law, joined his efforts to those of Maurice. Personal interviews got them no further. In the first draft of reconciliation occurred the words 'submission at mercy'. Philip crossed out 'at mercy'[1] but agreed to discuss submission on terms. The Emperor flatly refused all terms. Philip continued to hesitate. He began to make more far-reaching offers. The agent Ebeleben passed them on to the Electors, to Arras and Doctor Seld who was gradually taking the place of Naves, since dead. On June 2nd a document was laid before Charles in which the Electors sought for the assurance that after his surrender the Landgrave would not be subject to 'a death sentence or imprisonment for life'. The Emperor, the ultimate judge of all their entreaties, approved this document.

But the Electors were interpreting Charles's approval far more widely than they should, when they hastened to tell the Landgrave that, according to the articles, he would not suffer 'either in body or possessions, either by imprisonment or otherwise'. And so Philip came to meet the Emperor in all good faith, while the Electors irresponsibly negotiated, pretending that they had understood, from the document which the Bishop of Arras had formulated, something very different from what was written in it. It was strange that the Landgrave did not recall how little use Maurice's intervention had been to the Duke of Brunswick.

So Philip came to his fate. On the morning of June 19th he had an interview with Arras, and found that the articles had been stiffened. The Electors talked him out of his fears. They had asked Charles in vain to give his hand to the prince if he fell on his knees before him. Yet in spite of this check, they calmed the Landgrave.

In the evening at about 6 o'clock, the great drama began.

---

[1] The full German formula is 'auf Gnade und Ungnade'. The English equivalent for this is, to surrender 'at mercy'. In the German, Philip crossed out 'Ungnade' only (TRANSLATOR'S note).

Charles was on his throne, surrounded by a splendid group of courtiers. The Landgrave was requested to kneel while his Chancellor read out an apology. The Emperor made answer, using Seld as his spokesman. The answer was couched in the pre-arranged terms, and clearly stated that the Landgrave should not suffer life-long imprisonment; everyone heard it. Charles gave Philip no permission to rise. When at last he got up of his own accord, the Emperor did not give him his hand.

But the Duke of Alva invited him to supper, with both the Electors. After the meal Philip was taken into a separate room. The Electors complained. Maurice went further, became almost violent, and insisted, in spite of warnings, on spending the night with his father-in-law. But the Emperor stood to his rights. Perhaps he was recalling his own bitter experiences with another royal prisoner, King Francis. On the 21st he said openly to the Electors that he considered the Landgrave's own person as the only adequate hostage for the execution of the peace terms.

Charles had reached his goal, and that without further bloodshed. Accompanied by the two leaders of the Schmalkaldic League, both his prisoners, he went to the Diet at Augsburg. The Bishop of Arras wrote to tell Queen Mary that an attack on the towns of north Germany would not now be worth making, for the booty would hardly cover the pay of the troops. The Emperor was going another way to find money. He contemplated forming an Imperial League on the lines of the Swabian League. He had his eye on two Swabian towns for its nucleus, Ulm and Augsburg.

THE IMPERIAL CONSTITUTION AND THE LOW COUNTRIES. THE STRUGGLE OVER THE COUNCIL AND THE 'INTERIM'

Charles had combined a universal and a particular theory into his idea of an Imperial League. He wished to strengthen his position on the military and the financial side, to develop the imperial constitution in the direction of autocracy.

Since the thirteenth century the imperial constitution had been breathlessly trying to keep pace with the development of urban and territorial states. Kings and Emperors made use of the same

573

weapon as towns and princes — the bond of a league or confederation in the interests of internal peace. The peace of the land was no longer threatened by some isolated criminal, but by individual princes who sought, by means of feuds and alliances, to build up their own power, or to defend themselves. The towns did the same. The Swabian League, which had existed in south Germany from 1487 until 1533, had been a tool of Hapsburg policy, of an imperial policy such as Charles himself understood.

Charles had grown up to this idea. He and his councillors rightly thought of the German constitution in terms of a League or confederation. But even then it needed some sort of an executive. Periodical Diets, owing to the incidence of the subsidies, led to division rather than unity. On the other hand an Imperial League with subsidies and payments made in the Emperor's name would at least guarantee general peace, since it would be a visible organ of imperial administration.

In the middle of the war, in that letter which he wrote to Ferdinand on January 9th, 1547, Charles laid bare this project. On June 13th he opened negotiations for its realization at Ulm. His commissioners were the Cardinal Bishop of Augsburg, Margrave Hans of Kustrin, Johann von Lierre and Heinrich Hass. The negotiations did not go smoothly. The Estates answered the imperial commissioner with counter-suggestions, and did not agree with them to any extent.

The whole question was next referred to the Diet at Augsburg. Charles returned from Saxony to open it in person. He was determined to draw every possible advantage from the stirring events in which he had taken part during the last year. But he could not disregard the very serious alterations beyond the German frontier and their probable repercussions. On January 28th, 1547, Henry VIII of England had died. The Vatican seriously believed that it could use the occasion to gather the Catholic states of Europe together against the English, but the death of Francis I on March 31st forced them to postpone the plan. Strange indeed were the changes in the policy of the aged Pope, a prey to jealousy and fear; he had first deserted the Emperor and then sought his help again, although at the same time opposing him at the council. Nothing more offensive or likely to annoy Charles could have been thought of, than the Pope's commission to the legates on February 17th

1547, to move the transference of the council to Bologna. And when the legates obeyed his instructions, Paul wrote to Charles on March 11th, hypocritically stating that he had had nothing whatever to do with their action. Even Juan de Vega was stung to fury. At the imperial Court there was unmistakable tension. The nuncio was referred to Charles's ministers, for the Emperor was afraid that, if he saw him personally, he might give vent to angry phrases, which however true, would be most impolitic. Charles was no longer trying to check the ebullient temperament of youth, but a deep-seated irritation, the growth of many years, which he felt he could no longer control. On practical points he refused to give in. He told his ambassadors in Rome to protest solemnly against any act performed by the council at Bologna.

This was the situation on July 4th, 1547, when the legate, Cardinal Sfondrato, was received in audience by the Emperor at Bamberg. Charles had come up the Saale from Halle, on his way across Franconia to Augsburg. The Emperor refused to listen to the suggested plot against England. Germany was more important to him, and after his last experiences of the Pope's friendship, he had little or no desire to interfere in other people's business. To soothe him, the legate suggested that the council could be moved back to Trent, if the Germans would definitely undertake to submit to it. In the meantime the German bishops could go to Bologna. At this Charles fell into such a rage that Sfondrato timorously asked whether he had better withdraw. Charles retorted dryly that he could do as he pleased.

The results of Sfondrato's conversations with the Emperor and his ministers were startling. He fared as Cervino had done long before. The rage and righteous indignation of the Emperor, the unanimity of the Court in the same outlook, could not fail to make an impression on the legate. He advised the Pope to change his tactics. Since France showed no sign of supporting papal policy, the Cardinals urged the Pope to let the council return to Trent. But the obstinate old man refused, and on September 15th a solemn session was held in Bologna.

Mendoza thought of protesting. He spoke openly of his intention and was strengthened in it by the Emperor. Charles declared that unless the Pope changed his resolution, he would call a new council himself and begin on the reform of the Church.

In this mood Charles opened the Diet of Augsburg on September 1st, 1547. The ceremony was performed with that splendour which he had so often used as a cover for his inner weakness. The main subjects to be discussed were those which the Emperor had so often mentioned in his letters to his brother, the *Reichskammergericht*, the League, and the Church question.

The administration of justice, the first object of political rule, Charles wished to consolidate. It is true that he played small personal part in the details of its administration. For centuries to come the great criminal code which bears his name, the Carolina, was to be fundamental to German justice, but Charles himself had nothing to do with its individual provisions. All the same, justice was very near to his heart. By the reform of the *Reichskammergericht* he meant to secure the nomination of its members and to arrange for the Estates to pay its cost. This was not unfair for the Estates had an interest in it, if only to prevent cases of general importance passing from its jurisdiction to that of the *Reichshofrat*.[1] Besides which if the *Reichskammergericht* could be set in order, its rulings would form an important standard against which to measure the justice of every day.

Charles managed to have his way in nearly all these points. The Estates seemed willing to acquiesce on the judicial point, in order to be able to defend themselves the more strongly when Charles came to questions which touched their religious belief and their political privileges.

The Church question was further complicated by the complete severance of the bond which bound the Pope to the Emperor. On September 10th the Pope's son, Pier Luigi Farnese, had fallen a victim to conspiracy. Ferrante Gonzaga had been vehemently hostile to him, the Doria too had made common cause with other enemies of the Farnese dynasty, and Pier Luigi had contributed to his own unpopularity by giving himself the airs of a great noble, upstart though he was. As a result of the conspiracy, Gonzaga resumed Piacenza, as a part of the duchy of Milan. The aged Pope was profoundly embittered. Meanwhile the confusion of spiritual and political values made the destruction of the Farnese dynasty also the destruction of the Church.

[1] A Court of Justice consisting of imperial Councillors: approximately equivalent to the English Court of Star Chamber (TRANSLATOR's note).

Paul III threw himself into the arms of France and sought the help of Venice to complete a League. All the ambitions for the liberation of Italy, which had come to so ignominious an end twenty years before, flourished again, and on the imperial side they were talking of occupying the papal states, as the Hohenstaufen had done, or as Charles himself had done in 1526.

In Augsburg on October 18th Charles issued a formal proclamation. He decreed that the council should go back to Trent, and called upon 'the estates who adhered to the Augustana to appear at the said council'. Last of all he asked the Diet to consider how 'the Estates were to live together in peace until they came to the said council'. In accordance with a demand originally made at another Diet a quarter of a century before, the princes now at last agreed to appear before the council. Only the towns raised objections, to which Charles had to give some consideration.

On November 6th, 1547, almost exactly eighteen months after his first mission, Madruzzo left Augsburg for Rome as the Emperor's messenger. On November 25th he saw the Pope, with Farnese and Mendoza. Paul received somewhat contradictory answers from them. Cardinal del Monte sharply defended the rights of the council. Mendoza offered to protest but at length it was decided that all decisions should be referred to the assembly at Bologna. This, when it came, was clear and consistent, but it repudiated all attempts to come to an understanding with the Germans.

Now the Emperor made ready to publish his long-prepared Protestation in Bologna and in Rome. On January 16th, 1548, his procurators Francisco Vargas and Doctor Velasco appeared before the assembled fathers of the council at Bologna in order to deliver their protest in all formality. They were allowed to come in as the fathers did not wish to appear to throw any obstacles in the way of free speech. They embarked at once on long and threatening speeches, ending with the words: 'We tell you explicitly, that our Emperor will defy all the attacks to which you and your Pope have exposed the Church; he will take the Church under his own protection and will do all that his imperial office, his rights and his duty dictate.' Cardinal Monte replied with unruffled dignity. But the fathers in general gained an uncomfortable feeling from what had passed, and felt inclined, within themselves, to revise their original proud decision against the Emperor's requests.

In Rome Diego Mendoza repeated the imperial Protestation to the assembled Cardinals. He did not spare the person of the Pope. Paul III fell back on written replies, and looked about him for advice. The world was to wait long for any concrete result. For the time being the council was quiescent.

This served as a preliminary for the *Interim*, or, more fully, the imperial '*Declaration of how things are to be managed in the Holy Roman Empire, touching the question of religion, until the general council can be held*', which had been published with the recess of June 30th. The twenty-six articles of which this Declaration is composed reveal how profound was Charles's desire that his name should be coupled, if not with the actual return of Germany to the Catholic fold, then at least with its preliminaries, with the arrangement of a tolerable settlement. He had worked to no other end for the last seventeen years. Any attempt to settle the problem of German Protestantism by a piece of paper was bound to fail; Charles's attempt was further invalidated in that it arose partly at least from his anger at the utter failure of Pope and council. At such a time he needed all his courage and political flair; intrepidity and a fine sense of the political situation was necessary, and the declaration had little of either. Yet, inadequate as it was, Charles's policy was nobler, more conscientious, and in reality more practical than the painful dynastic policy of the Farnese, or the cold attitude of the Catholic theologians and canonists. These latter were prepared to risk the destruction of Christianity in the effort to subject one party, either by orders or by force. But the inadequacy of the compromise was clear. The Protestants would certainly not accept the re-establishment of the ancient Church, together with the doctrines which the council had all too lightly formulated. They would not accept saints, masses, images and the sacramental teaching of the Catholics. The bounds of the possible had been reached when a compromise had been made in 1539 over Transubstantiation, but now the Protestants were expected to agree to the celebration of the feast of Corpus Christi. On the other hand the clergy regarded the tacit acceptance of the secularization of Church land with the utmost suspicion. Other provisions were a modified permission for the marriage of priests and provision for the administration of the communion, sometimes, in both kinds. These reforms, although they were later to be stormily demanded by the Bavarian and Austrian gentry, and even on occasion, by their governments, seemed at the moment to be infringements of the rights of the Catholic Estates. They evoked the bitterest opposition. As always, Eck, the implacable Chancellor of Bavaria, made the most serious difficulties with the Emperor. Only when Charles explained to the Catholics that these provisions were only alternatives to the habitual usage, introduced purely for the convenience of the Protestant Estates, were they at length calmed.

But Charles gained nothing by his *Interim*. The imprisoned Elector of Saxony soon showed him how valueless it was by rejecting it to his face. Farther afield, nobody honoured it with the slightest attention. The constitution of the Church was already too loose to be affected by such general commands.

At the moment, however, all Charles wished to obtain was a temporary arrangement. He still believed that he would be able to persuade the Diet and certain leading princes to submit to the council. He was therefore all the more anxious that the council should be called as soon as possible, in the form he had promised. Until that time he wished to impose doctrines and forms of worship in accordance with his own beliefs, as well as certain disciplinary measures for the reform of the clergy. This again was a project which he could not successfully carry out within the framework of that old order, which Charles himself respected. An organization like the Church, a living organism, could not be reformed from without. The movement must come from within.

Yet the effort which Charles made is memorable. He showed himself by this right but hopeless ambition to be in harmony with so many other loyal and devout Christians, in the centuries before his own, and in the time to come. He was one of those who, clinging to the Church with his whole soul, was all the more cruelly alive to the sordid materialism of its spiritual pastors, to the growing contradiction between its teaching and the living world. He was one of those who give themselves up to dreams and hopes, as though righteous indignation, loving anxiety and goodwill alone were enough to change the world.

The Emperor could not altogether believe that such success as he had, had been bought by force alone. He knew that he could not master spiritual things in such a manner. But he had long realized that force, not reason or contract, was the ultimate test of the validity of every act and every right. In conflicts lasting for more than thirty years he knew that force alone had kept his lands at peace, restored Spain and Italy to his control, kept the Turks at bay, preserved and enlarged the Netherlands, and last of all brought Germany — or so he thought — under his control.

He wished to confirm and prolong his power. Two ways seemed open to him. He could either develop the constitution to suit him or identify the Empire with his own dynasty. During the year 1547-8 his thoughts found this channel, and he imagined that he would best achieve his dynastic end by forming a League in the old traditional German fashion. When this failed, and only then, did he look about for some other way.

His councillors spared no pains to maintain and develop the League theory which had come into being at Ulm. But in the winter of 1547-8 at Augsburg, negotiations in the council chamber dragged wearily on, their course changing with the changing moods of the Diet, and their goal never apparently any nearer. Charles quite openly demanded a strong army under imperial control; this hardly reconciled the Estates to the proposed League, through whose help the Emperor hoped to obtain the means and the men. Charles's ministers thought that the idea was more popular among the smaller than among the greater Estates. But the dissemination of the League idea did little save cause ill-feeling in the deliberations of the princes. Annoyed by the un-friendly behaviour of the Electors in the council of princes, in February 1548 Charles once again referred the solution of his problem to a mixed council. This action set the seal of failure on the whole attempt.

All that remained of the plan was a 'subsidy'. This was voted to Charles in answer to a demand made on May 19th; it took the form of a 'Roman month'[1] for the recruiting of imperial troops which was to be paid into his reserve of gold. If Charles V could not achieve constitutional reform along monarchic lines at the very height of his power, it is clear that the days for such reform

___

[1] 128,000 Gulden: so-called because it was supposed to be the cost of the imperial army for a month (TRANSLATOR'S note).

had gone by. Perhaps, as so often happens in the physical world, a process already alive and developing was merely speeded up when an attempt was made to arrest it. The territorial principalities had gained great power in the Empire through their struggles with towns, knights and peasants, and above all through the religious movement. Yet they only realized their true strength, when Charles's attempt to coerce them brought them face to face with the constitutional problem.

The constitutional problem remained unsolved, for the Emperor himself was a territorial prince, who, if the need arose, would use his individual force against the Empire. To secure the increase of dynastic power by the exploitation of the imperial constitution, and to develop the individual territory in despite of the confederation, was the embarrassing quandary in which every royal landowner found himself. And what could a ruler do who, like Ferdinand, had lands lying all in the same district, of which some did and some did not belong to the Empire, or belonged only in part to the Empire, like Bohemia? In the Netherlands the situation was even more complicated. The duchies of Burgundy, Flanders and Artois did not belong to the Empire; the other provinces were part of the Empire, but the Burgundian state had completely severed them from it in administration. Both Emperor and Empire needed more clarity on points like these.

Charles V now tried to find a solution which would please all parties. Queen Mary initiated the plan in the instructions she gave to the imperial councillor Viglius van Zwichem on August 28th, 1547. She took into account all the old differences of opinion, but admitted that some of the provinces did indeed belong to the Westphalian Circle although she was in no position to say 'what relation the Westphalian bore to the Burgundian Circle', or what lands belonged to the latter.

A Burgundian treaty, drawn up on June 26th, 1548, in agreement with the imperial Estates, settled this question, and laid down the privileges of the Netherlands and their duties to the Empire. Henceforward all the Netherlands were to be considered as belonging to the Burgundian Circle, but were to be exempted from the jurisdiction of the *Reichskammergericht* and the authority of the Diet. They were, however, to participate in the defence of the Empire against foreigners, were to provide such troops and money as the Emperor wanted, and twice as much as an ordinary Elector. If the danger which threatened was from the Turks, then the Netherlands were to give three times as much. Charles arrived at these decisions by discussion and debate. They followed out the general line of his imperial policy — that of placing all the Hapsburg lands in the protection of the Empire, itself so rich a recruiting ground for armies, and arranging for them to pay for this privilege by supplying his brother with the money he so urgently needed in his wars on the Turk.

Unless we are much deceived these years form the climax of Charles's close relationship with Ferdinand. They co-operated both in politics and diplomacy, acted together in the Schmalkaldic war and finally reorganized their kingdoms to depend mutually upon each other.

THE DYNASTY AND CHARLES'S POLITICAL TESTAMENT OF 1548

In the preceding winter, on January 18th, 1548, Charles had once again taken up his pen to compose a testament for his son; 'because my weakness, and the dangers to my life which I have barely out-lived,' he wrote, 'seem to indicate that I should give you some advice in case of my death'. In this testament Charles could not too often exhort Philip to keep on good terms with his highly revered brother Ferdinand, and with his sons.

In this testament Charles openly declared that, at Ferdinand's request he had decided on the marriage of his elder daughter Mary to Ferdinand's eldest son, Maximilian. He went on to command Prince Philip to seek his uncle's advice on all questions of international policy, whenever the need should arise. He added that he himself had always done this in order to strengthen his own imperial authority, and called the last war to witness to its success. Philip, who figures in this document solely as King of Spain, was further told not to give financial aid in a Turkish war, for this affected only Germany and the Netherlands. 'In Germany', Charles tells his son, 'you will always find good soldiers if you pay them enough. If you cannot get enough in Germany, you may turn to the Swiss, but you must handle this people generously in accordance with the traditions of the Burgundian dynasty.'

This testament bears witness yet again to Charles's old beliefs, the backbone of his policy. But this time he develops them into a comprehensive picture of the whole European situation, and even considers the provinces on the farther shore of the Atlantic.

Seeing that human affairs are beset with doubt, I can give you no general rules save to trust in Almighty God. You will show this best by defending the faith. After all our trouble and labour in bringing back the German heretics, I have come to the conclusion that a general council is the only way. Even the German Estates have agreed to submit to it. Have a care, therefore, that the council continues, in all reverence to the Holy See. But proceed cautiously against the abuses of the Vatican when they affect your own lands. Make choice of worthy and learned men for parishes and benefices, for the greater glory of the Church and the quiet of your own conscience; choose such as will stay in their cure and perform their duties. Preserve peace and avoid war, unless you are forced to it in your own defence, for warfare is a heavy burden on our hereditary lands, which I have left to you not diminished in anything, but increased. Unhappily I have from time to time been forced to cede certain of the privileges of the Crown; you can try to regain them.

Peace will depend not so much on your actions as on those of others. It will be a difficult task for you to preserve it, seeing that God has bestowed so many great kingdoms and principalities on you. I therefore suggest the following things for your consideration. You yourself know how unreliable Pope Paul III is in all his treaties, how sadly he lacks all zeal for Christendom, and how ill he has acted in this affair of the council above all. Nevertheless, honour his position. The Pope is old; therefore take careful heed to the instructions which I have given my ambassador in Rome in case of an election. There will always be trouble with the Pope, in Naples, in Sicily, and in Castile on account of the Pragmatica.[1] Look to it. Keep a good understanding with the Venetians. I have done much for the Duke of Florence and he is grateful; he is also our kinsman since he married into the family of Toledo. The Duke of Ferrara leans to France: handle him cautiously. The Duke of Mantua is to be trusted: cherish him for he has suffered much in the wars. Genoa is the most important of all

[1] See *supra*, p. 496.

to us. Act shrewdly and skilfully in your dealings with it. Siena and Lucca, let us hope, will remain under the protection of the King of the Romans.

France has never kept faith and has always sought to do me hurt. The young King seems about to follow in his father's footsteps. But act cautiously and try to keep the peace for the weal of Christendom and your own subjects. The French will always be casting about for excuses to resume their royal claims on Naples, Flanders, Artois, Tournai and Milan. Never yield to them, not so much as an inch; they will take an ell. From the beginning of time these French Kings have been greedy for their neighbours' land. Defend Milan with good artillery, Naples with a good fleet, and remember that the French are discouraged if they do not immediately succeed in anything that they undertake. The Neapolitans are much given to revolt; let them be constantly reminded of how the French sacked their town. Apart from this, treat them with moderation. You can never manage without Spanish troops in Italy. Have a care to the maintenance of the border fortresses in Spain and Flanders, where the citadels of Ghent and Cambrai are the most important. In Franche Comté, whose neutrality has now been established against France, you will need the support of Switzerland and Austria. To preserve peace I have allowed my demands for our ancient hereditary land, for the duchy of Bourgogne, to drop. But do not altogether renounce your rights. Hesdin is not worth fighting for.

At the present time the French are emphatically refusing to give back to the Duke of Savoy the lands which they unjustly seized. I have always supported the Duke in his claim, not only because of the relationship of our two families, but for the better security of Italy. The French will use Piedmont as a base for raids on Italy, and will continue in their efforts to gain Milan and Naples. Do not let yourself be persuaded at any time to renounce Piedmont. The present situation, bad as it is, is better than a mistaken settlement. But if you give troops to the Duke to regain this land, do it with the utmost caution. Only if the French and English are fully engaged, and if you can get the help of the Swiss, will it be safe for you to send troops to Savoy. At the moment the troubles in Germany and the pacific policy of the regency in England make this impossible.

Charles went on to advise his son to maintain good relations with England through his present treaties, but not to take any part in the perennial disputes between England and France. So far as Scotland was concerned, the Emperor pointed out that the great thing was to be sure of freedom in trade. Philip's behaviour to Denmark had been defined by Charles's last treaties with that King. The Emperor dissuaded him from taking any part in the political schemes or distresses of the aged, imprisoned Christian II, although, for the sake of his daughter, he told him that he might seek to ease his captivity. It would be unwise, he added shrewdly, to have him set at liberty.

Next he particularly advised Philip to watch over his fleet. It was his best defence against pirates in the Mediterranean; it would keep the French from interfering in the Indies. Moreover, Philip should cultivate the friendship of Portugal for the same reasons. 'Do not cease to keep yourself well-informed of the state of these distant lands', Charles added, 'for the honour of God and the care of justice. Combat the abuses which have arisen in them.' Charles himself had but recently insisted on having a detailed report from the Viceroy, Antonio Mendoza.

Above all the Emperor urgently entreated his son to look about him for a new wife. 'You cannot be everywhere', he wrote, 'you must find good viceroys and such as will not overstep their instructions. You must not stoop to consider every complaint that is made against you, but you must not disregard them all. The best way is to hold your kingdoms together by making use of your own children. For this you will have to have more children and must contract a new marriage.' Charles went on to suggest the French King's daughter as a possible wife for Philip. She would be a living guarantee of peace and the treaties, and an instrument through whom the just rights of Savoy might be regained. If Philip could not have her, there was Jeanne d'Albret, always supposing that her family would abandon its claim to Navarre. Charles added that she was extremely attractive and very clever. A marriage with one of Ferdinand's daughters, or with Queen Eleonore's, would make no new friendship for the dynasty. As to the Infantas, the elder, Mary, must marry the Archduke Maximilian, the younger, Joanna, the King of Portugal.

It would be best for the Netherlands, Charles went on, if Queen

Mary, who had proved herself so excellent a governor, both in peace and war, should keep them for the present. On the other hand, she herself was asking to be relieved of the task. In that case, it might be a good plan to hand over the provinces to Maximilian and the Infanta as regents. But, Charles added, such an arrangement would be dangerous, if Maximilian were to be chiefly concerned for his own interests. It had better not be done until Philip could himself make personal contact with the Netherlands, and with the young Archduke.

> I commend to you most solemnly, [Charles ended] the execution of my will and codicils, as also those of the late Empress. I beseech God to care for you and lead you in His ways, so that He may take you in the end to His eternal glory. You have my blessing.

This testament of the Emperor's breathes the mellow atmosphere of old age. That same atmosphere surrounds another document of a different kind, dating from this year — the magnificent portrait, which Titian painted of the Emperor at Augsburg.

On a wooden chair covered with velvet, in front of a brocaded hanging, sits the Emperor. His pose is tired, he is relaxed, almost slumped into his chair. Yet his eyes are still alert. He sits in an open loggia, commanding a wide and strangely mournful landscape. This dreary prospect, with its grave and graceful lines, contrasting strongly with the bold, almost harsh composition of the foreground, evokes at once a feeling of awe, a sense as of something above the ordinary things of life. Here is the Emperor, the master of all the world; yet he sits before us in all simplicity, close to us, human, plainly dressed, simple, unposed. He is alone and sunk in thought. The face, the lips, the hands, whose action never alters in all his pictures, betray some narrowness, some indefinable rigidity of outlook. Yet everything about him bears witness to the self-possession, the inner intensity of his being. Years and cares have left their mark. It is hard to believe that this old and weary man is but forty-eight years old. Early he had learnt to think of the hour of his death; he had known shadows all his life — the mother who had never been for him but as one dead, the wife who died young. Illness had tormented him more than most men. He was sensitive, easily moved to excitement, by little things as well

CHARLES V
aged 48

as by great. He had striven honourably to control himself, to recognize his duties, to think out his measures carefully. Never for a moment had he forgotten his great responsibility towards God, towards his lands, towards the yet unborn princes of his transcendent line.

CHAPTER IV

DISILLUSIONMENT AND DEATH

Sailing up the Rhine in the summer of 1550, on his way to yet another Diet of Augsburg, Charles dictated on ship-board to his companion William van Male, the first pages of his life-story. Typically he began with a bald and direct statement of fact. 'After the death of King Philip there were several wars in the Netherlands in which the Emperor Maximilian, with his habitual courage, defeated the French.' With these words he opened his *Vita Nuova*, his autobiography, not because he personally had any recollection of those wars, but simply because it was undeniably a legal truth that his reign as a prince began at the moment of his father's death. On the journey, and later in Augsburg, he went on with these memoirs, piling year upon year, gradually enlarging the picture, forgetting nothing, no experience however homely or personal, which had had any meaning for him, no action, no grief, no joy, not even a journey or an attack of gout. He recorded all with the same pedantic accuracy. Yet as the story gradually drew near to the present time he became more and more engrossed in politics. His descriptions grew gradually more informative, more detailed, more critical. He described exhaustively, for instance, his more recent experiences, the settlement with Cleves, with France, with the Pope, with the German Protestants. It was as though in writing of them he became once more engrossed in what had happened. The wars of 1543, 1544, 1546, 1547 lived once again before his eyes. The memoirs became little more than a diary of the wars; he may even have had such a diary and used it as the basis of his autobiography. He lingered, but without prejudice, over the movements of the campaign, over councils of war and single engagements, over the errors of his opponents and of his own staff. Proudly he compiled this memorial of the brave days that were gone, a distant echo in words, of the actions which had been.

Charles's testament revealed all that was medieval in him — his devotion to religion and the Church, his contemplation of himself in the mirror of his son. But in his memoirs he revealed that other facet of his character, the Renaissance side. He laid stress here on actual facts; his style was pragmatic and kept close to the theories and manner of the humanist historians, who themselves took Livy, Sallust and Caesar for their models. His attitude to the wars, too, was of the Renaissance, and above all his approach to fame. It was as though his early aristocratic pride, the pride of the Burgundian nobleman, the longing for honour and glory had been transfigured into the desire to achieve immortality through history. Not for nothing did Charles take with him everywhere his cosmographers, his chroniclers, his historiographers, his poets and his painters. He prized very highly that historian of the Schmalkaldic war, Luis d'Avila, who had idealized his actions. Yet all the same he suffered some discomfort in his conscience at this development of his character, for later he asked the Jesuit Francisco Borgia whether this preoccupation with his own life were not a sin.

In spite of his many contacts with Renaissance culture, he never became a true man of the Renaissance. In vain did van Male hope that he would be asked to translate the autobiography into Latin for publication. The Emperor kept the pages under lock and key, and sent them in 1552 to his son in Spain. He mentioned them again later, and a Portuguese translation was made of them, but then they disappeared. Only the Portuguese version has survived.

From these memoirs we draw Charles's own dry account of what took place at the Augsburg Diet of 1548, on the eve of which we last took leave of him.

Before the King of the Romans left, their Majesties arranged among themselves for the marriage of the Emperor's elder daughter to the eldest son of the King his brother, he that is at present styled King of Bohemia. It was the Emperor's intention to send for his son, the Prince of Spain, so that he might himself see his lands and become acquainted with his subjects; he accordingly asked his royal brother and his royal son-in-law, to be graciously pleased to let this latter go to Spain, celebrate his marriage there and remain there during the absence of the prince, to govern the Spanish kingdoms in the Emperor's name. They agreed to this. Thereupon the King of Bohemia departed from Augsburg to go by way of

Italy, taking ship from Genoa, to Barcelona and thence by land to Valladolid, where the marriage was celebrated.

The King of the Romans left shortly after to attend to his own affairs. The Emperor stayed a few more days to set some outstanding problems in order. Then he too left. He placed 2000 Spaniards in the fortresses of Württemberg, but withdrew the troops from Augsburg itself. When everything had been arranged he took the road for Ulm, from which town also he withdrew the garrison in order to take some of it with him, and turned northwards to Speyer, thence down the Rhine to Cologne. This was the ninth time he had travelled down the Rhine and the eighth time he had come back to the Netherlands. He met his sister at Louvain, whence he proceeded to Brussels in order to devote himself to affairs of state, more especially to those touching the Netherlands.

The Emperor remained in Brussels from the end of September 1548 until May 1550, apart from one long tour of the Low Countries in the autumn of 1549. In June 1550 he came back to Germany. In the meantime his opinions on the future relationship between the two branches of the dynasty, if they had not fundamentally altered, had at last solidified in favour of one solution.

PRINCE PHILIP AND THE SPANISH SUCCESSION

In the wills which Charles had drawn up in 1543 and 1544, he was still uncertain of his plan for permanently uniting the Netherlands with the Empire. Since that time he had reorganized the relations between them. He had first planned that Maximilian should be governor, and then rejected that scheme in favour of the rulership of Philip. In return for this, Maximilian and the Infanta Mary were proclaimed regents in Spain on September 29th, 1548. In Spain, meanwhile, Maximilian had married Charles's elder daughter. In spite of the political storms which were to pass over them, the two lived happily in their union until death dissolved it: they had fifteen children. Yet in spite of his marriage and his wife, Maximilian had no happy recollections of his visit to Spain. Later on, he felt his absence all the more keenly because of the advantage which was taken of it in the Empire by the imperial family.

Don Philip first handed over the government to his cousin, and then, obeying his father's command, fitted out for himself a suite in the traditional and sumptuous style of old Burgundy. It was a fact on which chroniclers commented with some amazement. Titles and ceremonies were meticulously rearranged to suit the Low Countries, Castilian tradition being for the time being utterly sacrificed. Later, the formality, for which the Spanish Court came to be famous throughout Europe, derived not from the manners of Castile, but from those of the ancient duchy of Burgundy.

Philip's journey lay across Italy, then by Trent, Munich and Augsburg to the Rhine and the Netherlands. It was a triumphal progress rather than a voyage. Superb triumphal arches, like those which had once been raised to do honour to the victor of Tunis, were now erected to welcome the unknown heir to Charles's many crowns. The delicate, unwarlike, conscientious and not very lively youth received all these acclamations with embarrassment, a certain stiffness and a general lack of grace. The popular opinion was that he was haughty.

He found the Low Countries recovering from the ghastly experiences of the forties. Their English friendship was reacting unfavourably on their commercial relations with Scotland, but apart from this drawback, they were by now developing their own fleet to protect themselves against piracy. At peace with France on the one hand, they were also enjoying the fruits of the Burgundian treaty with Germany. The Estates seemed willing to vote the Emperor very considerable sums. Charles meanwhile completed the pragmatic sanction by which he united all of the hereditary lands, and extended an honourable welcome to his sister Eleonore, who, as widow of King Francis, had just withdrawn from France in tragic circumstances. Charles had placed his prisoners in safe keeping, Philip of Hesse at Malines, whence he soon made an abortive attempt at escape. The incident provoked wild political excitement, and induced Charles to avenge himself with the utmost rigour on all who had been concerned in it. About the same period Europe echoed to another political sensation, this time one which had no ultimate significance: the exiled Muley Hassan of Tunis made his appearance at Charles's Court.

Meanwhile the Duke of Arschot went out with a great following to meet the Prince of Spain at Bruchsal on the upper Rhine, and to accompany him on his entrance to the Netherlands. At Namur he was greeted by Philibert Emanuel of Savoy, a man who rejoiced in Charles's absolute confidence. At the Castle of Tervueren Queen Mary welcomed him, accompanied by the Duchess Christina of Lorraine. They entertained him with a review of troops, or more accurately with a mock-battle carried out in the convention of the time, with defiles, cannonades and processions. Philip entered Brussels riding between the Duke of Savoy and the Cardinal of Trent. Behind him came Alva, Arras, Egmont and Horn. Peacefully these four rode together behind the King and ruler who was to be. Little did they then foresee what the future held in store for them. In the next year William of Nassau, the youthful heir to the Prince of Orange, was to woo the daughter of Maximilian, Count of Buren. This was that celebrated Count of Buren who, on December 23rd, 1548, made ready to meet death with so many scenes of farewell, so many thanksgivings, such drinking of healths and general ceremony, that a whole generation of literature, sentimental and heroic, sprang from the event.

The Spanish prince presented a curious contrast to the richly clad, solid-looking Netherlanders. He had no natural gaiety, nothing of the freshness of youth. Wine made him sick and he fainted during a tournament. On the other hand he could not have his fill of religious ceremonies and walking in processions. Charles eyed his son with pride. He had already had him proclaimed his heir in Spain. On April 2nd, 1550, he repeated the ceremony for the Netherlands. But the *Joyeuse Entrée* of Prince Philip was to end in bitter tears. Charles's hope that his son might grow to understand the land and the people was not fulfilled. This did not prevent the Emperor from seeking to re-live his own life in his son, to make him the repository of his future. With such passionate love did he follow the young man's career that he laid the widest plans for him during these next years, and thought even of securing him the imperial throne.

Contemporaries even whispered into King Ferdinand's ears that Charles was trying to prevent his succession to the imperial throne, and perhaps would take from him his title as King of the Romans. But the substance of Charles's new plan, although original was not so unfair as this. Charles still intended Ferdinand to succeed him in the Empire; but he now wanted Philip to succeed

Ferdinand, and Maximilian, Ferdinand's son, to succeed only on Philip's death. Charles justified this policy to himself by pretending that it would ensure dynastic unity and the universal power of the family. He felt that such unity could only be guaranteed by some kind of legal arrangement, as that the two branches of the family should hold the imperial title alternately. Yet before judging Charles's attitude too ungenerously, it is only fair to remember what he had already done to secure the unity of the dynasty, and to prevent too serious a division of the family inheritance. He had been ready to defy tradition and pass over his own son's claims, in order to secure to Ferdinand the title, King of the Romans. But this incident was now forgotten or taken for granted, and it was comprehensible enough that Ferdinand and his sons resented the idea that the imperial succession was to be taken from them and given back to Philip.

Charles's plan was the climax of his life-work. He felt that the world power of his family would rest on firm foundations, only if he could transfer the idea of inheritance from his territorial possessions to the imperial title itself. Then and only then would the scattered lands of the Hapsburg be united and sanctified under the holy mantle of Empire. On such foundations the building could rise, perfect in symmetry and strength, as kings and queens, princes and princesses, rulers and viceroys, all scions of the same illustrious line, were established in land after land, in province after province.

The theory that the imperial crown could be inherited had made intermittent and spontaneous appearances in German history, as soon as any one dynasty became firmly established. But when, in an excess of zeal for his dynasty, an Emperor attempted to gain legal recognition for the almost accomplished fact, he unleashed the angry opposition of the princes. This was true above all if the Emperor called in foreign powers to his aid. Henry VI had striven to gain his end with the help of Naples and had failed. Charles V was now to make another attempt, with the help of Spain. But before Charles's plan could mature, before he could present it to the Electors, it had already withered. The Austrian branch would have none of it. Ferdinand and his sons, naturally enough, were unanimous in their disapproval. They were supported by all their councillors and servants, a race in whom the age-old traditional jealousies between Courts flourished. They cried out on the bitter humiliation which it would be to them to be shouldered out of the imperial succession. Maximilian, curiously enough, who was the chief obstacle and the main sufferer from Charles's scheme, was not only the object of his father's melancholy care, but gained, by his determined opposition to the plan, a considerable prestige among his adherents and throughout the Empire. Charles's behaviour, by making Maximilian popular, did much to ensure the heredity of the imperial crown in the dynasty, although not in the way he himself wanted.

Since the beginning of 1550 Charles, Ferdinand and Mary — for the Queen proved to be indispensable in such family discussions — had been deliberating gravely. Mary believed profoundly in the dynastic principle and was devoted to the Emperor. On May 1st she employed every grace she had to win over Ferdinand, imploring him not to stand in the way of a legal guarantee of the unification of the whole family, by opposing the election of Philip as King of the Romans. Charles supported his own arguments by ably summing up the points in their favour as against the objections.

These discussions of the succession problem took an almost academic form, so that it is interesting to study a typical schedule of arguments concerning the future protection of the dynasty. The paper is undated, but probably belongs to a slightly later period in the argument than Mary's appeal to Ferdinand. Five questions were raised on this schedule, all were then answered by the dialectical method, and at the end a few rather lame conclusions were deduced. 'Is it necessary', thus ran the argument, 'to regulate the inheritance while the Emperor and King of the Romans are both alive?' The answer to this was not difficult: doubtless it was necessary, so that the danger of a double election should be avoided and no impotent or heretical person should ascend the throne. The next question was: 'What is to be expected of a successor?' Here the answer was somewhat longer. The successor must be a person with very considerable power of his own, as well as all the virtues proper to a king, for the Empire was not rich in resources and had many dangerous neighbours like the French and the Turks. 'Where can such a prince be found?' the schedule next cogently inquired. The immediate answer to this was: only in the House of Hapsburg.

This contention was proved by a rapid review of all the other ruling houses of Germany. 'Is it essential', the questionnaire unrelentingly pursued, 'to keep the imperial dignity in that family?' Again the answer was an emphatic affirmative, in spite of all the burdens which the family must thereby take upon its own hereditary lands, and the gold which it must send from Spain to the Empire. Great as were these sacrifices, the Hapsburg dynasty had always shown itself ready to bear the burdens of Christendom at its own expense. Nor, the argument speciously proceeded, would the decretals against making the Empire heritable be violated by its continuance in the Hapsburg family; the election was always supposed to fall on the best man, and the members of the Hapsburg family alone had an inner vocation to the office. 'And who, in the last resort, is the better man, the future King of Bohemia and Hungary, or the King of Spain and the Netherlands?'

This was the crucial question, and the compiler of the schedule proceeded to solve it with amazing candour. The first essential, he argued, was that the two princes should remain friends, so that, as the common saying goes, 'one hand can help to wash the other'. Maximilian's advantages were the proximity of his own hereditary lands, his friendship with the German princes, his knowledge of the language, and his experience in war and peace. Philip, on the contrary, held sway in remote countries, governed fortresses in Spain, the Indies, Italy and Africa, was unfamiliar both with the people and the language, and had grown unpopular, because the Spanish soldiers in the Empire were unpopular. Against this, it might of course be urged that Italy was the other hand of the Empire, the seat of the imperial throne and of the Papacy, which could only be adequately protected by a prince owning land in Italy. It might also be argued that France could not be checked save from Italy and the Netherlands. As for the general dislike of the Spanish soldiers, soldiers were seldom angels; Philip's education abroad and ignorance of German could be remedied, as the same defects had been remedied in Ferdinand, who had become a good German. Under the wise guidance of his father, Philip would learn how to govern his kingdoms in peace and freedom, the world over.

The schedule concluded with the statement that it would be useless to deceive oneself as to the difficulties of the plan, but just as many difficulties had been surmounted before Ferdinand had been elected King of the Romans. The essential factor was, and would always be, that their Majesties and their children should be united in love and harmony.

Just now these very qualities were conspicuously absent.

The two monarchs met at Augsburg several weeks before the Diet. The Emperor, who had brought Philip with him, tried to force the initiative on Ferdinand. Ferdinand evaded it. What he already knew of his brother's intentions, together with the removal of his own eldest son to Spain, made him obstinate and distrustful, and hindered his freedom of action. When Arras became insistent and Queen Mary added her entreaties by letter, Ferdinand even demanded that Maximilian be recalled from Spain. Nothing seemed to move him. Charles sent for Mary. She arrived on September 10th but could do nothing with Ferdinand. Maximilian kept his rights: the discussions were called off: the Queen withdrew.

This was Charles's first disappointment. He had imagined that things would be easier. The autumn days dragged drearily on. The Estates made answer on August 20th to the propositions of July 26th. In these Charles had brought forward the council, the *Interim* and the pacification of the Empire. But the opposition was stronger than it had been two years before. On August 27th Granvelle died, and, as men reported, the Emperor seemed to 'have lost his own soul'. The skilful Bishop of Arras had not his father's prestige. The Schmalkaldic war was not yet wholly quenched: round Bremen the troops of the Counts of Oldenburg and Mansfeld were still active; Magdeburg held out, provoking anger and astonishment from the imperial party. The city was a hot-bed of Protestant discontent, for it maintained itself against the *Interim* and against the attacks made on it by the surrounding principality. At the Diet no better solution could be suggested than that the Elector Maurice should execute the ban against Magdeburg. Money was to be granted to him which was later to be made good by a special vote in the Estates. The business was accomplished in the end, although not without ill-feeling and protests. In October Charles's troubles were once again aggravated by an attack of gout.

In November he sent the imperial Vice-chancellor, Seld, to

speak seriously to the Estates. They gave in, but their distrust of the Spaniards was growing, and they were now learning to couple the black name of the Bishop of Arras with this party. In December they at length agreed, under pressure, that they would send representatives to the council which a new Pope was making ready to reassemble at Trent.

The election of Cardinal del Monte to the Papacy had amazed the world. The imperial party had tried to push the election of the Englishman, Reginald Pole, and had, as Mendoza's dispatches show, very nearly achieved their object. But the French turned the balance in favour of Cardinal del Monte, who became Pope as Julius III and proved, from the beginning, far more favourable to the Emperor than anyone had reason to hope. He sent Pedro de Toledo immediately to the imperial Court as nuncio, and later Pighino, Archbishop of Siponto. In the late summer this latter was already carrying on negotiations in Augsburg. They came to an agreement about the council, although the problem of Parma and Piacenza was still a source of anxiety, for the Farnese family clung to France for help.

Little by little the French government drifted back to its old position of hostility to the Emperor, in Germany, in Italy, at the Vatican, on the Flemish border and in the Mediterranean. They had in their agent, Marillac, an acute observer of all that happened both in the imperial surroundings at Augsburg, and in the Empire at large. Apart from a very occasional miscalculation, he kept the French King well posted of all that passed. The French government had once stood the friend of Chaireddin Barbarossa; it now extended its patronage to another sea-robber, no less bold. This was Dragut, who had himself once been a galley-slave; but he had been enfranchised, had risen to mastery himself, and now plagued the kingdoms of Naples and Sicily in his own ships, a bold and desperate leader. In this very autumn of 1550 on September 10th, the Viceroy Juan de Vega and Andrea Doria had launched a successful attack on his headquarters at Monastir and Mohadia south of Tunis, in the same latitude as Malta. The victories, greeted with wild enthusiasm, were unhappily wiped out in the following year.

Charles was thus again all but overwhelmed with the perennial cares of his immense dominions, when he at last decided to resume the family discussions for the arrangement of the succession. Their progress was hindered by Ferdinand's not unjustifiable desire to acquire Transylvania, which involved him in fresh troubles with the Turks, so that he had to make renewed demands for financial help. Charles saw in this merely an unwelcome diversion of those subsidies, which he had received to quell Magdeburg and his last opponents in the Lower Saxon Circle.

On December 10th Maximilian arrived at Augsburg. On his way from Spain, he had been sought out more than once by French embassies, making him every offer of friendship. At Augsburg he assumed an attitude of reserve towards the Emperor and his plans. He avoided Prince Philip altogether. He and his Austrian party believed in all good faith that they were defending rights which had been their own for many years. And Charles, charming as he could sometimes be, was not the man to smooth away family disagreements with an airy gesture. In the narrow rooms of the great gabled houses of Augsburg, the two groups of the divided family seemed to step warily round and round each other, without coming to an agreement or an issue. In the end they even began to discuss the business by letter rather than by word of mouth, a development which usually betokened the final stage of tension in an argument. Now that the estrangement of the princes was apparent, now that irrevocable words had actually been committed to paper, reconciliation seemed out of the question. The only hope left was that Mary would be able to resolve their differences.

On December 16th Charles wrote to her, a long and despairing letter, concluding with a postscript in his own hand. The very writing was tremulous with sorrow and anxiety. He had not written the body of the letter himself, not so much for fear of tiring his hand, as because the recapitulation of all these quarrels excited his nerves too much. He declared that he was ready to die of vexation. He had not in all his life had to face so much obstinacy, not from the late King of France, nor from the present one, nor from the Connétable. And the worst of it was, he lamented, that Ferdinand did not appear to take things at all to heart. He hoped, Charles piously added, that God of His mercy would give his brother better thoughts and himself more patience; he besought Mary, if she could not help, at least to comfort him.

Mary answered the appeal by coming in person, and the wrangle began afresh. Like the earlier discussions, it took place in the house of the Fugger family. To crown all, the interminable argument over subsidies to fight the Turk had been tenfold embittered by tension in Württemberg. Ferdinand, as the liege lord of the old Duke Ulrich, had initiated a legal action against him for his part in the Schmalkaldic war. Before the cause could be decided, on November 6th, Duke Ulrich died. Charles himself now stepped forward on behalf of the heir, Duke Christopher, and protested that further occupation of the country was impossible owing to the great expense. Ferdinand was thus once again forced to relinquish Württemberg.

Of all these embittered discussions between the brothers, a little packet of documents has survived: notes, jottings, memoranda, heads of arguments. The greater number are in the hand of Queen Mary or King Ferdinand. The whole matter was argued in the closest secrecy. Try as they might to interpret an occasional hint, an unguarded gesture, neither councillors nor foreign ambassadors ever discovered anything to the point. Even now it is impossible to follow the quarrel through its every phase. We can but trace the main outline, and we know the ultimate result as it was written out by the brothers and sister in their own hands, on March 9th, 1551.

In this document Ferdinand agreed that when he was Emperor he would use his influence with the Electors to have Philip made King of the Romans, provided Maximilian was chosen for Philip's successor at the same time. If this last stipulation were to hinder Philip's election, Ferdinand undertook not to press it. In the preliminary negotiations, Ferdinand had displayed a very different attitude, suggesting that the prospect of Maximilian's election must be used to calm the fears of the Electoral College.

Philip in his turn undertook to assist Ferdinand against all enemies and rebels in the hereditary lands, and promised to support him in calming the religious troubles. This might be effected through the council, always supposing it was still sitting. Ferdinand promised, when he was Emperor, to appoint his nephew governor of Italy, in return for a promise that Philip would fulfil his duties conscientiously; he was also to renounce his right of bestowing fiefs of the Empire, and to refrain from disposing of the great fiefs of Mantua, Montferrat, Piedmont, Florence and the imperial fief of Ferrara. After his election as King of the Romans, Philip was to marry a daughter of Ferdinand.

Even Mary realized that Maximilian could hardly be expected to enter into any agreement on these terms, and no written contract was required of him. They contented themselves by asking for his verbal consent, and one of Queen Mary's letters shows that he gave them all the satisfaction which could be expected.

On May 26th Prince Philip took leave of his father to go back to Spain. A popular joke declared that Charles tried to buy the tears of the people for his son's departure by generously distributing Indian gold. At Genoa, Philip met Maximilian who had gone to fetch his bride back to Germany. She, in the meantime, had become the mother of their first child, Anna, who was much later, as the fourth wife of Philip, himself her uncle, to be the mother of his only surviving son and heir.

The Emperor passed the rest of the summer at Augsburg, retiring to Innsbruck only at the end of August. Here he was visited by his daughter and son-in-law, Mary and Maximilian, on their return from Spain.

But in the heart of Germany storm was gathering. It broke while Charles was at Innsbruck.

STRAWS IN THE WIND. THE 'INTERIM' AND THE COUNCIL. THE LEAGUE OF PRINCES AND HENRY II OF FRANCE

Charles was still at Augsburg when he heard of the success or failure of his first overtures to the German Electors. He had already approached them about the coming imperial election, although the fact itself was in the distant future. Charles had arranged to handle the Rhenish Electors, Ferdinand to canvass Saxony and Brandenburg. Each prince was to act in the name of his brother as well as his own. This was the means by which the German princes and their ministers came to know of the Hapsburg plan. Unhappily things went badly from the beginning. The proper ambassador for the business was Doctor Gienger, but he was ill and Ferdinand could not send him. Instead he worried Charles with so many meticulous inquiries as to whom he was to send instead, that the Emperor imagined that he was again trying to get out of the plan. The trouble was at length smoothed away and they sent Schlick to Joachim and Maurice, the Vice-chancellor of the Empire, Seld, to Cologne and Mainz, Veltwyk to the Elector Palatine, and the lord of Lierre to Treves. But whatever the quality and skill of the ambassadors, the result was always the same. Courteously but firmly, the Electors rejected the proposal.

The aged Elector, Frederick of the Palatinate, took the opportunity to pour out a tale of past recollections, boasting to Veltwyk that he had been the great man at the election of Charles and Maximilian. But he did not forget to add his views on the irritation which the Spanish troops had evoked in the Empire, nor on the annoyance which Don Luis d'Avila had caused with his arrogant book about the Schmalkaldic war.

The Electors of Mainz and Treves were already on their way to Trent.

This at least had resulted from Charles's unrelenting obstinacy. The council had been called back to Trent and reopened on May 1st, 1551. Not only the leading German prelates went to it, but Protestant princes and towns sent representatives. On October 22nd the ambassadors of Württemberg arrived, on November 11th the historian of the Reformation, John Sleidan, appeared to represent Strasbourg and a group of other towns. On January 9th the plenipotentiary of the Elector Maurice himself made his appearance.

But what could the participation of a few Protestants achieve at this eleventh hour? The Vatican had loitered too long before applying the salve of a council to the sore; and at the last minute, in spite of Charles's entreaties, the Pope disregarded his intentions. The German Estates sought to satisfy their Emperor's demands, but the sending of delegates to the council, so far from showing that they were ready for reconciliation, was no more than a solemn demonstration of the now established breach.

At the thirteenth session, on October 11th, they confirmed the doctrine concerning the Blessed Sacrament, but at the express wish of the Emperor they postponed the question of communion for young children and of the cup for the laity. Decisions on confession and extreme unction followed. It was in the nature of things impossible to revise the fundamental decretals which had hitherto been issued. The only important move made by the Protestants at Trent was, typically enough — a protest.

For long enough now the ultimate decision in this religious and political problem had lain with Germany. The Council of Trent was the servant of the Catholic Church and the Counter-Reformation. It was too late to stem the German Reformation. To use his own words, Charles's last hope was gone.

Meanwhile those ecclesiastical regulations which he had issued to establish peace in Germany, exacerbated the opposition. Charles's opponents whetted their anger on them almost daily. Everyone recognized that the *Interim* was an insufficient half-measure. The belief was not confined to theologians and pastors; it was expressed in the halls of the nobility, in the sitting-rooms of burghers, in the countryside among peasants and travellers. The *Interim* was the object of laughter and scorn, and of every ignominy which men could devise.

The popular mood bred resourcefulness and courage, but it did not bring forth any decision for the future. Opposition was rife in the Lower Saxon Circle, from Bremen to Magdeburg, in all the coastlands from Friesland to Prussia, but there was still nothing to give substance to the theory.

Maurice had agreed to carry out the ban against Magdeburg, if he might subsequently become the patron of the city. His mission gave him the excuse both to raise troops and to stay away from the Diet. To all appearances he was the Emperor's tool, and the opponents of Charles, the Margrave Hans of Küstrin, Duke Albert of Prussia, and Duke John Albert of Mecklenburg, who had formed themselves into a league on February 26th, 1550, regarded him as their chief enemy. They intended to relieve Magdeburg. When Maurice heard that they had begun to recruit in the Bishopric of Verden he set off as early as January 1551, and with relentless resolution seized all of their troops whom he could use, and scattered the rest. Charles praised him warmly for his promptitude.

As early as February, Hans of Küstrin grasped the essential fact that Maurice, like himself, was fundamentally hostile to imperial policy; in the course of the next few months he realized the immense superiority in arms of this young, malleable and vigorous leader. Acting on broad principles, they entered into alliance. The bait with which Maurice was tempted, was the freeing of his father-in-law the Landgrave of Hesse. This too worked with the Hessian ministers. All alike were agreed in the necessity of throwing off this 'bestial, intolerable and continual servitude, like that of Spain'. Acting without the knowledge of the Landgrave and of his own initiative, Maurice contemplated a French alliance. Of the old anti-imperial league, there remained John Albert of Mecklenburg and Hans of Küstrin. To this nucleus another was soon added, Margrave Albert of Branden-burg-Kulmbach, a boisterous soldier whose name alone spread terror. He once again gave force to the old theory of Protestantism as a war on the landed prelates.

For many years, and more particularly since the attack on Württemberg, nothing had frightened Charles so much as a projected alliance between France and the princes. Their separation in 1543-4 had been the cause of his greatest victories; their alliance might endanger his very life. Even in history there are occasional examples of poetic justice. Such a one now came to pass. The Lochau heath had been the scene of Charles's great victory over John Frederick of Saxony on April 24th, 1547. Here, at the hunting box which was later called Annaburg, early in October 1551, the French King's ambassador Jean de Fresse, Bishop of Bayonne, signed a treaty with the German princes. This treaty brought Charles to his fate.

There is neither space nor necessity to enter into all the details of those negotiations. They were not always easy, for Margrave Hans was meticulous and circumspect, Maurice impulsive and unscrupulous. The Hessians, too, had cause for complaint. 'The Devil', they wrote home, 'has interfered not once but a thousand times.' After a heated scene, the Margrave left on the evening of October 3rd, but Maurice, the Hessian councillors and the Bishop stood fast by their terms.

They agreed that the King of France was to pay 70,000 crowns a month, and 240,000 crowns for the first three months so that troops could be raised. In return for this, the document stated, 'it is thought good that His Majesty of France shall have possession of those towns, which although they have belonged to the Empire for all time, are yet not of German speech. These are Cammerich, Toul in Lorraine, Metz, Verdun, and any others of the same kind. These he shall govern in his right as Vicar of the Holy Roman Empire, to which office we shall use our powers to appoint his majesty. The Empire shall nevertheless maintain whatever jurisdiction it has over those towns'.

There was no question of the bishoprics; even the towns were not to be separated from the Empire but merely ruled over by the King as imperial Vicar. Yet, however the cession was phrased, it was a sacrifice of imperial land. The princes saw no other means of carrying on the war without which they despaired of reaching their goal, and so fell back on the dangerous expedient of ceding to the French policy of expansion.

The strategic plan which underlay this alliance with Henry II was that of severing Charles's connection with the Netherlands, and forming themselves a united front down the Rhine; this would give them the inner lines, and a defensive position from which they would be more able to attack the Emperor. 'We will march on the Emperor himself', they agreed.

After they had signed their treaty at Lochau, the princes issued an apologia in which they revealed not only the strategic base of their political alliance with France, but indicated that the originator of the scheme was Maurice of Saxony. In this manifesto, the German princes issued a challenge. 'For important reasons', they wrote, 'we hold it for right and proper, nay we advise and do most sincerely entreat that His Majesty in his own person and with a great following should come to meet us. In the last resort our two armies must fight each other, calling on God to decide between us. The cup must be drunk to the dregs ere it can be flung down.'

By the treaty of Chambord, on July 15th, 1552, the French King ratified the decisions of Lochau. The King of France issued a manifesto on February 3rd. The document was published at Fontainebleau, but it had been printed at Marburg in Hesse. On February 14th, Maurice and William of Hesse completed their military plans at Friedewalde in Hesse. While William was executing these, he wrote to his brother-in-law Maurice on March 15th, saying that he had just received news direct from the French King. Henry calculated that he would be at Toul on the 20th. 'Thence', wrote William, 'he intends to march at once for the Rhine, in so far as the towns of Metz, Toul and Verdun throw no obstacles in His Majesty's way.' The towns were thus considered not as goals in themselves, but as mere obstacles on the way to the Rhine.

Henry himself had indeed expressed a different opinion when he declared that he 'had enough to do in Italy and the Netherlands'. But he came to the Rhine in response to the entreaties of the German princes, and it was then that he recognized the importance of the Lorraine bishoprics as stepping-stones. He occupied each of them in turn, by intimidation or treachery, swiftly and almost without loss.

But what was the Emperor doing to defend himself?

Charles at first refused to listen to all rumours of a movement against him. With an overconfidence, compact of self-will and contempt for the princes, he smilingly waved aside the warnings of his more observant brother and sister. As early as the beginning of October, when the princes were holding their meetings with the Bishop of Bayonne in the hunting box on the Lochau heath, Mary wrote to warn Charles that something was afoot between Maurice, the young Landgrave of Hesse and the King of France. Ferdinand and Christopher of Württemberg warned him by letter and by their ambassadors. But Charles was confident in his contempt for the elder generation of German princes, whose conduct had indeed given him cause enough for despising them for the whole of the last decade. He was confident, too, in what he took to be the devoted loyalty of the younger princes. Here, too, his view was supported by some, at least, of the facts, for the princes of the Brandenburg dynasty did one by one drift back to his side. He asked Maurice to come and talk matters over with him. And Charles really thought that Maurice would accept the offer. So trusting was he of the Elector's loyalty.

Maurice, meanwhile, had long been in possession of Magdeburg, but for specious reasons he still continued to keep on foot the army which had been originally raised to reduce the city in Charles's name. By November 17th, 1551, he had completed his negotiations with the German princes and the French King, and issued one last appeal to the Emperor on behalf of his father-in-law, the

Landgrave Philip. Fate offered Charles one last opportunity. He rejected it.

On February 25th, Maurice's ambassadors excused their master for not coming to see the Emperor, on the grounds that the journey was dangerous, and repeated the request for Philip's release. Charles answered on March 4th that if Maurice would come, everything could be arranged. On March 17th Maurice again excused himself.

Gradually rumours took shape, facts emerged. Early in March the Elector of Mainz appealed to Queen Mary for help against the Hessians. But the warring princes did not march to the Rhine; they left the King of France, precariously perched, to keep watch on that. Turning away from Mainz, they headed southwards. In the second half of March matters moved speedily to an issue. On April 1st the princes were at Augsburg; on the 4th they entered the town. Ulm closed its gates. Now the army headed for Tyrol. At the eleventh hour, on April 6th, Charles tried to escape to the Netherlands. The Rhine was blocked by the French King. He fell back to Innsbruck, still apparently unable to grasp the fact that the rebellion was directed in bitter earnest against his own person.

Then the advance stopped. Maurice offered to treat.

LINZ AND PASSAU. MAURICE, FERDINAND AND THE EMPEROR

As early as March 3rd Charles had sent one of his leading courtiers, Joachim de Rye, lord of Balançon, a knight of the Order of the Golden Fleece, to his brother Ferdinand with an instruction which the Bishop of Arras had drawn up. In face of the growing rumours of insurrection in Germany he asked for advice and help. He did not feel that he should allow the Margrave Albert's obvious designs on Würzburg and Bamberg to deceive him as to the more general purport of the rebellion. Bewildered, he was sure that it must have more adherents than the princes alone, for the burghers of Augsburg had not been willing to give him financial help. He implored Ferdinand to listen to no councillors who sought to divert his attentions to the Turkish menace;

the insurrection in Germany was far more grave, for unless it could be stilled all hope of raising subsidies for war on the Turk would vanish. Money and troops could not be had; Charles implored Ferdinand to use every means at his disposal to persuade the rebels to peace. If Maurice and Albert complained of the *Interim* and the imperial attitude to religion, Charles advised Ferdinand to reply by reminding them of the benefits which they had received from the Emperor, and by pointing out how un-reliable the French alliance had proved to the Duke of Cleves. He might also enlarge on the moderation with which Charles had always acted in the religious question. No one knew better than Ferdinand how little Charles contemplated so gross a violation to the Golden Bull as the establishment of a hereditary right of the imperial throne; still less did the Emperor contemplate any infringement of the German Liberties. As for the occasional extension of his own lands, Charles justified his every act: he had but asserted his own undeniable rights in Gelderland, he had often explained the engrossment of Utrecht, and he had paid a high price for Lingen. Charles went on to suggest that the Margrave Albert, a bankrupt at best, could be bought off. As for Maurice's complaints of the imprisonment of the Landgrave, they were wholly unjustified. The Landgrave was a man who could not but make further trouble if he were set free. Moreover, Charles added, had he not offered to discuss this very point with Maurice personally?

More intricate than this open instruction was the secret instruc-tion which Charles sent with it. The secret instruction was based on a private fear that Ferdinand, who had never yet expressed the least sympathy for his brother in his present predicament, might himself be in some secret understanding with the rebels. Balançon was told to use his eyes, and if he saw the slightest indication of any such understanding, to urge Ferdinand most seriously to consider the absolute necessity of standing shoulder to shoulder with the Emperor. They were brothers and bound to one another: Ferdinand was making a grave error if he thought he could count on other people. Charles was not alone threatened; Ferdinand's position in the Empire, his right to the imperial throne were themselves at stake. Balançon was not to stop with Ferdinand. He was to seek out Maximilian and point out to him, too, how much this alliance between Maurice, the 'King of Saxony' and the French, threatened his own position. Maximilian might save the situation by intervening personally as a mediator, and thus win to himself great honour and reputation.

In spite of Ferdinand's growing discontent, Charles was unjustified in his suspicions. Far from betraying him, Ferdinand had written to Maurice on March 4th admonishing him to peace, and had later sent off the Chancellor of Bohemia, Heinrich Reuss von Plauen, to see him. On March 16th this latter joined Maurice at Leipzig and was able to arrange a conference at Linz for April 4th.

Maurice agreed to the meeting, but twice later asked for a postponement. With astonishing skill, he continued to play off each of the parties against the other. Having thoughtfully extracted a document from his Hessian allies, he displayed this shamelessly at Vienna, pretending to regret that his allies 'had gone somewhat too far with foreign princes'. But he contrived to maintain his reputation among his allies by his apparent reserve in dealing with Ferdinand's overtures, as well as by his subsequent actions.

On March 11th and 22nd the Emperor gave Balançon yet more instructions for the coming negotiations. Charles was ready to concede the release of the Landgrave, although only after the troops had been disbanded for a fortnight, and a guarantee given that they should not join the King of France. The religious settlement was to be that laid down in the last Diet. Charles added that no consideration in the world would induce him to act contrary to his conscience and duty. The whole instruction, down to the last details, filled a thick pamphlet.

Queen Mary now intervened from the Netherlands, sending her advice, together with a glowing appeal to King Ferdinand's loyalty. 'By God, Monseigneur', she wrote on April 9th, 'let bygones be bygones. I beseech you, Monseigneur, let your brother's troubles speak more eloquently to you than my words. Do not forget that His Majesty has never hesitated to come to your help whatever his own weakness. I implore you, Monseigneur, yet again and with all the strength I have, make haste to his help.'

Ferdinand indignantly repudiated the hints of his brother and sister against his own loyalty. The truth was that neither his present position nor his character, in this so unlike that of Charles, enabled him to attempt the impossible. Yet he did not neglect all obvious and reasonable steps to help his brother during the next months. He came to Linz from Pressburg, by way of Vienna, and on the way he sent his brother some more advice, this time for handling the Elector of Brandenburg and Hans of Küstrin. He also urged him to release John Frederick of Saxony. All this proves that although Ferdinand did not abandon his ancient alliance with his neighbour Maurice, he was busily trying to guarantee himself against him for the future.

On Easter Tuesday, April 19th, the negotiations opened at Linz. Ferdinand and his sons, the Elector Maurice, the Duke of Bavaria and the Bishop of Passau were all present. Charles's representatives were Rye and Lazarus von Schwendi. Maurice as usual stayed in the background, pushed his allies and the French into the foremost place, and amused himself by assuming, with more success than usual, his favourite role of mediator. He ingeniously suggested new demands to his own allies, so that, while apparently playing a moderate part himself, he would be sure of getting what he could out of the negotiations. In this way, demands which had begun modestly enough, were gradually heightened. Ferdinand did not feel that he could yield in Charles's name to all that the allies asked for the French King, for religion, for imperial government. Maurice, however, soon began to feel a sense of isolation, and asked for a larger meeting, in which he hoped to gain more support. Charles was nothing loath; he was playing for time. After some correspondence had been exchanged between Linz and Innsbruck, a second meeting was fixed at Passau for May 26th. The assistance of the princes of southern and western Germany was called in.

Maurice had realized that the conditions under which Charles was prepared to release the Landgrave Philip could not be fulfilled. His allies would never agree to disband their army before it had gained any serious victory. Moreover the only guarantee which Charles would give in the religious question was that a Diet should decide 'by what peaceful means the schism in religion might be healed'. This was to give an easy victory to the Catholic majority in the Diet. It was no guarantee at all. The preliminaries signed at Linz on May 6th had not in fact advanced the argument in the slightest. Perhaps that was inevitable. The main thing was that both parties had gained time.

Maurice had not spent those two weeks in negotiations alone. No truce prevented him from carrying out his military plans, and he had been busily making all ready for his march on Innsbruck. He had also sent an embassy to the French King to secure his participation in the negotiations at Passau. He postponed the armistice.

It was strange in the circumstances that he should have sent that embassy to France about the Passau meeting, for this must surely have endangered the payment of any more subsidies from that direction; if he were to invade Tyrol he had sore need of the money. He does not seem to have thought the matter out, or if he did, the subtleties of his policy elude us. He may have decided that the real issue was to be tried at Passau, and that the neutral powers would help him, the Rhinelanders for instance, who feared the French. But he could not hope to eradicate all fear of the Emperor in Germany, nor to check the violence of the Emperor's soldiers, unless he put him altogether out of action.

The risk he took was immense. Apart from the greater resources of Charles, he had yet another lever with which to put pressure on Maurice — the deposed Elector of Saxony. Maurice had to feel his way cautiously, step by step, between his ally France, whom he was double-crossing, and the Hapsburg princes, with whom he would have to reckon for a long time to come. His actions cannot all be explained on rational grounds. It is idle to attempt an explanation for every important decision in history, particularly in dealing with so complex a nature as Maurice. The logical explanation is not always the historic explanation. Yet the mainspring of Maurice's actions is sufficiently clear. Charles had made a firm stand at Linz, and it was accordingly necessary for Maurice to gain some visible success in order to strengthen his own position, and impress the weaker Estates. He therefore sent word to Margrave Albert to attack Nuremberg in May, and to enforce on Bamberg and Würzburg those notorious treaties by which the former disgorged 80,000 Gulden and let him occupy twenty villages, and the latter paid 220,000 Gulden. Maurice himself, with the rest of the army, turned across upper Swabia towards Füssen. Near Reutte they drove the imperial troops back into the gorges of Ehrenberg, surrounded and forced them to surrender. This was on May 19th. On the 23rd they entered Innsbruck.

The unprotected Court had fled over the Brenner. The Emperor marched from Eisack into the valley of the Rienz, thence over the watershed of Innichen into the valley of the Drave. On the 24th he was at Lienz, on the 27th at Villach, where he could turn either by way of Pontebba into Italy, or eastwards across Carniola into Styria. Bitter indeed to the aged Emperor, bred in all the traditions of chivalry and sovereignty, was this ignominious flight before his victorious enemies. But, as so often before in that long career, he collected his strength in this dark hour and took courage in remembering how great were still his resources. Letters and embassies went out over all Europe. Peace was made in Italy; 200,000 ducats came in from Naples; Anton Fugger, who accompanied the Court, offered 400,000 ducats and persuaded the Genoese to hold up their demands for re-payment.

The preparations for war which had not been completed were now set on foot once again. Margrave Hans of Küstrin was still at Maurice's side, but he had received a visit from the imperial field-marshal Hans Böcklin, the father-in-law of Schwendi. Hans was already out of sympathy with Maurice, whom his allies were beginning to call the 'Kinglet'. Had Charles but taken the occasion which offered and made certain religious concessions, he could have forged a knife to strike Maurice in the back. Hans was indignant at the manifesto issued by the leaders of Maurice's party, above all by the French. 'The devil may trust in you, for I shall not,' he scribbled in the margin. He asserted that the princes 'cared nothing for religion and still less for the word of God'. His own wishes coincided with the Emperor's overtures. He set about a formal negotiation for an imperial pension. Meanwhile, Ferdinand, too, was arming. Spanish and Italian troops were to come across the Alps. The Duke of Alva had been sent for from Spain.

Did the Emperor wish to strike once again and prevent the meeting at Passau? Such an act would have been neither in his own, nor in Ferdinand's, interest. Charles still regarded the French, not the princes, as his chief enemy. But he had to be stronger before he could attack them. By his long delay he was, as much as anything, gaining time, and thereby freedom of action, for himself at Passau.

Once again the curtain goes up on one of the great scenes of history.

Maurice of Saxony was great enough for the gigantic task awaiting him at Passau, and the Emperor was not unequal to his rival. Charles sent off on June 4th, a personal letter to Ferdinand and full instructions for Rye. The Vice-chancellor, Seld, was sent to help the latter. Charles still reserved all final decisions for his personal consideration. His chief point was that the demobilization of the army should precede the release of the Landgrave by a full fortnight, that the princes should repudiate the intervention of the French, and that the religious and political question should be referred to a Diet. Time was on Charles's side.

Maurice's action now underwent a significant change. He stepped forward openly as the champion of the most urgent demands of his allies. He defended the claims of the Landgrave and the French, refused to yield over the demobilization of the army, and voiced the general complaints of the princes in questions of political and religious liberty. This step converted him from a mere ambitious dilettante into an historic figure. He it was who, standing forth at Passau, gave the final form to the Reformation settlement. He it was who laid down the preliminaries, which were to be permanently enshrined three years later in the Peace of Augsburg.

With many a melancholy shake of the head, Ferdinand objected to the coming of a French ambassador. But when he came he let the Estates hear him. This proved the best solution in the end, for as soon as Jean de Fresse had spoken, he withdrew from Passau of his own free will. The French Bishop, with his long thin pointed nose, had awakened little sympathy among the princes. After he left, the French question presented few further difficulties. As in 1544, the princes almost unanimously abandoned the French alliance.

The release of the Landgrave was a knottier problem. Many suggestions were made in opposition to the fourteen day limit for demobilization laid down by Charles. Maurice and the princes persisted in their demand that the release and the demobilization take place simultaneously.

Maurice insisted, meanwhile, that neither a Diet nor a council were of any avail in solving the religious question, because the majority in them was always Catholic. Maurice went back to the solution which had been suggested in 1525 — a national gathering. If this gathering, too, proved incompetent to arrange a settlement, then Maurice demanded an 'outright, unconditional and perpetual peace'. Further discussion was put off to the coming Diet, but at Passau they reached the firm resolution that a definite peace must be made. As for the goods of the clergy, Maurice was ready to guarantee their property, so long as this referred only to the property they still possessed. By insisting on this Maurice all but wrecked the whole conference, but at length he allowed himself to be satisfied with a private promise from the King.

The neutral Estates, on the other hand, were unanimous on the political question. There was some hesitation about granting indemnity to all those who had participated in the last war, but there was no serious difference of opinion.

At the very end there was one more painful shock. Like the Emperor, the war-lords had withheld their final decision. Maurice did not make this clear until June 22nd, and then Ferdinand was forced to agree. The Elector left on the 24th to get the consent of his fellows in arms. In the interim he agreed to a truce. Secretly, Maurice had taken the precaution of asking Ferdinand to ask the Emperor not to liberate the deposed Elector of Saxony. It was a useless request for the old man had been freed some time before. He now followed in the imperial train of his own will.

The worst was yet to come. So far neither the Emperor nor Maurice's allies had recognized the terms.

Maurice made haste to the camp of his friends at Eichstätt. Margrave Albert burst out into one of his usual noisy rages and refused to listen to the terms. The Landgrave William of Hesse, though less noisy, was equally unreasonable, and Maurice had to waste time talking him over. John Albert of Mecklenburg wanted the French to be included. Maurice had therefore to make some reservations to the terms, although he felt that on the whole they would be accepted. On July 3rd Maurice returned to Passau to meet Ferdinand. He was told that Charles had unconditionally rejected the terms. Maurice was incensed, both in appearance and in fact. Charles's refusal did no good. The neutrals almost to a man sympathized with Maurice.

Ferdinand was in despair. Maurice had promised to help him against the Turks when the initial problem was settled, and the peril in that quarter grew from day to day. On the evening of the 8th Ferdinand hastened to Villach, and there implored Charles to give in. But to his brother's tears the Emperor opposed the strength of his unshaken convictions. Ferdinand might stand to lose his present and future safety: Charles stood to lose his immortal soul. In some points Charles was prepared to give in, but not in religion, and not over the government of the Empire. He would grant the Protestants unconditional peace only until the Diet met, and he reserved his judgment on the complaints made against imperial rule. The princes had no right to meddle in such matters. Ferdinand could do no more. In the pouring rain he took leave of his brother, to hurry across the hundred and twenty miles which divided him from Passau.

The onus of decision rested once again on Maurice and the war-lords. In the meantime they had been re-establishing their reputation in Germany by laying siege to Frankfort, garrisoned by the imperialists. To this town, therefore, on July 16th and 17th came the ambassadors of Ferdinand and the Estates.

The question was, would the princes accept the treaty now that Charles had taken the heart out of it? The princes had not been successful at Frankfort and their efforts to raise guns and ammunition in the neighbourhood had made them anything but popular. Yet at first the Landgrave William rejected the new terms. Later, however, he began to ask himself what was likely to become of his imprisoned father if he persisted in his refusal. Angry and disillusioned, Maurice nevertheless thought it better to accept. He had already severed his connection with France beyond recall, and engaged himself too far with the Hapsburg dynasty. In the meantime the Emperor was in arms and might at any moment unleash the deposed Elector to harry him. Maurice managed to talk over the young Landgrave. The others could be disregarded. On August 2nd Maurice and William gave their consent. On the 3rd Maurice struck the camp. The soldiers protested. Maurice incontinently had it set on fire. He himself marched southwards to join in the campaign against the Turks.

Now it was Charles's turn to have doubts. Only a minority of the rebels had accepted the terms, and dangers were still in the air. Ferdinand once more used all his persuasions on his brother, and this time not in vain. Charles ratified the treaty in the form in which Maurice and the Landgrave had accepted it at Munich on August 15th.

THE EMPEROR BEFORE METZ

Absorbed in the great decisions which were being made in Germany, we have been forced to overlook events which were happening farther afield. Charles's relations with Pope Julius III remained good; they even contemplated an alliance. It was true that Charles thought it wisest not to attend the council, close at hand though it was, lest any should think that he was exerting an undue influence. And for the rest he considered the council totally ineffective. At the news that the army was marching on Trent, the delegates scattered. Charles did not live to see them meet again.

The struggle for Parma and Piacenza still played an important part in the relations of Pope and Emperor. The old alliance between the Farnese and Henry II of France was still in force. But the Pope deprived Ottavio of all his rights over the fief of Parma on May 22nd, 1551, and thus became involved in a war with him. Julius relied on Charles to help him. Both combatants suffered from lack of funds, and in the winter of 1551-2 the Pope was willing enough to have peace with Ottavio and the French government. On April 29th peace was concluded, and Charles joined in the treaty on May 10th. But all the efforts of Julius to make a general peace between the King of France and the Emperor came to nothing. Henry II fulfilled his obligations under the treaty of Chambord, marched on the Rhine and made himself fast in the episcopal cities of Lorraine; the pirate Dragut appeared before Naples, acting in conjunction with the French ambassador Aramont; Ferdinand was dragged into another Turkish war in defence of Hungary and Transylvania. To fill Charles's bitter cup to the brim, the Sienese, with French help, drove out the imperial garrison. Henry II took over the patronage of the town, acting through Cardinal d'Este, before the Viceroy of Naples had yet made up his mind to traverse the papal states and come to the rescue.

Charles was once again at war with France on every front. Even on the Flemish border the usual hostilities had broken out. Round Hesdin, Thérouanne, Renty, troops marched and counter-marched. At Luxembourg, Yvoy, Damvillers and Montmédy trouble was rife.

For the future history of Europe by far the most important event was Henry II's seizure of Metz. This town, like nearly all the great episcopal cities of Germany, was proud to call itself a *free* city, but a free city *of the Empire*. It carried the imperial eagle in its coat of arms. The government of the city had long been narrowly aristocratic, confined to the few so-called 'Paraige' families. These great patricians had their magnificent, if middle-class, houses in the town — such as the Hôtel St. Livier which stands to-day — and their lordships and lands in the country round about. But in religion even these families were divided. One of the oldest families of all, the Heu, were half Protestant, half Catholic. The Protestants, no less than their opponent the Catholic imperial Bishop, Cardinal Lenoncourt, were anxious for their town to continue a part of the Empire. But conversely, the Bishop, like most of the Paraige families, was in sympathy with France. With such divisions in cultural, religious and political interests, the people of Metz set great store by their neutrality, in particular in all quarrels concerning the Netherlands. The Netherlands lay very close indeed to the lands of Metz; in those days it must not be forgotten that the Netherlands included the bulwark of Luxembourg, stretching as far to the south of Thion-ville as the village of Marange. As early as 1543 Charles had sent one of his ministers from the Low Countries, Boisot, to Metz to warn the burghers against Protestant tendencies, and to remind them of their duties to the Empire. In the Empire, Charles included the Netherlands. But now the territorial aggression of France had all but reached Metz from the south, spreading out across that divided frontier district, honeycombed with greater and lesser principalities, spiritual and temporal. When the French government claimed the lordship of Goin and the abbey of Gorze, its policy had brought it to the very gates of Metz. In April 1552 the Connétable of France marched across Lorraine, making himself master there in despite of the widowed Duchess Christina. The imperial garrison at Gorze resisted; he bombarded the place with his artillery, forced a surrender, marched in and slaughtered the garrison.

The decisive moment was yet to come. Marching on, the Connétable asked the terrified city of Metz to give quarters to his army of 38,000 men in the surrounding country, and to allow him and his suite to lodge within their walls. They agreed, but Montmorency marched in with 1500 of his best troops, instead of a handful of servants. This was a flat abuse of confidence and an exploitation of the city's weakness. The people would have done better to close their gates, as the burghers of Strasbourg had done. They had trusted to their neutrality and had not even armed themselves. Now it was too late. The garrison did not again leave the town. Shortly after the King himself followed in the wake of his army and appointed the Duke of Guise governor. Guise lost no time in converting the town into a fortress of considerable pretensions.

The town had long outgrown its walls, and Guise now made use of these, together with the suburbs which stretched out across the neighbouring high ground, to construct a modern fortress. His actions were characterized by barbarous ruthlessness, but he followed out an old French tradition in disguising his procedure under legal forms. He pulled down all the suburbs, more especially those which later became Montigny and Sablon, the districts where the celebrated abbeys of St. Arnulf, St. Symphorian, St. Peter, and St. Clement lay in the open country-side. At the ancient monastery of St. Arnulf, Charlemagne's wife, Hildegard, lay buried, with his son Lewis the Pious and fifteen other members of his dynasty. These were carried away to be buried with great pomp in the new monastery of St. Arnulf within the city. Guise thus contrived to flatter the pride of the citizens and divert their attention.

The inner citadel was strengthened, as the outlying houses were razed. All the buildings which had sprung up against or near the walls were destroyed; the fortifications were completed and modernized, and stores of building materials, with wood, planks, sacks and poles were laid in. Queen Mary heard of all these things through her generals and spies. Later, when she gave advice to Charles, she relied much on this foreknowledge.

The Emperor meanwhile had marched as far as Strasbourg. On his way he had gone through Munich, Augsburg and Ulm, and traversed Alsace, showing himself everywhere friendly, gracious and grateful for the loyalty of his people. In Lower Alsace he was joined by fresh troops, and he was now hesitating, wondering what step to take next. Years before, in the late summer of 1541, he had insisted on attacking Algiers although the season was too far advanced, because he had not been able to face disbanding his great armaments unused. So at this time he felt impelled to deliver a counter-attack, however late the season, against those who had struck so shrewd a blow at him.

From Weissenburg, on September 23rd, he wrote to the Queen. The letter, which has but recently come to light, gives a clear picture of his situation. Charles thanked her for her answer to his previous questions. He had heard in the meantime from Count Egmont, who was commanding the army in Luxembourg, that the Margrave Albert, who had been harrying the Rhenish bishoprics, Treves in particular, for some months past, had now marched on Metz. He took this to be the decisive moment in the campaign. The great question which he was asking himself, and which he now laid before his sister, was whether or not he should pursue the Margrave. Metz was a town of immense importance to the French, and he might try to take it 'by sapping and storm. From this city they (the French) will have a clear road to the Rhine and so will be able to cut off my communications from south Germany to the Netherlands, besides which they can threaten Thionville and the whole province of Luxembourg. From Metz, too, they can tamper with the communications between the Netherlands and Franche Comté. Their fortifications cannot yet be finished so that we might have good hope of taking the town'.

In marching on Metz, Charles was considering above all the interests of his dynastic lands — south Germany, Franche Comté, the Netherlands.

On September 28th Mary decisively dissuaded any attack on Metz. She very sensibly proposed that the troops should go into winter quarters in Treves and Lorraine, while the campaign was postponed until the coming spring. Charles would not listen to her advice. He preferred that of his own chief military adviser, the Duke of Alva, who had hastened from Spain to join him. Fatal decision! Alva was strengthened in his scheme for attacking Metz by a new and unexpected incident.

Charles had marched out to meet the last enemies who were still in arms against him. The treaty concluded at Passau left only the Margrave Albert Alcibiades and the King of France. The Margrave Albert Alcibiades and his army were to the immediate military situation as Metz was to the political future: both blocked Charles's communications from south to north, both threatened Luxembourg.

What a victory would it not be, if Charles could turn this dangerous enemy, the Margrave, into a political friend! The power of Charles's opponents would thus be halved, his own doubled. This was the tempting prospect which now opened before the Duke of Alva. By October 8th certain offers had been made to him through an intermediary, the Duke of Nassau-Saarbrücken. On October 15th Alva sent Arras to urge the Emperor to conciliate the Margrave. It would have been rash indeed to march on Metz with Albert Alcibiades ready to fall on his flank, and it would have been difficult to arrange for forces in the Netherlands or the great bishoprics to keep watch on him. But, so Alva thought — if the Margrave could but be won over — Charles might gain a peace from France on terms more favourable 'than ever prince was granted up to this present'.

The Margrave set his price very high. He demanded that the notorious treaties which he had forced on Würzburg and Bamberg in May should be confirmed. Charles had of course previously cancelled them. The Emperor could not conceal from himself that to grant such a confirmation would be to fail in his duty and perhaps to commit a grave political error. But he may well have calculated that if he could prevent the Margrave from doing any more harm at the moment, he could deal with his pretensions effectively after the reduction of Metz, and his own final victory. In any case he gave in to the temptation, and on October 24th confirmed the treaty. On November 10th Schwendi brought his negotiations with the Margrave to a successful conclusion; Albert Alcibiades marched over to the imperial side with 15,000 men.

The Emperor was not comfortable about it. He had to exercise some self-control, and force himself to give the Margrave his hand at their first meeting. His conscience gave him little rest. In a moving letter to Queen Mary on November 13th, he poured out his troubles. 'We were all very much discouraged', he said, 'even the Duke of Alva who was always in favour of making every effort for an understanding. I gave in because I saw that the only alternative was to disband my army, which would have meant that all my expense had been in vain. May God send a blessing on us. If we fail now it will be serious indeed.' Alva meanwhile had spoken to Bassompierre, the French governor of Lorraine, and had derived the impression that, after the capture of the Duke of Aumâle by the Margrave, the French were inclined to peace. 'God knows', Charles went on, 'what thoughts go through my head since I was forced into this agreement with the Margrave, but needs must when the devil drives, *necessité n'a point de loi.*'

And so the Emperor advanced on Metz. The Margrave remained on the left bank of the Moselle, acting as a loose auxiliary force. The imperial army was in the south-east and the troops of the Duke of Egmont, de Boussu and others in the north-east.

On its narrow tongue of land, protected by steep banks, between the rivers Moselle and Seille, Metz was a fortress not difficult to defend. It was not easy to storm it from the north and west, across the broad arm of the Moselle, nor from the east up the steep banks of the Sille. A reconnoitring party attempted to attack it on the side of the Porte Sainte-Barbe, but this too was found to be impracticable. The army from the Netherlands therefore camped on the right banks of the Seille and Moselle, at St. Julien. The main army crossed the Seille by the bridge at Magny and tried to attack Metz from the flat ground in the south. The fortifications in this quarter, stretching from the high corner which was later to be the citadel, across the Moselle and down to the so-called Deutsche Tor on the Seille, were relatively weak. But the Duke of Guise had long devoted himself to them, placed his own lodging in this part of the town, and given a good example to his workmen by himself wielding pick and shovel among them. The outworks of the fortifications stretched well beyond the walls, so that it was long before Charles's men were in close range of the walls. For weeks the fighting was mostly in the exposed country round about.

The imperialists tried to reach the fortifications by digging parallel saps, under cover of a bombardment from their well-entrenched batteries. On November 20th, a cold, clear day, Charles himself, who had been held back by illness at Thionville, at length joined his troops. Mounted on a white palfrey, he reviewed the army. He could be clearly distinguished from the town, where the besieged garrison kept a careful diary of each day's events. The last stage of the siege was now at hand. On November 23rd Charles directed all his guns on that part of the wall just west of the Porte Champenoise. On the 24th his thirty-six cannon fired no less than 1448 shots into the town — or so the besieged calculated. They even recognized in the artillery the workmanship of Juan Manrique.

But Charles was still unsuccessful. Twenty feet of the corner bulwark of the Tour d'Enfer collapsed because a cannon ball hit it at its weakest point, the chimney. Great parts of the city wall were shattered and the Emperor's men rushed on the breaches with loud cries. But as soon as the dust and smoke cleared they saw that behind the broken ramparts was an inner wall, stronger than the outer and newly built.

The weather was bad, with rain, snow and bitter cold. The soldiers who came from the south suffered all the more terribly because their quarters in the ruined suburbs were miserable indeed. The besieged had comfortable lodgings and plenty to eat within the town, for all useless mouths had been ruthlessly expelled.

For the first half of December the imperialists did not slacken in their efforts to storm the shattered walls. In vain. Only one alternative presented itself. The defences could be mined. Here and there the besieging army was fairly close to the walls. Underneath the Tour d'Enfer the besieged could already hear that faint ominous tapping which is so familiar to every man who has attempted to counter-mine in a war of sieges. But although mine and counter-mine were laid, the town did not fall.

The Duke of Guise did not confine his defence to mere military technicalities. He was a magnificent leader in the moral sense. He encouraged and organized his men. But the weather, too, was his ally. On Charles's side every heart was sinking. Charles

THE STRUGGLE FOR GERMANY

himself was lodged at the castle of La Horgne, the remains of which are to this day used as a farm-house. He was anxious about the condition of the Netherlands, and as, unhappily, there was no shortage in his diet, his health was plaguing him as usual. The damp, cold and continual exertions increased his ailments. His highly educated chamberlain, van Male, complained bitterly in a letter to de Praet. Charles's doctors, he said, were hopelessly weak-minded, Queen Mary spoiled him, and he himself was so uncontrolled that even in the early morning he would be quaffing iced beer. He himself had often argued with him, telling him that men of the hardiest constitutions could not digest the stuff, but all to no avail.

Gradually at Charles's headquarters all hope of success vanished. 'The Emperor is thinking of abandoning everything and going back to Spain,' wrote the Bishop of Arras to Queen Mary on December 17th. But on Christmas Day there seemed to be a ray of hope. 'So often the Emperor has had strokes of luck in his moments of worst danger, and when they were least expected. God grant it now.'

The miracle did not happen. Instead depression and mutiny spread in the imperial forces. They cried out on the Duke of Alva who had led them to this hopeless and murderous siege. Charles, as always, remained resigned and calm, but saw in the early days of January 1553, that he must raise the siege. He struck camp without further trouble. He himself remained at Thionville until January 13th. On February 6th he was again in Brussels.

THE EMPEROR WITHDRAWS FROM GERMANY

At Innsbruck the storm had first broken over Charles. At Metz it overwhelmed him. He had with difficulty recovered from the shock of his flight from Innsbruck. He could not recover from the shock of his defeat at Metz. Once again the traditional policy of Burgundy, the seizure of Lorraine, had failed. Charles V had failed before Metz, like his ancestor Charles the Bold, before Nancy. Imperial policy collapsed. The Emperor even lost confidence in himself. It was as though Heaven had deserted him. When he signed the Treaty of Passau he had already felt that, in

622

certain individual matters, both spiritual and temporal, he had gone further than he should in granting concessions. The confirmation of the Margrave's treaty with Bamberg and Würzburg, which he had previously annulled, robbed him of his rest. During the next months he went so far as to dictate to the Vicechancellor, Seld, his revocation of the treaties of Metz and Passau. The document in which he did this reflects his own views of the events of the year 1552.

Charles began with the statement that he already knew of the private understanding between Maurice, Albert and France at the time of their siege of Magdeburg in 1551. But, the Emperor continued, although he had faced rebellion before, he had never faced so much deceit. The princes had hitherto suited their words to their deeds. As things went on Charles heard more of Maurice's complaints about the Landgrave's imprisonment, about religion and the council, although 'many people said that for the Duke's own person neither religion was of any importance. We for our part were only furthering the council so as to restore unity to our beloved Christian faith'.

The document goes on to explain that Maurice offered to come to see Charles, but then gave up the visit for a trivial excuse. Instead he recruited troops and published the most inflammatory manifestos. Negotiations at Linz and Passau followed, while, in spite of the truce, Maurice invaded Tyrol, and plundered the imperial baggage. The French attacked at the same time and the Turks advanced, boasting that they had an understanding with the French.

Maurice did not make it clear until he had been at Passau for some time that he was not acting for all the rebels. Charles had been compelled to accept the treaty because of the urgent entreaty of King Ferdinand, himself threatened by the Turks, and of the loyal Estates, 'who showed themselves lacking in courage and hope'. He had, however, excepted two clauses which affected his conscience and his rights as a sovereign, 'thereupon Duke Maurice, for his part agreed to disband all his troops or to let them join the King our brother'. But at an outside estimate, Charles continued, not more than half had joined the King. The rest stayed 'with the Margrave, who with their help horribly wasted the bishoprics of Mainz, Treves and Speyer'. Others joined the French or the gentry of Brunswick. In such circumstances it would have been only reasonable not to have importuned the Emperor at Passau for indemnity for all these.

On his way to Metz, Charles went on, he had news that the Margrave was threatening the peaceful Estates of the Empire, and this left him no choice save to negotiate with him. It was the lesser of two evils.

The treaties of Passau and Metz were a tissue of injustices which only force had compelled him to accept. He hoped now with the help of the imperial Estates to make all these things good again. But should he die first, or should he achieve nothing in his deliberations with the Estates, then, he continued, 'we wish once again to ratify and confirm anything in the above-mentioned treaties which may reasonably and justly be confirmed, our own interests and the interests of our posterity notwithstanding. But apart from these clauses, we hereby protest and declare before God and all the world, that whatever there may be in either of these treaties against God, against justice, against the decrees and laws of the Holy Roman Empire or of ourselves, and against common justice, was got from us by force and the machinations of the wicked and shall be utterly cancelled, withdrawn and wiped out'.

At Ferdinand's request this proclamation was never published. It bears no date. Rumours circulated at the imperial Court that Charles intended to annul the Treaty of Passau, but on December 29th, 1553, Ferdinand reaffirmed his own part therein, and hinted that he expected some further recognition for the part he had played and the sacrifices he had made. He added the traditional postscript to his letter: 'God knows I have no other desire save to serve Your Majesty in all obedience.' Yet Charles himself came very near to publishing his renunciation of the treaty, for his agreement with the Margrave had aroused so much ill-feeling in Germany. The Estates of both religions, and the Austrian councillor John Ulrich Zasius in particular, regarded all that Charles had done since the treaty with resentment and displeasure. How did Charles reconcile his great preparations for war with his leniency first to one prince or town of the Empire and then to another? Suspicion was rife. No one could seriously believe that at fifty-three Charles was a man broken in body and spirit. He had often been ill, and had now been ill for a long time, but he had so often before made unexpected and swift recoveries that they regarded nothing as impossible.

Maurice in particular, the most restless and observant spectator of Charles's political actions, took note of everything. The deposed Elector John Frederick and his sons, seemed to Maurice's anxious eyes to be gaining a suspicious self-confidence. Was Charles planning to make use of them? Or was the Spanish succession to be forcibly imposed as soon as the Emperor had recovered from the shock of Metz? Why, after so criminally restoring the Margrave to a favoured position, did he let him recruit troops and rage across Franconia? Maurice watched the princes of south and western Germany move gradually into union, until they formed in March the League of Heidelberg for mutual defence. He himself, on March 24th, entered into alliance with Henry of Wolfenbüttel; on May 6th he formed the League of Eger with Bohemia and some of its neighbour states. These were preparations against something; but against what? Were they arming against the growing uncertainty, against the disturbers of the peace, or against the Emperor himself? Yet in reliable documents there is no trace of any plan of the Emperor's to use the Margrave against his old enemies, or to enforce the Spanish succession. Nor is there any reason to suppose that Maurice had any more glorious ambition than the preservation of his own rights.

Yet events moved towards a decision of universal significance. The German Estates grasped the essential fact that they must stand together if they wished to preserve the territorial power which they had acquired during the last thirty years. For years they had been quarrelling, on paper or in arms. The Catholics from the first had urged Charles to war, without themselves having the least intention of helping him. The Emperor, on the other hand, partly from necessity, partly from inclination, had long sought to obtain his ends by peaceful means. His failure had been an object lesson to them all. The way to the peace of Augsburg lay open.

Maurice had himself thought of the formula — 'an unconditional and perpetual peace'. Since Passau his political stature seemed to have grown. He knew very well what he was about when he helped Ferdinand against the Turks. Yet his actions were not based on statecraft alone. He had no doubts as to the motive of his own action when, with Henry of Brunswick, he turned his arms at last against the 'mad Margrave', well-knowing the Margrave to be the Emperor's ally. Maurice felt that he was fighting and subduing in the Margrave Albert the destructive forces of that worn-out and venal *canaille* of German society, the robber-barons. The class had grown intolerable in the temporal principalities of the Reformation. On July 11th, 1553, he broke the Margrave at Sievershausen. Merciful fate took him in the hour of his greatest victory. He died in the shadow of the Margrave's captured banners. All the sins of his life were atoned by this heroic death. It was the climax of his career. The future could have held no more for him.

The Emperor, too, threw open the road to religious peace. He did not yet abdicate, but he withdrew altogether from German affairs and left them to his brother. He invited the Pope to the Diet, but he himself issued his memorable refusal to attend on June 8th, 1554. His refusal, as he himself asserted, was made in all good faith, 'as is seemly between brothers, and with the additional plea that you pry out no hidden reason for my conduct. My reason is only this question of religion, in regard to which I have an unconquerable scruple, which I have already told you by word of mouth at Villach when we were together'. Charles added that he did not doubt Ferdinand's unwillingness to enter into any concession to which he, as a Christian prince, could not agree in all conscience. To prove that he had not lost interest he drew up a schedule of all the articles which might be of importance to the Diet.

Like the reflections on the treaties of Passau and Metz, this document has survived, in the handwriting of the Vice-chancellor, George Sigismund Seld, himself a man of Augsburg. After long service abroad he had entered Bavarian service, but on the death of Naves he had become indispensable in the imperial chancellery, and during the last years had grown personally very dear to Charles. This schedule illuminates for us once again, in a manner which is sympathetic to, and yet not wholly uncritical of, imperial policy, the attitude in which Charles approached his Empire and its problems, above all the religious question. It serves the purpose of a political testament for Germany, of an epilogue to the reign.

The Catholic princes were characterized, as they had been in 1530, as purely self-seeking. The spiritual princes, according to this document, hated the thought of reform, and doubtless that had been the reason for which God had smitten them in the last war. The Pope, the cardinals, and their superficially conducted council came in for much sharp criticism. The old tendency to come as far as possible to meet the Protestants by discussions on a basis of parity is still obvious in this document. It was thought to be the best way towards unity and peace. In 1530, Seld argued on this point, thirteen clauses had remained in doubt between the two parties. But in 1541 at Worms and Regensburg, not more than five or six remained unsolved. This was but an outward sign, he admitted, but it was typical. The history of all heresies proved, he went on to say, that they lost strength with time. Witness the Arian and Utraquist heresies. The *Interim* had been a failure — Seld admitted as much — but the reform of the clergy would be an excellent thing. Naturally Charles could hardly 'drag the resisting prelates by the hair' to agree to it. The Lutherans, Seld continued, would not agree to a council like that at Trent. Many devout men thought that the council had never been truly free. Foreign powers would not send delegates, and therefore the imperialists — by which term in this context Seld meant the Protestants — felt that they lacked support. On the other hand a national council would have no canonical validity, and provincial synods were able to deal with disciplinary matters only. Diets had never yet done anything except postpone the decision.

Of temporal things Seld declared that the authority of the Estates had increased, that of the Emperor dwindled. His power rested on the hereditary lands, but these were attacked and threatened on all sides by Turks, French and Moors. Neither the imperial ban nor the action of individual circles had the least effect in preserving peace. 'The subsidy voted in 1548 was rich enough, but owing to the impertinence of Maurice it was wasted in the reduction of Magdeburg.' The Swabian League had been in itself a good thing, but many leagues in Germany would be but a further element of unrest. As for Charles's treatment of the Margrave, the Emperor's critics failed to realize how difficult the position had been, because of the revolt of the princes. It would be best, Seld advised, to arrange the disposition of land as it was in 1552.

Last of all the document discussed the complaints of the Estates against the imperial government — the employment of foreigners, the introduction of foreign soldiers and the delay in public business. Seld admitted that Charles had often delayed. But for the rest, he pointed out that Charles had always had German vice-chancellors, while it would be absurd to suggest that he should exclude the most eminent ministers of his other lands from discussion of German affairs. Possibly Charles had alienated imperial lands by bestowing the fiefs of Milan and Siena on his son, but he had increased the Empire by adding Genoa, Florence and Piacenza. The complaints of the princes that their privileges have been attacked were, he asserted, groundless. The Emperor had no intention of making the imperial throne hereditary. He had given much time and thought to settling internal conflict between the Estates, such as the disagreement between Württemberg and Austria, and the quarrel between Hesse and Nassau which he had been trying to resolve for many years. If the Emperor had acted harshly towards the Landgrave, he had paid for his mistake.

This schedule was to serve as a guide to Charles's representatives at the Diet. Their chief office was to support Ferdinand, and they had to know beforehand what points were likely to be raised. They had no responsibility for the direction of affairs. Charles once again assured Ferdinand that he trusted that implicitly to him. In April 1555 he wrote once more, explaining that for his own person he must register a formal protest against anything which 'could infringe, hurt, weaken or burden our ancient, true, Christian and Catholic faith'. He referred Ferdinand to their conversation at Villach and subsequent correspondence. He asked that he should be consulted, or even furnished with a list of preliminaries for the settlement of the religious problem.

Only at Ferdinand's urgent entreaty did Charles continue to carry the imperial title for so long. Ferdinand himself felt the need of having some ultimate authority to which he could appeal in a crisis. This was the only reason that the final imperial recognition of equal rights for the adherents of the Confession of Augsburg went out under the name of the Emperor Charles V.

In fact he had nothing to do with the recognition of two parallel religions in Germany, nor with anything else decided at Augsburg in 1555. The religious settlement was not the last act in the reign of Charles V. It was the first in the reign of Ferdinand I.

THE EMPEROR ABDICATES AND RETURNS TO SPAIN

When Maximilian and his wife Mary left Spain, Prince Philip once more took over the regency in the usual form, acting on imperial instructions of June 23rd, 1551. Philip stayed in the country for the next three years. He was then called away to play his part in a great historic drama. This time, acting in his own name, he appointed as his representative in Spain his sister Joanna, widow of the Infant of Portugal, and mother of the heir, Don Sebastian. Thus, each in turn, Charles's three children had governed Spain.

On the day following the issue of his instructions to Joanna, Philip set off to England to solemnize his marriage to the Queen. Mary, the eldest daughter of Henry VIII and the cousin of the Emperor, had succeeded to the throne on the death of her half-brother Edward VI on July 6th, 1553. She needed the support of a strong foreign power to protect her against potential opposition in the country. The Emperor's agent, Simon Renard, had promised her every assistance. The help which he had previously given in establishing her legitimacy and in upholding the old Church encouraged her to rely on him. Above all, as soon as Philip had given his agreement, he was anxious to marry her to his son. On October 30th the Queen's betrothal to the absent Infant of Spain took place with the greatest solemnity. The ceremony was performed in the Privy Council and the host was elevated in the presence of the imperial ambassador. Mary's Spanish and Catholic blood may have stirred within her, recognizing in the heir to Spain the husband chosen for her by God.

Ferdinand was at the same time trying to secure her hand for his own second son. But once again his children had to give place to his brother's. The event did not altogether sweeten Ferdinand's views. Yet the King of the Romans admitted himself willing to withdraw and he may have had some consolation in Charles's assurance that he would regard Philip's English marriage as a substitute for his succession in the Empire. As things now stood, the Electors would never agree to Philip's succession in Germany. Ferdinand's elder son lamented his father's docility in a letter to his brother-in-law, Albert of Bavaria. 'God grant', he wrote, 'that His Majesty will one day stand up to His Imperial Majesty and not always show himself so chicken-hearted as he has hitherto. I am perpetually astonished at the blindness of His Majesty; he will not see how unfraternally and how falsely His Imperial Majesty is treating us.'

The Emperor had long considered Margaret of France for Philip's second wife. Later the negotiations for his marriage to Eleonore's daughter, Mary of Portugal, had gone some distance, but were broken off because of the great prospects which opened before the imperial family in England. Philip sailed for England with seventy ships and the Duke of Alva as master of his household. Charles had recently had him proclaimed King of Naples so that he too, like his wife, should bear a royal title. On July 25th, 1554, Philip and Mary were betrothed at Winchester. Great prospects of expansion unrolled themselves before the Hapsburg dynasty.

The event decided Charles to rearrange the inheritance of the dynastic lands. He did this in his fifth and last Testament, dated June 6th, 1554. It was followed later only by a series of lesser codicils. The Testament was conceived in the grandiose and melancholy style of Charles's closing years, the mood in which he was to withdraw from the world to seek his last rest. He could not go until he had seen his dynasty confirmed in the new and splendid possessions which he had given it. He began by commending his soul to God, and asked that he might be buried at the side of his wife at Granada. He ordered 30,000 masses for his soul and the distribution of 30,000 ducats in alms. He commanded his heirs to execute his will as well as those of his grandparents Maximilian and Mary, and to pay all the debts which had accumulated, out of the revenues of the three great knightly orders of Spain. For the quiet of his conscience he ordered an inquiry into his rights over Piacenza and Navarre.

He charged Philip to remember his duty to God and Holy Church, to further the Inquisition, to care for justice, to look after his people and to protect the humble and weak against powerful nobles and grandees. Other ideas which had early engaged Charles's attention emerge again. The Inquisitors, he suggested, should be given canonicates so that they did not have to live on the confiscation of goods from the accused. The domain rights of the Crown should be won back wherever possible.

He advised Philip to establish primogeniture in the male line for Spain and to appoint regents for Don Carlos, who had lost his mother at birth. The children of Philip's marriage with Mary were to rule in England, with certain modifications if they should have only a daughter.

The Testament reckoned on the new and boundless prospects of the dynasty. If England and the Netherlands were united under one hand, and strongly supported by Spain and the Empire, France could be strangled out of existence. These plans of the Hapsburg dynasty were the true explanation of the war-lust of Henry II of France and his generals, and of the still more violent opposition of Pope Paul IV, of the Neapolitan family of Caraffa. He followed Julius III on June 23rd, 1555, after the brief pontificate of Marcellus. Paul IV saw that the papal states would soon be shut in on all sides by Hapsburg power, while no other monarch could be called in to redress the balance.

Meanwhile Charles's overwhelming desire for rest, his melancholy thoughts of death, urged him onwards to complete a plan which he had long had in mind. This was to divest himself of all his powers of government, to remove himself from all temporal authority. Dangers on all sides postponed his decision month after month.

French troops crossed the frontiers in several places and took Marienburg, Bouvines, Dinant. Philibert Emanuel of Savoy, now commander-in-chief of the imperial forces, moved against them. The Emperor himself followed in his litter and took part in the relief of Renty. At the same time grave news came from Italy. The Marquis of Marignano and Duke Cosimo of Florence were forced to take arms against the French and their old enemy Pietro Strozzi. They drove back the French as far as Siena which was defended by Blaise de Montluc. After many anxious months they at length won a great victory, and on April 2nd, 1555, Siena fell. But this did not alter the hostile attitude of France.

The Queen of England attempted to mediate between the Emperor and the French King at Gravelines, but without success. The French ambassador, copying the technique of his predecessor on a like occasion forty years earlier, at once abandoned all talk of the immediate present and took refuge in generalities. He wanted not only Piedmont and Savoy but Asti and Milan for the young Duke of Orleans. This was the third generation of princes bearing this title for whom such demands had been made. He wanted Navarre for the Duke of Vendôme, Antoine de Bourbon. The imperialists, on the other hand, suggested that the question of Savoy and Piedmont should be settled by a marriage between Philibert Emanuel and a sister of Henry II. In return Don Carlos was to keep Milan and marry Elisabeth of France. All the negotiations led to nothing and after a brief truce the war broke out afresh.

Meanwhile in Italy Paul IV arose like a latter-day Gregory VII or Innocent III. He was a harsh, ascetic, passionate man, a man of great words, intoxicated by his new position as prince of the Church. In his attitude to reform and to politics, he was a radical. He belonged to the group of Italian thinkers who still believed that their land might be set free, and for the last time in the century we find these ideas filling the political world of Italy. But he never succeeded in rising above the private feuds of his own family, nor yet did he find means to liberate himself from the Spaniards, save by calling in the French. He declared that the Spaniards were nothing but the spawn of Jews and Moors, and when he was told that the imperial ambassador Bernardino Mendoza was a brother of the well-known Diego Mendoza, he said that he wished to know no more about his character: that was enough. Blindly and determinedly he trusted in the French; at Naples, he regarded them as naturalized Italians. He wanted to liberate Florence: he hated the Colonna and the Medici, tried to elevate the Sforza and Santa Fiore. He extended a warm welcome to the French ambassadors, Lansac and the Cardinal of Lorraine. His policy reached a climax in his secret treaty with this latter, signed on December 15th, 1555, by which Naples was to be ceded to a son of the French King. Sicily was to be given to Venice at the same time, for by Italy the Pope understood the four states only, Milan, Venice, Naples and the Papacy.

Charles, too, was now in earnest. He sent the Duke of Alva to Italy and published to all the world that if the Pope did not make an end of his follies, he too would consider himself free to act as he chose, before God and man. Once again, as they had done thirty years before, the imperial forces threatened the papal states and Rome.

In the midst of these quarrels, which seemed like a return to the first struggling years of his reign, Charles decided to abdicate. Many events worked to the same end: his mother had died on April 13th, 1555; Philip's wife, the English Queen, proved barren, and thus condemned the whole of his northern scheme to collapse. This latter failure may have had some effect in securing the peace of Augsburg. All increased Charles's resolution to withdraw.

On October 22nd, 1555, he began by resigning his sovereignty of the Order of the Golden Fleece. On the 25th he abdicated his rulership of the Netherlands to Philip in the great hall of the castle at Brussels. All the great men of the land were solemnly assembled when Charles made his entrance, leaning on the shoulder of Prince William of Orange. He was surrounded by the knights of the Golden Fleece, the councillors and ministers of the Netherlands, the provincial governors, Philibert Emanuel of Savoy, Christina of Lorraine, the young Archduke Ferdinand of Austria, King Philip, Queen Eleonore and Queen Mary.

The councillor, Philibert of Brussels, announced the imperial intention of abdicating and thus gave the sign for the solemn ceremony to begin. Charles himself rose to his feet. He held a few notes in his hand, and, consulting these from time to time in his habitual manner, delivered a brief summary of his life. Forty years before, in this same room, he reminded them he had been declared of age. Later he had been called upon to succeed his grandfather Ferdinand in Spain, his grandfather Maximilian in the Empire. He had found Christendom torn in pieces and beset with foes, against whom he had fought for the greater part of his life. Nine times he had visited Germany, six times Spain, four times France, twice Africa, and twice England. Now he was preparing to make his last journey, to Spain. He was deeply grieved to think that he could not leave his people in peace as he had always wished. He had set all on this hope, his life, his repose, and every resource at his disposal. But his forces were failing, his health was gone. Even before he made his last journey to the Empire, he had known that he was at the end of his strength. Yet the unceasing anxiety and unrest of Christendom had driven him on to risk all that he had in the game. After the King of France and several of the German princes had failed in their attack on him, he had tried to regain Metz, but it was too late in the winter and the cold, wet and snow had brought the enterprise to nothing. It was in God's hand to give or to withhold success. He thanked God that He had so often helped him. At this present hour he was tired even to death and desired only to give his own lands to King Philip, the Empire to Ferdinand.

Next followed the last scene of all, a scene so moving that all present wept. Charles exhorted his son to stand fast in the faith of his fathers, to care for peace and justice. He himself had often erred, out of youth, out of self-will, out of weakness. But he had never wilfully wronged any man. If he had done so unwittingly he asked forgiveness.

White and exhausted, the Emperor sank down into his chair.

Nothing was heard in the great hall but the stifled sobbing of the audience. Tears coursed down the cheeks of the noble ladies and down the Emperor's own. Philip threw himself on his knees in front of his father, and took the oath which the aged Emperor had asked. Charles raised him to his feet and tenderly embraced him. Then the prince turned to the assembly, apologized for his inability to speak their language fluently, and asked the Bishop of Arras to read out his speech. Queen Mary next spoke, taking her leave of the lands over which she had ruled. She had decided to follow her brother and Queen Eleonore to Spain. The two Queens were both exhausted after long and weary lives in the heat and glare of the state. Mary above all had worn herself out in her brother's service. The Emperor thanked her for all she had done in a voice laden with emotion.

We may search the annals of history in vain for such another scene, for such another generation of princes as these of the Hapsburg dynasty, who were ready of their own free will to retire from the scene of their sovereignty. The splendid radiance of the High Renaissance seems to shine even through the events

634

of history. At what other time, in what other continent, was so great a scene so greatly played?

After his abdication from the Netherlands, Charles abdicated his sovereignty over Castile, Aragon, Sicily and the Indies on January 16th, 1556. Recently the account of these proceedings has come to light. This time the scene was played out not in the great hall but in Charles's private apartments. The circle was smaller, the atmosphere the same. Charles spoke again of the abdication which he had performed on October 25th, but this time he laid greater emphasis on his wish to live wholly in the service of God. Once again he bore witness to the fact that he belonged essentially to an age now dead, an age which felt that God was to be served best not in affairs of state, but in solitude and contemplation. The old Emperor entrusted to his son a casket containing his will and codicils, and spoke of this document with an explicit reference to the instructions he had given Philip in 1543, when he had forbidden him to ransom him if he should be taken prisoner. For the rest, he added that although he was neither *letrado* nor jurist, he remembered that he had read in St. Augustine that wills were only valid on the death of the testator. Only a few more months were left to him, and he wished to spend them atoning for his sins and clearing his conscience.

His formal abdication of the crowns of Castile, Leon and the Indies were next read out from written documents by notaries, using the Spanish language. Vargas read out the abdication of Aragon, the Islands and Sicily, in Latin. When he gave up the Netherlands, he had laid down his presidency of the Golden Fleece; now, on resigning Spain, he laid down his mastership of the three great orders, Santiago, Calatrava, and Alcantara — all in favour of Philip.

During these days of abdication, Charles occupied, for quiet, an elegant little house in the park of his castle. Perhaps there was something symbolic even in this. Here, too, he lived when he signed the truce of Vaucelles with France, and until it was ratified. Here, too, he received the new ambassador, Admiral Coligny and read his credentials. Charles's fingers were so badly swollen with gout that he could with difficulty untie the string which tied the document. Making light of his now vanishing strength, he laughingly told Coligny that he too had once been a gallant cavalier and vain of his person. He recalled how proudly he had ridden into Naples in 1536.

Now and again in history chance brings about a dramatic juxtaposition. Coligny was to be the dominant figure of the Huguenot revolt in France, the Prince of Orange was to be the champion of the Protestant Netherlands. Both were with the great Catholic Emperor during his last days in the Low Countries. Both played a part in the closing scenes of his political life, in the passing of the greatest figure of the older generation.

Maximilian and Charles's daughter Mary came to say good-bye. Charles had longed for their coming and often spoke of it. He wanted to see his brother Ferdinand once again. But this could not be. Instead he had to send the Prince of Orange on September 12th, 1556, with a letter, in which he gave the imperial throne to his brother. He assured him that his fraternal love remained unaltered, and left to him the choice of a decisive moment to make the change public. Not until February 1558, did the Electors agree to Charles's abdication and accept the elevation of Ferdinand. Another stout document had been drawn up to settle the Spanish succession and prepare a warm alliance between Ferdinand and Philip. But it seems that there was no further serious discussion of this point, nor any attempt to re-introduce the idea of Philip's succession to the imperial throne.

In Spain, meantime, the new King had been proclaimed. Banners were hung out and proclamations read. The first grandee of the land, the child Don Carlos, did homage to his absent father. Standing before the royal standard, unfurled above him, he cried out, 'Castilla, Castilla, por el rey Don Felipe!'

Charles left Brussels on August 8th, 1556. Philip went with him as far as Ghent. On August 28th they parted, never again to meet. As so often before Charles sailed from the coast of Zeeland, and twenty-six ships followed him, bearing the two Queens and a great train of Spaniards. The imperial ship was richly fitted with everything needful to his comfort. On September 28th they disembarked at Laredo, a small port to the east of Santander. From here they went by way of Burgos to Valladolid. Charles would attend no formal receptions. Only at Carbezon, not far from

Valladolid, his grandchild Don Carlos was allowed to see him. In spite of his wish to avoid solemnities, the people of Burgos rang the bells and set lights in their windows. The Constable of Castile came out to meet him. In Valladolid itself Charles received the regent, his younger daughter Joanna. Then he hurried southwards over the pass of Tornavacas, over the precipitous mountain paths to the province of Estremadura, the basin of the river Tagus west of Toledo.

The Court settled down at first in the Vera de Plasencia, the slopes of those hills which lie open to the southern sun and are sheltered from the north by the Sierra de Gredos; they lived at Jarandilla, a castle belonging to Don Garcia Alvarez de Toledo, Count of Oropesa. It was a fine autumn and Charles paid visits to Seville and Granada, recalling perhaps the times he had spent there as a young man, soon after his wedding. He took infinite pleasure in looking out from the windows and balconies of his rooms on the flowers and fruit below him in the mellow sunshine. On November 21st he paid his first visit to the monastery of San Jeronimo de Yuste, next to which his own imperial villa was to be built.

SAN JERONIMO DE YUSTE

Once only in all his latter years had Charles visited the south, Seville, Cordova, Granada. Once he had landed at Cartagena coming back from Algiers. Then he had travelled to Madrid by way of Murcia, Albacete and Ocaña. Once he had visited Valencia to receive homage. But much of the country was still unknown to him. He had spent the greater part of his time in old Castile, in the country surrounding Valladolid where the Cortes met, at Tordesillas, Palencia, Tudela and Burgos. Hence he had sometimes travelled up the Douro by way of Aranda, Catalayud, to Saragossa and farther on to the Cortes in Monzon, or by way of Montserrat to the ports of Barcelona and Palamos. Often too he had stayed in the Tagus valley and near Madrid, whence too he had travelled the roads to Saragossa, Catalayud and Siguenza. He was well known to the people of the towns of Alcala and Aranjuez on the Tagus, and he had been often seen farther down the river at Toledo, Talavera and Oropesa. From Oropesa a road, which he had traversed, went south by way of Sierra to the chief cloister of the Jeromites, Santa Maria of Guadaloupe. Westwards from Oropesa and comparatively close to this chief province of Old Castile, lay Jarandilla and the monastery of San Jeronimo de Yuste. Charles had come, therefore, to no uncharted wilderness, but to a quiet backwater but a little way from paths which he and his Court had often trod, not far from the country where his dear Empress had lived and died.

The order of St. Jerome belongs essentially to Spain. Yet it had close connections with many other monastic orders, followed the rule of St. Augustine in the main, and was predominantly contemplative. It was one of the richest orders in the kingdoms, and kept watch over many celebrated relics, like those at Guadaloupe. Many Spanish Kings lay buried in its monastic churches.

These considerations may have partly influenced Charles's decision to build himself a residence next to San Jeronimo. The monastery could be seen from the windows and terraces of Jarandilla, and the courtiers, who did not look forward to the retirement, noticed with anxiety that even in fine weather the mists hung about the towers and buildings of the monastery, which was almost blotted out when the heavy rains from the south smote against the mountain wall. But when Charles traced out the foundations of his villa on November 25th, they were relieved to find the site more sunny and pleasant than they had anticipated. It seemed that San Jeronimo would be after all a beautiful and quiet spot, retired from the world.

On February 5th, 1557, the Court moved into its new residence.

Judging by the spacious standards of the late Renaissance Charles's villa was as modest as it could well be. Four well-lit rooms occupied each of its two floors. The abbey church was situated just behind the villa, a little higher up the slope of the hill, so that one of the upper rooms of the villa could open into it. Charles could thus pass straight into the church, and from his room he could even see the south side of the high altar. On the east and west pleasant terraces were built to catch the sun, and here Charles used often to sit in the open air. On the south, between a plantation of trees, and a small wood, a wide prospect met the eyes. The plaisance was closed about by walls, and the

638

grounds were enlivened with tiny brooks and cascades, which refreshed plants and men alike.

The interior of the villa was rich with costly hangings, tapestries from the Netherlands, embroidered scenes and paintings in oils, statues and curious jewels, clocks and scientific instruments, beautiful and luxurious furniture. Charles had no intention of leading the life of an ascetic and a monk. Nor had he any external connection with the monastery, although everything was arranged to suit the Emperor's great need for quiet, and the sense of repose and contemplation for which his age cried out.

The great train of courtiers and servants were lodged either in a wing of the monastery or in the neighbouring village of Quacos. As well as the master of the household, Don Luis Mendez de Quijada, lord of Villa Garcia, Charles kept with him his secretary Martin de Gaztelu, his physician, Doctor Mathys of Bruges, and his old companion William van Male. He had also many servants, readers, assistants and priests. All these men were ardent letter-writers, and of all Charles's life we have not so much detailed knowledge as we have of this one short period. His physical condition, his daily activities, the letters he wrote and the visits he received, all are known to us.

Several monks, brought from other monasteries on account of their beautiful voices or other gifts, served the Emperor as well as his own suite. But he kept his own confessor, Juan de Regla, with whom he often spent many hours in religious discussion. His library was small, but he did not deny himself worldly literature as well as more serious works like Boethius and St. Augustine. He had brought his astronomical books, his maps and his Caesar with him, as well as the *Deeds of Charles the Bold* by the Burgundian Olivier de la Marche, and his own personal notebooks and journals of his travels. He had persuaded the Inquisition to give him permission to read a French translation of the Bible, as its study in the vernacular was otherwise not allowed.

The little Court of fifty people was able to live comfortably on its pension of 20,000 ducats a year, more especially as the Regent often sent presents when she was in the neighbourhood. Certain domestic animals were kept also, and the larder could be filled from time to time by hunting. Guests had to stay in Quacos or at Jarandilla. Only when the two Queens, to Charles's joy, paid him a visit, did he make an exception and give them a room in his villa.

The monastic peace of Yuste was not utterly undisturbed. Philip, Joanna, and the Emperor's old servants, were all too much in the habit of taking his advice not to honour him with continual reports of all that had happened, and to storm him with letters and requests for good counsel. Like the distant rumble of a cannonade, the sound of the great world without echoed, now loud, now soft, in the ears of the old Emperor. He had lived too long and too passionately in the world itself to be altogether unmoved by such noises.

Now and again an urgent embassy or message would persuade him to intervene personally once more. But he obstinately refused to take up the reins of government either in Spain or elsewhere.

The French broke the truce of Vaucelles: Paul IV openly opposed all Charles's adherents in the Cardinals' College and throughout Italy: the Duke of Alva invaded the papal states to protect Spain's interests and Spain's friends. Soon after these events Charles expressed his vehement disapproval of a truce which he felt had been too rashly signed, and which was likely to drive Paul IV and his family only the more towards the French alliance. He urged Joanna, the Queen-regent of Spain, to defend the frontier and gave her advice as to how to do it.

His fears came true. The alliance of the Pope and the French King proved a serious danger to the young Philip, and Charles again impatiently intervened. At the end of March 1557 Philip's councillor and confidant, Ruy Gomez, later Duke of Eboli, appeared at the Emperor's Court for help and advice. Charles was angry at the delay and dishonesty shown by the *Casa de Contratacion* in raising money for his son, and began to turn about him with such vigour that he had soon raised many hundreds of thousands of ducats. These resources, with the success of Alva and the attitude of Cosimo de' Medici, turned the balance in Italy against the French party, led by Guise, Brissac and the Duke of Ferrara. Philibert Emanuel and Count Egmont, meanwhile, on August 10th, 1557, won the most celebrated tactical victory of the century at St. Quentin on the Flemish frontier. There was nothing of the monk in Charles's passionate participation in all these events.

Next a family conflict broke out in Portugal. It was doubtful whether Charles's sister Katherine, the widow of the last King, John III, was to be regent, or Charles's daughter Joanna, the mother of the young heir. Charles gave his judgment in favour of Katherine, partly no doubt because he felt that while Philip was away Joanna could not be spared from Spain.

Charles also took care to provide for the possibility of the little King's death. If Don Sebastian of Portugal did not grow up, only two members of the Portuguese dynasty would be left, the Cardinal-Infant Henry, and the Infanta Mary, Eleonore's daughter by her first husband. Charles sent as ambassador to Portugal, Father Francisco Borgia. He had once been marshal of the Court to the Empress, and had then been known as Duke of Gandia, but he had abandoned all his titles when he entered the Society of Jesus. This ambassador was to obtain from Queen Katherine her consent to the accession of Don Carlos, should Don Sebastian die. The little Don Carlos of Spain was in fact the heir to Portugal, after the present King, for both his mother and grandmother had been Princesses of that land. Feeling in Portugal was such as to give Queen Katherine the excuse to withhold her consent. But whether he succeeded or not, it was interesting that Charles, in his anxiety for the future of the peninsula, should have formulated the Pan-Iberian idea. His son Philip was to bring the dream to pass, and to gain with the Portuguese throne, all her colonies the world over.

We need not linger over events at Yuste itself. They have been recorded in countless writings of monks and courtiers. Queen Eleonore, who had lived to see her daughter Mary once again, her darling wish, died at Talaveruela in February 1558. Queen Mary, more than ever alone, visited her brother once again and stayed until March 16th. At Philip's wish Charles had declared that he would let Mary be regent in the Netherlands once more, and as his own health grew worse he was greatly rejoiced to find that she was willing to go. But her health too prevented her from ever again taking over the reins of government. Charles's anxiety for the Netherlands came to an end when on July 13th Egmont's great victory over the French, under de Thermes at Gravelines, prevented them from breaking through from Dunkirk to Calais. Now at last peace over all Europe was in sight. In the following year the Peace of Câteau Cambrensis was to set the seal on the long struggle, and bring about the temporary cessation of war between France and Spain.

Quijada lived part of the time away from Yuste with his wife Magdalena Ulloa at Villagarcia. In their house the little son of Barbara Blomberg was growing up. He had been entrusted at first to the musician Massi to look after, and at this time he was still called Jeronimo. Magdalena followed her husband to Quacos in the summer of 1558. The boy came with her. He was still not recognized as Charles's son, but when he appeared about the Court, performing the duties of a page, his lively blue eyes and fresh fair complexion filled his father with a new joy. He wrote a special codicil ensuring his future and leaving a legacy to his mother.

In the summer Charles contracted a serious cold, complicated by a severe general attack of gout. It may have been caused by his habitual neglect of diet, or by his casual disregard of all necessary precaution against the treacherously cold winds of the early morning. The last painful weeks dragged by, and reports from Yuste grew melancholy. At one time Charles celebrated a requiem mass for his father and grandfather, an act which gave rise to the legend that he had arranged and watched his own funeral obsequies.

Charles suffered so much from his gout that he would have no more visits. He even refused to see the regent Joanna. His old friend Don Luis d'Avila happened to be in the neighbourhood and was allowed to come to him. He was now the Grand Controller of the order of Alcantara. By chance, too, a messenger from Philip turned out to be a preacher whom Charles had once known, Carranza, now Archbishop of Toledo. He appeared at Yuste when Charles was already dying. Power of attorney had been rapidly made out in favour of the secretary Gaztelu, and in the next days a codicil was drawn up giving Charles's last wishes for the payment of his servants and the disposition of his personal effects. The Emperor wished to be buried under the high altar at San Jeronimo itself, with the Empress beside him. But he left the final arrangement to Philip. He admonished Philip and Joanna to proceed sternly against the Lutherans, of whom two dangerous nests had just been smoked out at Seville and Valladolid.

Both these had been founded by theologians whom Charles had once cherished, and whom he had taken with him to Germany. Constantin Ponce de Leon and Augustin Cazalla. Almost to his last breath Charles was busied with this, the worst problem of all his life, the rock on which he had foundered in Germany.

The letters of Doctor Mathys give a day to day account of Charles's illness. He was delighted with a plate of fresh fruit, but if this was not to be had he continued, to the physicians' despair, to indulge himself with whatever took his fancy. Towards the middle of September they gave up all hope of his recovery. They began to talk of extreme unction. The faithful Quijada objected to it for as long as he dared. But when Charles became so weak, that he was expected to die at any hour, he had to yield to the inevitable. Charles listened with passionate devotion to the whole series of services which the Catholic Church has prepared for the consolation of the dying. Following an old tradition, he had consecrated tapers from Montserrat ready to take in his hand at the last, and the little crucifix which the Empress had held in her dying hand. The Archbishop of Toledo pressed it between his fingers, reminding the Emperor at the same moment that Christ's death was the only source of mercy for sinners. The Catholic d'Avila, overhearing, thought this a very Protestant sentiment, and the Archbishop was to be reminded of it later when he stood his trial by the Inquisition. One of the monks from the monastery found a word more in sympathy with the orthodoxy of those who watched at Charles's bedside. It was Saint Matthew's Day, and he connected this with the Emperor's own birthday, the feast of that saint's brother-apostle, Saint Matthias. In the protection of these two apostles, he said, Charles could go with confidence into the everlasting. On September 21st the Emperor died.

He had gone to his end borne up by his faith and confident in his God. Until the last he had shown himself to be essentially imbued with that medieval spirit of devotion, the spirit to which his life had borne witness. He gave himself up to all the austere and lesser works of atonement, and was anxious to secure through the intercession of his monks and through his charity to the poor of the country, through masses for his soul and all the other provisions of his will, the rich salvation which the Church had laid up for her sons. In his last codicil he ordered that Titian's great 'Gloria', the magnificent picture of the Trinity which had been painted to his order, and which was one of the most valuable of his treasures, should be given to the High Altar of the monastic Church of San Jeronimo. No other act bears such startling witness to the grandeur and profundity of the Emperor's devotion. The great canvas depicts the Holy Trinity enthroned in the heights of heaven. At their side stands the Mother of God. About and before them crowd the heavenly hosts, angels, saints and blessed ones. Among these holy ones, already wrapt in contemplation of the God-head, the Emperor dared to have himself depicted. At his side kneels his wife. Both are accompanied by angels, both are shown as already in the state of ultimate blessedness. The imperial crown lies discarded at their feet. This was the proudest and yet the humblest expression of the idea which had guided Charles's life. He knew that he had been called by God's all-highest will. The picture and his whole career are like some stupendous vision of the great period of the Catholic Church, of the Trecento, to which the Counter-Reformation, in spite of the dividing gulf of the Renaissance, was yet inwardly very near.

Once again our thoughts go back to the Emperor's youth, to his Dutch teacher Adrian of Utrecht, who later became Pope, to the Chancellor Gattinara whose imperial theory was no other than that dreamed of by Dante — a world-order with Pope and Emperor each in his sphere, each filled with a sense of profound responsibility towards all Christendom. According to his abilities, but with unflagging devotion, Charles had lived all his life in the pursuance of this idea. He was a man, with the daily weaknesses and caprices of his kind, yet in the permanent motives of his desire, in the courage of his convictions, something more than a man, a great figure in the history of the world.

Contemporary Europe felt that a great man had passed. They measured him by the breadth of his lands and the grandeur of his actions. Soon, too, they judged him by the wisdom of his political testament, for it was shortly after made known. For his son and successor, he became in course of time the object of almost idolatrous admiration. In the prime of his life, King Philip built the great monastery of the Escorial, dedicated to Saint Laurence, on whose day the battle of St. Quentin had been fought. He intended to use it as his chief residence. In this most magnificent of royal tombs he collected in the year 1574 the remains of all the princes of his family, of his own and the preceding generation. They lie there still, Charles V and Isabella of Portugal, close by Charles's mother Queen Joanna, their own infant children, Hernando and Juan, their daughter-in-law Mary of Portugal, and the two royal sisters, Eleonore of France and Mary of Hungary.

INDEX

INDEX

INDEX

INDEX

INDEX

INDEX

Margaret of France, daughter of Francis I, 425, 474, 519, 532, 630
—— of York, widow of Charles the Bold, 33
Marignano, battle of, 74
—— marquis of, 631
Marillac, 359, 597
Mark, Eberhard de la, 104, 150, 162, 468
—— Robert de la, 75, 150, 155
Marliano, Lodovico, 85, 126, 133
Marmier, Hugo, 104
Marne, campaign on the, 514ff
Marnix, Jean de, 46, 104
Marnol, 474
Marquina, Pedro, 536, 537, 541
Marseilles, 218, 351, 380
Marta, Santa, 338
Mary, daughter of Charles V, 325, 430, 438, 516, 590, 600, 629, 636
—— of Austria, daughter of Ferdinand, 423
—— of Burgundy (See Burgundy)
—— of Hungary, regent of the Netherlands, 43, 54, 140, 248, 296, 306, 309, 321f, 343, 346, 355, 365, 381, 384f, 408ff, 414f, 425, 426ff, 439, 460, 472ff, 476ff, 529, 547, 558, 581, 592, 594, 596, 598f, 618, 622, 633
—— of Portugal, daughter of Eleonore, 532, 641
Massarelli, Angelo, 531
Mathys, Dr., 639, 643
—— John, 356
St. Mauris, 395, 532, 546
Maximilian I, Emperor, 21, 24, 33f, 40f, 46, 51f, 71, 74f, 77, 91, 101, 431, 636; his debts, 137; his character, 96f
—— later Emperor, 516, 561, 582, 585-6, 590ff, 598f, 608, 629f
Mecklenburg, dukes of, 354, 602, 613
Medios frutas, 465, 479
Meit, Conrad, 45, 288
Melanchthon, Philip, 296, 307, 310, 437, 441f, 446ff, 530
Memling, Hans, 28
Mendoza, Antonio, 585
—— Diego, ambassador to Venice, 497f, 531, 534ff, 566, 577f
—— —— Duke of Infantado, 265
—— —— Viceroy of Valencia, 148
—— Hurtado de, family, 64
—— Iñigo, 279
—— Lope, 167
—— Rodrigo, marquis of Zenete, 148
Mercedes, 145
Merklin, Balthasar, provost of Waldkirch, 187, 266, 299
Mesa, Bernardino de, Bishop of Elne and later of Badajoz, 116, 162
Messina, 368
Metz, 505, 515, 604f, 616ff
Mexico, 173ff
Michelangelo, 230, 288
Mignanello, Fabio, 418, 528
Milan, 50, 165, 202, 213, 216, 220f, 231, 256f, 369f, 376, 399f, 430, 438f, 497f
—— Francesco Sforza, duke of, 152, 202, 217, 240f, 267f, 287, 369 (See also Alternatives)
Miltitz, Karl von, 111
Minden, 444
Mocenigo, 416f
Mohacz, battle of, 247
Moluccas, 170, 221, 463
Mömpelagard, 330
Moncada, Hugo de, 73, 235, 240, 243, 262, 270
Monluc, Blaise de, 475, 631
Monte, Giovanni Maria del, Cardinal, 534, 577 (See also Julius III)
Montepulciano, 471, 474
Montezuma, 175f
Montferrat, 344

Montmorency, Anne de, 227, 236, 345, 380, 386, 617
Montpelier, 92, 108
Monzon, 476 (See also Cortes of Aragon)
Moors (See Moriscoes)
Moriscoes, 68f, 148, 200
Morone, Girolamo, 228f; nuncio and cardinal, 418, 435, 437, 448
Mota, Dr. Pedro Ruiz, 49, 85
Mühlberg, 567-9
Mulert, Dr. Gerhard, 355
Muley Hassan, 360, 367

Najera, Abbot, 147, 222
Naples, kingdom and city of, 73, 109, 115, 139, 149, 151, 156, 218, 221, 268, 270f, 276, 280, 368f, 583, 632
Narvaez, Pamfilo, 175, 336
Nassau-Breda, Engelbert of, 37
Nassau-Dillenburg, Henry of, 37, 55, 58f, 104, 127, 155, 177, 196, 252, 261, 302, 345, 362, 380, 385
—— —— William of, his brother, 302
—— —— William of, his nephew, 592, 633, 636
Nationality, 66, 97f, 193, 346, 602
National meeting for religious reform, 185, 305, 446, 613
Naturel, Philibert, 155
Nausea, Frederick, 438
Navagero, 252, 269
Navarre, kingdom of, 71f, 73, 155, 156, 478 (See also Albret)
Navarro, Pedro, 68, 72, 203, 268
Naves, Johann von, 409, 434, 439, 449, 466, 510, 527, 546
Netherlands, 23ff, 190, 482, 504-5; relations of, with France, 33, 517ff; with the Empire, 581f, 590f; inheritance of, 516, 520, 591; finances and administration of, 322, 460-1; Estates of, 322-3, 384f, 479; nobility of, 36f; towns and commerce, 23, 190, 412; the Church, 26, 545, 548; religious feeling in, 356, 476
Nice, truce of, 387f
Nogarola, Count, 359
Noircarmes, 345, 362
Norway, 141, 323
Noyon, treaty of, 75f, 116
Nuremberg, Diets at, 184f, 499

Obernburger, 546
Ofen-Pest (Buda-Pest), 444, 451-2
Oldenburg, Christopher of, 355, 552, 554, 571, 596
Olivier de la Marche, 27, 30
Orange (See Chalon)
Orleans, Duke of (See France)
Orley, Barend van, 46, 165
Orsini, Cardinal-legate, 108f, 251
Osiander, Andreas, 437
Oslo, 323
Osorno, Don Garcia Fernandez Manrique, Count of, 493
Oxe, Torben, 141

Pacheco, Family, 65
—— Pedro, 534
Pachs, Pedro, 148
Pack, Otto von, 297
Padilla, 144, 146
Palacios Rubios, 74
Palamos, 494
Palatinate, Frederick, Count Palatine, later Elector of the, 52, 55, 78f, 103, 184, 299, 354-5, 362, 397, 446; his relations with Denmark, 402, 411, 449, 471f; his policy as Elector, 512, 531, 540f, 559, 601
—— Lewis, Elector of the, 246, 297f, 438, 447
—— Wolfgang, Count Palatine, 499

653

INDEX

INDEX